Advance praise for *Imperfect Partners*

"For the United States, Southeast Asia is one of the most important and least understood parts of the world. Scot Marciel draws on his vast diplomatic experience to bring a wealth of illuminating stories, hard-earned insights, and wise analysis to bear on a region that will help determine our capacity to deal with the most pressing issues of the 21st century: climate and migration, trade and development, the future of democracy, and America's competition with China. *Imperfect Partners* is an indispensable resource for anyone seeking to understand Southeast Asia and America's relationship with its countries and people."
—**Ben Rhodes**, former deputy national security advisor and
 author of *After the Fall*

"Drawing on his 35 years of diplomatic experience, Scot Marciel has written an illuminating survey of the United States' relations with Southeast Asia. With service in Hong Kong, the Philippines, and Vietnam, ambassadorships to Indonesia, Burma, and the ten-member ASEAN group of countries, as well as numerous policy positions at the Department of State, the author brings to bear a highly practical understanding of the region combined with a profound grasp of its history. This is an excellent primer on a part of the world whose significance has grown substantially in recent years with the rise of neighboring China."
—**John Negroponte**, career diplomat, former U.S. Permanent
 Representative to the United Nations and the first director of
 national intelligence

"Ambassador Scot Marciel has written a gem of a book. Using his 35-plus years of diplomatic service living in and working with the nations of Southeast Asia, Scot tells a compelling story of the relationship between the United States and these countries and highlights their diversity and strategic importance to the United States. His thoughtfully researched account is brought to life with fascinating insights and captivating, on-the-scene anecdotes. Whether trekking through jungles to observe Philippine elections, landing in Vietnam to help open the U.S. Embassy, or visiting Rohingya communities in Myanmar, Scot has experienced the nations of Southeast Asia at their core. *Imperfect Partners* is a must-read for U.S. policymakers, business leaders, academics, humanitarians, and everyday Americans engaging with the nations of Southeast Asia."
—**Kristie Kenney**, former State Department counselor and U.S.
 ambassador to Thailand, the Philippines, and Ecuador

Imperfect Partners

IMPERFECT PARTNERS

The United States and Southeast Asia

Scot Marciel

Stanford | Walter H. Shorenstein
Asia-Pacific Research Center
Freeman Spogli Institute

ROWMAN & LITTLEFIELD
Lanham • Boulder • New York • London

Shorenstein APARC addresses critical issues affecting the countries of Asia, their regional and global affairs, and U.S.-Asia relations. As Stanford University's hub for the interdisciplinary study of contemporary Asia, we produce policy-relevant research, provide education and training to students, scholars, and practitioners, and strengthen dialogue and cooperation between counterparts in the Asia-Pacific and the United States.

Walter H. Shorenstein Asia-Pacific Research Center
Stanford University
616 Jane Stanford Way, Encina Hall
Stanford, CA 94305-6055
650-723-9741 | aparc.fsi.stanford.edu

Published by Rowman & Littlefield
An imprint of The Rowman & Littlefield Publishing Group, Inc.
4501 Forbes Boulevard, Lanham, MD 20706
www.rowman.com

86–90 Paul Street, London EC2A 4NE, United Kingdom

Library of Congress Cataloging-in-Publication Data Is Available

ISBN 978-1-5381-7894-2 (cloth)
ISBN 978-1-5381-7895-9 (paper)
ISBN 978-1-5381-7896-6 (eBook)

Contents

Part III. Countries in Transition

Part IV. ASEAN, China, and the United States

Foreword

This book is truly a labor of love. Every chapter—nearly every page—conveys Scot Marciel's deep affection and understanding of the peoples, cultures, and countries of Southeast Asia. Through my years working with him on the tricky issues in that important region, I came to learn that the feeling was mutual! Respect and affection for Ambassador Marciel were instantly evident throughout the region, even in those countries where U.S. diplomats had the greatest challenges. Every chapter of this wonderful book is rich with deep insight born of the author's extensive experience, strong relationships, perceptive and inquisitive mind, and intense study of the region and its issues. At the same time, it is a highly personal and engrossing voyage that we are privileged to share, as Scot recounts his adventures, from snake-liquor-infused breakfasts with communist cadres in Vietnam to policy debates with the secretary of state.

Scot and I each joined the Department of State as Foreign Service Officers in the same year—1985. But other than casual encounters, our paths did not really cross until 2008, when I returned from overseas and took up an assignment in the department's Bureau of East Asian and Pacific Affairs (EAP) at the end of the George W. Bush administration. Scot then held a senior position in the bureau; he had recently been named as America's Washington-based ambassador to the Association of Southeast Asian Nations (ASEAN)—an organization I would later come to know well. Not only was he the first U.S. ambassador to the organization, but the United States was the first non-ASEAN nation ever to name an ambassador to the association. He was newly confirmed in this position when we began working together and I was instantly impressed by Scot's passionate advocacy for expanded U.S. engagement with ASEAN and its member states, as well as his extraordinary familiarity with the complexities of the region.

It is not unusual in the Foreign Service to work alongside an impressive colleague with deep knowledge and enthusiasm for a particular part of the world. Nor was Scot the only officer I knew who could artfully work the system to get smart and timely policy decisions from the stodgy bureaucracy (although he was certainly one of the best!). The things that set Scot apart included his amazing sense of humor, his ability to stay focused on the things that truly mattered, his unflappable calm amid near-constant commotion, and—most importantly— his care and mentorship of more junior staff. I had these extraordinary qualities in mind when several years later I became the EAP assistant secretary and asked Scot, who was wrapping up his assignment as ambassador to Indonesia, to come back to headquarters as the number two in the bureau. I had many, many occasions over the next three years to be grateful that he said yes.

Imperfect Partners is part memoir and part foreign policy study— a fascinating hybrid that combines lucid explanations of the important issues that Scot dealt with and a highly personal chronicle of his memorable adventures. The book is refreshing and believable in large part because the author does not flinch from describing America's own imperfections, both in the messy business of making foreign policy, and as seen as seen through the eyes of our Asian interlocutors when diplomats like Scot try to implement those policies.

As loyal as they come, Scot Marciel nonetheless recognized, even as a young diplomat on his first overseas assignment in the Philippines, that the best laid plans of Washington's much-vaunted interagency policy committee would not survive the first brush with reality. Sitting at a conference table in the basement of the White House, it had been easy to decide that the United States would simply pressure the Filipino strongman Ferdinand Marcos to implement reforms that would enable a democratic transition to a new, legitimate government. But in the field, talking to the Filipino people and dealing with the reality of the Marcos regime, Scot could see that "reform" was not in the cards. Events quickly proved him right, and we are treated in this book to a dramatic street-level, first-hand account of the extraordinary exercise of "People Power" by the citizens of the Philippines, as well as the behind-the-scenes policy debates and maneuvering of top American officials.

This book reflects Scot's direct involvement in some of the most consequential turning points in America's relationships with Vietnam, Burma, Thailand, and other Southeast Asian states. His personal bond with an Indonesian furniture-retailer-turned-governor, for example, later served to jump-start a new era in U.S.-Indonesia relations when that governor—Joko Widodo—became president. Who other than Scot Marciel could have convinced the secretary of state to fly forty-plus hours roundtrip in an Air Force plane just to attend the inauguration in Jakarta—a gesture that paid huge dividends for the United States? Who other than Scot had the credibility with all the critical players in Burma, as well as with key policymakers back home, to ensure the United States remained positively engaged in promoting reform and reconciliation at the same time it was leading the campaign to end Burma's brutal mistreatment of the minority Rohingya community?

Yet, *Imperfect Partners* is far more than a collection of war stories (although there are some doozies). It is a deeply thoughtful analysis of the challenges facing the United States in the region and a set of well-reasoned recommendations on the policy choices available to today's decision-makers in Washington. Like the rest of this captivating book, Scot's proposals are down-to-earth, sensible, and eminently wise. In particular, I commend the insightful discussion of the underappreciated impact of U.S. assistance on so-called nontraditional security threats such as disease, extreme weather, and water security. Long before the outbreak of COVID-19, Scot had been involved in helping Southeast Asian nations contend with SARS, with devastating typhoons, and with illegal fishing. He lays out a compelling case for how U.S. support now in these areas benefits American interests, above and beyond the humanitarian rationale. His advice about focusing on Southeast Asian youth should be heeded in Washington as well. The United States should be seizing the opportunity to influence and engage in a dynamic region with a digitally savvy population, roughly half of whom—over three hundred million people—are under the age of thirty.

It would be hard to find another book that conveys, with nearly the authority or the modesty of Scot Marciel, the realities of diplomacy, the policy process, the personalities, and the interest groups that have shaped the course of U.S.-Southeast Asian relations. *Imperfect Partners* sheds great light on people and events of profound historical significance. But more importantly, this book offers a roadmap for how we should understand and approach the challenges of today and the opportunities of tomorrow.

Daniel R. Russel
Vice President for International Security and Diplomacy
Asia Society Policy Institute

Acknowledgments

I want to thank a number of people who put in a lot of time and effort to help me with this book, offering ideas that helped me shape it, reading and commenting on draft chapters, and encouraging me to believe that I could actually finish the book. This is in addition to the many colleagues and friends who allowed me to interview them for the book.

Specifically, I want to thank, in no particular order, Adam Schwarz, Professor Catharin Dalpino, Ambassador Kristie Kenney, Ambassador Patrick Murphy, Ben Rhodes, Ambassador Bill Heidt, Andy Rothman, Richard Childress, Melissa Brown, Bill Flens, Ambassador Nina Hachigian, Lionel Johnson, David Galbraith, Alyce Abadalla, and Ambassador Bob Blake for taking time to read and provide helpful comments on many of my draft chapters. Collectively, they saved me from multiple errors of fact and memory, pointed out flaws of logic and organization, and reminded me of many key points that I had failed to include. None of them, of course, is responsible for any errors or flawed analysis in the book—those are all on me.

I also want to thank Professor Gi-Wook Shin and Professor Don Emmerson of the Walter H. Shorenstein Asia Pacific Research Center, part of the Freeman Spogli Institute at Stanford University, for welcoming me to the center, encouraging me to write this book, supporting my research and writing, and offering many ideas and suggestions that helped me frame and focus my thoughts.

The U.S. Department of State has reviewed this manuscript prior to publication. The opinions and characterizations in this piece are those of the author, and do not necessarily represent official positions of the United States government.

Scot Marciel
November 2022
Stanford, California

Abbreviations

AA	Arakan Army
ACMECS	Ayeyawaddy-Chao Phraya-Mekong Economic Cooperation Strategy
AEC	ASEAN Economic Community
AFP	Armed Forces of the Philippines
AFTA	ASEAN Free Trade Agreement
AIIB	Asian Infrastructure Investment Bank
APEC	Asia Pacific Economic Coordination
APSC	ASEAN Political and Security Community
ARF	ASEAN Regional Forum
ARMM	Autonomous Region of Muslim Mindanao
ARSA	Arakan Rohingya Salvation Army
ASEAN	Association of Southeast Asian Nations
ASG	Abu Sayyaf Group
ASSC	ASEAN Socio Cultural Community
ATA	Anti-Terrorism Assistance
BIA	Burmese Independence Army
BRI	Belt and Road Initiative
BRR	Badan Rehabilitasi dan Rekonstruksi
BSPP	Burma Socialist Programme Party
CDC	Center for Disease Control
CMEC	China-Myanmar Economic Corridor

CNRP	Cambodia National Rescue Party
COC	Code of Conduct
COMELEC	Commission on Elections
CPP	Cambodian People's Party
CPP	Communist Party of the Philippines
CPTPP	Comprehensive and Progressive Agreement for Trans-Pacific Partnership
DFC	Development Finance Corporation
DOC	Declaration of Conduct
EAO	ethnic armed organization
EAP	Bureau of East Asian and Pacific Affairs (in the U.S. State Department)
EAS	East Asia Summit
ECLR	Malaysian East Coast Light Rail
EDCA	Enhanced Defense Cooperation Agreement
EDL	Electricite du Laos
EEZ	exclusive economic zone
FPNCC	Federal Political Negotiation and Consultative Committee
FUNCINPEC	National United Front for an Independent, Neutral, Peaceful and Cooperative Cambodia
GAM	Gerakan Aceh Merdeka, or Free Aceh Movement
GDP	gross domestic product
ICJ	International Court of Justice
ICMI	Indonesian Association of Muslim Intellectuals
IDP	internally displaced person
IMET	International Military Education Training
IPEF	Indo-Pacific Economic Framework for Prosperity
ITLOS	International Tribunal on the Law of the Sea
JI	Jemaah Islamiyah (movement)
JMSU	Joint Marine Seismic Undertaking
JSOTF-P	Joint Special Operations Task Force–Philippines
JTF-FA	Joint Task Force Full Accounting
KIA	Kachin Independence Army
KIO	Kachin Independence Organization
KNU	Karen National Union

KPK	Komisi Pemberantasan Korupsi, or Corruption Eradication Commission
KPNLF	Khmer People's National Liberation Front
LMC	Lancang-Mekong Cooperation
MCC	Millennium Challenge Corporation
MIA	missing in action
MILF	Moro Islamic Liberation Front
MLSA	Mutual Logistics Support Agreement
MNDAA	Myanmar National Democracy Alliance Army
MNLF	Moro National Liberation Front
MPR	Majelis Permusyawaratan Rakyat, or People's Consultative Assembly
NAFTA	North American Free Trade Agreement
NAMFREL	National Movement for Free Elections
NBI	National Bureau of Investigation
NDAA	National Democracy Alliance Army
NGO	non-governmental organization
NLD	National League for Democracy
NPA	New People's Army
NSC	National Security Council
NU	Nadhlatul Ulama
NUG	National Unity Government
ODP	Orderly Departure Program
PACOM	U.S. Pacific Command
PAD	People's Alliance for Democracy
PDI	Indonesian Democratic Party
PDI-P	Partai Demokrasi Indonesia Perjuangan (Indonesian Democratic Party of Struggle)
PKI	Partai Komunis Indonesia (Indonesian Communist Party)
PKP	Philippine Communist Party
PNI	Indonesia Nationalist Party
POW	prisoner of war
PPP	People's Power Party
RAM	Reform of the Armed Forces Movement
RCEP	Regional Comprehensive Economic Partnership

SAC	State Administrative Council
SBY	Susilo Bambang Yudhoyono
SDN	Specially Designated Nationals
SEATO	Southeast Asia Treaty Organization
SEZ	special economic zone
SLORC	State Law and Order Restoration Council
SPDC	State Peace and Development Council
SRP	Sam Rainsy Party
TAC	Treaty of Amity and Cooperation
TAF	Transaction Advisory Fund
TIFA	Trade and Investment Framework Agreement
TNI	Tentara Nasional Indonesia (Indonesian Armed Forces)
TPP	Trans-Pacific Partnership
UNCLOS	UN Convention on the Law of the Sea
UNTAC	UN Transitional Authority for Cambodia
USAID	U.S. Agency for International Development
USDA	Union Solidary and Development Association
USDP	Union Solidarity and Development Party
UWSA	United Wa State Army
VFA	Visiting Forces Agreement
WHO	World Health Organization
WTO	World Trade Organization

Chronology of Scot Marciel's Diplomatic Assignments on Southeast Asia

1985–86	Vice Consul at the U.S. Embassy in the Philippines. Served as observer for 1986 "snap" elections and witnessed the "People Power" revolution.
1987–89	Economic Officer at the U.S. Consulate General in São Paulo, Brazil.
1990–92	Laos Desk Officer in the State Department's Office of Vietnam, Laos, and Cambodian Affairs, working on POW/MIA issues, refugee matters, and early steps toward normalization of relations with Vietnam.
1993–96	First U.S. diplomat to work in Hanoi since the end of the Vietnam War. Led initial U.S. Department of State Office, then served as Chief of the Political-Economic Section at the U.S. Liaison Office and then at the U.S. Embassy. Deeply involved in normalization and development of diplomatic relations.
1996–99	Economic officer at the U.S. Consulate General in Hong Kong during the territory's reversion to Chinese rule and the Asian Financial Crisis.
1999–2001	Deputy Director of the State Department's Office of Monetary Affairs, engaged in debt relief and the U.S. response to economic crises in Indonesia, Turkey, Argentina, and elsewhere.
2001–04	Economic Counselor at the U.S. Embassy in Turkey.
2004–05	Director of the State Department's Office of Southern European Affairs.

2005–06   Director of the State Department's Office of Mainland Southeast Asia, responsible for relations with Vietnam, Laos, Cambodia, Thailand, and Burma.

2006–07   Director of the State Department's Office of Maritime Southeast Asia, responsible for relations with Indonesia, Philippines, Malaysia, Singapore, and Brunei.

2007–10   Deputy Assistant Secretary of State for East Asia and the Pacific, responsible for relations with Southeast Asia. Beginning in 2008, served concurrently as the first U.S. Ambassador for ASEAN Affairs, based in Washington, DC.

2010–13   U.S. Ambassador to Indonesia.

2013–16   Principal Deputy Assistant Secretary of State for East Asia and the Pacific, responsible for relations with Southeast Asia.

2016–20   U.S. Ambassador to Myanmar.

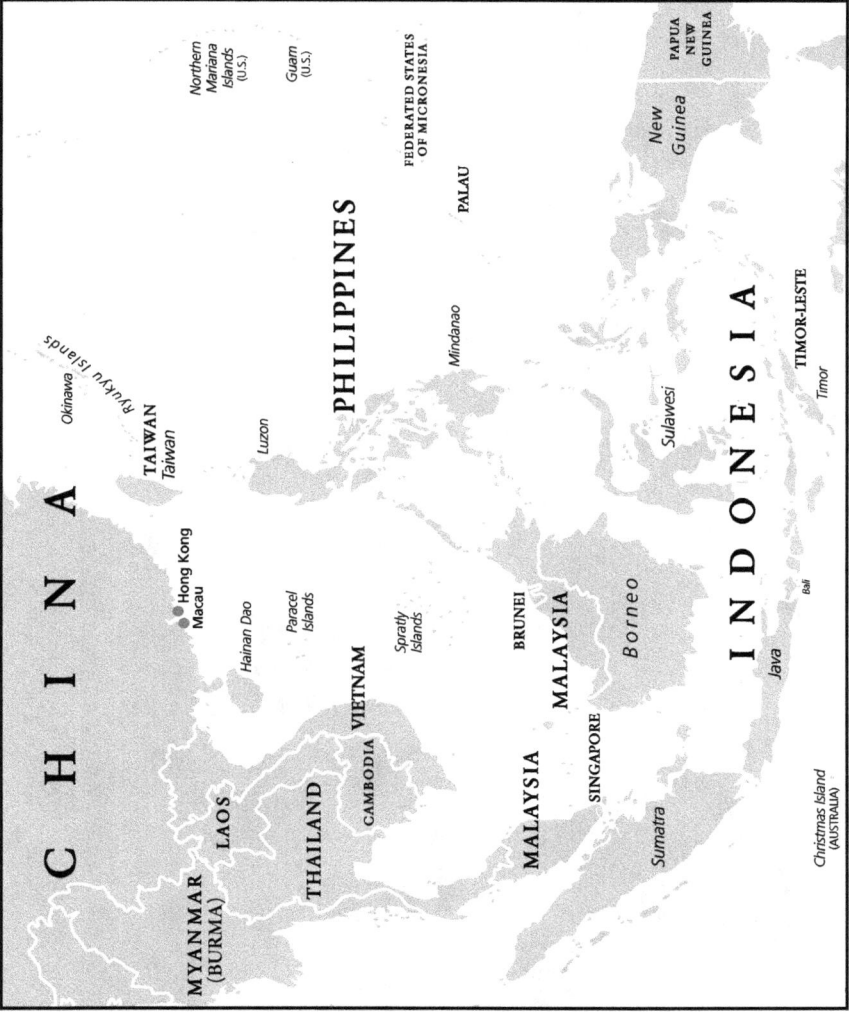

Imperfect Partners

Introduction

The writer Patrick Winn called Southeast Asia "heaven for the compulsively curious."[1] Lucky for me, because through a combination of accident, good fortune, and a few random decisions I have spent a good part of the past thirty-seven years working in or on the region as an American diplomat. There has been a certain Forrest Gump element to my journey, as I have been able to witness and participate in some remarkable events, and meet many incredible men and women who, in big ways and small, have helped shape the future for their countries and the region.

My introduction to the region was the Philippines in the dying days of the Ferdinand Marcos regime. I saw insurgency, corruption, injustice, and poverty, but also a people's yearning for democracy and the triumph of People Power. I was fortunate to go to Hanoi to help reestablish relations with our former enemy Vietnam and to participate in the difficult and impressive shift from foe to friend. I spent three years in newly democratic Indonesia, where change clashed with vested interests, and watched a young politician rise by offering good governance. I joined the euphoria of Aung San Suu Kyi's inauguration in Myanmar and struggled to find solutions to the tragedy of unending ethnic conflict and the forced exodus of the Rohingya.

I also have been constantly reminded of the tremendous diversity in the region; it might be a unit geographically (to some degree), but the

---

1 Patrick Winn, *Hello, Shadowlands: Inside the Meth Fiefdoms, Rebel Hideouts and Bomb-Scarred Party Towns of Southeast Asia* (UK, Icon Books, Ltd., 2019), prologue.

histories, cultures, languages, forms of government, and attitudes vary widely from country to country. That is why I am wary of the label Southeast Asian "expert." I like the term "aficionado" more, as it suggests great interest without assuming full understanding.

During years in Washington, I assisted in efforts to modernize our longstanding alliances with Thailand and the Philippines, to continue building the relationship with Vietnam, and to reassure ever-wary friends in the region of the United States' continuing commitment in the face of a rising China that saw the region as its sphere of influence. I served as the United States' first ambassador for the Association of Southeast Asian Nations (ASEAN)—the regional grouping that brings together ten Southeast Asian countries—and worked to help colleagues and the American public understand Southeast Asia and its rising importance to us.

Southeast Asia *is* important. The ten ASEAN states are home to 650 million people, nearly matching the combined populations of the United States and European Union. Several of these nations lie between China and India, while others straddle the crucial trade routes between East and West. Southeast Asia is home to the world's largest Muslim-majority population (Indonesia), to tens of millions of Buddhists, and to one of the world's biggest Catholic populations (Philippines). It could have become the second front in the war on terror but managed to avoid that fate. A handful of Southeast Asian countries have claims in the South China Sea, where China is using its might to try to assert control and sovereignty—despite the weakness of its claims—over vast reaches of island-dotted sea in a clear test of the international community's willingness and ability to insist that nations follow international law and practice.

Few people realize the size or importance of Southeast Asia's economy, or know of its remarkable potential. The ten Southeast Asian nations that collectively make up ASEAN saw their collective gross domestic product (GDP) grow five-fold between 2000 and 2018, reaching $3 trillion. Combined they would be the world's fifth-largest economy and one of its largest exporters. They are the United States' fourth-largest export market, and home to more U.S. investment than China, Japan, India, and Korea combined. GDP growth averaged more than 5 percent yearly in 2000-08, and the percentage of the population living in poverty fell from 47 percent in 1990 to 14 percent in 2015. The region's demographics are a strength, with one-third of the population under twenty years of age and only 7.5 percent over sixty-five.[2] With its youthful population (in sharp contrast to the aging populations of northern Asia), consistently high economic growth rates, and impressive digital connectivity, there is good reason to expect Southeast Asia to become an even more important part of the world economy in the coming years. While the COVID-19 pandemic is setting back the region's economies, as it is those in the rest of the world, Vietnam and other Southeast Asian nations are also positioning themselves to benefit from the nascent diversification of manufacturing out of China and as potential tech start-up hotspots.

A few problems threaten this bright future, however. First, despite strong popular demand for greater democracy and better governance, the powerful elites who dominate many Southeast Asian countries have largely been able to maintain their grip on power, sometimes taking small steps to accommodate public demands but doing little to share real power or allow the creation of institutions that would fight corruption, offer justice, or provide for accountability. This weakness in political development holds the region back. Indonesia has moved the farthest down the democratic path, though it still faces many challenges, including endemic corruption and the risk of more political clashes between Islamists and secularists. Others, such as Thailand, have regressed, though even there we see continued public demands for greater democracy and reform. Most recently, Myanmar, after a surprising if flawed democratic opening, has suffered a major setback in the form of a military coup and subsequent brutal crackdown on protestors.

Second, ethnic and religious differences continue to cause tension, division, and even violence in several Southeast Asian countries. Myanmar is the most obvious case, as some two dozen ethnic armed groups continue their decades-old struggle for greater autonomy from the ethnic Bamar-dominated central government, while intolerant religious nationalists claiming to be defending Buddhism promote division and helped create an environment in which many considered it acceptable for the military to drive the Rohingya population out of the

---

2 Data from U.S.-ASEAN Business Council Website, https://www.usasean.org/why -asean, and ASEANStats Website, Infographics on ASEAN Socio-Demographic and Economic Indicators, https://www.aseanstats.org/infographics/socio-demographic -and-economic/.

country. Separatist movements in southern Thailand and the southern Philippines have persisted, with minority Muslim populations (who in the case of Thailand are also ethnic Malay) fighting for independence or autonomy. Indonesia has largely tamed its separatist elements, save in Papua, but like Myanmar is struggling to prevent a small hardline and intolerant element within the majority religion from spreading its divisive and dangerous message. As is true throughout the world, the threat of religious- or ethnic-based nationalism warrants close attention.

These problems demand attention for obvious reasons, but also because they leave at least some of the countries in the region more vulnerable to unwanted outside influence than they otherwise would be. Widespread corruption among entrenched political and economic elites in some countries, for example, not only frustrates and upsets the public at large, but also results in shady deals with unscrupulous foreign interests that further entrench the elite, distort the economy, and in some cases chip away at sovereignty. Religious and ethnic tensions can cross borders, but also invite in outside actors—e.g., foreign terrorists or extremist elements—who can engage in violence and exacerbate existing domestic tensions.

The risk of excessive Chinese influence poses yet another challenge to Southeast Asia's otherwise promising outlook. The issue here is not China's rise per se, as that has brought important economic benefits to Southeast Asia. Rather, the concern is the growing evidence that some Chinese policies and activities pose a threat to the sovereignty and full independence of Southeast Asian nations. China is using its economic clout to attain a level of leverage over its neighbors that could greatly limit their freedom of maneuver; in some cases it is going further, using its physical might to assert its will. The latter is most obvious in the South China Sea, but one can also see it in the Mekong, where Chinese upstream hydropower projects are giving it power over essential water flows to the riverine Southeast Asian countries.

Along its borders with Laos (officially, the Lao People's Democratic Republic) and Myanmar, China is physically encroaching on its neighbors, through a combination of undocumented Chinese migration, nontransparent deals with corrupt local businesses or officials, and establishment of economic zones that appear to be de facto Chinese settlements, full of Chinese workers, using Chinese currency and payment systems, and effectively off-limits to local law enforcement. In Myanmar, the Chinese are supplying weapons to insurgent groups and turning a blind eye to shipments of precursor chemicals that international criminal syndicates are using to produce and distribute massive amounts of methamphetamines while undermining government authority. The relationship with China is hugely important to all of Southeast Asia and managing it effectively, while maintaining full independence of action, will be both difficult and essential.

This brings us to Southeast Asia's relations with the United States, the focal point of this book. The United States has cooperated closely with Southeast Asia in the economic, political, security, and cultural realms over the years, bringing significant benefits to both sides of the Pacific. Still, my friends in the region often talk about how the United States does not truly understand Southeast Asia or how to engage effectively with it. They are not wrong. At least for as long as I have been working in the region, we—myself included—have struggled to understand it and to figure out how best to plug into it.

Part of the problem is the very notion of Southeast Asia as a region. People who have not spent a lot of time in the area tend to think that it represents a community with some kind of shared history, ethos, and outlook. It does not. The nations of the region have different histories, cultures, and religions; different levels of economic development, different legal and political systems, and different foreign policies. For outsiders, the clubby, informal, and friendly ASEAN meetings suggest a level of intimacy and like-mindedness that does not really exist, outside of foreign ministries. In fact, the countries of the region established ASEAN back in 1967 largely to manage friction and mistrust among themselves, fearing that clashes between them would invite the great powers to intervene and interfere. The one thing all ten ASEAN members can agree on is that they are vulnerable to the great powers and need to work together as much as possible to preserve their national and regional autonomy, and to amplify their collective voice so as to have a say in what happens in their environs.

A second contributing factor is the lack of U.S. expertise on the region. If a U.S. diplomat is assigned to Japan, China, or Korea, he or she can read hundreds if not thousands of books and turn to countless experts for knowledge and advice. That is not the case for Southeast Asia, both due to the dearth of quality books and experts in general and because knowledge or expertise in a specific country does not necessarily help very much in the country next door. These days, there are a huge number of academics and think tankers studying, speaking, and writing on China, but only a handful covering Southeast Asia. At Stanford's Walter H. Shorenstein Asia-Pacific Research Center, for example, there are more than a dozen people studying and writing on various aspects of China right now. There are two of us working on all of Southeast Asia.

Third, and related to the above items, since the end of the Vietnam War, official Washington has largely viewed Southeast Asia as a sideshow, except when a crisis or natural disaster hits. Foreign policy elites have tended to focus on the Middle East and Europe, at least until recently, often for good reason. With a few important exceptions, Asia policy has been dominated by China or Japan experts, who like many of us have a hard time figuring out whether to deal with Southeast Asia as a unit or as a collection of vaguely similar but confusingly different states. When they venture into ASEAN meetings, hoping to find Southeast Asian coherence and clarity, they usually depart disappointed and revert to focusing on one or more bilateral relationships in the region that have caught their attention.

A fundamental problem in trying to get consistent top-level Washington engagement and strategic focus is that, while Southeast Asia is important strategically, politically, culturally, and economically, it does not offer an easy handgrip for the uninitiated in the form of a dominant player or a powerful regional organization. To refer to the overused analogy of Europe, Southeast Asia boasts neither a Germany nor a Brussels. Indonesia is by far the biggest player, and is the one country capable of throwing its weight around in the region. With rare exceptions, however, it chooses not to do so. It is not the Indonesian way, and that probably makes most of its neighbors happy. ASEAN is a useful institution, but it is not the European Commission, nor was it ever intended to be.

Moreover, with the exception of Singapore and Vietnam, the Southeast Asian governments do not work Washington very well, and sometimes are not particularly willing or able U.S. partners. Washington policymakers are constantly pulled in many directions, and—if a country is not either incredibly important or in crisis—they are hesitant to invest significant time and resources in working on it, absent clear signs that the other country is interested and at least reasonably capable of making increased engagement productive.

For Washington policymakers, then, it is easy to base Asia policy largely on the actions and approaches of the big players—China, Japan, Korea, and Australia—and to deal with Southeast Asia episodically and, as I noted, as a sideshow. We Southeast Asian hands often joke about the look we get from Northeast Asia hands whenever we pipe up about the importance of Southeast Asia.

This was not always the case. During the Cold War, the conflicts in Laos and then Vietnam dominated the Washington foreign policy agenda. We focused intensively on—and invested heavily in—supporting our allies and friends against the threat of communist expansion, mostly on the Southeast Asia mainland but also in places such as Indonesia. When the Vietnam War ended, many in the United States felt that we had focused *too much* on Southeast Asia, and so there was a perhaps inevitable decline in U.S. engagement. To the extent policymakers did look at the region post-1975, they continued to view developments through the Cold War prism. We worked closely with ASEAN to counter what we saw as Soviet-backed Vietnamese aggression in Cambodia, and engaged heavily in the Philippines—home to critical U.S. bases—to push longtime ally Ferdinand Marcos to reform and, when that failed, to encourage his departure and a peaceful democratic transition in the face of a growing communist insurgency.

With the fall of the Soviet Union and end of the Cold War, we lost our strategic prism for the region. We established and then developed relations with an emerging Vietnam, which was important and temporarily reinvigorated our interest in the region, but that was more about healing our own internal wounds and ending Cambodia's tragedy than it was grand strategy. Over the next twenty years or so, strategic interests fell to the wayside and were replaced by a strong push for democratic reform and greater respect for human rights, along with more attention to bilateral trade issues. This approach was understandable, given the absence of a strategic rival, but it meant long-term relationships and even alliances did not keep Washington from playing hardball on shorter-term economic and human rights issues. U.S. attention to the region was intermittent, as crises and problems elsewhere in the world demanded Washington's involvement.

When the Asia Financial Crisis hit in 1997–98, the United States—with a few exceptions—did not jump in to offer substantial assistance, but supported the International Monetary Fund's orthodox approach, which in the region was seen as particularly bitter. Indonesia's democratic transition—and the violent turmoil and risk of disintegration that accompanied it—captured our attention for a while because of the country's overwhelming importance and the interest of then assistant secretary of state Stanley Roth, but it has been difficult to sustain. The September 11 attacks focused our attention on the region—particularly Indonesia and the Philippines—as a potential second front in the war on terror, but that was fleeting, as the George W. Bush administration devoted much of its foreign policy energy to the Middle East and Afghanistan. Overall, while generally maintaining good relations with most of the region, we tended to measure countries and adjust the quality of our relationships—including with our treaty allies—based on their progress, or lack thereof, on democratic and human rights grounds. Again, Vietnam and Singapore stood out as exceptions, as they managed to maintain our interest and engagement despite the lack of political reform.

We have pushed democracy and human rights so hard because they represent our fundamental values, but also because we believed—and I continue to believe—that the people of the region want greater democracy and the ability to exercise their fundamental rights, not to mention better and more transparent governance. Long-term U.S. support for human rights, democracy, and improved governance overall has been a force for good in the region, and helps explain much of the goodwill the United States enjoys. The emerging democratic trends we saw in the region in the 1980s and 1990s gave us hope and created high expectations that, for the most part, have not been met. The region's failure to live up to these expectations has frustrated and disappointed Washington policymakers. Our tendency to react strongly to setbacks in these areas, along with our inconsistent engagement, has sometimes disappointed our erstwhile partners in the region.

After the Cold War, we saw a substantial increase in influence over policymaking toward the region by a number of individuals and organizations that normally would play only a marginal role in U.S. foreign policy. Congress largely took control of Burma policy via legislation, and key congressional staffers played an outsized role in determining policy toward Cambodia and even Indonesia. Also, with the increased focus on democracy and human rights, nongovernmental advocacy groups gained substantial influence, using their connections and their public messaging to insist upon tough U.S. responses to democratic backsliding and human rights problems. Congress passed legislation mandating that the executive branch do more to monitor and to rank—and if need be to sanction—countries for failing to cooperate sufficiently with the United States on trafficking in persons, religious freedom, and other matters.

The Obama administration introduced the "pivot," later known as the "rebalance." The administration's foreign policy team recognized that for years Washington had neglected Asia, particularly Southeast Asia, because of its intense focus on Iraq, Afghanistan, and the broader

Middle East. They decided to pay more attention to the region. The result was that, after years of episodic engagement, the United States showed up and engaged consistently with ASEAN and its member states. It signed ASEAN's Treaty of Amity and Cooperation, participated actively at ASEAN-hosted regional meetings, launched annual U.S.-ASEAN Leaders meetings, joined the East Asia Summit, and continued to negotiate the Trans-Pacific Partnership trade deal. It was a good move, though it did not constitute a full strategic shift. U.S. assistance to the region increased only marginally and remained a fraction of what we spend in Africa, the Middle East, or Latin America. The United States stepped up our efforts to support the ASEAN claimant states on the South China Sea issue, but stopped short of any direct confrontation with Beijing when China began muscling its way into others' exclusive economic zones.

China's growing role and increasing assertiveness—and concerns that it has sought to establish overwhelming influence if not domination of Southeast Asia—has restored more of a strategic focus to the U.S. approach to the region in recent years. That approach, however, has suffered from a couple of major faults. First, while on the one hand recognizing the strategic importance of working with all ten ASEAN members to help them maintain maximum maneuvering room and autonomy, much of official Washington—including Congress—has continued to calibrate U.S. willingness to engage and work with countries based on their progress or lack thereof on democratic reform and respect for human rights. Sometimes the United States ends up pulling back sharply on engagement or even imposing sanctions, undermining the strategic goal of maintaining regular dialogue and interaction. Striking the right balance on these matters is challenging, but I have seen too many Washington players fail to accept that there is a trade-off.

Also, the United States has not been willing to put its money where its mouth is. Outside of the Pentagon budget, U.S. funds for assistance and the all-important exchange and education programs are a pittance. U.S. assistance is often effective in bringing real benefits to communities, as well as improved governance, but it is insufficient. Nobody is suggesting the United States should try to match China dollar for yuan, but it could and should do a lot better.

Third, U.S. strategy has lacked a sustained trade pillar. Like everywhere, trade and other economic relations matter enormously in Southeast Asia, and have a direct impact on the level of influence we and other outside powers enjoy. If Washington is not going to pursue some successor of the Trans-Pacific Partnership, it needs to come up with *some* trade strategy for Southeast Asia. Regardless of your feelings about the partnership, you cannot fight something with nothing.

Last and most important, the U.S. approach toward Southeast Asia cannot be simply a corollary of its China strategy. The United States needs to engage and build closer partnerships with Southeast Asia on the region's own merits and based on a positive agenda. I am convinced that, despite our many differences and the fact that we have often disappointed each other—we have been imperfect partners—the United States shares with Southeast Asian governments and publics many interests, especially ensuring the full independence and autonomy of all of the countries and the region as a whole. There also is a significant reservoir of goodwill in the region toward the United States.

Think about it in terms of physics. Southeast Asia consists of a number of countries of modest mass (mass being defined here as military, economic, diplomatic, and demographic clout), and one—Indonesia—of somewhat greater mass. One does not have to be anti-Chinese to understand that, as China's mass grows, the only way to resist its gravitational pull—and thus ensure freedom of maneuver and genuine autonomy for the region and the individual states—is for the Southeast Asians to strengthen themselves, and for other major players (i.e., the United States, along with key partners such as Japan, Australia, and India) to provide a balancing gravitational pull. It is not a matter of turning ASEAN into an anti-China group, which is a nonstarter anyway. Rather, it is a matter of the Southeast Asians doing all they can to increase their individual and collective strength and cohesion, and for the United States (along with allies and friends) to help ensure their freedom of movement by providing a reliable magnetic pull of its own. This will require tending not only to the bilateral relationships, but also ensuring a consistent focus on engaging wisely and effectively in the alphabet soup of regional ASEAN-centered fora that are easy for Americans to play down but that are of critical importance.

This book is an attempt to share some of what I have experienced in and learned about the region and U.S. engagement with the region over the past thirty-seven years. It is not meant to be a comprehensive study of the region, or an encyclopedic review of U.S. relations with all countries in the region. Rather, it is more of a collection of observations, analysis, and thoughts on the region and U.S. policy based on my own experiences, supplemented by research and discussions with current and former colleagues and counterparts. As a result, it necessarily focuses heavily on my assignments in the Philippines, Vietnam, Indonesia, Myanmar, and as ambassador for ASEAN affairs, though it also will cover key issues that I dealt with from Washington. The book includes a fair amount of history, because many of our policy mistakes have come from a failure to understand that history. It also discusses important domestic developments in the region, and the interplay between those developments and U.S. policy. My hope is that, by tracing the key happenings in the region and in some of our relationships over the past few decades, I can flesh out some of the ideas noted above and offer a few modest thoughts on the way ahead.

Given my role, the perspective is necessarily one of an American diplomat who has dealt with the challenges of working with foreign governments and within my own. And, as my Indonesian friends would say, I apologize in advance for anything I write that is not accurate or causes offense.

I. The Allies

CHAPTER ONE

A Troubled Ally

The Philippines under Marcos

It was well after midnight, in the early hours of February 23, 1986. I had just dropped off my girlfriend (now my wife) at her parents' house in the suburb of Marikina and was driving home down Epifanio de los Santos Avenue—commonly known as EDSA—one of the main thoroughfares through metropolitan Manila. Normally, few people were on the streets this late, but as I crossed through a major intersection, there were swarms of people gathering near two downtown military facilities, Camp Aguinaldo and Camp Crame. I assumed they must be preparing for a protest, since demonstrations were common in those days as people rallied against longtime president and dictator Ferdinand Marcos's perceived stealing of the presidential election held a few weeks earlier.

Early the next morning, a colleague called to tell me that Defense Minister Juan Ponce Enrile and Constabulary Chief General Fidel Ramos had turned against Marcos and were supporting Marcos's electoral opponent, Cory Aquino. It turned out that Enrile, Ramos, and their troops had holed up in camps Aguinaldo and Crame the previous night, and—in response to a public plea by influential Catholic cardinal Jaime Sin—crowds of people had begun flocking to the area to offer their support. Thus began what became known as the Philippine People Power revolution, which resulted in the ouster of Marcos and the restoration of democracy just a few days later. Remarkably, I had driven right through the early stages of this historic revolt and been largely oblivious—not an auspicious beginning to a career in which success depends heavily on one's powers of observation and awareness.

I had arrived in Manila ten months earlier to begin my diplomatic career and, as it turned out, my decades-long engagement with Southeast Asia. I had written my master's thesis on U.S. human rights policy in the Philippines, so had been delighted to volunteer for the posting when it showed up on the list of assignments available to our entry-level class of foreign service officers. It was not a sought-after posting for first-tour officers: inevitably, 90 percent of the job would be conducting visa interviews, because Manila processed a huge number of visa applications. I ignored that downside, thinking maybe I would be fortunate enough to see the end of the Marcos dictatorship. (This was less prescience than hope, to be sure.)

My first reaction to Manila was sensory overload. Not in the sense of the clichés about the exotic, spice-scented, coconut tree–swaying tropics, but rather an overwhelming combination of noise, traffic, pollution, and sweaty heat. Manila at the time was home to some seven million people, and they all seemed to be on the street at once, occupying everything from luxury sedans to smoke-belching buses to the omnipresent *jeepneys*, in which perhaps a dozen Filipinos would cram themselves into an impossibly small pair of benches behind the cab. It did not take long to see deep and widespread poverty, whether in the notorious slums or among the child beggars on Roxas Boulevard, the main road along Manila Bay connecting my apartment to the U.S. embassy. It also did not take long to notice the uniformed guards—usually armed with assault rifles—in front of virtually every business. Guns were everywhere in the city, and across the country.

The Colonial Legacy

The Philippines in the mid-1980s was both an important U.S. treaty ally and a country that, in the words of Assistant Secretary of State for East Asia and the Pacific Paul Wolfowitz, was in "deep trouble."[1] The U.S.-Philippine alliance had been born out of a unique history: the Philippines had been a U.S. colony, and the two nations' histories had been intertwined for a century. After more than three centuries of Spanish colonial rule, Filipinos under Emilio Aguinaldo were fighting

---

1 *Administration Review of U.S. Policy Toward the Philippines: Hearing Before the Comm. on Foreign Relations*, 99th Cong. (October 30, 1985) (statement of Paul D. Wolfowitz).

for independence in the late 1890s. When the United States launched a war against Spain in 1898—mostly over Cuba, where residents also were fighting for independence—the Philippines became an important part of the campaign. A U.S. fleet under Commodore George Dewey won a decisive victory over the Spanish fleet in Manila Bay, and President McKinley followed up by sending U.S. troops to the Philippines. The Filipino rebels expected the United States to support their independence struggle and were enraged when instead the Philippines was taken as a colony (by Spain's cession under the Treaty of Paris). Many Filipinos were unwilling to accept a new colonizer. The result was three years of often brutal fighting between the United States and Filipinos that left the former in charge as a colonial power.

The United States ruled the Philippines fully until 1935, when it granted the Philippines limited autonomy ahead of full independence in 1946. During the period of colonial rule, with all the inevitable negatives colonization brings, the United States did introduce free education (in English) and offered duty-free status to imports from the Philippines. This led to heavy Philippine dependence on the United States for trade and investment, with U.S. trade accounting for well over half of Philippine total trade in the period leading up to independence. The colonial period also resulted in initial Filipino immigration to the United States, which over time created a significant Filipino American population.

The combination of Spanish and American rule of a largely ethnic-Malay population produced a unique culture, which one Filipino friend described as "Malay, with three hundred years of heavy Spanish-Catholic influence, and a thin veneer of Americana on top." Many of us at the embassy noticed the Spanish-Catholic influence, not only in terms of names, language, and religion, but also in the form of land-based oligarchies and politics that in many ways resembled Latin America more than the rest of Southeast Asia.

The Philippines saw heavy fighting during World War II, starting with the Japanese defeat of combined U.S. and Philippine forces on the Bataan Peninsula and Corregidor Island, the former the starting point for the brutal Bataan Death March, the latter the site of General Douglas MacArthur's escape and his resulting "I shall return" vow (actually offered in Australia, not the Philippines). Four years of combat culminated in the Battle of Manila, which left the city more damaged than any other city in the war, other than Warsaw. My late father-in-law recalled running through the streets of the city as a child with his family trying to escape the fighting in early 1945, only to turn around and see his father killed by a bomb.

The United States granted the Philippines full independence in 1946, and in 1947 the two countries signed an agreement that gave the United States the right to several bases, most notably Subic Bay naval base and Clark Air Base, which were for years the largest U.S. overseas bases in the world. Successive U.S. administrations viewed these bases as critical strategic assets throughout the Cold War, and the United States made heavy use of them during the Vietnam War.

The alliance and relationship went beyond these bases, however. Despite the ugliness of colonial rule, the colonial era and the experience of World War II ensured the two nations had a considerable period of shared history. U.S. cultural influence, for good or bad, was and is remarkably heavy, with many Filipinos listening to U.S. music, watching U.S. movies and television, and otherwise feeling a strong attachment to things American. Even the ubiquitous jeepneys, the gaudy minibuses that ferry so many Filipinos around, trace their history to surplus U.S. jeeps from World War II. Immigration has played a huge role in this shared history, with some four million Filipinos living in the United States[2] and some 350,000 Americans living in the Philippines in 2016.

A View into Philippine Reality

Working in the embassy's massive consular section gave my colleagues and me full exposure to many aspects of this unique relationship. Every day we interviewed hundreds of Filipinos who were seeking visas to travel to, work or study in, or immigrate to the United States. In fact, it seemed that nearly everyone we met wanted to go to the United States. Sadly, holding a U.S. visa was a status symbol. I still recall meeting Filipinos who would proudly whip out their passports to show off their valid U.S. visa. Those who did not yet have visas would regularly evince strong interest in obtaining one.

I found the widespread affection and attachment to the United States both flattering and unhealthy. The country even boasted a political party whose platform was to make the Philippines America's fifty-first

2 "Filipinos in the U.S. Fact Sheet: Filipino Population in the United States, 2000–2015," Pew Research Center Social and Demographic Trends, https://www.pew socialtrends.org/fact-sheet/asian-americans-filipinos-in-the-u-s/.

state. It is the only country where I have lived that I thought suffered from a shortage of nationalism. There was and still is a small but vocal nationalist element, which manifested itself in support for or at least admiration of leftist political movements, opposition to U.S. bases, and regular demonstrations in front of our embassy, some of which turned violent. Still, the overwhelming majority seemed more interested in obtaining visas than in demonstrating. Some of this was love of the United States; a lot of it was the result of a miserable economy and desperation for greater opportunity. Millions of Filipinos were working abroad, often in difficult conditions, sending money home each month to support their families. In addition to thousands of bona fide tourists and immigrants, each year tens of thousands of Filipinos sought tourist/business visas with the intent of going *tago ng tago* (staying and working illegally in the United States).

The huge demand for U.S. visas led to the development of a cottage industry of individuals and companies who offered "help" to Filipinos anxious to obtain visas. Some of this was legal, if troubling, such as advising visa applicants what to wear and what to say in their visa interviews. Some went far beyond that, offering fraudulent documents, fake visas, and even fake passports, or arranging fraudulent marriages or engagements to facilitate immigration. To combat this fraud, the consular section had established an anti-fraud unit, with two U.S. officers and six Filipino investigators. I spent one year running that section, which gave me an unvarnished view of the seamy underside of corruption and law enforcement in the Philippines.

All of us in the consular section knew that a significant portion of visa applicants presented fraudulent documentation on income, savings, property, and employment, all of which were important evidence of significant economic ties to the Philippines (since U.S. immigration law presumes would-be travelers are impending immigrants unless they can demonstrate sufficient ties to their home nation). One day, I decided to run a test. We sought to verify all the documents that applicants presented to our visa officers. We were stunned to find out that every document we reviewed turned out to be fraudulent—every single one.

The real question—and the one that mattered most in terms of understanding conditions in the Philippines—was why everyone brought fraudulent bank and income documents. The answer, in brief, was the systemic corruption and bad governance that pervaded the country. People did not put money into bank accounts because they did not trust the banks or did not want the government to know they had money. They did not declare their income because they did not want to pay taxes. While no one really likes paying taxes, the difference in the Philippines was that people were convinced their tax dollars would simply be funneled into the pockets of corrupt politicians. Plus, as some Filipino friends told me, they already paid enough in "informal taxes," meaning bribes. So nearly everyone hid their income and their savings to keep them out of the hands of the corrupt system.

The anti-fraud job also introduced me to the Philippine law enforcement and justice systems. They were corrupt and, in the case of law enforcement, often brutal. A couple of anecdotes will explain. The first involved the National Bureau of Investigation (NBI), modeled on the FBI. I worked regularly with the NBI, so there was nothing unusual about receiving a call from them asking me to go to their nearby headquarters to talk with an alleged people smuggler they had just arrested. I drove over, walked into the office, and saw them using a stun gun on the poor guy, who was writhing on the ground in his own vomit. I shouted at my NBI contacts to stop, imagining headlines the next day of "U.S. Vice Consul Participates in Torture Session." They looked at me like I was crazy, since this was apparently normal practice for them.

The most infamous people smuggler was Manuel "Nonoy" Bala, who was wanted in the United States for his crimes. We worked diligently with local authorities to ascertain his whereabouts and encourage his arrest but got nowhere. One of my contacts, who was one of many well-armed individuals who had only a vague affiliation with the military or police, had been pursuing Bala for weeks. One day, he came to my office to tell me that he could not arrest Bala (because he had too much protection and would be released almost immediately), but he could kill him. He asked me what he should do. Alarmed at his casual tone, I swore and said, "No, don't kill him. He's an alien smuggler, not a murderer or terrorist."

The job put me in regular contact with the Manila police, and in particular with a senior police officer who worked out of the Western Police District[3] headquarters. We used to meet from time to time for a beer, over which he would often tell me the reality of how the police operated. He explained that, because the justice system simply did not work, the only way the police could keep crime under control was to go out every now and then and kill a bunch of criminals. He was so matter-of-fact about it that it was shocking. He was equally shocked

---

3 Now known as the Manila Police District.

that I had a hard time accepting their methods. I concluded early on—and continue to believe now—that a strong, independent judicial system is perhaps the most important element of democracy and good governance. The lack thereof—which is the norm in Southeast Asia—has been and remains an enormous hindrance to development.

These stories are by themselves small things, but I include them because they reflect to a significant extent the ills of the Philippines in the mid-1980s. As Paul Wolfowitz had said, the country was in "deep trouble." Some of its problems had been simmering for decades. Others were, if not new, growing in magnitude.

The Oligarchy

One of those ills or flaws was (and is) the enormous power and influence of the oligarchy, a group of fewer than a hundred political clans that—with some changes among them—has dominated politics and the economy for decades. And this is not just a Manila-based political elite. Rather, it is based on the power and influence of large landowners throughout the country who have built their own economic and political fiefdoms, and used their power to keep the state and national bureaucracy weak and even beholden to them. One Philippine political scientist has argued that this system began with U.S. colonizers, who found it easiest to work with existing large landowners and enabled those landowners to dominate the initial legislative institutions set up before independence.[4]

I saw these fiefdoms firsthand in my travels around the country from 1985 to 1986, for example when I accompanied our consul general on a late 1985 visit to Marawi, the capital of Lanao del Sur Province on the southern island of Mindanao. (This is the same Marawi that was the site of intense and deadly combat between the Philippine armed forces and ISIS-affiliated extremists in 2017.) Our host was Governor Ali Dimaporo, a Marcos-aligned warlord. He had first been elected congressman in 1949 and had served on-and-off again as congressman and governor in the region since then. Many viewed him as the most powerful politician in Mindanao. He had forged a close alliance with Marcos back in 1965, and as governor (Marcos appointed him to the

---

4 Wilfrido V. Villacorta, "The Curse of the Weak State: Leadership Imperatives for the Ramos Government," *Contemporary Southeast Asia* 16, no. 1 (June 1994): 67–92, https://www.jstor.org/stable/25798233.

job in 1976) he bragged about regularly delivering large numbers of votes for Marcos during every election. Some even joked that he produced more Marcos votes than there were actual voters in Lanao del Sur. Dimaporo also boasted a large private army, known as the "barracudas." One analyst of Mindanao politics said of Dimaporo that "the three G's of Philippine politics, guns, goons and gold, swirl around him with manic abandon."[5]

Dimaporo greeted us warmly. At sixty-seven years of age, slightly stooped and balding, he did not look at first glance like the fierce warlord I had expected. He did, however, have a certain gravitas, and in every way acted like a man who was used to being in charge. He introduced us to his family (there were rumors he had several wives), and proudly showed off his well-equipped private military force. Marawi was, without a doubt, "Dimaporo territory," and would remain so for many years. When Dimaporo passed away nearly twenty years after we met him, his wife was serving as the province's governor and his son as a member of congress.

And then, of course, there was the Marcos family, which had its base in the province of Ilocos Norte in Luzon, the country's most populous island and home to the capital of Manila. Ilocos Norte and Ilocos Sur, as well as Cagayan Province to the east, are home to the Ilocanos, one of the many distinct groups with their own language that highlight the tribal nature of the country. I was able to visit in mid-1985, again accompanying our consul general. The highlight of the visit was a luncheon hosted by vice governor and Marcos ally Roque Ablan at his mother's house in Laoag, the provincial capital. While a dozen or so of us dined at the main table, hundreds of members of the public came to enjoy free food in the palatial estate. Ablan explained that his mother fed the public daily, which was part of the reason his family was so loved.

Seated across from me was the twenty-eight-year-old governor, Ferdinand "Bongbong" Marcos Jr., the only son of the president and Imelda. He looked really young to be governor, even though we were about the same age, and largely deferred to Ablan when the talk turned to politics and governance. Perhaps because of our closeness in age, he spent much of the lunch talking with me about life in the United States

---

5 John Unson, "ARMM Mourns Dimaporo's Death," *Philstar Global*, April 22, 2004, https://www.philstar.com/headlines/2004/04/22/247143/armm-mourns-dima poro146s-death

and (with no sense of irony) his belief in democracy. Thirteen years later, Bongbong ran for and was elected governor of the province. He later was elected to congress representing Ilocos Norte's second district, succeeding his sister. He then was elected to the senate, with his mother taking his seat in congress, and narrowly lost the race for vice president in 2016. Just before this book went to print, Marcos won a landslide victory in the Philippine presidential elections and was expected to take office on June 30, 2022.

The presence and influence of this oligarchy had a profound impact on the country. Politically, it not only reduced competition, but it led to fear, abuse, and injustice on a regular basis. Powerful governors, mayors, and other oligarch members were said to "own" judges, or at least to be able to bribe them easily. Many also had their own private security forces, which were often brutal and almost always immune from justice. Economically, the system perpetuated high levels of income inequality. Figures from the early 1990s showed that the top 5.5 percent of all landowning families owned 44 percent of all tillable land, and the richest 15 percent of all families accounted for more than 52 percent of national income.[6] A 1984 World Bank study came up with similar numbers, finding that 20 percent of families controlled 59 percent of income, while approximately half of all rural families lived below the poverty line.[7] According to the Institute for Public Democracy, between sixty and one hundred families effectively controlled all elective positions at the national level.[8]

Communist Insurgency

The oligarchy, inequality, injustice, and corruption endemic in the Philippines fueled the rise of the communist New People's Army (NPA), which grew from a small group at its founding in March 1969 to an increasingly powerful force that threatened the country's stability in the 1980s and remains active today. The NPA was born out of the newly formed Communist Party of the Philippines (CPP), which had split from

---

6 Jose Almonte, "The Philippines Rejoins Asia," paper presented to the Singapore Institute of International Affairs and the National University of Singapore Society, June 11, 1993, 13, cited in Villacorta, "Curse of the Weak State."

7 Cited in Stanley Karnow, "After Marcos, More of the Same?" *New York Times*, November 18, 1985.

8 Almonte, "The Philippines Rejoins Asia," cited in Villacorta, "Curse of the Weak State."

the more orthodox Philippine Communist Party (PKP), which in turn included the remnants of the defeated *Hukbalahap* communist insurgency of the 1950s. The CPP and NPA made clear that their goal was to overthrow the Marcos regime, eliminate the vestiges of imperial (i.e., U.S.) influence, and dramatically reform the country's socioeconomic structure.

When I arrived in the Philippines in early 1985, the NPA was very active, with regular clashes between it and the military. In 1984, Assistant Secretary of Defense Richard Armitage estimated that the NPA boasted some ten thousand armed members, ten thousand active sympathizers, and was responsible for perhaps two thousand deaths that year.[9] Aligned with the CPP/NPA were an eclectic mix of leftist groups, including labor unions and student groups. These groups supplied the demonstrators who regularly protested in front of our embassy, calling for the end of U.S. bases, the overthrow of President Marcos, and an end to the oligarchy that ruled the country.

By that time, the U.S. government and the embassy were sufficiently concerned about the growth and potential of the NPA to establish a provincial reporting program. Two-officer embassy teams were each assigned to cover one or two key provinces so that we could collectively gain a better understanding of the NPA's presence and activity, as well as the effectiveness of the government's counterinsurgency campaign. For us new officers, it was a great opportunity to get out of the consular section to travel and contribute to reporting and analysis.

I was assigned, along with a colleague, to cover Cagayan and Isabela provinces in northeastern Luzon. The area was known as "Enrile territory" after Juan Ponce Enrile, Marcos's defense secretary and the dominant political figure in these two provinces. Over the course of fifteen to eighteen months, we traveled five or six times to the region. Since flights were irregular, I often made the full-day drive north from Manila. My favorite part was winding through the green hills of Nueva Ecija Province and through its capital, Cabanatuan, site of the POW camp that held the survivors of the Bataan Death March until their dramatic rescue in January 1945.[10]

---

9 F. A. Mediansky, "The New People's Army: A Nation-Wide Insurgency in the Philippines," *Contemporary Southeast Asia* 8, no. 1 (June 1986): 1–17, https:/www.jstor.org/stable/25797879.

10 This rescue was dramatized as *The Great Raid*, a 2005 film.

Because it was virtually impossible to schedule meetings ahead of time due to the inadequacy of phone connections, we often just showed up and asked for meetings at the last minute. Fortunately, we usually were able to see a good collection of officials and others. The governors and mayors predictably gave us good-news stories, usually while explaining all they were doing to help their people. A common occurrence would be for our meeting with, say, a mayor to be interrupted by a local citizen in need, who would approach the mayor and ask for assistance. Inevitably, the mayor would pull a wad of cash from his pocket and pass it to the individual, who would bow and offer profuse thanks. I always wondered whether they asked themselves how the mayor, whose official salary was miniscule, had so much money to dole out. I used to marvel at the lack of embarrassment or shame on the part of the mayors, who were clearly proud of how they were helping their citizens. This was classic, retail-level patronage politics, and it was how the system worked.

We found the local priests well informed and more willing than many others to talk about real issues. At the time, the Catholic Church in the country was in the middle of a transformation from a relatively conservative political force to one increasingly opposed to the Marcos government. It is hard to say how many priests were sympathetic to the CPP/NPA; there was an element of "liberation theology" present, but I would not hazard a guess at how widespread it was. Still, priests often seemed to have a sense of whether and to what extent NPA forces were around and would often share general if not precise information with us. I remember one time meeting a priest in a room full of congregants. I asked him whether there were any NPA around. He said "Yes, there are some here in this room," and everyone laughed. Fortunately for me, at the time the NPA was not targeting Americans, so we felt less of a threat from them than we did from some of the "goons" associated with local political figures. (Sadly, this changed shortly after I left the Philippines. In 1989, an NPA team assassinated our defense attaché, Colonel James Rowe, as he left his house in Manila. Rowe was a true American hero, having been one of the very few U.S. soldiers in the Vietnam War to have escaped from Viet Cong captivity.)

The Moros and Mindanao

The NPA was not the only insurgency active at the time. In the south, the government was grappling with an armed movement seeking autonomy for the Moros, the name for Muslims who inhabit much of the southern island of Mindanao and the smaller islands of the adjacent Sulu Archipelago and who make up about 5 percent of the country's population. This insurgency had a long history. Islam had found its way to the southern Philippines in the late fourteenth century, at the same time it entered what is now Indonesia and Malaysia. The Spanish (and Catholicism) came more than a century later, but never managed to assert full control over the Muslim areas of the south. Some argue (credibly, in my view) that the protracted conflict between the Spanish in the north and the Muslims in the south created the distrust and hostility that continues to this day. During the pre-independence period, President Manuel Quezon decided to pursue a policy of "no special treatment" for the Muslim south (meaning there would be no effort to afford the region any kind of special autonomy or status), and even encouraged Christian farmers to migrate to predominantly Muslim regions. This policy, which continued in one form or another for decades, changed the demographics, making the previously majority Muslims a minority in Mindanao, a reality that fueled resentment and anger.

In 1971, Nur Misuari and a few others formed the Moro National Liberation Front (MNLF) to fight for what they called a *Bangsamoro* (Moro nation) homeland. Fighting escalated in 1974, at which time the MNLF fielded an estimated thirty thousand troops, eventually leading to the Tripoli Agreement of 1976 (the Libyans had been supporting the MNLF). The agreement called for limited autonomy for thirteen provinces in Mindanao and Sulu, but quickly broke down amid a resumption in fighting. After years of mixed conflict and negotiations, the ascent of the Cory Aquino administration in 1986 led to a new constitution in 1987 that included a provision on autonomy. The Philippine Congress then passed a law in 1989 that called for an Autonomous Region of Muslim Mindanao (ARMM) in the provinces of Sulu, Tawi-Tawi, Lanao del Sur and Maguindanao. Implementation moved slowly and fighting continued until September 1996, when President Fidel Ramos signed with the MNLF a "Final Peace Agreement." The agreement called for the establishment of a Southern Philippine Commission for Peace and Development, which in turn was to lead to a new autonomous ARMM government in 1998. The MNLF, however, had splintered back in 1984, with the Moro Islamic Liberation Front (MILF) breaking away over its desire to press for both independence and the establishment of Islamic law. The MILF and the even newer Abu Sayyaf Group (established in 1991) refused to sign the "final" peace agreement and continued fighting.

During my time in the Philippines, there were regular battles between the Armed Forces of the Philippines (AFP) and the MNLF/MILF in Mindanao and in the Sulu Archipelago. The Moros did not threaten the stability of the country, but—together with the NPA—made significant parts of Mindanao challenging not only for local communities but also for economic development. Lawlessness had long dominated in many areas affected by the fighting, and it was obvious to many that some of the ostensible rebels felt comfortable straddling the line between ideology and theology, and criminality. In June 1986 my girlfriend and I felt safe enough to travel to Zamboanga, a prominent Muslim-majority city on the southwest tip of Mindanao, and from there venture out on a day trip to tiny, idyllic Santa Cruz Island, just a short boat ride away. We did not think too much about it until the next month, when rebels-turned-criminals kidnapped a Swiss tourist and his Filipina girlfriend who were visiting the very same island. The companion was released after about a week to help secure a ransom, and the tourist gained his freedom eighty-one days later after a harrowing experience.

Dictatorship

Of course, apart from the oligarch and the insurgencies, the other important ill plaguing the Philippines at that time was the shift from democracy to a repressive, corrupt dictatorship. Ferdinand Marcos had risen to power through the House of Representatives and then the Senate before winning the 1965 presidential election. He was reelected in 1969, but then declared martial law on September 21, 1972, enabling him to stay in power indefinitely (Marcos would not have been able to seek a third presidential term in 1973 under the Philippine Constitution). Marcos claimed martial law was needed against the threat of a growing communist/leftist uprising and the Moro separatist insurgency.

Initially, martial law enjoyed some popular support, as Marcos pledged to tackle corruption, weaken the oligarchy, and go after the communist rebels. While he did take some steps, his main achievement through the decade was to solidify his role as dictator, imprisoning opponents, silencing dissent, and taking away essential freedoms. Under martial law, Marcos oversaw severe and widespread violations of human rights, including extrajudicial killings, torture, and "disappearances." According to Amnesty International, from 1972 through 1981, the Marcos regime and its allies arrested some 70,000 people, tortured 34,000, and killed 3,200.[11] The Philippines even had its own chilling term for extrajudicial killings: "salvaging." Many of the violations were carried out by the military, the constabulary, or the police. Others were the work of so-called goons on behalf of Marcos or local warlords and political leaders.

Economically, Marcos turned to what became known as crony capitalism, weakening some of the old oligarchs and using state authority and revenue to shift resources and opportunities to family members and business leaders close to him. The combination of rising commodity prices, new investment incentives, establishment of an export-processing zone, and improved agriculture production (due in part to the introduction of new rice varieties) meant the economy grew some 7 percent annually in the five years after the declaration of martial law, but this rate proved unsustainable. Later in the decade, as the global economy weakened, Marcos turned increasingly to foreign loans (hence increased debt) to keep the economy moving.[12]

Growing Problems

As the Philippines entered the 1980s, the country suffered from growing problems. The NPA and CPP had momentum, benefiting from continued inequality, injustice, and human rights violations. Perhaps more importantly, the economy faced mounting challenges. Foreign debt had tripled between 1974 and 1978, as exports and foreign investment growth slowed while debt service grew. The debt service might have been manageable had it not been for the second oil price shock in 1979–80. The Marcos government responded by ratcheting up spending, but this blew up the budget deficit and increased the current account deficit to 8 percent of GDP in 1982–83.[13]

11 Amnesty International, "Philippines: Restore Respect for Human Rights on 46th Anniversary of Martial Law," Public Statement ASA 35/9139/2018, September 21, 2018, https://www.amnesty.org/en/documents/asa35/9139/2018/en/.

12 Ronald E. Dolan, "Martial Law and Its Aftermath (1972–86)," in *Philippines: A Country Study* (Washington, DC: GPO for the Library of Congress, 1991), http://countrystudies.us/philippines/57.htm.

13 Robert S. Dohner and Ponciano Intal, Jr., "Debt Crisis and Adjustment in the Philippines," in *Developing Country Debt and World Economy*, ed. Jeffrey D. Sachs (Chicago: University of Chicago Press, 1989).

The resulting balance of payments problems led the International Monetary Fund to demand painful measures to restore stability. These measures, which included a sharp decrease in the money supply, eased the balance of payments problems but exacted a high cost in terms of output and employment. From 1983 to 1985, total investment expenditures fell by half, and per capita income fell a stunning 15 percent.[14]

This economic crisis was not just bad luck. It resulted in large measure from Marcos's brand of crony capitalism, which over the past dozen years had stifled competition, siphoned a growing portion of government revenues into Marcos family or crony companies, and fundamentally distorted the overall economy, discouraging investment and producing instead capital flight.

Others have documented in detail how crony capitalism under Marcos worked, but a few examples, highlighted in a 1984 study by a team of University of the Philippines economists, warrant mention. Sugar and coconuts ranked as two of the country's largest agricultural industries and employed a huge number of workers. In the 1970s, Marcos established a tax on the production of coconuts, paid by farmers, ostensibly to fund the Philippine Coconut Authority and to finance a coconut replanting scheme. The money was deposited, interest free, in Marcos crony Eduardo "Danding" Cojuangco's United Coconut Planters Bank, which then charged farmers 8 percent to borrow. The contract for the replanting program went to another Cojuangco company. His coconut milling company enjoyed a near monopoly on crop purchases; at one point his mills controlled 82 percent of the industry. Another of his outfits, Unicom, had been granted a monopoly on the export of coconut products. All this diverted huge amounts of money from poor farmers to Cojuangco.[15]

Marcos gave control of the sugar industry to another crony, Roberto Benedicto, in the mid-1970s. The president issued decrees that de facto nationalized the domestic and foreign trade in sugar. He put Benedicto in charge of the National Sugar Commission, a regulatory body, and the National Sugar Trading Corporation, which he then granted a monopoly to buy sugar from Philippine farmers and to market it at home and abroad. Benedicto also owned two banks that financed the sugar business. Farmers and independent analysts complained that this

---

14 Dohner and Intal, "Debt Crisis and Adjustment in the Philippines."
15 William Branigin, "'Crony Capitalism' Blamed for Economic Crisis," *Washington Post*, August 16, 1984.

monopoly penalized farmers, offered no accountability for Benedicto's use of the funds, and left a number of farmers unpaid while the crony raked in millions.[16]

Marcos did not invent crony capitalism. He simply took it to new heights. He diverted state resources to cronies, and/or granted them exclusive trading rights, with virtually no accountability. These practices were so widespread that they distorted the entire economy, hurting farmers and discouraging investment from non-crony companies. As one economic study put it, "Massive corruption and distortion/diversion of assets had macroeconomic consequences."[17] The 1984 report blamed the weak economy on the concentration of power in crony hands and the use of the government to "dispense economic privileges to small factions in the private sector."[18]

And this does not even get at the massive corruption of the Marcos family itself. When I was there, people referred to Imelda Marcos as "Madam Ten Percent," as she was said to skim that amount from government contracts. Marcos himself was alleged to have made tens of millions of dollars off a contract awarded to Westinghouse to build a nuclear plant in Bataan (it was never built). When Marcos fled the country in 1986, Philippine officials estimated his family's wealth at some $10 billion. Years later, when Swiss courts authorized the release of hundreds of millions of dollars of Marcos family deposits, the court determined that the vast majority of those funds were of "criminal origin."[19]

Rising Opposition

By 1983, all these factors—rising insurgencies, a weakening economy, continuing abuse, injustice and inequality, and growing unhappiness with Marcos and his cronies' massive corruption—had sapped Marcos's support and raised concerns about the country's stability. In addition, Marcos's health began to decline precipitously. He secretly underwent a kidney transplant in mid-1983.[20] As early as 1980, American

---

16 Brannigan, "'Crony Capitalism' Blamed for Economic Crisis."
17 Dohner and Intal, "Debt Crisis and Adjustment in the Philippines."
18 Brannigan, "'Crony Capitalism' Blamed for Economic Crisis."
19 Stolen Asset Recovery Initiative (STAR), "Asset Recovery Watch Database," http://star.worldbank.org.
20 Raymond Bonner, *Waltzing with a Dictator: The Marcoses and the Making of American Policy* (New York: Times Books, 1987), 340.

analyst Richard Kessler raised the question of whether the Philippines might become the next Iran, i.e., might Marcos fall like the Shah had.[21]

A growing number of business elites already had shifted into opposition to the regime, in part because of their unhappiness about declining business and patronage opportunities as Marcos funneled resources to his cronies. Some of these business leaders banded together to form the Makati Business Club, which pushed for change. The Catholic Church, under the leadership of Cardinal Sin, also had moved into outright opposition. Growing concern that a continuation of the weakening Marcos regime could enable the communists to gain control added to the fear and to the demand for change.

Then things got worse. Benigno "Ninoy" Aquino, the scion of a wealthy landowning family and a longtime Marcos rival who emerged in the early 1970s as a leading opposition figure, was among the first opposition politicians arrested when Marcos declared martial law in 1972. The regime threw the kitchen sink at him, charging him with everything from murder to subversion. In 1977, a military court convicted him and sentenced him to death by firing squad. After he suffered two heart attacks in prison, Imelda Marcos intervened and offered him a chance to go to the United States for medical treatment. Aquino agreed and received treatment, but then stayed with his family in the United States, where he continued his fierce criticism of the Marcos regime.

In August 1983, Aquino decided to return to the Philippines, even though he was aware of the risks. After multiple delays as Marcos worked to prevent his return, Aquino landed on a China Airlines flight on August 13, 1983. A few minutes later, he was gunned down on the tarmac, as was his alleged assassin, Rolando Galman. His murder sparked global outrage and accelerated the development of a broader, more united political opposition to the Marcos regime. Although we did not know it at the time, it marked the beginning of the end for Marcos.

Growing U.S. Concern

The assassination also fueled growing doubts in Washington about Marcos and the longstanding U.S. policy of supporting him. When I arrived in Manila in early 1985, the Reagan administration's stated

---

21 Richard J. Kessler, "The Philippines: The Next Iran?" *Asian Affairs: An American Review* 7, no. 3 (Jan–Feb, 1980): 148–60.

policy—the result of an interagency policy review completed a few months earlier—was to continue to support the Marcos government, but to insist upon economic, political, and military reforms leading to an eventual political transition. It made sense on paper, perhaps, but—in my view—not in reality. I remember a conversation, a few months after I arrived, with Scott Halford, the embassy's political counselor. I asked him why we were still supporting Marcos. His response reflected the party line: "We are pressuring him to reform." When I followed up by asking what Marcos had done in the past few years that might inspire confidence that he had the capability for reform, the answer was that he had not done anything. I was convinced our policy was wrong.

I am making the policy options at the time sound more simplistic than they were. It would have been easy for someone on the outside to propose that since Marcos was a dictator and clearly destined to fall, the United States should abandon him. Although technically I was not on the outside, since I was a U.S. government employee, my position was so low that my views had little or no impact. So I had the luxury of being morally righteous. For those who had responsibility for our policy, though, it was more complicated. Marcos had been a strong ally for decades. If we tossed him aside, what message would that send to our other allies, particularly in the aftermath of the fall of Saigon, of the Shah, and of Somoza in Nicaragua (all of which gave rise to regimes hostile to the United States)? In the absence of a strong, coherent opposition, would Marcos's downfall make things better or worse? Might the NPA be able to take over? And what about our bases? Remember, this was still the Cold War, and we were in a global competition with the Soviet Union. Our bases and our alliance with the Philippines were important assets, and we genuinely feared the communist NPA could take over the country.

My unhappiness with our policy also reflected the gap between what those of us at junior levels in the field believed was the view in Washington and what policymakers actually were thinking and saying in quiet conversations. Those involved in Washington policy discussions at the time have insisted that they were not under any illusions about Marcos, but had to be very careful, given the high stakes involved. The late 1984 policy review, according to *New York Times* reporting, had determined that Marcos was both "part of the problem" and "part of the solution."[22] By mid-1985, it was becoming increasingly clear to

---

22 Leslie Gelb, "Marcos Reported to Lose Support in Administration," *New York Times*, January 26, 1986. Gelb's story presumably was quoting from an early draft

many in the administration that Marcos was not going to make the necessary reforms. Michael Armacost, under secretary of state for political affairs and ambassador to Manila until 1984, reportedly was pushing to withdraw U.S. support from the dictator.[23]

Others at the National Security Council (NSC), the State Department, and the Department of Defense, however, felt it was premature. They put forward four arguments: (1) that Filipinos, not Americans, should be the ones to force a change; (2) that, while the Catholic Church and the Makati business community had turned against Marcos, the all-important military had not; (3) the legal opposition had not "congealed," in Assistant Secretary of Defense Rich Armitage's words;[24] and (4) a premature "push" from Washington could backfire, leading a declining Marcos to delegate more power to Imelda and Armed Forces chief of staff General Fabian Ver, who presumably would take a hardline stance against any attempt at change, which in turn could lead to civil war. In other words, it was not that the administration held out false hope that Marcos would change. Rather, it recognized that Marcos needed to go, but it would be necessary to wait for the right time and the right dynamics to develop inside the Philippines before taking any action.[25] Key Washington players were in constant contact with our embassy to monitor and assess the situation.

The U.S. embassy in Manila is enormous. It is housed in a beautiful old colonial building right on Manila Bay, with a veranda just off the ambassador's office overlooking that bay. Our ambassador during

---

of the National Security Directive, which was leaked to the press. The final version dropped the specific language about Marcos being "part of the problem" and "part of the solution," but subsequent policy statements suggested that conclusion still drove U.S. policy. The directive was declassified in 2005: "NSDD 163 United States Policy towards the Philippines," National Archives Catalog, February 20, 1985, https://catalog.archives.gov/id/6879758.

23 Various media reports indicate that Armacost was one of at least a handful of State Department officials who favored ousting Marcos. See, for example, Stanley Karnow, "Reagan and the Philippines: Setting Marcos Adrift," *New York Times*, March 19, 1989. Columnists Evans and Novak named Armacost the "ringleader" of the anti-Marcos effort in an early 1986 *Washington Post* column. Rowland Evans and Robert Novak, "The Philippines Struggle," *Washington Post*, February 22, 1986.

24 William E. Kline, "The Fall of Marcos," Case Study, Kennedy School of Government, Harvard University, 1988. (Hard copy obtained by author.)

25 Telephone interview with former NSC Asian affairs director Richard Childress, August 3, 2020.

my tenure there was the highly regarded Steve Bosworth. In addition to having a first-rate mind and temperament, Bosworth looked and acted the part. Tall, angular, with white hair and glasses befitting his background as an economist, Bosworth was thoughtful, but also a man of few words. In those days of what I call the "imperial ambassador," lowly junior officers such as myself were intimidated by him (at least I was). Years later, when we were both in different roles and I got to know him, I found him warm and affable. He had not changed; I had just gained enough years and experience not to be so intimidated.

The embassy, like Washington policymakers, was struggling to find the right policy balance in a sticky situation. Everyone wanted a return to democracy and broad-based reform, hence the official policy of pushing exactly that. We had some leverage, particularly in the form of large amounts of assistance, including military aid, as well as the influence of the U.S. voice. Marcos also had leverage, however: he could reconsider U.S. bases in the Philippines, and there was the threat of chaos and even a communist takeover if he were pushed out.

The question of how to manage this difficult balancing act came into public view during an October 1985 Senate Foreign Relations Committee hearing to "review" U.S. policy toward the Philippines. The hearing made crystal clear the grave concern in Washington that a continuation of the status quo—i.e., more Marcos without reform—could well lead to a communist takeover.[26]

The committee chairman, Senator Richard Lugar, opened the discussion by referring to Assistant Secretary of State Wolfowitz's congressional testimony earlier in the year, in which Wolfowitz stated that U.S. policy rested on the premise that fundamental political, economic, and military reforms were essential if stability in the Philippines was to be maintained. He asked whether we were seeing such reforms (1).

Senator Alan Cranston, ranking minority member, spoke in sharper tones. "We are here today because there is a gathering storm in the Philippines. It is a storm which threatens democracy in that former American colony, a storm which threatens our important bases in the Philippines, a storm which threatens American security interests throughout the Pacific rim" (3).

Cranston warned of the risk, if reforms were not carried out, of a military takeover by "an indigenous Maoist force," and stated that "it

---

26 The summary of the hearing is based on and the page numbers that follow refer to *Administration Review of U.S. Policy Toward the Philippines.*

is clear that in the Philippines there are all the makings for the United States of another Vietnam, another Iran, another Nicaragua" (3).

In his opening statement, Wolfowitz made his point about the Philippines being in "deep trouble." He warned that critical U.S. interests were at stake, as a communist takeover of the Philippines would threaten stability in all East Asia (4). He noted that the administration had made "unmistakably clear" to President Marcos the need for urgent and deep reform, adding that the administration believed such reform was essential to prevent a communist victory (5). Assistant Secretary of Defense Richard Armitage echoed Wolfowitz's language, stressing that the U.S. concern went far beyond our military bases. The administration's primary concern, he explained, was that the "Philippines remains a stable and democratically oriented ally and a bulwark of freedom in Southeast Asia" (39). Both officials offered some hope that the policy was working, arguing that they were seeing some modest reforms, including in the military, but also conceded that the reforms to date were insufficient.

Just a few weeks earlier, President Reagan had sent Nevada senator Paul Laxalt to Manila as his personal emissary to assess the situation and to highlight the administration's growing concern directly to Marcos. Ambassador Bosworth had been communicating this concern to Marcos and those around him, but Reagan thought sending his friend, Senator Laxalt, as a personal emissary would erase any doubts the presidential palace might have about Washington's views. In subsequent phone calls between Washington and Manila, Laxalt told Marcos that "there is an almost uniform feeling that you have lost the support of your people . . . ." In a separate conversation, Marcos hinted that he might call a "snap" election to prove that the Philippine people still supported him.[27]

Snap Elections

Less than a week after the Senate hearing. Marcos announced that the Philippines would hold early "snap elections" for president in early 1986. Tellingly, he made the announcement on U.S. television, and invited the United States to send election observers. Marcos presumably thought he could count on his control of the state machinery, and the

---

27 Paul Laxalt, "My Conversations with Ferdinand Marcos: A Lesson in Personal Diplomacy," *Policy Review* 37 (Summer 1986): 2–5.

lack of time for the fractious opposition to organize, to win the election, restore his legitimacy, and ease the pressure from Washington.

The opposition was not organized, though it had done better than expected in the May 1984 National Assembly elections. Longtime politician Salvador Laurel had already announced his candidacy, but he lacked popularity as he was seen (rightly) as another old-style politician. Cory Aquino, thrust into the limelight by her husband's assassination, was the obvious choice, but—as someone who had never been in the forefront of politics—she hesitated. Over the next few weeks, she decided to run, and various players—including Cardinal Sin—played key roles in convincing Laurel to drop his candidacy and run as her vice-presidential candidate.

Within the embassy, most of us believed Aquino would win easily if the vote were fair. As one colleague put it, all she had to do was stand up in front of a microphone and shout, "That man killed my husband." The $64,000 question was, How fair would the election be? I heard some Marcos supporters say, with undue confidence, that he would simply "buy" the votes of the farmers, as he had done in the past. The ambassador and his team quickly organized an embassy-wide election observation plan, in which those of us who had been traveling regularly to particular provinces would return to those provinces as observers, in many cases accompanied by officers from Washington or other posts who had volunteered to help. In addition, Senator Lugar led a large observer team from Capitol Hill.

More importantly, the Filipinos themselves—led by the business community—had organized a nongovernmental observation group, known as NAMFREL (the National Movement for Free Elections), to offer a neutral alternative to the official Commission on Elections (COMELEC), which was widely seen as controlled by Marcos and thus not credible. Also of critical importance, in my view, was the omnipresent Cardinal Sin's message to voters: he said that taking money from Marcos's machine, which many would do, did not obligate them to vote for Marcos. In other words, he was telling them that they were not bound by the Philippine practice of *utang na loob* (basically, a favor for a favor).

Observing the Elections

Just ahead of the elections, scheduled for February 7, I boarded a U.S. Navy helicopter with a colleague from Washington, flew up to Subic

Bay to pick up a radio operator (no cell phones in those days!), and then flew on to Isabela Province in northeastern Luzon. Flying over the mountains, the crew advised us to sit on helmets, as the NPA sometimes took potshots at helicopters. We spent the day before the elections talking to priests, NAMFREL members, and local officials, trying to gauge the environment. Then, on election day, we went from polling station to polling station to monitor what was happening. The actual voting seemed to go well in the area we were in, but the big concern would be in the transport of the ballot boxes and the actual counting.

We took a short side trip into neighboring Quirino, which was a subprovince dominated by the Marcos machine. We had not been there very long before we were warned that we were not welcome and "escorted" out of the region by a pickup truck full of heavily armed goons. Having a truckload of notoriously undisciplined, heavily armed men following you on narrow roads in a remote, forested area is somewhat discomfiting, to say the least.

Still, the lasting image in my mind from that day is not the Quirino joy ride, but came from later in the day, when we were gathered at a local office in Isabela Province where ballot boxes from outlying polling stations were being collected. We heard shouting outside, and rushed out to see a poor farmer, apparently one of a few tasked with shepherding a ballot box from a nearby village, refusing to surrender that ballot box to local officials until he was safely inside the office and in full view of witnesses. I think of that man often whenever I hear someone suggest that poor people do not care about democracy.

A Contested Outcome

The greater drama happened elsewhere. NAMFREL did superb work guarding ballot boxes and attempted to do a rapid tally of the results to prevent manipulation later on. NAMFREL's tally showed Aquino with a comfortable lead. COMELEC's tally, however, had Marcos ahead. There were widespread allegations of fraud, intimidation, and manipulation of voter lists. Senator Lugar issued a statement claiming that between 10 and 40 percent of the voters had been disenfranchised. Two days after the election, thirty-five COMELEC employees staged a dramatic walkout to protest what they said were discrepancies between their figures and those officially announced, indicating significant fraud. On February 15, the Marcos-dominated National Assembly, ignoring the widespread, credible allegations of substantial fraud, proclaimed Marcos and his vice-presidential candidate, Arturo Tolentino, winners. The Catholic Church issued a strong statement condemning the "unparalleled fraudulence" that took place in the election and vote counting.[28] The next day, Cory Aquino spoke to a huge rally at Luneta Park in Manila and called for a campaign of civil disobedience.

The results left Washington struggling. While three visiting U.S. senators echoed the Catholic Church's assessment of widespread fraud, President Reagan hedged. On February 11, he expressed concern about reports of fraud, but suggested—despite the lack of evidence—that both sides might have engaged in problematic behavior. Ambassador Bosworth quickly went to see a very upset Cory Aquino and urged her to be patient, as Washington would come around. Bosworth was right. On February 15, the White House issued a statement saying that ". . . the elections were marred by widespread fraud and violence perpetrated largely by the ruling party."[29]

The president sent legendary diplomat Phil Habib to Manila to assess the situation. As a junior officer, I was not privy to Habib's conversations, but I recall vividly when the ambassador brought Habib to brief the embassy team in a large town hall format. Habib wondered aloud whether there might be room to negotiate a Marcos-Aquino power-sharing agreement. I thought this was absurd and, forgetting my place, voiced my opinion to Habib and the entire room, arguing that there was zero chance such an arrangement would work and that even proposing it would alienate the Filipino people. I was out of line, but fortunately was never chastised for my inopportune outburst. I later learned that Ambassador Bosworth had sent a series of classified messages to Washington arguing vigorously that we needed to be on the right side of history, and that meant abandoning support for Marcos in favor of Aquino, widely seen as having won the election. I also learned that Habib returned to Washington with a clear message that Aquino had won and Marcos needed to go.[30]

---

28 John Burgess and William Branigan, "Roman Catholic Bishops Condemn 'Fraudulence' of Philippines Election," *Washington Post*, February 15, 1986.
29 Kline, "The Fall of Marcos," 22.
30 Telephone interview with Richard Childress, director of Asian affairs in the National Security Council during the Reagan administration, August 21, 2020.

People Power

While Washington debated what to do, events in Manila moved ahead. A group of officers known as the Reform of the Armed Forces Movement (RAM) had emerged in 1982, led by Col. Gregorio "Gringo" Honasan and Lt. Col. "Red" Kapunan. (I would come to know Kapunan more than thirty years later, when we both served as our countries' ambassadors to Myanmar.) While some have labeled the movement as simply opportunistic, an embassy colleague who at the time was in close contact with its leaders argues that it was born at least in part out of a sense of altruism and of growing frustration with what they perceived as the incompetence and corruption of many generals, most notably Armed Forces chief Fabian Ver. Some of the RAM group had seen heavy fighting—and witnessed comrades dying—in battles with the MNLF, and they were angry that nobody at the top seemed to care. The group was associated with, if not fostered by, Defense Secretary Juan Ponce Enrile (Honasan commanded the Defense Department's own security force), who had been engaged in a behind-the-scenes power struggle with Imelda Marcos and General Ver as President Marcos's health declined. It is possible and perhaps likely that, at least for Enrile, this was more about power and patronage than democracy. Anyway, Enrile had encouraged this RAM movement, the members of which saw their future aligned with him and not with Imelda and Fabian Ver.

Various credible reports indicate that RAM leaders, along with Enrile, decided to engineer a coup on February 23. Ver, however, caught wind of the plan, consulted with Marcos, and planned to arrest the coup plotters. Enrile was tipped off and decided to move preemptively. He called Fidel Ramos, who agreed to join him at Camp Aguinaldo, where in front of the press late on February 22 they announced their resignations, said they did not think Marcos had won the election, and called on Marcos to respect the will of the people. They also appealed to others in the armed forces, the constabulary, and the police to join them in upholding the constitution. Shortly thereafter, Cardinal Sin spoke on Radio Veritas to urge the public to go to camps Aguinaldo and Crame to support and protect Ramos, Enrile, and their troops. Tens of thousands went that night (this is what I saw driving home late that night).

The next few days brought more high drama. On February 23, loyalist soldiers moved toward camps Aguinaldo and Crame, but stopped when confronted by large civilian crowds, estimated at three to four hundred thousand. Over the next day or two, there was incredible tension as people along EDSA and elsewhere placed themselves in harm's way between loyalist and rebel forces. The now-iconic images of nuns kneeling in front of tanks, offering flowers, tell the story. Everyone, embassy personnel included, wondered whether and when the loyalist forces would attack, and how many soldiers would defect to Enrile and Ramos.

On February 23 morning, a colleague and I drove to the embassy and asked what we could do to help as the embassy monitored the situation. We were first sent to Mendiola Bridge, near Malacañang Palace (the presidential residence), where soldiers and police were facing a large but peaceful crowd. At least twice the security forces opened up water cannons on the demonstrators, who would flee briefly and then return. A few hours later, I was sent to the airport to report on an incoming flight of troops. I saw a military plane land and troops disembarking. I sauntered out onto the tarmac and sought out the commander to ask which side the troops were on. He glared at me, told me it was not safe for me to be there, and stalked off to a waiting convoy of trucks.

In Washington, senior administration officials met virtually nonstop to shape the administration's response, with a heavy emphasis on avoiding violence and finding a way out for Marcos. Longtime Marcos assistant Alex Melchor, who had grown disillusioned with him, had arrived in Washington on February 20, and over the coming days met with several senior administration officials in his personal capacity (i.e., not at Marcos's behest) to discuss a Marcos "departure scenario."[31]

On Sunday, February 23 (early morning Feb. 24 in Manila), key Washington players gathered at Secretary of State George Shultz's house to hear from just-returned Phil Habib and to discuss policy options. Defense Secretary Caspar Weinberger, NSC advisor John Poindexter, and CIA deputy director Bob Gates attended, as did Rich Armitage and Paul Wolfowitz. They all agreed Marcos needed to go and presented that consensus view to the president at a White House meeting later that afternoon. Reagan agreed, and subsequently approved a

---

31 Telephone interview with Richard Childress, August 21, 2020; and Peter F. Schaefer, "Setting the Record Straight on Marcos's Fall," *Asian Wall Street Journal Weekly*, February 19, 1996.

White House statement urging President Marcos not to attack Enrile and Ramos.[32]

On February 24 in Manila, Ambassador Bosworth read the White House statement to President Marcos, who was upset but still refused to give up. General Ver and Army Commander General Josephus Ramas ordered loyalist forces to attack the EDSA compounds, and General Fidel Ramos called for more civilians to come to the area. A flight of ostensibly loyalist troops aboard military helicopters approached Camp Crame, presumably with orders to attack, but then landed inside the camp and defected. Throughout the day, there was more posturing and movements, and more defections, but no significant fighting. Tens of thousands of Filipinos remained in the streets, both protesting against Marcos and supporting Aquino and the troops who were demanding the president step down. Although tension and the threat of violence remained high, the demonstrators in that very Filipino way somehow found ways to stop and enjoy a plate of hot *pancit* (noodles) or some other favorite. I always wondered where all that fresh hot food came from in the middle of a mass protest.

Following discussions between Bosworth and Paul Wolfowitz, the State Department drafted and the White House approved another statement on February 24, saying that it was "futile" for the Marcos regime to try to stay in power, and calling for a "peaceful transition to a new government."[33]

Still not convinced, President Marcos called Senator Laxalt and asked if he should resign. Laxalt asked for time to consult with Reagan, which he did in the afternoon of February 24 (early morning Feb. 25 in Manila). He then called Marcos back and said, "The time has come."[34] Marcos nonetheless insisted on proceeding with his official inauguration, but it was clear that this was nothing more than a face-saving exercise. Cory Aquino held her own inauguration ceremony the same day. There was still concern that General Ver might try to stay on and fight. He had reached out via a former CIA station chief to ask how Washington would react if he unleashed the military. According to NSC Asian affairs director Dick Childress, the message back was clear: "If you use force, there will not be a seat on the plane for you [to leave the country]."[35]

---

32 Karnow, "Reagan and the Philippines."

33 Kline, "The Fall of Marcos," 24.

34 Laxalt, "My Conversations with Ferdinand Marcos."

35 Interview with Richard Childress, August 21, 2020.

That evening, Marcos, his family, Ver, and his close advisors departed on U.S. helicopters to Clark Airfield, from which they were flown to Guam and then Hawaii. The drama was mostly, but not completely, over. Some of Marcos's loyal Presidential Security Guard forces left Malacañang Palace on a U.S. Navy boat that had motored a few miles up the Pasig River from Manila Bay to evacuate them. On the way out, the nervous guard elements took control of the boat. The U.S. Navy officer commanding the boat radioed the embassy and was connected to Ambassador Bosworth. I happened to be nearby and could overhear part of the conversation. In one of the most remarkable leadership displays I have ever seen, Bosworth asked the U.S. officer to put the guard commander on the radio. Then I heard Bosworth say the following: "I understand you have taken control of our boat. This is what you are going to do. You are going to put down your weapons and return control of the boat to the U.S. Navy. They will ensure you get out safely. Do you understand?"[36] End of conversation.

A few hours later, as the city celebrated, a few of us from the embassy decided to go to Malacañang Palace to see what was happening. We walked onto the palace grounds, which were filled with tens of thousands of Filipinos who were celebrating and looting. I remember seeing people run out of the palace carrying paintings and clothes. We quickly realized that we were the only Americans there, and that—given Washington's longtime support for Marcos—being at the palace was not a particularly good idea. We headed for the exits, but it was so crowded that it was almost impossible to move, like being caught in a strong ocean current. Fortunately, we eventually made it out, and returned to the embassy. When we arrived, a crowd of Filipinos had gathered outside the gates, checking cars to make sure no one was sneaking in Marcos family members or cronies. They checked our car and let us pass. The trip to the palace was foolish, but it did allow us to witness an historic moment.

Democracy Restored

The next several days were full of celebration for many Filipinos, but there was a lot of work to do. Marcos's departure had been necessary, but it was far from sufficient. Other than the Marcos family itself, all the problems that had existed—corruption, injustice, insurgency,

---

36 These may not have been his exact words, but they are at least close.

economic weakness, a flawed military, and the rule of the oligarchy—remained. The question was, How much could Cory Aquino, someone with no political or governance experience, accomplish? Put another way, Would the revolt against Marcos lead to the systemic change the country needed? I heard many Filipinos saying some variation of "Marcos is gone, so now things will improve." I was not so sure. After all, much as we all bought into the story of mass protests forcing Marcos out, to a certain extent it was the Manila elite—with public support—that had ousted him.

Aquino brought in a broad new cabinet, established in March 1986 the Constitutional Commission to draft a new law of the land, canceled local elections that had been scheduled for May, and instead appointed hundreds of provincial and local officials. She abolished and repealed a number of repressive laws and decrees, including one that allowed for arbitrary detention, and restored a significant amount of freedom. She reached out to leftists, releasing political prisoners and offering dialogue. She installed highly respected businessman Jamie Ongpin as finance minister, and with him developed an ambitious program to reform taxes, deregulate business, and begin to dismantle the Marcos-era monopolies. She was able to return the economy, which had declined sharply the previous two years, to modest growth. And she established the Presidential Commission on Good Government to go after Marcos's ill-gotten wealth.

Her government soon found itself struggling against multiple challenges. First, her cabinet, made up of a range of ambitious political figures from different parties across the ideological spectrum, quickly began squabbling and maneuvering for position, hindering effective policymaking and implementation. This reflected in part the tendency in the Philippines—and elsewhere in the region, I later learned—for political parties to be based on personalities rather than policies, i.e., for parties to be established as political vehicles for ambitious would-be leaders rather than to reflect particular ideological views.

Aquino's appointment of provincial and local officials proved divisive, with many struggling to gain acceptance. Her reliance on a political ally, Aquilino Pimental, to fill most of the local jobs turned out to be particularly divisive, as others within the fractious government felt he was using this power to build his own political base. The radical left, taking advantage of greater democratic space, began making life difficult, with leftist unions organizing a wave of labor strikes that hit the economy and business confidence hard. Meanwhile, the NPA renewed its operations in the countryside. Elements of the military, particularly the RAM movement that had helped push Marcos out, remained troublesome, warning that their patience with what they perceived as Aquino's ineffective approach toward the NPA would quickly wane.

In July 1986, Marcos loyalists, led by his former running mate, Arturo Tolentino, and accompanied by nearly five hundred soldiers, occupied the historic Manila Hotel in a bungled coup attempt. Tolentino took an oath as acting president and designated a cabinet, but the operation never went beyond that. Still, it was a sign of things to come. A separate coup attempt, linked to Enrile, was quashed before it began in November of the same year, leading Aquino to fire the longtime defense secretary. A number of other attempted coups or unauthorized military operations occurred over the next several months, culminating in a serious, violent coup attempt by RAM, led by Col. "Gringo" Honasan in August 1987. The Aquino administration would suffer three more coup attempts by the end of 1990. None of the coups succeeded, but they severely damaged both investor confidence and the government's credibility, and lent an aura of weakness to the Aquino administration.

Marcos's departure had also fueled a growing and emotional debate within the country about the future of U.S. bases, the agreement for which had to be renewed by 1992. Leftists predictably called for an end to the bases, arguing that they represented a colonial legacy and left the country overly dependent on the United States. Others joined in the call for different reasons, with some pointing out that the bases were responsible for the exploitation of thousands of Filipinas who worked as prostitutes in the bars and clubs around the bases. The "bargirls" themselves demonstrated in favor of keeping the bases, upon which their livelihoods depended. I understood their position, but at the same time found it tragic.

I departed the Philippines in November 1986, a time when most people—including many in the embassy—remained optimistic. The People Power Revolution's success in toppling Marcos had been a huge positive step for the country. It was a rare example of people, through nonviolent means, forcing out a dictator. Moreover, despite the coup attempts, the Philippines had restored democracy, and had in Cory Aquino a leader who was honest, decent, and committed to maintaining and strengthening democracy and freedoms. The embassy, under Ambassador Bosworth's leadership, had navigated skillfully through treacherous currents, avoiding rash decisions while staying true to U.S.

values and persuading a cautious Washington to shift course in what, in hindsight, was the right move to protect U.S. strategic interests and also support the Philippines' return to democracy.

Major questions, as I was departing the Philippines, were whether the success of People Power would translate over time into real, systemic change in the way the country was run, whether it would spur similar democratic transitions elsewhere in the region, and whether we and the Filipinos would be able to find a way to maintain our bases and our alliance when the base agreement ended in 1991.

CHAPTER TWO

A Bumpy Ride

U.S.-Philippine Ties since the People Power Revolution

A few months shy of twenty years after I had left the Philippines, I returned to the country for the first time in mid-2006 as director of the Office of Maritime Southeast Asian Affairs.[1] After the hope of People Power and several years of stability and growth under President Fidel Ramos in the mid-1990s, the Philippines once again appeared to be the sick man of Southeast Asia. Its politics suffered from seemingly nonstop scandal and intrigue, with occasional coup attempts. Its economy trailed those of its neighbors. Its military remained weak and ineffective. And it still faced the multiple insurgencies, oligarchic control, injustice, and violence that had plagued it for decades. President Gloria Macapagal-Arroyo's (2001–10) support for President George W. Bush's global war on terror had injected some positivity into the bilateral relationship, but even that effort was undermined by widespread allegations of corruption, her dalliance with Beijing, and her 2004 decision to withdraw the small Philippine military contingent from Iraq. In Washington, despite the always-warm feelings toward the Philippine people and interest in combatting terrorism, there was little sense of true alliance and a general lack of enthusiasm for investing heavily in it.

Over the next fifteen years, the Philippines—and our alliance—would be a veritable roller-coaster ride, with wild shifts both in the leadership from Malacañang Palace and in the quality of our bilateral relationship. The Philippines would go from a virtual afterthought, in alliance terms, to a reasonably serious, strategic partner willing to

---

1 The office is part of the Bureau of East Asian and Pacific Affairs in the U.S. Department of State.

stand up to China's bullying, only to shift once again to become a giant question mark.

The Bases

When I left Manila in 1986, the future of the huge U.S. bases in the country had been in doubt. The original ninety-nine-year deal codified in the 1947 Military Bases Agreement had been amended in 1966 to end in 1991. President George H. W. Bush appointed former assistant secretary of defense and respected Asia hand Richard Armitage to serve as "special negotiator" for what clearly were going to be difficult negotiations in pursuit of a new agreement. On the Philippine side, President Cory Aquino (1986–92) faced pressure from a loud nationalist movement, well represented in the Philippine Senate, that argued the bases were a legacy of colonialism and dependence on the United States, and did little to protect Philippine interests. Other opponents pointed to the bases' negative social impact, noting widespread prostitution and other vices in the areas around the facilities. The 1990 decision of the U.S. Congress to reduce assistance (compared to requested levels) only added to the pressure on Aquino, who showed her irritation by refusing to meet Defense Secretary Dick Cheney during his visit to the country in February of that year.

On the U.S. side, the end of the Cold War and significant budget constraints combined to lessen the enthusiasm in both the administration and Congress to commit large amounts of assistance in return for continued use of the bases. Some in Congress resented the notion of paying "rent" for bases that were meant to bolster Philippine security as well as ours, and pushed back on Philippine complaints over the precise amounts of aid to be offered, noting that the country ranked among the largest U.S. aid recipients in the world.

Testifying later in front of Congress, Armitage summarized the challenges he faced going into the negotiations. He said the administration knew the talks would be tough, and was prepared to walk away if necessary. The Aquino government, he added, seemed unsure whether it wanted the bases, but was adamant that—if there was going to be a new agreement—Washington was going to have to "pay handsomely" for it. Armitage alluded to the end of the Cold War and noted, "It had not become obvious to our Filipino friends that the Philippines was no longer in this new world the center of strategic thinking, and that the

American people were not willing to bear any burden or to pay any price for the use of Philippine facilities."[2]

Nonetheless, the negotiations made progress, and by spring 1991 seemed to be heading toward an agreement under which the United States would provide some $360 million annually in assistance in return for use of the bases for at least another decade. Fate intervened, however, in the form of the massive volcanic eruption of Mt. Pinatubo in June, which decimated Clark Air Base and caused significant damage to Subic Bay naval base. Under those circumstances, Armitage later testified, there was no way the United States could provide the same level of assistance. In July, negotiators settled on a lesser amount— some $200 million per year—with the understanding that Clark was unusable for the foreseeable future.[3]

On August 27, 1991, the United States and the Philippines signed the agreement in the form of a Treaty of Friendship, Cooperation and Security, but as a treaty it needed the Philippine Senate's approval. Facing strong nationalist sentiment, the upper house on September 16, 1991, voted twelve to eleven against the treaty. Since approval would have required a two-thirds majority in favor, the vote was not as close as it seemed. After the vote, President Aquino toyed with the idea of going over the Senate's head via a national referendum but ended up not pursuing that option. As a result, on November 24, 1992, the last U.S. ship sailed out of Subic Bay, and new Philippine president Fidel Ramos (1992–98) raised his country's flag over what had been our last base in Southeast Asia.

Personally, I had mixed feelings. As a U.S. official who thought our security presence in the region played an important and positive role, of course I wanted us to be able to maintain our bases. On the other hand, I had some sympathy for the argument that the bases were a hangover from the colonial era and needed to go so Filipinos could feel fully independent. Also, it was impossible not to be troubled by the pervasive prostitution and other social ills that had developed around the bases.

Unfortunately, the way the process played out, with many Filipinos feeling that we had not been generous enough in our assistance, and

---

2 *The Philippine Bases Treaty: Hearing before the Subcommittee on Asia and Pacific Affairs of the Comm. on Foreign Affairs*, 102nd Cong. (September 25, 1991) (statement of Richard L. Armitage).

3 *The Philippine Bases Treaty* (statement of Richard L. Armitage).

with the Philippine Senate voting down the treaty amid a lot of harsh, nationalist rhetoric, there were plenty of raw feelings on both sides at the end. As Ambassador Richard Solomon later recalled, "There was an attitude of, 'Well, if they're not interested in treating us in an appropriate way, the hell with them. If they want us to go, we'll go. Goodbye.' There was a lot of bad blood in that situation." Solomon added that, in his view, many in the Pentagon were "fed up" with the Philippines, and were not unhappy to walk away from the bases.[4] With the Soviet Union no longer a threat, neither side appeared to be thinking strategically or long-term about the implications of the withdrawal.

There was nonetheless hope in some quarters that, based on the 1951 Mutual Defense Treaty, which provided the legal basis for our alliance, the Philippines would continue to allow U.S. ships and sailors some access to Philippine ports. Strong domestic opposition in the Philippines, however, greatly limited military-to-military cooperation, as did the absence of a status of forces agreement.

It took the discovery in 1995 that China had established a presence on Mischief Reef, in the South China Sea, to prompt Manila and Washington to take another look at the security relationship.[5] The Chinese authorities clearly saw an opportunity to press their luck in the aftermath of the U.S. withdrawal from the bases, amid a low point in the bilateral security relationship.

Shortly after learning of the Chinese presence, Manila began discussions with Washington about bolstering security cooperation. These talks resulted in the 1998 signing and the 1999 ratification of the Visiting Forces Agreement (VFA), which allowed U.S. servicemen and women to enter the Philippines to participate in joint exercises and other mutually agreed-upon activities. In 2000, U.S. and Philippine forces jointly conducted Exercise Balikatan in the Philippines, the first joint exercise in many years and an event that quickly became an important annual opportunity for our militaries to work together.

---

4 Liz Dee, "In Politics, Pinatubo and the Pentagon: The Closure of Subic Bay," Association for Diplomatic Studies and Training, May 31, 2016, https://adst.org/2016/05/politics-pinatubo-pentagon-closure-subic-bay-philippines/.

5 Mischief Reef is a small shoal about 120 miles west of the Philippine island of Palawan. The Philippines has claimed sovereignty over it historically, and insists it is part of its exclusive economic zone. The reef also, however, falls within China's so-called nine-dash line, a vast area of the South China Sea over which China asserts sovereignty based on "historical rights."

Politics and Scandals

Philippine president Joseph Estrada (1998–2001), who had ridden a populist wave into office in the 1998 elections, had been among the strongest opponents of the 1991 bases agreement. As president, nevertheless, Estrada supported the VFA and a strong bilateral relationship with the United States. His administration, however, quickly floundered amid widespread charges of corruption and numerous leaks to the press about his poor work habits and excessive drinking. In fact, when he visited Washington in August 2000, the Philippine embassy insisted that his planned meeting with President Clinton take place before noon, prompting whispers within the Washington policy community that the embassy was afraid Estrada might not be in good shape if the meeting took place after lunch.

Back in Manila, Estrada faced not only rapidly declining popular support but also accusations of receiving millions of pesos from illegal operations of *jueteng*, a Philippine numbers game. The legal case against him gained momentum, resulting in an impeachment trial held by the Philippine Senate in January 2001. During the trial, a slim majority of Philippine senators—mostly allies of Estrada—voted on national television not to open an envelope said to contain details of large deposits to Estrada's personal bank account. The vote prompted Senate president Aquilino Pimental and eight other senators to walk out of the building, and thousands of Filipinos to take to the streets in protest in what quickly was dubbed "People Power II." Over the next few days, from January 17 to 20, the number of protestors swelled, and the Armed Forces of the Philippines (AFP) withdrew their support from Estrada. Finally, the Supreme Court ruled that "the welfare of the people is the supreme law," in effect providing a legal basis for Estrada to be removed from office. Estrada argued that these actions were unconstitutional, but agreed in the interest of national reconciliation to resign in favor of Vice President Gloria Macapagal-Arroyo.[6]

The "soft coup," as some termed it, against Estrada was controversial inside and outside the country. Some praised it as reaffirming the country's democratic spirit, à la the People Power uprising against Ferdinand Marcos in 1986. Many welcomed the removal from office

---

6 Seth Mydans, "'People Power II' Doesn't Give Filipinos the Same Glow," *New York Times*, February 5, 2001.

of a man whose hedonistic lifestyle, corruption, and mismanagement was an embarrassment. Others, however, expressed concern about the legally questionable ousting of a man who had been elected fairly by the country's voters, and feared the implications if popular movements to overturn election results became a habit. Still others noted that the Manila elites, in effect, had overthrown a president elected largely by the country's impoverished majority.[7]

All of these problems highlighted a country that remained beset by many of the same problems that had led to Marcos's demise fifteen years earlier: a big rich-poor divide; endemic corruption; the military's continued role in politics; and a lack of public trust in the country's democratic institutions, which led some to believe the only solution was to take matters into their own hands via attempted coups or new "People Power" movements. Underlying all of this was the country's poor economic performance. Where the Philippines and Thailand had enjoyed nearly identical gross domestic product (GDP) per capita levels in 1970 and 1980, by 1990 Philippine GDP per capita had barely increased, while Thailand's had doubled (from 1980 levels). In 2000, Thailand's per capita GDP remained twice that of the Philippines.[8]

A small number of powerful families—political dynasties—continued to dominate Philippine political and economic life. The new president, Gloria Macapagal-Arroyo, reflected this reality, as the daughter of a former president. She entered office and quickly became emmeshed in a series of controversies and scandals that tainted her leadership throughout the decade. To begin with, many of Estrada's supporters did not accept the legitimacy of her ascent to the office. When a Philippine court (the *Sandiganbayan*) ordered Estrada's arrest in April 2001, thousands of his supporters demonstrated at the EDSA shrine in what they called "People Power III." On May 1, they tried to force their way into Malacañang Palace. The security forces responded with force, and there were numerous casualties.

In July 2003, after months of rumors about alleged military plotting, a few hundred members of the armed forces took over an apartment building in Makati (Metropolitan Manila) in an effort to instigate an uprising against the president. The rebels claimed they were

---

7 Mydans, "'People Power II'."
8 Cielito F. Habito, "Divergent Twins: PH and Thailand," *Philippine Daily Inquirer*, September 2, 2017, https://opinion.inquirer.net/106791/divergent-twins-ph-thailand#ixzz6WMdXJBs3.

acting against Arroyo's corruption and her alleged intent to declare martial law. The authorities negotiated an end to this rebellion after only eighteen hours, with no bloodshed, but the event highlighted both widespread unhappiness with the president and the precarious state of Philippine democracy.

Despite low approval ratings and near-constant allegations of corruption, many linked to her husband, Arroyo managed to squeak out a narrow victory over actor Fernando Poe in the 2004 presidential elections. She won less than 40 percent of the popular vote, however, and even that was put into doubt amid widespread complaints of cheating that culminated a year later, when the "Hello Garci" scandal erupted. In a nutshell, authorities had uncovered a recording of a pre-election phone call between Arroyo and an election (COMELEC) official, Virgilio Garcillano (hence "Garci"), during which the president stated that she needed to win by at least one million votes. The implication of cheating kicked off investigations and impeachment efforts in both 2005 and 2006, both of which failed, and led former president and supporter Cory Aquino to call for her resignation.

The political controversies and scandals did not let up. In 2006, Arroyo declared a brief state of emergency in response to a military coup attempt. Around the same time, her effort to promote constitutional reform—charter change or, in Philippine slang "Cha Cha"—fueled more political battling, as her opponents accused her of trying to overcome the constitutional prohibition against running for re-election and turned the issue into a debate about her fitness for the office. In 2007, Arroyo came under fire for her husband's alleged role in a $329 million telecommunications deal with China's ZTE Corporation. Various players testified that the deal involved enormous kickbacks engineered by Mike Arroyo.

Along with the scandals, Arroyo presided over a period of modest and uneven economic growth, with GDP rising by an annual average of 4.6 percent during the decade. That was not terrible, but the country underperformed compared to many of its neighbors. Moreover, the poverty rate rose slightly, exacerbating the inequality that had long plagued the Philippines.

The decade-long turbulence that rocked Philippine politics starting in 2000—on top of years of political and economic troubles—affected the bilateral relationship with us in at least two major ways. First, it gave ammunition to those in Washington who viewed the country as a severely flawed partner not worthy of substantial U.S. attention.

Second, it handicapped Manila's ability to grapple with two challenges to Philippine and U.S. security interests.

Counterterrorism Efforts

In May 2001, just a few months after Arroyo took office, the extremist Abu Sayyaf Group (ASG) kidnapped some twenty tourists, including three U.S. citizens, from a resort on the island of Palawan. Abu Sayyaf beheaded one of the Americans a few months later, and kept the other two as hostages for more than a year before a Philippine military operation rescued one but resulted in the death of the second.

By then, President Arroyo had fully signed on to President George W. Bush's global war on terror, and the two governments began a period of close counterterror cooperation. As part of Operation Enduring Freedom, Washington in 2002 dispatched some six hundred U.S. military personnel to the Philippines to serve as advisors to the Philippine military as it pursued terrorists in western Mindanao and the Sulu Archipelago. The U.S. effort, known as Joint Special Operations Task Force–Philippines (JSOTF-P), aimed to provide the training, equipment, and tactical advice that the Philippine military needed to carry out operations, but without entangling U.S. forces in actual combat. The U.S. forces, whose presence the 1998 VFA made possible, operated out of the southern city of Zamboanga, where they sought to keep a low profile. The two countries also signed a Mutual Logistics Support Agreement (MLSA), which allowed the United States to stage equipment temporarily on Philippine bases.

In 2003, President Arroyo further bolstered the alliance by sending some 150 Philippine medics and humanitarian workers to Iraq as part of the "Coalition of the Willing." During a May visit to Washington that year, Arroyo praised U.S. leadership: "There may be others who might feel timid or hostile about U.S. leadership in the war against terrorism," Arroyo said. "We believe that U.S. leadership and engagement with the U.S. makes the world a safer place for all of us to live in."[9] President Bush, in turn, named the Philippines a Major Non-NATO Ally, and pledged to support a joint review of Philippine military requirements, with an eye toward assisting the country's military modernization.

---

9 Jim Garamone, "Philippines to Become Major Non-NATO Ally, Bush Says," American Forces Press Service, May 19, 2003.

The United States sharply increased military assistance to Manila from only $10 million in 2001 to $50 million in 2003, while nearly doubling total assistance of all types to $203 million.[10] Washington gave the AFP access to the U.S. military's excess defense articles program, under which the U.S. Defense Department transferred to Manila a C-130 transport aircraft, a Coast Guard patrol boat, a special-forces landing craft, Huey helicopters, and thousands of rifles.[11] While this might not seem like much to those in the trade, it provided a major boost for the underequipped Philippine military. Also, the two sides stepped up training and joint exercises, focusing on building the Philippine counterinsurgency and counterterror capacity. The United States also agreed to train three counterterrorism units (Light Reaction Companies) that would form the AFP's first special forces units.

A year later, Manila ignored strong Washington protestations and pulled its troops from Iraq under intense domestic political pressure after a Filipino truck driver, Angelino dela Cruz, was abducted in July 2004 by Iraqi radicals, who threatened to kill him unless Filipino forces left the country. Washington had stressed that giving in to the kidnappers' demands would only encourage further kidnappings, but Arroyo decided the political storm at home if dela Cruz were killed would be more than she could bear. The withdrawal caused much upset in Washington, and instantly cooled the bilateral relationship. General John P. Abizaid, who commanded U.S. troops in the Middle East, said, "It is regrettable we lose a member of the coalition and regrettable countries are making decisions that would appear to be appeasing terrorists as opposed to standing up to them."[12] The State Department called Ambassador Frank Ricciardone back for consultations, as the Bush administration reassessed bilateral relations.[13]

---

10 Data from foreignassistance.gov.
11 Renato Cruz de Castro, "The Revitalized U.S.-Philippine Security Relations: A Ghost from the Cold War or an Alliance for the 21st Century," *Asian Survey* 43, no. 6 (Nov-Dec 2003): 921, https://www.jstor.org/stable/10.1525/as.2003.43.6.971; and Leslie Wayne, "Free to a Good Country," *New York Times*, October 31, 2006.
12 James Glanz, "Hostage Is Freed After Philippine Troops Are Withdrawn from Iraq," *New York Times*, July 21, 2004.
13 Mely Caballero-Anthony, "Beyond the Iraq Hostage Crisis: Re-Assessing US-Philippine Relations," Institute of Defence and Strategic Studies, Commentaries, July 28, 2004, https://www.rsis.edu.sg/rsis-publication/nts/626-beyond-the-iraq -hostage-crisis/#.WQ1RiIiGPIU, cited in Jeremy Chiang, "Philippine Foreign Policy in the 21st Century: the Influence of Double- Asymmetric Structure" (conference paper, ISA International Conference 2017, Hong Kong, China, June 15–17, 2017).

President Arroyo flew to Beijing just a few weeks later, sending—presumably deliberately—a clear message that she had other options if the United States chose to downgrade the bilateral relationship. This transparent "play the Chinese card" only added to the sense in Washington that she—and perhaps the Philippines—could not be trusted. It also led the influential Heritage Foundation to write a scathing article blasting Arroyo as the "weakest leader in the region," and questioning the wisdom of further U.S. military assistance.[14]

Despite this downturn, Washington policymakers decided that it was in the U.S. interest to continue to support the Philippines' effort to defeat the ASG and other militant forces in the southern Philippines. After all, this occurred during the period of heightened concern that Southeast Asia as a whole—particularly Indonesia and the Philippines—could become a second front in the global war on terror. Although military and other assistance declined by a modest amount, that move was driven by the annual budget realities as much as by any disappointment with the Philippines.

On the ground, the AFP and their U.S. advisors faced a tough challenge. The ASG operated in remote, rough terrain on the islands of Jolo and Bacilan in the Sulu Archipelago, as well as in parts of western Mindanao. There, they enjoyed at least tacit support from elements of the population who had never fully bought into Manila's rule. The fact that there were three armed groups in the region posed a major problem for the counterterror effort. The ASG, which benefited from the support of the extremist Jemaah Islamiyah (JI) movement in Indonesia, operated as a terrorist group and had been recognized as such by Washington. Some militants, particularly in JI, doubted the religious motivation of Abu Sayyaf's leaders, implying they were driven more by criminal intent than religious passion. That did not change the fact that ASG carried out a large number of appalling terrorist acts. For example, it claimed responsibility for the February 2004 bombing of *SuperFerry 14* off the coast of Manila, killing 116 people. A year later, on Valentine's Day, the group detonated bombs in Makati, Davao, and General Santos City, killing several and wounding some 150, including children.

Two other armed movements—the Moro National Liberation Front (MNLF) and Moro Islamic Liberation Front (MILF)—operated in many of the same areas as ASG. These movements drew from the same Moro

---

14 Dana Dillon, "Arroyo's Policies Disappoint," Heritage Foundation, October 7, 2004, https://www.heritage.org/defense/commentary/arroyos-policies-disappoint.

population pool as the ASG, but operated more as separatist insurgents than terrorists. The government had concluded an agreement with MNLF in the 1990s and was negotiating with MILF off and on through Arroyo's tenure as president. In theory, the U.S. target was the ASG, as they were the terrorists with links to some of the worst international actors. In practice, however, elements of the MNLF and the MILF sometimes fell in with or otherwise worked with the ASG, making it difficult to distinguish them. Some members of the MNLF worked closely with ASG in the Sulu Archipelago. The MILF, meanwhile, engaged in a series of heavy clashes with the Philippine military, with deaths in the hundreds. It was all too easy, particularly for outsiders, to group them all together as "Muslim extremists."

Throughout the decade, the U.S.-backed Philippine military suffered some setbacks but also scored impressive victories, including the killing of Abu Sayyaf leader Khaddafy Janjalani in September 2006 and of another senior leader, Abu Sulaiman, in January 2007. Overall, there was a sense that the terrorists, while still capable of individual acts of major violence, were largely on the defensive. Despite that, it was not always easy to maintain support for the JSOTF-P effort. When I served as deputy assistant secretary of state for Southeast Asia in 2007–10, I—along with other colleagues—had to push back against suggestions by some in the Pentagon that we end the U.S. presence. Their argument was largely one of resources: with all that was happening in Iraq and Afghanistan, keeping several hundred special forces in the Philippines was hard to justify, as the argument went. Moreover, despite the successes, there was no end in sight.

I strongly disagreed. For a relatively modest investment of forces and money, we were helping an ally score numerous successes against a significant terrorist movement and keeping that movement on the defensive. Why would we give that up? It was not like we were doing so great in the counterterror fight elsewhere and the Philippines was the laggard. If anything, it was just the opposite. The debate never escalated to the most senior levels of government, and we succeeded in maintaining support for JSOTF-P.

In 2008, the Philippine authorities announced they had finally reached an agreement with MILF, which would be a huge step in reducing violence in the south and isolating the ASG. The deal, however, encountered opposition from some Christian communities in Mindanao, who feared coming under Moro/Muslim dominance, and also was challenged on constitutional grounds. Arroyo had failed to build political support for the agreement among key constituencies, particularly in Congress and among the affected Christian communities in Mindanao, ahead of its announcement. Once the opposition developed some momentum, she was too politically weak and/or lacked a game plan to counter it. As a result, the deal fell apart, and fighting resumed.

Despite important successes on the ground, the government's control over some areas, particularly Jolo and Basilan in the Sulu Archipelago, remained tenuous. In August 2009, for example, MNLF and ASG militants ambushed a Philippine patrol on the island of Basilan, killing twenty-three marines and soldiers, while losing thirty-one of their own. On the margins of a trip to the Philippines in 2009, I was invited by Ambassador Kristie Kenney to join her planned visit to Jolo for the opening of a new road on the island. I first flew to Zamboanga, where JSOTF-P personnel picked me up at the airport in an unmarked vehicle and took me to the Philippine military base that housed them. The soldier who picked me up at the airport could not believe I had vacationed in the city some twenty-five years earlier—it was impossible to imagine in 2009.

I slept in a shipping-container-turned-bedroom, and headed out by U.S. Apache helicopter early the next morning. Flying over the turquoise waters of the Sulu Sea, I found it difficult to reconcile the idyllic beauty of the area with its well-earned reputation for violence and brutality.

On Jolo, I met up with Ambassador Kenney, and along with various Philippine officials we trudged along the newly built road on foot, accompanied by hundreds of heavily armed troops. The heat was oppressive, and the poverty was harsh. The presence and demeanor of the troops reinforced my feeling that the threat from the ASG (and perhaps others) was real. It felt as if we were in occupied territory.

Flirtation with China

While the Arroyo administration invested heavily in the counterterrorism partnership, it took a softer approach toward the other major security challenge at that time, the increasingly aggressive Chinese posturing in the South China Sea. During Arroyo's 2004 visit to Beijing, shortly after the Iraq hostage fiasco, she had surprised Washington and many others by agreeing to set aside the two countries' dispute over the South China Sea and have the Chinese and Philippine national oil companies conduct a joint seismic study—the Joint Marine Seismic Undertaking (JMSU)—in the area. As noted Southeast Asia observer Barry Wain put it at the time:

> The Philippine government has broken ranks with the Association of Southeast Asian Nations, which was dealing with China as a bloc on the South China Sea issue. . . . [It] also has made breathtaking concessions in agreeing to the area for study, including parts of its own continental shelf not even claimed by China and Vietnam. Through its actions, Manila has given a certain legitimacy to China's legally spurious "historic claim" to most of the South China Sea.[15]

Arroyo's visit sparked a flurry of high-level exchanges, including Philippine defense secretary Avelino Cruz's November 2004 trip to Beijing, during which he signed a Memorandum of Understanding on Defense Cooperation and agreed on an annual bilateral security dialogue. The following April, Chinese president Hu Jintao visited Manila, where he and Arroyo publicly reaffirmed their shared commitment to closer ties and to cooperation in developing the South China Sea.

During her tenure, Arroyo made a total of nine official visits to China, signing dozens of bilateral agreements and making clear that she thought cooperating with China was the Philippine's best option. In Manila, there were constant rumors that her husband, Mike Arroyo, was lining his pockets through corrupt deals with Chinese entities. The most noteworthy was a $329 million telecommunications deal with the ZTE Corporation. The project aimed to build a national broadband network, but the high cost allegedly included tens of millions of dollars in kickbacks. The public uproar in the Philippines as reports of this deal leaked was such that President Arroyo had to cancel it. This and other allegations of corruption connected to Arroyo's commercial deals with China raised growing concerns in the Philippines. Indirectly, those concerns contributed to the Philippine Congress passing the Archipelagic Baseline Act of 2010, legislation that "delineated Philippine sovereign interests and restricted the government from entering into future JMSU-like agreements without due process and transparency."[16]

---

15 Barry Wain, "Manila's Bungle in the South China Sea," *Far Eastern Economic Review* 171, no. 1 (Jan/Feb 2008): 45–48.

16 Alex S. Boardo, "Enhanced Defense Cooperation Agreement: Aquino III's Balancing Strategy with the United States against China" (master's thesis, Naval Postgraduate School, 2017), http://hdl.handle.net/10945/52958.

In Washington, we were fully aware of but not unduly concerned about President Arroyo's efforts to bolster ties with China. After all, nearly all Southeast Asian nations were following a similar path, in the aftermath of what was being called Beijing's "charm offensive" and in the context of dramatically increasing trade between China and its southern neighbors. Also, we remained confident that the Philippine nation as a whole was much more in favor of a closer relationship with the United States than with China. We were, however, troubled by the Arroyo administration's naivete concerning the South China Sea. There was no chance, we knew, that China would agree to joint development in any areas other than those where its claims were the weakest. In other words, China was playing the old "what's mine is mine, and what's yours is (half) mine too" game.

Challenges in the Relationship

While not fretting unnecessarily over Manila's flirtation with Beijing, we made sure we were bringing our "A" game to the Philippines. Working closely with Ambassador Kenney in Manila and U.S. Pacific Command (PACOM) in Hawaii, we maintained support for JSOTF-P's excellent work and launched an initiative—aimed at those in the Philippine military and bureaucracy who were less enamored than Arroyo of China's actions in the South China Sea—to enhance the Philippine's capacity to monitor and patrol its maritime areas. Using funding authorized by the Pentagon for countering security threats (the so-called 1207 account), the State Department funded the construction of a series of radar installations in key spots on the Philippine coast, significantly improving the ability of authorities in those locations to see who was doing what in their coastal waters.

We also continued well-funded U.S. Agency for International Development (USAID) programs to promote inclusive economic development, including—per Ambassador Kenney's strong recommendation—substantial amounts for the country's restive south. This was not money primarily aimed at winning hearts and minds, but rather, in anticipation of a possible peace deal with the MILF, attempting to help local communities create economic conditions that could absorb a large contingent of demobilized, armed fighters. I would see later, in Aceh, Indonesia, the problems that can develop when armed men who have been fighting for years suddenly find themselves at peace, but in an area with few good jobs.

In addition to these activities, it is important to mention the day-to-day work that our embassy was doing to shore up the favorable views that the vast majority of Filipinos harbored toward the United States. In the policy world, not to mention academia, we tend to give short shrift to this work, but it really matters. In all of our embassies, our teams implement a wide variety of exchange and outreach programs, plus engage in constant messaging, to tell the story about what the United States is doing as a good partner. Some of it is through traditional and social media or other communications, but often it is what I call "retail diplomacy," reaching out and touching people in a way that leaves them feeling positive about America. Ambassador Kenney happened to be a star at this, with a very active Twitter following, regular appearances on Philippine television, and seemingly nonstop personal engagements throughout the country. This might seem small to those who have not done diplomacy firsthand, but I promise you it is of huge importance.

Sometimes months or even years of effective public diplomacy can be undermined or even undone by one incident. That is what we faced in the Philippines just as I was taking over the portfolio. A U.S. Marine, Lance Corporal Daniel Smith, was accused in December 2005 of raping a Filipina (originally identified by the pseudonym "Nicole") in a van while other Marines allegedly cheered him on. In addition to the unimaginable human tragedy, the case also threatened severe damage to the bilateral relationship, particularly on the military side. The Philippine public demanded Smith face trial and punishment under the Philippine judicial system. Our military, skeptical of the objectivity of the Philippine judicial system, particularly in such a high-profile case, objected vehemently to that idea. The VFA, which is supposed to govern such cases, is complicated. It states that the United States does not have to turn over an accused offender to the Philippine authorities unless the crime is of "particular significance" to the Philippines. It also allows the United States to maintain custody of the accused until the end of all legal proceedings.

After a year of legal proceedings, a Makati City court found Corporal Smith guilty of rape in December 2006 and sentenced him to approximately forty years in prison. The court ordered him confined at the Makati City jail. In close consultation with us at State and with PACOM, however, Ambassador Kenney had been working with Philippine foreign secretary Alberto Romulo on an arrangement to allow Smith to remain in U.S. custody pending his appeal of the conviction. The day after Smith's conviction, that agreement became active, and

Smith was transferred to our embassy. The decision provoked an outcry from the Philippine public, as for many it smacked of the colonial
era. It was, however, consistent with the terms of the VFA, and also essential to keep our military from reconsidering its ability to work with
its Philippine counterparts.

The case remained an irritant in the relationship for some time,
and also created practical problems for our embassy, which did not
have the facilities to house and monitor someone in Corporal Smith's
situation. In February 2009, the Philippine Supreme Court ruled that
Smith's transfer to the embassy had violated the terms of the VFA, but it
did not explicitly demand he be returned to Philippine custody. Shortly
thereafter, "Nicole" submitted a letter recanting her allegations, fired
her lawyer, and left for the United States. In April of that year, an ap-
peals court acquitted Smith, and the embassy and PACOM moved him
out of the country the next day.[17]

As we dealt with the Smith case, we faced pressure on the home
front over the continued substantial number of extrajudicial killings
in the Philippines. What had been known as "salvaging" during the
Marcos years continued, with an extremely high number of political
murders. After declining somewhat during the late 1980s and 1990s,
such killings rose significantly in the 2004–07 period, prompting the
Asia Foundation to call the country a "world leader in extrajudicial
killings" in a 2010 report.[18] UN special rapporteur Philip Alston visited
the country in February 2007, and concluded that politically motivated
killings were "widespread" and included government-sanctioned murders of civil society activists as well as the work of a "vigilante death
squad" in the southern city of Davao. He later reported to the UN
Human Rights Council that extrajudicial killings had peaked at 220
in 2007.[19] He and the Asia Foundation both found that leftist-oriented
civil society activists topped the list of victims, though many journal-

---

17 Reynaldo Santos, Jr., "Looking Back: Daniel Smith and the Subic Rape Case,"
Rappler, December 1, 2015, https://www.rappler.com/newsbreak/iq/looking-back
-daniel-smith-subic-rape-case.
18 Al A. Parreño, *Report on the Philippine Extrajudicial Killings (2001-Aug, 2010)*
(Manila: USAID/Asia Foundation, 2011), https://www.loc.gov/item/2012330478/.
19 UN Human Rights Council, Promotion and Protection of All Human Rights,
Civil, Political, Economic, Social and Cultural Rights, Including the Right to Devel-
opment: Report of the Special Rapporteur on Extrajudicial, Summary or Arbitrary
Executions, Philip Alston. Addendum. Follow-Up to Country Recommendations—
Philippines, A/HRC/11/2/Add.8 (April 29, 2009).

ists—usually local radio personalities—also found themselves targeted. The targeting of journalists led Reporters Without Borders to drop the Philippines to 142nd place in its global ranking of press freedoms.[20]

Very few of these murders resulted in prosecutions, but everyone believed that the vast majority were carried out by military or police, or in some cases by gunmen at the behest of local politicians. The communist New People's Army also committed such murders, but not nearly as many as government or government-aligned forces. It was clear to us that security forces were killing people they considered communist sympathizers, and that powerful political clans were eliminating people who were "causing trouble," whether as journalists, critics, or political opponents. Our embassy in Manila pushed the government hard to take stronger action to stop the murders and to hold accountable the murderers. My colleagues and I did the same on our regular visits to the Philippines and in our conversations with the Philippine ambassador in Washington. Usually, they responded by agreeing there was a problem but arguing there was little they could do because witnesses refused to testify (for good reason).

In March 2007, the Senate Foreign Relations Committee held hearings on this problem, as a number of senators wanted to highlight the issue and press the administration to do more. Deputy Assistant Secretary of State Eric John, in his testimony, readily acknowledged the problem and laid out all that we were doing to press for a solution, but there was no way to paint a good picture of what was happening.[21] Extrajudicial killings—and an almost complete lack of accountability—were a huge problem in the 1980s under Marcos, in the 2000s under Arroyo, and—as we will see—during President Duterte's tenure. The impunity with which government and other powerful actors have been able to kill people they see as opponents ranks as one of the Philippines' most intractable problems, and reflects a broken justice system and a high tolerance among some political leaders for political violence.

On November 23, 2009, Esmael Mangudadatu, a candidate for governor in the province of Maguindanao (in Mindanao), sent a convoy of cars full of women and journalists to file his candidacy papers in the provincial capital of Shariff Aguak. Mangudadatu sent women and

---

20 Parreño, *Report on the Philippine Extrajudicial Killings.*
21 *Extrajudicial Killings in the Philippines: Strategies to End the Violence. Hearing before the Senate Foreign Relations Full Comm.*, 110th Cong. (March 14, 2007) (statement of Eric G. John). Author was present at the hearing.

journalists on the theory that his opponent, Andal Ampatuan, son of the longtime governor and de facto warlord of the province, would not harm such a group. He was wrong. When the convoy reached the Ampatuan's eponymous hometown, a group of gunmen ambushed it, killing dozens in the initial spray of bullets and then mercilessly hunting down and killing the survivors. It was a massacre, with fifty-seven people, including some thirty journalists, killed. Among the dead were Mangudadatu's wife and two of his sisters.[22] I thought at the time that, if the Philippines failed to bring the perpetrators to justice, there really was no hope for the place. A decade later, a Philippine judge found Andal Ampatuan, Jr. and several accomplices guilty of murder and sentenced them to life in prison. It was slow justice, but at least it was justice.

Reinvigorating the Alliance

The tumultuous Arroyo presidency ended in June 2010, when Benigno "Noynoy" Aquino took office after winning a significant victory over former president Joseph Estrada and other candidates in national elections held a month earlier. The son of assassinated opposition leader Benigno "Ninoy" Aquino and President Cory Aquino, Noynoy's victory was as much the result of a tidal wave of public emotion following his popular mother's death in late 2009 as it was of the nation's belief in him. In Washington, where I was preparing to leave for assignment in Indonesia, I—along with many others—saw his election as unlikely to lead to major change, given his modest record of past success and the fact that his election was based more on family connections than on a clear program of action. I should have been more optimistic.

I will defer to Filipinos to judge Aquino's presidency overall, but from our perspective his six-year rule produced substantial economic gains, some much-needed political stability, and a significant strengthening of our bilateral alliance. Aquino entered office promising to tackle corruption and reduce poverty. Throughout his tenure, he largely avoided charges of personal corruption and was generally seen as honest, though his administration had its share of corruption scandals. He

---

22 Dan Murphy, "Philippines Massacre: The Story Behind the Accused Ampatuan Clan," *Christian Science Monitor*, November 24, 2009, https://www.csmonitor .com/World/Global-News/2009/1124/philippines-massacre-the-story-behind-the -accused-ampatuan-clan.

also avoided major political turmoil, in that there were no coups or attempted "people power" efforts to overthrow him. In that sense, he offered some stability and a reasonably high degree of popular support, despite some legitimate criticism over his handling of a major typhoon in 2013 and some other failings. Also, Aquino put together a talented cabinet that, in our view, supported what we believed were his genuine efforts to improve governance, build stronger institutions, and improve the lives of the masses.

In an effort finally to end the decades-long Moro insurgency in the south, President Aquino held secret talks in Tokyo with MILF leader Murad Ibrahim in August 2011, resulting in new negotiations that produced the Framework Agreement on the Bangsamoro in October 2012 and the 2014 Comprehensive Agreement on the Bangsamoro, which was to end all fighting between the Armed Forces of the Philippines and the MILF and put in place a "Bangsamoro" to replace the old Autonomous Region of Muslim Mindanao, which had proven ineffective. Implementation, however, depended on passage of legislation known as the Bangsamoro Basic Law.

This legislation stalled due to a major clash between the army and the MILF in January 2015. In what became known as the Mamasapano Incident, Philippine National Police forces entered Mamasapano, in Maguindanao Province, to try to kill or capture a high-profile JI terrorist named Zulkifli bin Hir, aka "Marwan," who was staying with a breakaway MILF group. The police killed Marwan, but their action set off a major clash with the MILF that led resulted in the death of thirty-five police commandos. This disastrous outcome prompted a huge public outcry and fueled opposition to the peace agreement with the MILF.

On the economic front, Aquino enacted reforms that significantly improved the economy. His administration increased government revenue through more efficient collection, boosted foreign direct investment substantially, increased foreign exchange reserves, and—by helping the country achieve an investment grade credit rating—brought interest rates down sharply. It streamlined bureaucracy to enhance competitiveness, and made some gains against corruption. As a result, economic growth, which had averaged between 4 and 5 percent the previous decade, rose to an annual average of 6.2 percent during his tenure.

We could see the change in terms of U.S. business attitudes. After years if not decades of being bearish on Philippine prospects, more U.S. business executives working in the region began pointing to the Philippines as a country of interest. In numerous visits to the country and in discussions with groups such as the US-ASEAN Business Council, I witnessed a steady increase in interest and optimism about the Philippine economy.

Critics rightly noted that this enhanced growth did not reduce poverty rates, and many Filipinos complained that in reality it did not seem like the economy had grown as fast as the numbers suggested. Karl Kendrick Chua, the World Bank chief economist in the Philippines, defended the government's economic efforts while noting that it would take more time to reduce inequality. "On the whole, Aquino has been very positive for the Philippines. But then, the country came from decades of difficulties so you cannot expect to fix 6 decades of difficulty in just 6 years," Chua said.[23]

Aquino's presidency coincided with the Obama administration's "rebalance" to Asia, which involved, among other things, more engagement and investment in our relationships with ASEAN and its member states, including the Philippines. When President Aquino met President Obama in New York in September 2010, Obama affirmed his desire to strengthen the bilateral relationship, and Aquino agreed. During that same trip, the two governments signed a five-year compact under which the U.S. Millennium Challenge Corporation would provide $434 million in assistance—over and above our already significant USAID program—designed specifically to promote broad-based, inclusive growth in the Philippines.

Six months later, in March 2011, two Chinese patrol boats harassed a Philippine Department of Energy–contracted ship that was surveying oil and gas prospects near Reed Bank, which lies only eighty miles west of the Philippine island of Palawan. Manila protested, noting that Reed Bank was not even part of the disputed Spratly Islands. The Chinese dismissed the protest, asserting that it was "indisputable" that all the Spratly Islands and the surrounding maritime domain belonged to China. This incident, combined with numerous smaller examples of assertive Chinese behavior in the South China Sea, highlighted to the Aquino administration both the value of the U.S. alliance and the country's own severely lacking maritime capabilities.

Back in 2003, presidents Bush and Arroyo had agreed to a review of Philippine military capabilities and needs. That review led to the

---

23 Chris Schnabel, "Beyond the Numbers: How Aquino Fueled the Economy," Rappler, June 17, 2016, https://rappler.com/business/economy/president-aquino -economy-legacy.

establishment of two programs deemed essential to bilateral military cooperation: the Philippine Defense Reform program, and the AFP's Capability Upgrade Program. The former focused on organizational and management reform; the latter emphasized building the country's external defense capacity, which had long lagged behind internal security as a priority. But even the latter, however, focused on building internal security capabilities during its first phase (through 2012), only after which it would switch to emphasize external and specifically maritime defense capacity.[24]

By 2011 and 2012, the combination of years of inadequate defense spending, focus on internal security, and a corrupt and convoluted procurement process meant that the Philippine military was woefully unprepared to deal with challenges in the South China Sea. According to its own 2007 assessment, the military only had a few ships capable of conducting maritime patrols, and those vessels lacked even anti-aircraft/anti-submarine capabilities. The air force was in no better shape, and was using *trainer planes* to perform territorial defense missions.[25]

President Aquino called for renewed efforts to modernize Philippine naval and air forces, but given continuing severe budget constraints also looked to the United States to help fill the gap. In late January 2011, even before the Reed Bank incident, the two countries held the first Bilateral Strategic Dialogue. At that dialogue, Assistant Secretary of State for East Asian and Pacific Affairs Kurt Campbell affirmed that "the Obama administration was committed to boost[ing] the Philippine military's capacities to patrol its waters as part of a larger goal of keeping Asian sea lanes open." In the following weeks, Washington and Manila established working groups to consider further cooperation in several fields, including maritime security.[26] Later that year, Secretary of State Hillary Clinton visited Manila, where she reaffirmed the U.S. commitment to the Philippines.

Let me explain U.S. thinking here. Nobody seriously thought that, even with U.S. assistance, the Philippines (or Vietnam or Malaysia) would be able to match China's military might in the South China Sea. Washington was not interested in promoting a futile arms race. Rather,

---

24 Walter Lohman and Renato De Castro, "U.S.–Philippines Partnership in the Cause of Maritime Defense," Heritage Foundation, August 8, 2011, https://www.heritage.org/asia/report/us-philippines-partnership-the-cause-maritime-defense.
25 Lohman and De Castro, "U.S.–Philippines Partnership."
26 Lohman and De Castro, "U.S.–Philippines Partnership."

it saw how Beijing took advantage of the almost total absence of maritime awareness and capability among the other nations involved in the South China Sea dispute to assert its presence through the deployment of small patrol boats and ships. The United States wanted to help these countries build sufficient capacity to (a) know what was happening in their own coastal waters and exclusive economic zones, and (b) have some capacity to patrol and show a presence in those waters and offer at least a minimal level of protection to their fisherman or oil exploration operations.

In that context, the Obama administration approved the transfer of three former U.S. Coast Guard *Hamilton*-class cutters through the Pentagon's Excess Defense Articles program. While small by U.S. Navy standards, the cutters would immediately become the largest ships in the Philippine Navy. Washington also continued to support the construction of listening and communication stations along the Philippine coast, designed to enable the AFP to monitor maritime activity in the South China and Sulu seas (for the latter, counterterrorism was a larger priority).

Things escalated in April 2012, when two Chinese maritime surveillance ships intervened to stop the Philippine Navy's *Gregorio Del Pilar*—one of the recently transferred U.S. Coast Guard cutters—from arresting a group of Chinese fishermen engaged in illegal fishing and poaching at Scarborough Shoal, a disputed area but one in which Philippine authorities had exercised control for some time. A tense confrontation followed over the following weeks, as bilateral negotiations failed and China sent more ships to the shoal. The Filipinos demanded China pull back. China expressed outrage that the Philippines had "escalated" the situation by using a navy ship to do law enforcement work. Filipino diplomats flew to Washington to consult. There, administration officials reaffirmed their support but did not clarify whether the United States agreed that the 1951 Mutual Defense Treaty—the legal basis for and bedrock of the alliance—applied to this disputed area. The Filipinos were disappointed, as the lack of clarity on this matter had been a cause for concern in Manila for years.

With no effective channels of communication between Manila and Beijing, Assistant Secretary Kurt Campbell tried to broker a deal to end the standoff. After intense negotiations, Campbell thought he had agreement from both Manila and Beijing to a coordinated pullback from the area. Manila certainly believed there was a deal, and so in the latter part of June (some ten weeks after the initial incident) withdrew its ships, expecting China to reciprocate. China did not, and thus took administrative control of Scarborough Shoal from the Philippines. It was a huge setback for the Philippines, and for the United States.[27] To this day, some in the Philippines hold the United States at least partly responsible for their "loss" of Scarborough Shoal, the argument being that a firm U.S. stance at that time—including an explicit statement that the Shoal fell under the 1951 treaty—could have forced the Chinese to pull back.

The Philippines turned to ASEAN for support, raising the matter during the July 2012 ASEAN Regional Forum Summit. The Chinese, however, could count on support from the host, Cambodia, upon which it continued to lavish large amounts of unconditional assistance. With that, plus China's vague promise finally to start ASEAN-China talks on a long-sought code of conduct for the South China Sea, ASEAN for the first time failed even to issue an end-of-summit communiqué that might have offered support to Manila.[28]

The failure here belonged to ASEAN, and to Cambodia specifically, but it also reflected Manila's stunning lack of pull within the organization. As one of the five original ASEAN members and the region's second-largest nation (by population size), the Philippines should be a powerful voice within ASEAN. It is not, and has not been for some time. This reflects, in part, Manila's narrowly focused diplomacy, which in my experience has tended to emphasize the relationship with Washington and, to some extent, with Beijing and Tokyo, with much less attention paid to ASEAN. According to a few ASEAN insiders with whom I have spoken, President Aquino himself tended to have a short attention span at the long, inefficient ASEAN summit meetings, and so did not endear himself to his counterparts. Others in ASEAN complained that the Philippines failed to consult adequately with its ASEAN counterparts ahead of the summit, turning instead to Washington to help it solve the problem. From the outside, reliance on a slow-moving, consensus-driven, cautious ASEAN rather than turning to major outside players might be maddening, but in the region, it is considered essential.

27 Michael Green, Kathleen Hicks, Zack Cooper, John Schaus, and Jake Douglas, "Counter-Coercion Series: Scarborough Shoal Standoff," Asia Maritime Transparency Initiative, Center for Strategic and International Studies, May 22, 2017, https://amti.csis.org/counter-co-scarborough-standoff.
28 Ely Ratner, "Learning the Lessons of Scarborough Shoal," National Interest, November 21, 2013, https://nationalinterest.org/commentary/learning-the-lessons-scarborough-reef-9442.

A few months after the summit, as Manila and Beijing continued to discuss Scarborough Shoal, Chinese officials reportedly told their Philippine counterparts not to involve the United States or pursue international legal action. The Aquino administration rejected this appeal, and instead took steps that demonstrated an unexpected willingness to stand up to China's bullying. First, the Philippine Congress passed the AFP Modernization Act to bolster its military capabilities, seeking a "minimum credible defense." Second, and of great importance, in January 2013 it filed a challenge to Chinese actions in the South China Sea at the UN Permanent Court of Arbitration under the UN Convention on the Law of the Sea (UNCLOS). This shift from its previous diplomatic reliance on ASEAN probably reflected frustration over that institution's failure to support Manila during the 2012 summit. Third, it accelerated efforts to facilitate a stronger U.S. presence in the region and specifically in the Philippines.

The filing of the UNCLOS case marked a significant change in the approach of the claimants and, frankly, took some courage on the part of the Filipinos, given China's known hostility toward any such legal action (China preferred bilateral negotiations, where its strength would have the advantage). In brief, the Philippine filing asked the Permanent Court of Arbitration to find that China's "nine-dash line"—which asserted "historical rights" over much of the South China Sea—had no basis under UNCLOS. It also asked the court to determine whether certain disputed land features constituted islands or rocks, or were submerged. This mattered greatly because only land features that are determined to be "islands" generate a two-hundred-mile exclusive economic zone. If they are determined to be rocks or submerged features, they would generate only a twelve-mile territorial sea (for rocks) or nothing (for submerged features). Put another way, if the court ruled against China's nine-dash line and found that none of the disputed land features constituted islands (which we expected would be the case), then the area under dispute, at least according to international law, would shrink dramatically, and much of China's claims over maritime areas would be found to have no basis in international law. The Philippine filing also asked the court to affirm that China had no right to block Filipinos from fishing around Scarborough Shoal.

The United States strongly supported the Philippine UNCLOS case, even though it had not ratified UNCLOS, because in addition to opposing Beijing's attempt to assert its sovereignty via force, the United States believed that most of China's extensive maritime claims, as shown on its nine-dash-line map, had no basis in international law. We saw the legal case as a way to line up international law and much of the international community not against China per se, but against an aggressive Chinese effort to illegally assert its sovereignty over a vast area. The goal was to create more pressure on Beijing to back off. On a broader level, we also were arguing that China was undermining international law and practice through many of its actions, and that the international community needed to put pressure on Beijing to conform to the same rules all the rest of us were following (and which had benefited China itself greatly over the years).

In August 2013, I returned to Washington as principal deputy assistant secretary responsible for Southeast Asia, and immediately began working with new East Asia and Pacific assistant secretary Danny Russel and National Security Council (NSC) colleagues to encourage ASEAN nations as well as international partners to speak out in support of the Philippine action at The Hague. This became a top priority for Asia-focused policymakers that summer and fall, and we succeeded in garnering a high degree of international support for the case. We were not lobbying the court, but rather arguing that legal proceedings were an appropriate way to address at least some aspects of the contentious South China Sea disputes. The Chinese disagreed, and made clear they would not accept any ruling by the tribunal (presumably unless it ruled in their favor).

The same month that I resumed work in Washington, we initiated negotiations with the Philippines on the Enhanced Defense Cooperation Agreement (EDCA). The negotiations were the outgrowth of a series of discussions over the previous two years in which Philippine authorities—recognizing that even the enhanced maritime capacity they were working with us to build would not be sufficient—began to discuss ways in which more U.S. forces and equipment could be present in the country.

In August 2011, the joint Mutual Defense/Security Engagement Board had agreed to develop ideas for enhancing cooperation, particularly in the maritime arena, including but not limited to possible rotation of U.S. maritime assets through the Philippines. During the January 2012 Bilateral Security Dialogue in Washington, Philippine officials expressed support for a greater U.S. military presence. Two months later, Manila announced President Aquino wanted to host more U.S. troops on a rotational basis, as well as to step up ship visits and joint exercises. Aquino met with President Obama in Washington in June, and reiterated his desire for more U.S. support. After the Chinese in effect told the Filipinos they would just have to accept Chinese control of Scarborough Shoal, Manila decided it needed to pursue an agreement that would facilitate a greater U.S. military presence.[29]

Negotiations would take eight rounds over eight months. The biggest challenge was to find language that would allow U.S. forces to enjoy regular access to Philippine bases without violating the Philippine Constitution's prohibition on foreign military bases or triggering the Philippine public's understandable concerns about the agreement infringing on their sovereignty. Defense Secretary Chuck Hagel, during his late August 2013 visit to the Philippines, hinted at the likely solution direction by stating, "The United States does not seek permanent bases in the Philippines that would represent a return to an outdated Cold War mentality. . . . Instead, we're using a new model of military to military cooperation befitting two great allies and friends. I'm looking to increase our rotational presence here . . . ."[30] Once Washington and Manila agreed on this conceptual approach, the most difficult issues concerned the duration of the agreement (it ended up being for ten years) as well as various provisions the Philippine government needed to assure its public and its Congress that the agreement would not give the U.S. military either de facto control of Philippine bases or the right to take actions without Philippine approval.

In the middle of the negotiations, super typhoon Haiyan (also known as Yolanda) struck the central Philippines on November 8, 2013, killing thousands, displacing millions, and causing catastrophic physical damage. The typhoon was one of the strongest ever recorded, with winds of nearly 200 mph. It also produced a massive storm surge of more than seven meters (twenty-three feet), all but wiping out the city of Tacloban (pop. 240,000) on Leyte Island. In an already poor part of the country, millions lost not only their homes but also their livelihoods. The infrastructure was devastated.

In the days ahead of Haiyan making landfall, we were already preparing to respond, in close coordination with Embassy Manila, USAID,

29 Renato Cruz de Castro, "The 21st Century Philippine-US Enhanced Defense Cooperation Agreement (EDCA): The Philippines Policy in Facilitating the Obama Administration's Strategic Pivot to Asia," *Korean Journal of Defense Analysis* 26, no. 4 (December 2014): 427–44.

30 Manuel Mogato, "Hagel Assures Philippines No New Permanent Bases," Reuters, August 30, 2013, https://www.reuters.com/article/philippines-usa/hagel-assures -philippines-no-new-permanent-u-s-bases-idINL4N0GV1OZ20130830.

and PACOM. Because massive storms and earthquakes usually severely damage the local infrastructure, one of the biggest immediate problems in responding is logistics: how to get relief to areas when roads, bridges, and airports are not functioning. That is when our military's incredible logistical capacity pays huge dividends. USAID's Office of Foreign Disaster Assistance also has tremendous expertise and experience, and works effectively with our military.

So, while we set up a twenty-four-hour task force at the State Department to coordinate things from our end, our embassy in Manila coordinated on its end. A USAID disaster response team somehow got to Leyte ahead of all other official relief teams and quickly began assessing damage and needs, so that those supplies most needed would have priority. It also coordinated closely with the Philippine government, the UN, and nongovernmental organizations active in the relief effort. Within a short period, the U.S. government arranged for five USAID airlifts to deliver urgently needed relief supplies. U.S. Marines already on the ground in the Philippines responded quickly as well, using C-130s and MV-22 Ospreys to carry relief supplies to Tacloban and other areas. PACOM sent the USS *George Washington* Carrier Strike Group to the Philippines to bolster search and rescue operations, provide medical care, and deliver supplies via its twenty-one helicopters. Overall, the U.S. government provided $37 million in urgent relief and humanitarian assistance, in addition to providing vital logistical and airlift capacity in the initial weeks after the storm.[31]

The U.S. government did this because it was the right thing to do. If its help is requested when a major natural disaster strikes, the United States will offer this kind of assistance to any country. On November 19 I testified at a Senate Foreign Relations Committee hearing on our response to the typhoon and was proud to be able to describe our efforts and our commitment to helping our Filipino friends. We did not do it to win favor with the Filipinos, but there is no doubt that the speed and effectiveness of our response added to the positive views the vast majority of Filipinos held of the United States.

Those warm feelings were then and remain today a critical element in our bilateral alliance, arguably more important than the details of how our militaries work together. A Pew survey in 2015 found that

---

31 Office of the Press Secretary, White House, "Fact Sheet: U.S. Response to Typhoon Haiyan," news release, November 19, 2013, https://obamawhitehouse .archives.gov/the-press-office/2013/11/19/fact-sheet-us-response-typhoon-haiyan.

more than 90 percent of Filipinos viewed the United States favorably, a number that is virtually unmatched around the world.[32]

The boost to Philippine public opinion of the United States emanating from our response to the typhoon probably played a role in allowing us to conclude and sign the EDCA. We had been working for months toward conclusion of the deal in expectation that a signing ceremony would highlight President Obama's scheduled visit to Manila in late April 2014. Just days ahead of his arrival, Foreign Secretary Albert Del Rosario—a strong advocate of the agreement and the alliance—told Ambassador Phil Goldberg that he worried Aquino would not approve the deal. In Washington, where hyper-caffeinated angst is the norm, the worry level shot up.

The problem lay less in any specific provisions than in President Aquino's concern about a possible domestic political backlash. Many in Washington, myself included, routinely underestimated the Philippine public's concerns about sovereignty and wariness toward any deal that might hint of a return to the old days of bases and perceived U.S. domination. I do not know whether most Filipinos shared those concerns, but certainly a significant and vocal minority did. It did not help that the draft EDCA we had presented to Manila was essentially a template agreement we used around the world. It did not offer the Filipinos much in terms of negotiating room, and that led some in the leadership to feel uncomfortable about it.

Ambassador Goldberg recognized this, and quickly engaged key players around Aquino, listening to their concerns and suggesting minor tweaks to address them and to ensure the Filipinos understood they had a genuine say in the text. His efforts paid off. Aquino signed off on the deal. Phil Goldberg and Philippine defense secretary Voltaire Gazmin signed the EDCA on April 28, 2014, just a few hours before President Obama arrived in Manila. It was a big step forward. NSC senior director for Asia Evan Medeiros called it "the most significant defense agreement that the United States has concluded with the Philippines in decades."[33] Under Aquino, the alliance had been revitalized. We were back to being strong strategic partners.

---

32 "America's Global Image," Pew Research Center, June 23, 2015, https://www.pewresearch.org/global/2015/06/23/1-americas-global-image/.

33 Thomas Maresca, "Obama Visits Philippines," *USA Today*, April 27, 2014, https://www.usatoday.com/story/news/world/2014/04/27/us-philippines-defense-pact/8299491/

In brief, the agreement allowed for U.S. forces to rotate through a se-lect number of Philippine military bases and to pre-position equipment at those bases. It also anticipated that the United States would invest to upgrade the capabilities of the bases and to enhance U.S.-Philippine military interoperability. In other words, it provided for an enhanced U.S. military presence and closer bilateral cooperation while recogniz-ing Philippine sovereignty concerns and the need to be attentive to Phil-ippine public sensitivity.

Beijing's actions leading up to the signing only highlighted the need for the agreement. In March, Chinese Coast Guard vessels prevented Philippine ships from supplying a handful of the country's Marines sta-tioned aboard a rusting Philippine Navy ship, the *Sierra Madre*, which had been beached on the Second Thomas Shoal back in 1999. Second Thomas Shoal is little more than a rock, well within the Philippine ex-clusive economic zone, that is submerged at high tide, but it nonetheless was subject of a dispute between China and the Philippines. Beijing jus-tified blocking the resupply by claiming the Philippines intended to use the supplies to build up the site, which in the Chinese view would violate the 2002 China-ASEAN Declaration of Conduct on the South China Sea.

In Washington, we saw the Chinese move as dangerous and pro-vocative, yet another sign of Beijing's willingness to use force to assert its will. In our view, given all the sensitivities and tension in the South China Sea, it was important that no party use force or coercion to try to gain an advantage. We viewed this as separate from the question of resolving disputes over sovereignty. It was a matter of avoiding acts that could spark conflict, and of pushing back against China's "might makes right" approach. We issued a statement criticizing China's "pro-vocative" interference in the Philippine attempt to maintain the status quo, and noted that the status quo predated the 2002 Declaration of Conduct.[34]

The Filipinos urgently needed to resupply the Marines on the *Sierra Madre*. We did not see much strategic value in the ship's presence, but at this point allowing the Chinese to, in effect, force the Philippines to abandon the outpost was not acceptable. The Filipinos conducted a few airdrops of supplies, but that approach was not sustainable. After much internal discussion between State, NSC, and the Defense

---

34 Zachary Keck, "Second Thomas Shoal Tensions Intensify," *The Diplomat*, March 13, 2014, https://thediplomat.com/2014/03/second-thomas-shoal-tensions -intensify/

Department, NSC staff asked President Obama to call President Xi Jinping to, among other things, stress the need to avoid the use of force around Second Thomas Shoal. We also agreed to work with PACOM to provide some "safe" support for Philippine efforts to maintain—but not to build on—the ship and its small Marine detachment. A few weeks later, a U.S. Air Force P-8 airplane flew over the site as two private Philippine boats evaded Chinese vessels and successfully resupplied the *Sierra Madre*.

After the typhoon, we and our Filipino counterparts continued our efforts to implement the EDCA and to strengthen the bilateral relationship even further. As China continued its assertive behavior in the South China Sea and began building artificial islands and putting military installations on them, we committed in July 2015 to provide nearly $40 million to the Philippines as part of the new Maritime Security Initiative for Southeast Asia (which also aimed to provide help to Vietnam and Malaysia). In bilateral talks with the Philippines, we expanded the rotational presence of U.S. military forces to five bases, including one on Palawan, the main island closest to the disputed Spratly Islands. In April 2016, U.S. aircraft operating out of Clark Airfield under the EDCA flew near Scarborough Shoal in a clear demonstration of our presence. That same month, at the conclusion of our annual *Balikatan* joint exercises, visiting Defense Secretary Ash Carter highlighted our "ironclad" commitment to the Philippines.[35]

The purpose of Carter's language was to reassure Philippine authorities who remained concerned about our unwillingness to state explicitly that the 1951 Mutual Defense Treaty applied to the disputed areas of the South China Sea. Without revealing sensitive information, I can say that we had multiple discussions about this in Washington, and there was concern about the possibility of putting ourselves in a situation in which we could be pulled into an active conflict with China not of our own choosing.

I left for my assignment in Myanmar in March 2016, feeling that—after many ups and downs—both the Philippines' domestic situation and our bilateral alliance were moving in a positive direction. We had

---

35 Sheena Chestnut Greitens, "The U.S.-Philippine Alliance in a Year of Transition: Challenges and Opportunities," working paper, Brookings Institution, May 2016, https://www.brookings.edu/wp-content/uploads/2016/11/fp_20160713 _philippines_alliance.pdf.

put serious substance into the military alliance, with a rotating presence of forces and sustained high levels of assistance and joint exercises, even as JSOTF-P's operation wound down. The political and diplomatic relationships were sound, and confidence levels in Washington vis-à-vis Manila had increased.

An Abrupt Shift

In May 2016, Filipino voters elected brash, populist Davao mayor Rodrigo Duterte to succeed the outgoing Nonoy Aquino, ushering in yet another abrupt shift in the style and tone of leadership out of Malacañang Palace. In a country still dominated by elites from a handful of powerful oligarchic families and still suffering from widespread poverty and inequality, Duterte's populist, hands-on style and vow to get tough on corruption and crime appealed to many voters.

Immediately upon entering office, Duterte unleashed a violent "war on drugs," openly saying that drug dealers and users who did not surrender themselves would be hunted down and killed on the streets. "My order is shoot to kill you," he said on August 6. "I don't care about human rights, you'd better believe me."[36] In his first few months in office, his own national police chief publicly stated that police forces had killed several hundred drug peddlers, and claimed "vigilantes" had killed several thousand more.

When the United States criticized the obvious human rights abuses, Duterte fired back, calling both our ambassador and President Obama "sons of bitches," and threatening to turn away from the U.S. alliance. In October 2016, he made a state visit to China, where he announced the Philippines' "separation" from the United States and signed a series of agreements with President Xi Jinping, winning commitments from Beijing for some $24 billion in soft loans and investment pledges. Tellingly, Duterte did not raise (at least publicly) the Philippines' high-profile legal case at The Hague against China's actions in the South China Sea, which had resulted in an overwhelming repudiation of China's claims. Instead, he said he would set the ruling aside and try to

---

36 Barbara Demick, "Rodrigo Duterte's Campaign of Terror in the Philippines," *New Yorker*, August 26, 2016, https://www.newyorker.com/news/news-desk/rodrigo-dutertes-campaign-of-terror-in-the-philippines.

resolve the disputes through bilateral dialogue, which is what China had wanted all along.[37]

In Washington, policymakers felt another case of "Philippine whiplash," as Duterte shifted his country's policy dramatically and blasted the United States crudely and loudly. Duterte's views on the United States, which appeared to be deeply personal and consistently antagonistic, were out of step with those of the rest of the country. At the same time, Duterte was then—and has remained—extremely popular with his electorate. Given these realities, Washington wisely chose not to do battle with Duterte, but instead to focus on maintaining and even building on our strong relations with the rest of the country, including many senior officials in the Duterte administration.

Throughout the Duterte presidency, Washington sought to maintain steady, consistent engagement with the Philippines, and support for all those in the country who continued to promote democratic values, strong institutions, and broad-based economic development. As is the case in most of the region, the United States channels a significant amount of its assistance through quality civil society organizations. In places such as the Philippines, civil society members have bravely pushed for reform, transparency, greater justice, accountability, and for the rights of women and members of the LGBTQ community, often at significant personal risk.

More broadly, the United States continued its assistance programs, including support for military modernization as well as economic development, and worked with the Duterte administration whenever possible on major strategic issues, such as when China's aggressive actions in the South China Sea went beyond what even Duterte found acceptable.

Washington also jumped in to assist when ISIS-linked extremists seized the city of Marawi in Mindanao in 2017. I had visited Marawi in 1985, when warlord Ali Dimaporo dominated the area, and again in 2008, when Ambassador Kenney and I witnessed anti-American demonstrations and felt the tension in the air as religious hardliners worked to gain influence in the city. We of course had no idea how bad things were going to get several years later.

---

37 Richard Javad Heyderian, "Philippine President Duterte's Pivotal Visit to China," China-US Focus, October 26, 2016, https://www.chinausfocus.com/foreign-policy/philippine-president-dutertes-pivotal-visit-to-china.

In 2016, ISIS in Syria had publicly named Isnilon Hapilon its leader in the Philippines. Hapilon was leader of an Abu Sayyaf faction and one of the terrorists responsible for the 2001 kidnapping of three Americans (and more than a dozen Filipinos). He and his group had earlier pledged allegiance to ISIS, solidifying worrisome links with the most extreme Middle East terrorist group. In May 2017, AFP troops entered Marawi looking for Hapilon, who was believed to be hiding there. The troops ran into fierce resistance from hundreds of militants, who took over the city and raised the ISIS flag. This led to a brutal five-month siege, during which much of the city's population was forced to evacuate and a significant portion of the city was destroyed. The prolonged urban conflict, which made the headlines globally on an almost-daily basis, resulted in some nine hundred terrorists killed, including Hapilon, along with approximately 150 Philippine troops and dozens of civilians.

It was a scary reminder that the terrorist threat in Southeast Asia remained very real. The United States, despite the cooling of relations with the Duterte administration, offered tangible and important assistance in the siege of Marawi. The Pentagon publicly confirmed that U.S. Special Forces elements, while avoiding conflict, were providing training and other technical assistance, including aerial surveillance, electronic eavesdropping, and communications.[38]

President Duterte used his popular support to go after his opponents, taking legal action against journalists such as Rappler's Maria Ressa and opposition politicians such as Senator Leila DeLima, who, at the time of this writing, had spent five years in jail on drug charges that many believe were trumped up to silence her. In Duterte's final year of his six-year presidential term, Philippine civil society remained under threat, as extrajudicial killings targeted many who advocated for human rights. Duterte also continued to pursue his drug war, resulting in thousands of killings, but, in the eyes of some of his supporters, also effectively reducing crime.

On foreign policy, Duterte leaned away from Washington and toward China, criticizing the U.S. refusal to state explicitly that the 1951 Mutual Defense Treaty applied to disputed areas in the South China Sea. In late 2018, Philippine national defense secretary Delfin Lorenzana called for a review of that treaty and implied it could be

---

38 Neil Jerome Morales and Simon Lews, "U.S. Joins Battle as Philippines Takes Losses in Besieged City," Reuters, June 9, 2017, http://reut.rs/2rbCIhe.

canceled. Duterte himself visited China five times as president, while avoiding Washington. Starting in mid-2019, his infatuation with China appeared to diminish to some extent, with the Philippines declining to pursue joint development in the disputed Reed Bank area and new foreign minister Teddy Locsin taking a more pro-U.S. position than his predecessor had. Secretary of State Mike Pompeo's March 2019 comments, in which he for the first time explicitly stated that the 1951 defense treaty applied to the South China Sea, certainly helped.

If the past twenty years have been a roller-coaster in terms of the bilateral relationship, then 2020 was a particularly intense up-and-down ride. In January, President Duterte threatened to cancel the VFA—which governs all U.S. military presence in the country—unless Washington reversed its decision to cancel Duterte ally Senator Ronald Dela Rosa's U.S. visa. A month later, the Foreign Ministry delivered a note to the U.S. embassy formally notifying us of the government's intention to end the agreement after the required 180-day "cooling off" period. On June 1, the ministry notified the embassy that Manila wished to "freeze" that 180-day countdown, as those around Duterte debated the wisdom of pulling out of the accord.

In July 2020, Foreign Secretary Teddy Locsin, in an official statement, called on China to honor the 2016 Permanent Court of Arbitration ruling on the UNCLOS case, marking the first time since that ruling that Manila had spoken out forcefully in support of it.[39] A month later, following Mike Pompeo's statement declaring that the United States had determined that China's vast maritime claims were illegal, Defense Secretary Lorenzana announced that President Duterte had decided the Philippines would not participate in any joint maritime exercises beyond its twelve-mile territorial seas.[40] Lorenzana's statement in effect endorsed China's position, so was a major step backwards. At the September ASEAN Summit, Foreign Secretary Locsin again stepped for-

---

39 Teodoro L. Locsin, Jr., "Statement of Secretary of Foreign Affairs Teodoro L. Locsin, Jr. on the 4th Anniversary of the Issuance of the Award in the South China Sea Arbitration," Department of Foreign Affairs, Philippine National Government Portal, July 12, 2020, https://dfa.gov.ph/dfa-news/statements-and -advisoriesupdate/27140-statement-of-secretary-of-foreign-affairs-teodoro-l-locsin -jr-on-the-4th-anniversary-of-the-issuance-of-the-award-in-the-south-china-sea -arbitration.

40 Kathrin Hille and John Reed, "US's Tougher Stance on South China Sea Undermined by Philippines," *Financial Times*, August 16, 2020, https://www.ft.com/ content/8537751f-2ffd-4d78-b6bb-2b3beb5230c3.

ward, making a strong statement welcoming the U.S. presence in the region and pointing a finger at China.[41] Speaking to the UN General Assembly's annual meeting in late September 2020, President Duterte made his strongest statement to date, insisting that the 2016 Court ruling was international law and that all countries must abide by it.[42] A few days earlier, Foreign Secretary Locsin had explicitly stated that, if China attacked Philippine forces in the South China Sea, he would call Washington and activate the 1951 Mutual Defense Treaty. Locsin also took the opportunity to blame the Obama administration for having allowed China to take control of Scarborough Shoal in 2012.[43]

In July 2021, having twice more extended the freeze on the 180-day countdown to end the VFA, President Duterte reversed his January 2020 decision to terminate the agreement, publicly announcing that the deal was back in force. Washington breathed a sigh of relief, pleased that a significant threat to the alliance had been removed.

Whatever else one might think of Duterte's foreign policy, there is no doubt that it ended the brief period under President Aquino during which the bilateral alliance seemed to be a genuine strategic partnership. On the domestic front, Duterte accentuated the country's longstanding lack of accountability on human rights and continued the unfortunate practice of pursuing legal action against political opponents and critics.

While not a member of the Philippines' traditional oligarchy, Duterte did little to change the dominance of the country's political family dynasties. After the 2019 elections, some 14 of the 24 national senators belonged to a powerful clan, as did 162 of 300 House of Representative members. Sixty of 81 governors hail from political families, and 40 are related to members of the House. In the Marcos family stronghold of Ilocos Norte, governor Matthew Marcos Manotoc succeeded his mother, Imee Marcos (daughter of Ferdinand and Imelda), who was elected senator. Another Marcos family member, Eugenio Angelo

41 "Philippines Welcomes U.S. Presence to Maintain Order in South China Sea," Radio Free Asia, August 26, 2020, https://www.rfa.org/english/news/china/presence-08262020183240.html.

42 Sebastian Strangio, "In UN Speech, Duterte Stiffens Philippines' Stance on the South China Sea" The Diplomat, September 23, 2020, https://thediplomat.com/2020/09/in-un-speech-duterte-stiffens-philippines-stance-on-the-south-china-sea/.

43 Roy Mabaso, "Locsin to Call Washington if Filipino Vessel Attacked in West PH Sea," Manila Bulletin, August 26, 2020, https://mb.com.ph/2020/08/26/locsin-to-call-washington-if-filipino-vessel-is-attacked-in-west-ph-sea/.

Marcos Barba, won election as the House representative, and another, Michael Marcos Keon, served as mayor of the provincial capital of Laoag. Cecile Araneta Marcos became the province's vice governor. [44]

When I look at the Philippines since the glory days of People Power in 1986, it is clear that, despite some important economic progress and continued democratic elections, the country still has not addressed the fundamental challenges of the dominance of the oligarchy, the huge gap between the rich and the poor, widespread political violence, and impunity for the powerful. There has been some progress in dealing with the issue of Moro separatism, but there is more work to do. On the positive side of the ledger, many Filipinos in government, civil society, and the press continue to push for reform and progress. There is hope in the next generation.

The Way Forward

U.S. policymakers should remember that the Philippines occupies a uniquely strategic location in Southeast Asia, and also boasts one of the most pro-American populations in the world. Despite the challenges, the United States needs to continue to invest in the relationship. Washington will have to accept that progress likely will remain slow and uneven, and that the alliance relationship will bounce back and forth, depending in good part on who is running the Philippines. The military relationship with the Philippines remains central to U.S. presence and strategy in the region, so Washington needs to cultivate it carefully to maintain access while remaining sensitive to the legitimate sovereignty concerns in the country.

The recipe calls for strategic patience, defined not as inaction but as not overreacting to sudden shifts or public blasts by any future Philippine leaders, plus continued support for pro-reform elements and further efforts to build on the strong public support for the relationship. Washington will need to work with Manila to find ways to strengthen trade and investment ties, which have lagged. Bilateral trade is only some $29 billion, less than half of U.S.-Vietnam trade and considerably below our trade levels with Malaysia, Thailand, and even Indonesia. Manila can do more to reduce trade restrictions and improve

---

44 Michael Bueza and Gloria Marie Castro, "MAP: Major Political Families in PH After the 2019 Elections," Rappler, August 30, 2019, https://www.rappler.com/newsbreak/in-depth/map-major-political-families-philippines-after-elections-2019.

the business environment, but the United States should look for every opportunity to build what should be a more powerful pillar of the relationship.

On the Philippine side, it would be helpful to invest more in the relationship with ASEAN. ASEAN membership is an important asset, and the Philippines could benefit substantially—including in its efforts in the South China Sea—by being seen as a more consistently serious partner in the institution. The country would also be wise to encourage—whether in government or in universities and think tanks—its capacity for long-term strategic thinking, which over time might allow it to plot a more steady and effective foreign policy course.

CHAPTER THREE

Great and Good Friends

The United States and Thailand

While the United States and the Philippines have been on a roller-coaster ride of sorts, proponents of U.S.-Thai relations have been discussing, in various forms and for many years, how to revitalize an alliance that seems to have lost its way. In 1989, the U.S-Thai Bilateral Forum agreed that it was a "new era" in the relationship and warned particularly of Thai concerns about the lack of U.S. sensitivity to their interests.[1] In 2010, a National Bureau of Asia Research seminar worried about the strong sense of drift in the alliance.[2] In 2018, both the Center for Strategic and International Studies and the Asia Foundation highlighted that the relationship had declined and needed revitalization.[3] In an interview for the Asia Foundation program, former U.S. ambassador to Thailand Eric John said, "Since the end of the Cold War, the relationship has been on autopilot

1 Clark D. Neher and Wiwat Mungkandi, *U.S.-Thailand Relations in a New International Era* (Berkeley, CA: Institute of East Asian Studies, University of California at Berkeley, 1990).

2 National Bureau of Asian Research and Georgetown University, *The United States-Thailand Alliance: Reinvigorating the Partnership*," U.S.-Thailand Alliance Workshop report, April 28, 2010, https://www.nbr.org/wp-content/uploads/pdfs/events/us_thai_alliance_2010_report.pdf.

3 Brian Harding, "Moving the U.S.-Thailand Alliance Forward," CSIS commentary, August 7, 2018, https://www.csis.org/analaysis/moving-us-thailand-alliance-forward; and Thomas Parks and Benjamin Zawacki, *The Future of Thai-U.S. Relations: Views of Thai and American Leaders on the Bilateral Relationship and Ways Forward*, white paper (San Francisco, CA: Asia Foundation, August 2018), https://asiafoundation.org/wp-content/uploads/2018/08/The-Future-of-Thai-U.S.-Relations.pdf.

with neither nation putting forth a lot of effort, a kind of drift into irrelevance for both sides."[4]

For the past fifteen years, these worries about the alliance have been paralleled by U.S. concerns about the Thai political situation. What seemed to many Americans and Thai in the 1990s to be steady and even inexorable movement toward stronger democracy became in the early 2000s a period of intense political polarization, producing two coups that set back prospects for democracy and political stability in a country long hailed as a Southeast Asian success story. These political problems—and particularly the coups—did not cause the drift in the bilateral relationship, but they exacerbated it.

I first went to Thailand as a tourist in 1985 and immediately fell in love with the place. I trekked up to Chiang Rai and the Thai-Lao-Burma border in the northeast, a part of the country that was beautiful but still very undeveloped. The food everywhere was incredible, even on the overnight train from Bangkok to Chiang Mai. I have been back probably fifty times, as a part-time resident while commuting to and from Hanoi in the early 1990s, as a Washington policymaker working on the region, and as ambassador to Myanmar. Although I was never assigned there for more than six weeks at a time, I felt like Thailand was my home away from home in Southeast Asia.

For those of us long involved in Southeast Asian matters, Thailand always has played a central role, both in the region itself and as a key U.S. partner. Through the Cold War and as the United States came to terms with Vietnam, Laos, and Cambodia in the early 1990s, during Indonesia's upheaval in the late 1990s and early 2000s, amid Myanmar's long struggle for peace and freedom, whenever natural disasters struck the region, and during many discussions with and about the region, U.S. officials have counted on Thailand not only as a close ally, but as a constructive and effective diplomatic player and a source of stability and consistency in an often-turbulent region. So the challenges of the past few decades—the seeming drift in the alliance and U.S. concerns over Thai domestic political developments—have been a source of frustration and disappointment.

To understand how these twin challenges developed, it is important to review the history, both of the relationship and of Thai politics. One has to begin with the fact that the Thai kingdom, long known as Siam, is the only Southeast Asian nation never to have been colonized. The

---

4 Parks and Zawacki, *Future of Thai-U.S. Relations*, 14.

Thai are immensely proud of this fact. It reflects diplomatic skill, but also the Thai knack or penchant for playing off major powers against one another and for accommodating external demands *only to the necessary extent* while resisting capitulation. The country's long practice of hedging among the major players has been called "bamboo diplomacy," suggesting a willingness or ability to bend with the wind but not to break.

The U.S.-Thai relationship goes back a long way. The two countries established relations in 1818 and signed a Treaty of Amity and Friendship in 1833, the first such treaty the United States had signed with any Asian nation. Thai colleagues like to remind their U.S. counterparts that in March 1861 King Mongkut sent a letter to President James Buchanan offering two domesticated elephants as gifts to be used as beasts of burden. (In lore, the offer was of elephants to help with the civil war, which is not true.) President Lincoln, who had taken office by the time the king's letter arrived, politely declined in a response in which he memorably addressed the king as "Great and Good Friend."[5]

In a strange, roundabout way, the Second World War—or rather its immediate aftermath—strengthened the relationship. After Japanese forces entered the kingdom, the Thai government allied with Tokyo and declared war on the United Kingdom. Bangkok instructed its ambassador in Washington to deliver a declaration of war on the United States as well, but the ambassador "lost" the message. At the end of the war, the United Kingdom wanted to extract some measure of punishment, but Washington rejected that and chose not to treat Thailand as an enemy.

Thailand by that time was no longer an absolute monarchy. In 1932, conservative elements in the military joined forces temporarily with leftists to execute a bloodless coup and promulgate a new constitution that made Thailand a constitutional monarchy. After the war, the Thai authorities allowed a free press as well as, for the first time, political parties that competed in a democratic election in 1946. That year also marked the ascension of Bhumibol Adulyadej to the throne, after his predecessor died under mysterious circumstances. King Bhumibol, who had been born in Cambridge, Massachusetts, went on to reign for more than seventy years, during which he played a huge role in Thai life.

---

5 "History of the U.S. and Thailand," U.S. Embassy & Consulate in Thailand, http://th.usembassy.gov/our-relationship/policy-history/io/.

Thai politics over the following decade involved a series of coups by rival groups, all of which were closely tied to the country's powerful military and bureaucracy. Political parties and the parliament generally were not powerful forces, nor was public opinion, and the military/ bureaucracy largely set and implemented policy. The king at that time enjoyed popular support but was not yet the powerful influence he would become in the years ahead.

In 1957, Field Marshal Sarit Thanarat, the Thai Army's commander-in-chief, staged yet another coup. Sarit served as prime minister until his death in 1963. His emergence coincided with the steady rise in influence and popularity of the king. Paul Handley, author of the controversial book *The King Never Smiles*, argues that Sarit and those around him made a deliberate decision to elevate the king's public persona, and to wrap military in the mantle of an increasingly popular and prestigious monarchy. Sarit reintroduced the royal language, provided funds to the palace, and publicly associated the king with many of the government's activities.[6] He also strengthened the country's *l'ese majeste* laws, making it a crime to criticize the king.

The Cold War Alliance

The military dominated Thai politics from the time of Sarit's coup until 1973. This period also marked the apex in U.S.-Thai alliance relations. Spooked by Mao Zedong's victory in China in 1949, the Soviet and Chinese-backed North Korean attack on South Korea in 1950, and the Viet Minh's defeat of the French at Dien Bien Phu in 1954, Thai authorities shifted from their traditional neutral stance to a pro-West position to counter the communist threat.

Thailand sent troops to Korea to join UN forces seeking to repel the North Korean advance. In 1954, it signed the Manila Pact, which created the U.S.-led Southeast Asia Treaty Organization (SEATO), establishing a legal basis for its new alliance with the United States. SEATO's headquarters was placed in Bangkok. (Other SEATO members were the Philippines, Pakistan, the United Kingdom, France, Australia, and New Zealand.) Between 1950 and 1956, the United States and Thailand signed agreements on education and culture, economic and technical cooperation,

---

6 Kevin Hewison, "A Book, the King and the 2006 Coup," review of *The King Never Smiles. A Biography of Thailand's Bhumibol Adulyadej*, by Paul Handley, *Journal of Contemporary Asia* 38, no 1 (February 2008): 190–211.

and military assistance. The United States also launched the Fulbright Program in Thailand in 1950, enhancing educational ties. Washington helped Thailand secure the World Bank's first-ever loan to a Southeast Asian nation, dispatched a Military Advisory Assistance Group to the country, and stepped up military assistance. From 1951 until 1972, U.S. military assistance consistently accounted for at least 25 percent and sometimes as much as 50 percent of Thailand's military budget.[7]

The United States saw Thailand as a bulwark against communist expansion in the region and a potential model of national (and eventually democratic) development. The Thai, in turn, saw the alliance as the best way to preserve their security and independence in the face of significant communist threats, and also a way to bolster their own economic and military capacity. This set of common interests, and the close cooperation born of it, produced a remarkably strong and effective alliance over the next few decades.

In the late 1950s and early 1960s, both Thailand and the United States saw the situation in Laos as the major external threat. Both wanted tiny, impoverished, landlocked Laos to be a buffer (along with Cambodia and South Vietnam) between China and North Vietnam and the rest of the region, including of course Thailand. Laos was riven by civil war, with the North Vietnamese and Chinese backing the communist Pathet Lao. In his early 1961 meeting with the incoming president, John F. Kennedy, President Eisenhower highlighted the Laos crisis, warning his successor that he might have to consider military intervention to prevent the fall of "the cork in the bottle" (Laos) to communism. If Laos fell, he warned, it would be "the beginning of the loss of most of East Asia."[8]

For the Thai, if the Pathet Lao prevailed, communist forces would be just across the Mekong River from the kingdom, specifically the country's northeast, which was isolated, poor, and—the Thai worried—vulnerable to communist elements. It did not help that the Communist Party of Thailand announced in 1961 that it was launching an armed

7 Gregory V. Raymond, "Strategic Culture and Thailand's Response to Vietnam's Occupation of Cambodia, 1979–1989: A Cold War Epilogue," *Journal of Cold War Studies* 22, no. 1 (Winter 2020): 4–45.

8 U.S. Department of State, "Memorandum for the Record," January 19, 1961, *Foreign Relations of the United States, 1961–1963* (24 vols., Washington, D.C. 1988-1996, 24: 21), cited in Edmund. F. Wehrle, "'A Good, Bad Deal': John F. Kennedy, W. Averell Harriman, and the Neutralization of Laos, 1961-1962." *Pacific Historical Review* 67, no. 3 (1998): 349–77, www.jstor.org/stable/3641753.

struggle inside the country, though insurgent activity was minimal until 1965.

The Kennedy administration adopted a two-pronged approach to the Lao crisis, holding international negotiations in Geneva to try to reach a deal with the Soviet Union to ensure Laos' neutrality, while stepping up efforts to bolster Thailand's security capacity. A 1960 military assistance agreement, along with the king's successful visit to the United States that same year, had further bolstered the bilateral relationship, and the United States stepped up the flow of military assistance to Bangkok. During the king's visit, he and President Eisenhower issued a joint communiqué that reaffirmed ". . . the unwavering determination of the United States fully to honor its Treaty commitments undertaken in the cause of collective security."[9]

An even more important step occurred during Thai foreign minister Thanat Khoman's March 1962 visit to Washington. In an effort to reassure the perennially worried Thai, who were extremely wary of Washington's support for the Geneva negotiations, Secretary of State Dean Rusk and Thanat signed what became known as the Rusk-Thanat Agreement, which reaffirmed the U.S. commitment to Thai security and made clear that the commitment did not depend on the Manila Pact (which many interpreted as requiring the agreement of all SEATO members before forces could be deployed).[10]

In May 1962, amid negotiations in Geneva, the Pathet Lao scored a major victory over government troops in Nam Tha Province in Laos, alarming both the Thai and the United States. Prime Minister Sarit immediately sent Thai forces to the border and President Kennedy deployed 6,500 U.S. troops to Thailand. This marked the first U.S. combat troop presence in Southeast Asia since World War II, and the first time Thailand had voluntarily accepted foreign troops on its soil.[11] Kennedy withdrew the troops once the Geneva talks produced an agreement, but a precedent had been set. The Thai were not happy with the Ge-

---

9 *United States Security Agreements and Commitments Abroad: Kingdom of Thailand. Hearings Before the Subcommittee on United States Security Agreements and Commitments Abroad of the Comm. on Foreign Relations*, 91st Cong. (November 10, 1969) (statement of Ambassador Leonard Unger).

10 Arne Kislenko, "A Not So Silent Partner: Thailand's Role in Covert Operations, Counter-Insurgency, and the Wars in Indochina," *Journal of Conflict Studies* 24, no. 1 (2004): 65–96.

11 Kislenko, "A Not So Silent Partner."

neva accords, believing they were not likely to succeed in stopping the Pathet Lao. Thus early on doubts arose among the Thai about the U.S. commitment to its protection.

Nonetheless, over the next few years, the two countries worked closely to counter the threat from Laos. The details could fill a book, but in brief they involved U.S. training of Thai counterinsurgency forces, and U.S. and Thai training of and support for Lao government forces, some of it covert. The Thai government allowed U.S. forces to use its bases to launch airstrikes against Vietnamese sanctuaries and supply lines in Laos, and removed the previous requirement for prior notification of those strikes. Thai "volunteers" also worked directly with Lao forces against the Pathet Lao.

After the Gulf of Tonkin incident in August 1964, Bangkok and Washington began to shift their focus to Vietnam. The two governments agreed to upgrade some Thai airbases and to station U.S F-100 aircraft in Thailand. Following North Vietnamese attacks on Pleiku in early 1965, which prompted President Johnson to deploy U.S. combat forces to Vietnam, the Thai agreed to an expanded U.S. presence and allowed the United States to begin systematically bombing Vietnamese targets from Thai bases.[12]

There was no formal agreement allowing U.S. use of the bases, nor was there a status of forces agreement governing the presence of U.S. troops. Thai authorities insisted that the bases were fully Thai, but in practice did not vigorously monitor or regulate U.S. use of those bases. For its part, the United States continued to increase military assistance to Thailand and carried out significant construction activities to expand existing bases and build new ones. This culminated in the early 1966 completion of the sprawling airbase at Utapao, which was capable of launching B-52s. Utapao quickly became a major locus of operations for U.S. bombing runs.

By the end of 1965, there were 9,000 U.S. Air Force personnel stationed in Thailand, and some 200 aircraft. A year later, those numbers rose to 25,000 and 400, and they reached highs of 50,000 personnel and approximately 600 aircraft by 1968–69. Bangkok also sent some 11,000 Thai troops to Vietnam to support the South Vietnamese

---

12 Unger, *United States Security Agreements and Commitments Abroad: Kingdom of Thailand.*

government.[13] Thailand had become essential to U.S. prosecution of the war in Vietnam.

Thailand's increasingly clear support for U.S. efforts, as well as its own direct involvement, coincided with or perhaps caused increased Chinese support for the kingdom's communist insurgency. From 1965 to 1966 insurgent activity picked up significantly, causing serious concern in both Bangkok and Washington. The United States estimated in 1968 the insurgents numbered some two thousand, bolstered by steady propaganda via Chinese-funded radio stations. Ambassador Graham Martin expressed concern that the insurgency was starting to look "too much like Vietnam."[14] In response, the U.S. boosted training of and support for Thai counterinsurgency forces, which were able to gain the upper hand against the insurgents.

Doubts Creep In

The year 1969 marked a high point in terms of numbers of U.S. forces in Thailand and Thai forces in Vietnam. Over the next few years, however, several developments led the Thai—who had long harbored concerns about U.S. reliability—increasingly to doubt America's commitment. First, President Nixon proclaimed the Nixon (Guam) Doctrine, under which the United States would begin to turn over more of the actual fighting of communist forces to regional governments. This was directed at South Vietnam but also affected Thailand. The United States began to draw down its forces in Thailand, but also to reach out to Beijing for the first time. In September 1969, the war-weary U.S. Senate passed a resolution stating that, in the event of conflict in Thailand, no U.S. troops should be sent.

By 1972, the United States had established relations with the People's Republic of China and was deep in peace negotiations with the North Vietnamese in Paris. In 1973, those talks produced the Paris Peace Accords to end the war, and the United States moved to pull its combat forces out of Vietnam. As this happened, the Thai withdrew their own forces out of Vietnam and began negotiating the withdrawal of all U.S forces from Thailand.

---

13 Unger, *United States Security Agreements and Commitments Abroad: Kingdom of Thailand.*
14 Kislenko, "A Not So Silent Partner," 77.

Events accelerated. North Vietnamese forces attacked the south in force in spring 1975 and captured Saigon on April 30. Communist forces also seized control of Cambodia and Laos, while the United States—tired of the war and with President Ford lacking congressional support to intervene—stood by. Privately, the Thai were near panic, holding a National Security Council meeting shortly after Saigon fell to contemplate what they would do if Vietnamese forces did not stop but instead turned west toward Thailand.[15] Publicly they reacted sharply, with Foreign Minister Thanat telling the press: "If anything, the April capitulation of Phnom Penh and Saigon, by dealing a heavy blow to the U.S. position in the whole of Asia, raised doubts about how effectively it will play its future role as a responsible regional power."[16] The Thai normalized relations with Beijing in July 1975 and watched the last U.S. forces depart their country in March 1976. Before that happened, however, one additional incident damaged the bilateral relationship. When the Khmer Rouge seized the U.S. container ship *Mayaguez* in May 1975, the United States sent forces out of Utapao to try to rescue the crew without consulting or even informing the Thai authorities, which angered the government and resulted in Thai protests.[17]

Thus ended the period of greatest trust and cooperation in the relationship, at least on the Thai side. The alliance continued, but arguably Americans now looked at it more fondly than the Thai did. For the United States, the Thai had been exceptional allies, allowing U.S. forces to operate with significant freedom out of their bases and hosting thousands of American GIs on rest and recreation visits. The Thai had also benefited immensely, both from U.S. protection and from the vast sums both the U.S. government and visiting GIs spent in the country. Many close relationships had been built and endured. Still, the rapid U.S. withdrawal from the region created serious doubts among

---

15 Telephone interview with Catharin Dalpino, Georgetown University, August 6, 2020.

16 Kenneth S. Harbin, "The Expanding Sino-Thai Military Relationship: Implications for U.S. Policy in Thailand," (master's thesis, Naval Postgraduate School, December 1990), https://Calhoun.nps.edu/bitstream/handle/10945/27592/90Dec_Harbin.pdf

17 Lewis M. Stern, "Diverging Roads: 21st-century U.S.-Thai Defense Relations," *Strategic Forum* 241 (June 2009), Institute for National Strategic Studies, National Defense University, https://ciaotest.cc.columbia.edu/wps/inss/0017418/f_0017418_14900.pdf.

Thai policymakers, who would increasingly hedge their bets even while continuing to work with Washington.

The way in which the Thai managed the alliance, even at its peak, warrants attention, because it reflected longstanding Thai concerns with safeguarding their sovereignty or avoiding the perception among their own citizens that they were turning the country over to the Americans. As noted above, the Thai allowed U.S. forces to operate freely but avoided any formal agreement and insisted that U.S. forces only use Thai facilities and not build their own. It was America's first taste of the "Thai way," which (in my simple definition) meant a remarkable pragmatism and willingness to accommodate external interests to a degree as long as nothing is written down and all can be plausibly denied. The United States, in turn, did not interfere in or worry unduly about Thai domestic politics, despite the lack of democracy.

But Thai politics were evolving nonetheless. In late 1973 security forces bloodily suppressed student demonstrations, killing more than one hundred people. The resulting public uproar forced Prime Minister Thanom Kittikachorn to resign and leave the country. The king, for the first time, stepped in and named a former university rector, Judge Sanya Dharmasakti, as interim prime minister to oversee the drafting of a new constitution. The resulting 1974 document moved Thailand into a brief period of democratic rule that ended with yet another military coup in late 1976. For most of the next fifteen years, the military ruled, but with the king and an elected parliament playing more influential roles than they had in the past.

Focus on Cambodia

Vietnam's December 1978 invasion and occupation of Cambodia presented a new threat to Thailand and ASEAN. The Singapore government publicly warned, "What is happening in Cambodia today could happen to us tomorrow . . . and Thailand is on the frontline."[18] Vietnamese troops were now right on the Thai border. The Thai swung into action, reaching out to the Chinese (who supported the Khmer Rouge government and opposed Vietnam's invasion), the United States, and ASEAN.

The Thai worked feverishly through diplomatic channels to deny recognition to the Hanoi-installed government and to pressure Vietnam to withdraw. Prime Minister Prem Tinsulanonda and Foreign

---

18 Raymond, "Strategic Culture and Thailand's Response."

Minister Siddhi Savetsila worked to create a Cambodian resistance that would be acceptable to both China and the rest of ASEAN. In June 1982 a coalition of opposition groups came together as the Coalition Government of Democratic Kampuchea. The Chinese began to funnel weapons to the opposition through Thailand and in 1986 began selling arms to Thailand; they also ended their support for the Communist Party of Thailand, severely weakening the insurgent effort.[19]

Washington also stepped in, flexing the alliance's muscles for the first time in several years. After a Vietnamese incursion into Thailand in June 1980, Washington quickly airlifted supplies, including artillery, to Thailand. In 1982 Defense Secretary Caspar Weinberger visited Bangkok and reaffirmed that the United States remained bound by the Manila Pact and the 1962 Rusk-Thanat agreement to defend Thailand. The United States increased military assistance with an arms sales program that enabled Thailand to buy weapons at low interest rates. Over the next few years, U.S. military assistance grew to $100 million per year, and a 1985 memorandum of understanding provided the Thai with a stockpile of ammunition for use in the event of an emergency, the first such U.S. arrangement outside of NATO and South Korea. The two allies began a series of joint and combined training exercises centered on the annual Cobra Gold exercises.[20]

The shared goal of pushing the Vietnamese out of Cambodia, in the context of the continuing Cold War and Soviet support for Vietnam, kept the alliance reasonably healthy through the 1980s. Senior U.S. and Thai diplomats and other officials worked closely together on the diplomatic front to deny the Phnom Penh regime legitimacy and to keep the pressure on Vietnam. It was not a return to the heights of the 1960s alliance, as the Thai had diversified their security and diplomatic engagements to include China and ASEAN, but it remained a good and important relationship that contributed to the conclusion of a Cambodian peace agreement in 1991 and the Vietnamese withdrawal from the country.[21]

I visited Thailand several times in the early 1990s as part of my work on the Vietnam, Laos, and Cambodia desk, and those visits offered

---

19 Raymond, "Strategic Culture and Thailand's Response," and Harbin, "The Expanding Sino-Thai Military Relationship."
20 Muthiah Alagappa, *The National Security of Developing States: Lessons from Thailand* (Dover, MA: Auburn House Publishing Company, 1987), 107–13.
21 Telephone interview with Richard Childress, August 21, 2020.

a sense of the closeness of our relationship. First, Thailand was the jumping-off point for any travel into the old Indochina, and our embassy in Bangkok worked closely with the Thai to monitor the situation in all three countries. The Thai had been unenthusiastic hosts of hundreds of thousands of Vietnamese, Lao, and Cambodian refugees after 1975, and thousands still remained in Thai refugee camps, not to mention all the refugees from Burma. I remember crossing the Mekong from Vientiane to Udorn, where we still maintained a consulate, and from there traveling to visit a Hmong refugee camp on Thai soil. We were working with the Thai on a huge range of issues—counternarcotics programs, refugee resettlement, monitoring of conflict in Burma, regional health threats, and of course regional security and diplomacy. Thailand served as our hub for mainland Southeast Asia, and we had comfortable and good relations with a huge swath of the Thai government, military, and public. This was reflected in our enormous embassy, which housed dozens of departments and agencies, many with regional responsibilities.

A New Era

The end of the Cold War and the Vietnamese withdrawal from Cambodia were important achievements, but they also eliminated the external threat that had been the primary motivating factor behind the alliance. Not just in Thailand but more broadly, Washington shifted from a Cold War focus to one that emphasized economic issues and human rights, including reducing our large trade deficit and promoting democracy and good governance. We had always pursued these goals, but they took on added importance in the absence of a major foreign threat. This shift of approach in Washington, combined with domestic Thai factors, resulted in a series of irritants during the 1990s that tested the bilateral relationship.

In February 1991 Prime Minister Chatichai Choonhavan's government, which had been democratically elected in 1988, was toppled in a coup. The coup leaders promised elections and appointed the respected technocrat Anand Panyarachun as prime minister. Following elections in early 1992, General Suchinda Kraprayoon, who had helped instigate the coup and who had not stood for election, pushed his way into the premiership. His move kicked off large-scale protests beginning in April that the army brutally repressed in what became known as Bloody May. The king, by now a powerful force in the country, intervened and compelled Suchinda to resign. The king reappointed Anand as interim prime minister until new elections in September 1992, which returned Thailand to a democratically elected government for the next fifteen years.

The United States reacted quickly to both the 1991 coup and Bloody May, cutting off aid in response to the former and canceling the Cobra Gold exercise in response to the latter. The aid cutoff was mandated by U.S. law; the Cobra Gold cancellation was appropriate, given the military's harsh repression of Thai demonstrators. Nonetheless, some in the Thai military saw the U.S. actions as a sign that Washington could not be counted on.

Around the same time and unrelated to the above actions, U.S. trade officials began pressing the Thai harder on a series of commercial disputes, particularly concerns about intellectual property rights. Washington listed Thailand as a "priority country" on intellectual property rights, suggesting trade action if Thailand did not address U.S. concerns. The United States was separating its trade policy from its alliance relationship; the latter did not preclude tough action on the former.

In 1994 Thailand rejected a U.S. proposal to pre-position military equipment in the Gulf of Thailand, presumably due to concerns about upsetting neighbors (China) or provoking domestic criticism for being too accommodating to foreign interests.[22]

Most importantly, when the Asian Financial Crisis hit Thailand hard in 1997, causing a deep recession, market turmoil, and high unemployment, the Thai hoped and expected that Washington would offer help. However, Washington did not join Japan, Australia, and others in contributing to an August 1997 International Monetary Fund–led rescue package for Thailand. Many Thai were upset, and to this day look back on the crisis as a time when their ally failed to help. Adding to their annoyance was the U.S. inflexibility to renegotiate the terms of an impending F-18 fighter purchase, necessitated by cuts to the Thai military budget in response to the financial crisis. The F-18 deal fell apart in the end. The following year, the U.S. decision to support the Canadian candidate to lead the World Trade Organization over Thai candidate Supachai Panitchpakdi further damaged an already strained relationship.[23]

---

22 Stern, "Diverging Roads: 21st-century U.S.-Thai Defense Relations."
23 Stern, "Diverging Roads: 21st-century U.S.-Thai Defense Relations."

By 2000 ties had cooled considerably from the glory days of the past. Some Thai had begun to complain that, despite their status as an ally, Washington was not treating Thailand any better or differently than it treated any other country. Meanwhile, domestic politics in Thailand had taken an important turn.

The Rise of Thaksin

In the aftermath of the 1991 coup and 1992 demonstrations/elections, momentum in favor of greater democracy grew, fueled by a more active civil society, a growing and better educated middle class, and a global sense that democracy was on the march. The Thai began drafting a new constitution, much of which former prime minister Anand personally oversaw. Despite Anand's relatively conservative reputation, this document would be the country's most democratic constitution. It created conditions for a strong executive but also offered the possibility that a popular party with a strong leader could take control of government without coalition partners. (Part of the goal was to end the era of weak coalition governments that could not complete their terms.) The constitution included a series of checks and balances to prevent such a leader from amassing too much power and also established a constitutional court. The drafting process was very democratic. Many of the traditional elites—the military, big business, the bureaucracy, and some around the palace—did not like it because it would harm their interests. It nonetheless passed in a referendum in 1997, in part because many Thai feared that failure to promulgate it would deepen the already severe crisis the country was facing over the economy.[24]

The new constitution led to the rise of a new and powerful politician, Thaksin Shinawatra. A Sino-Thai billionaire businessman who had previously served in the Royal Thai Police, Thaksin turned out to be a revolutionary politician in the Thai context. Instead of appealing just to the Bangkok elite, who had always decided everything political in the country, Thaksin used modern political tools and tactics to reach out to the long-neglected rural poor, particularly in the heavily populated north and northeast of the country. He convinced rural Thai in those regions that they had a stake at what happened at the national level. He appealed to the Thai sense of national humiliation for having

---

24 Telephone interview with Ambassador Skip Boyce, August 10, 2020.

started the Asian Financial Crisis by promising to repay the IMF loans early. He promised affordable healthcare for all and loans for farmers. His party, *Thai Rak Thai* (Thai Love Thai), won big in the 2001 elections, and Thaksin became prime minister.

In that position, Thaksin delivered on many of his promises. His government did repay the IMF loan early. It did provide healthcare at reasonable cost, devolved more power to local governments, and provided low-cost financing to villagers. Thaksin also did things that Thai politicians just did not do. After his inauguration, he took his wife to Starbucks in his Porsche. He rode a public bus. He also hired a team that pored over the 1997 constitution, looking for every provision and loophole he could use to amass more power.

Thaksin's populist economic policy, known as "Thaksinomics," featured cheap credit and heavy government spending; it successfully stimulated the economy, which was still recovering from the financial crisis of a few years earlier. Economic growth rose from 2.2 percent in 2001 to almost 7 percent in 2003 and 6.1 percent in 2004, and foreign investment grew significantly. The poverty rate dropped from 15.6 percent in 2002 to 9.8 percent in 2005, according to the World Bank.[25]

Thaksin's popularity, political talents, and the strong economy ensured his Thai Rak Thai party won an absolute majority in the 2005 parliamentary elections, the first time that had happened in Thailand. When I arrived on the Mainland Southeast Asia desk a short time after the elections, Thaksin appeared dominant in Thai politics, though there were signs of growing opposition as well. In my initial visits to Thailand during that time, I saw how impressively the country had developed over the previous ten to fifteen years. Bangkok had boomed, but even more impressive was the significant infrastructure development in the previously impoverished areas of the north and northeast, as well as the rapid growth of manufacturing and exports. I still have photographs from my 1985 visit to the northeast that show deep poverty and very low levels of development, at least in some areas. The contrast when I returned twenty years later was stark, in a good way.

Not everything was rosy, however. In 2003, Thaksin launched a "war against drugs," which might have made sense in theory but which in practice resulted in as many as 2,800 extrajudicial killings by security forces. In 2005, the UN Human Rights Committee expressed concern

---

25 "World Bank Open Data," World Bank, https://data.worldbank.org.

about "the extraordinarily large number of killings" associated with the drug war.[26]

Also under Thaksin, long-simmering resentment in the country's three southernmost provinces erupted in 2004 into a violent insurgency that over the next decade would take result in some six thousand deaths. The roots of the conflict go back to Thailand's 1909 absorption of the previously independent Patani Sultanate, followed by decades of Thai authorities trying to assimilate the largely Malay-Muslim population into Thai culture. Violence flared from time to time over the decades, but the situation had been relatively calm since the early 1980s, due at least in part to a deal that had been struck between Prime Minister Prem Tinsulanonda and elites in the south, and the Prem government's shift away from a heavy-handed assimilation approach to a softer strategy.

Under Thaksin, the region saw a significant upsurge in violence, particularly beginning in 2004. The reasons are complex, but longtime Thailand observer Duncan McCargo has argued convincingly that at least some of the upsurge was attributable to Thaksin's effort to replace the governance network that Prem had established with his own for political reasons.[27] In any case, the increased violence contributed to a tearing of the social fabric, particularly between Malay-Muslim and Thai-Buddhist communities in the region, and over time undermined Thaksin's political support.

Increasing Cooperation

Despite these problems, in mid-2005 the bilateral relationship looked somewhat more promising than it did several years earlier. Washington was pleased with Thailand's decade-plus development as a democracy and with its support on regional and global security issues. The Bush administration had launched negotiations with the Thai on a free trade agreement, which had the potential to expand two-way trade and to bolster the overall bilateral relationship. It also approved the sale of advanced air-to-air missiles for Thailand's F-16 fighters in 2001. President Bush designated Thailand a Major Non-NATO Ally in 2003, which

---

26 "Thailand's 'War on Drugs,'" Human Rights Watch, March 12, 2008, https://www.hrw.org/news/2008/03/12/thailands-war-drugs.

27 Duncan McCargo, "Thaksin and the Resurgence of Violence in the Thai South: Network Monarchy Strikes Back?" *Critical Asian Studies* 38, no. 1 (2006): 39–71.

allowed the Thai greater access to U.S. foreign and military assistance, including credit guarantees for major weapons purchases. Thaksin approved the reopening of Utapao airbase and a major naval base at Sattahip, and Thailand became an important logistical hub for our operations in Afghanistan and Iraq, as well as for disaster relief efforts. The Thai themselves contributed a few hundred troops—mostly medical personnel and engineers—to support reconstruction efforts in Afghanistan and Iraq, though Thaksin withdrew Thai forces from Iraq in late 2004 due to Thai public opposition.[28]

The Thai also were assisting efforts to fight terrorism, bolstering cooperation with the CIA to the point of establishing a Counter Terrorism Intelligence Center in 2001. The high point came in 2003, with the Thai arrest of Riduan Isamuddin, a.k.a. Hambali, the suspected leader of Jemaah Islamiyah, just outside of Bangkok. The Thai agreed to transfer Hambali to U.S. custody. At the same time, U.S. officials were viewing with concern the resurgence of a violent insurgency in the country's south. It was an internal matter, but Washington watched carefully for any signs that outside terrorist groups might try to infiltrate and take over the movement.

U.S.-Thai cooperation in responding to the horrific December 2004 tsunami, which hit southern Thailand as well as Indonesia and other areas, highlighted a continuing and underappreciated element of the relationship. The Thai allowed us to use Utapao as a logistical hub for relief operations that focused on Indonesia, which had suffered devastating losses. They did the same in 2008, when Cyclone Nargis hit Myanmar, killing more than 150,000 people.

As deputy assistant secretary responsible for Southeast Asia, I was in Singapore for a meeting with ASEAN the week after Nargis hit; there I received a call from EAP Principal Deputy Assistant Secretary Glyn Davies asking me to go to Bangkok to meet up with Admiral Tim Keating, the PACOM commander, and USAID administrator Henrietta Holsman Fore for a trip to Yangon to offer assistance to the military government there. I flew to Bangkok and then joined Ambassador to Thailand Eric John for the drive to Utapao. Ambassador John explained that Keating, Fore, and I would fly a U.S. C-130 transport plane from Utapao carrying a modest amount of U.S. Thai relief supplies. Thai General Nipat

---

28 Emma Chanlett-Avery and Ben Dolven, "Thailand: Background and U.S. Relations," in *Thailand: Conditions, Issues and U.S. Relations*, ed. Kenny N. Kade (New York: Novinka, 2014), 17–18.

Thonglek would accompany us to—as he explained on the flight—help ease Burmese concerns that the United States might have a hidden agenda. To me, this was a wonderful example of a good partnership—a U.S. aircraft carrying senior U.S. officials flying out of a Thai airbase, accompanied by a senior Thai military official who would help "grease the skids" in Yangon. It did not hurt that, at the same time, former Thai foreign minister Surin Pitsuwan, who was ASEAN's secretary-general, was pressing the Myanmar authorities to accept international assistance. Within a few weeks, U.S. C-130s were flying several relief flights a week from Utapao to Yangon; U.S. aircraft ended up making 185 of these flights over the next several months.

Political Turmoil and Disappointment

Unfortunately, Thai domestic politics had turned messy, setting back not only Thai democracy but also any momentum in the bilateral relationship. In 2005, Thaksin faced rising criticism over corruption scandals involving his cabinet ministers, violence in the south, the abuses and extrajudicial killings associated with his anti-drug campaign, and his autocratic tendencies, including alleged intimidation of the media. There was a sense that, after Thai Rak Thai's landslide electoral victory earlier in the year, Thaksin and his party were acting with increasing arrogance. He and his team used their encyclopedic understanding of the 1997 constitution to begin running roughshod over the institutions that were meant to keep executive power in check. The prime minister's visits to rural areas, particularly in the north and northeast, where he was very popular, began to erode the military's power base. Perhaps more alarming to many, Thaksin's behavior—particularly during these rural visits—suggested that he was attempting to put himself on the same plane as the king, or at least was vying with the king for popular support.

Thaksin clashed with the palace network, led by former prime minister and head of the King's Privy Council, Prem Tinsulanonda. He came to be opposed by many of the old elite—old Sino-Thai money, intellectuals, and some in the military. As Kevin Hewison put it, Thaksin's "egoism, drive, aggression and failure to adequately observe the hierarchies of the Thai power structure earned him multiple enemies and identified him as a danger to the old oligarchy."[29] Then, in early 2006,

---

29 Kevin Hewison, "Thaksin Shinawatra and the Reshaping of Thai Politics," *Contemporary Politics* 16, no. 2 (June 2010): 128.

Thaksin sold his telecom conglomerate, Shincorp, to Singapore's state-owned Temasek Holdings and reportedly paid no tax on the $1.9 billion sale price. This gave his opponents valuable ammunition.

Beginning in early 2006, demonstrations organized by the so-called People's Alliance for Democracy (PAD) began in Bangkok. They included multiple factions but came to be dominated by media titan Sondhi Limthongkul. The demonstrations grew large and constant, with protestors—who came to be known as the "yellow shirts"—accusing Thaksin of corruption, nepotism, anti-democratic behavior, and disloyalty to the king. Thaksin always insisted he was loyal to the king, but his actions allowed his opponents to portray him as a threat to the monarchy.

In response to growing calls for his ouster, and increased criticism from the palace, Thaksin announced early elections to be held in April 2006 to try to restore his mandate. The opposition boycotted. Thak Rak Thai won, but the opposition pointed to the party's relatively unimpressive showing to argue that Thaksin had not won the mandate he had sought. Moreover, the PAD questioned the validity of the election based on technicalities. In other words, voting resolved nothing. The king stepped in and asked the Constitutional Court to rule on the validity of the elections. The court subsequently declared the elections invalid based on the positioning of the voting booths and called for new elections to be held in November.

We in Washington watched all of this in a state of bewilderment. We knew Thaksin enjoyed significant popularity and believed he had been fairly elected in 2001 and again in 2005. At the same time, we understood, based on our embassy's reporting and our own regular conversations with knowledgeable observers, that the anti-Thaksin protests had some legitimate concerns. Thaksin did seem to be undermining checks and balances, he did operate with an authoritarian streak, and he had overseen human rights violations in his fight against drugs. For us, however, it was hard to think of a better way than free elections to resolve such fundamental political disputes.

The 2006 Coup

We, along with many others, expected Thaksin's continued popularity in rural areas to carry his Thai Rak Thai party to victory in November. The Thai military, however, had other ideas. On September 19, 2006, while Thaksin was attending the UN General Assembly in New York, the military staged a coup, the eighteenth since the establishment of Thailand's constitutional monarchy in 1932. The coup leaders promised elections to quickly return power to the people, after the drafting of a new, interim constitution. Until then, they named former army commander Surayud Chulanont interim prime minister.

We saw the coup as a major setback for Thailand and the relationship. The official State Department response was that we were "disappointed" in the coup and urged restoration of civilian rule as soon as possible. White House spokesman Tony Snow stated, "We hope those who mounted it [the coup] will make good, and make good swiftly, on their promises to restore democracy."[30]

Whenever there is a coup or other major democratic setback in any country, but particularly in a country that is a close friend and ally, the fact of the coup sets off at least two lines of action: a cutoff of certain forms of assistance, which is mandated by law in the case of a coup; and, more informally and unofficially, intense pressure from various U.S. domestic constituency groups that are seeking to shape the broader administration response. That includes some in Congress and the media and even within the executive branch, as well as human rights groups, who demand a tough U.S. response to show our unhappiness and to try to force the offending party to change course. It also often involves other groups—sometimes including our military—who emphasize our longer-term, strategic interests in maintaining good relations with the country, and so urge a softer response. The relevant regional bureau of the State Department, in close coordination with our embassy, works with the NSC and other relevant agencies to try to chart a course that (a) respects U.S. law, (b) recognizes the need not to continue "business as usual," and (c) tries to avoid significant damage to our long-term strategic and economic interests.

Washington interagency discussions after the Thai coup in 2006 reflected this dynamic. As required by Section 508 of the Foreign Operations Appropriations Act, the State Department on September 28 announced suspension of several aid programs that provided funds for financing of equipment and weapons purchases, education and training, and peacekeeping operations. Washington also suspended funds under the so-called 1206 program, which allowed the State Department to

---

30 "Thailand's King Gives Blessing to Coup," CNN, September 20, 2006, https://www.cnn.com/2006/WORLD/asiapcf/09/20/thailand.coup.king/.

use Defense Department funds to provide counterterrorism assistance. The total amount suspended was some $29 million. As I recall the discussions, there was not a lot of internal debate within the administration about whether to suspend these programs—it was a requirement under our law.

The debate ensued over what, if any, additional steps the United States should take to show its displeasure. Some groups in and out of government wanted us to take a hands-off approach—i.e., sharply limit our interaction with the new government as a way of showing our disapproval and maintaining our credibility as a force for democracy. Thus, when our capable and experienced ambassador, Skip Boyce, who knew Thailand as well as anyone in the U.S. government, went in to see Surayud shortly after the coup, there was immediate criticism and blowback, including from some within the administration. EAP assistant secretary Chris Hill defended Skip in the face of criticism from NSC officials. Skip had, after all, used the meeting with Surayud to stress the importance of an early return to democracy.

In the end, the administration suspended both U.S. security assistance and free trade agreement (FTA) talks until a democratically elected government returned to office, but decided to go ahead with the Cobra Gold military exercise in February 2007. The security assistance cutoff was legislatively mandated, as I have noted. The FTA talks, frankly, were not going well anyway, due to significant opposition among elements of the Thai public. We hoped that a new, elected Thai government might resume them with vigor, but it was pretty clear that the lack of public support for the agreement had doomed it. We debated Cobra Gold, but the Pentagon (with EAP support) won the argument by stressing that the exercise was not a favor to Thailand but rather of great significance to our regional security efforts (since it was multilateral) and of much value to our own military, as the exercise could not be replicated elsewhere.

In Thailand it seemed the U.S. response was either too hard or too soft, depending on whom one asked. Prominent academic Thitinan Pongsudhirak argued that Thailand "got off lightly in the West," noting what he called the "perfunctory" suspension of security assistance.[31] During my regular visits to Thailand in 2006 and 2007, a

---

31 Thitinan Pongsudhirak, "The Geopolitical Ripples From Thailand's Coup," *Nikkei Asia*, July 31, 2014, https://asia.nikkei.com/Politics/Thitinan-Pong sudhirak-The-geopolitical-ripples-of-Thailand-s-coup.

number of Thai friends quietly scolded me for what they perceived as the insufficiently strong U.S. response to the coup. On the other hand, the Thai military and other anti-Thaksin elements complained that we should have been more understanding, and recognized why the coup was "necessary." To them, our response was yet another example of why Thailand could not fully count on the United States as a security partner.

Increased Political Polarization

The coup-makers intended to use the period right after the coup to "fix" Thai politics by making it impossible for Thaksin to return to power. They failed. Instead, the coup if anything intensified the country's political polarization, resulting in alternating periods of intense turmoil and suppressed political activity. The result has been a virtual halt in Thailand's political development and an intense inward focus that greatly limited Bangkok's normally significant role in the region, all the way up to the present day. Over the next several years, Thailand would go through a dizzying period of large-scale, sometimes violent protests, elections, court action to overturn election results and remove politicians from power, and a deep, painful division within Thai society, all of which would culminate in another coup in 2014.

The post-Thaksin interim government committed to producing a new constitution and running elections. In May 2007 a constitutional tribunal ruled that Thaksin's Thai Rak Thai party had violated election rules in 2006, and therefore must disband. The court also banned Thaksin and 110 party executives from politics for five years, while acquitting the opposition Democrat Party of all election-related charges. Pro-Thaksin elements, however, did not go away. Rather, they formed a new party, the People's Power Party (PPP), and swept to victory in the December 2007 elections. The parliament elected PPP leader Samak Sundaravej as prime minister and set about pursuing what most saw as a Thaksin-directed policy platform, including calling for amendments to the 2007 constitution. Thaksin, who had stayed abroad after September 2006 coup, returned.

By May 2008 the "yellow shirts" had returned to the streets, arguing that the Samak government was a Thaksin proxy and was trying to engineer his return to power. They staged sit-ins at government offices and steadily ramped up protests, some of which turned violent.

In October protestors laid siege to parliament. In late November they occupied Bangkok's two airports, shutting them down for a week.

I was in Bangkok that August as thousands of PAD demonstrators occupied Prime Minister Samak's office, forcing him to work from a military base in north Bangkok. It was striking to see modern, developed Bangkok—which had for years seemed an oasis of stability in a chaotic region—struggling to function amid constant street protests. I remember thinking that, much as we support the right of people to protest peacefully, the demonstrations had crossed the line into lawlessness; i.e., the right to peaceful assembly does not equate to the right to occupy government buildings or airports by force. (I understand the irony of an American diplomat saying this after the January 2021 events in Washington, DC.)

Meanwhile, anti-Thaksin elements turned to the judiciary again, this time to challenge the 2007 election results, Thaksin himself, and those around him. In a series of legal cases, the courts (a) found Samak guilty of illegally taking money for appearances on a television cooking show while serving as prime minister, forcing him out of office; (b) banned deputy party leader Youngyuth Tiyapairat from politics for five years for alleged vote buying; (c) ruled that Foreign Minister Noppadon Pattama and the entire cabinet had violated the constitution by failing to ask parliament to approve a diplomatic agreement with Cambodia; and (d) convicted Thaksin of corruption charges, leading him to (again) flee the country.

Finally, the constitutional court banned the PPP for alleged electoral misdemeanors, and forced the PPP government out of office. In December 2008, Democrat Party leader Abhisit Vejjajiva pulled enough votes from former PPP lawmakers to get himself elected prime minister, ending for the moment Thaksin's dominance.[32]

Abhisit was an interesting figure. Born and educated in the United Kingdom, Abhisit's fluent English, Oxford accent, and upper-class background sometimes seemed to enable him to connect better with Western diplomats than with the working class and poor of Thailand. His support, and that of the Democrat Party, came largely from Thailand's south and the Bangkok elite and middle class. He in particular struggled to win votes from the north and northeast, and from the poor

---

32 Seth Mydans, "Thai Parliament Selects New Prime Minister," *New York Times*, December 15, 2008; and Hewison, "Thaksin Shinawatra and the Reshaping of Thai Politics."

and working class. In my meetings with him, he always came across as moderate and thoughtful. Many Thai, however, found his politics and his speeches uninspiring.

Not long after Abhisit took office, pro-Thaksin groups—known as the "red shirts" in contrast to the anti-Thaksin "yellow shirts"—took to the streets, blasting Abhisit as not having been democratically elected and using many of the same tactics the yellow shirts had used. Significant protests began in March 2009 with a series of sit-ins outside government offices and soon escalated. In April 2009 they forced cancellation of the annual ASEAN East Asia Summit in Pattaya, compelling Thai authorities to evacuate foreign leaders by helicopter. It was a massive embarrassment for the government and underlined the perilous state of politics in Thailand at the time.

Throughout this period, those of us in Washington were struggling with how to respond to the political paralysis and constant street demonstrations. Our ambassador in Thailand, Eric John, and his team were in constant contact with all parties, urging dialogue and restraint. I visited any number of times throughout 2007–10 in my role as deputy assistant secretary responsible for Southeast Asia. Always, I would talk to a wide range of voices, trying to understand the dynamics and see what we, as a foreign government, could do to encourage a peaceful and democratic resolution. We were careful not to side with the yellow shirts or the red shirts—I even avoided wearing a red or yellow tie when I was visiting—but many Thai saw us as biased toward Thaksin because we consistently advocated for elections as the best way to let the Thai people determine their future leaders.

Anti-Thaksin elements dismissed us as naïve, implying that Thaksin had so rigged the system that they could not defeat him in an election. Longtime Thai friends and contacts bemoaned the situation, but also insisted that the polarization inside the country had reached such intense levels that even families and close friends had split. As longtime Thailand observer Kevin Hewison put it, the division was profound, and centered on Thaksin. ". . . Thaksin's supporters see him as being up against an establishment that refuses to dispense justice to Thaksin or those who voted for him and his party. Meanwhile, opponents view Thaksin as the embodiment of evil, cunning, and treachery, who sought to control the state and oppress the people for his own gain."[33]

---

33 Hewison, "Thaksin Shinawatra and the Reshaping of Thai Politics," 120.

The anti-Thaksin crowd portrayed their efforts as necessary for the protection of the monarchy, accusing Thaksin of being against the king. While Thaksin insisted that was not true, he did regular political battle with people around the palace, led by head of the Privy Council, Prem Tinsulanonda. A longtime Thailand watcher with excellent contacts on all sides told me he convinced Thaksin—after he had left the country upon his conviction in 2008—to accept a potential deal whereby he could return to Thailand and avoid jail time in return for committing to stay out of politics, period. When this individual ran this proposed compromise by people affiliated with the palace, they said Thaksin could return, but he would have to go to jail. No deal.

In Washington, my colleagues and I spoke regularly to congressional staffers, others in the administration, and friends in the think-tank community, explaining the situation as best we could and welcoming ideas, but also pushing back against the Washington tendency to believe that, if there is a problem overseas that has not been solved, it is because the State Department is not trying hard enough.

While dealing with Thailand's political polarization, we faced other issues that affected the relationship. Most notably, we were pressing the Thai to extradite Viktor Bout, a notorious Russian arms dealer known as the "Merchant of Death." Working with U.S. law enforcement agencies, the Thai had arrested him in March 2008 but subsequently stalled on our request for extradition. In mid-2009 a Thai court ruled against extradition, leading a senior U.S. embassy official to say the ruling left him "disappointed and mystified."[34] The Thai clearly feared upsetting their relationship with Russia, which raised eyebrows in Washington, given that U.S. officials had made clear to their treaty allies in Bangkok how important the extradition was. Finally, in November 2010, the Thai agreed to extradite Bout, ending the mini-crisis.

In Bangkok, protests, marred by occasional violence, ebbed and flowed throughout the rest of 2009. A new wave of demonstrations began in March 2010. Tens of thousands of red shirts occupied Bangkok's downtown and—copying the tactics of yellow shirts in 2008—even stormed parliament. The situation deteriorated rapidly, with constant protests and red-shirt demonstrators occupying parts of the city for nine weeks beginning in March. On April 10, at least four soldiers and

---

34 Douglas Farah, "Foreign Policy: Something Wicked . . . This Way Does Not Come Often," NPR, August 12, 2009, https://www.npr.org/templates/story/story .php?storyId=111799310.

seventeen civilians were killed in clashes as the army tried to disperse the red shirts.

During this period, we were being flooded with advice from "experts" on Thailand, usually advocating that we side with the red shirts (as more democratic). There was a near-consensus in the administration that we should not take sides, and we did not, but we did continue to encourage dialogue. In early May EAP assistant secretary Kurt Campbell invited a few respected former officials from the pro-Thaksin camp and the Abhisit government to breakfast in Bangkok, to hear their views about any possible way out of the difficult situation. The government officials decided in the end not to attend, and Foreign Minister Kasit Piromya criticized our "interference."[35] On May 19, 2010, armored vehicles and troops stormed red-shirt protestors' encampments, bringing a bloody and shocking end to the weeks of turmoil and violence. The toll from the move against the protestors was high—some ninety dead and two thousand wounded. The authorities arrested a number of red-shirt leaders.

I left Washington to serve as ambassador to Indonesia a few months later but tried to follow developments in Thailand from Jakarta. In 2011, in yet another attempt to resolve the political impasse, Thailand held new elections, with the same results as the previous several elections: the pro-Thaksin Pheu Thai party, led by Thaksin's sister, Yingluck Shinawatra, won a large victory.

Some in the Thai elite and Democrat Party had initially reacted to the Pheu Thai party's decision to place Yingluck in the leadership position by deriding her as a businesswomen with no political experience who would not offer much competition on the campaign trail. She turned out to be a surprisingly effective campaigner. Her warmth and charm allowed her to connect with voters, and helped ensure she and her party swept to victory.

As prime minister, Yingluck put together a moderate cabinet and moved cautiously. She called for an amnesty for those—red shirt and yellow shirt alike—who had been arrested in connection with the demonstrations of the past few years, prompting opposition accusations that the true goal of the amnesty was to allow Thaksin back into Thailand and Thai politics.

---

35 Emma Chanlett-Avery, *Thailand: Background and U.S. Relations*, Congressional Research Service RL32593, February 8, 2011, 6, https://crsreports.congress.gov/product/pdf/RL/RL32593.

U.S. officials tried to take advantage of the return to some semblance of calm and normalcy postelection by working with the new government on a range of regional and bilateral matters. Yingluck expressed some interest in joining the Trans Pacific Partnership negotiations, but there was little optimism among either the Thai or U.S. trade negotiators that Thailand would be willing and able to make the trade commitments that the partnership demanded. When I returned to Washington in mid-2013 to serve as EAP principal deputy assistant secretary, the Thai embassy in Washington and those around Yingluck were lobbying for a White House invitation, ostensibly to celebrate the 180th anniversary of the signing of the Treaty of Amity and Friendship, but more transparently to bolster Yingluck's standing. The State Department, Pentagon, and NSC all were willing, but it is quite hard to add more leader visits to an already packed White House schedule. The truth is that we did not make it a priority.

Opposition protests took off again in late 2013, led by a group calling itself the People's Democratic Reform Committee. The group was protesting the proposed amnesty bill, but continued their demonstrations even when the government agreed not to pursue that legislation. Yingluck called elections for February 14, 2014. Committee demonstrators tried to block people from voting, but many did nonetheless. Pheu Thai again was victorious but had no time to celebrate. The Constitutional Court nullified the elections in March, and then in early May removed Yingluck from office for dereliction of duty and abuse of power, all linked to her transfer of a security officer back in 2011.

The 2014 Coup and an Alliance Low Point

Also in May, the military declared martial law, but at the same time invited representatives from all parties to try to negotiate a political solution at the Army Club in Bangkok. On the second day, Army Commander Prayut Chan-ocha apparently lost patience with the slow pace of the talks and sent in soldiers to detain the negotiators while he announced to the public that he was taking power. It was yet another coup. Prayut claimed the military had seized power because the country needed "to reform the political structure, the economy, and the society."[36]

---

36 Kate Hodal, "Coup Needed for Thailand 'To Love and Be at Peace Again'— Army Chief," *The Guardian*, May 23, 2014, https://www.theguardian.com/

The coup was strange. First, it made little sense to us for the military to bring political leaders together to try to negotiate a solution and then to stage a coup a day later. Second, unlike the 2006 coup, the military engaged in heavy and even scary repression. It hooded and handcuffed cabinet members, holding them incommunicado for up to a week and in some cases ransacking their homes. The military leaders banned gatherings of more than five people, shut down websites, and ordered some two hundred academics, activists, and journalists to report to army headquarters for possible arrest.

We reacted firmly to the coup. Secretary of State John Kerry said bluntly that there was "no justification" for it, and that it would have "negative implications" for our relationship with Thailand, particularly the military.[37] He added that we would review our assistance and our engagements with the Thai. The truth was that we were deeply frustrated with the coup. As I said in congressional testimony in June 2014, we understood Thailand was suffering from intense political polarization "over Thaksin's role but also over some more fundamental issues such as the role of the Bangkok elite versus that of people in rural areas, particularly in the north and the northeast." I stressed, however, that we did not see how a coup would resolve anything. Moreover, I noted that, unlike the 2006 military usurpation of power, this time the generals were engaged in significant repression of fundamental liberties and also seemed inclined to stay in power for a longer period. As a result, we could not continue with business as usual, and in fact had already suspended substantial military assistance and pulled back on planned high-level engagements and training opportunities.[38]

A few months after the coup, Professor Thitinan wrote that, in international eyes, the pro-coup argument "had a less convincing ring to it" than it had in 2006, when we and others understood that some of Thaksin's actions were problematic.[39] In this case, we could see no credible argument that the Yingluck government was veering toward an anti-democratic or autocratic path, and it certainly had been duly elected. Rather, the purpose of the coup was, to put it bluntly, to avoid the "mistakes" of the previous coup, which had failed to "fix" Thai

world/2014/may/22/military-coup-thailand-peace-general-prayuth-chan-ocha.
37 David Brunnstrom and Arshad Muhammed, "Thai Coup Draws Swift Condemnation; U.S. Says Reviewing Aid," Reuters, May 22, 2014, http://reut.rs/1jaOisq.
38 *Thailand: A Democracy in Peril: Hearing Before the Subcomm. on Asia and the Pacific*, 113th Cong. (June 24, 2014) (statement of Scot Marciel).
39 Pongsudhirak, "The Geopolitical Ripples From Thailand's Coup."

politics, and to stay in power as long as was necessary to reshape the country's political institutions to the point that the Thaksin "threat" would be eliminated for good.

The military was making a bad situation worse by being highly repressive, arresting opponents, prohibiting any public criticism and many public meetings, intimidating the media, blocking websites, and ratcheting up use of the kingdom's draconian lèse-majesté laws to prosecute anyone whose comments could be seen as critical of the monarchy. The repression, perhaps helped by a general exhaustion many Thai felt from the seemingly endless demonstrations and chaos in the streets, meant that public opposition to the coup and the military government was muted—much more so than I would have expected after so many years of watching the democratic spirit develop in the Thai public.

Many in Thailand—in the new government and among the Bangkok elite but also including some in the American business community—reacted critically to the firm U.S. stance on the coup, claiming again that Washington just did not understand why the coup was necessary. The U.S. embassy—and particularly Ambassador Kristie Kenney—faced particularly harsh criticism, some of which was misogynistic. Kenney's effective use of Twitter and popularity among many Thai only added to the criticism she faced. It did not win the Thai any friends in Washington, for sure, and made even those of us who were big supporters of the relationship begin to question it.

During my visits to Thailand, I reminded my friends, in private conversations, that they had criticized us several years earlier for not standing up strongly enough for democracy during the previous coup. This is different, they said. The coup really was needed to restore order and ensure Thaksin did not regain power. Many contacts in the Democrat Party welcomed the coup initially, though their enthusiasm waned as they realized that the military had no intention of turning power over to them either. In fact, the coup was to some extent both an anti-politician and anti–political party move, not simply an anti-Thaksin act. I had lunch with former prime minister Abhisit in New York some months after the coup. He was careful about what he said, but it was clear from the conversation that things had not gone the way he and his party had expected.

Even today, there is much debate over what drove events, including the coup. Certainly, a good chunk of it revolved around Thaksin—people either supported him or thought he was a threat. But it goes deeper than that. With Thailand's economic development had come growing demand from previously disenfranchised Thai, particularly in rural areas, to have their voices heard in the country's political and economic decisions. Many in the Bangkok-based elite just did not want that to happen. It was a fundamental disagreement over political power. The knowledge of the likely imminent passing of the king—who had towered over the country for so long—added to the tension. Conservative elements feared the king's demise might create an opportunity for Thaksin to return to power, courtesy of some oft-rumored deal with the crown prince. As one colleague put it, there was a sense in Bangkok that whoever had power when the king passed would be in a strong position to retain it, so ensuring neither Thaksin nor his sister were in power became paramount for some.

After taking initial steps to respond to the coup, we had to determine how we would engage longer term, given that General Prayut and company seemed to be in no hurry to surrender power. In Washington, we tried to navigate between an excessively harsh policy that would undermine our long-term alliance and relationship and one that would not be true to our values or supportive of all the people in Thailand who felt, correctly, that their vote had been ignored and their rights curtailed. In multiple meetings of the Deputies Committee (an NSC-chaired meeting at the deputy-secretary level) that Ambassador Kenney joined via video, usually in the middle of the night Bangkok time, State, Defense, Treasury, the Office of the United States Trade Representative, and NSC representatives discussed and debated how best to proceed. We knew that there was little we could do that would fundamentally alter the political situation in Thailand, nor could we return to business as usual absent some political progress. At the same time, Thailand was a longtime friend and ally; we could not just walk away in a huff. We had major interests there—security, health, and law enforcement cooperation, and an important regional partnership.

The biggest debates were over Cobra Gold. Some argued for suspending our participation, saying to continue with it would send exactly the wrong message. Others, led by the military but including those of us in EAP, argued that Cobra Gold was critical to our interests in the entire region. We insisted that pulling out of the exercise would raise serious questions among our other partners in the region about our dependability, at precisely the time we needed to reassure them because of China's aggressive posture in the South China Sea. The deputies agreed to scaled-down U.S. participation in the next Cobra Gold exercise in

February 2015, which was either a smart compromise or a waffling approach that would make no one happy, depending on whom one asked.

While we debated grand strategy, other elements of our system continued on autopilot. Among them: the annual Trafficking in Persons Report, which assigns countries to tiers based on the extent to which they are working to combat human trafficking. In 2015, the State Department ranked Thailand as tier 3—the poorest possible ranking. I can say from working within the bureaucracy that these decisions are not part of some grand strategy, and more often than not are in conflict with any grand strategy the United States might have. The Thai, of course, did not believe that. They assumed that the low ranking was simply another way for Washington to hit at them in response to the coup.

The Thai played the China card openly, in effect telling us that our policy was pushing them toward China, and of course Beijing was moving aggressively to try to take advantage of the situation. The Thai already had built a defense relationship with China and now turned to Beijing for support. The Chinese, who had already overtaken the United States as Thailand's largest trading partner (in 2010), were happy to oblige. They offered to supply the Thai military with tanks and diesel submarines, invited more Thai officers to study and train in China, and ramped up already considerable joint exercises with various branches of the Thai military. Politically, Beijing sent Premier Li Keqiang to Bangkok in late 2014 to reaffirm their support and to sign to major economic deals, including for development of a $12 billion Chinese-funded railway.

In January 2015, Assistant Secretary of State Danny Russel visited Bangkok, the highest-ranking U.S. official to travel to Thailand since the coup. In addition to his official meetings, he was to give a speech, which would allow us to present our views on the current situation and the bilateral relationship to the Thai public. We worked long and hard to produce a speech that was nuanced, sensitive to Thai concerns, and appreciative of the long-standing relationship, but also noted our concerns about restrictions on civil liberties and a narrow, top-down political process going forward. In an indication of how far apart we and many of the Thai were, however, Danny's remarks—which I thought struck just the right tone—prompted a furious response from the Thai government, which accused us of meddling in their affairs and harming the country's reputation. They no doubt were particularly sensitive to Danny's comments expressing concern about the impeachment of and criminal charges filed against former prime minister Yingluck just a few days before the speech.[40]

Many in Thailand also complained bitterly about what they perceived to be a double standard: we had ignored a military coup in Egypt in mid-2013 for strategic reasons, in their view, but chose not to ignore their coup, even though they were a Major Non-NATO Ally. The Thai ambassador and many Thai contacts constantly hammered that point home. There was little we could say in response. They also were angry that the White House had welcomed the head of Vietnam's repressive communist party but insisted on distancing itself from long-time ally Thailand because of the coup. Again, they thought we were being inconsistent.

The low point in bilateral relations arguably was in December 2015, when Thai authorities announced that our new ambassador, Glyn Davies, was being investigated for allegedly insulting the king. Glyn's "error," it seemed, had been to note in a public speech at the Foreign Correspondents Club of Thailand the very long sentences being given to some of those found guilty of violating Thailand's strict lèse-majesté laws. My colleagues and I in Washington, who had worked closely with Glyn for years and considered him one of our very best diplomats, were aghast at the Thai move. Cooler heads in Thailand apparently recognized that proceeding with this case would be a major mistake, and in a very Thai way made it go away.

The King's Demise and Change in Washington

The king's passing in late 2016 brought grief to millions of Thai and led to a one-year official mourning period, which meant further delays in holding elections. Politics, however, continued. Crown Prince Vajiralongkorn ascended the throne some two months after his father's death and quickly showed his intention to play a significant role in politics. After an April 2017 referendum approved the military-drafted constitution, which was designed to keep political parties weak and the military strong, the new king asked that it be amended to, among other things, give him control of the Crown Property Bureau, which manages the enormous holdings of the monarchy.

---

40 In September 2017, a Thai court would find former prime minister Yingluck Shinawatra guilty of "dereliction of duty" for her alleged role in a rice-pledging scheme, a month after Yingluck would jump bail and flee the country.

Meanwhile, a new administration took office in Washington, one focused more on China and less on human rights. In October President Donald Trump welcomed Prime Minister Prayut Chan-ocha to the White House, amid pledges to revitalize the relationship. Washington lifted the prohibition on arms sales to Thailand, which agreed to buy Apache helicopters and Stryker armored vehicles. The U.S. administration's moves received praise in some quarters as recognizing geopolitical realities, and criticism in others for implying acceptance of a military coup and government. There are no easy answers in situations like this. If "pulling back" from the relationship does not produce positive results, in terms of a return to democracy, within a reasonable amount of time, then Washington is left with an awkward choice of continuing to distance itself and watching the relationship deteriorate, or resuming something close to business as usual.

After numerous delays, Thailand finally held elections under its new constitution in March 2019. The constitution weakened political parties and offered a powerful role for various oversight bodies populated by people the military appointed, as well as an appointed upper house (Senate). The election results themselves were disputed, with Pheu Thai initially declaring that it had won a majority, only to be told it had not. Courtesy of controversial apportionment of parliamentary seats, Prayut Chan-ocha's Palang Pacharat party was able to cobble together a coalition that—together with the 250 appointed seats in the upper house—produced a narrow majority that put Prayut back in power as the elected prime minister. Simply put, it was not a triumph of democracy, but it did result in an elected government. This, among other things, allowed Washington to resume security assistance.[41]

Multiple elections, street violence, two coups, and a couple of new constitutions have not resolved the Thai political problems, and it is hard to predict what happens next. For the past fifteen years, we have seen an almost-constant political battle between the old Bangkok-based establishment—the palace, the military, the bureaucracy, and some big businesses, supported by many educated elites—and the majority of the rest of the country (at least per the election results), including the predominantly rural north and northeast and some in the younger generation who are not as enthralled with the old ways as their parents.

41 "Military Government Chief Prayuth Chan-ocha Elected Thai PM," Al-Jazeera, June 6, 2019, https://aje.io/2hf3b.

The success of Thanathorn Juangroongruangkit's Future Forward party in the 2019 elections highlights, to some extent, this generational divide. Today, even as I write this, students are leading significant demonstrations in Bangkok against the government. More dramatically, they are even calling into question the role of the monarchy. In many ways, the Prayut government is simply trying to preserve a power arrangement that many people believe is obsolete—another example of a Southeast Asian elite clinging on to power. Many of the people I spoke to for this book believe change is coming, though they do not know when, how, or in what form.

Redefining the Relationship

As for the bilateral relationship, it has been impossible for the recent past to live up to the high expectations created during the alliance's glory days in the 1960s (even if those glory days might not have been as ideal as we remember). The people I know who understand Thailand and the relationship best say those days were an anomaly, and bilateral ties are now back to a more natural situation in which the Thai have diversified their relationships and are seeking a balance among the big powers.

Friends in academia tell me the Thai have been sending out feelers for years about their desire to redefine the alliance. That desire reflects the changing regional and global situation, in which there is no shared "adversary." It perhaps also suggests Thai questions about whether the current alliance, in practice, is less significant and meaningful than, say, the sort of strategic partnership the United States enjoys with Singapore, which many Thai see as receiving preferential treatment despite not being an ally.

Whether or not Washington and Bangkok initiate a formal dialogue to discuss these matters, it is important that the two governments sit down together to talk about the overall relationship, including the specific defense alliance. In doing so, there are a couple of points that the two governments might keep in mind.

One of the things Washington needs to do is to stop measuring the relationship against the halcyon days of the past and instead focus on the many ways the two countries can and should work together going forward. Second, U.S. officials need to understand that the Thai do not view the Chinese as a threat the way many in Washington do. They have a good relationship with China and are going to want to maintain that. A Thai journalist recently told a longtime American Southeast Asia hand that the Thai are "with you (the U.S.) on the weekdays and with the Chinese on the weekends." Third, the United States needs to ensure that it maintains regular, senior-level dialogue, even during rough patches or setbacks, such as what we have experienced vis-à-vis Thai politics in recent years. For their part, the Thai authorities could make a greater effort to encourage and welcome increased bilateral dialogue and offer their own ideas on ways in which the two countries can cooperate.

What might a "redefined" partnership or alliance look like? On the military alliance side, the two sides can build on existing cooperation, including exercises, training, and military equipment sales, but perhaps also add some new elements. For example, the two militaries have worked together previously on responding to natural disasters. Some years ago, the Thai floated the idea of making Utapao airbase a hub for such cooperation; Washington should explore whether and how to do that. Second, the dialogue could explore ways to use the annual Cobra Gold exercises as a springboard to promote broader regional security cooperation. Third, the United States and Thailand should resume regular high-level diplomat-military discussions to assess security and other risks and opportunities in the region, including the implications of a potential Chinese naval base in Cambodia.

The military partnership, whether in alliance form or not, will remain an essential component of the overall relationship, but it does not need to dominate it. Arguably, one of the most important elements of the effort going forward should be continuing to build on the very long and beneficial ties between the people of the United States and the people of Thailand, including in business. Economic and commercial ties are big and important, and there is room for them to grow. Thailand boasts the second largest economy in the region, after Indonesia. It already hosts substantial U.S. investment and is a major trading partner. Although FTA negotiations in the 2000s did not work out, there might be opportunities for even closer trade and investment links.

Beyond that, the United States and Thailand have an incredible ongoing history of connections of all types—family, students, exchange participants, tourists, university partnerships, and more. The U.S. embassy's highly successful exhibition to celebrate two hundred years of friendship—the 2018 "Great and Good Friends" exhibit—highlighted this longstanding partnership. Washington should redouble our efforts to bring Thai students to the United States, and U.S. students to Thailand, as well as build more university and research partnerships, and use Thailand as a hub for more regional people-to-people programs, particularly focused on the Mekong subregion.

Ideally, the United States can also revitalize its long practice of consulting regularly with the Thai on all manner of regional issues, taking advantage of their deep knowledge and insights and giving them the respect of being a true partner whose advice helps guide America. Washington might again look to Bangkok to be a partner of choice and a source of guidance in both the Mekong subregion and in ASEAN. Specifically, the two countries can continue and ideally expand their partnership in preserving the Mekong River ecosystem, in promoting development through Thailand's Ayeyewady-Chao Praya-Mekong Economic Cooperation Strategy, in tackling the large and growing regional narcotics problem, and in mitigating the impact of climate change. U.S.-Thai cooperation on health, including the great work done by the two militaries at the Armed Forces Research Institute of Medical Sciences, can and should be continued and ideally expanded.

The U.S. partnership with Thailand is imperfect, but the long, shared history, the still-significant reservoirs of goodwill, and the large number of common interests should allow the two countries—with patience and persistence, and recognition of each other's failings and sensitivities—to move from disappointment to a healthier, more productive, forward-looking partnership.

II. THE FORMER FOES

CHAPTER FOUR

From Enemies to Friends (Part 1)

Renewing Ties with Vietnam

If you ask U.S. foreign policy officials these days to name the Southeast Asian nation with which they most like to work, a surprising number will say Vietnam. In the summer of 2020, the two countries celebrated both the twenty-fifth anniversary of the normalization of bilateral ties and the remarkably positive trajectory of the relationship. On both sides, there is a palpable sense of wonder and satisfaction that the two countries have developed such a strong bond.

Normalization and the building of a genuine partnership were not inevitable. One only has to look at the lack of progress in rebuilding ties with Iran, whose anti-American revolution took place just four years after the fall of Saigon, to see that progress with Vietnam was not preordained. In the years after the Vietnam War, emotions on both sides were raw and there were significant, substantive issues that divided the two: American servicemen missing in action (MIAs); Agent Orange and unexploded ordinance; Vietnam's re-education camps and the exodus of "boat people;" Vietnam's invasion and occupation of Cambodia, as well as its alliance with the Soviet Union; and diametrically opposed ideologies.

The story of how the United States and Vietnam overcame these differences to reestablish diplomatic relations in 1995 and then continued building them to the point of becoming significant partners today is important, not only for the two countries but for what it tells us about the ingredients necessary to build stronger relations with others in the region. My involvement began in 1990, when I started working on the State Department's Vietnam, Laos, and Cambodia desk, but the story really begins in the 1970s.

The End of the War

The Paris Peace Accords, signed on January 27, 1973, were supposed to bring a formal end to the Vietnam War. They also included provisions for the release of all remaining prisoners of war (POWs), mutual efforts to share information on those missing in action, and U.S. support for the reconstruction of North Vietnam, with President Nixon suggesting an assistance figure of more than $3 billion. Problems began almost immediately. When, from February to March 1973, the Vietnamese released 591 U.S. POWs in Operation Homecoming, some in the United States raised concerns, believing there should have been more. Washington accused Hanoi of not being forthcoming with more information, either about potential POWs or about those missing in action.[1] This included those unaccounted for in Laos, most of whom had been lost in areas under the control of Vietnamese forces. (Much of the Ho Chi Minh Trail, through which Hanoi sent men and supplies south during the war, was in eastern Laos.) Then, in early 1975, North Vietnamese and Viet Cong troops launched an offensive that "liberated" Saigon and led to the unification of the country under communist rule—a clear violation of the accords.

Just months after the fall of Saigon, the U.S. House of Representatives established the Select Committee on Missing Persons in Southeast Asia, chaired by Congressman Sonny Montgomery. Montgomery led a committee trip to Hanoi in December 1975. The Vietnamese told Montgomery they had released all POWs and that gathering information on those missing was difficult. Montgomery told the Vietnamese that the U.S. offer of reconstruction assistance was not binding, but rather a "statement of intent" linked to Vietnam's implementation of the Paris Peace Accords, which in Washington's view Vietnam had violated. The committee returned to Washington saying they did not believe Vietnam was holding any POWs and that a full accounting of those missing was not possible.[2] (As of April 30, 1975, the United States listed a total of 2,583 Americans unaccounted for from the war in Vietnam, Laos, and

---

1 Paul Heer, "A Report on US-Vietnamese Talks on POWs/MIAs During the Nixon, Ford and Carter Administrations: Prepared for Richard Childress, National Security Council," September 23, 1985, declassified November 2007, https://www.cia.gov/readingroom/docs/DOC_0005359871.pdf.
2 Heer, "Report on US-Vietnamese Talks."

Cambodia.[3]) Further bilateral talks in 1976 went nowhere, with the United States accusing Vietnam of withholding information as leverage to extract economic aid, and Vietnam retorting that the United States was using the POW/MIA issue as an excuse not to provide promised assistance.

Early Effort to Normalize Falls Short

President Jimmy Carter entered office in early 1977 believing it was important to normalize relations with Vietnam as a way of helping to heal the deep domestic wounds the war had caused in the United States. At the same time, he felt sympathy for the families of the unaccounted-for servicemen and wanted to do what he could to address the issue. He asked United Auto Workers president Leonard Woodcock to lead a commission, which included Congressman Montgomery, that would go to Vietnam and Laos to try to obtain more information on MIAs.

The commission traveled to the region in March 1977. The Vietnamese told the commission they were interested in normalization but expected significant amounts of aid. The Vietnamese insisted again that they were not holding any U.S. POWs, and the commission concluded they were telling the truth.[4] Based in part on that conclusion, President Carter announced that he had accepted Vietnamese premier Pham Van Dong's invitation to resume normalization talks in Paris without preconditions.[5] The Woodcock commission's quick acceptance that the Vietnamese were not holding live prisoners, combined with continuing reports from departing Vietnamese refugees of possible "live sightings" of Americans, led some in the United States who were following the issue to conclude that the Carter administration was setting aside or even writing off the issue in the interest of speedy normalization.

Carter might have believed that normalization would create better conditions for cooperation on accounting going forward. He sent

---

3 According to the Defense POW/MIA Accounting Agency (DPAA), 2,646 individuals were listed as missing after Operation Homecoming. A total of 63 were accounted for between 1973 and April 30, 1975, resulting in the 2,583 unaccounted for figure as of that later date. "Progress in Vietnam," Factsheet, DPAA, November 20, 2020, https://www.dpaa.mil/Resources/Fact-Sheets/Article-View/Article/569613/progress-in-vietnam/

4 Heer, "Report on US-Vietnamese Talks."

5 Austin Scott, "U.S., Vietnam Set Talks to Establish Normal Relations," *Washington Post*, March 24, 1977.

Assistant Secretary of State for East Asia and the Pacific Richard Holbrooke to Paris for a series of talks on normalization in late 1977 and 1978. The two sides made some progress, but became hung up on Vietnamese demands for assistance. At one point, according to a member of the U.S. delegation with whom I recently spoke, Holbrooke went beyond his instructions to offer normalization outright. The Vietnamese demurred.[6] At another point, in the latter half of 1978, the Vietnamese reportedly offered to delink normalization from their longstanding demand for assistance.[7]

By that time, however, the United States had begun to sour on any rapprochement with Vietnam. In December 1978 the Vietnamese invaded and occupied Cambodia, pushing out the genocidal, Chinese-backed, and virulently anti-Vietnamese Khmer Rouge regime. They also expelled hundreds of thousands of ethnic Chinese residents (and others), resulting in the tragic exodus of the "boat people." In November they announced they had signed a Treaty of Friendship with the Soviet Union. Vietnam probably viewed all of this in terms of its own rapidly declining relationship with China. Washington saw it in the context of the U.S.-USSR Cold War and its ongoing efforts to normalize relations with China, which took precedence over establishing ties with Hanoi. The Carter administration abhorred the Khmer Rouge, but could not stomach an invasion by the Soviet-backed Vietnamese, nor the horrific plight of the boat people. The normalization talks with Vietnam ended, as did any prospect for cooperation on POW/MIA accounting or economic assistance. Deteriorating China-Vietnam relations, culminating in China's military incursion into northern Vietnam in 1979, only pushed Vietnam further into the Soviet camp (at a time when the USSR was invading Afghanistan), and turned the temperature in the U.S.-Vietnamese relationship even colder.

Cambodia and POW/MIA Accounting

The Reagan administration inherited this situation when it took office in 1981. It was focused on the Cold War and viewed Vietnam in that

---

6 Telephone interview with former ambassador and deputy assistant secretary of state Kenneth Quinn, July 27, 2020.
7 U.S. Department of Defense and Department of State, *Final Interagency Report of the Reagan Administration on the POW/MIA Issue in Southeast Asia*, January 19, 1989, Washington, DC (hard copy obtained by author).

context. At the same time, Reagan was deeply committed to addressing the POW/MIA issue, and instructed that it be elevated to the "highest national priority." He brought the families of the unaccounted-for
Americans—represented by the National League of Families of POW/
MIAS—fully into the interagency process on the issue, with the league's
executive director given access to classified information and a direct
voice in policy discussions. Tactically, the administration insisted that
the issue be pursued as "humanitarian," not linked to political issues.[8]
Washington made clear that Vietnamese withdrawal from Cambodia
was an essential condition for progress toward normalization, though
of course it was known that progress would be hard to achieve without
Vietnamese cooperation on POW/MIAs. In the meantime, the administration maintained a full trade embargo on Vietnam, blocked international financial institutions from lending to the country, and restricted
Vietnam's diplomats assigned to the United Nations in New York to a
twenty-five-mile zone around the UN.

Over the next few years, the administration sent several delegations
to Hanoi to try to spark cooperation on the POW/MIA issue. After a
hiatus in 1978–81, the two sides began regular technical-level talks
in 1982, resulting in some limited progress but also frequent halts in
cooperation as the Vietnamese sought to tie cooperation to political
goals. The Reagan administration insisted that POW/MIA cooperation
be delinked from those goals and that movement on normalization depended on Vietnamese withdrawal from Cambodia. The administration's own January 1989 report on the issue stated, "For the first five
years [of the administration], progress followed a 'two steps forward,
one step back' pattern . . ."[9]

Vietnam in the first decade after the fall of Saigon was a grim place.
The Communist Party unified the state, then instituted hardline Soviet-
style policies, collectivizing farms, nationalizing trade and business, and
sending an estimated four hundred thousand people associated with
the former Republic of Vietnam regime to re-education camps, where
conditions were harsh to brutal. The party tolerated no dissent and
oversaw a dire economic situation—Vietnam was one of the poorest

8 Richard T. Childress and Stephen J. Solarz, "Vietnam: Detours on the Road
to Normalization," in *Reversing Relations with Former Adversaries*, ed. C. Richard Nelson and Kenneth Weisbrode (Gainesville, FL: University Press of Florida,
1998), 94–95.
9 *Final Interagency Report of the Reagan Administration on the* POW/MIA *Issue in
Southeast Asia.*

countries in the world. As many as one million Vietnamese, including many ethnic Chinese, fled the country, with massive numbers leaving in 1978–79.[10] Most fled on treacherous boat journeys through waters plagued with storms and pirates. Many did not survive. In 1979, after Vietnam's neighbors said they would not accept any more refugees, the UN hosted a conference in Geneva in which the neighbors agreed to again be countries of "first asylum," in return for the United States and other Western countries agreeing to accept the "boat people" permanently as refugees. Vietnam agreed to a UN-proposed and administered Orderly Departure Program (ODP) that sought to bring some order and greater safety to the departure process.[11]

The situation began to improve slowly in late 1986, when the convergence of four factors led the Vietnamese Communist Party to adopt a policy of *doi moi* ("reform" or "renewal") at its 6th Party Congress. Those four factors were (1) the desperate domestic situation, including 700 percent inflation and deep poverty, which party leaders recognized posed a threat to their power; (2) the Soviet Union's sharp reduction in assistance to Hanoi, which exacerbated the economic problems and drove Vietnam to reduce its dependence on Moscow; (3) Gorbachev's initiation of political reforms (*perestroika*); and (4) the positive lesson of China's economic reforms, which began in the late 1970s. Under the party's general secretary, Nguyen Van Linh, Vietnam allowed farmers to till private plots, gave the green light for people to open small businesses, and even slightly broadened the parameters for permitted public debate.

As Vietnam initiated reforms, the White House looked to bolster what had been disappointing POW/MIA cooperation, while reaffirming its policy linking normalization to Vietnamese withdrawal from Cambodia. (In 1985, the administration had tweaked that policy to focus on Vietnamese support for a comprehensive peace agreement in Cambodia, as well as withdrawal of its troops.) NSC staff had been working through the Indonesians, who wanted to be helpful, to encourage greater Vietnamese cooperation. There were breakthroughs in 1984–1985, including agreement on crash site excavations and quiet

---

10 William Branigin, "Shotgun Wedding," *Washington Post*, April 23, 1985.

11 Committee on the Judiciary, Senate, U.S. Congress, *International Conference on Indo-Chinese Refugees: 1989, A Staff Report Prepared for the Use of the Subcommittee on Immigration and Refugee Affairs of the Committee on the Judiciary* (Washington, DC: US Government Printing Office, June 1989), https://babel .hathitrust.org/cgi/pt?id=pur1.32754078877192&view=1up&seq=1.

acknowledgment that Hanoi held remains (discussed more below), but then cooperation again ground to a halt.

Early Signs of Progress

In 1987 President Reagan appointed respected former chairman of the Joint Chiefs of Staff General John Vessey to be special emissary to Hanoi on the POW/MIA issue. Vessey, accompanied by NSC director for Asian Affairs Richard Childress and National League of Families executive director Ann Mills Griffiths, traveled to Hanoi in August 1987 to meet with Vietnamese foreign minister Nguyen Co Thach, who was a proponent of improving relations with the United States. Thach agreed to increased Vietnamese cooperation, and the U.S. delegation agreed to step up humanitarian assistance, including in areas such as prosthetics for disabled Vietnamese, another legacy of the war.

The pace of senior-level talks and cooperation on the POW/MIA issue picked up noticeably from that point on, though the road was far from smooth. Vietnam returned more remains and for the first time allowed joint U.S.-Vietnamese investigations and surveys of sites linked to unaccounted-for U.S. soldiers. It might not have been obvious at the time, but over the next several years it would be cooperation on the POW/MIA issue that allowed us to build a relationship with the Vietnamese authorities and eventually establish diplomatic relations.

It is worth saying a little more about Nguyen Co Thach's role in the normalization process. In an August 2020 webinar hosted by Vietnamese ambassador to the United States Ha Kim Ngoc, a number of Americans who had been deeply involved in the normalization process praised Thach's courage, vision, and persistence as critical to the development of bilateral relations.[12]

As noted above, Thach had agreed in the mid-1980s to increase POW/MIA cooperation. Even before that, however, he had engaged quietly on a number of occasions with key U.S. players, including Dick Childress and Ann Mills Griffiths. Griffiths had flown to New York to meet Thach in September 1983 and then brought together Childress and Thach shortly thereafter. The talks were kept quiet, but they led to a series of private Childress-Thach meetings that greatly increased each side's understanding of the other's interests, concerns, and constraints and created the

---

12 "Nguyen Co Thach: Breaker of Deadlocks, Builder of Ties" (webinar, hosted by the Vietnamese embassy, Washington, DC, August 28, 2020).

basis for future expanded cooperation. According to Childress, Thach at one point acknowledged that Vietnam was holding remains, but was afraid to release them for fear of the U.S. reaction. Childress urged him to release the remains over time, which Vietnam did, though there is still debate on whether it released all the remains it held.[13]

Then, in 1988, Thach reached out to former U.S. ambassador to Laos William Sullivan, whom he knew well from the earlier Paris and Geneva negotiations. Sullivan had left government and was now running the International Center in Washington; he remained well connected. Through Vietnam's ambassador to the United Kingdom, Thach invited Sullivan to visit Hanoi to discuss normalization. Sullivan had some discussions with the Vietnamese envoy in London, but the State Department was not ready to bless a trip until Vietnam took some steps on Cambodia. The blessing came in 1989, so Sullivan traveled to Hanoi with the International Center's Virginia Foote. Shortly after that, Sullivan established the U.S.-Vietnam Trade Council, which Foote led for several years.[14]

The council played an important bridging and unofficial communications role for the next several years. It began to bring over Vietnamese Foreign Ministry officials as fellows, without diplomatic status, so they could get to know Washington. One of those fellows was Le Bang, who over the next few years played a crucial role in normalization discussions as Vietnam's permanent representative to the UN in New York, and then became Vietnam's first ambassador to Washington in 1997. The Trade Council's creative approach of bringing Vietnamese diplomats to Washington without diplomatic status was to serve as a model for our own efforts a few years later.

The End of the Cold War Brings Opportunity

A couple of factors combined to create better prospects for movement toward normalization during the George H. W. Bush administration. First, the Soviet Union weakened and then collapsed, ending the Cold War. This both eliminated the bipolar prism through which the United States had viewed Vietnam and caused the Vietnamese to look for other foreign partners. Hanoi had heavily relied on Moscow, both strategically and economically. Its leaders realized they needed to bolster

13 Telephone interview with Richard Childress, August 21, 2020.
14 Telephone interview with Virginia Foote, August 6, 2020.

relations elsewhere and so showed greater willingness to work with the United States on a variety of issues.

Second, the Bush administration—particularly Assistant Secretary of State for East Asia and Pacific Richard Solomon and Deputy Assistant Secretary Ken Quinn—placed a high priority on achieving a comprehensive peace agreement in Cambodia, where the ongoing fighting between the Vietnamese-backed regime and the Khmer Rouge–dominated opposition had created both a humanitarian tragedy and a moral issue for Washington, which had held its nose and backed the opposition due to Cold War geostrategic concerns. (Quinn had spent six years in southern Vietnam during the war, and had been one of the first to report from the field on Khmer Rouge atrocities in neighboring Cambodia.) Solomon and Quinn were among the few who thought a peace agreement could be achieved, and they understood that Vietnam's support for such a deal was critical. Others in the administration, including Secretary of State James Baker and NSC advisor Brent Scowcroft, were pragmatists first and foremost, and were willing to engage Vietnam to further the Cambodian peace prospects as well as to achieve other goals.

One of those goals was to help those Vietnamese who had suffered for years from their association with the old South Vietnamese government and with the United States. In 1988, Congress passed legislation to allow so-called Amerasians (Vietnamese-born children of U.S. servicemen) to immigrate to the United States. In July 1989, the United States and Vietnam negotiated an agreement to facilitate the interviewing—and follow-on emigration to the United States—of current and former re-education camp detainees and their dependents under the UN-backed ODP. These individuals had been allowed, in theory, to emigrate since 1979, but in practice Vietnamese authorities had allowed only a small number of them to leave. Under the 1989 agreement, Vietnamese agreed both to release remaining detainees and expedite the emigration of those who the United States determined qualified under what became known as the "Humanitarian Operation" subprogram of ODP. Over the next several years, more than 165,000 former detainees and their immediate family members emigrated to the United States under this program.[15]

---

15 Alicia Campi, "From Refugees to Americans: Thirty Years of Vietnamese Immigration to the United States," *Immigration Daily*, https://www.ilw.com/articles/2006,0313-campi.shtm; and "Refugee Admissions Program for East Asia," fact

In mid-1990, when I joined the State Department's Vietnam, Laos, and Cambodia desk, Vietnam had largely withdrawn its troops from Cambodia, was beginning to implement the ODP "Humanitarian Operation," and was continuing solid if not great cooperation on the POW/MIA issue. There was talk of moving toward normalization of relations, but the administration made clear that movement would depend, among other things, on completion of a comprehensive Cambodian peace agreement.

The Internal U.S. Debate

At the time, a number of influential constituent groups were lining up either for or against normalization. Not surprisingly, the differing views reflected a continuation of the division the war had created within our country. POW/MIA family groups and some veterans' groups, such as the American Legion, argued against moving too quickly absent better Vietnamese cooperation on the accounting issue. Many Vietnamese Americans, a growing voice in the country, strongly opposed normalization with the communist regime that had been their enemy for so long and that continued to abuse human rights. On the other side stood some veterans who thought reconciliation would help heal America, and a number of humanitarian groups, some of which were responding purely to humanitarian concerns and others of which felt the United States had a moral obligation to help rebuild the country that it had bombed (and sprayed with Agent Orange) so heavily. The business community also began pushing more vociferously for an end to the embargo and establishment of diplomatic relations, arguing that the lack of ties was hurting U.S. business and workers. Last but not least, a small but highly influential group in Congress, led by senators John McCain and John Kerry,[16] became involved, working together to try to enable enough progress to allow for normalization.

Over the next few years, the Bush and then the Clinton administrations sought to move forward while carefully navigating the competing domestic interests. In September 1990, Secretary of State James Baker met in New York with Foreign Minister Nguyen Co Thach, the

---

sheet, U.S. Department of State archive, https://2001-2009.State.gov/g/prm/rls/fs/2004/28212.htm.

16 Senators Bob Kerrey and Patrick Leahy also played prominent roles, as did Congressman and former POW Pete Peterson.

highest-level bilateral meeting yet, and agreed to lay out steps that could lead to normalization. In the weeks and months that followed, a U.S. interagency group (including the State and Defense Departments, the NSC, and National League of Families executive director Ann Mills Griffiths) held a series of meetings to develop a series of actions Vietnam could take that would address Cambodia, refugees, and POW/MIA accounting, as well as positive moves Washington could make in response to Vietnamese progress. Over a series of difficult interagency discussions, these steps eventually were folded into what became known as the April 1991 "roadmap" to normalization.

I sat in on a number of these discussions and they were difficult and often emotional. Even speaking with participants today, nearly thirty years later, the feelings are still strong. One of the principals called the experience "a nightmare." While I would not say the Cambodia and refugee issues were easy (in terms of the interagency discussion), they were generally not too controversial within the Washington interagency community. The real debate surrounded the POW/MIA issue, where the differences were often profound, and reflected differing views on how much more Vietnam could cooperate.

Even today, it is impossible to write about this issue without annoying or angering at least some of the players who were involved, but I will try to be as fair and objective as possible. In a nutshell, some—particularly representing the National League of Families and the Defense Department—believed that the Vietnamese were *still* holding back both actual remains (reportedly held in a "warehouse"), as well as archival and other information that could help us account for at least some of the missing Americans. They wanted the roadmap to include language requiring the Vietnamese to "empty the warehouse," as one participant recalls (though that might not have been the exact language). Others, principally at the State Department but including some in the military, agreed the Vietnamese could and should do more, but were not convinced that Hanoi could easily produce either remains or useful information. They did not want the roadmap to include conditions the Vietnamese could not possibly meet. As a result, the debates were intense, even angry. And understandably so, because we were talking about U.S. servicemen who had been lost in the war, and their families, who had been suffering ever since from a lack of closure as well as grief.

My view is that the Vietnamese were holding back on information—and remains—through the 1980s, attempting to use them as a bargaining chip. I have not seen any solid evidence that this practice continued into the early 1990s. I do believe, however, that there were dedicated, patriotic Americans on both sides of the debate who were trying to do what they thought was best for the country and the families.

I cannot say the same, sadly, about a small number of Americans who shamelessly sought to exploit the issue for personal gain or maybe just because they wanted to see their names in the newspaper. During the 1980s, the notion that Vietnam (and/or Laos) was still holding live American prisoners took hold in the national psyche, through a combination of Rambo movies, hyped-up and irresponsible "rescue operations" carried out by private Americans, and various conspiracy theories arguing that successive U.S. administrations were for some reason "hiding" the truth about imprisoned Americans. Hanoi deserved some of the blame for this, because its failure to share information and address legitimate U.S. concerns helped create the environment in which these conspiracy theories could prosper. The truth is, however, that much of it was nothing more than money-making opportunism on the part of a small number of Americans. The POW/MIA families were the victims.

The Roadmap

In any event, in April 1991—after one more round of late-night interagency drama at the State Department that involved one principal walking out of the meeting in anger—Assistant Secretary of State Richard Solomon presented the roadmap to the Vietnamese permanent representative to the UN, Trinh Xuan Lang, in New York. The Vietnamese response was along the lines of "we neither accept it nor reject it."[17]

The Vietnamese were not about to formally accept a set of conditions, but the roadmap played a useful role in that it laid out a clear and reasonable way forward that both countries largely ended up following. The actual roadmap envisioned four phases, but there were two central elements: (1) normalization required agreement on and implementation of a comprehensive Cambodian peace agreement, with the "pace and scope" of movement toward normalization also depending on Vietnamese cooperation on POW/MIA accounting; and (2) the roadmap was less a series of quid pro quo actions than an outline of how, in response to progress by Vietnam, the United States would

---

17 Steven Greenhouse, "U.S. Open to Talks on Ties with Vietnam," *New York Times*, October 23, 1991.

move the bilateral relationship forward. In other words, the idea was to build trust both ways by responding to Vietnamese efforts with concrete U.S. steps.

In April 1991 Vietnam took a major step by agreeing to allow the United States to set up a POW/MIA accounting office in Hanoi (it opened in June). October saw more progress, as the Cambodian peace accords were signed in Paris. After the signing, Secretary of State Baker announced that the United States would ease constraints on U.S.-organized travel to Vietnam and lift the twenty-five-mile travel restriction on Vietnamese diplomats in New York. He also said we would begin direct talks with Vietnam on normalization, with progress on POW/MIA accounting the key condition for forward movement.[18] In 1992, Vietnam allowed the United States for the first time to investigate so-called live sighting reports (as the name would suggest, these were reports of possible U.S. POWs seen alive in Vietnam), and also allowed increased access to wartime archives. In response, the United States reestablished direct telecommunications links with Vietnam, offered $3 million in humanitarian aid (mostly for prosthetics for disabled Vietnamese), lifted most restrictions on U.S. NGO activity, and eased the trade embargo to allow transactions for "basic human needs."[19]

It was not all smooth sailing, however. In 1991, there were a number of reports suggesting American POWs might still be being held in Vietnam, Laos, or Cambodia, including three photographs allegedly of missing American POWs. In one particularly dramatic case, the spouse of one of the men said to be in the photo insisted that it was indeed her husband. All of us in government took these photographs very seriously and spent months trying to find out if they were legitimate, even if many of us were privately skeptical. Deputy Assistant Secretary of State Ken Quinn hopped on a plane immediately, flew to Hanoi, and impressed upon his Vietnamese interlocutors the urgency and importance of getting answers. It was an intense period. After some months, we were able to confirm that the photographs were hoaxes. They were real photographs, just not of Americans. Once again, someone had deliberately created a hoax, causing enormous consternation and, most tragically, falsely raising the hopes of family members.

---

18 Greenhouse, "U.S. Open to Talks on Ties with Vietnam."
19 Mark E. Manyin, *The Vietnam-U.S. Normalization Process*, CRS Issue Brief for Congress, Congressional Research Service, updated June 17, 2005, 3, https://fas.org/sgp/crs/row/IB98033.pdf.

In an effort to get to the bottom of the POW/MIA issue once and for all, the Senate in August 1991 established the Select Committee on POW/MIAS, chaired by Senator John Kerry and co-chaired by Senator Bob Smith, a New Hampshire senator who had suggested the Vietnamese were still holding live POWs. Over the next eighteen months, the committee investigated, held hearings, and asked the administration to turn over decades of relevant documents for review. I ended up doing a lot of the legwork of reviewing the State Department's documents and then funneling them up the chain to Secretary Baker, who approved releasing nearly all of them to the committee. There was no cover-up or conspiracy to be found in those or any other documents, but the transparency involved in releasing them was important to the public and certainly to the POW/MIA families. In March 1993, the Select Committee issued its final report, which included some criticism of past administrations' efforts on the issue but concluded that, while it was possible that a small number of POWs had remained behind after Operation Homecoming, there was "no compelling evidence" that any American POWs were still being held.[20]

By that time, the Clinton administration had entered office, and I was studying Vietnamese language at the State Department's Foreign Service Institute. Since we had no embassy in Hanoi, I went into language training not knowing if I would actually have an onward assignment in Vietnam. After all, a colleague around that time, Spence Richardson, had taken a year to study Korean in anticipation of the possible opening of a liaison office in Pyongyang. Needless to say, he never went.

A "Presence" in Hanoi

I was luckier. Midway through my one year of Vietnamese training, I was assigned to be the so-called Vietnam watcher at our embassy in Bangkok. So at least I would be in Bangkok, or so I thought. By early July 1993, things had progressed to the point that the administration

20 Mary H. Cooper, "U.S.-Vietnam Relations: Should the U.S. Normalize Relations with its Old Enemy?," CQ Researcher 3, issue 45, December 3, 1993, https://library.cqpress.com/cqresearcher/document.php?id=cqresrre1993120100. See also Select Committee on POW/MIA Affairs, POW/MIAS: Report of the Select Committee on POW/MIA Affairs, 103rd Congress, Report 103-1, January 13, 1993, https://fas.org/irp/congress/1993_rpt/pow-exec.html.

announced it would no longer oppose lending by international financial institutions to Vietnam. Then, a few weeks later, Assistant Secretary of State for East Asia and the Pacific Winston Lord, along with Deputy Secretary of Veterans Affairs Hershel Gober, led a delegation that included veterans' groups to Vietnam to push for even greater POW/MIA cooperation. They had good meetings and received more assurances of stepped-up efforts.

Several days later, Deputy Assistant Secretary of State Ken Quinn—the State Department's point man on Southeast Asia and a key player on Vietnam policy—called me at home to say the department needed me to go to Hanoi for an indefinite period to work in our military's POW/MIA office. He explained that Winston Lord had reached agreement with the veterans' groups for the State Department to send a few of its officers to Hanoi "temporarily" to handle all the congressional visitors and consular issues involving American citizens. This, he said, would free up the Joint Task Force Full Accounting (JTF-FA) team in Hanoi (the military unit charged with pursuing full accounting) to concentrate full-time on POW/MIA work. I was to lead this small team, which would work out of the JTF-FA office.

Ken made it clear that I and two colleagues who would follow me to Hanoi would be there without diplomatic immunity, which put us at some risk. He said the department would understand if we declined the assignment. None of us did. I cannot speak for my colleagues, but I did not feel particularly at risk, as the Vietnamese would have every incentive to ensure we were treated appropriately.

A few weeks later, my wife, three-month-old daughter, and I flew to Bangkok, where I spent a month or so waiting for specific instructions for Hanoi. The instructions came (written by NSC advisor Tony Lake, I was told) and they read mostly as a list of all the things I could not do. Perhaps most notably, I could not initiate calls on Vietnamese officials, or even consult with other diplomats (with the exception of the UK and Canadian ambassadors). I called Ken Quinn and complained, asking "What am I supposed to do?" His response: "Be a presence."

The reality was that the State Department wanted a small presence in Hanoi, partly to help manage all the visits by members of Congress and veterans' groups, but also to start scoping out the situation in Vietnam and specifically in Hanoi, and to send a signal to the Vietnamese that we hoped to move the relationship forward. Inevitably, of course, we would develop connections with Vietnamese counterparts as we worked together to handle visits. At the same time, the department severely constrained our activities because they did not want us to do anything to suggest we were de facto "normalizing" the relationship. We were following the Le Bang example of a few years earlier.

Leaving my wife and daughter in Bangkok, I flew to Hanoi in early August 1993. The flight itself reflected both the troubled history between our nations and the strange state of the relationship. Because the trade embargo remained in place, I would have to pay cash for everything in Hanoi, including long-term car rentals and hotel stays. So I carried nearly $50,000 in cash with me. The Embassy Bangkok finance officer who handed over the bundle of cash also warned me that I would be personally responsible for it if I were robbed or lost the money.

The Vietnam Airlines plane itself was pure white—not even the airline's name was painted on the fuselage. This was the bizarre by-product of U.S. Treasury rules governing the embargo that somehow made it possible for the airline to "wet lease" a handful of Airbus planes legally as long as the airline's name and logo were not displayed.

The flight also carried a living symbol of what our countries had gone through. Lewis Puller, Jr., son of Marine Corps legend "Chesty" Puller, had fought as a Marine in Vietnam. In late 1968, while seeking to evade an ambush, he stepped on a landmine. He survived, but with horrific injuries, including the loss of both legs, that left him in pain and wheelchair-bound for the rest of his life. He had written a book, *Fortunate Son*, that had won the Pulitzer Prize just a year before I met him. Now he was on this flight, returning to Vietnam for the first time as head of a charity devoted to healing the wounds of war on both sides. We spent the flight talking about his experience and what he hoped to do in Vietnam. Tragically, less than a year later, Puller would end his own life.

One of the desk officers from the Foreign Ministry's Americas department met me at Hanoi's Noi Bai airport and welcomed me on behalf of his government. A U.S. officer picked me up and drove me to the JTF-FA office, which was housed in a modest older villa and known (unfortunately) as "The Ranch." There I met detachment commander Lt. Col. John Cray and the rest of the team, and was given an office that would be home to us for the next eighteen months. A few weeks later I would be joined by two State Department colleagues.

True to Ken Quinn's comment that our role was to be "a presence," the State Department had not given us any equipment. Lt. Col. Cray was kind enough to loan us a couple of laptops, and we had a phone and a fax machine. That was it. There was no local staff. There were no secure communications links. Email was not yet used at the State Department, at least not globally. There was no diplomatic immunity. We were just there.

During the first few weeks, I hewed closely to my instructions, venturing out to call on the UK and Canadian ambassadors, making some basic administrative arrangements (all in my amateurish Vietnamese), and learning the details of the extraordinary work JTF-FA was doing on accountability. I spent a lot of time exploring the city and practicing my Vietnamese.

An Awakening Vietnam

Hanoi in those days was just beginning to emerge from its fully socialist days. The country was still extremely poor but the economy was growing. Any number of small mom-and-pop shops and markets had opened, coexisting with the still-plentiful state-run shops. The poorly stocked state-owned department store still claimed prime Hanoi real estate overlooking picturesque Hoan Kiem Lake in the heart of downtown. I ate several times in the state-owned Restaurant #75, where the food and service were what you would expect in a Soviet-style restaurant.

A handful of cars fought for space in narrow streets crowded with bicycles and a growing number of motorbikes. I used to marvel at how dozens of bicycles and motorbikes would converge on an intersection from two directions, with no stop signs or traffic lights, and the riders would magically and effortlessly navigate through unscathed. Whenever a brave or unwise foreigner would join the crossing on their bicycle, the Vietnamese automatically adjusted, allowing all to survive for another day and the foreigner to believe they had proven their cycling skills.

I stayed for nearly a year at the modest Saigon Hotel on Ly Tuong Kiet Street (like so many of Hanoi's streets, named after a national hero who had fought the Chinese in one of Vietnam's many wars with its northern neighbor). The hotel's amenities were, shall we say, limited, so I ate most of my meals at *pho* stalls or cheap local restaurants. I used to stop in regularly at a small kiosk at the end of the block that sold a limited supply of canned goods, most of which looked like they might have fallen off a truck some years earlier. On weekends, I would treat myself to a freshly made donut and coffee at a marvelous hole-in-the wall shop a few blocks away. It did not have a name (other than its address, 252 Hang Bong Street), but was run by a man who had studied to be a pastry chef in France. I would sit on one of the tiny plastic stools that were ubiquitous in Hanoi and read the English-language *Vietnam Investment Review* while enjoying my small feast.

Early on, I found that an older "cyclo" driver (cyclos were the Vietnamese equivalent of rickshaws) had been assigned to me, presumably by the Ministry of Interior. Whenever I was not working, he ferried me around the city, visiting temples and historic sites and introducing me to some of the best pho stalls and *bia hoi* (local draft beer poured out of questionable plastic tubes) spots.

What struck me then, and struck so many Americans then and later, was the friendliness of the Vietnamese people. There was none of the anti-American hostility we expected from the war era. Instead, everyone wanted to talk with Americans, and asked when we were coming back to Vietnam. A Western journalist friend, who was not from the United States, complained that the Vietnamese ignored him whenever he traveled with American journalists.

I have often wondered how to explain the lack of hostility. After all, we had bombed the hell out of Hanoi and much of the country. I will never forget a conversation with a Vietnamese driver who was taking a State Department delegation around Hanoi sometime in 1994 as we were looking at potential embassy sites. He let on at one point that most of his family had been killed by bombs during the war. I asked why he was so friendly, given that history. His response: "I'm not mad at America. It was war." On another occasion, a Vietnamese official responded to a similar question from an American military officer by saying, "We've been fighting the Chinese for two thousand years. The war with you was just a hiccup."

Early Engagements

Within weeks of my arrival, things began to pick up, as congressional and veterans' delegations came to Vietnam. I remember meeting a Veterans of Foreign Wars delegation, all of the members of which had served in Vietnam and were returning to the country for the first time since the war ended. Normally, the State Department did not manage visits by private groups, but because of the important role veterans' groups played in the nascent relationship with Vietnam, the State Department authorized us to do all we could to ensure their visit was productive. Anyway, we left the airport en route to the city on what was in those days a narrow, windy road through rice fields. As we passed women farmers irrigating their crops in their traditional, low-tech way, I looked back and saw one of the veterans gazing out the window. He shook his head, and—obviously thinking about the war—asked rhetorically "What were we doing here?"

The Vietnamese authorities understood how important these trips were and did their best to win over the visitors. Our counterparts at the Foreign Ministry, led by Americas desk director Nguyen Xuan Phong and including Ha Kim Ngoc (ambassador to the United States from 2018 until late 2021), were always extremely professional and responsive, as was the very capable deputy minister, Le Mai. Top officials regularly made themselves available to meet with important visitors, including veterans. Communist Party chief Do Muoi, an elderly man with limited formal education, was masterful in these meetings. It was not so much what he said, but rather his ability to express what seemed to be genuine empathy, especially toward visiting veterans. During one visit by a veterans' delegation, Do Muoi rose from his chair at the end of the meeting, and spoke individually with each of the Americans. When he got to the last veteran, a gentleman in a wheelchair, Do Muoi tearfully bent down and hugged him, shaking his head and saying, "We can never let this happen again." He promised the group that Vietnam would do everything possible to account for missing Americans, and hoped that the two countries could become fast friends.

It is hard to exaggerate how important and effective that kind of personal engagement can be in building trust. I often thought that it made little sense that people could, on the one hand, believe that Vietnamese authorities were capable of holding American prisoners in bamboo cages twenty years after the war, yet also accept as genuine the promise of a Vietnamese Communist Party leader to do everything possible to achieve the fullest possible accounting. But words matter, emotions matter, and sometimes bonds are formed in the most unlikely places.

I do not want to make it sound like everything was sweetness and light. For the most part, the Vietnamese authorities worked professionally and fairly with us, but they still had their hardliners and their suspicions and kept very close tabs on my colleagues and me. Just a few weeks after I arrived, I attended a small dinner the Vietnamese hosted for some Washington visitors. On the margins of the dinner, one of the

Interior Ministry[21] officials with whom we worked on the POW/MIA issue asked me how I was finding Hanoi. I began to describe some of my explorations of the city, listing the various places I had visited the previous Sunday. He listened with a big smile and then said, "I know." It was both funny and a clear reminder that they were keeping a close watch on us.

In January 1994 Admiral Charles Larson, the commander of U.S. Pacific Command (then known as CINCPAC, later as PACOM and now as INDOPACOM), visited Hanoi to support the JTF-FA team and to discuss the POW/MIA issue with the Vietnamese. He was by far the most senior U.S. military officer to visit Vietnam since the war. The Vietnamese hosted a small dinner for him at the Foreign Ministry's guest house, and a handful of Vietnamese military officers joined (which was rare). I sat at the end and took notes. The conversation started off stilted. Within minutes, however, participants on both sides were talking about the war, including where they had served and how they remembered certain battles. It turned out that a few had been on opposing sides in the same battle. As they discussed the battles, one could sense an actual bond forming across the table. It was remarkable, and in some ways symbolized how dealing with the tragedy of war could and would in many ways bring the two countries closer together over time.

The regular visits of senators and members of Congress were critical to the development of relations at the time. Senators Kerry and McCain each visited several times, and always were received at the highest levels. Both pushed the Vietnamese constantly to do more on POW/MIA accounting. Senator McCain would occasionally bristle when a Vietnamese interlocutor would make the mistake of reading canned talking points about how well Hanoi had treated American POWs, but the Vietnamese respected him greatly. They even rewrote the unwritten history of the monument commemorating his capture on the shore of Truc Bach Lake in Hanoi. The small cement marker was put up to celebrate the shooting down of his plane and his capture; later, as the Vietnamese sought to win over Americans, they talked about the monument almost as if it was a tribute to McCain, their former enemy turned friend. Everyone, especially McCain, knew the reality, but it was important to change the way we talked about each other if the relationship was to move forward.

---

21 The Interior Ministry was responsible for internal security, and would later become the Ministry of Public Security.

Lifting the Embargo

And the relationship did move forward. Vietnam extended cooperation on POW/MIA accounting, returning remains of U.S. servicemen, allowing more investigations of "live sighting reports," granting increased access to documents, expanding trilateral cooperation with Laos on MIA cases in Laos near the Vietnamese border, and working with JTF-FA to resolve so-called discrepancy cases. In late January 1994 the U.S. Senate passed a resolution urging the administration to lift the trade embargo, and on February 3 President Clinton did just that. In his remarks, he made it clear that he was taking this action in response to enhanced Vietnamese POW/MIA cooperation, and because he believed lifting it was the best way to ensure even greater progress on accountability going forward. Several veterans' groups and the National League of Families publicly criticized the decision, saying Vietnam had not yet done its part under the roadmap to warrant such a major U.S. step. They made clear their intention to press for greater Vietnamese cooperation before full normalization.[22] The Veterans of Foreign Wars, however, supported the move, arguing that it would facilitate further POW/MIA accounting.

The lifting of the embargo was good news but also proved somewhat embarrassing for me personally. Early on February 4, the German ambassador in Hanoi called to ask if I could stop by to see him. When I arrived in his office, he congratulated me on the good news. I asked him, What good news? He laughed loudly and shared the news about the embargo, which Bonn had passed to him overnight in a diplomatic telegram (this was before the days of instant news on the internet, and there was no CNN in Vietnam). Apparently, nobody in Washington thought that my colleagues and I needed to know that the president had lifted the embargo. When I called to inquire, I was told that the State Department had not informed me because they did not want me to talk with the press. My response is not printable.

The president also had announced that the United States and Vietnam would establish liaison offices in each other's capitals. A liaison office is sort of an intermediary step between no diplomatic relations and the establishment of embassies with ambassadors. For example, we had opened a liaison office in Beijing (which George H. W. Bush

---

22 Ruth Marcus and Thomas W. Lippman, "Clinton Lifts Vietnam Trade Embargo," *Washington Post*, February 4, 1994.

subsequently led) in 1973. This was big news, including for me personally, as it meant my assignment in Hanoi would go from temporary to "permanent" (as permanent as any diplomatic posting can be), so I would be able to bring my family over from Bangkok to join me.

Before we could open liaison offices, we needed to settle some "technical" issues: our claims for U.S. government-owned property seized by Vietnam in 1975; compensation for private property lost by U.S. private citizens, including Vietnamese Americans, at the end of the war; and an agreement that would ensure we would have consular access to any U.S. citizens arrested in Vietnam. Practically, we also needed to find a building to house our liaison office.

Over the next many months, we focused on these issues, while also continuing to press the Vietnamese to further strengthen POW/MIA cooperation. That meant a steady stream of delegations from Washington. Some were high-profile administration or congressional delegations coming to push on the POW/MIA issue. Others were more technical, focused on property, claims, and consular access. All were important.

It is worth saying a few words about the actual work on POW/MIA accounting. It involved many elements, including significant research, gaining and making use of access to Vietnamese archives, sending joint teams out to talk to locals in areas where Americans were lost to try to determine the site of a crash site or what happened to someone on the ground, and much more. One critical aspect—trying to recover actual remains, often from the sites of plane crashes twenty to twenty-five years earlier—required joint U.S. and Vietnamese teams to helicopter into often-remote areas and set up what amounted to archeological digs to try to recover remains or other identifying information. I went out on a couple of these operations and left with the greatest respect for those men and women doing the work. We knew it could be dangerous, as the helicopters often flew in rugged terrain, but it really hit home several years later, when in April 2001 a Vietnamese MI-17 helicopter bringing a joint team to a remote crash site in Quang Binh Province crashed, killing sixteen Vietnamese and American team members.[23]

All along, we had been operating with the most rudimentary communications with Washington: mostly phone calls and faxes. When we

---

23 "Vietnam Crash Kills 16, Pentagon Says," CNN, April 7, 2001, http://www.cnn
.com/2001/WORLD/asiapcf/southeast/04/07/vietnam.crash.02/

had sensitive meetings, or took notes on important policy-level discussions featuring Washington officials, we literally took notes on yellow legal pads. Then, every few weeks, one of us would fly to Bangkok and draft official, classified telegrams from those hand-scrawled notes, sending them in via Embassy Bangkok's secure communications channel to Washington. This was far from ideal, but it was the only way we could do our business.

As we pursued the various issues that were key to opening the liaison office and eventually establishing full diplomatic relations, the State Department sent reinforcements in the form of a few additional officers. We finally were given permission to hire one local staffer, who helped immensely (and greatly relieved our Foreign Ministry counterparts, who now had someone to talk with in the office who actually spoke their language properly).

Throughout 1994 the Vietnamese continued to bolster cooperation on POW/MIA accounting. After lengthy, often difficult negotiations, in early 1995 we reached an agreement on property, under which Vietnam would return several former U.S. government properties, and compensate us for the others in the form of cash or real estate. In that package, we received a beautiful, if dilapidated, villa that had been the Foreign Ministry's Foreign Press Center and later became the U.S. ambassador's residence. We also received an ungainly but new nine-story building on Lang Ha Street that was meant to serve as temporary home to our liaison office but remains the incredibly overcrowded U.S. embassy chancery twenty-five years later.

I still get grief from my colleagues over that building, because I was the one who found it. More accurately, my driver pointed it out to me one day as we were driving through the city. We had been looking in vain for months for a suitable building, but—given the dearth of modern office buildings—had grown tired of looking at pleasant but small old villas or abandoned embassies (my favorite being the former Bulgarian embassy, which was just awful). I stopped to look at the Lang Ha building, which was still under construction. A private company was building it with the intention of renting out individual floors to foreign companies. It was the best building around, and we were able to obtain it in the property deal.

We also reached agreement on private claims resulting from the loss of private property in 1975. Vietnam agreed to compensate private owners, as well as the Overseas Private Investment Corporation, to the tune of $209 million, with the money to be paid out of Vietnamese assets that Washington had frozen back in 1975.[24]

We had contentious negotiations over an agreement on consular access to American citizens, an essential part of the work of any diplomatic mission. The obstacle was Hanoi's insistence that Americans of Vietnamese descent were still Vietnamese citizens. We could not accept that, of course. In the end, we found a diplomatic solution: an agreement that granted us consular access to anyone who had entered Vietnam using a U.S. passport.

We had a small ceremony to mark the opening of the liaison office on January 28, 1995, and opened for business a few days later. The Vietnamese opened their office in Washington a few days after that. The next several months were a blur, as we managed visiting delegations, followed up on property matters, and continued to expand our network of contacts in Hanoi and the country. Meanwhile, the Vietnamese, who had re-established diplomatic ties with China in 1991, were reaching out to others in the region, joining ASEAN as a full member, and sending party chief Do Muoi to Japan and Australia. Vietnam's membership in ASEAN was a big deal. After all, concern about the spread of Soviet and Chinese-backed communism, personified by Ho Chi Minh and North Vietnam, had helped spur the establishment of the regional organization in 1967. For years, ASEAN's members—led by Thailand—had taken a strong stance against Vietnam's occupation of Cambodia, and worked closely with us and China to pressure Vietnam to withdraw.

Normalization

By mid-1995, President Clinton was leaning toward announcing the establishment of diplomatic ties, but—mindful of the criticism that he had avoided the draft—sent old friend Bill Richardson to Vietnam for one more assessment. Richardson returned, went directly to the White House, and told the president he should just do it. On July 11, President Clinton, flanked by senators Kerry and McCain, announced that the United States would establish formal diplomatic relations with Vietnam. The decision generated controversy, with longtime proponents cheering and others highly critical. On Capitol Hill, senators Bob

---

24 Manyin, *The Vietnam-U.S. Normalization Process.*

Dole and Trent Lott blasted the president's move as premature, while others welcomed it.

My view then and now was that it was the right move. One can always find reasons to delay, usually based on the argument that the other country has not yet done enough. The problem is that argument can be used in perpetuity—the Vietnamese would never do enough on POW/MIAs to satisfy everyone. At some point, leaders have to decide if there has been sufficient progress to warrant moving ahead, not necessarily as a reward, but more as a way to continue positive momentum. (There were echoes of this debate twenty years later when the Obama administration re-engaged with Myanmar.) I say that with great respect for some good friends who argued then—and continue to argue—that the Vietnamese at that point still had not done enough on POW/MIA cooperation, as defined in the roadmap, to justify establishment of diplomatic relations.

The president sent Secretary of State Warren Christopher to Hanoi in early August to launch the new chapter in the relationship. In a series of meetings with top Vietnamese officials, Christopher both expressed the U.S. desire to build a healthy relationship with Vietnam and addressed key issues of concern: POW/MIA accountability, human rights, and religious freedom. He then formally opened the U.S. embassy and announced that Desaix Anderson, a highly respected diplomat with long experience in Asia, would serve as chargé d'affaires pending nomination and confirmation of a U.S. ambassador.

Over the next year, we worked to build the foundations for what we hoped would be a broad and deep bilateral relationship. Desaix Anderson proved to be a superb choice, as the embassy team loved him and he knew how to work with the Vietnamese. Washington sent out more reinforcements, almost all of whom had served in Vietnam (in the military or the Foreign Service) back in the old days. They were all good people, but personally I thought it would have been wiser to include a greater number of people who would not look at Vietnam through the prism of the war.

I spent a fair amount of time looking at the economy and working with the small but growing U.S. business community. A handful of U.S. business "pioneers" had come out early, even before the lifting of the embargo, in hopes of being well placed to build once the embargo was lifted. The lifting of the embargo and then normalization of relations spurred even more to come. Many were, in my view, overly optimistic about business prospects at the time. That tends to be true whenever a new market opens. In the case of Vietnam, it was exacerbated by the unique emotional pull that Vietnam had (and has) on many Americans, because of the history. I met a number of visiting businessmen who had either served in Vietnam or whose lives had been shaped by it; I always felt it was hard for them to separate their business judgment from their personal views. Still, the American business community was growing, and even established an unofficial American chamber of commerce in 1995.

A number of other Americans were there to work on humanitarian matters. The country's deep poverty, combined with the destruction and damage from the war, meant there was more than enough to do. Beginning in 1989, the U.S. government had begun providing small amounts of humanitarian assistance for prosthetics and such. Private donors also contributed, supporting a growing number of U.S. and European NGOs. U.S. veterans such as Chuck Searcy played an important role. I got to know Chuck in 1995, when he came to Vietnam with the Vietnam Veterans of America Foundation to oversee a U.S. government–funded prosthetics project. In 1991 Searcy had started Project RENEW, an effort to clear unexploded ordinance in heavily damaged Quang Tri Province, but moved full-time to Hanoi four years later. He is still there.

Vietnam in 1995–96 presented a mixed picture. On the one hand, many of us thought that the pace of economic reform had slowed, and that the authorities were not doing enough to take advantage of the tremendous foreign business interest. The economy's dynamism was being undermined by corruption and the still-heavy role of state-owned enterprises. Politically, it remained an intolerant one-party state that did not allow independent media, labor, or civil society groups. The military and internal security forces, along with much of the Communist Party, remained conservative and deeply suspicious of us. In early 1996, the party launched a campaign against "social evils," focusing on prostitution, drugs, pornography, and massage parlors, but also going after anything that in their view might "harm" Vietnamese society. It was in many ways an effort to combat the foreign influences that inevitably accompanied the country's economic and diplomatic opening.

Hanoi had decided to allow a small number of foreign journalists to work in Vietnam, but it did so reluctantly and went out of its way to make their lives and jobs difficult. Journalists were regularly followed, any local staff had to report regularly to the authorities, and those they interviewed were at risk of being interrogated. Those who wrote articles considered too critical of the party/government might be called in for discussions, during which the authorities would remind them that the government could choose not to renew their visas.

The POW/MIA issue gave us virtually our only entrée to the military and police, as the Vietnamese POW/MIA interagency team included the Foreign Ministry, the Defense Ministry, and the Interior Ministry. Beyond those engagements, however, most of our efforts to reach out and engage these institutions or the Communist Party were rebuffed. In early 1996, I asked our local assistant to call the party's think tank, the Institute of Marx, Lenin, and Ho Chi Minh Thought, to request a courtesy call. They didn't know what to think, so they asked her why I wanted to visit. Just for fun, I told her to tell them I wanted to join the Communist Party. They agreed to the meeting and were polite, but made it clear they did not share my enthusiasm for a follow-up discussion.

These conservative elements, however, could not hide the remarkable dynamism of the country and the change it was propelling. In Hanoi, we could see the number of motorcycles and cars increasing rapidly, and new restaurants and shops opening daily. I still remember the day a real grocery store—with two aisles—opened, or the time an Australian launched a take-out barbecue restaurant with a Vietnamese partner. The economy was growing at 6–8 percent a year (it grew at an annual average rate of 7.9 percent in the 1990s). Poverty was falling significantly and people were getting wealthier, buying motorcycles, televisions, and refrigerators, in that order of priority.[25]

The change was even more noticeable in Ho Chi Minh City, which always boasted an entrepreneurial spirit. The city was hopping even then, and attracted foreign business interest much more than did Hanoi or elsewhere. Danang too was beginning to emerge, though more slowly.

There was change too in the countryside, particularly as farmers benefited from liberalized agricultural policies. Still, some places were going to need more time to develop. In late 1995, I took a week-long trip through the Central Highlands, which had seen some of the heaviest fighting of the war and remained impoverished. I flew to Danang,

---

25 John Thoburn, "Vietnam as a Role Model for Development," Research Paper No. 2009/30, United Nations University–World Institute for Development Economics Research, May 2009, http://citeseerx.ist.psu.edu/viewdoc/download?doi =10.1.1.395.5645&rep=rep1&type=pdf.

hired a car and driver, and drove to Kontum, Pleiku, and Ban Ma Thuot—household names to many Americans from the war. These towns had not seen many Americans, and certainly not U.S. officials, since the war. In each place, I called on the local People's Committee. They seemed surprised to see me traveling alone and greeted me politely but warily. As soon as I started speaking to them in Vietnamese, the mood would change, and usually within two or three minutes a bottle of whiskey would appear. The high point (or maybe low point) was when the People's Committee chairman of Pleiku unexpectedly joined me for breakfast the morning after we had imbibed a generous amount of whiskey together, and insisted we drink snake liquor along with the day-old fried eggs we were served.

We did not fully understand it at the time, but there was intense debate and jockeying for power among senior Vietnamese leaders during this time, in the lead-up to the 8th Party Congress in mid-1996. Vietnam for years had practiced rule by triumvirate—the general secretary of the party, a president, and a prime minister—usually representing different regions of the country. In the 1990s, those positions were held by three men with strong political bases: Do Muoi, who hailed from the north, was party chief and boasted a strong network in the party and among party activists and labor; President Le Duc Anh, born in the central region, had a powerful patronage network throughout the armed forces; Prime Minister Vo Van Kiet, a southerner, had more backing from reformers, the growing business community, and the country's south. They argued over policy, including the pace of reform, and over patronage. At the Party Congress, none was willing to retire unless the others did as well, so the needed leadership change was punted to 1998, when conservative compromise candidate Le Kha Phieu was chosen to lead the party. This mattered because the lack of strong leadership reflected itself in a lack of strong economic direction and reform. Combined with the 1997 financial crisis, the result was a significant decline in foreign investment and in GDP growth.

I departed Hanoi in mid-1996, with my last task managing NSC advisor Tony Lake's July whirlwind visit, during which he met General Secretary Do Muoi in Hanoi, President Le Duc Anh in Danang, and Prime Minister Vo Van Kiet in Ho Chi Minh City (plus visited a POW/MIA excavation site by helicopter and worked in a short trip to see his former house in Hue). I left satisfied with the progress in bilateral relations, but unsure how optimistic to be about Vietnam's future. In hindsight, I was too pessimistic. I put too much weight on the lack of reform momentum and the caution of the state, and insufficient weight on the energy and dynamism of Vietnam's young population. It seemed that every young Vietnamese person we met those days was working during the day and then going to school at night to learn English, computing, or business. I have not seen such energy and ambition anywhere else I have served.

CHAPTER FIVE

From Enemies to Friends (Part 2)

The Development of U.S.-Vietnam Relations

A few weeks after becoming director of the State Department's Mainland Southeast Asia office in mid-2005, I received a call from the political counselor at the Vietnamese embassy in Washington, Dang Dinh Quy. He introduced himself and invited me out for pho. Quy picked me up at the department in an old Plymouth and drove me to a pho shop just across the Potomac River, explaining that it was one of the few shops in the area that flew the correct Vietnamese flag (most insisted on flying the old South Vietnamese flag). Over bowls of noodles, Quy gave me a crash course in the current geopolitics of the region as seen from Hanoi and offered his suggestions on how Washington should view the situation.

The noodles were great, but the reason the lunch warrants a mention here is because it reflected two important qualities that have had a big impact on the development of U.S.-Vietnam relations since normalization, and have guaranteed relatively consistent senior-level Washington attention even during times when policymakers were largely neglecting Southeast Asia as a whole: Vietnam's keen geostrategic sense, and the talent Hanoi and its emissaries have shown for effectively working Washington at all levels. Quy and I had many conversations on the region during the next few years in Washington, and then continued them in Hanoi when he led the Foreign Ministry's Diplomatic Academy, where a new generation of strategically thinking diplomats were learning the trade. (Quy served in New York as Vietnam's permanent representative to the United Nations from 2018 until the end of 2021.)

Growing Relations 1996–2005

By 2005 the bilateral relationship already had developed significantly from 1996, even though Vietnam's reforms had slowed significantly during that period as conservatives within the Communist Party pushed back against what they considered excessive liberalization. Trade and economic relations had led the way. The draft bilateral trade agreement we had shared with Hanoi in May 1996 led to a formal trade deal in 2000 and the U.S. granting of normal trade relations in December 2001. This in turn sparked a sharp rise in bilateral merchandise trade from $1.5 billion in 2000 to nearly $8 billion in 2005 (it had been only $450 million in 1995).[1]

Political and diplomatic ties between Washington and Hanoi had grown as well. The two countries exchanged ambassadors in 1997, with President Clinton sending former POW Pete Peterson to Hanoi and Vietnam sending longtime diplomat Le Bang to Washington. In 1999, the United States opened a consulate general in Ho Chi Minh City, while Vietnam opened one in San Francisco. The two governments maintained consistent high-level engagement and steadily expanded the agenda of issues to discuss. President Clinton's 2000 visit to Vietnam marked a major step forward, despite then party chief Le Kha Phieu's unfortunate decision to lecture Clinton on the war during their meeting. Prime Minister Phan Van Khai became the first Vietnamese leader to visit Washington in 2005. Again, the visit marked a breakthrough, even if it was marred by a Vietnamese American protestor punching a Vietnamese official in the head outside the Willard Hotel in Washington.

Military and security ties, not surprisingly, were slower to develop, due to caution and wariness on the part of the Vietnamese security forces and Communist Party, as well as U.S. human rights concerns. In the 1990s we struggled to gain access to the then Ministry of Interior (later the Ministry of Public Security) and the military, or even the Communist Party. We were able to work with a handful of officials from the military and Ministry of Interior on POW/MIA accounting, but beyond that they largely rebuffed our efforts to build relationships. On the infrequent occasions when we landed a meeting, the discussions were vague and slightly uncomfortable.

---

1 U.S. Census Bureau, "Trade in Goods with Vietnam," https://www.census.gov/foreign-trade/balance/c5520.html#2000.

We began to make some progress in the early 2000s, no doubt driven by Hanoi's growing concerns about a rising China. Also helpful were some initial steps we took on war legacy issues important to Vietnam, such as President Clinton's agreement during his late 2000 visit to form a joint committee to pursue scientific research on the problem of Agent Orange/dioxin contamination. In 2002–03 we saw the initiation of working-level defense talks, focusing on war legacy issues such as demining as well as noncontroversial matters such as military medicine and search and rescue.

Human Rights and Religious Freedoms: Persistent Stumbling Blocks

During this period and up to the present, U.S. concerns about the twin issues of human rights and religious freedom have regularly cast a shadow over otherwise warming ties with Vietnam, and dealing with these serious issues has at times threatened to slow or even halt improvement in the relationship. Although Vietnam has made progress in many areas, its ruling Communist Party kept—and continues to keep— a tight lid on dissent, prohibiting independent media and squelching any efforts to push for independent organizations or multi-party democracy. In addition, Vietnam's restrictions on certain religious groups and activities, particularly in the sometimes-restive Central Highlands, caused it to land on the State Department's list of Countries of Particular Concern in 2004–05.[2] Key members of Congress, often spurred on by Vietnamese American constituents, spoke out regularly and strongly on these issues and called on U.S. administrations to curb growing bilateral relations until and unless Vietnam did more to improve its human rights situation.

All of us engaged with Vietnam have consistently raised these issues. During my regular visits to Vietnam in 2005–10, and again in 2013–16, human rights and religious freedom were always on the agenda. I remember visiting Hanoi in 2008 or 2009 and arranging through our consulate general in Ho Chi Minh City to visit a prominent dissident whom the authorities watched closely. Meeting with Foreign Ministry officials in Hanoi prior to flying south, I had a rather tense back-and-forth about meeting the dissident. I made it clear that we needed to be

---

2 U.S. presidents annually review all countries for violations of religious freedoms; those with severe violations are designated as Countries of Particular Concern.

able to see such people and that a Vietnamese decision to prevent the visit would hurt them much more than letting it take place. They reluctantly agreed, but we always worried that such visits, while helpful in some regards, could make life harder for those we visited, so we were cautious about them.

On many occasions the Vietnamese authorities have blocked activists from meeting with U.S. embassy officers or with visiting officials from Washington, or have harassed them after such meetings. They even prevented activists from meeting with visiting President Obama in 2016, causing the president to call out the government for its actions.

Nonetheless, I believe our constant focus on human rights and religious freedom enabled us to achieve some limited progress. The Vietnamese would occasionally release dissidents, though skeptical friends in the human rights community often asked whether these or others would simply be swept up again weeks or months later. We launched a regular bilateral dialogue on human rights, which continues today. And we did see real progress on religious freedom, which resulted in the State Department taking Vietnam off the list of Countries of Particular Concern in 2006.

I testified about this limited progress before the House Foreign Affairs Subcommittee on Human Rights in November 2007.[3] I explained the steps we had seen over the past few years, including new legislation and the release of all prisoners whose cases we had raised with the Vietnamese as being tied to religious freedom. I noted that the significant Catholic minority in the country could freely and regularly attend church services. I clearly did not satisfy some of the members, who forcefully criticized me (and through me the administration) for not doing enough on human rights. It is part of the job, but that hearing stands out in my mind as one of the toughest verbal beatings I have taken on any issue.

The challenge in countries such as Vietnam is that, while the United States is rightly concerned about the lack of democratic freedoms and respect for fundamental rights, it has a relatively limited ability to bring about change. Sure, Washington could refuse to engage Hanoi until it allows a more democratic system, but such an approach would

---

3 *Human Rights Concerns in Vietnam: Hearing before the Subcommittee on International Organizations, Human Rights and Oversight of the House Committee on Foreign Affairs*, 110th Cong. (November 6, 2007) (statement of Scot Marciel), https://www.govinfo.gov/content/pkg/CHRG-110hhrg38819/pdf/CHRG-110hhrg38819.pdf

(a) almost certainly be ineffective, and (b) leave us with no ability to advance our many other interests vis-à-vis Vietnam. Change, when it comes, will be the result of internal dynamics within the country, possibly even within the party. Until that happens, the best the United States can do is to continue to highlight the issue, support efforts to increase space for dialogue and debate, and encourage Vietnam's further integration into the world.

In some areas Vietnam has allowed expanded space for discussion and debate, and it has not banned social media like Facebook, though many in authority are wary of it. People do have greater access to information. During a late 2014 or early 2015 visit to Hanoi, for example, I met with a group of young people who, while not activists per se, were active in the business and broader world. When I asked them what their primary sources of news and information were, they responded the *Wall Street Journal*, Politico, and the like. I was surprised, but they assured me that access to these news sources was not a problem (though authorities do block certain "sensitive" articles).

Also, there is greater space than in the past for people to criticize the government or specific individuals, as long as they do it carefully. A Vietnamese official privately and informally explained to me recently that people could, for example, publicly call out officials involved in corruption. The trick was not to accuse the officials of corruption outright, but rather to note (on social media) that so-and-so had a remarkably nice house, or expensive car, or Rolex watch, letting others draw the appropriate conclusion about how the individual could afford such costly items.

Fundamentally, however, for all of its noteworthy progress on economic development and integrating into the world, Vietnam under the Communist Party has done very little to create a more democratic state or to grant its citizens critical political and civil liberties. It remains a repressive one-party state, and that fact is a regular source of tension in the relationship.

For their part, the Vietnamese authorities have been troubled by the actions of some groups within the Vietnamese American community. For example, Vietnamese officials would regularly raise with us concerns that Vietnamese American lobbying had led any number of localities throughout the United States to fly the old South Vietnamese flag whenever the occasion for a flag was warranted. The Vietnamese did not understand that, in our federal system, it was not easy or necessarily even possible for the State Department, or the federal government overall, to intervene and stop such practices. Hanoi also objected strongly to the activities of Viet Tan, a U.S.-based group that was founded in 1982 by remnants of the old South Vietnamese government. The group states that its mission is "to overcome dictatorship and build the foundation for sustainable democracy."[4] Vietnam in 2016 declared the Viet Tan a terrorist organization and warned that any Vietnamese found to be involved with it would be punished.

Continued Development of the Relationship

Importantly, while not glossing over these difficult issues, neither government has allowed them to define the overall relationship or prevent continued senior-level engagement and further progress in the overall bilateral relationship, even during periods when Washington tended to calibrate its relationships in Southeast Asia based on progress—or the lack thereof—on democracy and human rights. There are many reasons for this, starting with Vietnam's consistently effective outreach efforts in Washington, its knack for offering strategic perspectives that had been largely absent from the rest of the region, save Singapore, and the presence of significant constituencies supporting the relationship in Congress, the business community, and elsewhere.

Again, the commercial relationship has led the way in the development of the relationship. Vietnam's accession to the World Trade Organization in 2006, which we supported, ensured the rapid expansion of commerce continued. By 2019 bilateral trade in goods reached $77.5 billion, making Vietnam our thirteenth-largest trading partner and the United States Vietnam's fourth-largest partner.[5] There were problems, to be sure, as Hanoi complained about U.S. regulations that limited the import of Vietnamese catfish, and we have regularly reminded Hanoi that it enjoys a massive trade surplus with us. U.S. private investment also has soared, highlighted by Intel's 2007 decision to invest $1 billion to build its largest assembly and testing facility in Vietnam. Lengthy negotiations on the proposed Trans-Pacific Partnership (TPP) ended in Vietnamese disappointment when the United

---

4 "Vietnam Declares US-Based Activist Group Is a Terrorist Organization," *The Guardian*, October 7, 2016, https://www.theguardian.com/world/2016/oct/07/vietnam-viet-tan-terrorists-dissent.
5 "Vietnam," Office of the United States Trade Representative, https://ustr.gov/countries-regions/southeast-asia-pacific/vietnam.

States abandoned the effort for the TPP in early 2017, but trade relations have continued to grow nonetheless. In talking to U.S. business organizations in the summer of 2020, it was clear that U.S. business as a whole remains more bullish on Vietnam than almost anywhere else in Southeast Asia (Singapore is the perennial exception, given its status as a hub for U.S. business in the region).

This bullishness reflects Vietnam's impressive economic development and consistent commitment to integrating fully into the global economy. Between 2000 and 2017, the country's per capita GDP tripled, reaching more than $6,000 in 2017. Poverty rates, which had already dropped significantly by 2000, have fallen even further since then.[6] It is not just the numbers. One can see it in the streets, in the explosion of motorcycles and cars on the roads and of quality hotels and restaurants, and in the development of businesses that can compete internationally. Companies such as Vingroup, Viet-Jet, Vinamilk, and Sabeco now appear on places such as Forbes' "Best Over a Billion" list of top companies in the region. I saw this in Myanmar in 2016–20. Vietnamese companies were increasingly active there and opened the country's first modern shopping mall in 2015. In the past few years, Vietnam also has moved quickly and effectively to attract U.S. and other foreign companies seeking to diversify their manufacturing operations out of China, and has pulled in more such companies than any of its neighbors. Vietnam, particularly Ho Chi Minh City, also is aggressively promoting itself as a rising hotspot for digital start-ups.

Sustained engagement and dialogue have also facilitated growing diplomatic and political-security ties. Following Prime Minister Phan Van Khai's 2005 visit to Washington, the United States initiated a small International Military Education and Training program for Vietnam, and the following year Defense Secretary Rumsfeld visited Vietnam and authorized the sale of nonlethal defense articles. In 2008, at the end of the George W. Bush administration, we held our first-ever Bilateral Political, Security, and Defense Dialogue at the deputy minister level in Hanoi.

The momentum continued under the Obama administration, as the United States moved to "rebalance" toward Asia and both governments grew increasingly concerned about China's behavior, particularly its

---

6 "The Next Stage of US-Vietnam Relations: A Blueprint to Deepen Trade and Investment Ties," U.S. Chamber of Commerce, May 8, 2019, https://www.uschamber.com/report/the-next-stage-of-us-vietnam-relations-blueprint-deepen-trade-and-investment-ties.

aggressive actions in 2009 and 2010 to pursue its maritime and territorial claims in the South China Sea. Secretary of State Hillary Clinton's strong statement calling out the Chinese on those actions at the 2010 ASEAN Regional Forum (which Vietnam hosted) received a lot of attention, and probably helped convince the Vietnamese that Washington was serious about the issue. The two governments launched an annual Defense Policy Dialogue at the deputy minister of defense level in 2010, and in 2011 signed a memorandum of understanding on bilateral defense cooperation that listed five areas of cooperation, including maritime security.

Even then, not everything went smoothly. When newly arrived U.S. ambassador David Shear made his initial call on Deputy Defense Minister Nguyen Chi Vinh in mid-2011, Vinh reacted to Shear's mention of human rights by reminding the envoy of Vietnam's long war for independence and dislike of foreign interference. Shear countered that he was in Vietnam in large part because the United States valued Vietnam's independence and wanted to do all it could to help preserve it.[7] (That U.S. emphasis on helping Vietnam maintain full independence and sovereignty has been a cornerstone of the relationship ever since.) During her 2012 visit to Hanoi, Secretary of State Hillary Clinton publicly rapped the Vietnamese authorities on human rights, calling for greater freedom and directly linking any easing of our prohibition on weapons sales to progress on rights.[8]

These hiccups did not discourage further cooperation. In 2012 Defense Secretary Leon Panetta visited Vietnam, and, for the first time, the Vietnamese allowed him to visit Cam Ranh Bay.[9] The symbolism was not lost on anyone. In late 2013, Secretary of State John Kerry traveled to Hanoi and, with one eye on Chinese actions in the South China Sea, offered U.S. assistance to Vietnam on maritime issues. By this time, I had returned from Jakarta to serve as principal deputy assistant secretary in the East Asia and Pacific Bureau, responsible once again for Southeast Asia. One of my first tasks was to work with colleagues at the State Department, the Pentagon, and the NSC to win support within the administration and then on Capitol Hill for assistance to Vietnam

---

7 Telephone interview with former ambassador David Shear, July 28, 2020.
8 Patrick Barta and Vu Trong Khanh, "Clinton Presses Vietnam on Rights Record," *Wall Street Journal*, July 10, 2012.
9 Cam Ranh Bay was the premier U.S. naval base in the former Republic of Vietnam during the Vietnam War.

and other claimant nations to bolster their ability to monitor what was happening in their own coastal waters. We faced significant opposition due to human rights concerns, but we argued successfully that maritime assistance was both appropriate, given China's increasingly aggressive moves in the South China Sea, and unlikely to be used to violate human rights.

In 2013, the relationship received a further boost when President Obama and visiting Vietnamese president Truong Tan Sang launched the U.S.-Vietnam Comprehensive Partnership, under which the two countries agreed to work together in nine discreet areas. In less than twenty years, the United States and Vietnam had gone from distrust, embargo, and no diplomatic relations to a genuine partnership that involved cooperation across an ever-expanding range of issues.

The South China Sea Spurs Closer Security Ties

China upped the ante in the South China Sea in May 2014, sending a $1 billion mobile oil-drilling platform into disputed waters that Vietnam claimed as part of its exclusive economic zone. The Vietnamese were livid. They demanded China withdraw the rig and sent boats to the area, resulting in a series of low-level clashes between those boats and Chinese ships escorting the rig. The Vietnamese public, with its long history of pushing back against China, reacted angrily, and there were violent demonstrations targeting Chinese-owned factories in the country's south. China had to evacuate thousands of its citizens.

Although we had been careful not to take a position on the competing claims, we saw the Chinese move as aggressive and dangerous. Secretary Kerry told Chinese foreign minister Wang Yi the action was "provocative" and urged China to pull the rig back.[10] Hanoi sent Deputy Foreign Minister Ha Kim Ngoc to Washington as a special envoy to consult with us on next steps. Ambassador Nguyen Quoc Cuong hosted a small dinner for Ngoc with Assistant Secretary of State for East Asia and Pacific Danny Russel, NSC senior director for Asia Evan Medeiros, and me. Vietnamese permanent representative to the UN Le Hoai Trung also joined. We spent hours in intense discussions with these senior Vietnamese diplomats, who made it clear that China's ac-

---

10 "Kerry: China's Oil Rig in South China Sea 'Provocative,'" VOA News, May 13, 2014, https://www.voanews.com/a/kerry-chinas-oil-rig-in-south-china -sea-provocative/1913329.html.

tion had deeply upset Hanoi, and that Vietnam—as always—would not take it lying down. At one point, one of our Vietnamese interlocutors asserted that "Vietnam might be a small country, but we will defend ourselves even from big countries." Danny and I looked at each other and said, "Yeah, we know about that." The frankness and seriousness of the conversation was striking and highlighted just how far the relationship had come in a relatively short time. We were not allies, and we were not going to become allies, but we had become serious partners.

China eventually withdrew its rig, but its action had clearly harmed its relationship with Vietnam. It also had encouraged Washington players—including on Capitol Hill—to consider what more we could do to help Vietnam and other Southeast Asian partners build their maritime capabilities, not for combat but to have the capacity to patrol and monitor their offshore waters. Ahead of an early October 2014 visit to Washington by Vietnamese foreign minister Pham Binh Minh, the administration pushed for further steps to provide material support for Vietnam in the maritime arena. Once again, we faced opposition from human rights groups and some on Capitol Hill, but we argued that—if we wanted to be taken seriously in the region on geostrategic issues—we had to do more to support countries that were standing up to China. During Minh's visit, Secretary of State John Kerry announced that the United States would ease the prohibition on lethal weapons sales to allow for Vietnam to buy, on a case-by-case basis, lethal equipment for maritime surveillance and security. The move was partly symbolic, as Vietnam was unlikely to start buying large amounts of expensive U.S. equipment, but Hanoi warmly welcomed it.

While all of this was happening, the Vietnamese Foreign Ministry and others continuously encouraged us to do more to reach out to those elements in Hanoi that remained wary, even suspicious of the United States, specifically the Vietnamese Communist Party, as well as the Ministry of Public Security and the military. There were many in these institutions who continued to believe that the United States sought the overthrow of the regime. We had tried to build those ties before, but under Ambassador Shear the embassy redoubled its efforts, particularly via the party's International Relations Committee. At the same time, the embassy and we in Washington continued to stress to the Vietnamese that progress on human rights would facilitate closer relations, and would also be essential when it came time for congressional approval of the TPP trade agreement.

Landmark Party Chief Visit to Washington

In a February 2015 phone call with Foreign Minister Minh, Secretary of State Kerry invited Communist Party general secretary Nguyen Phu Trong to visit Washington.[11] The Vietnamese accepted and planned a June visit. Hanoi sent Politburo member and public security minister (later president) Tran Dai Quang to Washington in March for a series of meetings to, in effect, test the waters for Trong's visit. It was also the first visit ever by a Vietnamese public security minister. Ambassador Cuong called me a few days before Minister Quang was to arrive to ask me to join him in a private meeting with the minister that Saturday, March 15, so that I could informally give him a sense of what to expect. I drove out to the Marriott Hotel at Woodley Park in northwest Washington DC and spent a few hours both welcoming Quang and highlighting for him the key issues he would likely hear about during his visit, including of course human rights. His visit went well and encompassed a remarkable range of meetings, including with the State Department, Defense Department, CIA, FBI, and the NSC, as well as key members of Congress. The fact of his visit, as well as some of the details—even including the pre-meeting with me—highlighted once again the Vietnamese understanding of how to work Washington.

In the weeks leading up to the general secretary's visit, positive momentum continued to develop, as Defense Secretary Ash Carter visited Hanoi and signed a Joint Vision Statement with Defense Minister Phung Quang Thang that committed the two sides for the first time to pursue greater operational cooperation. Just before the general secretary arrived in Washington, there was minor drama at the White House, as at least one senior official questioned whether the president should hold yet another meeting with a top Vietnamese official, particularly one representing the Communist Party. Danny Russel, who previously had been the NSC's senior director for Asia, used his excellent rapport with top NSC officials to make the case for the meeting, and the opposition faded.

President Obama met with Nguyen Phu Trong in the Oval Office on July 7, 2015, forty years after the end of the Vietnam War and almost

---

11 Tra Mi, "Vietnam Plays Up U.S. Invitation to Communist Party Chief," VOA News, February 17, 2015, https://www.voanews.com/a/vietnam-united-states -invitation-communist-party-chief/2648251.html.

exactly twenty years after the establishment of diplomatic relations. I sat in on the meeting, in which the two leaders acknowledged both the difficult history and the significant progress that had been made in the relationship. Obama made it clear that the United States would continue to speak out on human rights, but at the same time deftly eased Vietnamese concerns by emphasizing that the United States respected their right to have their own political system. The Vietnamese delegation left very pleased. I was in Hanoi just a few weeks later, accompanying Dr. Jill Biden, and the mood among top Vietnamese officials remained buoyant.

President Obama followed up on the general secretary's visit by making his own trip 2016 to Hanoi, where he announced the full lifting of the prohibition on weapons sales to Vietnam. Even though Vietnam has yet to buy any major weapons systems from the United States—it would be hard to shift from its longtime supplier Russia—Obama's move sent an important symbolic message.

Relations Under the Trump Administration

The momentum continued into the Trump administration, despite President Trump's decision—immediately upon taking office—to withdraw from the TPP trade agreement. That withdrawal stung Vietnam, which understood the strategic consequences of a U.S. pullback from economic engagement with the region. Nonetheless, the Vietnamese moved quickly to engage and build relationships with the new administration. Prime Minister Nguyen Xuan Phuc traveled to Washington in May 2017, becoming the first Southeast Asian leader to visit the new president. Phuc and Trump issued a joint statement reaffirming their commitment to building closer cooperation. Later in 2017, President Trump visited Vietnam for the Asia-Pacific Economic Cooperation Leaders' Meeting, returning in 2019 for both bilateral discussions and his second meeting with North Korean leader Kim Jong-Un. The security relationship continued to develop, as Secretary of Defense James Mattis visited Vietnam twice in 2018 and U.S. aircraft carriers twice made port calls in Danang (in 2018 and 2020).

The Trump administration's focus on its global trade deficit, specifically its large deficit with Vietnam, caused some bumps in the road. In 2019, President Trump called Vietnam "the worst abuser" on trade, after which his administration imposed high duties on some categories of steel imports from Vietnam. The administration determined in late 2020 that Vietnam was a "currency manipulator" and slapped some preliminary tariffs on Vietnamese car and truck tires. These issues led some in Vietnam to look forward to the new Biden administration, which they hoped would follow a different path on trade matters, even though Vietnamese in general were more supportive of Trump than many in Southeast Asia, because of his tough stance on China.

Despite the problems over trade, the Biden administration entered office in early 2021 inheriting a strong and growing bilateral partnership. The enthusiasm and high-level engagement in July 2020 celebrations marking the twenty-fifth anniversary of the establishment of diplomatic ties highlighted both the strength of the relationship and the enthusiasm both countries appear to feel about it going forward. Although there were no dramatic developments in the relationship during the first year of the Biden administration, the United States dropped Vietnam from the list of "currency manipulators," and both Vice President Kamala Harris and Secretary of Defense Lloyd Austin visited Hanoi.

Growing Education and Humanitarian Ties

Good official relations are essential, but broader nongovernmental links, including businesses, universities, and NGOs, also have played an important role in the development of increasingly close bilateral ties. U.S. NGOs led the way, beginning to work in Vietnam well before normalization and steadily expanding their work in humanitarian and other areas. In 2008, a senior Vietnamese official estimated that fully one-third of all international NGOs in the country were from the United States.[12] They not only have done important work but have also helped forge personal ties that have been critical.

Education links have also boomed. Vietnam War veteran Tommy Valley, founder of the Vietnam Program at Harvard University's Ash Center, set up the Fulbright Economic Teaching Program in partnership with the University of Economics in Ho Chi Minh City in 1994. For two decades, that program offered courses but also an environment

---

12 Bui The Giang, "Vietnam-U.S. Political and People-To-People relations: A Brief Overview," in *Dialogue on U.S.-Vietnam Relations Ten Years After Normalization*, ed. Catharin E. Dalpino (Washington, DC: Asia Foundation, 2005).

where Vietnamese could discuss economic reform and other public policy issues among themselves and with visiting U.S. professors. In 2015, the Vietnamese authorities granted a license to the Fulbright University of Vietnam, the first private university in the country. The Fulbright Economic Teaching Program merged into the university as the Fulbright School of Public Policy and Management, and now offers the country's first master of public policy degree.

Meanwhile, thousands of Vietnamese have flocked to the United States to study at American universities. In 2019, nearly twenty-five thousand Vietnamese students were enrolled in U.S. higher education institutions, making Vietnam the sixth-largest source of foreign students in the United States.[13] The U.S. government has invested heavily in education, most notably through the Vietnam Education Foundation. Established by legislation authored by senators Kerry and McCain, the foundation offers scholarships to Vietnamese students pursuing advanced degrees in science and math. Since 2003, the foundation has supported some six hundred students in their studies.[14]

Veterans such as Tommy Vallely, both as individuals and as part of organizations, have also played an important role, sometimes through humanitarian work but often just trying to heal the wounds of war on an individual basis. In 2012, for example, a U.S. veteran who had fought in Vietnam, Robert Frazure, decided to return the wartime diary he had found on the body of a Vietnamese soldier after a battle in 1966. With the help of the Public Broadcasting Service, Frazure sent the diary back to Vietnam, where visiting Defense Secretary Leon Panetta handed it over Vietnamese officials, who returned it to the soldier's family.[15] This seemingly small move, and others like it, generated enormous media attention throughout Vietnam and added an emotional

13 "Number of Vietnamese Students in the U.S. Increases for 18th Straight Year," U.S. Embassy & Consulate in Vietnam, November 19, 2019, https://vn.usembassy.gov/number-of-vietnamese-higher-education-students-in-the-united-states-increases-for-18th-straight-year/; and Mark A. Ashwill, "Vietnamese Student Enrollment in the U.S. Holds Steady," University World News, February 8, 2020, https://www.universityworldnews.com/post.php?story=20200205124654543.

14 Office of the Press Secretary, The White House, "Fact Sheet: United States-Vietnam Education Cooperation," May 25, 2016, https://obamawhitehouse.archives.gov/the-press-office/2016/05/25/fact-sheet-united-states-vietnam-education-cooperation.

15 "Vietnam Soldier's War Diary Returned to Family," *Bangkok Post*, September 22, 2012, https://www.bangkokpost.com/world/313459/vietnam-soldier-war-diary-returned-to-family.

element to a growing relationship that no amount of official discussions can provide.

More broadly, efforts to deal with the humanitarian issues that the war produced have been absolutely essential to building public support in both countries for closer relations. For the United States, obtaining the maximum Vietnamese cooperation to achieve the fullest possible accounting for our POW/MIAs has dominated. The Vietnamese initially pressed for substantial aid for postwar reconstruction, but as noted earlier the United States pushed back, pointing out that it was Vietnam that had violated the Paris Peace Accords that called for such aid. Since at least the early 1990s, the Vietnamese have shifted their focus to seeking assistance in clearing landmines and unexploded ordinance and in dealing with the health and environmental impact of the substantial amount of Agent Orange the U.S. military sprayed in the country during the war, as well as assistance in finding the remains of the many Vietnamese soldiers who were killed during the war but whose remains could not be found because of the wartime circumstances.

The United States has gradually increased its humanitarian assistance, including millions of dollars from the Leahy War Victims Fund, which beginning in 1989 funneled money through the U.S. government to groups such as the Vietnam Veterans of America Foundation to assist Vietnamese victims of landmines and unexploded ordinance.

Agent Orange

Senator Leahy also has been a strong supporter of programs to deal with the health and environmental impact of Agent Orange. During the war, the U.S. military sprayed an estimated twenty million gallons of defoliants, including Agent Orange, as a way to deprive the Viet Cong and North Vietnamese Army of cover (and food). Agent Orange includes dioxin, a highly toxic chemical that can have serious health and environmental effects.[16]

The Agent Orange issue has been contentious from the beginning. The Vietnamese insisted that the United States needed to help both treat those affected by Agent Orange and assist in disposing of so-called hotspots, where they claimed that heavy concentrations of

---

16 Michael F. Martin, *U.S. Agent Orange/Dioxin Assistance to Vietnam*, Congressional Research Service R44268, updated February 21, 2019, https://crsreports.congress.gov/product/pdf/R/R44268/20.

dioxin rendered land uninhabitable and even toxic. Washington was cautious, both because of legal liability issues (former U.S. servicemen also had filed legal claims based on exposure to Agent Orange) and because of concern that Vietnam was blaming Agent Orange for causing virtually every disability in the country.

Over time, with the support of key members of Congress and individuals in the private sector, we were able to find ways to talk about and then deal with the problem. There had been some modest progress on the government-to-government side between 2002 and 2006, with the establishment of a joint advisory group and a small U.S. Environmental Protection Agency program with the Vietnamese Academy of Science and Technology and Ministry of National Defense that led to creation of a joint dioxin research laboratory in Hanoi in 2005. Also, Pentagon experts met with their Vietnamese counterparts to share information on our own experience with dioxin as well as on how and where we had used and stored Agent Orange during the war.[17]

In 2007, the Ford Foundation and the Aspen Institute helped establish a U.S.-Vietnam Dialogue Group, consisting of prominent educators, scientists, and public figures, to try to increase understanding of the issue and help the governments find a way to deal with an issue with which they were still struggling. This private sector effort merged with growing interest on Capitol Hill. I was called to testify twice, in 2008 and 2009, in front of the House Foreign Affairs Subcommittee on Asia about what the administration was doing to help Vietnam on Agent Orange. In my 2009 testimony, I was able to point to a total of $44 million in U.S. assistance since 1989 to help Vietnamese with disabilities, regardless of the cause (this language allowed us to avoid the question of whether a particular individual's disability was the result of Agent Orange). I welcomed congressional appropriation (via supplemental budgets) of $3 million each in FY 2007 and FY 2009 to address the environmental and health impacts of Agent Orange, noting that we were spending roughly one-third of that on health, and most of the rest

---

17 *Our Forgotten Responsibility: What Can We Do to Help Victims of Agent Orange: Hearing before the Subcommittee on Asia, Pacific, and the Global Environment Subcommittee of the Committee on Foreign Affairs*, 110th Cong. (May 15, 2008) (statement of Scot Marciel), https://www.govinfo.gov/app/details/CHRG-110hhrg42425/CHRG-110hhrg42425.

on initial work on environmental remediation of a dioxin hotspot in Danang.[18]

The pace of cooperation grew rapidly after that. By the end of 2020, Congress had appropriated nearly $390 million to help address Agent Orange.[19] Some of that went for health, but the bulk went for the environmental remediation of Danang. I visited the Danang remediation project in 2015, a year after Senator Leahy had visited to launch it. I am not knowledgeable enough on the science front to explain it properly, but in simple terms it involved technology that heated the affected soil sufficiently to render the dioxin harmless, or at least significantly less harmful. In May 2016, President Obama, meeting with Vietnamese president Tran Dai Quang, looked forward to the completion of the Danang project (done in 2017) and initiation of a much bigger project to clean up the old Bien Hoa Air Base near Ho Chi Minh City. The United States Agency for International Development launched that project in 2019, a remarkable step given that for years our internal discussions in Washington had assessed that Bien Hoa was too big and expensive for us to tackle.[20]

The Ingredients of a Positive Relationship

Our ability to work with the Vietnamese on issues such as Agent Orange, unexploded ordinance, and POW/MIA accounting has been essential to creating the public support in both countries for closer ties. I have already discussed this on the U.S. side, but public opinion on the Vietnamese side also mattered. Sure, it is not a democracy, but that does not mean Hanoi's leaders can ignore public sentiment. U.S. assistance and support on legacy of war issues has helped build Vietnamese

---

18 *Agent Orange: What Efforts Are Being Made to Address the Continuing Impact of Dioxin in Vietnam? Hearing Before the Subcommittee on Asia, the Pacific and the Global Environment of the Committee on Foreign Affairs*, 111th Cong. (June 4, 2009) (statement of Scot Marciel), https://www.govinfo.gov/content/pkg/CHRG-111hhrg50112/pdf/CHRG-111hhrg50112.pdf.

19 Michael F. Martin, *U.S. Agent Orange/Dioxin Assistance to Vietnam*, Congressional Research Service R44268, updated January 15, 2021, https://fas.org/sgp/crs/row/R44268.pdf.

20 Amruta Byatnal, "USAID Begins New Round of Agent Orange Cleanup in Vietnam," Devex, January 8, 2020, https://www.devex.com/news/usaid-begins-new-round-of-agent-orange-cleanup-in-vietnam-96222.

public support for the relationship and also allowed the development of many personal relationships that have buttressed bilateral ties. As Vietnamese ambassador to the United States Ha Kim Ngoc put it during a July 2020 Stimson Center discussion on legacies of the war, "It seems that the vicious war . . . could divide our countries forever. But addressing war legacy issues has become (the) glue connecting our two people closer. After all, the gamechanger is the determination by both sides to leave the past behind and look forward to the future."[21]

Several other factors help explain why this relationship has prospered, even during times when Washington has largely been focused elsewhere. First and foremost is China. I have said for years, only half in jest, that everything in Vietnam can be explained by some combination of China, power, and money. Vietnam's strategic concern about China has been and remains huge. Despite some ideological and party-to-party ties, the Vietnamese in general are, at a minimum, very wary of China. This was true even during the war, but at that time the United States did not appreciate it and saw the war as a Moscow-Beijing–supported communist effort. Even when I was serving in Hanoi twenty-five years ago, my conversations with the China watchers at the Foreign Ministry always followed the same script. I would ask about relations with China. They would say relations were good. Then I would ask about Chinese maritime and territorial claims in the South China Sea, and my interlocutor's face and tone would instantly change, and he (it was always a man) would angrily complain about China's unacceptable claims and behavior.

Vietnamese concern has only grown with time, as China's power and reach has expanded. The Vietnamese are realistic, so they know they need to maintain reasonably good ties with Beijing, and they generally do. Also, some in the leadership probably have felt more kinship, ideologically at least, with China than with us. At the same time, they know that the Vietnamese public as a whole is anti-Chinese, so the leaders have to be mindful not to be seen as leaning toward China. Then party chief Le Kha Phieu lost support ahead of the 2001 Communist Party Congress in part because he was seen as tilting too much toward Beijing. Prime Minister Nguyen Tan Dung, according to at least one senior U.S. official at the time, was openly playing the U.S. card in the lead-up

21 "The U.S.-Vietnam Relationship and War Legacies: 25 Years into Normalization" (Stimson Center meeting, July 15, 2020, virtual). Highlights at https://www.stimson .org/2020/the-us-vietnam-relationship-and-war-legacies-looking-to-the-future/.

to the 2016 Party Congress (though tellingly, it did not prevent him from losing his seat over corruption and nepotism allegations).

Money is the second factor, and I do not mean personal enrichment (though that might be a factor too). Vietnam's leaders have been committed for at least thirty years to seeing the country develop rapidly, whether as a means to stay in power or just because they see development as a good thing. They recognized early on that the best way to achieve development was to (a) enact domestic reforms, and (b) integrate into the world economy, with a particular focus on expanding commerce with the United States. So they supported the Bilateral Trade Agreement, pushed to join the WTO, and then decided to pursue negotiations to join the TPP. One former U.S. trade official with whom I spoke recalled a meeting with Prime Minister Dung to gauge his interest in the TPP, during which Dung made clear Vietnam was interested. "It was like pushing on an open door." Vietnam negotiated the TPP agreement with us, even though it would have required them to make very difficult and—for them—threatening reforms, especially on labor. There was fierce debate within the Vietnamese leadership over this very issue, but in the end the party decided that the benefits of further tying themselves to the United States and the global trading system—and diversifying away from economic dependence on China—was worth the risk. For the United States, Vietnam's openness to business has kept U.S. companies relatively bullish for years, even though it is not that easy to do business there. The results, in terms of the trade and investment numbers, speak for themselves.

Another key is pragmatism. This is necessarily subjective, but in my experience the Vietnamese tend to be pragmatic. They did not like the roadmap we offered in 1991, but they realized it was the only way forward toward normalization, so they followed it, more or less. They did not like our pressure on religious freedom in the early 2000s, but were willing to adjust their approach and grant more religious freedom because they clearly saw it as in their interest. They had rather openly rooted for Senator John McCain to win the 2008 presidential election but moved quickly after the election to reach out to the new Obama administration. As one longtime observer of Vietnam told me recently, the Vietnamese know what their interests are. They have a vision. And they do a pretty good job of following that vision, no matter what it takes.

The Vietnamese, like Americans, focus more on results than on process. In this, they stand out from many of their Southeast Asian neighbors. I do not mean other Southeast Asians do not care about results, but in some other cultures the process is as important as the outcome. I do not think that is the case with the Vietnamese. They want to achieve something. I remember representing the United States at an ASEAN-hosted meeting of senior officials to discuss regional matters, back in 2008 or 2009. In a series of bilateral meetings with the ASEAN representatives ahead of the main meeting, I laid out U.S. goals for the meeting and pushed for some concrete results. Many of my interlocutors nodded, and acknowledged the value of concrete results, but emphasized also the importance of avoiding any confrontations or actions that might upset any others. My Vietnamese counterpart, Pham Quang Vinh (later ambassador to Washington), took a different approach. He greeted me, sat down, and said, "Here are the five things we need to accomplish in the meeting." He briefly described each one, and then concluded with "Let's achieve these results, then we'll go have a beer." It was a classic Vietnamese no-nonsense (other than the beer) approach. The Vietnamese might have a different vision for ASEAN than the United States does, to the extent Washington has one at all, but the two governments share a desire to see the institution develop and play a more active role. U.S.-Vietnamese cooperation in regional fora, including ASEAN, the East Asia Summit, and the Lower Mekong Initiative, has grown steadily over the past decade, and there is opportunity to do much more.

Finally, to finish where I started this chapter, the Vietnamese know how to work Washington, and maybe Americans in general, and how to present a strategic picture of the region that U.S. policymakers find useful. Some might even say that the Vietnamese knew how to work American public opinion during the war, and helped win support among some segments of the American public for an early end to the conflict. They have continued to be proactive in engaging not only senior U.S. officials but official Washington at all levels, as well as the business community, NGOs, Congress, and other interest groups. They recognized, more than most of their Southeast Asian colleagues, that being passive in Washington does not work. You have to fight for attention, and for engagement. They do, and they do it very effectively.

Of course, the Vietnamese start with a unique advantage. A lot of Americans, and a lot of U.S. officials, are fascinated by Vietnam. Some of this—maybe a lot of it—is due to the history, which is ironic but true. The tragedy of the war also bound us together. The story of building a relationship with a country with which we fought a bitter war is very appealing to many Americans. Plus, a lot of U.S. officials like working with the Vietnamese. Despite our significant differences and the fact that the Vietnamese are tough negotiators, there is a sense among many of my official colleagues that it is possible to get things done with the Vietnamese. This is partly the result of Hanoi's pragmatism, but also the relative effectiveness of their bureaucracy in sharing information and coordinating among ministries (something that is rare in the region). When U.S. delegations visit Vietnam for talks on any subject, they can be sure that everyone they meet with will have been fully briefed on the substance of the previous meeting, even if it is with another ministry. That makes a huge difference. I cannot stress enough how important the prospect of achieving something concrete is when you are trying to convince someone to get on a plane to fly twenty-four hours across the Pacific. As a result, it has never been hard to convince senior U.S. officials to travel to or meet with Vietnamese counterparts. Particularly during times when Washington is focused elsewhere in the world, that is a big advantage.

Realistic Goals

To close on a cautionary note, it is important for policymakers, particularly in Washington, not to assume that the positive trajectory in the bilateral relationship, along with Vietnam's obvious concern about China, will lead to anything akin to an alliance relationship. I know some have visions of U.S. warships operating out of Cam Ranh Bay. That is unlikely. Much as they worry about China, the pragmatism of Vietnamese leaders will ensure they avoid going so far vis-à-vis the United States as to infuriate Beijing. That will be especially true as long as the Vietnamese harbor some doubts about U.S. reliability and commitment to the region.

Also, despite all the progress, there remain in Hanoi any number of conservative individuals and institutions that will continue to apply the brakes to the relationship with Washington. On our end, concerns about human rights and the lack of democratic reform will limit the relationship to some extent. One also has to wonder whether at some point the very energetic younger generation of Vietnam will demand more political space and freedom, creating domestic political problems that so far Hanoi has managed to avoid.

The important point is that the relationship, even short of an alliance, is profoundly in both countries' interests. Washington benefits from a strong, fully independent Vietnam that is playing an increasingly important role in the region, while the close relationship with Washington gives Hanoi much-needed leverage vis-à-vis China. The booming commercial ties help both countries, while the growing education and people-to-people links build constituencies that will help ensure the durability of the overall partnership.

CHAPTER SIX

Tragedy and Disappointment

Cambodia since the War

The photographs at Cambodia's Tuol Sleng Genocide Museum are haunting—hundreds of men, women, and children captured on film as they faced torture and death at the hands of the Khmer Rouge. As I toured the museum with Deputy Secretary of State John Negroponte in the fall of 2008, looking at photograph after photograph of people whose faces revealed the anguish, shock, and fear they must have felt, I choked up and cried. Whenever I think of Cambodia, I remember those photos and wonder how a society that has had its very soul ripped apart manages to function at all.

Beyond its tragic history, Cambodia warrants a chapter in this book because its relationship with the United States over time has reflected the evolution as well as the disappointments of the broader U.S. approach toward Southeast Asia. During the Cold War, the United States viewed Cambodia initially through the prism of confronting global communism as manifested in the Vietnam War, and then via the lens of preventing Soviet-backed expansion in the form of what Washington referred to as the Vietnamese-backed Heng Samrin regime. After the Cold War and the 1991 Cambodian Peace Accords, the United States invested heavily in support of Cambodia's democratic experiment and reacted sharply when Hun Sen took the country off the democratic course. More recently, Hun Sen's Machiavellian politics and tilt toward China have created even more animus toward him in Washington, particularly on Capitol Hill.

Caught up in A Bigger Struggle

The story begins in the heart of the Cold War in the 1960s, when Cambodia found itself caught up in a nascent indigenous communist insurgency, the Vietnam War, and the global great power rivalry. Prince Norodom Sihanouk, who had returned from exile to lead the country following its independence in 1953, maneuvered to try to maintain the country's neutrality, first leaning somewhat toward the United States but then—in the later 1960s—breaking ties with Washington and leaning more toward North Vietnam.

By that time North Vietnamese troops were operating inside Cambodian territory, using the eastern part of the country to maintain troops and bring supplies into South Vietnam through the Ho Chi Minh Trail. Sihanouk had little choice but to accommodate the Vietnamese, so he stayed quiet while publicly protesting U.S. and South Vietnamese cross-border incursions targeting the North Vietnamese. Over time, Sihanouk's authoritarian behavior and willingness to accommodate the Vietnamese resulted in him losing some domestic support.

In March 1970 a pro-U.S. general, Lon Nol, ousted Sihanouk. The move was widely called a coup, even though the National Assembly had voted to strip the prince of power.[1] Lon Nol vowed to rid the country of Vietnamese communist forces, but his own military performed poorly. In Washington, the Nixon administration believed the Vietnamese and Vietnamese-backed forces were gaining the upper hand in Cambodia and that Phnom Penh could fall, which would endanger the administration's Vietnamization policy. As a result, the United States stepped up military aid and in May 1970, together with South Vietnamese forces, launched a major incursion into Cambodia to hit North Vietnamese forces and try to cut off North Vietnamese supply routes. When that failed, Nixon lifted restrictions on U.S. bombing, which resulted in a massive bombing campaign that extended beyond the border region.[2]

---

1 Andrew Nachemson, "Remembering Cambodia's 1970 Coup," *The Diplomat*, March 20, 2020, https://thediplomat.com/2020/03/remembering-cambodias-1970 -coup/.

2 Taylor Owen and Ben Kiernan, "Bombs Over Cambodia," *The Walrus*, October 2006, https://gsp.yale.edu/sites/default/files/walrus_cambodiabombing_octo6.pdf; and Office of the Historian, "Foreign Relations, 1969–1976, Vietnam, January

After his ouster Prince Sihanouk threw his support behind the Khmer Rouge, an indigenous Maoist movement that had been operating with limited success since the early 1960s. The combination of Sihanouk's continued popularity in much of the countryside and support from Hanoi and Beijing helped the Khmer Rouge gain strength. Some observers have argued persuasively that the extended U.S. bombing campaign also fueled the Khmer Rouge's rise, as it alienated the population and drove the insurgents further west toward Phnom Penh.[3] By 1971–72, the Lon Nol government had lost control of much of the countryside, and the sharp reduction of U.S. support for Lon Nol after the 1973 Vietnam peace agreement added to the insurgents' momentum.

The Khmer Rouge Era

On April 17, 1975, the Khmer Rouge occupied Phnom Penh and ushered in a four-year period of absolute horror. On the very day they took the capital, they began forcibly herding the entire population out of the city in a disastrous move to try to create a new, agrarian society. The U.S. Holocaust Memorial Museum's description sums it up best:

> By the afternoon of that very first day, soldiers using bullhorns began ordering the city's two million residents into the countryside. Houses and schools were emptied at gunpoint, with shots fired if people did not move fast enough. Not even hospitals were spared, with patients forced into the streets. Families split apart as children lost sight of parents in the confusion of the exodus. Thousands of people died in the chaos along jammed roads leading from the capital. Friends and relatives were made to leave behind the bodies and trudge on, carrying what few possessions they could.[4]

The Khmer Rouge closed schools, libraries, and religious institutions, and opened torture centers such as Tuol Sleng. They mercilessly eliminated anyone who did not conform to their bizarre vision. Over the next four years, the Khmer Rouge would either directly murder or

---

1969–1970," U.S. Department of State Archive, https://2001-2009.state.gov/r/pa/ho/frus/nixon/vi/64033.htm.
3 See, for example, William Shawcross, *Sideshow: Kissinger, Nixon and the Destruction of Cambodia* (New York: Simon and Schuster, 1979).
4 "Day One: April 17, 1975," United States Holocaust Memorial Museum, https://www.ushmm.org/genocide-prevention/countries/cambodia/case-study/violence/day-one.

otherwise be responsible for the deaths of some 1.5 to 2 million Cambodians, perhaps 25–30 percent of the country's population, in what arguably was the world's worst mass killing since the Holocaust.[5]

Others have written at length about the horrors of the Khmer Rouge period. It is hard to wrap one's head around the notion of a government killing a quarter of its own population, no matter how many times one hears the numbers. What always stands out to me is that the Khmer Rouge shattered the collective psyche of the entire society, wounding it so deeply that it is remarkable the country is able to operate at all.

Some four decades later, over dinner in a Phnom Penh restaurant, a senior Cambodian Foreign Ministry official opened up to me about his own experience during those years. The Khmer Rouge had separated him from his wife, sending each to work in the fields in remote rural areas. He did not think he would survive, let alone ever see his wife again. They had no way to communicate with each other, or even to know if the other was alive. When the Vietnamese drove out the Khmer Rouge, he found himself walking dozens of miles to return home. When he arrived, he saw his wife, who had just made her way back for the first time in more than three years. As he put it, "We were among the lucky ones."

Washington's Cold War View

From the early 1960s until 1975, successive U.S. administrations had largely viewed Cambodia through the lens of the Vietnam War, which of course was all about the global Cold War battle against Soviet- and Chinese-backed communist expansion. It was not that the United States did not care about Cambodia. It just was secondary to Vietnam. Official Washington treated Cambodia as a "sideshow," a term memorialized in William Shawcross's damning indictment of U.S. policy at the time.[6]

The Khmer Rouge rule coincided with a period in which the United States, humiliated by the loss of Vietnam and deeply divided over the war, wanted to have as little as possible to do with the old Indochina. To the extent that Washington paid attention, its focus remained on

---

5 "Cambodia 1975–1979," United States Holocaust Memorial Museum, https://www.ushmm.org/genocide-prevention/countries/cambodia/case-study/introduction/cambodia-1975.
6 Shawcross, *Sideshow.*

countering Soviet-backed Vietnam, even if it meant working with the Khmer Rouge. Secretary of State Henry Kissinger told Thai foreign minister Chatichai Choonhavan in November 1975 that, while the United States considered the Khmer Rouge to be "murderous thugs," Washington "would not let that stand in our way" in trying to improve relations, as the U.S. strategic goal was to make Cambodia and Laos barriers to further Vietnamese expansion.[7] A few weeks later, during a meeting between President Ford and Indonesia's President Suharto, Kissinger offered a similar but more nuanced take, acknowledging that the Khmer Rouge regime was bad but emphasizing the U.S. interest in Cambodia preserving its independence vis-à-vis Vietnam.[8]

To be fair to Kissinger, because the Khmer Rouge cut off the country from the world, the scale of the regime's executions and other deprivations was not as clear in late 1975 and early 1976 as it would later become. The publication of more and more credible reports of mass murder in 1976 and 1977 coincided with the advent of the Carter administration, which made human rights a foreign policy priority. The Carter administration issued increasingly strong statements condemning the Khmer Rouge's behavior, culminating in President Carter's April 1978 statement labeling the Khmer Rouge the "worst violator of human rights in the world today."[9]

The Carter administration supported tough UN resolutions calling out the Khmer Rouge and demanding an end to human rights violations, but it also continued to emphasize the importance of Cambodia remaining independent from Vietnam. This reflected the big power rivalries at the time. By the mid to late 1970s, China and the Soviet Union were increasingly at odds, and the United States was building a new relationship with China. China supported the Khmer Rouge, while

---

7 "Memorandum of Conversation, Secretary's Meeting with Foreign Minister Chatichai of Thailand," November 26, 1975, declassified July 27, 2004, National Security Archive, George Washington University, https://nsarchive2.gwu.edu/NSAEBB/NSAEBB193/HAK-11-26-75.pdf.
8 Document 141, "Telegram 14946 from the Embassy in Indonesia to the Department of State, December 6, 1975, 1000Z," in *Foreign Relations of the United States, 1969–1976, Volume E–12, Documents on East and Southeast Asia, 1973–1976,* ed. Bradley Lynn Coleman, David Goldman, and David Nickles (Washington: Government Printing Office, 2010), https://history.state.gov/historicaldocuments/frus1969-76ve12/d141.
9 "International Response to Khmer Rouge Rule," United States Holocaust Memorial Museum, https://www.ushmm.org/genocide-prevention/countries/cambodia/case-study/violence/international-response.

the Soviet Union supported Vietnam. The United States despised the Khmer Rouge but in the Cold War context was also deeply concerned about the threat of Soviet-backed Vietnamese expansion.

This policy dilemma revealed itself publicly in early 1979 in the first official State Department reaction to Vietnam's Christmas Day 1978 invasion of Cambodia. Spokesman Hodding Carter said that "while the United States takes great exception to the human rights record of the government of Kampuchea [the official name of Cambodia] we, as a matter of principle, do not feel that unilateral intervention against the regime by any third power is justified."[10]

Supporting the Opposition

When Vietnam occupied Cambodia and installed a pro-Hanoi regime led by former Khmer Rouge officials Heng Samrin and Hun Sen, the United States, China, and Thailand, along with many other ASEAN nations, saw the issue as Soviet-backed Vietnamese aggression rather than the removal of a genocidal regime. Washington, Beijing, and Bangkok led efforts to oppose the new Cambodian government and to support an unholy opposition alliance that included Prince Sihanouk's royalist party, the National United Front for an Independent, Neutral, Peaceful and Cooperative Cambodia (FUNCINPEC), the rightist Khmer People's National Liberation Front (KPNLF), led by longtime political figure Son Sann, and the Khmer Rouge.

From 1979 until the end of the Cold War, Washington's primary focus vis-à-vis Cambodia remained putting maximum pressure on Vietnam to withdraw from Cambodia, even if that meant implicitly working with the Khmer Rouge. The United States, along with China and ASEAN, blocked the Vietnamese-installed regime in Phnom Penh from taking Cambodia's seat at the UN, insisting that first the Khmer Rouge and then the broad opposition alliance including the Khmer Rouge occupy the UN chair. Washington also provided military assistance to the non–Khmer Rouge elements of the opposition, while turning a blind eye to Chinese and Thai direct support to the Khmer Rouge. Jimmy Carter's national security advisor, Zbigniew Brzezinski, acknowledged as much when he told journalist Elizabeth Becker in

---

10 Elizabeth Becker, "Vietnamese Invasion of Cambodia Draws Criticism by U.S.," *Washington Post*, January 4, 1979.

1979, "I encouraged the Chinese to support Pol Pot. Pol Pot was an abomination. We could never support him, but China could."[11]

The Reagan administration tweaked the policy to emphasize that it was supporting the non–Khmer Rouge elements of the opposition, but overall its focus remained on pushing back against Soviet-backed Vietnamese expansionism. For U.S. policy, Cambodia became a part of the Reagan Doctrine, which supported so-called freedom fighters against Soviet-backed leftist or communist regimes in places such as Nicaragua, Angola, Mozambique, and of course Cambodia.

By 1990, when I joined the Vietnam, Laos, and Cambodia desk, the Cold War was coming to an end. Vietnam was looking to normalize relations with the United States and had withdrawn its troops from Cambodia. Washington could view Cambodia less as a Cold War issue and more as a devastated country that needed peace and, ideally, democracy. The George H. W. Bush administration—increasingly uncomfortable with Washington's indirect support for the Khmer Rouge—had made the effort to achieve a Cambodia peace agreement a top priority. Led by Assistant Secretary of State Richard Solomon, Deputy Assistant Secretary Ken Quinn, and future ambassador to Cambodia Charlie Twining, the administration redoubled efforts to work with ASEAN—particularly Indonesia—as well as with Vietnam and with the other permanent Security Council members to finalize an agreement.

The Peace Accords and Hope for Democracy

The effort culminated in the October 1991 signing of the Paris Peace Accords on Cambodia. Under the agreement, the four Cambodian parties to the conflict—the Vietnamese-backed Cambodian People's Party (CPP) regime in Phnom Penh, the Khmer Rouge, the KPNLF, and the FUNCINPEC—agreed to allow the United Nations to play a substantial role, assuming administrative control of much of the government machinery, supervising significant demobilization and disarmament of the various armed forces, and conducting a nationwide election to determine a new, democratic government. It was an ambitious vision that the United States and other sponsors of the agreement invested in heavily, both financially and emotionally. In hindsight, it is easy to criticize the agreement's designers as overly optimistic about the willingness

---

11 Elizabeth Becker, *When the War Was Over: Cambodia and the Khmer Rouge* (New York: Simon and Schuster, 1986), 435.

of the various Cambodian parties to implement their commitments, though one wonders whether there were better alternatives.

The agreement ran into trouble almost from the beginning. The fundamental problem was that the two most powerful factions—the Khmer Rouge and the CPP—had signed the agreement only under great international pressure. There had not been any actual reconciliation between the two. In addition, UN funding and bureaucratic delays meant that the UN Transitional Authority for Cambodia (UNTAC), which was to take over much of the interim administration from the CPP, was delayed in arriving and never really took sufficient control of the country's administration. Third, the UN proved too weak to disarm and demobilize either the Khmer Rouge or the CPP's forces. By early 1992, the Khmer Rouge were refusing to cooperate with UNTAC and gradually withdrew from the agreement to renew fighting.

Despite these problems, UNTAC succeeded in running competitive nationwide elections in 1993, with some 90 percent turnout. FUNCINPEC won a plurality, just shy of 50 percent of the vote, with the CPP coming in second. Hun Sen refused to accept the results, however, claiming election irregularities. He ratcheted up the pressure by engineering a secessionist threat in the provinces east of the Mekong River. Eventually, the various players worked out a deal under which FUNCINPEC's Prince Ranariddh (Sihanouk's son) would be "First Prime Minister" and the CPP's Hun Sen would be "Second Prime Minister." Most of the writing about this period suggests that Hun Sen used his control over a significant number of armed forces to force the UN and FUNCINPEC to accept this deal. Some, however, argue that, under the country's new constitution, FUNCINPEC was compelled to strike some kind of deal with CPP in order to garner the votes in parliament for a new government.[12]

In those early days, Washington policymakers did not have a good sense of the power dynamics within the CPP. When I was on the desk in 1990–92, we often referred to the CPP-led government as "the Heng Samrin regime." As of 1990, Heng Samrin was chairman of the Council of State and secretary-general of the People's Revolutionary Party, which changed its name to the CPP in 1991. We also knew that Chea Sim, who became president of the CPP in 1991, had significant influence. It soon became clear that Hun Sen had garnered the most power

12 Telephone interview with former U.S. official involved in Cambodian affairs during the period, January 7, 2021.

within the party, though Heng Samrin and Chea Sim continued to hold important positions.

From 1993 to 1997, the two parties (CPP and FUNCINPEC) and leaders coexisted uneasily as each party retained control over its own armed forces and built parallel networks inside the state machinery. It was just a matter of time before it fell apart. Tension built in 1996 and 1997, ahead of planned 1997 commune and 1998 parliamentary elections. Both the CPP and FUNCINPEC attempted to bolster their forces by recruiting Khmer Rouge soldiers. In March 1997 a grenade attack, widely believed to have been carried out by Hun Sen's bodyguards, shattered a demonstration led by opposition leader Sam Rainsy, a former FUNCINPEC finance minister who had been pushed out for his aggressive anti-corruption efforts. The attack killed several people.[13]

Hun Sen Assumes Control

Then, in early July 1997, CPP and FUNCINPEC forces clashed, leading to significant fighting that resulted in a CPP victory and Prince Ranariddh fleeing the country to avoid arrest. Hun Sen emerged as Cambodia's paramount leader. Again, the bulk of the writing about this incident labels Hun Sen and the CPP as the aggressor. A minority, including at least a couple of U.S. officials working on Cambodia at the time, argue that it was not that clear-cut and that FUNCINPEC at a minimum shared significant responsibility for the fighting.

The United States, Japan, and several other countries condemned the violence and suspended nonhumanitarian assistance. Over the next several months, they pressed Hun Sen to allow the scheduled 1998 national elections to proceed freely. Japan brokered an agreement under which Prince Ranariddh returned and competed in the elections. After widespread reports of CPP violence and intimidation in the lead-up to the elections, the CPP won a narrow victory over the FUNCINPEC, ensuring Hun Sen would retain his role as prime minister. Prince Ranariddh became speaker of parliament, which allowed at least the semblance of representative government to continue. In 1998, the U.S. Congress added language to the foreign affairs appropriations bill prohibiting U.S. direct assistance to the Cambodian government (though not to

---

13 See, for example, Sopheng Cheang, "Cambodia Marks 20 Years Since Deadly Grenade Attack," Associated Press, March 30, 2017, https://apnews.com/article/02 7b9bb8504e40d48d83d695bfaefcbd.

the country), due to the political violence and Hun Sen's de facto 1997 coup.

Ever since then Hun Sen has skillfully and sometimes ruthlessly maintained power, using a combination of patronage politics, electoral intimidation and violence, arrests and threatened arrests of political opponents, as well as some genuine popular support garnered from the country's overall stability and economic development, to fend off threats to his rule. For example, in the 2003 national elections—which were an improvement over those of 1998 but still flawed—Hun Sen's CPP won 73 of 123 seats in parliament, short of the two-thirds majority needed to form a government on its own. The opposition FUNCINPEC and Sam Rainsy Party (SRP) refused to join the CPP to form a government until and unless Hun Sen stepped down. Hun Sen refused, and in 2004 the CPP-dominated National Assembly added a clause to the constitution that forced a vote on a new government. The assembly elected a coalition government, with Hun Sen as prime minister and Prince Ranariddh once again serving as speaker of parliament. The SRP denounced the added constitutional clause as unconstitutional.[14]

In early 2005, Hun Sen filed a defamation lawsuit against Sam Rainsy and the National Assembly voted to strip Rainsy and two of his SRP colleagues of parliamentary immunity. Rainsy and Chea Poch fled the country, but Cheam Channy was arrested, prosecuted, and convicted of creating an illegal armed force. In December 2005 Sam Rainsy was convicted in absentia of defamation against government leaders. A few months later, ahead of a February 2006 meeting of foreign donors, King Norodom Sihamoni (who had succeeded his father, King Sihanouk, in 2004) pardoned Rainsy, Poch, and Channy at Hun Sen's request.[15] This prosecute-convict-pardon cycle would become a regular Hun Sen practice in the years to come.

That same month, the National Assembly passed a law allowing a government to be formed based on a majority vote in the assembly, as opposed to the previous two-thirds requirement. Prince Ranariddh resigned as speaker of the National Assembly in protest, which prompted Hun Sen to engineer the election of a more accommodating figure to replace Ranariddh as head of FUNCINPEC.[16]

---

14 "Cambodia: Events of 2006," Human Rights Watch, https://www.hrw.org/world-report/2007/country-chapters/cambodia.
15 "Cambodia: Events of 2006."
16 "Cambodia: Events of 2006."

The CPP Remains Dominant as the Economy Grows

By this point, FUNCINPEC was declining as a political force, with the opposition to Hun Sen being led by the SRP and activist Kem Sokha's Human Rights Party. The CPP, however, remained dominant, boosted by its strong-arm tactics but also the country's relative political stability and solid economic performance. Although Cambodia remained poor, it had enjoyed relatively good economic growth since the early 1990s, with annual rates reaching more than 6 percent in 2006–07.

Strong textile exports helped fuel that growth. In 2007, they accounted for an estimated 80 percent of the country's total exports and employed more than three hundred thousand people. Textile exports to the United States alone accounted for some 60 percent of total export revenue in 2008. Cambodia benefited under the U.S. Generalized System of Preferences as well as a 1999 bilateral agreement that increased import quotas for Cambodian textiles in return for progress in protecting labor rights. Over 97 percent of U.S. imports from Cambodia at the time were textiles and apparel.[17]

U.S. policy at the time sought to promote both broad-based economic development and greater democracy. When I took over as director of the Office of Mainland Southeast Asia in 2005, it was clear to me (and most everyone else) that our policy was achieving much more success on the economic front than on the political side. The question for us was what more, if anything, we could do to encourage further progress politically. Hun Sen's "coup" in 1997 had greatly disappointed many in Washington, crushing hopes that Cambodia might enjoy a truly democratic future.

Pushing for Democratic Space

A big part of the challenge involved the rapid ups and downs in the amount of democratic space Hun Sen allowed in Cambodia. For example, as noted above, the government prosecuted Sam Rainsy and others in his party (and stripped them of parliamentary immunity) in 2005. Politically, things looked grim. In early 2006, however, Hun Sen

---

17 Thomas Lum, *Cambodia: Background and U.S. Relations*, Congressional Research Service RL32986, April 30, 2009, 7–8, https://crsreports.congress.gov/product/pdf/RL/RL32986.

adopted a softer approach. In addition to choreographing their pardon, he ordered the freeing of other political prisoners and eliminated jail time as punishment in defamation cases. This softer approach continued through 2007 and the U.S. government responded with stepped-up engagement.

In early 2008 congressional testimony, I noted that "the relationship between the United States and Cambodia has been steadily improving, based in part on the progress that Cambodia itself has made." I pointed to positive developments in several areas: "The strengthening of civil society and democratic processes, improvements in the fight against human trafficking, progress on efforts to bring several Khmer Rouge leaders to justice, and increasing religious tolerance." I added that "we have seen an increase in space for political activity which has allowed for an active political opposition and an increasingly dynamic civil society. Cambodia's April 2007 commune-level elections were peaceful and generally positive." I pointed out that this progress had led to the first U.S. Navy ship visits to Cambodia in thirty years as well as the launch of a Peace Corps program.[18]

Around the same time, ambassador to Cambodia Joe Mussomelli stated that, due to Cambodia's positive steps, "the U.S. was able to restore military-to-military ties, the U.S. Congress removed restrictions that prohibited us from directly funding Cambodian government projects, and we have seen a myriad of high level U.S. government officials visit Cambodia to meet with its leaders and civil society representatives."[19]

In the 2008 national elections, the CPP won a major victory, taking 90 of the 123 seats. The opposition complained of fraud, but most observers concluded that the elections—while flawed—were better organized technically and suffered less violence and intimidation than previous elections. The CPP's victory can be attributed to strong economic growth (nearly 10 percent annually at the time), effective use of patronage and the state machinery, and probably a nationalist boost: just before the elections the government announced it had resolved, in

18 *An Overview of Cambodia and Debt Recycling: How Can the U.S. Be of Assistance? Hearing Before the Subcomm. on Asia, the Pacific, and the Global Environment of the Comm. on Foreign Affairs*, 100th Cong. (February 14, 2008) (statement of Scot Marciel), https://www.govinfo.gov/content/pkg/CHRG-110hhrg40746/pdf/CHRG-110hhrg40746.pdf.

19 "Ask the Ambassador," January 11, 2008, U.S. Department of State Archive, https://2001-2009.state.gov/r/pa/ei/ask/99222.htm.

Cambodia's favor, a major disagreement with Thailand over an historic site on the border.

In late 2009, Hun Sen returned to his earlier, tougher tactics, accusing Sam Rainsy of using fake maps to criticize the government for purportedly surrendering territory to Vietnam, fueling already-strong anti-Vietnamese sentiment in the country. We were not happy with Rainsy's anti-Vietnam rhetoric. I remember meeting him in Phnom Penh and urging him to soften his tone, rather than risk provoking anti-Vietnamese sentiment. On the other hand, we strongly opposed Hun Sen's legal action against Rainsy, which clearly sought to weaken the prime minister's primary political rival. The National Assembly once again stripped Rainsy of parliamentary immunity and he went into exile ahead of his 2010 conviction in absentia.

Despite this setback, the Obama administration—committed to its pivot or rebalance and mindful of Cambodia's growing ties with China—continued its dialogue with the government and its policy of greater engagement. Secretary of State Hillary Clinton visited Cambodia in 2010 and 2012 (the latter to attend a meeting of the ASEAN Regional Forum), and President Obama visited in 2012 to attend the Cambodia-hosted East Asian Summit, the first presidential visit ever to the country. Obama met with Hun Sen and urged him to release political prisoners and allow opposition parties to operate more freely. Years later, many in the CPP remained bitter about Obama's high-profile critique of the government during his visit.

The U.S. military continued to expand its cooperation with its Cambodian counterparts. In 2012, a U.S. Navy ship visited the port of Sihanoukville, and U.S. and Cambodian naval elements participated for the third year in a row in a naval exercise called CARAT (Cooperation Afloat Readiness and Training). The two militaries also conducted bilateral peacekeeping exercises. During this period I visited Cambodia regularly, always meeting with the government, opposition figures, and the country's remarkably active and impressive civil society. We also began a broad, multi-agency bilateral dialogue at my level, which engendered a surprising amount of interest and buy-in from Cambodian officials.

We were not under any illusions that Hun Sen was going to become a Jeffersonian democrat, but we believed engagement offered the best hope of preserving at least a modest amount of democratic space and of building longer-term relationships with Cambodian individuals and institutions that, over time, might be able to move the country in a more positive direction. We continued to provide substantial assistance, the bulk of which went to support civil society, economic development, and improved governance. We also reached out to build relationships with others around Hun Sen, including his son, Hun Manet, a West Point graduate who might be in line to succeed his father. All the while, we maintained close contact with the democratic opposition, always highlighting the importance of political competition and discouraging moves to restrict the operating space for political parties, the independent media, and civil society.

The Khmer Rouge Tribunal

The United States also placed a high priority on supporting and encouraging the work of the Khmer Rouge Tribunal, an independent court that had been established jointly by the UN and Cambodia in 2007 to pursue justice for the victims of the Khmer Rouge. The United States, along with France and Japan, provided much of the funding and diplomatic support for the tribunal. It has been subject to much criticism for its cost ($300 million), slow pace of work, and meager results (it only convicted three Khmer Rouge officials in eleven years).[20] The Hun Sen government opposed further prosecutions and created continuous problems for the tribunal. The lack of cases and convictions have raised questions about whether the cost and effort were worthwhile.

The fact that the tribunal met and deliberated in Cambodia, with a fair amount of transparency that allowed many ordinary Cambodians to follow its work, and that it convicted three Khmer Rouge members, including two top officials, made it a very valuable effort, in my view. When I visited the tribunal, dozens of people—victims or relatives of victims—were attending the sessions, wanting and perhaps needing to see some justice after so many years of pain. Youk Chhang, the remarkable man who founded and runs the Documentation Center of Cambodia (which keeps records of the Khmer Rouge era), told the *New York Times*, "They have established a culture of debate in this broken society, and any talk about the tribunal is extremely important for Cambodia." The *Times* story added that, during the tribunal's operation, Cambodia for the first time included a chapter on the Khmer

---

20 See, for example, Peter Maguire, "The Khmer Rouge Trials: The Good, the Bad, and the Ugly," *The Diplomat*, November 14, 2018, https://thediplomat.com/2018/11/the-khmer-rouge-trials-the-good-the-bad-and-the-ugly/.

Rouge era in the country's high school curriculum, ensuring that the younger generation would know what happened.[21] I am not an expert on accountability or transitional justice, but in my view truth and fact-telling about horrors such as the Khmer Rouge genocide are essential, whether or not justice through legal means is attained.

Hun Sen Tilts Toward China

The 2012 ASEAN Summit turned out to be notable not just for President Obama's participation but for the Cambodian government's decision to block—in an unprecedented step—an ASEAN statement. The move clearly was made at China's behest, as China opposed any statement that discussed ASEAN concerns about the South China Sea. Everyone knew that China's influence in Cambodia had grown significantly in the past several years, as evidenced by Cambodia's decision to deport fourteen Uighur asylum seekers back to China in late 2009, but the 2012 summit highlighted clearly how willing Hun Sen was to toe the Chinese line, even if that meant alienating his ASEAN brethren. The irony of Hun Sen turning to China, which had been the Khmer Rouge's most fervent supporter for many years, was striking.

China had been building its relationship with Cambodia for some time. Although Beijing had been a mortal enemy of the Vietnamese-backed Cambodian regime in the 1980s and had a longstanding close relationship with Prince Sihanouk, Chinese leaders recognized in the mid to late 1990s that Hun Sen and the CPP were the key players in the country and so worked hard to build a relationship with them. China's efforts included generous amounts of assistance, regular visits, and a practice of not criticizing human rights violations or anti-democratic behavior.

Elections and Hope for Change

Back on the domestic front, Cambodia's 2013 national elections turned out to be very competitive, as the normally fractious opposition worked together to form the Cambodia National Rescue Party (CNRP), with Sam Rainsy as president and Kem Sokha as vice president. Under international pressure, Hun Sen asked King Norodom Sihamoni to

---

21 Seth Mydans, "11 Years, $300 Million, and 3 Convictions: Was the Khmer Rouge Tribunal Worth It?," *New York Times*, April 10, 2017.

pardon Sam Rainsy, allowing him to return in mid-July 2013, just ten days ahead of the elections. With Rainsy back, the CNRP party won 55 of 123 seats, while the CPP suffered a net loss of 22 seats, keeping only 68. The CNRP nonetheless rejected the results, claiming widespread fraud had robbed it of an absolute majority and the right to form a new government.

The opposition organized large protests and boycotted parliament for a year. Initially, the CNRP's demands focused on investigating alleged election fraud, but when it became clear that would not happen, the party emphasized reforming the National Election Commission. After a year of protests and boycotts, the CPP and CNRP reached agreement in July 2014 on a set of election commission reforms that would allow the CNRP to return to parliament. While Sam Rainsy and other CNRP members argued that they had achieved much of what they wanted, the reality was that they had felt increasingly pressured—including by the arrest of several prominent party members earlier in the month—to take whatever deal they could get.

During my regular visits during this period there was a sense in our embassy, among other foreign observers, and among at least some Cambodians, that time was on the side of the opposition, as the younger generation appeared to be moving away from the CPP and toward the CNRP. While the older generation, remembering the Khmer Rouge era, might have placed more weight on the CPP's ability to maintain stability and achieve solid growth, a growing percentage of younger people were chafing at the corruption, nepotism, and violence of CPP rule. Government and CPP land-grabs also had become a big issue for many people, highlighting the government's corruption and failure to stop CPP insiders and cronies from stealing land from people. The prospect of more competitive politics argued for continued engagement and maximum diplomatic efforts to maintain as much democratic space as possible in the country.

Hun Sen Goes After the Opposition and the United States

Hun Sen and his CPP compatriots must have seen the same trend, because by 2015 they began taking aggressive steps to ensure their continued hold on power. In 2015, the National Assembly passed legislation that imposed new restrictions and requirements on civil society, which had been almost uniformly opposed to CPP rule. From 2015 to 2017, according to the Department of State, authorities arrested some twenty-five members of the opposition on various political charges.[22] Authorities charged Sam Rainsy with defamation in 2015, leading him to flee once again into exile.

Hun Sen's growing repression made his participation in President Obama's January 2016 Sunnylands summit with ASEAN leaders problematic, as there were calls to exclude the prime minister from the event. Obama understood that meeting with ASEAN was an all-or-nothing proposition. If we had tried to exclude any leader or country, the other ASEAN members would not have come. Hun Sen came and, as the *Phnom Penh Post* put it, got "his photo op with Obama."[23] Unfortunately, his participation in the meeting did not change his approach toward politics back home.

In June 2016, government critic Kem Ley was murdered in what many thought was a government-backed crime.[24] Over the next few years, Hun Sen combined unprecedented repression with a sharp increase in anti-U.S. rhetoric. In 2017, Cambodia postponed the annual Angkor Sentinel military exercise with the United States, ostensibly because of the need to focus on local elections that year. The government also expelled the National Democratic Institute for failing to register appropriately, while government media accused the group of conspiring with the CNRP to overthrow the government. It closed numerous radio stations that sold air time to Voice of America and Radio Free Asia, and Radio Free Asia felt compelled to close its Phnom Penh office. In September 2017 the government closed the *Cambodia Daily*, an independent newspaper that had been one of the few media outlets to offer criticism of the government.[25]

Also in September, the government arrested Kem Sokha on accusations of conspiring with the United States to overthrow the

---

22 U.S. Department of State, "Country Reports on Human Rights Practices for 2017: Cambodia," April 20, 2018.

23 Charles Rollett, "PM Gets His Photo-Op with Obama as Cambodian-Americans Protest," *Phnom Penh Post*, February 17, 2016, https://www.phnompenhpost.com/national/pm-gets-his-photo-op-obama-cambodian-americans-protest.

24 "Killer of Activist Kem Ley Sentenced to Life," BBC News, March 23, 2017, https://www.bbc.com/news/world-asia-39362264.

25 Thomas Lum, *Cambodia: Background and U.S. Relations*, Congressional Research Service R44037, updated January 28, 2019, https://fas.org/sgp/crs/row/R44037.pdf.

government, a claim U.S. ambassador Bill Heidt called "absurd."[26] In November 2017, the Cambodian Supreme Court ordered the dissolution of the CNRP for allegedly seeking to topple the government. The court banned a hundred CNRP members from politics for five years, and vacated all fifty-five CNRP-won seats in the National Assembly, turning those seats over to more docile "opposition" parties such as FUNCINPEC. Longtime journalist/analyst Sebastian Strangio, who had worked in Cambodia for years, noted that the harsh repression appeared to signal a break with the CPP's longstanding practice of alternating between repression and political easing: "They seem to be tearing up the rules by which Cambodia's pseudo-democracy has run for the past 25 years."[27]

A Downward Spiral

All of this proved too much for Washington, as Hun Sen's authoritarian actions had reached new levels, as had his anti-American rhetoric and actions. In November 2017 the Trump administration suspended assistance intended for the 2018 national elections, and the U.S. Senate passed a resolution urging the administration to impose sanctions on Cambodian officials implicated in political repression. In December, the administration announced that it would not issue visas to officials involved in undermining democracy.

The downward spiral continued in 2018 and 2019. With the opposition emasculated, the CPP won every seat in the 2018 National Assembly elections, a major departure from past elections that were flawed but still allowed for competition. The CPP continued to hound its opponents in the CNRP, the media, and civil society, including filing treason charges against Sam Rainsy and other opposition members.

The United States imposed new sanctions on Cambodia and also accused the government of signing a secret deal with Beijing to allow China's military access to Ream Naval Base, while turning down a U.S. offer to conduct renovations at that facility. Cambodia strongly

---

26 Ananth Baliga and Mech Dara, "U.S. Envoy Calls Government Claims 'Absurd,'" *Phnom Penh Post*, September 13, 2017, https://www.phnompenhpost.com/national/us-envoy-calls-government-claims-absurd.

27 David Boyle, "Cambodia Arrest Opposition Leader, Alleges Treason," VOA News, September 2, 2017, https://www.voanews.com/a/cambodia-arrests-opposition-leader-alleges-treason/4013099.html.

denied the allegation, but it continues to roil the relationship, and has also caused some distress among some of Cambodia's ASEAN neighbors. One prominent former Singaporean official has even suggested ASEAN consider expelling Cambodia if the country continues to align so tightly with Beijing.[28] On the U.S. side, Vice President Mike Pence sent a letter to Hun Sen directly expressing concern about the reported deal with China.[29]

The decline in relations has been so steep that some outside observers have urged the United States to adopt a new approach. For example, journalist Sebastian Strangio penned an op-ed in mid-2020 advising Washington that its approach of pressuring Hun Sen was backfiring and pushing the country further into China's pocket. While not defending the CPP, he stressed the need to understand that, from Hun Sen's point of view, the United States was targeting his country for special treatment, in terms of pressure for democracy and human rights, compared to its willingness to engage other authoritarian states in the neighborhood and despite Washington's own record of bombing Cambodia during the Vietnam War.[30]

By design or by accident, Washington sent mixed signals to Cambodia over the last year of the Trump administration. President Trump sent a letter to Hun Sen in November 2020 stating that the United States did not seek regime change but also urging the prime minister to return the country to the democratic path. Hun Sen welcomed the letter in some of his most positive comments on the United States in years. Around the same time, however, U.S. lawmakers wrote to Secretary of State Mike Pompeo urging the United States to impose additional sanctions on Cambodia over its democratic backsliding and calling for the United States to consider following Europe's lead in withdrawing trade preferences from Cambodia.[31]

---

28 David Hutt, "Time to Boot Cambodia Out of ASEAN," *Asia Times*, October 28, 2020, https://asiatimes.com/2020/10/time-to-boot-cambodia-out-of-asean/.

29 Timothy R. Heath, "The Ramifications of China's Reported Naval Base in Cambodia," RAND Blog, RAND Corporation, August 7, 2019, https://www.rand.org/blog/2019/08/the-ramifications-of-chinas-reported-naval-base-in.html.

30 Sebastian Strangio, "The World According to the CPP," *The Diplomat*, July 23, 2020, https://www.sebastianstrangio.com/2020/07/23/the-world-according-to-cambodias-cpp/.

31 Sopheng Cheang, "Cambodia's Leader Relieved Trump Doesn't Seek Regime Change," ABC News, November 27, 2019, https://abcnews.go.com/US/wireStory/cambodias-hun-sen-tells-trump-welcomes-relations-67340590.

A Policy Dilemma

Looking back, watching and assessing Cambodia's internal politics—and the U.S. approach to Cambodia—over the past twenty-five years has been like watching the same film loop again and again, with only small changes between every showing. Hun Sen has allowed a modest amount of competitive politics and opposition but has responded to every serious threat to his hold on power with threats, intimidation, and legal action against his opponents. His control over the state machinery, including the courts, has meant that the opposition has been playing with a stacked deck for decades. As the United States, and the West more generally, has stepped up pressure and criticism, he has responded by turning increasingly to China, which offers aid and investment, as well as political support. China does not condition its support on better politics and governance, but rather on Cambodian willingness to accommodate and support China's strategic interests.

During this period, the United States has oscillated between trying to work with Hun Sen and trying to pressure him. Neither has proven particularly effective. The Obama years, which saw the most engagement, might have improved the tone of relations, but that did not stop Hun Sen from supporting China's position in the South China Sea or going after his domestic opponents. Since 2017, Hun Sen's harsh repression and his increasing alignment with Beijing have pushed Washington both to ramp up pressure and to try to engage.

The truth is that, for U.S. policymakers, there is no easy answer. For many in Washington, Hun Sen has become a nemesis. The anti–Hun Sen sentiment is particularly strong in certain corners of the U.S. Senate, where Hun Sen's behavior is seen—with some justification—as a betrayal of so much of what the Cambodian people and the international community have worked for during the past thirty years. This disappointment, even anger, has produced strong pressure for sanctions to try to change Hun Sen's behavior.

Taking the Long View

Sanctions and other punitive measures, however, are unlikely to be effective, particularly as long as China is willing to step into the trade, aid, and investment void as needed. The United States needs to take the long view on Cambodia (sort of like the Philippines under Duterte or

Myanmar during the often-disappointing pre-coup period). Hun Sen is not likely to change, but he also will not be around forever. That does not mean his successor will come from the opposition. Recently, the prime minister has taken steps to groom a successor generation within the CPP, promoting younger people into key positions and asking well-regarded economy and finance minister Aung Pornmoniroth to represent him at the 2020 ASEAN Summit.[32] In late 2021, Hun Sen publicly stated that he would support his son, Hun Manet, to succeed him.[33]

For Washington, all of this highlights the importance of maintaining a dialogue with the government and CPP—including on democracy and human rights—and finding areas of potential common interest, such as protecting the Mekong River, while avoiding punitive measures born out of anger and frustration. After all, if we can engage with the communist-led Vietnamese government, why not with the CCP? It also means, without question, continuing to engage with the political opposition and encouraging all efforts to maintain the maximum amount of democratic space in the country.

Washington also should continue assistance and trade preferences to promote broad-based development and to support civil society and other positive forces within the country. This means more quiet diplomacy rather than public statements. And it should continue working with other ASEAN nations discreetly to consider ways to encourage Cambodia not to dive deeper into China's pocket. Gaining agreement for such a "soft" approach will be a tough sell in Washington, particularly on Capitol Hill, but it is the least bad of the options out there.

As the United States moves forward, it is important to remember that, even though Hun Sen and the senior CPP leadership have clearly sided with China, many in Cambodia's younger generation continue to look to the United States as a potential partner and contributor to the country. Cambodians do not want to be isolated or overly dependent on China, and many would welcome more engagement with the United States. Washington needs to stay focused on the long game and as much as possible avoid letting shorter-term disappointments and frustrations cause it to give up hope on the country.

---

32 Luke Hunt, "Aun Pornmoniroth Emerges as Potential Future Cambodian Prime Minister," *The Diplomat*, November 24, 2020, https://thediplomat.com/2020/11/aun-pornmoniroth-emerges-as-potential-future-cambodian-prime-minister/.

33 Prak Chan Thul, "Cambodian Leader Hun Sen Says Backs Eldest Son to Succeed Him," Reuters, https://www.reuters.com/world/asia-pacific/cambodian-leader-hun-sen-says-backs-eldest-son-succeed-him-2021-12-02/.

III. COUNTRIES IN TRANSITION

CHAPTER SEVEN

From Sukarno to Suharto to SBY

Dealing with ASEAN's Giant

Although Indonesia is the world's fourth-largest country (by population) and the linchpin of Southeast Asia, it is also a country that Americans, for the most part, neither know much about nor have invested heavily in. A country of some 270 million people, 85–90 percent of whom follow Islam, Indonesia is home to the world's largest Muslim population and ranks as its third-largest democracy. Its 17,000 islands stretch from the Indian Ocean into the Pacific, straddle strategically important ocean straits, and boast natural resources that are the envy of much of the world.

As part of the "pivot" or "rebalance," and in response to Jakarta's proposal to develop a bilateral comprehensive partnership, the Obama administration in 2009 placed a priority on strengthening U.S. relations with Indonesia, a nation deeply steeped in a history of nonalignment and, particularly since September 11, 2001, wary of U.S. policy toward the Muslim world. Over the next few years, we would try to turn what had been a cordial but not overly close relationship into a genuine partnership, while also doing all we could to support the Indonesian people's efforts to overcome the legacies of their authoritarian past, further develop their democracy, and accelerate economic progress.

When President Obama took office in early 2009, Indonesia was preparing to hold national elections that would further consolidate its democracy, making it a compelling partner for the United States and—as Indonesians liked to say—an excellent example for those who questioned whether Islam and democracy could coexist. Indonesian president Susilo Bambang Yudhoyono, who would win re-election decisively in July of that year, served as an example in a different way: a former general who had retired from the military, won a free and fair election, and governed as a democrat.

A decade earlier, Indonesia had been on the verge of chaos. The 1997–98 Asian Financial Crisis had devastated its economy, sparking a political crisis that forced President Suharto—who had dominated the nation politically for three decades—out of office. Over the next few years, Indonesia struggled to implement democratic reforms as it faced continuing economic crises, terrorist attacks, outbreaks of ethnic and religious violence, and separatist insurgencies that resulted in one province's secession and led to warnings that Indonesia could become the next Yugoslavia and/or the second front in the global war on terror.

It was difficult to find optimists among observers of Indonesia in 1999–2002. By 2010, when I arrived to begin my assignment as U.S. ambassador, the tables had turned, and foreigners in particular expressed sometimes unbridled optimism, especially about the economy. Investment bankers led the charge, telling audiences at countless Jakarta seminars—in outbursts of economic determinism that would have made Marx proud—that Indonesia's economy would surpass that of Germany within fifteen years. Most Indonesians, aware of the weaknesses of their political and economic system, tended to be more cautious.

Now, more than a decade later, the level of optimism has declined, with more than a few analysts expressing concern about possible democratic backsliding and an economy that has not performed quite to earlier high expectations. Similarly, many observers have concluded that U.S.-Indonesian relations have underperformed. In a region that has seen its share of democratic disappointment, and ups and downs in its relations with the United States, it is useful to take another look at Indonesia's democratic transition and its struggle for unity and stability, and to assess the U.S.-Indonesian relationship during that period and going forward.

Building a Nation

Like many other former colonies, Indonesia can trace some of its challenges back to the pre-independence period, when the Dutch East India Company pasted together a collection of kingdoms and societies scattered across thousands of miles of islands to establish the Dutch East Indies. They did not create a nation. They simply administered a very diverse region as one colony because it was convenient for them.

Fortunately, the founders of modern Indonesia—particularly Sukarno and Mohammed Hatta—made some important decisions back in the 1920s, two decades before independence, that proved crucial to their ability to forge one nation out of this sprawling archipelago. First, they avoided what might have been the easy call to center the nation around the long-dominant Javanese kingdom and culture, eschewing the complex Javanese language in favor of the easier and more politically neutral choice of Malay, a widely known trading language in the region. Creating a true national language is absolutely critical in building a nation, and it was a wise choice.

Second, the Indonesia Nationalist Party (PNI) that they founded emphasized from its beginning the goal of creating a new "Indonesian" identity that "transcended and encompassed" all of the societies and communities living under the Indonesian roof.[1] Sukarno in particular would later receive a lot of criticism—much of it valid—for his leadership, but he and Hatta deserve respect and admiration for these early decisions, which proved crucial in creating a sense of Indonesian nationalism that, with some notable exceptions, has helped hold the country together through very difficult times.

When Indonesia finally won independence in 1949, Sukarno and Hatta had to build on this start to try to create a true nation. As Adam Schwarz describes in his landmark *A Nation in Waiting,* the initial big political debate was over what kind of nation it was going to be, including whether it would be an Islamic state or a more secular country.[2] After much discussion, Sukarno—stuck between pressure for an Islamic state and the need to keep the outer islands (which tend to have larger non-Muslim populations) satisfied—weighed in with a uniquely Indonesian solution: the concept of *Pancasila,* whose five elements included the idea of a belief in one God (without defining whose God), along with justice and civility among people, unity, democracy through de-

---

1 David Joel Steinberg, ed., *In Search of Southeast Asia: A Modern History* (Honolulu: University of Hawaii Press, 1985), cited in Adam Schwarz, *A Nation in Waiting,* 2nd ed. (Boulder, Colorado: Westview Press, 2000), 4.

2 Schwarz, *A Nation in Waiting,* 10. Schwarz describes the Indonesian debate of the time in much more detail, arguing that there were actually three schools of thought about how to proceed.

liberation and consensus among representatives, and social justice. Although the Islamists were very unhappy and the role of Islam remains a hot topic even today, Sukarno's "solution" allowed the country to move forward.

The Sukarno Era

Sukarno's force of personality enabled him to dominate Indonesian politics for a generation, but the period of parliamentary democracy in the 1950s was marked by instability and a number of regional revolts, which reflected both unhappiness over what outlying regions saw as Javanese political and economic dominance as well as, in some cases, concern about the growing power of the Indonesian Communist Party (PKI). In a bid to end this instability and consolidate his power, Sukarno in 1959 suspended the constitution and launched "Guided Democracy," which in effect meant a much more powerful president and executive branch. The military at the same time initiated its *dwifungsi* practice, establishing a parallel structure of governance from the national down to the local level. This practice would continue for forty years, giving the military a significant role in governance.

Sukarno relied on an odd coalition of Islamists, nationalists (including the army), and the PKI for political support and took the economy down a socialist path that was to prove economically disastrous. Abroad, he adopted an aggressive nationalism and helped launch the global Non-Aligned Movement, which pursued a brand of anti-colonialism that had an anti-Western tint (because, of course, the colonial powers had been from the West). He put heavy pressure on the Netherlands to surrender the remote eastern province of Irian Jaya (now Papua), which it still controlled, to Indonesia. By 1963–65, Sukarno had gone even further, calling for a Jakarta-Phnom Penh-Hanoi-Peking-Pyongyang axis, and launching a violent confrontation (the *konfrontasi*) against the newly established Federation of Malaysia, which the Indonesian leader viewed as a British neocolonial effort to constrain Indonesia's ambitions. He even briefly pulled Indonesia out of the United Nations in protest of its recognition of Malaysia.

Although the United States had been the first country to recognize independent Indonesia, Washington's relations with the Sukarno regime proved difficult. Rattled by Sukarno's dalliance with local communists, the CIA covertly backed regional rebels in Sumatra in the late 1950s (fifty years later, Indonesians would regularly remind me about this). President Kennedy shifted tactics, trying to win over Sukarno and the Indonesian military by increasing economic and military assistance and negotiating a deal that "gave" Indonesia interim control over Irian Jaya pending the results of a 1969 referendum (the "Act of Free Choice") that turned out to be a Jakarta-controlled "unanimous" vote in favor of becoming an Indonesian province.[3]

As Sukarno moved increasingly to the left, Washington's concern grew. Recall that this was during the height of the Cold War and just as the United States was about to send combat troops to Vietnam. In 1963, the U.S. Congress cut off aid to Jakarta, over the Kennedy administration's objections, because of Sukarno's aggressive leftist stance. Threatened with this action, the Indonesian leader famously said shortly before the Capitol Hill debate that the United States "could go to hell with its aid."[4]

1965—A Dangerous Year

By 1965, Sukarno had turned to the PKI for even more support, causing the two other pillars of his "coalition"—the military and Muslim groups—to become more anxious. Late on the night of September 30, one of the most memorable dates in Indonesian history, a group of leftist officers kidnapped and killed six military generals and a lieutenant in a strange and still-debated *putsch*. The military quickly quelled the revolt, blamed the pro-Sukarno PKI, and used the opportunity to wipe out the communists. Over the following months, the military worked with anti-communist groups to carry out one of the worst cases of mass murder in modern history, butchering an estimated five hundred thousand suspected communists in a bloodbath that literally caused rivers to turn red.

While the bloody purge of suspected communists proceeded, Sukarno lingered on as president, scrambling to find a way to stay in power. It was not to be. General Suharto, the commander of the Army's

---

3 Richard Chauvel, *Constructing Papuan Nationalism: History, Ethnicity, and Adaptation*, *Policy Studies* 14 (Washington, D.C.: East-West Center, 2005), 9–10, https://www.eastwestcenter.org/sites/default/files/private/PS014.pdf.
4 "Aid for Indonesia Barred in Senate; Sukarno Scored in Debate on Tower's Amendment," *New York Times*, August 14, 1964.

strategic reserve and hitherto largely unknown outside of the military, emerged as the dominant player and gradually eased Sukarno out. By mid-1966, Suharto had taken effective control, and by 1967 had become "acting president."

Washington was not unduly troubled by the violence, which—in the context of the Vietnam War and the anxiety of the Cold War—it saw as perhaps necessary in the war against communism. In fact, later research has confirmed that the U.S. embassy in Indonesia provided the military with lists of suspected communists. Writing in mid-1966, legendary *New York Times* columnist James Reston noted Washington's satisfaction. "The savage transformation of Indonesia from a pro-Chinese policy under Sukarno to a defiantly anti-communist policy under General Suharto is the most important of these [hopeful] developments. Washington is being careful not to claim any credit. . . but this does not mean Washington had nothing to do with it."[5]

Suharto Launches the New Order

Suharto would go on to dominate Indonesian politics for the next thirty years. In 1996 the news magazine *Asiaweek* called him the "Most Powerful Man in Asia."[6] That might have been an overstatement, but it gives a sense of his importance. Others have written excellent books on Suharto and his "New Order."[7] I limit myself to summarizing some of the main elements of his rule, particularly those that have posed the biggest obstacles to the country's later democratic transition, and to highlighting key developments in the U.S.-Indonesia relationship during this period.

---

5 James Reston, "Washington: A Gleam of Light in Asia," *New York Times,* June 19, 1966, quoted in Vincent Bevins, "What the United States Did in Indonesia," *The Atlantic,* October 20, 2017, https://www.theatlantic.com/international/archive/2017/10/the-indonesia-documents-and-the-us-agenda/543534/.

6 *Asiaweek,* July 5, 1966, cited in Stefan Eklot, *Indonesian Politics in Crisis: The Long Fall of Suharto 1996–98,* (Copenhagen: Nordic Institute of Asian Studies, 1999), http://www.diva-portal.org/smash/get/diva2:842567/FULLTEXT01.pdf.

7 See, for example, Michael R. J. Vatikiotis, *Indonesian Politics Under Suharto: The Rise and Fall of the New Order* (New York and Oxon: Routledge, 1993); David Jenkins, *Suharto and His Generals: Indonesian Military Politics 1975–1983,* Monograph Series No. 64 (Ithaca: Cornell Modern Indonesia Project, 1984); and Schwarz, *A Nation in Waiting.*

As Adam Schwarz has written, Suharto designed his New Order primarily to restore order and stability to the country.[8] After purging the military and bureaucracy of suspected communists and Sukarno supporters, he worked to build a stronger state, focused on economic development, and limited public participation in politics. He developed a corporatist model of governing in which nearly all institutions—even outside of government—were at least somewhat beholden to him.

Suharto did not ban civilian politics, but he created a system in which civilian politicians could not compete with him, sort of like Thailand's General Prayut after 2014. The idea seemed to be that, after a period of instability and chaos, the people should largely stay at home and let the leaders govern. They could vote every five years, but otherwise were to be seen, not heard.

Suharto forced nine political parties to dissolve and in their place created two others—the United Development Party (largely for Islam-oriented politicians) and the Indonesian Democratic Party (for nationalists and non-Muslims). He required these parties to pledge fealty to Pancasila, and neither was able to function as a true opposition. The parties existed to give the appearance of democracy where in fact there was none.

In 1967, Suharto created Golkar (*Golongan Karya*, or literally "functional groups") to serve as the regime's electoral platform. It was not a party, but a collection of groups, including labor, peasants, and—importantly—the military. By defining the military as a functional group, Suharto gave it standing to participate actively in politics and thus institutionalized the *dwifungsi* system.

Parliament (the MPR[9]), which elected the president, consisted of two houses. The lower house, or DPR,[10] consisted of 500 members, of whom 400 were elected and 100 were military (similar to Myanmar's system before the 2021 coup). Suharto, however, appointed all 500 members of the upper house, ensuring he controlled at least 600 of the 1,000 members.

By 1985, Suharto had gained even greater control, tightening censorship and otherwise restricting—if not eliminating—political activities that he did not oversee. He also managed an elaborate system

---

8 Schwarz, *A Nation in Waiting*, 28–29.
9 *Majelis Permusyawaratan Rakyat*, or People's Consultative Assembly.
10 *Dewan Perwakilan Rakyat*, or People's Representative Council.

of patronage that he used to ensure loyalty and to buy off potential troublemakers or opponents. Although his regime was capable of brutal acts, Suharto preferred to manage or avoid confrontation by attempting to bring nearly all political actors into his big and well-controlled tent. (As we shall see, this "big tent" concept continued, albeit under different circumstances, into Indonesia's democratic era.) As David Jenkins writes, Suharto "had established himself as the paramount figure in a society in which deference to authority is deeply rooted."[11]

Economic Reform and Progress

Suharto inherited an economy in shambles. Sukarno's socialist bent, nationalist rhetoric, expropriation of foreign investments, and general disinterest in the economy had resulted in very high levels of inflation, capital flight, underutilized factories, and broad decline. On a human level, friends who were in Indonesia at the time describe heartbreaking poverty and widespread malnutrition—people were suffering.

Suharto turned to a group of U.S.-educated technocrats to run the economy and supported largely pragmatic policies to reverse the economy's decline and raise living standards. Within a few years, the technocrats had stabilized the macroeconomic picture, rebuilt relations with foreign donors and international development institutions, and returned the country to growth.

Powered by oil revenue—courtesy of the two oil shocks of the 1970s—and a steady inflow of foreign (largely Japanese) investment, the economy grew by an average of more than 7 percent annually from 1968 to 1981. It softened through much of the 1980s but then returned to strong growth at the end of the decade. From 1967 to 1987, the economy grew by an average of nearly 5 percent, with per capita income increasing 4 percent a year. The government invested substantially in improved infrastructure, including roads, telephone lines, and electricity production. The country, which had become the world's largest rice importer under Sukarno in 1960–64, increased production sufficiently to be able to feed itself. Partly as a result, the World Bank in 1990 estimated that the proportion of the population living in absolute

---

11 David Jenkins, *Suharto and His Generals*, 13–14, quoted in Schwarz, *A Nation in Waiting*, 37.

poverty had fallen by 41 percentage points between 1970 and 1987, the fastest decline among all the nations studied.[12]

Patronage and Corruption

Suharto and those around him used the inflows of money from high oil prices and Japanese investment to pay for their patronage politics and to subsidize the nation's inefficient domestic industry. Although the technocrats around him tried to liberalize and promote competition, for political reasons Suharto directed resources and favors to relatives, and to cronies, many of whom were ethnic Chinese. This corruption and the associated economic distortions detracted somewhat from what was otherwise a period of solid economic progress, but—at least until the last few years of the Suharto era—did not rise to the catastrophic levels of the crony capitalism employed by Philippine president Ferdinand Marcos.

Suharto worked closely with ethnic Chinese businessmen for a couple of reasons, but the most important was because they posed no threat or challenge to him politically. The Chinese had long been both favored and discriminated against in Indonesia. Under the Dutch, they were granted certain preferential commercial privileges but were segregated socially. They lived in their own neighborhoods and went to their own schools. Suharto forced them to assimilate, encouraging them to take Indonesian names and closing Chinese language schools and all but one newspaper. Despite this attempt at forced assimilation, because of ethnic Chinese domination of the economy, they faced resentment from the rest of the population that could and would easily erupt into anti-Chinese violence. During my time in Indonesia, decades later, the ethnic Chinese business elite dominated the lists of richest Indonesians, but—in my experience—were always very aware of their vulnerability.

---

12 World Bank, *World Development Report 1990: Poverty* (Oxford University Press, 1990), 45–47, https://openknowledge.worldbank.org/bitstream/handle/10986/5973/WDR%201990%20-%20English.pdf. See also Indermit S. Gill, Ana Revenda, and Christian Zeballos, "Grow, Invest, Insure: A Game Plan to End Extreme Poverty by 2030" (Policy Research Working Paper no. 7892, World Bank, November 2016), 8, https://openknowledge.worldbank.org/bitstream/handle/10986/25694/WPS7892.pdf, and Schwarz, *A Nation in Waiting*, 58.

Suharto in the Middle

In the late 1980s and early 1990s, Suharto began to worry about his support among the military's nationalist elements, who increasingly were criticizing his family's corruption. He saw an opportunity in the revival of religious awareness and practice among the country's Muslim majority. As Muslim groups demanded a larger voice in the country's politics, Suharto established the Indonesian Association of Muslim Intellectuals (*Ikatan Cendekiawan Muslim Indonesia*, or ICMI), to try to coopt the movement and build political support to offset his declining relations with the military. He put loyalist B. J. Habibie in charge to ensure the ICMI did not become a platform for more assertive individuals.

Over the next several years, Indonesia saw a delicate political dance between Suharto, the military, rival Muslim groups, and nationalist politicians. In one corner were the traditional military leaders, who tended to be nationalist and wary of political Islam. In another was Nahdlatul Ulama (NU), a Java-based Muslim mass organization with tens of millions of followers. NU, led by Abdurrahman Wahid (also known as Gus Dur), represented traditional and generally rural Islam in Indonesia, which followed a syncretic and tolerant Islam that meshed with traditional beliefs. Wahid saw ICMI as a threat to democracy and a rival. He also was an outspoken critic of Suharto. In a third corner was ICMI, whose members tended to represent another Muslim mass organization, Muhammadiyah. Muhammadiyah follows what scholars call a more modernist strain of Islam, but in the Indonesian context that meant a less syncretic practice that called on followers to hew closer to the Qur'an. In the mid-1990s, the secular nationalist Indonesian Democratic Party (PDI), led by Megawati Sukarnoputri (daughter of Sukarno), began to stir, occupying a fourth corner.

Suharto, of course, was in the middle, always playing the different groups off against one other. In the early 1990s, he began placing Islamist-leaning officers, including his son-in-law Prabowo Subianto, into key military positions, creating a split between the "red and white" (nationalist) and "green" (Islamist) officers. In 1996 he maneuvered Megawati out of the PDI leadership in a blatant power display that created tremendous anger among her followers. Many of those followers rallied behind Megawati at PDI headquarters in Jakarta, where on July 22 a large group of thugs—widely believed to be either military or associated with the military—brutally attacked them.[13] In the months that followed, a series of violent riots—variously believed to have been initiated by Islamists in the military and/or ICMI—struck NU-dominated areas in Java in what was seen as an attempt to undermine Wahid. Suharto used this opportunity to convince Wahid to support Golkar in the 1997 parliamentary elections, in return for the president's de facto endorsement of Wahid's leadership of NU.[14]

Golkar won big in the 1997 elections, but the obvious fraud involved in the electoral process, combined with Suharto's earlier blatant ouster of Megawati from the PDI leadership, ended up making him and Golkar look even more corrupt and, arguably, more vulnerable than before. This was happening at a time when the Suharto family nepotism and corruption—they had skimmed at least $10 billion and possibly much more from the Indonesian economy—had become so extensive and well known that he was losing popular support anyway.[15]

The stage was set for the Asian Financial Crisis, which would be the spark that fueled the revolt that ended Suharto's long reign. Before getting into that, however, it is useful to look at how Suharto changed Indonesian foreign policy and to explore the U.S.-Indonesian relationship during this period.

U.S.-Indonesia Relations Under Suharto

After assuming the presidency, Suharto moved quickly to shift Indonesia's foreign policy back to a moderate, anti-communist approach. He did not abandon the country's nonaligned stance, but leaned West, particularly in the battle against communism. He ended Sukarno's confrontation with his immediate neighbors, paving the way for the establishment of ASEAN in 1967. Relations with the United States, which had cooled considerably under Sukarno, returned to a more normal state of affairs as the U.S. government welcomed the renewed stability

---

13 See Eklot, *Indonesian Politics in Crisis*, chapter 2.
14 Eklot, *Indonesian Politics in Crisis*, chapter 3.
15 Estimates of the Suharto family's wealth range from $10 to $40 billion. See, for example, Keith B. Richburg, "Cashing in on Years in Power," *Washington Post,* May 22, 1998; "Suharto's Family 'Must Return Looted Wealth'," Transparency International, May 24, 1998, https://www.transparency.org/en/press/suhartos-family -must-return-looted-wealth#; and "Suharto's Fortune," BBC News, September 28, 2000, http://news.bbc.co.uk/2/hi/asia-pacific/864355.stm.

and improved economy under Suharto, not to mention the end of Indonesia's flirtation with communism at home and abroad. Washington resumed military and economic assistance, and the two governments worked out an informal arrangement that enabled U.S. Navy vessels to sail through the strategically important Sunda and Malacca straits in or alongside the Indonesian archipelago.[16]

Indonesia's 1975 invasion and annexation of East Timor, the former Portuguese colony that shared an island with Indonesia's province of West Timor, dealt a major blow to the country's image. The invasion prompted violent resistance, and in the resulting conflict the Indonesian military committed significant human rights violations. In the United States, these abuses triggered a steady stream of criticism from human rights groups and some on Capitol Hill, but the Cold War environment militated against a significant shift by Washington away from support and engagement.

In the 1980s we worked closely and effectively with the Indonesian foreign ministry on two Southeast Asia matters, both involving what we used to call Indochina. As noted in chapter 4, NSC Asia advisor Dick Childress sought and won Jakarta's help in persuading Hanoi to engage more productively with us on the POW/MIA accounting issue. Later in the decade, Indonesia played a prominent role—sometimes as host of meetings—in the discussions that led to the Cambodian Peace Accords in September 1991. In both cases, Washington found the Indonesians to be pragmatic, helpful, and effective.

In the early 1990s, the U.S. Navy—having lost access to Subic Bay naval base in the Philippines—negotiated an arrangement to give it access to the Indonesian port city of Surabaya for ship repair. That deal ran into resistance from the U.S. Congress, which was outraged by the Indonesian Army's November 1991 massacre of Timorese protestors in Dili, the East Timor capital.[17] Although Suharto sacked the regional military commander as well as the East Timor commander, these rare accountability measures failed to satisfy critics, including on Capitol Hill. So began a long tussle between U.S. administrations, which in the post–Cold War world were focused on democracy and human rights

---

16 Larry Niksch, *Indonesia: U.S. Relations with the Indonesian Military*, Congressional Research Service 98-677 F, August 10, 1998, https://www.everycrsreport.com/files/19980810_98-677_ccc717c388e29caae32d5e71103fe52381077691.pdf.

17 Niksch, *Indonesia: U.S. Relations with the Indonesian Military*.

but also wanted to preserve ties with the Indonesian military, and key players on Capitol Hill and in the human rights community, who wanted to end or at least sharply reduce those ties because of human rights violations.

I will not go into all the details of the battles here. Suffice it to say that, from 1992 through the fall of Suharto in 1998, Congress consistently voted to enact partial or total bans on U.S. International Military Education Training (IMET) programs and/or arms sales for the Indonesian military. The George H. W. Bush administration expressed concerns about the human rights abuses but for the most part opposed congressional restrictions.

The Clinton administration, which generally had shifted U.S. diplomacy away from Cold War strategic thinking to a greater emphasis on democracy promotion and trade, listed Indonesia as one of the "ten big emerging markets" in the world and thus focused on commercial opportunities. It was willing to accept some but not all congressional restrictions on security assistance, arguing that too many restrictions would undermine our broader interests in Indonesia as well as our ability to build relationships with and influence the behavior of officers within the Indonesian military. Nonetheless, Congress did block IMET funding for Indonesia in 1993 and prohibited the sale of lethal weapons and equipment for crowd control in 1994.

In 1996, the Clinton administration succeeded in persuading Congress to restore IMET funding to Indonesia, albeit with several conditions. It also proposed the sale of F-16s (originally meant for Pakistan), but that fell through due to congressional opposition in the aftermath of the violent attacks against opposition leader Megawati Sukarnoputri's supporters in Jakarta in July 1996.[18]

The Asian Financial Crisis

A year later, the Asian Financial Crisis hit Indonesia hard. Within weeks of the crisis emerging in Thailand, the Indonesian rupiah began to fall, exposing significant weaknesses in the country's financial system and greater private debt (owed in ever more expensive dollars) than was thought. By October 1997, Indonesia reached agreement with the IMF for a significant loan that sought to stabilize the macroeconomy while also forcing structural reforms that IMF experts thought were

---

18 Niksch, *Indonesia: U.S. Relations with the Indonesian Military.*

essential. At the same time, the United States, together with Japan and other allies, was putting together a multi-billion-dollar package of support as well. The international support brought short-term relief, but doubts about the government's willingness to implement the tough reforms—plus Suharto's end-of-year decision to take a ten-day "health holiday"—added to concerns.

Then in January the president submitted a budget proposal that seemed divorced from reality, causing another wave of panic selling of the rupiah and forcing Jakarta to go back to the IMF for another loan in January. The IMF has been criticized for the strict conditionality it attached to the loan, but in fact many of the conditions were recommended by Suharto's own economic technocrats. By then, inflation was soaring, job losses were mounting, and the agricultural sector was being hit at the same time by the worst drought in memory. Suffering, including malnutrition, mounted, as did student protests.[19]

Ahead of the March 1998 MPR presidential elections, which normally would involve a rubber-stamping of Suharto's rule, Muhammadiyah leader Amien Rais suggested the formation of an opposition political alliance between him, Megawati, and his rival Abdurrahman Wahid. With pressure rising, some around Suharto turned to scapegoating the ethnic Chinese, particularly prominent businessman Sofjan Wanandi, leading to a series of anti-Chinese riots. Suharto began sharply criticizing the IMF and turned to U.S. economist Steven Hanke, who was promoting the unorthodox concept of a currency board to stabilize the economy. President Clinton called Suharto on February 21 to urge him to ignore Hanke's advice and stick with the IMF.[20]

As the election neared, the military cracked down on demonstrators, abducting several protest leaders. On March 10 the MPR duly elected

---

19 For more detailed discussions of the financial crisis in Indonesia, see Stephen Sherlock, "Crisis in Indonesia: Economy, Society and Politics," Parliament of Australia Current Issues Brief 13 1997–98, April 8, 1998, https://www.aph.gov .au/About_Parliament/Parliamentary_Departments/Parliamentary_Library/ Publications_Archive/CIB/CIB9798/98cib13; Schwarz, *A Nation in Waiting*, 337–45; Eklot, *Indonesian Politics in Crisis*, 96–121; and "Asian Financial Crisis in Indonesia," Indonesia Investments, https://www.indonesia-investments.com/culture/ economy/asian-financial-crisis/item246.

20 Reuters, "Clinton and Suharto Talk," *New York Times,* February 22, 1998; and Krithika Varagur, "Declassified Files Provide Insight into Indonesia's Democratic Transition," Voice of America, July 24, 2018, https://www.voanews.com/ east-asia-pacific/declassified-files-provide-insight-indonesias-democratic-transition.

Suharto, with B. J. Habibie as vice president. Suharto named an anti-reform cabinet, including his daughter, Tutut, and longtime crony Bob Hasan, making it clear to all that he had no intention of implementing the structural reforms that the IMF demanded but that would undermine his crony friends and family.

Growing Protests

The student protests continued to grow, as did the number of abductions of protest leaders. On May 12 soldiers opened fire on students protesting at Trisakti University in Jakarta, killing four. The next day thousands of protestors gathered near the university, where both Megawati and Amien Rais spoke to them. The following days saw a number of anti-Chinese riots, with numerous murders and women raped, often in plain view of the security forces, who did not intervene. It is widely believed that senior figures in the Indonesian military instigated this violence.

By May 18 huge crowds of demonstrators had largely taken over the parliament and were demanding Suharto's resignation and an end to corruption, nepotism, and human rights violations. Although Prabowo and some others in the military favored a harder line, military elements near the parliament did not suppress or interfere in the demonstrations, suggesting that they were ambivalent at most to Suharto's fate. The house speaker called for Suharto to resign. The handwriting was on the wall.

Suharto dithered for a few days, suggesting at one point he might establish a reform cabinet. It was too late. On May 20, Secretary of State Madeleine Albright publicly called for him to "engage in a historic act of statesmanship," i.e., resign.[21] That evening, fourteen members of the Indonesian cabinet wrote to Suharto calling on him to resign. A short while later, Armed Forces chief Wiranto visited Suharto at his home. Wiranto, who was a nationalist and wary of Vice President Habibie, said he would support a transfer of power to the vice president if Suharto agreed to let him transfer General Prabowo, head of the army's strategic reserve, to another position. Wiranto and Prabowo were rivals, and Wiranto wanted the Islamic-leaning Prabowo far from

---

21 Thomas W. Lippman, "Albright Encourages Suharto to Leave Office," *Washington Post*, May 21, 1998.

the seat of power. Suharto agreed and the next day announced his resignation, turning power over to B. J. Habibie.[22]

Throughout the crisis, Washington's primary focus was on avoiding massive violence or chaos, while encouraging longer-term political and economic reform. By mid-May, the Clinton administration had recognized that Suharto had to go, as made clear by Secretary Albright's May 20 statement. Following Suharto's resignation, President Clinton, in a White House statement, welcomed Suharto's decision as "an opportunity to begin a process leading to a real democratic transition for Indonesia." He urged Indonesian authorities "to move forward promptly with a peaceful process that enjoys broad public support."[23]

Suharto's fall brought Indonesia into a new era that would be known as *reformasi,* or reform. The hope of many Indonesians—and certainly of Washington—was that this would result in a transition to a democratic system that respected human rights, some form of federalism or decentralization to help manage the centrifugal forces in many of the country's regions, progress toward rule of law and control of rampant corruption, and an end or at least diminution of the military's role in politics. In addition, of course, there was an urgent need to restore economic stability and growth and to meet the urgent humanitarian needs of a population reeling from severe economic crisis.

An Unlikely Leader

One immediate question was whether and to what extent newly installed President Habibie could or would begin the reform process. Unlike Cory Aquino in the Philippines, who took over from Ferdinand Marcos in 1986 with the legitimacy born of a national election, Habibie had no mandate and in fact was looked on with suspicion by democracy activists, opposition parties, and much of the military.

Habibie was an unlikely leader. A German-educated engineer, he was known more for his interest in building an indigenous industrial/technology industry—including aircraft production—than for his political acumen. I got to know him a dozen or so years later. Like many others, I found him pleasant, open, and quirky.

22 Eklot, *Indonesian Politics in Crisis,* 210–13.
23 Keith B. Richburg, "Suharto Resigns, Names Successor," *Washington Post,* May 21, 1998.

Habibie nonetheless deserves credit for some important decisions and actions in the immediate post-Suharto period that moved the country further down the democratic reform path and that eventually—and painfully—led to resolution of the East Timor issue. One longtime Indonesia observer told me Habibie was the "unsung hero" of the country's democratic transition.[24] Recognizing the need for a government with a clear mandate and popular legitimacy, he pushed to move up national elections from 2003 to 1999. He also supported a special session of the MPR in late 1998 to approve constitutional amendments, including one that would allow for the earlier elections, another limiting the president to two five-year terms, and a third authorizing decentralization—a critical issue in a country facing separatist pressure in outlying regions unhappy with Jakarta's excessive control of power and resources. Surprisingly, he even offered to let the people of East Timor decide their future via a popular referendum, something the Indonesian military strongly opposed.

Habibie allowed the formation of political parties, relaxed restrictions on the press, and began releasing political prisoners. He also kickstarted economic reforms, making the central bank independent, establishing a bank restructuring agency to deal with the financial sector crisis, and promoting a new law on fiscal decentralization, which paralleled government and political decentralization. After declining by more than 13 percent in 1998, the Indonesian economy achieved modest growth in 1999, providing some hope for a longer-term recovery.

The Next Yugoslavia?

Despite these positive steps, Indonesia during the first few years of *reformasi* faced significant challenges. The economy remained in deep recession. There were almost no trusted institutions or political leaders capable of filling the power vacuum caused by Suharto's abrupt departure, nor was there a clear political path forward. The military enjoyed the trust of the public but did not want to take the lead politically. Long-simmering separatist insurgencies in Aceh (at the northern tip of Sumatra), Papua (in the country's far east), and elsewhere gained momentum, while pressure for East Timor independence grew. Bloody Muslim-Christian clashes in places such as Ambon and Poso in central and eastern Indonesia, egged on by Laskar Jihadi militants flooding

---

24 Telephone interview with Professor Karl Jackson, August 4, 2020.

to the areas, added to the sense of chaos and turmoil. Horrific fighting between local ethnic groups and Madurese migrants in Kalimantan completed the picture. Many in Washington and Indonesia feared Indonesia might not survive as a country—the "next Yugoslavia," some predicted, with all the violence and bloodshed that suggested.[25]

In Washington, the Indonesia crisis dominated the work of the State Department's East Asia and Pacific Bureau and commanded the attention of more senior leaders in that department, Pentagon, Treasury, and the White House. It was a time when the U.S. government generally was not paying much attention to Southeast Asia, but the risk of a country as big and important as Indonesia "blowing up"—as well as the possibility that it might emerge as a democracy—meant that Washington was interested and engaged. The U.S. goal at that point was simple: we wanted Indonesia to hold together, continue its democratic and economic reforms, and of course find peaceful solutions to the many conflicts it faced.

In August 1999, despite a campaign of intimidation by the Indonesian military, the people of East Timor in a referendum voted overwhelmingly against an Indonesian autonomy proposal and in favor of independence. Indonesian military–backed militias went on a rampage, killing, looting, and burning on a massive scale, and forcibly relocating thousands of Timorese to Indonesian West Timor. The unbridled violence and clear involvement of Indonesian security forces triggered an international outcry, including from the United States, that severely damaged Indonesia's standing at a time when the country desperately needed help.

The Clinton administration put intense pressure on the Indonesian government and military to end the violence, restore calm, and accept international peacekeepers. President Clinton accused the Indonesian military of "aiding and abetting" the violence and announced he was suspending military-to-military engagement. Chairman of the Joint Chiefs of Staff General Henry Shelton called Indonesian Armed Forces (TNI)[26] commander Wiranto twice in one week in September to make it absolutely clear that, if Indonesia did not do the right thing, it risked becoming an international pariah. The day after the second phone call,

---

25 For example, see David Armstrong, "The Next Yugoslavia? The Fragmentation of Indonesia," *Diplomacy and Statecraft* 15, no. 4 (December 1, 2004): 783–808, https://doi.org/10.1080/09592290490886865.
26 Tentara Nasional Indonesia.

Wiranto visited Timor, after which he called Shelton back to advise that he would recommend his government accept international peacekeepers, which it did.[27] A month later, the Indonesian parliament voted to "accept" East Timor's independence. (East Timor later would change its name officially to Timor-Leste.)

That same month, October 1999, Indonesia held its first truly competitive national elections in decades, choosing representatives to the MPR, which would then elect the new president. The election pitted Megawati Sukarnoputri's secular, nationalist PDI-P against Habibie's Golkar (now transformed into a true political party); other prominent contenders were the NU-dominated PKB, the Muhammediyah-dominated PAN, and the Islamist PPP.[28] The PDI-P won the most votes, but the Islamist-oriented parties, together with some in the military and anti-Megawati elements in Golkar, rallied behind Abdurrahman Wahid in the MPR to make him the surprise victor.

Gus Dur

Abdurrahman Wahid, better known at home as Gus Dur, was a uniquely Indonesian figure. As the leader of Nahdlatul Ulama, he represented better than almost anyone Indonesia's tolerant, syncretic brand of Islam. A pious Muslim, he was wary of political Islam and was a global spokesman for tolerance and respecting diversity. In Jakarta in late 2010, I attended the ceremony marking the one-year anniversary of his death. Thousands of people from all over the country attended; my wife and I were among only a handful of foreigners in a very crowded setting. At one point, concerned that the U.S. government's representative in Indonesia might feel uncomfortable surrounded by thousands of devout Muslims, an acquaintance leaned over and whispered to me: "Don't worry. These are Gus Dur's followers. They will protect you with their lives."

Mindful of the risks of polarization between Islamists and nationalists, President Wahid quickly moved to support Megawati for vice

---

27 Dana Priest and Bradley Graham, "E. Timor Killings Renew Debate on U.S.-Indonesia Military Ties," *Washington Post*, Sept 14, 1999.
28 PDI-P: *Partai Demokrasi Indonesia Perjuangan*, or Indonesian Democratic Party of Struggle; PKB: Partai Kebangkitan Bangsa, or National Awakening Party; PAN: *Partai Amanat Nasional*, or National Mandate Party; PPP: *Partai Persatuan Pembangunan*, or United Development Party (a.k.a. Development Unity Party).

president, a position she won, creating an awkward team at the top. In typical Indonesian fashion, he invited in representatives from all the main parties to his cabinet, focusing more on political unity—at least superficial unity—than on being able to deliver on a specific set of policies.

Early on, the new president took a series of important steps to promote his vision of tolerance and unity, ending restrictions on the use of the Chinese language and Chinese schools, changing Irian Jaya's name to Papua to show respect to its inhabitants, beginning negotiations with Acehnese separatists, and even traveling to East Timor, where he apologized to the people for the suffering they had endured. In early 2000, Wahid managed to push General Wiranto, one of the most powerful people in the country and a man closely associated with the military's abuses in East Timor, out of his position as leader of the military. He disbanded *Bakorstanas*, the much-maligned internal security organization, released the remaining political prisoners, and oversaw a tremendous increase in freedom of the press, association, and speech, along with the rapid development of civil society organizations.[29]

Washington Tries to Strike a Balance

For U.S. policymakers, the challenge was how to deal with the combination of very bad developments—particularly the Indonesian military's encouragement of mass violence in East Timor—and very good developments, including successful elections, multiple reforms, and a significant increase in freedom for the Indonesian people. We saw a similar situation in Myanmar twelve to fifteen years later, when numerous and unexpected positive developments coincided with the country's appalling treatment of the Rohingya. These situations pose a dilemma, especially because in Washington the voices of those who are (rightly) calling out the bad tend to be louder than those who are praising the good.

Separate congressional hearings on East Timor and on Indonesia in February 2000 highlighted this conundrum. The Timor hearing understandably focused on the actions of the Indonesian military, producing demands for accountability and justice, and reinforcing support for the prohibition on most military-to-military activities that Congress had

---

29 Human Rights Watch, "Indonesia: Abdurrahman Wahid's Human Rights Legacy," July 27, 2001, https://www.hrw.org/news/2001/07/27/indonesia-abdurrahman-wahids-human-rights-legacy#.

imposed in late 1999.[30] The Indonesia hearing focused on the bigger *reformasi* picture, including questions on whether the United States should review its position on Papua, where there was a significant separatist movement. Assistant Secretary of State for East Asia and the Pacific Stanley Roth laid out the administration's position:

> . . . the starting point for U.S. policy is the preservation of the territorial integrity of Indonesia. That is the position that President Clinton has articulated to President Wahid on his visit here. . . . East Timor was *sui generis* by virtue of its different legal status and the fact that its incorporation was never accepted by anyone. . . . So we are simply not looking at re-opening this issue [of Papua's status]. . . . I think there is a need for accountability as much in Papua as there is in Aceh and Timor. . . . But I think one also has to look at the over-arching national interest of whether we want to be a party to the disintegration of Indonesia, which I think would have devastating consequences for stability in all of Southeast Asia."[31]

Roth and Treasury Under Secretary Tim Geithner, testifying at the same hearing, laid out the administration's plan to help Indonesia move forward. Roth stressed the administration's near-doubling of assistance to Indonesia to help it begin to build democratic institutions. Geithner highlighted U.S. support for rescheduling of Indonesia's massive foreign debt, further loans from international financial institutions, and Treasury technical assistance in areas such as debt management and bank restructuring.[32]

Military Reform, Human Rights and Accountability

For Washington, a key question was the extent to which Indonesia could achieve military reform and accountability for past human rights

---

30 *East Timor: A New Beginning? Joint Hearing Before the Subcommittee on Asia and the Pacific of the House Committee of International Relations and the Subcommittee on East Asian and Pacific Affairs of the Committee on Foreign Relations*, 106th Cong. (February 10, 2000), https://www.govinfo.gov/content/pkg/CHRG-106jhrg67455/html/CHRG-106jhrg67455.htm.

31 *Indonesia: Confronting the Political and Economic Crises: Hearing Before the Subcommittee on Asia and the Pacific of the Committee on International Relations*, 106th Cong. (February 16, 2000) (statement of Stanley Roth), https://www.govinfo.gov/content/pkg/CHRG-106hhrg64418/html/CHRG-106hhrg64418.htm.

32 *Indonesia: Confronting the Political and Economic Crises* (statement of Timothy F. Geithner).

violations. Congress, in its annual appropriations language, consistently conditioned security assistance on accountability. Domestic pressure in Indonesia was growing as well, as the new media and political freedoms allowed people to gain a much better appreciation of the military's role in human rights violations, whether against democracy activists or insurgents in Aceh, Papua, and elsewhere.

Some critical reform was beginning. Most importantly, the military as an institution agreed to step back from politics. Also, Habibie took the important step of separating the police from the military. The number of parliamentary seats reserved for the military was reduced (they did maintain a hundred seats for some time), and a group of reform-minded officers advocated a "New Paradigm," under which military officers would no longer be placed in civilian bureaucratic positions, as they had been under Suharto. Starting in April 1999, officers could only accept such positions if they first retired from the military. President Wahid put a civilian, Juwono Sudarsono, in the defense minister position, while removing Wiranto from his post.

Accountability proved a harder nut to crack. The military had no tradition or practice of holding human rights abusers accountable. Even years later, Indonesians would often tell me that, in their culture, forgiveness trumped accountability. The Habibie and Wahid governments initiated some steps, but they faltered. For example, Habibie established an investigative committee that in November 1999 presented a lengthy report on military violence in Aceh. The report highlighted five cases where evidence was compelling of human rights violations, but only implicated mid-level officers.[33]

Indonesia established a Commission for Human Rights Violations in East Timor, which paralleled a UN investigation. In January 2000 both investigations implicated senior Indonesian civilian and military officials in the human rights abuses in Timor. The Indonesian commission specifically named General Wiranto. President Wahid refused to cooperate with any international criminal prosecution, insisting that this was a domestic matter and that Indonesia would pursue accountability. Indonesia set up a special human rights court to handle the process. Wahid, however, undermined the effort by promising to pardon Wiranto if he were found guilty. In the end, the Indonesian court process was widely criticized as grossly inadequate, as it gave mild punishments

---

33 Harold Crouch, "Indonesia: Democratization and the Threat of Disintegration," *Southeast Asian Affairs* 2000, 115–133, https://www.jstor.org/stable/27912247.

to a few mid-level officials but did not pursue others.[34] This failure to pursue accountability was to be an irritant in U.S.-Indonesian relations for years and was a key factor in the U.S. Congress in 1999–2001 imposing legislative conditions on the resumption of security assistance.

There also was, at least initially, little progress on two other areas of military reform: the military's role in business and its territorial command structure. For years, the military had engaged in a wide variety of businesses, many legal but some not, that undermined civilian control and accountability and also created conflicts of interest as well as opportunities for corruption and human rights abuses. Parliament passed a law in late 2004 requiring the military to surrender its businesses within five years, but implementation was repeatedly delayed.

As part of the *dwifungsi* system, the military also had established a system of territorial commands, in which military commands operated as parallel governance structures throughout the country. This system continued during *reformasi*, as the military insisted its presence throughout the country was necessary to maintain national unity, and civilian politicians in the end proved unwilling to force a change.

Gus Dur Impeached—Megawati Takes Over

Meanwhile, President Wahid was facing mounting challenges in Jakarta. In poor health, nearly blind, and increasingly focused on political maneuvering among the elite, Wahid failed to implement a coherent, effective economic policy and gradually alienated many of his political partners, particularly Vice President Megawati, Amien Rais, and many in the still-powerful military. Parliament voted overwhelmingly to censure him twice in early 2001 based on corruption allegations and by mid-year moved to impeach him. He fought back, warning of chaos if he was pushed out, calling on the military to restore order, and—as a last gasp—declaring a state of emergency and ordering parliament to close. In an important sign, the military refused to back him and parliament ignored him, voting instead to impeach him and replace him with Megawati Sukarnoputri.

In Washington the overwhelming sentiment was one of relief that the Wahid-Megawati transition had been peaceful, and that the military had chosen not to intervene (to protect Wahid or otherwise). Megawati did not enter office with a clear plan of governance and

---

34 Crouch, "Indonesia: Democratization and the Threat of Disintegration."

reform. She was more of a tactical politician than a strategic leader, and she delegated a lot of decision-making to her cabinet. Many saw her as more a symbol of anti-Suharto democracy—and Indonesia's secular nationalism—than a substantive leader. During her time in office, she rarely spoke to the nation. She was well known for her patience, which some termed stubbornness. I got to know Megawati reasonably well a decade later. In private conversations she was open and friendly, but rarely offered any substantive thoughts on policy matters or even the direction of the country, other than stressing the importance of preserving the diversity and tolerance that her party represented.

Although the military had been wary of Megawati for years because of her opposition to Suharto, she recognized that her weak support among Islamist political parties—due to her strong secular nationalism—left her with little choice but to lean on the armed forces politically. This political calculation, combined with her and her party's longstanding support for national unity (and thus lack of sympathy for separatist movements in Aceh and Papua), meant that she did not pursue military reform or accountability, nor did she try to constrain the military when it launched major offensives against separatists in Aceh. In fact, Megawati declared martial law in Aceh in May 2003, as the military sent some thirty-five thousand troops to the province to combat the Gerakan Aceh Merdeka (GAM, or Free Aceh Movement).

It was not just the armed forces to which Megawati turned, however. Rather than install a cabinet full of decisive reformers who might have pushed *reformasi* ahead more boldly, the new president turned to many figures from the Suharto era. Indonesian analyst Jeffrey Winters offered a particularly critical comment on this aspect of her leadership:

> She embraces the status-quo bureaucracy. She has personally embraced around her a lot of people who are directly—and I mean deeply connected—to the New Order. And it's not as if they forced themselves on her. They are a reflection of her desire to surround herself with people, which in her view, will know how to run the place and so on. And that means that she has essentially returned to what was, rather than what could be.[35]

It sounds a lot like what many would say about Aung San Suu Kyi in Myanmar fifteen years later.

---

35 Quoted in "Analysts Review Megawati's First Year in Office," Voice of America, July 23, 2002, https://www.voanews.com/a/a-13-a-2002-07-23-35-analysts-66291942/541271.html.

Megawati's tenure nonetheless saw a further consolidation of democratic trends and implementation of constitutional and other reforms that had been approved in 1999–2001. She also did appoint some important reformers to cabinet positions, most notably Attorney General Marzuki Darusman. Decentralization proceeded, as did the transition from indirect to direct elections for president and for regional officials. Independent media and civil society grew stronger, playing a more prominent role in public debates. After the turbulence of the 1998–2001 period, many people welcomed a sense of calm and stability. Megawati restored relations with the IMF, leading to the release of a much-needed $5 billion loan disbursement in late 2001.[36] By 2004 Indonesia's economy, while still weak, had recovered sufficiently that it no longer needed to rely on IMF loans or debt rescheduling. Growth had reached 5 percent, which was an improvement but still inadequate. President Megawati also visited a number of ASEAN member states, which Jakarta had neglected the past few years, reassuring her neighbors that Indonesia intended to play a regional role.

Indonesia's decentralization of power merits a few more words. Some devolution of authority and responsibility was critical to keeping the country together, but the political elite worried that shifting power to the provinces could actually encourage separatist tendencies in some areas. They decided instead to bypass the provincial level and devolve power to the district (*kabupaten*) level. This move made a lot of sense politically, but it came at a significant economic cost, as district-level governments were woefully unprepared to handle the new responsibilities, and the process resulted in a web of inconsistent and often contradictory regulations across the country.

Interestingly, the communal conflicts that had plagued Indonesia since Suharto's fall—particularly Muslim-Christian clashes in Poso and Ambon and ethnic conflict in Kalimantan—declined markedly during Megawati's tenure. The most plausible argument I have heard for this decline is that it was a combination of local peace-building efforts, better policing by the security forces—which had been accused of standing by or even contributing to conflicts in some cases—and perhaps the general calming of the overall political environment in the country.

---

36 Catharin E. Dalpino, "Indonesia at the Crossroads," Brookings Policy Brief 89, September 30, 2001, https://www.brookings.edu/research/indonesia-at-the-crossroads/.

The War on Terror

Two months after assuming the presidency, Megawati planned to travel to Washington to meet with President Bush. A week before her arrival, terrorists staged the September 11 attacks in the United States. She and President Bush agreed her visit should proceed, no doubt recognizing the opportunity presented by the leader of the world's largest Muslim-majority nation standing side by side with the leader of the United States. Megawati offered her condolences to the American people and expressed general support for U.S. efforts to pursue terrorists. She and Bush issued a joint statement vowing to "open a new era of bilateral cooperation based on shared democratic values and a common interest in promoting regional stability and prosperity."[37] Both Muhammadiyah and NU issued strong statements denouncing the attacks, and many Indonesians echoed those thoughts.

As the United States moved into Afghanistan to pursue al-Qaeda, however, Indonesian support wavered. Megawati noted that no nation had the right to attack another. More broadly, the U.S. pursuit of the global war on terror—including its operations in Afghanistan and Iraq—touched a couple of raw nerves among Indonesians. First, the powerful nonaligned gene in Indonesia's DNA—baked into the collective mindset by years of Sukarno's anti-West speeches—and the history of U.S. intervention in their country in earlier days makes many Indonesians wary of unilateral military action, particularly by the United States. Second, a lot of Indonesians opposed U.S. policy in the Middle East, particularly its strong support for Israel, and feared that the United States would use the terror attacks to target Islam writ large. By late 2002, a Pew survey would show that a solid majority of Indonesians opposed the U.S. intervention in Afghanistan and the global war on terror. Megawati's own vice president, Hamzah Haz, had responded to the 9/11 attacks by suggesting they might help the United States "cleanse its sins."[38] (He also said there were no terrorists in Indone-

---

37 Walter Lohman, "U.S.-Indonesian Relations: Built for Endurance, Not Speed," Heritage Foundation, March 5, 2010.

38 Anthony L. Smith, "Reluctant Partner: Indonesia's Response to U.S. Security Policies," Asia Pacific Center for Security Studies, March 2003, https://apps.dtic.mil/dtic/tr/fulltext/u2/a592297.pdf.

sia.) In a new democracy, Megawati had to tread carefully in light of these public views.

The September 11 attacks and the threat of terrorism highlighted to many in Washington the importance of Indonesia, particularly its democratic transition and lack of popular support for extremism. Many in the capital saw Indonesia's so-called moderate Islam as a potential example or model for the broader Muslim world, bolstering support for further assistance and closer ties. The Pentagon and the Bush administration in general wanted to take some steps to rebuild the military-to-military relationship but faced continued opposition from Congress, which in 2002 added more legislative conditions to the use of any funds to train or arm the Indonesian military.[39] Indonesian authorities themselves had mixed views on renewed military-to-military engagement. On the one hand, some in the military really wanted it. On the other hand, many Indonesians blamed the United States (along with Australia) for the loss of East Timor, and several civilian and military leaders—including presidents Wahid and Megawati—found the U.S. conditions imposed on the resumption of military-to-military relations unjust and humiliating. The Indonesians were willing to move forward, but they were also proud.

Nonetheless, the two sides took some small steps to begin to rebuild military ties. In February 2002 the United States and Indonesia held two days of security talks, which the *Washington Post* called the "most significant" talks between the two militaries since 1999.[40] Two months later, Defense Secretary Rumsfeld hosted Indonesian defense minister Matori Abdul Djalil in Washington, after which Rumsfeld told the press that the administration was interested in finding ways to work with Congress to reestablish appropriate military ties.[41]

A couple of developments over the next few years combined to accelerate progress. First, Indonesia was rocked by a series of domestic terror attacks, starting with coordinated terrorist bombing attacks in Bali in October 2002, which killed hundreds of mostly foreign tourists. Until then, Indonesian authorities had been hesitant to deal with

---

39 Kurt Biddle, "Indonesia-U.S. Military Ties," *Inside Indonesia,* July 29, 2007, https://www.insideindonesia.org/indonesia-us-military-ties-2.
40 "U.S., Indonesia Rebuilding Military Ties; Meetings on Terrorism, Piracy Are First Since Sanctions for E. Timor Violence," *Washington Post,* April 25, 2002.
41 "Resuming U.S.-Indonesia Military Ties," International Crisis Group Indonesia Briefing, May 21, 2002, https://www.refworld.org/pdfid/3c21b11a4.pdf.

the threat of terrorism, failing through ineptitude or lack of will to arrest known terrorists and largely neglecting the risks. The Bali bombing forced them to acknowledge an al-Qaida presence (in the form of its affiliate Jemaah Islamiyah) in the country. Subsequent major JI attacks against the Marriott Hotel and Australian embassy in Jakarta reinforced the country's vulnerability, raising concerns in Washington that Indonesia—along with the southern Philippines—could become a major front in the war on terror. This concern added to Washington's focus and interest in engaging. Even before the first Bali bombing, Secretary of State Powell had visited Jakarta and offered assistance to the security forces—mostly the police—to counter this threat.[42]

Democracy Consolidated

The second development, a massive tsunami that hit Indonesia in December 2004, was preceded by critically important national elections. The July 2004 elections were the first national elections held in the truly democratic era (the 1999 elections had taken place during Habibie's tenure), as well as the first direct elections for the presidency. Megawati ran for re-election, and in late 2003 and even into early 2004 winning a second term looked like a sure thing.

Her aloofness and the odor of corruption around the first family (particularly her husband, Taufik Kemas), however, along with the economy's continued weakness, caused her popularity to drop. Also, former general Susilo Bambang Yudhoyono, who had only recently served in Megawati's cabinet, where he earned a reputation as a steady, capable minister, decided at the last minute to establish the Democrat Party and to run against his former boss. His party barely reached the necessary 5 percent threshold in the April 2004 parliamentary elections to nominate him as a candidate, but once nominated he quickly became a formidable opponent.

In addition to Yudhoyono, Megawati's main rivals included former military commander Wiranto, Vice President Hamzah Haz, and Amien Rais. Remarkably, Wiranto—who a UN-backed court in East Timor had indicted for war crimes—ran with Abdurrahman Wahid's brother, Salahuddin Wahid, who was deputy chair of the National Commission

---

42 Todd. S. Purdam, "U.S. to Resume Aid to Train Indonesia's Military Forces," *New York Times*, August 3, 2002.

on Human Rights. Politics in Indonesia makes strange bedfellows, for sure.

The elections proceeded freely and fairly, with Yudhoyono and running mate Jusuf Kalla winning a plurality in the first round and then soundly defeating Megawati in the run-off. Megawati pouted and refused to concede but did nothing to prevent a smooth and orderly transition. Although Yudhoyono was a former general, his election did not suggest a return to the old days or to a powerful military. Even when he had been in uniform, he had shown himself to be a reformer. During U.S. Pacific Commander Admiral Dennis Blair's 2000 visit—at a time when the U.S. military was pressing the TNI hard on accountability—Yudhoyono had sensed Blair's frustration with his official meetings. Just before the U.S. delegation departed, the general found an opportunity to speak his own mind to his U.S. counterparts. He urged them to be patient, insisting that there were many like him who were trying to change the way the Indonesian military worked. As president, Yudhoyono proved himself to be a genuine democrat, not an advocate for the military to regain its political power. In hindsight, his election—in the first direct national elections—represented Indonesia's consolidation of democracy.

Yudhoyono, best known by his initials, SBY, entered office in October 2004 amid high expectations, due to his reputation as a solid, reform-minded individual who had promised to tackle corruption, strengthen the economy, and continue to build democratic institutions, while also raising the country's profile in regional and global affairs. He included in his cabinet, especially in key economic positions, a number of respected technocrats.

The Tsunami

Yudhoyono had only been in office for two months when a massive tsunami devastated large parts of Aceh Province, killing more than 160,000 people (plus tens of thousands more in Thailand and elsewhere) and destroying much of the province's already-limited infrastructure. The United States quickly offered to assist. Yudhoyono overruled nationalist elements in the military and welcomed U.S. assistance, which poured in. U.S. ambassador Lynn Pascoe asked Vice President Jusuf Kalla what Indonesia needed. Kalla said helicopters. Pascoe then spoke with U.S. Pacific Commander Thomas Fargo, who confirmed that the aircraft carrier USS *Abraham Lincoln* was nearby and available to help with its seventeen helicopters.[43] Within a few days, U.S. Navy helicopters were delivering relief supplies and helping ferry around Indonesian disaster relief personnel. The photos and television images of U.S. military personnel working side by side with Indonesian counterparts reached millions of Indonesians and by all accounts had a profound and positive impact on the Indonesian public's view of the United States, creating a more conducive domestic environment for closer relations with the United States. The visit and fundraising efforts by former presidents George H. W. Bush and Bill Clinton reinforced the positive U.S. role in helping Indonesia respond to the disaster.

The United States went on to contribute hundreds of millions of dollars for relief and reconstruction, providing immediate help to thousands and rebuilding hundreds of houses and a key highway along the Aceh Coast. I drove that entire rebuilt highway several years later with the Acehnese governor and former separatist fighter Irwandi Yusuf to celebrate its reopening and to show that the United States delivered on its promises.

In addition to moving quickly to welcome international assistance, SBY wisely established a special independent agency, the Badan Rehabilitasi dan Rekonstruksi, to coordinate relief and reconstruction, and appointed a highly respected technocrat, Kuntoro Mangkusubroto, to run it. The international community responded generously, and Kuntoro's agency worked exceptionally well, producing a recovery that was better than one would have expected. Many viewed the agency as the "gold standard" of post-disaster responses, thanks to Kuntoro's effective management and a lot of hard work by many others. Yudhoyono's leadership in this crisis also enabled him to solidify his place as the country's leader early in his term.

Yudhoyono's First Term

Beyond responding to the tsunami, Yudhoyono in his first term succeeded in increasing economic growth, reducing debt levels, and raising foreign reserves. The country felt stable, the military largely behaved, and citizens enjoyed increased prosperity and broad freedoms. Freedom House listed Indonesia as one of the region's few "fully free"

---

43 Telephone interview with former ambassador Lynn Pascoe, October 7, 2020.

nations, a remarkable change from just a handful of years earlier.[44] Under Yudhoyono, there was a sense that Indonesia's democracy was increasingly well entrenched and that the country was on a positive trajectory. SBY also made Indonesia more of an international player, engaging on the world stage, bringing the country into the G-20, and promoting active diplomacy in the region.

One of Yudhoyono's biggest achievements was achieving peace in Aceh. Actually, a lot of the credit deserved to go to his vice president, Jusuf Kalla, who had quietly restarted negotiations with the GAM separatists just after entering office. Almost immediately after the tsunami hit, the GAM called a unilateral ceasefire, which the government reciprocated. With help from former Finnish prime minister Martti Ahtisaari, government and GAM negotiators managed to conclude a peace deal in July 2005 that kept Aceh as part of Indonesia but gave it special autonomy in many areas. By the end of 2006, former GAM separatists were running the Aceh government, an incredibly rapid and dramatic turnaround. There have been plenty of criticisms of the subsequent Acehnese governments, particularly regarding the application of sharia law, but the agreement ended a brutal thirty-year insurgency that produced tens of thousands of casualties and massive human rights abuses.

It was around this time that I began visiting Indonesia for the first time, initially as director of the Office of Maritime Southeast Asia and then as deputy assistant secretary for the region. During my first few visits, a couple of things struck me. First, Indonesia—which had been overwhelmed by crises and instability for several years—had transformed into a normal, stable country. Second, it was a functioning democracy, with greater freedom than almost any other country in Southeast Asia. Third, Indonesian civil society had developed into a remarkable, positive force, a true pillar of democracy. The presence of mass organizations Nadhlatul Ulama and Muhammediyah gave civil society a good start, but hundreds of other independent organizations rose in the *reformasi* period. I always asked the embassy to end my visit schedule with a meeting with civil society representatives, because those meetings enabled me to depart the country feeling hopeful about its future. It was not because the people I met were satisfied. Civil

---

44 Freedom House, *Freedom in the World 2009* (Lanham, Maryland: Rowman & Littlefield, 2009), https://freedomhouse.org/sites/default/files/2020-02/Freedom _in_the_World_2009_complete_book.pdf.

society rarely is. Rather, it was the fact that they were able to operate with what appeared to be full freedom and were determined to push for greater reform, transparency, and freedom.

Good Bilateral Relations

We enjoyed a good bilateral relationship during this period. At the top, presidents Bush and Yudhoyono met a number of times, always stressing their shared commitment to democracy and tolerance. In congressional testimony in March 2005, Deputy Assistant Secretary of State Marie Huhtala praised Indonesia's democratic reforms and said the Bush administration believed "the success of Indonesia as a pluralistic and democratic state is essential to the peace and prosperity of the Southeast Asian region." She added that "we want to do everything possible to help Indonesia succeed and our relationship develop to its full potential."[45] President Bush pledged a multi-year $157 million assistance program to help Indonesia improve basic education. Washington also announced that the newly democratic Indonesia had qualified to receive a Millennium Challenge Corporation compact, which promised a substantial injection of assistance aimed at bolstering broad-based economic growth. In addition, the U.S. government was providing assistance to the Indonesian police, both to promote broad organizational and operational reform and more specifically to support its counterterror squad, known as Detachment 88.

Detachment 88 (or Det 88, for short) began to achieve significant success in the mid- to late 2000s, arresting or killing a significant number of Indonesian terrorists, including very prominent members of Jemaah Islamiyah. Detachment 88's efforts, along with the dramatic decline in Muslim-Christian communal conflict since 1999–2000, eased concerns that Indonesia would become a major terrorist hub. We supported the detachment through funding via the State Department's Anti-Terrorism Assistance (ATA) program.[46]

---

45 *Indonesia in Transition: Recent Developments and Implications for U.S. Policy, Hearing before the Subcommittee on Asia and the Pacific of the Committee on International Relations* (March 10, 2005) (statement of Marie Huhtala), https://2001-2009.state.gov/p/eap/rls/rm/2005/43242.htm.
46 Det 88 got its name from people confusing the ATA acronym for the phonetically similar number 88, so what might have been "Det ATA" became Det 88.

We could support the police because, as a separate institution, it did not face the same congressional restrictions as the Indonesian military. Even vis-à-vis the military, however, we were able to ratchet up engagement and training slowly through the decade. In 2005, the Bush administration invoked the national interest waiver in congressional appropriations language to allow it to resume military training (the IMET program), and later to offer Foreign Military Financing and allow the export of defense equipment to Indonesia. Administration officials argued that Indonesia's great strides in establishing democracy, its improved human rights record, need to combat terrorism, and overall strategic importance warranted such moves, despite the continued lack of progress on accountability for past human rights violations. They also asserted that reestablishing security ties would enable improved relationships between the two militaries and encourage greater professionalization of the Indonesian military.[47]

Not everything was rosy, however. On the U.S. side, we still faced congressional opposition to rebuilding the military-to-military relationship and wariness about the still-deep corruption of the Indonesian political system and bureaucracy. On the Indonesian side, opposition to the global war on terror and to U.S. interventions in Iraq and Afghanistan, combined with continued hostility to our broader Middle East policy, placed constraints on how much Indonesia could work with us. Related to this was a sense among key elements of the public that the United States was anti-Islam.

President Obama and a New Opportunity

In that sense, President Obama's 2008 election created an opportunity. President Bush had been a good partner for Indonesia, but he was too closely associated in Indonesian eyes with the war on terror and "anti-Muslim" sentiment to be viewed favorably by the masses. President Obama, on the other hand, offered a different message, and immediately appealed to many Indonesians. The fact that he had lived in Indonesia as a child for several years no doubt contributed to the much more favorable view Indonesians held of him.

---

47 *U.S.-Indonesia Relations, Hearing before the Subcommittee on East Asian and Pacific Affairs of the Committee on Foreign Relations*, 109th Cong. (September 15, 2005) (statement of Eric G. John), https://www.foreign.senate.gov/imo/media/doc/JohnTestimony050915.pdf.

President Yudhoyono recognized this, and in November 2008—
shortly after President Obama's election—suggested the two countries
establish a "Comprehensive Partnership." We presented this to incoming Secretary of State Hillary Clinton as an important opportunity, and
strongly recommended she and the president agree to pursue such a
partnership. Clinton traveled to Jakarta on her very first overseas trip as
secretary, in February 2009, and there committed with Indonesian foreign minister Hasan Wirajuda to build a Comprehensive Partnership.

When we returned to Washington, I was tasked with working with
Indonesian foreign ministry director General Retno Marsudi—who
would go on to serve as foreign minister—to turn the concept into
a reality. For the Indonesians, the partnership was part of a broader
effort to reach out and enhance their relationships with several big
powers and, in doing so, to be seen as a major regional power. In my
conversations with Marsudi, she also made it clear that they wanted
to expand our partnership beyond security and terrorism issues, which
had dominated during the Bush administration but which remained
sensitive domestically for the Yudhoyono administration.

We saw the partnership as an opportunity to bolster not only the bilateral relationship, but our ability to work with Indonesia to promote
everything from regional security to democracy and human rights to
work on climate change. Indonesia had joined the G-20 in 2008. Under Yudhoyono, Indonesia also had resumed its natural role as ASEAN's
leader and in that organization was pushing hard to set standards and
expectations on democratic practices and respect for human rights.
Yudhoyono, who very much wanted a role for himself and his country
on the global stage, also had embraced Hasan Wirajuda's initiative to
establish the Bali Democracy Forum, an annual meeting at which democracies and those who aspired to democracy could exchange views
and ideas. As Minister Wirajuda explained to me later, Indonesia would
not push democracy the way the United States did, but by hosting a
nonthreatening democracy meeting every year would seek to create a
normative standard that all countries should try to achieve. Finally, we
saw the partnership as a way to highlight the diversity and respect for
religious freedom that we and Indonesia shared.

Director General Marsudi and I spent the good part of a year negotiating the terms of the Comprehensive Partnership. The initial Indonesian proposal had been quite far from what we were seeking: reflecting
our different approaches, the Indonesian idea was more aspirational,
where we sought more concrete actions and results. Also, it was critical

for Indonesia politically that the partnership be absolutely clear about mutual respect for sovereignty and independence, something we had no problem accepting.

We worked well together. Marsudi was smart, open, pragmatic, and focused on results. She could be a bit brusque by Indonesian standards, but by Washington standards she was all charm. In the end, we produced a Partnership document that outlined cooperation around three pillars: political and security; economic and development; and sociocultural, education, science, and technology. We developed a Plan of Action under which six working groups would meet and come up with initiatives to enhance cooperation on energy, security, trade and investment, democracy and civil society, education, and climate and environment. We anticipated the secretary of state and foreign minister would cochair an annual joint commission meeting to hear about and assess progress and maintain momentum.

Because President Obama had lived in their country as a child, some Indonesians had wildly unrealistic expectations of how much time and attention he would devote as president to their country. Many seemed to expect he would visit in his first days as president and that he would deliver his much-anticipated speech to the Muslim world in Jakarta. They were disappointed when he chose Cairo instead, and even more when he twice had to postpone his planned visit to Indonesia (once because of problems passing his healthcare bill and a second time because of the Gulf oil spill).

Obstacles Remain

Despite all the positive vibrations surrounding the relationship, some fundamental problems remained. As noted above, although I saw little anti-Americanism, many Indonesians remained somewhat wary of the United States, due to a perception that the United States was anti-Muslim or that we harbored a hidden agenda to weaken them. For example, we had been negotiating since 2007 to resume our Peace Corps program, which Sukarno had ended more than forty years earlier. The Indonesian authorities insisted they wanted it, but they also wanted to impose numerous restrictions and start it off very small and contained. It was clear that they worried that Peace Corps volunteers would turn out to be spies, or be a source of problems, the way they thought Australian volunteers had been in East Timor and Western missionaries in

Papua, or that the Indonesian public would react negatively to their presence. It was only in late 2009 that we finally reached agreement, enabling the program to restart in mid-2010. It would quickly become a huge hit among Indonesians, with governors lining up to ask for volunteers to be sent to their regions.

Another sore point concerned our inability to work with the Indonesian Special Forces, Kopassus. We had largely ended the restrictions on military-to-military engagement by then, except for with Kopassus, which had a well-deserved reputation for abusing human rights. Under the Leahy Amendment, we could only provide training to a unit if we could "vet" it and determine that it—or its members—had not committed significant human rights violations, unless there had been accountability for such violations. In the case of Kopassus, State Department lawyers argued that, because its field "units" were pulled together from different Kopassus battalions on an operation-by-operation basis, and all the battalions had been involved in human rights abuses, there was no such thing as a "clean" Kopassus unit. I spent nearly two years in Washington working with the lawyers, the Pentagon, and others to try to find—or get the Indonesians to create—a unit that we could legitimately determine to be clean, all to no avail. In early 2010, our embassy in Jakarta reported that this could be a deal-breaker for an Obama visit, as President Yudhoyono stated it would be difficult for such a visit to be "successful" without some breakthrough on the Kopassus front.

For the Indonesians, this was less about wanting training for Kopassus and more a matter of "face" and pride. How could President Yudhoyono enter a Comprehensive Partnership with us if we were unwilling to work with the military's most elite—in their view—unit because of things that had happened years before? For us, we understood that the Indonesian military remained a powerful force and a key factor in regional security. Our sanctions against the TNI over the past decade were justifiable on moral grounds, for sure, but they meant that we had no relationship with an entire generation of rising Indonesian officers, who had developed a pretty big chip on their shoulder toward us because of our sanctions. It would be hard to sustain a good, broad-based relationship with the country if this continued. Moreover, while the Pentagon sometimes exaggerated how much of a positive impact our engagement and training might have, our military modeled and taught good behavior, which was better than many other militaries would offer.

The Indonesians did not make it easy. We learned that they had assigned an officer notorious for his alleged past involvement in human
rights abuses to be the Kopassus deputy commander. In a series of discussions over some months, Ambassador Cameron Hume and I—during multiple visits—had quietly urged the TNI to find a way to move
this officer out of Kopassus, saying it would be impossible for us to
move forward if he remained in place. One day, we learned by happen-
stance that the officer had been transferred. In true Indonesian fashion,
it was done so quietly that hardly anyone—including us—knew. In July
2010, Secretary of Defense Robert M. Gates, perhaps realizing that our
internal bureaucratic debate might never be resolved, bit the bullet and
announced that we would reengage with Kopassus.[48]

---

48 Elisabeth Bumiller and Norimitsu Onishi, "U.S. Lifts Ban on Indonesian Special
Forces Unit," *New York Times,* July 22, 2010.

CHAPTER EIGHT

Building a Partnership

U.S.-Indonesian Ties since 2010

In August 2010 I took up my assignment as ambassador in Jakarta, tasked with helping to build a true partnership on the ground and supporting Indonesia's continuing reform process. In my many pre-departure meetings with senior administration officials and on Capitol Hill, I received a long list of instructions and pieces of advice. My immediate boss, Kurt Campbell, summed it up best: "Scot, this is an important job. Don't screw it up."

I arrived in an Indonesia that had made great strides over the past decade. Dozens of political parties competed openly and freely in regular free and fair elections, the most recent of which had resulted in President Yudhoyono's re-election in 2009. People enjoyed substantial freedom, while the independent media and civil society flourished. Economic growth had reached 6 percent annually and the middle class was growing strongly. The country had tamed its communal conflicts and separatist insurgencies, save one in Papua, and the talk was of Indonesia's remarkable success rather than the risk of Balkanization.

One of the most impressive things I saw—and a key reason for Indonesia's ability to avoid the disintegration that many had feared—was the strong sense of nation throughout the country, other than perhaps in Papua. People would proudly say they were Javanese, Sundanese, Batak, Bugis, or Madurese, but it did not take away from the fact that they also felt themselves to be Indonesians. Everyone spoke the Indonesian language, and—this really struck me—joined enthusiastically in singing the national anthem whenever it was played. The military reflected the country's diversity; it was not a Javanese-dominated institution. This might seem like small stuff, but it was a tribute to the work that Indonesia's founders and subsequent leaders had done, and it was a critical glue that had helped hold the country together through difficult times. It also stood in stark contrast to what I would see years later in Myanmar.

Under President Yudhoyono, Indonesia also had become a more important player on the regional and global stage. In addition to playing an active role in ASEAN and the G-20, Indonesia had come to the forefront in discussions of climate change. Indonesia was one of the world's largest emitters of greenhouse gases (much of it due to the burning of forests), and SBY wanted the country to take a leadership position on the issue. He cohosted, with the UN, the annual UN Climate Change Conference in 2007 and announced at the 2009 G-20 summit a significant emissions reductions target of 26 percent below business as usual by 2020. He established a National Climate Change Council and worked to implement the UN's Reducing Emissions from Deforestation and Forest Degradation (REDD+) initiative in the country. We and the rest of the world were delighted to see Indonesia taking such an active position on the subject, even if it struggled to turn its positive rhetoric into reality.

Indonesia's Continuing Challenges

I could also see that Indonesia still had a lot of work to do. Although democracy and freedom seemed well entrenched, the quality of governance remained poor. Corruption remained endemic among politicians and in the bureaucracy, with Indonesia ranking a poor 110th out of 180 countries in Transparency International's corruption perception index. Parliament had transformed itself from a rubber stamp to an open, active institution, but remained populated by many members of the old, Suharto-era elite. The country's devolution of authority and resources to the district level had done political wonders, but many district governments and officials were corrupt and/or lacked the capacity to carry out their work.

The judicial and law enforcement systems also needed major overhauls. The courts were notoriously corrupt and inefficient, providing ordinary Indonesians with little hope of justice. The police welcomed their independence from the military, but also were widely regarded as deeply corrupt and often abusive.

Continuing low-level conflict in remote Papua highlighted Jakarta's inability to win over this long-restive region. Despite major investments by Freeport, a U.S. company, and British Petroleum, and a significantly increased flow of funds from Jakarta to the province, residents complained of deep poverty, the lack of progress, high rates of HIV/AIDS, and regular abuses by the armed forces. These abuses were an irritant in the bilateral relationship as well.

Economically, the country's solid growth rate masked continuing inequality and important weaknesses. First, the growth rate itself was artificially bolstered by unsustainably high commodity prices, while the economy had become increasingly reliant on natural resource exploitation over manufacturing. Achieving more sustainable growth would require significant structural reforms to streamline excessive and often contradictory regulations and reduce barriers to trade, as well as greater efforts to improve the country's infrastructure and combat corruption. Also, the country's reliance on resource extraction and on palm oil plantations (which were connected to the widespread use of fires to clear land) posed major environmental problems, which the entire region could see every year when organized burning produced a haze that blanketed Indonesia and its neighbors. Malnutrition and stunting remained major problems, particular in some of the more remote regions of the country. The healthcare system poorly served the public, in part because everyone who could afford it went to Singapore for treatment, reducing pressure on the government to invest in quality care at home.

The country also faced the difficult challenge of dealing with an evolving view of Islam in Indonesia and in the world. In my view, this question involved at least three distinct elements: the longstanding debate between "Islamists" and "secularists" over the appropriate role for Islam in governance and law; the problem of a small but vocal group that was promoting an intolerant brand of Islam; and, on the extreme end, the continued threat of terrorism. I saw the first issue as a legitimate political debate. The other two were more matters of rule of law and effective governance.

Some U.S. visitors would express concern about what they saw as the growing Islamization of the country. When I asked them to explain, they would point to the growing number of women wearing hijabs or of politicians making references to Islamic scripture and the like. I thought these concerns were largely misplaced. Being pious did not make one intolerant or an extremist. Also, unlike Turkey, where wearing a hijab often was a political statement, in Indonesia I did not see much of a connection between headscarves and politics. Women wore headscarves for many reasons. I remember attending an event in Jakarta with Coordinating Minister for Economic Affairs Hatta Rajasa. As always in Indonesia, there was music—a small jazz ensemble, including a young woman wearing a hijab, blue jeans, and boots playing the saxophone. I told the minister that many Americans would be confused about what this woman represented. He laughed and said, "This is Indonesia, not Saudi Arabia."

Looking at this picture of a complex Indonesia, the question for U.S. policymakers was what our role should be. I believed strongly that Indonesians had produced their own remarkable democratic transition, and they would have to determine their own path forward. We needed to stay out of the debate, particularly about Islam. What we could do was to support the people and organizations that were promoting reform and dialogue, and where appropriate provide training and assistance to boost the capabilities of important institutions. It also involved doing all we could to build stronger, durable ties between our two governments but also our two societies. Without public support, it would be difficult to sustain a productive partnership.

In practice, that meant continuing our assistance to improve the quality and effectiveness of the Indonesian police as an institution separate from the military, maintaining and ideally expanding our health and nutrition programs to help the country address malnutrition and stunting, supporting the country's effective and highly popular Corruption Eradication Commission (Komisi Pemberantasan Korupsi, or KPK), encouraging continued economic reform, and doing what we could to strengthen Indonesia's vibrant civil society, an essential pillar of its democracy. Vis-à-vis the military, we needed to continue to build relationships and provide quality training and education, while also stressing the importance of accountability for human rights violations. It also meant working together as much as possible to build a stronger economic relationship and to find regional and global issues on which we could cooperate.

President Obama's Visit

Although the bilateral relationship looked promising, I knew we faced one major liability: a lot of Indonesians thought we were anti-Muslim.

That is a big problem in a country with more than two hundred million Muslims. President Obama's election and rhetoric had helped, but the wariness and suspicion remained. Indonesian friends would point to what they considered to be our unconditional support for Israel, our interventions in Iraq and Afghanistan, and our post-September 11 imposition of new procedures for many Muslim visitors to our country, which for many Indonesians involved long waits for visas and/or being pulled aside for secondary screening every time they went through U.S. immigration.

If we were going to sustain a closer relationship, we had to address this problem. We were not going to change our policy in the Middle East, but we could show Indonesians firsthand what the United States was all about. The first step would be to make sure that President Obama's twice-postponed visit happened. The third attempt would be in October 2010, when the president would be traveling to India. Just days ahead of his scheduled arrival, Indonesia's Mt. Merapi—in central Java—began to erupt, putting thousands of Indonesian lives and the president's planned trip at risk. Vice President Boediono called me to ask if U.S. seismologists could help their Indonesian counterparts determine the right course of action to protect the people who lived around the volcano. We immediately connected the experts, who had a history of working together. Our scientists confirmed what the Indonesian experts were recommending—they needed to evacuate people quickly. The government took the advice, evacuated people, and saved thousands of lives.

That still left Obama's trip in question. Under Secretary Bill Burns called me from New Delhi to ask whether I was confident that, if Air Force One landed in Jakarta, it would be able to take off again (the risk being if the ash cloud floated over Jakarta). I took a deep breath and told him that I was confident, based on everything we had heard and seen to date. Fortunately, the Air Force One crew agreed, and the president flew into Jakarta a couple of days later.

It is hard to describe how big a deal Obama's visit was. As much as Indonesian politicians, government officials, and media personalities tried to play down how much it meant (mostly out of national pride, I think), they could not hide the fact that a lot of Indonesians felt a special connection to the president because of his previous time in their country. The excitement was palpable.

The president went directly from the airport to the presidential palace, where he held a warm and substantive discussion with President

Yudhoyono. The two talked openly and easily about how far Indonesia had come, but even more about how our two large, diverse democracies could work together on everything from security to economics and climate change to healing the divide between the Muslim world and the West. Presidents Obama and Yudhoyono shared a strong interest in bolstering the relationship, as each had personal ties to the other country, cared about international relations, and saw opportunities in cooperation between the world's second- and third-largest democracies.

It was President Obama's speech at the University of Indonesia on the second day of his visit, however, that stole the show. The place was packed with a who's who of Indonesian politicians, business leaders, activists, and academics. Obama's speech, which Deputy National Security Advisor Ben Rhodes wrote with input from the president, was brilliant. He talked about his time in Indonesia and spoke about Indonesia's own vision of itself as a tolerant, diverse, and democratic society, mixing in just enough Indonesian words and sayings to warm the hearts of everyone there. Many of the attendees were in tears as they got up to leave after the speech, which was replayed time and again on local TV stations. Several friends told me afterward that they recognized what the president was doing—by reminding Indonesians of the vision they had set for their country, he was gently encouraging them not to be pulled off that path by those who preached intolerance and division, without lecturing or criticizing. It was a master class in diplomacy.

The Comprehensive Partnership

The two presidents also formally launched the bilateral Comprehensive Partnership, which we had spent the past eighteen months developing. To direct and oversee the partnership, the U.S. secretary of state and Indonesian foreign minister were to cochair a Joint Commission, which would meet annually to review progress and address any concerns or problems. Foreign Minister Marty Natalegawa had visited Washington in September 2010 to cochair the first such meeting with Secretary Clinton. The discussions were open and constructive, including a mix of purely bilateral matters as well as a lengthy conversation over lunch on how the countries could work together on regional and global issues. Secretary Clinton and Foreign Minister Natalegawa got along well, with the secretary in particular valuing the foreign minister's advice on developments in Southeast Asia and on the South China Sea in particular.

We formed joint interministerial working groups that were to work throughout the year to ensure we put meat on the bones of the partnership. These working groups covered trade and investment, the security relationship, climate and the environment, education, and human rights and civil society. Secretary Clinton visited Jakarta in 2011 for the second Joint Commission meeting, which saw progress from some of the working groups but less from others. After 2011, we sometimes struggled to maintain the same level of participation, not because of any particular problem, but because it is often hard to sustain the enthusiasm for such annual engagements.

Addressing the Indonesian Public's Concerns about Us

To build on the momentum from the president's visit and ensure a positive environment for building the Comprehensive Partnership, I told the embassy team that we were going to focus on public diplomacy. By that I did not mean propaganda. Rather, we would use our public diplomacy tools to try to reduce the Indonesian public's concerns about U.S. policies (including those toward the Muslim world) and to build support among the public for closer cooperation with us. That involved using our exchange programs to give young Indonesians an opportunity to participate in programs in the United States, expanding our own travel and engagement throughout the country, focusing particularly on schools and *pesantrens* (Islamic schools), and making full use of our brand spanking new American Center—the unique, high-tech @america, housed in one of Indonesia's most popular shopping malls—to build rapport with Indonesia's younger generation.

Most importantly, it meant reversing the decade-long decline in the number of Indonesians studying at U.S. universities. Anyone who has practiced diplomacy for the United States for long knows that our universities are one of our greatest assets. People who come to America to study receive a great education, gain a deep understanding of our culture and values, and—with rare exception—remain lifelong friends of the United States. They also contribute to the financial health of our education system. The combination of the 1997–98 financial crisis, which greatly reduced Indonesian incomes, greater competition from places such as Australia and Singapore, and America's perceived anti-Muslim bias had resulted in a decline in Indonesian student numbers from some twelve thousand pre-crisis to under seven thousand in 2009.[1]

We had made higher education cooperation an essential component of the bilateral Comprehensive Partnership, with presidents Obama and Yudhoyono announcing in June 2010 the establishment of a Higher Education Partnership.[2] Under that partnership, the United States committed to boost funding for education exchanges and scholarships and to promote university partnerships. Our job at the embassy was to translate that commitment into reality. We made it our top priority throughout my tenure. We invited U.S. universities to visit, increased the number of scholarships, and visited dozens if not hundreds of Indonesian schools to highlight U.S. educational opportunities and explain that—contrary to popular belief—it was not difficult for legitimate students to get visas to study in America.

We invested a lot of time and effort into what I called "retail diplomacy"—reaching out to individual schools, groups, and people to engage directly. I will give one example. In early 2011, the *New York Times* published a story about @america. The article was mostly positive, but it noted that one Indonesian high school student whom the correspondent interviewed at the center spoke about her dream to study at a U.S. university, but then said: "I believe that America hates Muslims, and I'm a Muslim," she said. "I still believe that after coming here."[3]

I saw an opportunity. We called Islamic High School #4 in south Jakarta, which was where the student who was quoted studied, and asked if we could visit. They were surprised, but agreed. A few days later, we showed up. The school principal greeted us warmly and invited us into the auditorium, which was packed with students. Before we had a chance to make our presentation, a handful of students—boys and girls—climbed on the stage, picked up instruments, and played a couple of Michael Jackson songs for us. It was one of the things I loved about Indonesia—we go to an Islamic high school expecting a sober,

---

1 "All Places of Origin," Open Doors, Institute of International Education, https://opendoorsdata.org/data/international-students/all-places-of-origin/.

2 "Fact Sheet: U.S.-Indonesia Education Partnership," U.S. Embassy & Consulates in Indonesia, https://id.usembassy.gov/our-relationship/policy-history/embassy-fact-sheets/fact-sheet-u-s-indonesia-education-partnership/.

3 Norimitsu Onishi, "U.S. Updates the Brand It Promotes in Indonesia," *New York Times*, March 5, 2011.

wary crowd, and they immediately expose all of our not-so-hidden biases by warmly welcoming us and playing U.S. pop music for us, headscarves and all. It could not have been warmer. We talked about religion in America, including our rapidly growing Muslim population, and highlighted education opportunities. I met privately with the student who had been quoted in the *New York Times* story to apologize for embarrassing her with the visit and to say that, no matter what she thought of us, we still wanted her to study in our country.

I think our efforts—supported by groups such as the U.S.-Indonesia Society—had an impact. We reversed the decline in the number of Indonesians studying in the United States, and actually saw the numbers rise nearly 30 percent over the next several years. We supplemented that by sending promising young Indonesians to the United States on shorter tours, including via the U.S.-government-funded YES (Youth Exchange and Study) program, which brought Muslim youth from around the world together at Temple University for programs on diversity and tolerance. I cannot overstate the impact such programs have. One recent alum of the Temple program told me excitedly that "it changed my life." He was now working full time for a local Muslim organization that was seeking to counter intolerant hate speech coming from some hardline groups.

Sometimes the world upsets your best plans and programs. In September 2012, widespread media reporting about an amateurish, ugly American-made anti-Muslim video called "The Innocence of Muslims" set off huge and sometimes violent protests in the Muslim world. The reaction in Indonesia was not as severe as in some countries, but it was bad. People were angry and we could feel the heat building. I called Din Samsuddin, the U.S.-educated leader of Muhammediyah, and asked if he would issue a statement calling for calm. He did. I met with top NU officials, who also urged their followers to refrain from violence. I invited a group of some of the most conservative clerics to my house to discuss the video. I was impressed they came and we had a good discussion, in which I tried to explain how freedom of the media in America meant the government could not stop even ugly, prejudiced messages. Finally, I met with the Jakarta police chief, who promised to protect the embassy. We still faced some sizeable protests that degenerated into violence, including demonstrators hurling Molotov cocktails over the embassy walls, but the authorities protected us well and the vast majority of Indonesians expressed their disappointment peacefully. Still, it undermined so much of what we were trying to do.

The 2010 Wikileaks release of hundreds of thousands of telegrams from U.S. embassies around the world, including Embassy Jakarta, offered another unexpected challenge. Although the leaked messages from Jakarta, which dated from the period before I arrived, were not nearly as concerning as some others around the world, they still included some messages that were embarrassing to President Yudhoyono. I had never found SBY prickly or difficult. In fact, he was always warm and friendly to me. Still, no leader would appreciate the public release of potentially embarrassing information.

Foreign Minister Marty Natalegawa called me into his office to complain about the released documents. I have to say, he handled it about as well as I could have hoped. Always the calm and thoughtful professional, the minister told me privately that he would tell the press, immediately after our meeting, that he had strongly protested the leaked reports, making it clear that they were not acceptable. He asked me how I wanted to handle the matter. I told him that I would tell the press (since I would also have the opportunity to speak) that embassies report a lot of raw data and information, including unsubstantiated reports, which is one of the reasons those reports are not meant for public consumption. He agreed that was both accurate and useful to share and that it was in both governments' interests to move past the issue quickly. We then spoke to the press, answered some questions, and the media soon lost interest.

Building an Economic Partnership

On a more positive note, we were able to move ahead on our Millennium Challenge Corporation (MCC) program, which had been announced back in 2005 as a major initiative to help Indonesia achieve sustained inclusive economic growth. When I arrived at post, I found that the MCC-Indonesian negotiations had reached an impasse, and the MCC was so frustrated that it was considering abandoning the project. That would have been a disaster. Our team worked intensively over the next six months to smooth ruffled feathers on both sides and find a way forward. Finally, in November 2011, Secretary Clinton, who was accompanying President Obama to the East Asia Summit meeting in Bali, joined the signing ceremony to launch the five-year, $600 million program, which would fund small-scale clean energy projects, a nutrition program to counter stunting, and modernization of Indonesia's creaky government procurement program.[4] It was a great way we could contribute to Indonesia's economy while promoting health and transparency.

Indonesia's economy was performing pretty well, but that did not translate into good trade and investment relations. Historically, U.S. investment in the country had focused heavily on natural resources, which was a sore spot with Indonesians. Having been colonized by a private Dutch company that mostly was interested in their natural resources, it is not surprising that Indonesians have a strong nationalist streak vis-à-vis foreign investment, particularly in the resource sector. In the U.S. case, much of the animus has long been directed at Freeport-McMoran's massive copper mine on top of a remote mountain in Papua. Many Indonesians railed at Freeport for allegedly having struck a corrupt deal with Suharto (in the 1960s), for damaging the environment, and—in their view—for taking Indonesia's resources without adequate compensation. In fact, Freeport regularly paid huge amounts of taxes and employed thousands of local Papuans, yet it appeared to be one of the only companies in the country to face public scrutiny over its environmental record and tax payments.

More broadly, Indonesia continued to lean toward protectionism on trade and investment, putting in place any number of import restrictions and running an investment approval process that was long, tedious, and seemingly arbitrary. Some of this reflected the longstanding protectionist mindset of many Indonesians, but it was reinforced by the political clout of Indonesian conglomerates, which flourished in part by discouraging competition. This reality, along with continued high levels of corruption, discouraged U.S. investors. The result was that U.S. investment and bilateral trade remained far below what they could and should have been. Although bilateral trade grew solidly from 2000 through 2013, it subsequently plateaued at the $27–28 billion level. In 2019, bilateral trade in goods totaled less than $28 billion, just over one-third of U.S-Vietnam trade and one-half of U.S.-Thailand trade levels.[5] We struggled for three years to reduce protectionist barriers.

---

4 U.S. Embassy in Indonesia, "U.S. Signs Millennium Challenge Corporation Compact with Indonesia to Support Economic Growth," November 22, 2011, https://www.povertyactionlab.org/sites/default/files/Embassy%20of%20US%20Jakarta%20-%20MCC%20signs%20contact%20to%20support%20economic%20growth.pdf.

5 All figures from "Indonesia," Office of the United States Trade Representative, https://ustr.gov/countries-regions/southeast-asia-pacific/indonesia.

We scored occasional victories, but we failed to put much of a dent in Indonesia's default protectionist thinking.

In fact, as Yudhoyono's second term proceeded, the president turned more and more to protectionist measures, increasing restrictions on foreign investment and adding nontariff barriers in an apparent effort to mitigate rising criticism over his party's corruption scandals. SBY had promoted a solid reform agenda in his first term, but in his second term he disappointed. His second cabinet featured few reformers, and the president himself seemed more concerned with maintaining political unity and stability than pushing through much-needed economic reforms.

The Security Relationship

We made more progress on the security relationship. Police reform moved slowly, but our support to Detachment 88 continued to pay dividends, as the unit kept terrorist elements on the defensive. The lesson, to me, was that, while changing the mindset and approach of a huge organization such as a national police force is inevitably going to be slow and painful, it is possible to achieve success if you work with a smaller subunit, provided that subunit has strong leadership that buys into the ideas we promote. Detachment 88 had that kind of leadership. The Pentagon, particularly the Special Forces, pushed gently for a more active role against terrorism in Indonesia, but I pushed back. Indonesia would not welcome U.S. boots on the ground, and we wanted to encourage the Indonesian police, rather than the military, to take the lead on the issue.

Military relations also developed, as Indonesia's military stayed out of politics and looked increasingly to shift its focus from internal security to defending the country from external threats. We also had to build relationships with an entire generation of Indonesian officers who had risen during the period in which we had largely cut off military-to-military engagement. These officers did not know us and, in some cases, harbored resentment due to our previous sanctions on human rights grounds. It would take years to develop these relationships and we needed to get started. We were steadily expanding the number of U.S.-Indonesian military exercises, while also offering education and equipment.

In 2012, we provided funding to enable Indonesia to repair and upgrade its aging C-130 fleet and also transferred the first of eight refurbished F-16 fighters. After some difficult discussions with skeptics on Capitol Hill, we also were able to finalize the sale of eight Apache helicopters. Quietly, we continued to press the military on human rights. In October 2010, a video popped up on the internet showing Indonesian soldiers torturing a couple of Papuans. It was awful. I went to see Defense Minister Purnomo Yusgiantoro, who was still working to assert his control over the TNI. He agreed the soldiers' actions were unacceptable, but asked for time for the military's accountability mechanism to work. When a military court found the soldiers guilty, but sentenced them to only eight to ten months in prison, after which they would return to the military, I went back to see Purnomo again. I told him the result was not good enough, and would make it very difficult for us to keep working with the military. He said he could not overrule the military court, so I asked about administrative actions. Could he at least dismiss the soldiers from the military? We went back and forth over several weeks, until Purnomo finally agreed he could ensure the men would never wear a military uniform again. It is hard to change mindsets.

I have to share one funny story about Minister Purnomo, who was an open and engaging partner. On the margins of an Indonesian-hosted ASEAN Regional Forum meeting, he invited me to join him and some colleagues for an evening of karaoke. The minister and a series of generals and admirals took turns singing, all of them performing remarkably well. Purnomo turned to me and said, "It's your turn." I demurred, explaining that I was a terrible singer. He insisted, saying he was sure I was fine. Eventually, I went on stage and fumbled my way through a song. When I returned to my seat, Purnomo looked at me and said, with a big smile, "You were right. You really are a terrible singer."

Assessing Indonesia and the Partnership in 2013

As I finished my assignment in mid-2013, I felt that the partnership was developing well, despite the inevitable challenges. Bilateral trade was growing, albeit slowly, U.S. companies had recently won some major contracts in transportation and energy, the security relationship was expanding rapidly, and the combination of the Peace Corps program and the growing number of Indonesians studying in the United States was bolstering the all-important people-to-people relationship.

Moreover, throughout the Obama and SBY presidencies, there was a sense in both Washington and Jakarta that the relationship was improving, trust was growing, and we were working together better than we had in the past. The Joint Commission helped develop and solidify relationships covering a broad range of issues, particularly in areas such as the environment, energy, and education, but also importantly in the security sector. It was the kind of progress that does not generate headlines, but over time makes an important difference. The question was whether we could sustain it

While we worked to strengthen the bilateral relationship, we needed to remain realistic in one important respect. In keeping with its tradition, Indonesia would remain studiously nonaligned and independent, as reflected in its "thousand friends and zero enemies" diplomacy. Our goal was not to "win over" Indonesia to the U.S. side, but rather to support its development as a strong, prosperous, and independent democracy in which the Indonesian public thought well enough of the United States to support a close partnership with us. I used to say that a successful Indonesia that often disagreed with us was better for the United States than a weak Indonesia that always agreed with us. Likewise, we did not need to worry too much about Indonesia aligning with China. It was the one Southeast Asian nation with sufficient mass to fend off big power pressure.

Assessing Indonesia's domestic situation was more complicated. The pace of reform clearly had slowed during President Yudhoyono's second term. The naturally cautious and indecisive leader had, like most of his predecessors, followed a "big tent" approach, focusing more on keeping what he considered to be a politically divided country united than on pushing an ambitious agenda. While staying true to democratic values, he bent over backwards to avoid political controversy, staying silent as critics (including the Indonesia police) attacked the KPK or hardline Muslim groups targeted Christian churches and the small Ahmadiyyah community. Despite growing budget pressures, he chose not to lift fuel subsidies. He also did little to address the country's growing infrastructure problems, allowing feasibility studies on various projects to collect dust rather than take the risk of pushing them forward. His own party faced numerous corruption scandals, which weakened his standing and damaged his popular support.

Despite these problems, a couple of factors left me feeling reasonably optimistic about the country. First, looking back fifteen years, it was remarkable how far Indonesia had come. Some reform fatigue was almost inevitable. Second, the Indonesian people continued to enjoy widespread freedom, and the country was stable and growing. Third, civil society and the independent media—two essential pillars of democracy—were strong and active. Finally, there were encouraging signs that a new generation of political leaders, not tied to the New Order era, might be emerging.

The Jokowi Factor

Joko Widodo, better known as Jokowi, the governor of Jakarta, stood out among this new crop of politicians. I had met him in 2011, when he had already made a name for himself as mayor of the central Java city of Solo. My wife and I visited and spent a day with the mayor and his wife. The former furniture manufacturer explained his ideas of governance, which fundamentally revolved around getting things done and making life easier for local businesses and residents. He talked, for example, about how he had dramatically reduced the time and expense required for people and businesses to get basic documents simply by creating a transparent, open process. When I asked if that had been difficult, he gave what came to be one of his standard lines: "No, it just requires political will." He talked about how he had convinced reluctant street vendors to move to a new purpose-built market by meeting with them every week for a year, gradually winning their trust.

Jokowi had risen quickly, using his reputation as an honest man of the people who brought good governance to win election as governor of Jakarta in 2012 on Megawati's PDI-P party ticket. As governor, he continued to build his reputation by getting things done—including finally starting the long-delayed and desperately needed city mass transit project—and by constantly checking up on the Jakarta region's notoriously inefficient bureaucrats. He made daily trips (*blusukans*) to Jakarta's slums, where he would talk with average people, listening and also describing what he hoped to do.

I accompanied Jokowi on one of these famous *blusukan* trips. In his car en route to that day's destination, I asked him whether anything could be done to deal with the increasingly damaging floods that hit the city during the rainy season. He said the answer was to dredge Jakarta's canals. I asked if he needed foreign assistance to get that done. He said no. They had sufficient funds, it was just a matter of getting the work done. I asked how he planned to tackle that job. Jokowi smiled and said it was easy. He was going to call the director of the regional government-owned dredging company, tell him that he needed to dredge a certain canal right away, and then advise him that he—the governor—would meet the director at the canal at eight o'clock the next morning to get started.

It was hard not to like and admire him. He was honest, and he was getting things done. Despite his somewhat shy, quiet demeanor, Jokowi had confidence and sharp political skills. As his profile grew and people started talking about him as a presidential candidate, he faced the challenge of managing his relationship with PDI-P chief Megawati, who presumably would not take kindly to this upstart politician stealing the limelight (and the candidacy) from her. I witnessed the two interacting a couple of times, once at a small private dinner and a second time at Megawati's home, where my wife and I had gone to pay respects following the death of her husband. In both cases, Jokowi showed deference but did not kowtow. When someone asked him whether he would run for president, he would smile and say, "Ask *Ibu* Megawati."

A small but growing number of other local leaders, often city mayors, seeing Jokowi's rise, followed his example of focusing on good, results-oriented governance. It highlighted to me that voters could indeed reward good governance, and also that decentralization—particularly the creation of hundreds of mayoral positions—had created a sort of training ground for up-and-coming politicians. Indonesia needed this, as the existing national political and governing class continued to perform poorly, with corruption still endemic despite the KPK's remarkable success in prosecuting corrupt officials and putting them behind bars.

The Battle Over Corruption

Indonesia's Parliament had established the Corruption Eradication Commission in 2003, during the heart of the *reformasi* period. The KPK had independent authority to surveil, investigate, and prosecute. With that power and a dedicated staff, it had achieved a 100 percent successful prosecution rate, jailing dozens of parliamentarians, governors, mayors, and officials. Its success earned it plenty of enemies, including in parliament and the police. Starting particularly in 2009, parliament several times threatened to cut its budget or weaken its powers, while the police—a notoriously corrupt institution—went after KPK staff, including investigators.[6]

Many powerful institutions were aligned against the KPK, but it counted on one important ally—strong public support. Civil society groups rallied demonstrators to demand parliament back off from its attempts to weaken the KPK, and to pressure political leaders to rein in the police. When the police went to the KPK headquarters to try to arrest one of its leading investigators, hundreds of Indonesians went to the site to support the KPK and block police access. We tried to help where we could, visiting KPK headquarters regularly, offering training in investigation tactics and procedures, and telling the press afterwards how great it was to have such an institution protecting the Indonesian people. It was the Indonesian public, however, that deserved the credit for keeping the KPK alive and strong in this fundamental test of public interest versus vested interests.

President Jokowi

In 2014 I returned to Jakarta, accompanying Secretary of State John Kerry to attend Jokowi's inauguration as president of Indonesia. EAP assistant secretary Danny Russel and I had encouraged Kerry to attend, arguing that the presidential inauguration for one of the world's biggest democracies—and its largest Muslim-majority nation—warranted traveling halfway around the world. That was especially true because the Indonesian public had rejected a hardline nationalist candidate in favor of a candidate who represented tolerance and good governance.

Acknowledging public demand, Megawati had picked Jokowi to lead the PDI-P ticket against former general Prabowo Subianto, whose Gerinda party had won the backing of Golkar (although a good chunk of Golkar supported Jokowi) and Islamist parties. Despite his deeply problematic human rights background, Prabowo won support by portraying himself as a defender of Islam and a "strong" leader, in contrast with the indecisive Yudyohono. Prabowo's campaign tried to portray Jokowi as weak on Islam and on defending national unity, with some

---

6 Norimitsu Onishi, "Corruption Fighters Rouse Resistance in Indonesia," *New York Times,*" July 25, 2009.

in Prabowo's camp even claiming he was ethnic Chinese and Christian. After a hard-fought campaign, Jokowi won a narrow victory.

Although Jokowi had won by campaigning as a new kind of politician, not connected to the corrupt, entrenched elite, his picks for cabinet positions looked to many Indonesians like a return to the past. He named as defense minister a conservative military man, Ryamizard Ryacudu, ending fourteen consecutive years of a civilian leading that ministry. He chose a handful of highly political people close to former president Megawati, including her daughter Puan Maharani, to other cabinet positions. And he picked for the new position of chief of staff Luhut Panjaitan, a former army general.

Initially, some observers portrayed Jokowi as politically weak, beholden to Megawati, and thus forced to accept people he did not necessarily want in his cabinet. That might have been true to some extent, but it also might have been a very Javanese way of moving forward—the "big tent" approach of bringing in a broad range of people in order to have the political strength to move forward, however slowly. Luhut Panjaitan, while a former general, was also a political figure in his own right and someone who Jokowi had partnered with in business years earlier. Back in 2012 and 2013, Luhut had made clear to me on multiple occasions that he had signed on fully to the Jokowi train. His presence gave the new president an experienced right-hand man he trusted, which was absolutely essential to his ability to govern.

Jokowi was not a visionary reformer or strategic thinker. Rather, he was a tactical politician who had earned his way to the top by being pragmatic and getting things done. He was a "build this road" kind of politician who saw good governance as delivering on government services for the public, in sharp contrast to his more politically focused predecessors SBY, Megawati, and Gus Dur. As president, he focused on maintaining political stability and trying to improve living standards by tackling Indonesia's massive infrastructure deficit and cutting the red tape that strangled business, while also boosting spending on education and health. As Benjamin Bland has written, Jokowi approached the presidency in many ways just as you would expect a former small businessman to do.[7]

During his first term, Jokowi won plaudits for pushing forward a number of important infrastructure projects and for implementing a

---

7 Ben Bland, *A Man of Contradictions: Joko Widodo and the Struggle to Remake Indonesia*, Lowy Institute Paper (Australia: Penguin Random House Australia, 2020).

series of reform packages designed to cut red tape and facilitate business investment. His administration sharply boosted infrastructure spending and continued projects such as the Jakarta mass transit system (Jarkarta MRT), the first leg of which opened in early 2019, and the Trans-Java Highway, which also opened in early 2019. A series of reform packages boosted Indonesia's ranking on the World Bank Ease of Doing Business Index from 120th in 2013–14 to 72nd in 2017, although it has since stagnated.[8]

Jokowi did not succeed in returning economic growth to 7 percent, as he had promised during his campaign. The economy did, however, grow at 5 percent annually, which most considered a success given the weakness of the global economy and the decline in commodity prices, which were so important to Indonesia's economy. Jokowi's administration also put in place key social welfare programs, such as a national health card.

Not surprisingly, Jokowi was not as enthralled by foreign policy and Indonesia's regional and global role as his predecessor had been. He would be pragmatic, focusing on how foreign partners could support his goal of building Indonesia's economy. His choice for foreign minister—the able, pragmatic Retno Marsudi—reflected this. So did his pledge to make Indonesia a "maritime fulcrum," i.e., to refocus the country's attention on the waters that surrounded it, rebuilding marine infrastructure and highlighting Indonesia's place as the bridge between the Indian and Pacific oceans.

Obama invited President Jokowi to Washington in 2015. We looked forward to it with much anticipation—a meeting of two men who had risen from modest backgrounds and aroused great expectations with their elections. Some in Indonesia even called Jokowi "Indonesia's Obama." The meeting itself did not produce the kind of instant chemistry we might have hoped for—Jokowi's soft-spoken, almost shy, manner militated against that. Still, the two leaders got along well and announced they would "upgrade" the Comprehensive Partnership to a Strategic Partnership. Some of that, honestly, was just political semantics, but the leaders agreed to step up cooperation in the maritime sphere—related in part to China's increasing encroachment in Indonesia's EEZ near Natuna Island—and to work together more broadly on

---

8 "Jokowi Asks BKPM to Improve Indonesia's Ranking in EODB Index," IDN Financials, October 31, 2019, https://www.idnfinancials.com/archive/news/29792/Jokowi-asks-BKPM-to-improve-Indonesias-ranking-in-EODB-index.

the world stage. They also vowed to do more economically, promoting trade and investment, including in the energy sector.

Democratic Backsliding?

Politically, a number of critics—particularly in Australia, for whom Indonesia is hugely important—raised concerns that Jokowi in his first term allowed, if not encouraged, democratic backsliding.[9] They noted that he stood idly by while parliament passed legislation weakening the Corruption Eradication Commission, prompting large demonstrations. He also did nothing when Islamists took to the streets to protest against Jakarta governor Basuki Tjahaja Purnama (better known as Ahok)—Jokowi's vice governor when he had been governor—after he made a politically clumsy comment about what the Qur'an had to say about Muslims voting for non-Muslims. These demonstrations, which brought out hundreds of thousands of people, led to Ahok—an ethnic Chinese Christian—being prosecuted, convicted, and imprisoned for blasphemy. The critics also have raised concerns about the power of Islamic groups and about Jokowi's unwillingness to stand up to them. On top of that, some analysts—including some in Washington—have lamented what they see as Jokowi's tendency to allow retired military figures to play an increased role in politics, and the arrest of some critics on what seem to be political charges.

Despite these concerns, Jokowi won re-election in 2019, defeating rival Prabowo again, this time by a larger margin. Prabowo again ran on a hardline, nationalist platform, again portraying himself as a strong defender of Islam and railing like a populist against the elites. Jokowi ran on his accomplishments and his still-strong record as an honest man who got things done. He sought to counter attacks on his commitment to Islam by choosing as his running mate[10] Islamist Ma'ruf Amin, who had been among the leaders of the street campaign against Ahok.

---

9 See, for example, Tim Lindsey, "Is Indonesia Retreating from Democracy?", *The Conversation*," July 8, 2018, https://theconversation.com/is-indonesia-retreating -from-democracy-99211; and Ben Bland, "Politics in Indonesia: Resilient Elections, Defective Democracy," Lowy Institute, April 20, 2019, https://www.lowyinstitute .org/publications/politics-indonesia-resilient-elections-defective-democracy.

10 Jusuf Kalla, Jokowi's previous vice president, had already served two terms in the position and was ineligible to run.

Analysts struggled to characterize the election results. Some, such as the *New York Times*, saw Jokowi's re-election as a rare victory for moderate secularists against populist nationalists.[11] Others, however, warned that Jokowi—while certainly more moderate than Prabowo—was at a minimum excessively accommodating of intolerant and anti-democratic voices, and that Indonesia could be returning to a neo-Suharto period. Al-Jazeera ran the headline "A Revolution Betrayed."[12]

Jokowi's Second Term

In his second term, Jokowi has so far doubled down on his economics-first approach, reaffirming the priority he places on improving Indonesia's infrastructure and trying to streamline regulations to improve the business environment, while investing in human capital and job creation.

Jokowi presumably recognized that the 5 percent annual growth rate Indonesia has enjoyed over the past several years has not been sufficient to propel the economy forward as rapidly as needed, given deep poverty and a rapidly growing labor force (the benefit and the challenge of Indonesia's "demographic dividend"). The problem, in a nutshell, is that infrastructure is still lacking, corruption and red tape remain problematic, and the country's economic mindset is still more nationalist and protectionist than global and supply-chain oriented. The mindset is reflected in the small number of truly global Indonesian companies, the lack of Indonesian investment abroad, still-low trade and inward investment numbers, and low productivity. The country's weak education system does not help. There is too little research and development, a stunningly low number of Indonesian-originated patents and trademarks, and no Indonesian universities ranked in the world's top eight hundred higher education institutions. Investors complain about the difficulty of hiring quality staff.

After his re-election, Jokowi sought to address some of these problems, particularly excessive and overlapping local regulations, through passage of the so-called Omnibus Bill, which was designed to reduce

---

11 Bryan Denton, "With Joko Widodo's Re-election, Indonesia Bucks Global Tilt Toward Strongmen," *New York Times,* May 21, 2019.

12 Richard Javan Heyderian, "A Revolution Betrayed: The Tragedy of Indonesia's Jokowi," *Al Jazeera,* November 24, 2019, https://www.aljazeera.com/opinions/2019/11/24/a-revolution-betrayed-the-tragedy-of-indonesias-jokowi.

red tape and encourage investment in part by re-centralizing some reg-ulatory authority. Many in civil society, labor, and elsewhere criticized the legislation as too friendly to business and complained that it was rushed through without sufficient public consultation. Many others, however, particularly in the business community, welcomed the legisla-tion as long overdue and potentially very helpful in terms of improv-ing the business environment and making Indonesia a more attractive investment destination. They have also applauded the speedy introduc-tion of implementing regulations for the bill, though many are hold-ing off on final judgment pending actual implementation. The strategic advisory outfit Asia Group Advisors called the legislation, if it does not end up watered down in implementation, "the single largest economic reform initiative in Indonesia since . . . 1998."[13]

Jokowi also announced bold plans to move the Indonesian capital from Jakarta to the island of Kalimantan.[14] The idea makes sense in a lot of ways, as Jakarta is overcrowded, at risk from rising seas (the city itself is sinking), while shifting the capital to Kalimantan could over time bolster economic development there. Some, however, have blasted the idea as impractical, too expensive, and poorly considered, and in their view another example of Jokowi's tendency to make gut deci-sions, rather than go through lengthy analyses and studies.

Critics also had a field day with the Jokowi administration's initial (mis)handling of the COVID-19 pandemic. Concerned about the eco-nomic impact of any lockdowns or other stringent actions, President Jokowi delayed containment measures and later admitted that the gov-ernment had hidden data to prevent public panic. Sadly, COVID-19 cases and deaths increased rapidly, making Indonesia the hardest-hit country in the region. The government finally declared a national health emer-gency and put in place social distancing measures, but the country was hit very hard by the delta variant in mid-2021 and again (though with fewer fatalities) by the Omicron variant in early 2022.[15]

13 "Indonesia's Omnibus Law on Job Creation," Asia Group Advisors, March 19, 2021, https://asiagroupadvisors.com/insights/indonesia's-omnibus-law-on-job-cre ation/70.

14 In January 2022 the name of the new capital was announced to be Nusantara. Rebecca Ratcliffe, "Indonesian Names New Capital Nusantara, Replacing Sinking Jarkarta," *The Guardian*, January 18, 2022.

15 Sebastian Strangio, "Indonesia Breaks Daily COVID-19 Record As Omicron Surge Continues," *The Diplomat*, February 16, 2022, https://thediplomat.com/ 2022/02/indonesia-breaks-daily-covid-19-record-as-omicron-surge-continues/.

On the political side, many analysts continue to be concerned with signs of democratic backsliding. Such concerns grew when Jokowi invited Prabowo into his cabinet as defense minister, along with former military commander Wiranto. To many, it seemed that Jokowi was turning his back on human rights and on the spirit of *reformasi*. A number of analysts have warned of Jokowi's overreliance on the military itself, as well as on retired military officers whom he has appointed to senior positions. Recent efforts to amend the criminal code to, among other things, criminalize insulting the president, prompted large student protests and significant concern from the media and other observers. Freedom House has steadily lowered Indonesia's ranking on its World Freedom Index, dropping it from a score of 65 in 2017 to 61 in 2020.[16]

More recently, President Jokowi has been accused of trying to build a family dynasty, as he supported the candidacy of his son for mayor of Solo and his son-in-law for mayor of Medan. Then, in early 2021, President Jokowi's chief of staff, former general Moeldoko, attempted to take over control of the Democratic Party in a controversial party congress in Medan. The move, which if it held would have eliminated one of only two of the country's opposition parties, prompted a strong reaction from Democratic Party founder and former president SBY, who labeled it an "act of treason."[17] Most observers believe Moeldoko could not have made this move without Jokowi's blessing, despite the latter's denial. The takeover bid raised fears that Jokowi was trying to eliminate all effective opposition, potentially paving the way for him to run again for president in 2024, despite the constitution's two-term limit (Jokowi denied this). In the end, the government blocked Moeldoko's takeover attempt, and the courts confirmed that decision.

These developments have prompted a series of warnings from a range of Indonesian and foreign analysts, with headlines such as "Generals Gaining Ground," "Deepening Polarization and Democratic Decline in

---

16 Natalie Sambhi, "Generals Gaining Ground: Civil-Military Relations and Democracy in Indonesia," Brookings, January 22, 2021, https://www.brookings.edu/articles/generals-gaining-ground-civil-military-relations-and-democracy-in-indonesia/.

17 *Chandni Vasandani and Amanda Hodge*, "Indonesia Moves Closer to One-Party Rule as Jokowi Aide Takes Over Opposition," *The Australian*, March 8, 2021, https://www.theaustralian.com.au/world/indonesia-moves-closer-to-oneparty-rule-as-jokowi-aide-takes-over-opposition/news-story/3b880e108efaaef3d996cac36a127942.

Indonesia," and "Indonesia's Democracy under Challenge."[18] One analyst went so far as to claim: "There is now scholarly consensus that Indonesia's democracy has not just stagnated but is regressing."[19] It is not clear that there is such a consensus, but the trend is in that direction.

In my view, Jokowi is acting like a politician, and particularly like an Indonesian politician.

Just as his predecessors did, Jokowi is choosing the "big tent" approach to governing, accommodating some conservative and anti-reform elements politically in order to focus on infrastructure development and other economic steps he believes are essential, and will be his legacy. He also is living with the fact that Indonesia chose, during the early days of *reformasi,* evolution rather than revolution. This choice, or development if you prefer, probably saved the country considerable bloodshed, but it also meant that many figures and practices from the Suharto days have continued, undermining reform momentum. We can see similar developments or choices elsewhere in the region—the Philippines after Marcos, and even Myanmar following its political opening.

Also, Jokowi has been careful not to lean too far in any direction. Criticized for standing by while Islamists went after Ahok and then for bringing in one of those Islamists as his vice president, he has subsequently gone after some hardline Islamist groups, largely sidelined his vice president, and appointed Ahok to an important position as head of Pertamina, the country's state-owned oil company. The Corruption Eradication Commission, which seemed to be weakening significantly, has recently detained two of Jokowi's ministers. The point is not that everything is fine, but rather that the trend might not be as dire as some suggest.

It is reasonable and appropriate to be worried about some of the political trends we are seeing in Indonesia, but we also need to look at it in the regional and global context. In a time of rising populism, nationalism, authoritarianism, and political polarization, Indonesian voters have consistently rejected Islamists and hardline nationalists in favor of more moderate secularists. It is the freest and most democratic

---

18 See Sambhi, "Generals Gaining Ground"; Eve Warburton, "Deepening Polarization and Democratic Decline in Indonesia," Carnegie Endowment, August 18, 2020, https://carnegieendowment.org/2020/08/18/deepening-polarization-and-democratic-decline-in-indonesia-pub-82435; and Deasy Simandjuntak, "Indonesia's Democracy Under Challenge," East Asia Forum, January 30, 2020, https://www.eastasiaforum.org/2020/01/30/indonesias-democracy-under-challenge/.
19 Sambhi, "Generals Gaining Ground."

country in Southeast Asia. That freedom and the explosion of social media have also given intolerant hardliners a voice, which they have used effectively to mobilize support. This is a concern, but it is hardly unique to Indonesia.

Bilateral Relations During the Jokowi-Trump Era

The consensus among close observers of the U.S.-Indonesia relationship is that it has fallen short of expectations over the past several years, particularly during the Trump administration's tenure. On the Indonesian side, analyst Evan Laksmana noted in early 2021 that "relations have grown lethargic in recent years," while Andreyka Natalegawa a few years earlier concluded that bilateral ties were "not reaching their potential."[20] On the U.S. side, Joshua Kurlantzick lamented in 2018 that the relationship has "long underperformed its potential," while Amy Searight found that bilateral ties "chronically underperformed."[21]

A couple of factors explain the failure of the bilateral relationship to take off the way I and many others hoped it would. First, leadership matters, and neither President Jokowi nor President Trump shared their predecessors' strong personal interest in bilateral ties. Jokowi certainly was not anti-American. I spent enough time with him to know. Rather, as noted above, he saw foreign relations first and foremost in terms of how much any particular relationship could contribute to his goal of bolstering economic performance, particularly via infrastructure and other investments. Throughout most of his tenure, he has seen—with some justification—less willingness or ability from the United States in this area than from China, Japan, or some other partners. Trump, for his part, pursued an "America First" agenda, and largely saw Indonesia—indeed all of Southeast Asia—through the lens of U.S.-China

---

20 Evan Laksamana, "Advancing the US-Indonesia Defense Relationship," East Asia Forum, January 19, 2021, https://www.eastasiaforum.org/2021/01/19/advancing-the -US-Indonesia-Defense-Relationship; and Andreyka Natalegawa, "Enhancing the U.S.-Indonesia Strategic Partnership," csis, July 9, 2018, https://www .csis.org/analysis/enhancing-us-indonesia-strategic-partnership.

21 Amy Searight, "Jokowi 2.0: Policy, Politics, and Prospects for Reform," csis, October 18, 2019, https://www.csis.org/analysis/jokowi-20-policy-politics-and -prospects-reform; and Joshua Kurlantzick, "Keeping the U.S.-Indonesia Relationship Moving Forward," Council on Foreign Relations, Council Special Report no. 81, February 2018, https://cdn.cfr.org/sites/default/files/report_pdf/CSR81 _Kurlantzick_Indonesia_With%20Cover.pdf.

competition. Since Jokowi was not inclined to play a strong leadership role in ASEAN or to push back against China as vigorously as Washington might have wanted, the Trump administration's interest in the relationship lacked enthusiasm.

Partly as a result, there has not been a leader-level bilateral visit since Jokowi's 2015 trip to Washington. Moreover, Trump skipped most of the ASEAN leader-level meetings, so had little opportunity to engage Jokowi in that setting. The annual foreign minister–level strategic dialogue envisioned in the 2015 Strategic Partnership ran out of gas quickly, with no meeting at all during the last few years. There was a flurry of senior-level visits in the last few months of the Trump administration—including Secretary of State Pompeo to Jakarta, Defense Minister Prabowo to Washington, and Coordinating Minister Luhut Panjaitan to Washington. These were positives, but many saw them as too little, too late to make up for the lack of senior-level engagement in the preceding three-and-a-half years.

In addition, trade and investment relations failed to make much progress over the past few years. Trade levels, as noted earlier, have stagnated since 2013. Also, the Trump administration won a World Trade Organization case against Indonesia in 2017 (though that case began much earlier) and sought hundreds of millions of dollars in penalties. It also launched a review of Indonesia's eligibility for Generalized System of Preferences trade privileges (which fortunately ended in a decision to renew that eligibility). The Indonesian government, while implementing some important reforms and talking about its desire for more investment, put pressure on major U.S. investors, particularly Freeport, that resulted in the surrender of the majority share of Freeport Indonesia to an Indonesian state-owned enterprise.

The security relationship fared somewhat better, as the two militaries have continued to expand the number of joint exercises they engage in each year. The United States lifted its last restrictions on military-to-military activities in 2017 and continued to pursue training and weapons sales. In 2018, the U.S. transferred the remainder of the twenty-four F-16s that it had agreed to sell to Indonesia years earlier. The late 2020 visit by Defense Minister Prabowo, who previously had been deemed ineligible for a U.S. visa, gave the defense relationship an additional boost, even if it upset human rights advocates.

More broadly, the two governments had different views on some key international issues. Many Indonesians saw the United States as reneging on its global leadership role, including by withdrawing from the Paris Climate Change Agreement, and were not happy with what they saw as President Trump's anti-Muslim sentiments. They also disagreed with the Trump administration's policy toward the Middle East, particularly its unwavering support for Israel. Within the region, Indonesia saw the U.S. pushback against China, particularly via the Quad, as troubling and even dangerous. Jakarta took the lead within ASEAN in countering Washington's Free and Open Indo-Pacific strategy, which they saw as targeting China, with their own vision, which was more inclusive. The Indonesian public's view of the United States turned more negative, and the number of Indonesians studying in the United States declined noticeably. For their part, Trump administration officials were frustrated by what they saw as Indonesia's unwillingness to push back against problematic Chinese behavior. They also misjudged Indonesia, for example, by proposing that Indonesia host U.S. spy planes—a total nonstarter—or attempting to condition Development Finance Corporation investments on changes in Indonesia's policy toward Israel.

Some in Washington have expressed concern that Jokowi has been too willing to rely on China for infrastructure investments. China has been, after all, aggressively pushing projects throughout the region, offering massive financing and having state-owned companies ready to carry out projects, whether commercially viable or not. To be fair, China sometimes has been the only option, as many Western private companies were not willing to invest in these projects, the multilateral development banks' loans were heavily conditioned and moved painfully slowly, and Indonesian companies often lacked the capital, expertise, or interest. Jokowi is not necessarily pro-China, but China often has offered financing that he could not get elsewhere. Over time, Jokowi has cooled somewhat toward Beijing, the result of economic nationalism at home and China's increasing forays into Indonesia's EEZ around Natuna Island. Still, absent better options, he will continue to rely on China for infrastructure development support more than we and many Indonesians would have liked.

Despite these negatives, it is important to stress that, at the end of 2020, the U.S.-Indonesian relationship was not bad. It just was not as strong or positive as many thought it could have been. The question, at the end of the year, was what would be possible to achieve post-Trump. The Biden administration got off to a slow start on this front, with the Indonesians unhappy that both Vice President Kamala Harris and Secretary of Defense Lloyd Austin "skipped" Jakarta during their initial trips to Southeast Asia. By the end of 2021, President Biden's meeting with President Jokowi (on the margins of a climate meeting in Scotland) and Secretary of State Tony Blinken's visit to Jakarta, along with Foreign Minister Marsudi's earlier visit to Washington, had given a much-needed boost to the relationship.

The Relationship Going Forward

U.S.-Indonesian ties lie somewhere between the drifting apart of the U.S.-Thailand alliance and the consistently positive trajectory of the U.S.-Vietnam relationship. From Washington's point of view, Indonesia has succeeded in holding itself together and becoming a more prosperous and free democracy. It also has been a good, if limited, partner. The disappointment has largely been in the economic sector, where Indonesia's protectionism and corruption have discouraged trade and U.S. investment. Some in Washington who do not know Indonesia's historical commitment to nonalignment or recognize the benefits the economic relationship with China bring to the country also have been disappointed that it does not take a tougher line on China.

In 2018 analyst Josh Kurlantzick, in noting the relationship's underperformance, called for a shift to a more transactional relationship focused on areas of mutual interest, such as pushing back on piracy and on Chinese assertiveness in the South China Sea.[22] I agree that the relationship has underperformed compared to the high expectations set a decade ago; we had unrealistic expectations of how fast Indonesia would implement economic reforms and how durable President Yudhoyono's desire for the country to play a global role would be. They no doubt had unrealistic expectations of us as well.

I do not, however, agree on shifting to a more transactional approach, at least not for the longer term. Our strategy should be to continue building the foundations of a durable, healthy partnership, recognizing it is going to be a slow and sometimes disappointing journey. Strengthening the economic partnership will be key. To begin with, the United States should expand recent efforts to play a role in Indonesia's crucial infrastructure projects using some of the new tools Congress has approved, such as the Development Finance Corporation, and working with partners such as Japan to offer transparent, high-quality projects that will stand in contrast to those China has been offering. I appreciate that this is hard, but if the United States cannot find some

22 Kurlantzick, "Keeping the U.S.-Indonesia Relationship Moving Forward."

way to break through on this front, it will struggle to maintain, let alone strengthen, the quality of the bilateral relationship.

There is also more to be done to promote trade and investment. During a recent U.S.-Indonesia investment summit, the U.S. Chamber of Commerce and American Chamber of Commerce in Indonesia expressed hope for trade and investment expansion but noted that "the full economic potential of the U.S.-Indonesia relationship can only be realized through continued efforts by the Indonesian government to reduce trade barriers, protect innovation, promote regulatory transparency, and enhance structural reforms."[23] Indonesia's Job Creation Act, an omnibus bill passed in October 2020, if implemented reasonably well, should encourage more U.S. companies to pursue infrastructure and other investments, but Jakarta needs to do more to reduce protectionist measures. President Jokowi himself has sent mixed messages, recently telling Indonesians they should "love Indonesian goods, hate foreign products."[24]

One area of opportunity is Indonesia's burgeoning start-up scene. In the past several years, Indonesian entrepreneurs have developed several start-up unicorns, such as Go-Jek, Tokopedia, and Traveloka. Its digital economy is one of the fastest growing in the region. AppWorks partner Jessica Liu recently argued that Indonesia's digital ecosystem stands out in Southeast Asia, where it is perhaps behind only Singapore at this point.[25] Although most of the external funding to date has been Chinese or Japanese, U.S. companies such as Google, Microsoft, and Amazon are investing in building data centers to partner with companies such as Tokoepedia and Bukalapak. Most of the leaders in this sector are U.S.-educated and are developing closer ties with U.S. partners. This might be one of the most promising areas in which to develop the business/economic relationship.

23 "U.S. Chamber and AmCham Indonesia Convene Public and Private Sector Leaders for 8th Annual U.S.-Indonesia Investment Summit," U.S. Chamber of Commerce, December 11, 2020, https://www.uschamber.com/press-release/us-chamber -and-amcham-indonesia-convene-public-and-private-sector-leaders-8th-annual.
24 Kiki Siregar, "Indonesians Should 'Love Local Goods, Hate Foreign Products': President Jokowi," Channel News Asia, March 4, 2021, https://www .channelnewsasia.com/news/asia/indonesia-love-local-hate-foreign-products -jokowi-growth-14331276.
25 Judy Lin and Rodney Chan, "Singapore and Indonesia Lead in ASEAN Startup Scene, Says AppWorks Partner Jessica Liu," Digitimes, December 2, 2020, https:// www.digitimes.com/news/a20201201PD212.html.

There also are opportunities to work together more diplomatically, as long as Washington policymakers recognize and accept that Indonesia is going to remain firmly nonaligned and unwilling to join any initiatives that appear to target China. As we have seen in the aftermath of the 2021 Myanmar coup, Indonesia continues to stand up for democratic principles and has shown a willingness to take the lead diplomatically within ASEAN. Foreign Minister Marsudi did so during the Rohingya crisis in 2017–18, and again following the February 2021 coup. Washington and Jakarta do not need to form an explicit team in these areas, but there is much we can do together by exchanging ideas and, when appropriate, supporting Indonesia's diplomatic efforts in the region. With the Biden administration making climate change a priority, the United States and Indonesia can again partner in this area, both bilaterally and globally. It will be important to resume high-level visits, ideally by the presidents, and to hold regular cabinet-level discussions and meetings.

The United States needs to continue to invest in the military-to-military relationship, even inviting Defense Minister Prabowo to the United States (as then secretary of defense Mark Esper did in October 2020). Prabowo's record speaks for itself. The reason to invite him nonetheless is because the United States cannot build a relationship with other countries—or militaries—if we only talk with the people we like or who meet our standard. (I might sound hypocritical here, as I chose not to meet with Prabowo during my time in Indonesia. The difference is that Prabowo at that time held no official position, and I knew that he would use any meeting with me to claim that the United States had no issues with him as a potential president, which was not in fact the case. Now, he is a member of the cabinet of a democratically elected president. It is a different situation.)

The most important area in which to invest remains the Indonesian public, which while not anti-American continues to have some level of wariness about the United States, for all the reasons noted above. The more the Indonesian public supports or at least accepts close Jakarta-Washington ties, the more Indonesian leaders will cooperate with us. That is how democracy functions. To some extent, Indonesian attitudes toward us will remain hostage to our broader policy in the Middle East and our attitudes toward Islam. That is beyond the scope of this book.

Within those parameters, however, there is more Washington can do to build institutional relationships and win friends. For years, around the world, the United States has underfunded exchange and education programs, including scholarships, which are some of its best diplomatic tools. The current and future U.S. administrations should push harder for more resources to expand these programs and to build on nascent university-to-university partnerships. We should maintain and if possible expand our Peace Corps presence, and continue to support Indonesian civil society and independent media. By doing so, the United States promotes its values while also building trust and friendship. None of these ideas is revolutionary. It is more of the same, in some ways, but with an emphasis on *more* and on having the patience to engage consistently at all levels. In many ways, the recipe for building the relationship with Indonesia is the same as that for building U.S. ties with the entire region.

One of the biggest obstacles to progress is the lack of strong constituencies in both countries for the relationship. In Indonesia, the long history of nonalignment, plus concerns about U.S. policy toward the Middle East and Islam, are important factors. The military is a constituency of sorts, but even there the history of U.S. sanctions and disengagement means an entire generation of Indonesian officers had no U.S. connection. The United States is rebuilding that now, but more work is needed. In the United States, the general lack of knowledge and awareness of Indonesia's importance is the overriding factor, supplemented by a relatively weak business constituency, the result of a modest commercial relationship and Indonesia's historic lack of enthusiasm for foreign investment. U.S. think tanks and universities—potential constituencies—tend to focus their Asia attention on China, with India, Japan, and Vietnam getting most of what is left. The foreign policy establishment generally understands why Indonesia matters, but in the absence of a crisis there—à la 1998–2001—it is hard to get senior people to focus consistently on it, especially given the low likelihood of engagement producing quick, concrete results. Finally, unlike Vietnam and Singapore, Indonesia does not work Washington very well, despite having had effective ambassadors in recent years. A colleague argued that Indonesia is "strategically complacent," believing that its size protects it and that it does not need to take the initiative to win over countries like the United States.

One critical area, which might well be overtaken by events by the time this book sees the light of day, is the response to COVID-19. Indonesia has been hit hard and is looking to international partners for help and support. Through much of 2021, China's response appeared more vigorous than that of the United States. First, China managed the pandemic at home better than the United States did. Second, China aggressively promoted so-called vaccine diplomacy, sending large amounts of vaccine to Indonesia and conducting joint vaccine trials in the country. The United States stepped up its efforts in the latter half of 2021, sending nearly thirty million vaccine doses to Indonesia by the end of the year, according to USAID.[26] Going forward, it is essential that the United States continue to strengthen its health diplomacy in Indonesia, including by providing substantial amounts of COVID vaccine.

26 Swiny Andina, "The United States Donates Additional 3.3 Million COVID-19 Vaccines to Indonesia," December 19, 2021, Reliefweb, https://reliefweb.int/report/indonesia/united-states-donates-additional-33-million-covid-19-vaccines-indonesia.

CHAPTER NINE

The Cause

Burma/Myanmar under Military Rule

I arrived in Myanmar to take up my post as U.S. ambassador in late March 2016, one week before Aung San Suu Kyi's new, democratically elected government was to take office. In many ways, the country's transition from international pariah to at least partial democracy during the previous five years had been even more dramatic—and certainly more surprising—than Indonesia's fifteen years earlier. Expectations were high, both within the country and around the world.

When I departed more than four years later, in May 2020, those expectations—especially abroad—had been deflated, and Myanmar's standing had fallen sharply, at least in the West and the Muslim world. The main culprit was the military's brutal ethnic cleansing campaign—sadly defended or at least excused by Aung San Suu Kyi and much of the public—against the long-oppressed Rohingya community. Beyond that, the new elected government had failed to make progress on the country's desperately needed peace process. More surprisingly, it had chosen not to pursue much in the way of further political reform, even moving backwards in important areas such as freedom of assembly and the press. Myanmar's military had reasserted itself politically and was blatantly supporting hardline religious nationalists. Taking advantage of Western criticism, China had moved to expand its influence, and the once-promising U.S.-Myanmar relationship had cooled significantly. Although the majority of Myanmar people were enjoying much greater freedom and opportunity than they had under military rule, the reform effort had slowed considerably if not stalled completely in many areas, and the abuse inflicted on the Rohingya community had changed the way in which much of the rest of the world viewed the country.

Then, on February 1, 2021, the Myanmar military staged a coup, arresting Aung San Suu Kyi and many others, and dramatically setting the country back. The elected National League for Democracy (NLD) government might have disappointed in many ways, but the coup and subsequent military efforts to assert control constituted a disaster of the first order. The Myanmar public reacted with widespread protests and an impressive civil disobedience movement, to which the military responded with appalling and indiscriminate violence in an attempt to cow the population into submission. More than a year later, the military remains in power but faces widespread opposition and has been unable to assert full control or garner domestic or international legitimacy. Its brutal efforts to suppress opposition have failed and have also cost it what little respect it might have enjoyed, while also provoking a humanitarian disaster. The remnants of the NLD, along with others, have formed a National Unity Government, and numerous armed groups, known as People's Defense Forces, are actively fighting against the military, as are some ethnic armed groups. It is impossible to predict how things will play out, but as of the time of this writing the prospect is for more violence, further economic decline and humanitarian hardship, and continued instability for some time.

Indonesia and Myanmar Parallels

Although one has to be careful not to take it too far, there are interesting parallels between the Indonesian and Myanmar situations at the onset of reforms. Both boasted diverse populations with a dominant but not exclusive religion. Both had been under authoritarian and/or military rule for decades before unexpectedly beginning to reform. Both were highly centralized states that were vulnerable to centrifugal forces in the form of separatist movements. In both countries, the military played a major, institutionalized role in both internal security (targeting separatist movements) and in politics.

There were, of course, also many important differences. While Suharto was of the military, his rule over time became much less dependent on the military as an institution; in Myanmar, though, the institution of the military dominated, especially after 1988. Also, Myanmar's military rule had been more consistently repressive and brutal than Indonesia's. Its uniformed rulers had badly mismanaged the economy for decades, while Suharto at least produced significant economic growth and reduced poverty. Indonesia had never been as isolated as Myanmar; even at its low point internationally, during the East Timor crisis, Indonesia did not become a pariah nation.

An Unfinished Nation

Arguably the most important difference, however, was that Indonesia overall had a strong sense of nation, despite the separatist movements, whereas Myanmar did not. As I noted in chapter 7, Indonesia's founders had wisely established a national language that nearly everyone spoke and created a pre-independence movement that explicitly sought to create a national identity out of the country's diverse ethnic groups. The military reflected that diversity—one did not have to be from the dominant Javanese ethnic group to rise to senior levels.

Myanmar, on the other hand, remained—and remains to this day—what historian Thant Myint-U has called an "unfinished nation."[1] This lack of a sense of nation—and the identity politics that stem from it—remains at the root of many of the country's problems and conflicts to this day. While Washington (myself included) for many years saw the fundamental issue in Myanmar as democracy versus dictatorship, once you live in the country for a while you will likely conclude that—essential as democracy is—Myanmar's most difficult long-term challenge is to build a true sense of nation that incorporates all of its peoples and communities in a respectful and dignified manner. Of course, the 2021 military coup necessarily returned the fight against dictatorship to the forefront; however, it did not change the importance of tackling the longer-term challenge of building a shared sense of nation.

The story of how this came to be would require an entire volume, at least, but it is so important to understanding Myanmar today that I will try to hit some of the key points. The majority Burman or Bamar ethnic group has long dominated the country's central Irrawaddy (Ayeyarwady) River valley, while a large number of other ethnic groups have populated the more mountainous border areas that form an upside-down "U." Even in pre-colonial days, various Burmese kingdoms had only intermittent and incomplete control of many of these border areas. For example, the Rakhine in the west had boasted their own, often

---

1 Thant Myint-U, "Myanmar, An Unfinished Nation," *Nikkei Asia,* June 17, 2017, https://asia.nikkei.com/Politics/Myanmar-an-unfinished-nation.

powerful Arakan Kingdom, while various princes had governed the Shan Hills to the east.

The British did little to integrate the various ethnic groups or to create any sense of nation. In fact, they emphasized ethnic identity and division, categorizing different communities as "races" with certain characteristics and identifying specific regions by "race." They favored particular groups for different roles, relying for example on the "martial" Kachin and Karen to man the colonial army. They also divided the country by how they managed it—direct oversight over the lowlands, including the Bamar heartland, and indirect rule over the mountainous "Frontier Areas," which enjoyed greater autonomy and so generally had a more favorable view of the British than did the Bamar.

The British also brought in thousands of Indians to take important civil service positions and to help manage the economy. Millions more came of their own accord, seeking opportunity in a land that seemed more promising than their own. In the 1920s, two-thirds of Rangoon's population was Indian and the city competed with New York to be the world's largest immigration center.[2]

Intentionally or not, all of these steps had the effect of disempowering the majority Bamar, fueling resentment toward both the British and others seen to have benefited from colonial rule. A Bamar-dominated independence movement, which came to be led by Aung San, developed in the 1930s. It sought independence, first and foremost, but also a unitary state. The outbreak of World War II presented this movement with an opportunity. The fabled Thirty Comrades—nationalists led by Aung San—left Burma to obtain military training from Japan and then returned to lead their new Burmese Independence Army (BIA) in combat alongside the Japanese against the British. Meanwhile, Karen and Kachin units remained loyal to the British. In 1942, as the Japanese invading force pushed the British back to India, BIA forces encountered demobilized Karen soldiers in the Irrawaddy Delta, resulting in a series of massacres by the BIA and Karen revenge attacks.

When the tide of combat shifted a few years later and the Japanese were in full retreat, Aung San and company switched sides and joined the Allies. Post-war, Aung San used his domestic popularity and leadership of the BIA first to avoid arrest by the British (for having fought alongside Japan) and then to bargain for independence. Part of the agreement with London on independence was that the new army

2 Thant, "Myanmar, An Unfinished Nation."

would include roughly equal parts of previously pro-Japan BIA forces and pro-UK Karen and Kachin forces.

From World War to Internal Strife

The new nation barely had a moment of peace. A rival member of the Thirty Comrades conspired to assassinate Aung San and much of his cabinet in July 1947, and a second member led a communist insurgency that quickly threatened Rangoon. Only with the help of its Karen battalions was the Burma army able to fend off the communists. The Karen, however, wondered if they should be fighting for their own independence rather than for "Burma." They quickly fell under suspicion, resulting in the start of a conflict between the Burma army and the Karen National Union (KNU) that continues to this day.

In his brief time in de facto power (formal independence would only come in early 1948), Aung San tried to find a formula that would allow the new country to hold together. In early 1947 he met with Chin, Kachin, and Shan leaders in the town of Panglong, Shan State, to discuss a way forward. In the resulting Panglong Agreement, the Chin, Shan, and Kachin agreed to join the Union of Burma in return for significant autonomy and the right to secede in ten years if they were unhappy with the Union (the Kachin traded the right to secession for additional territory). They also agreed that the country's new constitution would create Shan, Kachin, and Karenni states, and a Chin territory. Unfortunately, ethnic communities outside of the Frontier Territories—the Karen, Arakan, and Mon, for example—were not included, so Panglong was only a partial deal.[3] Moreover, with Aung San's assassination, Burma's new leaders were not invested in the agreement and never delivered on the promised autonomy.

The 1950s offered parliamentary democracy but also political strife, instability, and any number of conflicts. In addition to the communists and the KNU, the Burma army had to fight Chinese Nationalist forces that had fled Mao's China and were—with U.S. support—seeking to regroup in eastern Shan State. By the early 1960s, this instability and Prime Minister U Nu's agreement to begin talks with the Shan,

3 Ye Htut, "Myanmar's Long Journey to Peace Starts in Panglong," *Straits Times,* August 31, 2016, https://www.straitstimes.com/opinion/myanmars-long-journey-to-peace-starts-in-panglong.

Karenni, and Chin on federalism prompted army commander General Ne Win to seize power, marking the onset of fifty years of military rule.

Ne Win's Coup

Ne Win's 1962 coup was primarily in response to political instability and the military's fear that talk of federalism could splinter the country, but it also was a Bamar nationalist move designed to restore the majority ethnic group to its previous dominant status. Ne Win forced hundreds of thousands of Indians to leave the country, shut off new immigration, kicked out many non-Indian foreigners, and rejected ethnic minority nationalism and autonomy.[4] He created a one-party state, led by his Burma Socialist Programme Party (BSPP), and offered his vision of a "Burmese Way to Socialism," which was isolationist, xenophobic, and Bamar-centric.

Over the next several decades, Ne Win and successor military rulers would reject any ideas of autonomy or federalism, insisting on a strong unitary state and engaging in regular battles with a variety of ethnic minority insurgent groups in the border areas. They also institutionalized deeply problematic concepts of ethnicity and identity. They accepted diversity in principle, but in practice pursued "Burmanization" of the country's history, language, education, and culture, pressuring all other ethnic groups to assimilate and suppressing attempts to develop or keep alive ethnic minority heritage. Rather than using institutions such as the military to integrate the country, as Indonesia had done, they ensured such institutions became the near-exclusive domain of the Bamar, who in their view were the only group that had unquestioned loyalty to the country.

Taing Yin Tha and Identity

The military also emphasized the concept of *taing yin tha* or "national races." This dangerous idea, which earlier had been used to promote unity among diverse indigenous communities, separated those ethnic groups that "belonged" in Burma from those that did not, with the

---

4 See Justin Wintle, *Perfect Hostage: A Life of Aung San Suu Kyi, Burma's Prisoner of Conscience* (New York: Skyhorse Publishing, 2007); and Thant Myint-U, *River of Lost Footsteps: Histories of Burma* (New York: Farrar, Straus and Giroux, 2006), chapter 12.

criteria ostensibly being whether said group existed in the country prior to the British arrival in 1824. In later years, the military would identify a rather arbitrary number of 135 major and minor ethnic groups that were *taing yin tha*, and introduce a constitutional provision that granted full citizenship to people based on whether they were a member of one of the national races (or "indigenous.")[5]

Today, these concepts of categorizing people by ethnicity and by whether or not they belong to an indigenous group loom large in everyday life and politics. When you meet an ethnic minority individual for the first time, chances are that he or she will identify by ethnicity and religion, not as a "Myanmar" person. Ethnic minorities tend to oppose proposals to remove ethnic and religious identifiers from government documents, seeing such proposals as yet one more effort to strip away their own heritage. People almost always include their ethnicity and religion not only on any government forms, but also on résumés and the like.

Identity is an even bigger challenge for those who are not *taing yin tha*. If you are Indian, Chinese, or Nepalese (Ghurka), obtaining basic documents, including passports, is a nightmare, even if your family has lived in the country for generations. In truly Orwellian fashion, people who might be part Indian, Chinese, or another nonindigenous community are required at immigration offices to wait in a "mixed blood" line. Similarly, people who do not fit neatly into the government's categories are often forced into one of them. For example, a friend who wrote on a passport application form that she was Bamar and Muslim was told by the immigration officer that she could not be both. If she was Bamar, she had to be Buddhist. When she insisted she was Muslim, the officer changed her ethnicity on the form to "Bengali."

All of this both reflects and is reflected in the overwhelming fear many people have that, if they are not vigilant, the survival of their ethnic group and/or religion will be threatened. Some of this is the inevitable fear that comes with living next to the two most populous countries in the world, China and India, but it goes beyond that. It relates in part to the great importance of Buddhism, particularly for the Bamar majority, and the fear that their Bamar Buddhist identity is at

---

5 For a detailed history and explanation of *taing yin tha,* see Nick Cheesman, "How in Myanmar 'National Races' Came to Surpass Citizenship and Exclude the Rohingya," *Journal of Contemporary Asia* 47, no. 3 (May 27, 2017): 461–83, https://doi.org/10.1080/00472336.2017.1297476.

risk. I cannot tell you how many times I have heard people point out that Afghanistan and Indonesia "used to be Buddhist," suggesting that, if the Bamar let down their guard for a moment, Muslims would take over and Burmese Buddhism would disappear. A Rakhine member of Parliament defended human rights violations against the Rohingya by telling me that he would support any means necessary to "protect my race." When one enters the Ministry of Labor, Immigration and Population in Nay Pyi Taw, one sees posted prominently the Immigration Department's motto: "The earth cannot swallow a race, but another race can."

This obsession with ethnic and religious identity—and the corresponding lack of a national identity—is Myanmar's original sin. One can blame the British, the military, or whomever, but it has been and remains a monumental challenge to the country's ability to become a complete nation that enjoys peace, stability, and democracy.

Ne Win's "Burmese Way to Socialism"

Prior to Ne Win's 1962 coup, Burma was struggling to make democracy work and, as noted above, faced separatist and communist insurgencies. On the other hand, its economy, civil service, and education system ranked pretty well relative to its neighbors, and it enjoyed some status as a regional airline hub as well as home to a Johns Hopkins University satellite campus. In other words, it was not in a state of disaster.

The coup, and the policies that Ne Win subsequently put in place, set the country on a downhill trajectory that lasted for decades. The coup leader's hyper-nationalism and fear of outside intervention led him to isolate the country, kick out the large Indian population—which included many able administrators and entrepreneurs—and nationalize businesses. He expelled foreign education institutions, including missionary schools, along with the Ford Foundation and Asia Foundation, and pursued a disastrous socialist-autarkic economic strategy that sent the country in the wrong direction. By 1987, Ne Win's economic policies had so impoverished Burma that it won admission to the United Nation's group of the world's "Least Developed Countries," officially marking it as one of the globe's ten poorest states.[6]

---

6 Committee for Development Planning, *Report on the Twenty-Third Session: Supplement No. 10*, E/1987/23, UN Economic and Social Committee, November 21–24, 1987, https://undocs.org/en/E/1987/23.

Politically, Ne Win arrested thousands of opponents, suppressed civil and political liberties, and imprisoned ethnic minority leaders, including the country's first president, Sao Shwe Thaik, who died in prison. In border areas, the Burma army, known as the *Tatmadaw*, pursued its brutal "four-cuts" strategy—cutting off food, funds, intelligence, and recruits—to try to defeat ethnic insurgent forces such as the Kachin Independence Organization (KIO), Shan State Army, the KNU, as well as the Chinese-backed Communist Party of Burma. The Communist Party of Burma eventually imploded in 1989, but ethnic insurgent groups continued to fight.

U.S.-Burmese Relations Under Ne Win

Prior to Burma's independence, U.S. interests had been limited to the work of Baptist missionaries, who were particularly active in the Kachin, Chin, and Karen regions of the country, and of course to Burma's strategically important position as a major supply route to China during World War II. The missionaries' work, along with the many schools they established and ran, produced memories and relationships that continue to matter today. Most Americans and Burmese are unaware of the country's World War II history, though it is still possible to find in Kachin a few veterans of the war-era Kachin Scouts, who fought bravely alongside U.S. soldiers against the Japanese. I met a handful of former Scouts in Myitkyina, the capital of Kachin State, in 2019. One invited me to return the following year to celebrate his hundredth birthday.

From independence through the early 1970s, Washington's policy toward Burma was a function of the Cold War, and particularly of the fear either that the new country's socialist-oriented leaders would lean too far toward China and communism, or that the country would fall to Chinese-backed communist aggression. Even after the 1962 coup, the primary American concern was that Ne Win would align with China and/or follow the Chinese line of criticizing the U.S. war in Vietnam. We did not care for his policies at home, but because of the Cold War kept our focus on the country's perceived vulnerability to communism.[7]

---

7 Kenton Clymer, *A Delicate Relationship: The United States and Burma/Myanmar since 1945* (New York: Cornell University Press, 2015).

Ne Win was cool toward the United States, but then he was cool toward almost all foreign countries. He closed the country off to the world and rebuffed efforts by Washington, Beijing, and others to woo him. He was particularly unhappy about the CIA's covert support for Chinese Nationalist (Guomindang) troops in Shan State, and about the slights he felt he had endured during his 1960 visit to the United States. President Johnson invited him to Washington in 1966 and gave him red-carpet treatment. That helped warm the relationship somewhat but did not fundamentally alter it.[8]

As U.S. relations with China developed in the 1970s, Washington's focus in Burma shifted more to narcotics. Burma had become one of the world's leading producers of opium and heroin. The history of how this happened is beyond the scope of this book, but in brief it revolved around various armed groups—ranging from the Chinese Nationalist forces who fled China after Mao's victory to 1980s drug kingpin Khun Sa's private army—taking advantage of the lawlessness, corruption, and conflict in the Golden Triangle (the area where Thailand, Laos, and Myanmar meet) to produce and market opium and heroin on a global scale. With that heroin reaching the streets of New York, Washington spent over $80 million during the late 1970s and 1980s to support the Burmese government's questionable anti-drug efforts, providing helicopters and planes as well as training. Because U.S.-Burma relations during this period remained cool—due to Ne Win's wariness of the United States and U.S. unhappiness with his repressive and destructive policies—narcotics cooperation provided one of the few channels of communication between the two governments.[9]

1988

The year 1988 marked a major turning point both for Burma and for U.S. policy toward it. After years of economic decline, Ne Win in late 1987 —allegedly on advice from his numerologist—abruptly withdrew currency notes from circulation, wiping out many people's limited savings and fueling the public's unhappiness with his rule. As inflation rose quickly in early 1988, a series of student-led demonstrations— some of which the army harshly suppressed—culminated in the historic August 8, 1988 (8-8-88) uprising, in which hundreds of thousands of

---

8 Clymer, *A Delicate Relationship*, 218–19.
9 Clymer, *A Delicate Relationship*, chapter 12.

people took to the streets to demand reform and democratic change. Aung San Suu Kyi, the daughter of independence hero Aung San but someone who had lived outside of the country for years, happened to be in the country at the time, visiting her ailing mother. Asked by protestors to use the power of her name and lineage to help the cause, she emerged as the top opposition leader, with her public arrival marked by a speech to an estimated five hundred thousand people at the historic Shwedagon Pagoda on August 26.

Ne Win had resigned in July, and for several weeks the military appeared unsure how to respond to the protests. Finally, in late September, the military asserted control and announced the formation of a new government, the ominously named State Law and Order Restoration Council (SLORC), led by General Saw Maung. The SLORC almost immediately began a violent crackdown on the protests. Within days the military killed an estimated three thousand demonstrators, arresting thousands more and causing others to flee to the border areas or into Thailand. The protests failed, but years later many people would point to 8-8-88 as the start of the country's march toward democracy.

Shortly after the crackdown, the SLORC surprisingly authorized political parties to form. A few days later, Aung San Suu Kyi and her colleagues formally registered the NLD party and began campaigning around the country. Continuing its schizophrenic approach, in July 1989 the SLORC placed Aung San Suu Kyi under house arrest, rounded up other NLD leaders, and then a few months later set parliamentary elections for the following May. The NLD won 60 percent of the vote and 80 percent of the seats. The official military party won only ten seats, the first of several times the military would be surprised to learn it was not popular. The SLORC responded by announcing that the elections had not really been for Parliament, but rather for members of a constitutional drafting body, and arrested most of the NLD candidates.[10]

The SLORC's actions in 1988–90 provoked outrage in many countries, including the United States. In Washington, the Reagan administration suspended military assistance immediately after the SLORC's brutal repression of the 1988 demonstrations. Over the next few years, Congress pushed for tougher measures, including sanctions, and the

---

10 "Burma: 20 Years After 1990 Elections, Democracy Still Denied," Human Rights Watch, May 26, 2010, https://www.hrw.org/news/2010/05/26/burma-20-years-after-1990-elections-democracy-still-denied.

Senate refused to confirm a new proposed U.S. ambassador to Rangoon, leaving our relations at the charge d'affaires level for more than twenty years. Although the Bush and Clinton administrations both initially resisted broad sanctions, congressional and later administration action put in place over the next several years a web of sanctions that banned new U.S. investment, greatly restricted imports from Burma, and required the United States to oppose loans from international financial institutions. The sanctions also included a list of individuals and organizations—added to a global grouping known as the Specially Designated Nationals (SDN) list—for whom any U.S. assets would be frozen and with whom Americans and U.S. companies could not do business.

Burma Becomes a Cause

From 1990 through 2007—coincidentally or not, the period during which Washington generally did not view Southeast Asia through a strategic lens—Congress effectively dominated U.S. policy toward Burma. It greatly limited what the executive branch could do (though in fairness there was little support in the executive branch for doing much) and framed the "Burma issue" almost totally as Aung San Suu Kyi and the NLD against the generals. Aung San Suu Kyi's courageous resistance to the military and role as symbol of the country's democracy movement won her the Nobel Peace Prize in 1991 and made her a global democracy icon. Her comments, when she would be released from house arrest for a while or was otherwise able to pass messages, greatly influenced Washington actions, including the application of sanctions and the U.S. decision not to recognize Burma's name change to Myanmar in 1989.[11]

Washington also had sympathy for the ethnic minority communities that were suffering so much from the military's brutal counterinsurgency campaigns, but few in Congress or the administration understood much about the complex set of insurgent groups, other than that they were fighting against a military we had determined was evil. The general expectation was that political reform leading to democracy and

---

11 For simplicity's sake, I am going to use the term "Myanmar" for the remainder of the chapter, as it is now widely recognized even by Aung San Suu Kyi and other pro-democracy politicians. Likewise, I will also use the now-standard English rendering of "Yangon," instead of "Rangoon."

a greatly reduced role for the military would facilitate peace with the ethnic minority groups.

The 1990s and 2000s also saw the development of what became known as the "Burma Lobby" in Washington, London, and elsewhere. This was an informal collection of individuals and groups that had adopted the Myanmar issue and devoted enormous effort and energy to pressing the U.S. and other governments to ratchet up pressure on the generals, including through sanctions. In Washington, the network included members of Congress, congressional staff, human rights groups, journalists, and other individuals with a strong interest in the country. They often were well connected with activists inside Myanmar, were in some cases very knowledgeable, and would come to wield significant influence over policy.

When I began as director of the Mainland Southeast Asia Office in mid-2005, Burma had become an international cause. Our policy was driven by a collective sense of outrage—which I shared—and a hope that sufficient international pressure eventually would force the generals to surrender power to Aung San Suu Kyi and her democratic following. We had almost no dialogue or engagement with the Myanmar military or government officials. Congress and the administration shared great concern about the overall lack of progress, continued human rights violations, and the country's growing economic and political reliance on China, but there were few ideas on what we might do differently and little appetite for a review of our policy. My first visit to the country, in late 2005, reflected our minimal engagement with the Myanmar authorities. As an office director, I was the most senior official the administration would allow to travel to Myanmar, and my only engagement with the government was a cursory meeting with a foreign ministry director general.

Years of Little Hope

Yangon in 2005–06 reminded me of a scene out of a 1950s Graham Greene novel. It was a city of dilapidated buildings and the light traffic that comes from people being unable to afford cars. There was none of the vibrancy one feels in Bangkok, Manila, or even 1990s Hanoi. Our embassy staff, working out of a run-down building downtown, looked out over a street embellished with anti-imperialist banners that one would have expected to see in Moscow or Havana in the 1960s.

My obligatory visits to NLD headquarters to see what remained of the party's leadership were depressing. The SLORC, which by then had wisely changed its name to the State Peace and Development Council (SPDC), had seen fit to release a couple of elderly party patrons from prison, as if that would convince people that the country was free and democratic. We would go to see these elderly gentlemen, always seated over an ancient wooden table on the second floor of their ramshackle party office. Special Branch officers who loitered across the street took pictures of everyone who entered or exited the office, including us. The "Uncles," as the NLD patrons were known, were courageous, but offered little hope and even less vision for what a future democratic Myanmar might look like.

One bright light in this otherwise dim picture was our American Center, the former United States Information Service library that for some reason the authorities did not shut down or block locals from entering. It was perhaps the only safe place in the city for people—mostly young people—to go, study, and talk freely. I vividly remember my first visit. The embassy had invited maybe fifteen to twenty activists and students to join me in a roundtable discussion. As they filtered into the room, each activist introduced themself to me, usually by telling me their name and then how many years they had spent in prison. It was both heartbreaking and inspiring. Many had spent more than a decade in prison, in horrific conditions, yet here they were taking risks again to talk about how they could help their country move forward. Years later, during different times, I would meet literally dozens of parliamentarians, government officials, professors, and activists who would tell me how much the American Center had meant to them during those most difficult times.

At the time, we struggled to see any sign that the regime would change its decades-old hardline approach. The new post–Ne Win military government had shifted away from socialism toward a sort of corrupt, kleptocratic capitalism, with any number of policies that simply made no sense if the goal was economic development. The regime set the official exchange rate for the *kyat* at an absurdly high level, making exports noncompetitive while allowing well-connected people to make a killing on the arbitrage between the official and black-market rates. Colonels and majors told farmers what to plant, when and how to fertilize their crops, and what price they would get for those crops. In one example of its bizarre policies, the SPDC in 2006 decreed that all farmers with an acre of land or more had to grow physic nuts (*jatropha*) to produce biofuel. The government, however, did not establish the facilities needed to process the nuts into biofuel, resulting in enormous waste and cost, most of which was borne by poor farmers. Economist Sean Turnell remarked, "The whole episode is illustrative of a more profound and pervasive system of centralized and often irrational decision making that lies at the heart of Burmese agriculture."[12]

Politically, after ignoring the 1990 parliamentary elections, the SPDC in 1992 established a National Convention that was to draw up a new constitution. The SPDC invited different parties to join, but the NLD withdrew from the process in 1995, calling it an undemocratic sham. The Convention was dormant from 1996 to 2003. In August 2003, Prime Minister General Khin Nyunt announced that the SPDC would revive the National Convention as part of the regime's seven-step "roadmap" to national reconciliation and "disciplined democracy." The plan was for the Convention to draft a new constitution, which would then be submitted to a national referendum for approval, after which the country would hold national elections. It was clear, however, that the military would be calling the shots throughout, and that the prospects of the roadmap leading to substantial, positive change were slim. As a result, the NLD and many ethnic minority groups boycotted the Convention.[13]

Khin Nyunt's announcement of the roadmap came just a few months after pro-regime thugs—led by members of the SLORC-inspired Union Solidarity and Development Association (USDA)—attacked an NLD convoy carrying party leader Aung San Suu Kyi near the town of Depayin, in central Myanmar. According to numerous reports, the attackers beat to death as many as seventy NLD members and supporters in an unprovoked and appalling attack from which Aung San Suu Kyi herself barely escaped. The regime, which had released Aung San Suu Kyi from house arrest a year earlier, placed her under arrest again, apparently for having allowed pro-regime elements to assault her convoy.[14] The incident provoked widespread condemnation around

12 Ed Cropley, "Myanmar's Nutty Scheme to Solve Energy Crisis," Reuters, March 11, 2008, https://www.reuters.com/article/idUSBKK16771520080312.
13 Wai Moe, "Junta Pushes the 'Seven-Step Roadmap' Forward Despite Flaws," Irrawaddy, December 3, 2007, https://www2.irrawaddy.com/article.php?art_id =9500.
14 Zarni Mann, "A Decade Later, Victims Still Seeking Depayin Massacre Justice," Irrawaddy, May 31, 2013, https://www.irrawaddy.com/news/burma/a-decade -later-victims-still-seeking-depayin-massacre-justice.html.

the world, even among normally reticent ASEAN neighbors. The SPDC's announcement of the roadmap probably was intended, in part, to respond to the global outrage.

Meanwhile, the military had pursued a two-pronged, divide-and-rule approach toward the many ethnic minority armed groups with which it had been fighting for years. On the one hand, General Khin Nyunt negotiated ceasefire agreements with several groups, including the powerful Kachin Independence Organization (KIO). On the other hand, it pursued other groups, including the KNU and Shan State Army, with its ruthless four-cuts tactics, literally burning, raping, and pillaging its way through territory controlled by those groups.[15] It encouraged factions within the insurgent groups to break away, offering arms and a virtual license to engage in illegal activities—especially drug and timber smuggling—in return for aligning with the military against their former brethren. In doing so, Khin Nyunt and company won some tactical victories, but also helped create a massive illegal economy—still there today—dominated by ruthless men with guns along much of the country's border with Thailand and China.

As a result of all of this conflict and massive human rights abuses, the State Department estimated in 2007 that there were over 140,000 refugees—the vast majority members of ethnic minority communities fleeing the military's offenses and egregious human rights abuses—from Myanmar living in camps in Thailand, along with some half-million internally displaced people.[16] This did not even count displaced and stateless Rohingya in Rakhine State and Bangladesh, a group that will be discussed later. So Myanmar in 2007 was a net exporter of refugees and drugs, adding to its status as one of the most troubled and troubling nations in the world.

In 2004, SPDC leader General Than Shwe purged and arrested General Khin Nyunt, placing him under house arrest for the next several years. Some had seen Khin Nyunt as offering the possibility for progress, as he had been one of the few generals willing to engage with foreign governments, had pursued ceasefire agreements with ethnic armed groups and, reportedly, had advocated for dialogue with Aung

---

15 See, for example, "License to Rape: The Burmese Military Regime's Use of Sexual Violence In the Ongoing War in Shan State," Shan Human Rights Foundation and Shan Women's Action Network, May 2002, https://www.peacewomen .org/sites/default/files/vaw_licensetorape_shrf_swan_2002_0.pdf.

16 Figures from "Southeast Asia," U.S. Department of State archives, https://2001-2009.state.gov/g/prm/108723.htm.

San Suu Kyi. Others remembered him as the man who had imprisoned thousands of his fellow countrymen, sentencing them to years of isola-tion and often torture in Myanmar's notorious prisons. Many years later, feelings toward him still ran strong. When Yangon chief minister Phyo Min Thein, who himself had been imprisoned by Khin Nyunt for fifteen years, paid respects to the former general at an event at the end of 2018, he was lambasted by activists. Min Ko Naing, the highly respected former leader of the 1988 student movement who had spent years in prison, wrote bitingly, "Never turn a murderer into someone respectful."[17]

In another bizarre move, the government in November 2005, with no advance notice, moved the capital from Yangon to Nay Pyi Taw, a new, artificial city that had been quietly built over the past few years in a sparsely populated area two hundred miles north of Yangon. We—and much of the world, including many people in Myanmar—learned about it when the government suddenly told bewildered civil servants to get on buses heading to a new capital and to leave their families behind in Yangon. Even ministers had received only forty-eight hours' notice. The Foreign Ministry informed diplomats after the move had begun and told them they were not welcome in the new capital. If they had business with the government, they could send a letter by fax! Various rumors flowed about the reasons behind the move: fear of their own people, concern that the United States would invade, and/or General Than Shwe's desire to follow the tradition of the old Burmese kings, who liked to build their own capitals. Whatever the reason, it added to the feeling that the SPDC was beyond hope.

This is where Myanmar stood in mid-2007. The generals remained in charge, led by the enigmatic Than Shwe. Aung San Suu Kyi remained isolated under house arrest, while thousands of other pro-democracy activists suffered in prison. The military continued its brutal counter-insurgency campaigns against ethnic armed groups, while encourag-ing corrupt, illegal business dealings along the borders. The economy showed few signs of life and much of the country remained mired in poverty, with broken education and health systems starved for cash while the military continued to buy weapons. The regime continued to ignore pleas for dialogue and reform from the various UN special

---

17 Quoted in Kyaw Phyo Tha, "Analysis: Kowtowing to the 'Prince of Evil,'" *Irra-waddy*, January 3, 2019, https://www.irrawaddy.com/news/analysis-kowtowing-prince-evil.html.

envoys sent by the UN secretary-general over the years, and from the West. Even Myanmar's ASEAN partners were frustrated enough by the military's unwillingness to change that they in effect forced it to give up its chairmanship of the group in 2006. Myanmar increasingly was leaning on China for support, and the Chinese were only too willing to help.

The Saffron Revolution

Then, in the summer of 2007, a rise in fuel prices sparked demonstrations, led initially by some of the former students who had been involved in the 1988 uprising. Over the next several weeks, the demonstrations grew and spread, as Buddhist monks—hugely influential in society—joined and often led the demonstrations. By mid-September, daily demonstrations of tens of thousands of people, in a movement dubbed the "Saffron Revolution" because of the color of the monks' robes, gave rise to hope that this could be a moment of democratic change. Many people thought the military would not open fire on Buddhist monks.

I had just returned from a visit to Yangon, where among others I had met former 1988 student leaders Min Ko Naing and Ko Ko Gyi. They, it turned out, would be among the first to be arrested during the Saffron Revolution, but the emergence of the monks offered hope nonetheless. When demonstrators were allowed to bypass police barricades on University Avenue in order to walk to Aung San Suu Kyi's house, where she greeted them over the house's walls, the feeling was electric. I allowed myself to feel hope. Then, on the evening of September 26, the military raided numerous monasteries, arresting thousands of monks. The next day, they cracked down on demonstrations in Yangon, using tear gas and live fire to brutally suppress the protests. It was a repeat of 1988, except this time the violence was captured on film and broadcast to the world.

In Washington, the reaction was strong and instantaneous. We already had viewed the SPDC as one of the world's worst regimes, and watching soldiers gun down monks on the street made people angry. There was enormous pressure to respond firmly. Laura Bush, the First Lady, had a personal interest in Myanmar, which only added to pressure from the White House to do something. Over the next twelve to fifteen months, I would spend 70 percent of my time on Myanmar issues, including attending near-weekly Myanmar meetings of the

Deputies Committee in the White House Situation Room as well as providing daily dawn telephone briefings to senior NSC staff.

In those weekly meetings, the deputies agreed on three lines of approach, all of which were meant to increase pressure on the SPDC generals to change their behavior, and none of which involved actually talking with the SPDC. The first line involved ratcheting up sanctions, including placing prominent SPDC officials on visa ban and asset freeze lists. Some participants wanted to force U.S. companies such as Chevron, which had invested in Myanmar before we banned such investments, to disinvest. A few colleagues and I spent hours in those meetings explaining why forced disinvestment actually would benefit the SPDC, as it could take over Chevron's share of the oil and gas industry for free (they no longer needed Chevron's technology to make it work). The deputies eventually accepted our argument.

The second line of approach required intensive lobbying efforts in foreign capitals, particularly in Asia, to try to persuade others to join us in our pressure campaign. The Europeans were generally like-minded, as were to some extent the Australians. We faced a tougher sell in Japan, Korea, India, and among Myanmar's ASEAN neighbors. They were not happy with the SPDC, for sure, but they also did not believe in a pure "stick" approach, arguing that engagement was the only way to gain influence. Some NSC officials argued that we should in effect boycott ASEAN meetings until and unless ASEAN disowned Myanmar, but my colleagues and I were able to persuade the deputies that such an approach would only damage our relations with the other nine ASEAN members.

The final line of approach involved working through the United Nations to put broader pressure on the SPDC. Part of the effort was to get the UN Security Council involved, a tough task given that China and Russia would have to agree to any action. After much negotiation, we worked out a reasonably strong UN Security Council statement that "deplored" the SPDC's use of violence and called for peaceful negotiations among the parties in the country. We also worked to support the efforts of the UN special envoy, Ibrahim Gambari, to try to facilitate some kind of internal dialogue. Gambari had an impossible task, as it turned out. The regime was not interested in any kind of dialogue, and after a while Gambari considered it a victory just to get a visa to visit the country. The more he tried to be "diplomatic" in order to stay in the game, the more frustrated Aung San Suu Kyi and others became with him. It finally got to the point that he was literally knocking on the door of her house in Yangon, and she was refusing to let him in.

Although the Bush administration believed in the cause and took a hard line vis-à-vis Myanmar, it was not hard enough for some. I met regularly with Washington-based human rights groups and other NGOs, and they consistently complained that we were not doing enough on the sanctions front, i.e., if we would just adopt this or that sanction, it might do the trick. There was zero reason to believe they were right, but they were adamant. Some on the Hill took a similar approach. I remember meeting with House staffers one afternoon. In a conversation that foretold debates a decade later in the context of the ethnic cleansing of the Rohingya, one staffer complained that I did not seem angry enough about the military's crackdown. He asked, "Where is the outrage?" I told him that anger was not a strategy. In fact, anger and frustration *were* driving our policy. It was a feeling that, if we just pressed hard enough, something would have to give. I fought against some of the particularly unhelpful ideas along those lines, but at least initially did not question the overall approach.

Of course, for some, our policy was too tough. Several of our Asian counterparts argued privately that, by taking such an aggressive approach, we were losing influence and pushing Myanmar closer to China. Nobody said it in so many words, but the argument in effect was that the fight for democracy in Myanmar was all but hopeless, and we should not abandon our other interests there for such a lost cause. Others argued that our punitive approach was unlikely to be effective. At a Senate Foreign Relations Asia Subcommittee hearing at which I testified, senators Webb and Kerry—both veterans of the Vietnam experience—questioned me aggressively on the administration's approach. They argued that sanctions alone would get us nowhere and that we should follow the example of our relationship with Vietnam, where engagement and dialogue had delivered more results than sanctions.[18]

Cyclone Nargis

Just six months later, on May 3, Cyclone Nargis tore into Myanmar's Irrawaddy Delta, killing more than one hundred thousand people and leaving a broad trail of utter destruction. President Bush, despite his

---

18 *Burma's Saffron Revolution: Hearing before the Subcommittee on East Asian and Pacific Affairs of the Committee on Foreign Relations*, 110th Cong. (October 3, 2007) (testimony of Scot Marciel), https://www.govinfo.gov/content/pkg/CHRG-110shrg44490/pdf/CHRG-110shrg44490.pdf.

intense dislike of the SPDC, focused on the damage and suffering, and immediately offered help. I accompanied PACOM Commander Admiral Tim Keating and USAID director Henrietta Holsman Fore to Yangon on May 12 to relay that assistance offer directly to SPDC authorities. We were met at the Yangon airport by Admiral Soe Thane. Soe Thane, who would go on to play a key role in the 2011–15 reforms, told me later that he had received instructions from the top to meet us and listen politely to what we had to say. He did that. Admiral Keating relayed President Bush's interest in helping and explained that he had ships not far offshore that could bring in aid by helicopters. Soe Thane's eyes widened when he heard that, and I imagined he was thinking that we wanted to use this as an excuse to invade. I asked Admiral Keating if he could allow Myanmar military personnel to ride in the choppers as a way to overcome the obvious lack of trust. He agreed, but it was still a bridge too far for the SPDC. They did not say no, but neither did they say yes. I had been in Asia long enough to know what that meant.

Just two days earlier, despite the enormous damage and confusion from the cyclone, the SPDC had gone ahead with a previously scheduled national referendum on the new draft constitution. It was approved overwhelmingly, though few deemed the vote credible. In testimony in front of the House Foreign Relations Asia Subcommittee on May 20,[19] speaking on behalf of the administration—I blasted the SPDC for proceeding with this referendum in the wake of the cyclone and for refusing to allow foreign experts to enter the country to help with relief. The administration's anger at the SPDC was again at a very high level. As reports came in of the SPDC arresting Myanmar citizens who tried to organize their own relief efforts, our frustration reached a peak.

Fortunately, ASEAN secretary general Surin Pitsuwan, supported by an emergency meeting of ASEAN foreign ministers that had ratcheted up regional pressure on Myanmar, won the SPDC's agreement to allow international aid to flow and some experts to enter the country. It was not perfect, but it was a marked improvement over the initial regime response.

---

19 *Burma in the Aftermath of Cyclone Nargis: Death, Displacement and Humanitarian Aid: Hearing before the Subcommittee on Asia, the Pacific and the Global Environment of the Committee on Foreign Affairs* (May 20, 2008) (testimony of Scot Marciel), https://www.govinfo.gov/content/pkg/CHRG-110hhrg42477/pdf/CHRG-110hhrg42477.pdf.

Until Cyclone Nargis, almost all of our Myanmar-related assistance had gone to groups and individuals outside the country. We supported independent media operating out of Thailand and Norway, and provided training to Myanmar activists in Thailand, in addition to humanitarian assistance to refugees and to health workers along the Thai-Myanmar border. We had been able to provide some cash grants to activists and civil society in the country via our embassy, but the amounts involved were very small. Now, in the aftermath of Nargis, we began to provide assistance inside the country. Initially, it was almost all via airlifts from Thailand, but over time we were able to direct funding to a nascent Myanmar civil society that had developed in response to the cyclone. After several months, when we felt immediate disaster-relief needs had largely been met, we faced some pressure from within the administration to end the assistance and return to the *status quo ante* of no aid. We pushed back and argued successfully that, by continuing to funnel assistance to Myanmar civil society, we had an opportunity to bolster a small but growing community that could contribute to real change in the country.

A New Approach

In January 2009, the Obama administration took office having committed to reach out and engage governments with which we had profound differences, provided that those governments showed a genuine interest in dialogue. This presented an opportunity for those of us working on Myanmar. With assistance from the Burma desk, I drafted a paper for incoming Secretary Hillary Clinton that argued for a new approach. We said that, while our past policy of heavy sanctions and pressure had been intellectually coherent and morally satisfying, it had not worked and was very unlikely to succeed in the future. We proposed that, without jettisoning our sanctions, we add engagement with Myanmar authorities to the policy mix. We were careful not to suggest that engagement alone would cause the SPDC to change its spots. Rather, engaging would allow us to build some relationships, improve our understanding of what was happening in the country, and thus better position ourselves to act effectively if and when a political opening occurred.

The reality was that, at that time, we knew almost nothing about the SPDC. We knew the names at the top of the leadership list: Than Shwe, Maung Aye, Thein Sein, Thura Shwe Mann, and the like. We had never met any of them, however, and even our embassy team had enjoyed only minimal contact with them or those immediately below them. We therefore mistakenly assumed that they all thought alike, at least in terms of openness to political reform.

Secretary Clinton welcomed our ideas and, in coordination with the White House, agreed to a full policy review. In February 2009, she publicly said that the administration was looking at options to improve its ability to promote progress in the country, noting that neither sanctions nor efforts to engage in the past had earned us significant influence. In late March our new Mainland Southeast Asia office director, Steve Blake, made a routine introductory visit to Myanmar. He visited the new capital, Nay Pyi Taw, where he surprisingly was granted a meeting with Foreign Minister Nyan Win. Subsequent accounts of that period have suggested that we sent Blake to Nay Pyi Taw as the opening gambit of our new engagement policy, but that was not the case. It was a routine visit of no policy significance on our side, though we took Nyan Win's decision to meet with him as a sign that the generals were interested in talking.

In the weeks that followed, I had the opportunity to meet Myanmar's permanent representative to the United Nations, Than Swe (no relation to General Than Shwe), who had come to Washington to participate in a broader East Asia Bureau meeting with representatives from ASEAN countries. Since the Myanmar charge d'affaires in Washington at the time was largely inactive and spoke no English, Than Swe seemed like a potentially better channel of communication. I began traveling to New York regularly to meet with him. He was well connected and surprisingly open, so we had frank and friendly conversations over many months that resulted in some minor positive steps (like the release of an arrested Myanmar American) and at least established a modest channel of communication.

Unfortunately, just as we were getting started, an American named John Yettaw decided to swim across Inya Lake in Yangon to Aung San Suu Kyi's residence, where she was under house arrest. The authorities detained him, but then decided to charge Aung San Suu Kyi for violating the terms of her house arrest. She went on trial in mid-May, just weeks before she was due, in theory, to be released from house arrest. Most observers, myself included, assumed the regime used Yettaw's strange swim as an excuse to keep her locked up ahead of the planned 2010 national elections.

In July 2009, while her trial was ongoing, newly confirmed assistant secretary Kurt Campbell, who would play a key role in Burma policy over the next few years, and I accompanied Secretary Clinton to the

ASEAN Regional Forum meetings in Phuket, Thailand. The secretary had given me the green light to meet informally with Myanmar foreign ministry officials on the margins of the meeting, and I had been authorized to tell them that we would consider lifting our investment ban if the regime released the opposition leader. Ahead of the meeting, I asked Clinton to let me go further and commit that we would lift the ban if they released her. After all, I argued, the offer that we would "consider" lifting it was pretty thin gruel. Secretary Clinton agreed, but then added, "You tell them that, if they imprison her, that's it. We will cut off all assistance." I gently pushed back, pointing out that the assistance was mostly going to support Myanmar civil society. Clinton said in no uncertain terms that she was having none of that and told me to make that clear to my interlocutors.

In any case, the regime followed the predictable route of convicting Aung San Suu Kyi and sentencing her to three years' imprisonment, though the court "generously" suspended half the sentence and allowed her to serve the remaining eighteen months under house arrest rather than in prison. It seemed yet another sign of the SPDC's unwillingness to compromise or to take even small steps that would have greatly improved its international standing.

In September, Secretary Clinton announced to the UN-hosted Friends of Burma group in New York that, as result of the administration's policy review, the United States would engage Myanmar at more senior levels, while holding on to existing sanctions. Both tools, she argued, were needed to try to achieve better results. She also said that the United States was open to easing sanctions and other restrictions should the authorities in Nay Pyi Taw show themselves willing to release Aung San Suu Kyi and take additional steps toward political opening.

Clinton's announcement followed by a month Senator Jim Webb's high-profile visit to Myanmar. The senator, who served as chair of the Asia Subcommittee of the Foreign Relations Committee and had for several years been a lone voice in Washington for more U.S. engagement with Burma, became the first American official to meet with General Than Shwe.[20] Although his visit was neither encouraged nor blessed by the administration, one has to assume that the SPDC—not understanding Washington any more than we understood Nay Pyi Taw—saw it as

---

20 Peter Walker, "Man Who Crossed Lake to Aung San Suu Kyi Home Leaves Burma," *The Guardian*, August 16, 2009, https://www.theguardian.com/world/2009/aug/16/john-yettaw-leaves-burma.

a positive sign from the United States. Senator Webb's visit and his consistent calls for a policy of engagement both nudged the administration forward and created political space for it to do so, both in Washington and in Nay Pyi Taw." The senator also succeeded in getting American citizen John Yettaw released from prison.

The Challenge of Initial Engagement

In November 2009, I accompanied Kurt Campbell on what would be the most senior-level administration visit to Myanmar in many years. As a condition for making the trip, we had insisted on being able to meet privately with Aung San Suu Kyi together with any other NLD leaders she wanted to include. The SPDC had agreed. When we arrived in Nay Pyi Taw, we learned that we would be able to see her, but not anyone else from the NLD. We took it as a sign of bad faith by the generals, and I advised Kurt that he should be firm in expressing our unhappiness with Prime Minister Thein Sein, whom we would meet the next day. Kurt followed that advice, and the meeting was somewhat stilted, uncomfortable, and disappointing. In hindsight, we were right to be unhappy, but I should have advised Kurt to express our unhappiness in a more subtle, Southeast Asian way.

The substance of the meeting with Thein Sein was otherwise predictable. Kurt laid out the administration's openness to engaging with Myanmar but made it clear that we hoped there would be progress in terms of release of political prisoners and the opening of some sort of broader national political dialogue that would include the NLD. Thein Sein took note of our ideas but was noncommittal, other than pointing to the national elections scheduled for 2010 as a major opportunity.

We met Aung San Suu Kyi at a nondescript Yangon hotel. She was still under house arrest, so Special Branch drove her to the hotel and waited for her outside. In the meeting, the opposition leader revealed both the charm and the steeliness (not toward us) that had made her such a formidable figure. She made it clear that she wanted to engage in dialogue with the military leaders and that she was not seeking revenge. The military, she said, had to be part of the solution. At the same time, she emphasized that there had to be tangible movement toward real civilian-led democracy; she was not looking for symbolic gestures.

The challenge with trips such as Kurt's is not only the substance but also the expectations. Diplomatic reality tells us that, after decades of minimal contact and very high levels of mistrust, one trip is very unlikely to change the trajectory dramatically. In fact, it would be ideal to make three or four trips to begin to build relationships and confidence before diving deeply into substance, especially on issues like fundamentally changing a country's political structure. The modern reality is, however, that—at least in Washington—people want instant results. It is madness, really, but that is the reality in which we operate. We tried in our post-trip briefings to the press and Capitol Hill to emphasize that the visit was the first step in what was likely to be a long process that might or might not produce positive results, but we could hear the clock ticking.

Kurt would return to Myanmar six months later for further discussions, and we also met senior Myanmar officials in New York and elsewhere, but as of mid-2010 there was little sign of movement inside the country. The policy debate in Washington centered on how we should consider Myanmar's planned November 2010 elections. On the one hand, it seemed clear that they would be significantly flawed. The regime's rules for participation led the NLD and several other key groups to announce they would boycott. On the other hand, a modest number of pro-democracy elements in the country decided to participate, arguing that it was the only opportunity to widen the political aperture. In the end, Secretary Clinton publicly called the process "deeply flawed," but we did not take a position on whether parties or individuals should boycott or position.

The elections proceeded and resulted in the pro-government Union Peace and Development Party (formed out of the old USDA movement) winning 76 percent of the seats in Parliament. The SPDC released Aung San Suu Kyi from house arrest a few days after the election. That was positive, but in our view did not presage any other significant change. The generals had kept her under wraps until they engineered the election outcome they wanted. Parliament "elected" former prime minister Thein Sein as president. Aung San Suu Kyi had told us a year earlier that she thought she could work with Thein Sein, but still our expectations were low.

Thein Sein Surprises

We were wrong, as were most Myanmar observers. Thein Sein gave a surprisingly open and reform-minded inauguration speech in March

2011, and within a few months began implementing important changes. In an unprecedented move, he invited Aung San Suu Kyi to meet with him in August, and the two began a dialogue that appeared to be genuine. That same month, he called for all ethnic armed organizations to join in a dialogue to try to end the country's decade-old civil wars. In September, Thein Sein announced that he was suspending the highly controversial Chinese-funded Myitsone Dam project in Kachin State. This was a stunning development and convinced a lot of skeptics that the change they were seeing in Myanmar was real, even if it was not clear how far the reforms would go.

By early 2012, the NLD was confident enough in the reform process that it decided to participate in parliamentary by-elections in April and won 43 of 45 open seats. Aung San Suu Kyi won one of those seats, bringing her to Nay Pyi Taw and highlighting the remarkable change in the country's political situation.

From 2012 to 2014, the Thein Sein government freed political prisoners, allowed the establishment of new political parties, eased restrictions on independent media and civil society, and carried out a wide range of economic reforms, including shifting to a market exchange rate. Internationally, the government opened up to the West, welcomed foreign experts and advice, and opened the door to foreign investors. Led by Minister Aung Min, the government's peace process produced a series of bilateral ceasefires, including with the powerful KNU and Restoration Council of Shan State (RCSS), and looked to be moving toward a potential nationwide ceasefire as an important stepping-stone to a national peace agreement.

The Obama administration reacted cautiously at first. In May 2011, Kurt Campbell gave a speech in which he expressed disappointment at what Washington had seen so far from the new government. A few days later, his principal deputy, Joe Yun, told a Congressional hearing that the administration was "not optimistic" that it would see any significant changes in the short term.

The mood began to change over the next several months. Despite setbacks such as the appearance near Myanmar of a ship believed to be carrying North Korean weapons and the military's breaking of the seventeen-year ceasefire with the Kachin Independent Organization, overall Myanmar's reform trajectory looked increasingly promising. Newly appointed special representative for Burma Derek Mitchell began traveling to Myanmar in late summer 2011, stepping up our engagement with both the Thein Sein government and the opposition.

Washington Responds

In November of that year, President Obama announced in Bali—on the margins of the Indonesia-hosted East Asia Summit meetings—that he had conferred with Aung San Suu Kyi the previous night and, based on that conversation, would send Secretary of State Clinton to Myanmar in a few weeks. He pointed to "flickers of progress" in Myanmar, and said the United States wanted to do everything possible to encourage further reform.[21]

A short time later, Hillary Clinton became the first U.S. secretary of state in fifty-six years to visit Myanmar, meeting with Aung San Suu Kyi in Yangon and with President Thein Sein in Nay Pyi Taw. She offered a carefully crafted, balanced message. The United States would encourage and support reforms, including by ending its opposition to international financial institution lending to Myanmar, initiating some small, targeted assistance programs within the country, and "considering" the possibility of exchanging ambassadors. At the same time, Washington's willingness to continue moving forward would depend on additional progress, including the release of remaining political prisoners and Myanmar ending its problematic military relationship with North Korea. She emphasized the need for further momentum behind the reform process.

For the next few years, the administration adopted what it called an "action-for-action" approach, in which Washington would ease sanctions and otherwise advance the relationship as it saw specific steps forward by Myanmar. Thus, following further releases of political prisoners and the successful April 2012 by-elections, Clinton announced five new steps: nominating an ambassador; opening a USAID mission; easing restrictions on U.S. NGO operations in the country; facilitating travel to the United States for pro-reform Myanmar officials; and beginning to ease restrictions on U.S. investments and financial service exports.

In September 2012, President Thein Sein and Aung San Suu Kyi both visited the United States (separately) around the UN General Assembly in New York. Aung San Suu Kyi naturally got most of the attention, but the administration ensured that President Thein Sein did

---

21 Brianna Lee, "During Clinton's Historic Visit to Burma, 'Flickers of Progress' Pave the Way for An End to Isolation," *Need to Know*, PBS, December 2, 2011.

not feel neglected. In his speech to the General Assembly, Thein Sein highlighted the country's recent reforms, including further release of political prisoners, the ending of pre-publication press censorship, and market-oriented economic reforms, while also pointing to earlier reforms to enable labor unions and promote worker rights.

During that visit and over the next several weeks, the administration eased constraints on Myanmar imports, implemented earlier decisions allowing it to support international financial institution lending, and further lifted restrictions on travel to the United States by key Myanmar officials. In October, the United States and Myanmar held their first Human Rights Dialogue in Nay Pyi Taw, with the United States represented by its assistant secretary of state for democracy, human rights and labor and a senior PACOM military officer (as a way to try to bring the Myanmar military into the human rights discussion).

How Best to Encourage Further Reform?

In November 2012, President Obama made a historic visit to Myanmar, meeting with President Thein Sein and Aung San Suu Kyi and speaking to a large audience at the University of Yangon. Consistent with past practice, the president sought to thread the needle between expressing support for the reform efforts to date and stressing the need for much more progress. Following his meeting with Thein Sein, Obama cautioned that the reforms to date were just the "first step" in a long road. After meeting with Aung San Suu Kyi, he made clear that U.S. policy was designed to "sustain the momentum for democratization."[22]

President Obama also touched on the biggest "fly in the ointment" in Myanmar's reform process. In Myanmar's Rakhine State, which lies on the border with Bangladesh, a horrific outbreak of violence between the ethnic Rakhine and Rohingya communities had occurred in June 2012, resulting in dozens of deaths and the displacement of tens of thousands of people. The violence highlighted the perilous state of the Rohingya, a Muslim community that had lived in Rakhine for generations but which the Myanmar government (and much of the public) viewed as illegal interlopers not deserving of rights. President Obama had decided to visit despite serious concerns over the treatment of the Rohingya,

---

22 "Remarks by President Obama and Daw Aung San Suu Kyi," White House, November 19, 2012, https://obamawhitehouse.archives.gov/the-press-office/2012/11/19/remarks-president-obama-and-daw-aung-san-suu-kyi.

with the administration believing that U.S. support for reform and re-formers offered the best chance of progress across the board. During his visit—and against the wishes of Myanmar authorities—he publicly highlighted our concerns about treatment of the Rohingya, calling for them to be treated with the same dignity as everyone else.[23]

As Myanmar continued to take two steps forward and one step back, some in Washington favored pushing forward with increased engage-ment, while others argued that we were moving too quickly. I happened to be in town for a brief visit a few months after Obama's Myanmar visit when I ran into a friend from a prominent human rights organiza-tion. He expressed concern that the administration was rushing ahead too quickly, noting all the problems that had not yet been resolved or even addressed in Myanmar. I disagreed, arguing that this was the first chance in fifty years for Myanmar to make progress, and we had to do everything we could to support the reform momentum. If we waited for Myanmar to fix all its problems before we did anything, we would lose any ability to influence developments.

Our brief conversation reflected a broader philosophical debate over not just policy toward Myanmar, but over how to support reform and change in any troubled nation. Smart and reasonable people can and will disagree on what is the best approach in any particular situation, but in the case of Myanmar the debate sometimes became bitter and personal, with some even implying willful neglect and bad faith on the part of those with whom they disagreed. As the saying goes, "In Wash-ington, if you want a friend, get a dog."

When I returned to Washington in mid-2013 to replace Joe Yun as principal deputy assistant secretary for East Asia and the Pacific, it was clear that Myanmar had come a long way, but equally clear that it still had a long way to go. On the positive side of the ledger, the country had gone from harshly repressive military dictatorship and pariah to a nascent, if seriously flawed, democracy in which most people enjoyed significantly greater freedom than they had only a few years earlier and much greater access to information (thanks to the government opening up the internet), and in which solid economic growth was beginning to bring greater prosperity to at least some people. A national peace process was underway that offered some hope of an end to sixty years of civil war.

---

23 Matt Spetalnick, Jeff Mason, "Obama Offers Praise, Pressure on Historic Myanmar Trip," Reuters, November 18, 2012, http://reut.rs/XUfFRR.

When I visited Myanmar in late 2013 for the first time in almost four years, I was stunned by the change. Physically, one could see lots of new construction and development, as well as much heavier traffic, which suggested increased prosperity for at least a portion of the population. More compelling, however, was that it no longer felt like a police state, though that was much less true for the Rohingya and in places where the military remained on the offensive against ethnic armed groups. People felt much freer to talk and share their views, opposition politicians—including Aung San Suu Kyi—were active inside and outside of parliament, civil society was operating pretty freely, and there was a sense of at least cautious optimism. Even in Nay Pyi Taw—which is a bizarrely designed government city with sixteen-lane, largely empty roads, ministry buildings purposely spaced far apart from each other, and a strong sense of emptiness—one could have real, substantive conversations. Parliamentary Speaker U Shwe Mann, a former high-ranking member of the SPDC, had emerged as an unlikely independent voice, much to the annoyance of President Thein Sein and many in the military.

The negative side of the ledger, unfortunately, was long. The 2008 constitution gave the military a guaranteed 25 percent of seats in parliament, which among other things constituted veto power over any proposed constitutional amendments. The military, despite going along with political reform to some extent, retained substantial power, remained unaccountable, and continued to engage in significant human rights violations regularly, particularly in the context of operations against ethnic armed groups. The military's lengthy ceasefire with the Kachin Independence Army (KIA) had ended in 2011, resulting in intense conflict and large numbers of displaced persons. The police and judiciary remained corrupt and largely incompetent, ensuring a lack of justice for all but the powerful and well connected. Ethnic minorities were still waiting for long-sought federalism, which would give them a much more significant voice in managing their affairs. And of course, the Rohingya community continued to languish, many in pitiful internally displaced person camps, without rights.

I went with Ambassador Derek Mitchell in early 2014 to see U Soe Thane, the former admiral who as minister in the president's office had become one of the key proponents of reform. I asked U Soe Thane how strong the reformers were within the cabinet. He laughed and said there were a few reformers, a few who were anti-reform, and the rest were waiting to see which way the wind blew. He made it clear that the reformists' hold on things was tenuous, and he stressed the need for continued U.S. support.

By 2014–15 Myanmar activists and some politicians were complaining that the reform momentum had slowed or even stalled. They pointed to the military's rejection of efforts to amend the constitution, the breakdown in the previously effective government-NGO political prisoner review committee, continuing arrests of peaceful protesters under the still-flawed peaceful assembly law, military violence against farmers seeking to recoup land that soldiers had previously confiscated, and the arrest and prosecution of several journalists. In late 2014, Aung San Suu Kyi complained that reforms had "stalled."[24] Although she did not mention the Rohingya, they also were continuing to suffer from severe institutionalized discrimination. Ahead of Secretary of State Kerry's August 2014 visit, House Foreign Affairs Committee chairman Ed Royce, in a letter to Kerry co-signed by dozens of his colleagues, argued that the administration was ignoring a number of concerning developments in its desire to move forward. The letter called for punitive measures, including re-imposition of certain sanctions.[25]

As has been the case in other countries that have shifted from authoritarian to more democratic systems, Myanmar's opening—including the liberalization of telecommunications, which led to explosive growth of social media, mostly Facebook—created opportunities not only for progress but also for groups to promote a much more troubling agenda. In Myanmar, nationalist Buddhist monks launched the "969 movement" to defend and promote Buddhism, particularly against the perceived threat of Islam. Over a few years, the 969 movement declined and was de facto replaced by the so-called Ma Ba Tha[26] movement, a widespread and diverse group of often influential monks who advocated for legislation and other efforts to "protect" Buddhism. Although Ma Ba Tha at the local level often provided useful community services and was not universally intolerant, it quickly became associated—especially internationally—with the views of some of its most hardline

24 "Aung San Suu Kyi: Reform Process 'Stalled,'" BBC News, November 5, 2014, https://www.bbc.com/news/world-asia-29919094.

25 Prashanth Parameswaran, "U.S. Policy on Myanmar Under Fire as Promise of Reform Dims," World Politics Review, October 7, 2014, https://www.world politicsreview.com/articles/14148/u-s-policy-on-myanmar-under-fire-as-promise -of-reform-dims.

26 Known in English as the Patriotic Association of Myanmar or the Organization for the Protection of Race and Religion, among other translations.

members, including the monk U Wirathu, whom *Time Magazine* famously featured on its cover as "The Face of Buddhist Terror."[27] In 2015 Myanmar's parliament passed four bills—colloquially known as the "Race and Religion Protection Laws"—that Ma Ba Tha had promoted, and that were widely viewed as targeting and discriminating against Muslims. Although the laws never were fully implemented, their passage added to the sense that reform was stalling, if not backsliding.

Myanmar, which had been forced by ASEAN back in 2006 to give up its scheduled chairmanship of that group, took advantage of its move out of pariah status to chair ASEAN and to host its annual summits in 2014. Because of that, President Obama again visited and used the opportunity to press Myanmar authorities to redouble their reform efforts. Obama stressed to Thein Sein the need to end the systematic persecution of the Rohingya and also highlighted the importance of amending the constitution to put it more in line with democratic principles. Although the tone of the visit was positive, administration officials were clear in their conversations with the media that they recognized that the early days of reform euphoria had given way to more difficult times. Deputy National Security Advisor Ben Rhodes told the *New York Times* that some reforms had continued, others had stalled or even moved backward, and that it was therefore a "mixed picture."[28] Ambassador Derek Mitchell stressed that the United States needed to be ". . . carefully engaged to promote change from the inside." He added that "We have no illusions about the challenges."[29]

2015: The Rohingya, Peace, and Elections

I was in daily touch with Derek throughout this period, and knew fully how concerned and frustrated he was, particularly with the lack of progress on the Rohingya issue. He, along with other like-minded diplomats and many visitors, constantly pressed the government to take

27 "The Face of Buddhist Terror," *Time,* July 1, 2013, http://content.time.com/time/covers/asia/0,16641,20130701,00.html.

28 "Press Briefing by Press Secretary Josh Earnest and Deputy National Security Advisor for Strategic Communications Ben Rhodes, 11/13/14," White House, https://obamawhitehouse.archives.gov/the-press-office/2014/11/13/press-briefing-press-secretary-josh-earnest-and-deputy-national-security.

29 Mark Landler and Thomas Fuller, "Obama Prods Myanmar Back Toward Democracy," *New York Times*, November 13, 2014.

steps to improve treatment for the Rohingya, but the reality was that little changed on the ground.

By mid-2015, hopes had shifted to the planned November national elections, which would be the NLD's first opportunity to compete in nationwide elections that we hoped would be free and fair. We poured a lot of money into technical support to ensure the elections were as free and fair as possible, and worked closely with the Union Election Commission and others to press for a fair and transparent process. Unlike in the 2010 elections, Myanmar authorities welcomed foreign observers. We and Congress both sent teams, as did the EU, Australia, and many others.

It was clear months ahead of the election that the race would come down to a battle between Thein Sein's Union Solidarity and Development Party (USDP), running on the success of their reforms over the past four years, versus Aung San Suu Kyi's NLD, running largely on her status as the longtime opposition leader and symbol of defiance and democracy. Her campaign message basically was: "I'm Aung San Suu Kyi. Trust me, and vote for the NLD." The USDP tried to paint her and the NLD as weak on protecting Buddhism. The NLD pushed back in part by deciding not to run any Muslim candidates. That decision, as well as Aung San Suu Kyi's refusal to speak up on behalf of the Rohingya, might have been smart politics in the short term, but it did not augur well for the future.

A month before the elections, Thein Sein hosted the highly anticipated signing of the Nationwide Ceasefire Agreement. The agreement, which had been negotiated over the past few years, had been designed to halt fighting, creating conditions for a political dialogue leading to a full peace agreement, which was expected to involve a federal structure that would give ethnic minority groups a much greater voice in running their affairs. Representatives from the ethnic armed organizations (EAOs) and the government/military had agreed on a text in March but could not overcome differences over which groups should be allowed to participate. The rebels insisted that the agreement include all EAOs (save the United Wa State Army and Nagaland rebels, who had no interest in joining). The military, however, rejected participation by three relatively new EAOs—the Kokang (formally the Myanmar National Democratic Alliance Army, or MNDAA), the Ta'ang National Liberation Army (TNLA), and the Arakan Army (AA)—on the grounds that they had not previously signed bilateral ceasefires. As a result, only eight EAOs were willing to sign the Nationwide Ceasefire Agreement. What

Thein Sein had hoped would be a big political win that would boost the USDP's electoral chances turned out to be a half-victory at best.

The elections were far from perfect—Rohingya and others were disenfranchised, some districts were deemed too insecure to allow voting, and so on—but in the broad scheme of things they were competitive and free. Millions of enthusiastic voters turned out and delivered a decisive victory to the NLD, which won 57 percent of the votes and nearly 80 percent of the elected seats in the national parliament (remember the military got 25 percent of the seats automatically, per the 2010 constitution). The USDP won less than 30 percent of the votes and an even smaller share of seats. Ethnic minority parties also fared poorly, as many voters in ethnic minority–dominated areas chose to vote strategically for the NLD as the best way to push the military-aligned USDP out of power.

In Yangon and other major cities, the election results prompted widespread celebrations and euphoria. For the first time in most people's lifetimes, they had been able to vote freely and choose the government they wanted. Although we had been studiously neutral in our engagement, there was no hiding the fact that nearly everyone in Washington with an interest in Myanmar also was celebrating. On November 9, 2015, with the 1990 election in mind, the big questions we were discussing were whether the military would honor the results and allow the transition to an NLD-led government to happen, and whether the military would agree to a constitutional amendment to allow Aung San Suu Kyi to become president.[30]

A few days after the election, President Thein Sein congratulated Aung San Suu Kyi on winning the election and committed to working with her to ensure a smooth transition. Military commander General Min Aung Hlaing likewise congratulated the NLD for winning the majority of the seats.[31] Over the next few months, neither the government nor the military did anything to threaten the transfer, but—in meetings with Aung San Suu Kyi—General Min Aung Hlaing rejected any constitutional change that would have allowed her to become president.

The new NLD-dominated parliament, which in an incredible turn included more than a hundred former political prisoners, began its

---

30 Article 59f specifies that individuals with foreign spouses or children cannot hold the position of president.
31 Annie Gowen, "Burmese President Congratulates Aung San Suu Kyi on Her Party's Lead in Elections," *Washington Post,* November 11, 2015.

session in February 2016. Unable to elect Aung San Suu Kyi president, the parliament chose instead her longtime aide, Htin Kyaw, and shortly thereafter voted to create a new position—state counsellor—that she would fill, in addition to being foreign minister. It was clear to all involved that, as state counsellor, Daw Suu (as she was often called) would run the government as a pseudo prime minister, and Htin Kyaw would follow her instructions. The military was angry with the creation of the new position and called the move unconstitutional. We and most of the international community—and no doubt the vast majority of the Myanmar public—were not upset. The military had created an artificial obstacle that prevented her from becoming president, but the election had given her a clear mandate to run the new government.

I had been nominated to replace Derek Mitchell as ambassador and hoped to get to Yangon before the new government took office in late March. My nomination was held up, however, due to disputes over sanctions. In response to complaints from our business community, Treasury had agreed—with interagency support—to allow U.S. companies to conduct trade operations through the main Yangon port, which was owned by a notorious crony on our sanctions list, Stephen Law. The solution was for Treasury to issue a general license that offered a narrow exemption from the ban on doing any business with Law or his companies. Unfortunately, Treasury was drafting this general license at the time I was going through my confirmation hearing and consulting with key senators, and I was prohibited from mentioning the forthcoming change in those discussions. When word of the general license leaked out, Senate Foreign Relations Asia Subcommittee chairman Cory Gardner was not happy that I had failed to mention this to him in the hearing or our private discussion. He put a hold on my nomination that took a while to resolve. Nonetheless, I was confirmed in time for my wife and I to arrive in Myanmar a few days before the new government's inauguration.

CHAPTER TEN

When Things Go South

The Aung San Suu Kyi Government

The mood in Yangon and Nay Pyi Taw in March 2016 was buoyant. Ahead of the NLD government's inauguration, expectations were high that the Aung San Suu Kyi–led government would reinvigorate the reform effort and the peace process, add to political and civil rights, and attract more desperately needed investment, especially from the West. We were more cautious on prospects for improved treatment of the Rohingya, because that issue had become such a third rail for Myanmar politicians.

As I made my initial calls as ambassador, I was struck by how many people, especially former political prisoners such as Yangon chief minister Phyo Min Thein and 1988 student movement leader Min Ko Naing, expressed their appreciation for U.S. support during the dark, pre-reform days. It had meant a lot to them, and they reciprocated with strongly positive feelings toward the United States. It reaffirmed to me the importance of always staying true to our values and supporting people who are struggling and sacrificing for freedom and democracy.

Although the new government took office with strong support and some remaining momentum from earlier reforms, it also faced a number of daunting challenges. It is worth briefly reviewing what at the time seemed to be the biggest obstacles to further progress.

- The military remained a constitutionally enabled powerful institution, with 25 percent of seats in parliament, which gave it the ability to block any constitutional amendments. The civilian government had little legal authority over the military, including its budget or its operations. Moreover, the commander-in-chief, under the constitution, had the right to name three powerful ministers: defense, home affairs, and border affairs (the latter had the lead role in promoting "development" in ethnic minority areas along the border). In addition, while the military had allowed a number of reforms to take place and accepted the most recent election results, it continued to see itself as a significant and legitimate political player, in fact as the one essential institution in the country. Moreover, it had not changed its behavior in the field and continued to commit significant human rights violations regularly and with impunity. Military-backed militias were operating in many border areas, misbehaving in all the ways undisciplined and unaccountable men with guns do. Finally, the military continued to play a major role in the economy, both through legal companies and through illegal activities, often in cahoots with militias, corrupt local businessmen, and others.

- The peace process appeared to have stalled after the October 2015 signing of the Nationwide Ceasefire Agreement. Other than the KNU, none of the most powerful EAOs had signed the agreement, and it was not clear how the new government would be able to chart a new path forward to bring in the non-signatories. More broadly, ethnic minority groups throughout the country, while generally supportive of Aung San Suu Kyi, wanted to see a change in how Nay Pyi Taw was going to work with them.

- The bureaucracy, the police, and the judiciary remained staffed largely by former military officers or military-appointed personnel. Aside from questions of loyalty, it was going to take a long time and a lot of work to change attitudes, reduce corruption, and develop a more service-oriented approach in these institutions. Moreover, the bureaucracy for decades had done little more than implement instructions from above; there was no system or culture within the bureaucracy of developing policy options, consulting with relevant stakeholders, or encouraging innovative thinking.

- The judiciary had no recent history of independence and was staffed largely by military-appointed judges who for years had taken guidance from military officials. More broadly, many laws were antiquated or inappropriate for a democratic government, and there was no strong, independent legal community.

- The NLD government had almost no experience in governing, as— through no fault of its own—it had been in opposition since its founding. This lack of experience, combined with a weak bureaucracy and the lack of strong institutions, would greatly complicate the new government's efforts.

- Meeting heightened economic expectations would be difficult. People had voted for the NLD because they wanted the military out and Aung San Suu Kyi in, but they also wanted better living standards. They would be patient for a while, but the NLD would have to show it could deliver economically. The window of opportunity—when Myanmar would be the "flavor of the month" among Western investors—would be limited.

- The election had given the NLD majorities in all but two regional and state legislatures, but the new government in Nay Pyi Taw would have to decide how much authority and responsibility it would grant to these legislatures and to the chief ministers (similar to U.S. governors) it would appoint. Also, the NLD would need to navigate its chief minister appointments carefully in Shan and Rakhine states, the two places where it did not win a majority.

- Aung San Suu Kyi would face enormous international pressure to address the institutionalized discrimination against the Rohingya community in Rakhine State. Some 140,000 Rohingya who had been displaced in the 2012 violence in the central part of the state near the capital of Sittwe remained in squalid internally displaced person (IDP) camps, with no rights and almost no access to education and health services. Others lived in their own villages, but also had few rights and faced severe restrictions on freedom of movement and access to health, education, and livelihoods. The status quo was not sustainable, but any move she made to improve conditions for the Rohingya would encounter strong opposition from the ethnic Rakhine, the military, and a considerable segment of society.

The Rohingya Issue Dominates

It did not take me long to run into the buzz saw of Myanmar identity politics, specifically vis-à-vis the Rohingya. I raised the Rohingya question in my first meeting with Aung San Suu Kyi, asking her how she planned to tackle it. She bristled slightly and complained that the world acted as if that were the only problem the country faced. She made clear that her top priority would be to re-energize the stalled peace process.

That certainly was a legitimate priority, but it was clear she was not anxious to address the politically fraught Rohingya problem.

In late April 2016, the embassy issued a statement lamenting the drowning—in a boat accident—of several Rohingya in Rakhine State. Mindful of the domestic audience, we "balanced" the statement by also expressing condolences for other losses of life around the same time in Rakhine. Since we had used the term "Rohingya" before, we were not prepared for the intensely hostile reaction our statement received. Nationalist monks and others demonstrated in front of the embassy, I received death threats, and some of our local staff were berated on the streets. During my introductory call on Home Affairs minister General Kyaw Swe in early May, he criticized me for using the term "Rohingya," saying I should "respect Myanmar's traditions." I responded that I had full respect for Myanmar's traditions, but Myanmar also needed to respect fundamental human rights. It was what we diplomats like to call a "frank" discussion.

It is almost impossible for outsiders to understand how or why the use of the simple term "Rohingya" is so toxic in Myanmar. Some of it is pure prejudice, but it goes beyond that. It relates to the population's view of national identity, and specifically to the question of so-called national races. To most people in Myanmar, using the term "Rohingya" to refer to the community of some 1.3 million people in Rakhine State, whose forefathers mostly came from the Chittagong region of Bangladesh, suggests that they are an indigenous group and thus have certain inherent political rights, including the right to citizenship and—this is more of a stretch—the right to some level of autonomy as an ethnic group.

For many people, having been exposed for years to propaganda about the threat to the nation and to Buddhism from the potential flood of Muslim immigrants from Bangladesh, it is not a big leap to believe that granting this community status as "indigenous" would lead to a massive influx of so-called Bengalis from Bangladesh that would upset the demographic balance and put their culture and their "race" at risk. This thinking explains the ongoing debate about when this community first came to Myanmar (remember, if they came before 1824, they would be a "national race") and the insistence of many that they are "illegal immigrants" or "Bengalis" (the latter implying they are foreign immigrants). It also explains that what to us in the West seems like a simple matter of calling the community by the name it prefers prompts such a hostile reaction. (I am not trying to justify the hostility to the use of the word "Rohingya," only to explain it.)

When I met with Aung San Suu Kyi again a few days after our statement, she raised the matter with me and asked me—diplomatically—not to use the term "Rohingya." She explained that she was not trying to argue the case for the term either way, but said its use led to emotional, even violent, reactions that made addressing the substance of the issue that much harder. I was noncommittal but thought she had made a fair point that warranted consideration.

Aung San Suu Kyi's request might not have been a big problem if it had stayed private, but someone in the foreign ministry decided to leak it to the press later that same week, just a day or two before I was to give my first major speech as ambassador. I avoided the subject in my remarks, but naturally the Western journalists present jumped all over it, asking if I would agree to Daw Suu's request. I waffled in the best diplomatic tradition, referring to the global U.S. practice of calling groups by the name they prefer but carefully avoiding use of the actual term "Rohingya." I thought I had skillfully escaped, but the next day Reuters and other news agencies published stories with headlines such as "New U.S. Ambassador to Myanmar Says He Will Keep Using Term 'Rohingya,'" and "U.S. Defies Myanmar Government Request to Stop Using Term Rohingya."[1] Those headlines won me some praise in the United States but stoked more anger and anti-Americanism in Myanmar.

Less than two weeks later, when Secretary of State John Kerry visited, I knew he would have to address the issue. I consulted with Assistant Secretary of State for East Asia and the Pacific Danny Russel, who arrived in Nay Pyi Taw shortly ahead of Kerry. We agreed that the secretary would need to use the term "Rohingya," but ideally in an artful way that we hoped would mitigate any public reaction. When Kerry met with Aung San Suu Kyi the next day, they discussed it along with a wide range of other issues, with the secretary emphasizing continued U.S. support for the NLD's reform efforts. During the follow-on press conference, Aung San Suu Kyi pounced on the inevitable "Rohingya"

1 See Antoni Slodkowski, "New U.S. Ambassador to Myanmar Says He Will Keep Using Term 'Rohingya,'" Reuters, May 10, 2016, http://reut.rs/1OdLIIh; and "U.S. Defies Myanmar Government Request to Stop Using Term Rohingya," The Guardian, May 11, 2016, https://www.theguardian.com/world/2016/may/11/us-defies-myanmar-government-rohingya-muslims.

question and offered what I thought was a superb answer. In brief, she said that, without prejudice to the question of what the community called itself, it was clear that outsiders using the term "Rohingya" caused great upset among many Myanmar people, but also that Myanmar people using the term "Bengali" (which was the politest word many in the country used for the Rohingya) was equally upsetting to many. She suggested that, to avoid getting bogged down on semantics, the government and diplomats should use the more neutral term "Rakhine Muslims," and focus on getting at the substantive issues.[2]

While any number of critics complained about the term "Rakhine Muslims," for the most part the state counsellor's remarks calmed the situation. This initial blow-up over the word "Rohingya" seemed to catalyze in Aung San Suu Kyi's mind that she could not put off the broader Rohingya issue. Daw Suu reached out to former UN secretary-general Kofi Annan and asked if he would be willing to lead an independent commission to study the matter and offer recommendations. Annan did his due diligence to make sure that the commission would be a genuine effort to address the problem, and then agreed to lead it. In August 2016 Aung San Suu Kyi announced the establishment of the Advisory Commission on Rakhine State, often referred to as the Annan commission or the Rakhine Advisory commission. Annan would serve as chair, and two international figures and two Myanmar figures would fill out the team.

The Aung San Suu Kyi Government

More broadly, in the first months after the democratic transition, the new government took charge, implemented some reforms, and outlined its goals. The first step had been to create the state counsellor role so that Aung San Suu Kyi had a position from which she could govern. That took a lot of effort and also set back relations with the military, but the leadership thought it was a worthwhile investment. In her first major speech in mid-April, Daw Suu laid out her priorities. At the top was national reconciliation, which turned out to mean reconciliation between the previous forces of oppression and the former opposition-turned-government. She chose not to purge the civil service of USDP and military officers but instead placed loyalists in ministry positions with instructions to try to make things work with their existing staff.

---

2 Lesley Wroughton, "Suu Kyi Calls for 'Space' to Address Myanmar's Rohingya Issue as Kerry Visits," Reuters, May 21, 2016, http://reut.rs/1qBUJ2H.

She also tried to establish good relations with the few military officers in minister positions, something she seems to have accomplished reasonably well. Overall, however, the civilian and military authorities largely failed to work well together, resulting in what many called a hybrid NLD-military government.

Aung San Suu Kyi listed the other top priorities as achieving peace, promoting rule of law, pursuing constitutional reform, and strengthening the country's nascent democracy. On the latter front, the NLD took several positive steps, dropping charges against some two hundred people who had been arrested for "crimes" such as unlawful demonstrations, pardoning eighty-three political prisoners, and repealing (via parliament) laws that had been used to suppress or target political activists. It took a little longer, but parliament also removed the oppressive legal requirement for people to register with local authorities if they wanted to stay overnight outside of their homes. On the other hand, the NLD did little to reform or develop the country's deeply problematic judicial system, failing to fill court vacancies or to improve legal training.

On the economic side, the government made some smart decisions to restore macroeconomic stability, which had suffered in 2014–15 as the Thein Sein administration had overspent ahead of the elections to the point that we thought the IMF might have to come in to help. This prudent, conservative economic approach was necessary, though it resulted in slower-than-anticipated growth. There was interest from foreign companies, including U.S. ones, but the government did little to take advantage of the window of opportunity to translate all the interest and support into tangible investment, offering no plan to improve the investment environment and virtually no communication about its intentions. In July 2016, Aung San Suu Kyi invited the business and diplomatic communities to Nay Pyi Taw to lay out her government's twelve-point economic program, but it was a big disappointment—little more than vague ideas of promoting various sectors without any specifics.[3]

The government's underwhelming initial performance on the economy—with the important exception of improving macroeconomic stability—reflected three broader weaknesses: (1) the new government's lack of governing experience and overreliance on new, unproven ministers who struggled to tame and manage their teams; (2) Aung San

---

3 Aye Thidar Kyaw and Claire Hammond, "Government Reveals 12-Point Economic Policy," *Myanmar Times*, July 29, 2016, https://www.mmtimes.com/business/21664-nld-12-point-economic-policy-announcement.html.

Suu Kyi's insistence on making many decisions that should have been delegated to ministers or even lower levels; and (3) the almost complete lack of strategic communications and messaging.

The first flaw was understandable. It was not the NLD's fault that most of its leaders had spent much of the past two decades in prison rather than gaining governing experience. The question was whether and to what extent they could improve. In my view, it was a mistake to parachute ministers into ministries by themselves. There was no way that, without a handful of loyal aides and staff to help them, they could set a new direction and ensure it was implemented.

The second weakness should not have surprised anyone, given Aung San Suu Kyi's known predilection for micromanagement. In any number of discussions with Washington visitors and people in Myanmar, I defended her from criticism on this point. I acknowledged that she was micromanaging and that it was a problem but argued that—if this was her worst flaw as a democratic leader—we should not complain too much. We also held out hope that, over time, she would delegate more.

Daw Suu's disinterest in communications and messaging caught us more by surprise. After all, she was a brilliant and often inspirational speaker and had used communications effectively for years as opposition leader. As de facto leader of the government, however, she chose not to speak much at all, nor did she promote messaging among others in the government. While she was often shown giving brief remarks at specific events, she made almost no effort to use her considerable communications skills and popularity to go on national television and offer the country any kind of vision or even to explain what the government was trying to do. It was baffling. I raised the matter with one of her closest advisors. He responded that she did not like giving speeches drafted by others and was too busy to write them herself. Surely, I thought, that could not have been the reason. I was still trying to figure this out when I left Yangon four years later. The best explanation I could come up with was that her vision of democracy involved the citizenry electing the government every four to five years and then just trusting the government to do the right thing, i.e., there was little need to communicate to the public regularly.

Aung San Suu Kyi had made the peace process a priority, both because the country desperately needed to end the civil wars that had plagued it for decades and because doing so would presumably strengthen her hand vis-à-vis the military on the question of constitutional reform. After all, the military's primary argument for maintaining such a powerful constitutional role was that it was the only institution that could hold the country together in the face of so many centrifugal forces. Recalling her father's Panglong Agreement nearly seventy years earlier, she called for a revival of the "Panglong spirit," and hosted the 21st Century Panglong Conference (also known as the Union Peace Conference) in Nay Pyi Taw at the end of August 2016.[4]

The meeting did not produce any breakthroughs, but it at least brought together nearly all of the players—the government, the military, the EAOs that had signed the 2015 ceasefire accord, and most of those that had not. Also, many welcomed the fact that the government broadcast the event—including speeches by EAO leaders—live to the nation, providing unprecedented transparency and visibility for the EAOs. There were complaints too: Daw Suu had announced the conference unilaterally rather than consulting with the EAOs first; there were perceived protocol slights and the like; several EAOs felt the preparations had been rushed to meet an artificial deadline; and, most importantly, the military had refused to allow the Ta'ang National Liberation Army, Kokang, and Arakan Army to join the conference. Nonetheless, many of the ethnic minority representatives with whom I spoke seemed pleased overall. There was a sense of cautious optimism.

That cautious optimism captured the general mood in the country at the time. There were many problems and some clear weaknesses in the new government, but most people understood the need for patience. It was going to take the NLD government time to figure out how to run the machinery of government and to work out a modus vivendi with the military. The government and parliament were continuing to eliminate or revise repressive laws, even if more slowly than many of us wanted. The military had allowed the transition to take place and appeared to be trying to work with the new government. It had not yet shown itself to be the across-the-board spoiler we would see in 2017–20.

Intensive Engagement and Support

Washington remained enthused about prospects for continued progress and reform, and that included much of Congress as well as the

---

4 "Myanmar's Peace Process: Getting to a Political Dialogue," International Crisis Group, Crisis Group Asia Briefing no. 149, October 19, 2016, https://www.crisisgroup.org/asia/south-east-asia/myanmar/myanmar-s-peace-process-getting-political-dialogue.

administration. We enjoyed good relations with the new government, with regular access to Aung San Suu Kyi and her ministers. There was a sense that we were all trying to move in the same direction. For the first six to nine months of the new government, we had almost weekly visits by senior administration officials and members of Congress, including Secretary Kerry, USAID director Gayle Smith, Export-Import Bank chair Fred Hochberg, multiple members of Congress, and many more. All emphasized to Aung San Suu Kyi and others in her government the strong U.S. support for democratic reform, economic development, and closer relations.

We had ratcheted up our assistance considerably over the past few years and were investing heavily in improved governance, healthcare, agriculture and economic reform, and civil society, while continuing to support the peace process. The one area where engagement remained severely limited was with the military. We had no senior-level military-to-military engagement, no training or military education programs, and only limited interaction, including agreeing with Thailand's suggestion to let a few Myanmar officers observe the humanitarian element of the annual Cobra Gold exercise. We had sought congressional support for a few years to start a small English-language training program, which we thought was a safe way to begin to engage and build relationships with mid-level officers, but Congress had rejected the idea. At Aung San Suu Kyi's request, we agreed to run any proposals for new military-to-military programs through the civilian government. Our intention was not to build traditional military-to-military ties, but to establish channels of communication and do what we could to encourage reform and improved behavior. Some longtime observers criticized our efforts as foolhardy, though few offered credible options for how to keep the powerful military from sabotaging the overall reform effort.

I met with General Min Aung Hlaing and his deputy, General Soe Win, multiple times to try to develop a relationship, and to encourage the military not to stand in the way of reforms and to end its offensive against the KIA in Kachin State. Over the past few years, Derek Mitchell, multiple senior Washington visitors, and I had consistently offered the same message to the military: we were open to building a military-to-military relationship, but we could only begin to do so to the extent that the military continued to support democratic reforms, worked toward peace, avoided any renewal of the relationship with North Korea, and increased respect for human rights.

From the outset, I found it difficult to build any kind of rapport with either of the generals. Min Aung Hlaing appeared superficially smooth, but any detailed conversation about peace and the ethnic minorities quickly revealed a high degree of Bamar chauvinism and a lack of interest in compromise. Later, when the Rohingya issue exploded, our conversations became even more difficult, as he betrayed an ugly prejudice against the Rohingya and a complete refusal to acknowledge the severe human rights violations the military had committed. Eventually, he would refuse to meet with me at all.

General Soe Win was a hardliner, though—unlike his boss—he was not deeply corrupt and did not tell obvious lies to my face. He saw himself as a soldier, not a politician. He was, however, uncompromising. I had many discussions with him about the peace process, particularly the deeply troubling conflict against the KIA in the northeast, and tried to persuade him that the ethnic minority communities had legitimate grievances. I suggested that it was difficult for both of us—him as an ethnic Bamar man in Myanmar and me as a white male in America—to understand and appreciate the feelings of discrimination and prejudice that others in our countries might have. I thought it was a good point. He absolutely did not get it.

I spoke with the generals at length about Rakhine State, warning that—while the Rohingya population itself was not quick to radicalize—outside elements, including al-Qaeda and ISIS, were using continued institutionalized discrimination and mistreatment of the Rohingya as a recruiting tool. It was conceivable, I argued, that such elements could decide to stage attacks inside Myanmar in response. (We were also worried that a small number of Rohingya at some point would resort to violence, but I did not say that to the generals for fear it would only add to their feeling that the Rohingya were a threat.) At one point, I discussed this with a senior police official, who shared my concerns but complained that Min Aung Hlaing "doesn't get it." He urged us to continue engaging with the senior general to try to get him to change his approach.

Lifting Sanctions

In July 2016 Deputy National Security Advisor Ben Rhodes visited, carrying with him a letter from President Obama inviting Aung San Suu Kyi to visit Washington in the coming months. In the weeks leading up to Ben's visit, I had been receiving regular entreaties from senior Myanmar economic officials urging us to lift our remaining economic sanctions. These NLD veterans, who acknowledged they had encouraged sanctions during the years of oppressive military rule, now argued that the remaining restrictive measures were hurting the economy and were a net negative for the reform effort. Aung San Suu Kyi herself, when the question had come up, had equivocated, telling us that she was not so worried about the sanctions and was confident we would lift them when we thought the time was right. On the other hand, she had been saying for a while that the key factor in determining whether the civilian side could gain supremacy over the military would be the government's success in delivering benefits, especially economic, to the people.

Since the reforms had begun in 2011, Washington had responded to progress by gradually easing and lifting the broad sanctions—including an import ban and a prohibition on new investments—that had been imposed via various laws and regulations starting in the 1990s. By mid-2016, the main remaining sanctions prohibited U.S. individuals and institutions from engaging in business or financial transactions with more than one hundred Myanmar individuals and companies remaining on the SDN list through the Burma Sanctions Program. For U.S. companies, the practical problem was that it took an extraordinary amount of due diligence to be confident that a business or individual with whom they might want to do business was not commercially linked with someone on the SDN list. In an opaque place like Myanmar, that was not easy to do. Also, while U.S. policy was to remove individuals and entities from the list as conditions warranted, in practice Treasury lacked the manpower to do so. There was broad agreement in Washington that a few such individuals should be dropped from the list, but it did not happen.

We had been discussing the issue within the embassy for several weeks. Based on our conversations with the U.S. business community, we had come to the view that our approach to date of gradually easing sanctions was ineffective. The problem, as some of the more outspoken members of the business community explained, was that for most major U.S. banks and corporations, sanctions were a binary matter. Either we had sanctions against a country or we did not. In the case of Myanmar, we had sanctions, and slicing little bits of them off every several months did not change that fact. Most major U.S. companies were not going to take the risk—and the legal risks were high, if they were found to have violated any sanctions, as were the reputational risks if international human rights groups drew attention to their engagements in Myanmar—to invest in or do business with a small-market country against which we were imposing sanctions, even if those sanctions had been eased to some extent. The fact of the sanctions had a particular impact on banking and payments that involved U.S. dollars or U.S. platforms such as Google Pay. Even though Treasury had granted a general license allowing such transactions through U.S. institutions, compliance officers in the United States remained wary, as the small market did not justify the potential risks, in their view.

During Ben Rhodes' visit, I told him that I thought we should lift the remaining sanctions. It was not about "rewarding" Myanmar or saying that the country had come far enough. Rather, it was about recognizing that the sanctions had achieved their primary objective in restoring elected government. Perhaps even more importantly, it was about eliminating an obstacle—one of the few that we controlled—to economic growth and development, and in doing so increasing the chances that the reform-minded NLD government would succeed and the darker forces in Myanmar would recede. Moreover, as the rest of the world stepped up investing in the country, should we not do what we could to encourage responsible U.S. investment, which should help in the country's fight for rule of law, against corruption, and for inclusive growth?

Ben said he would take the message back to Washington, but he cautioned that lifting the sanctions would only be feasible if Aung San Suu Kyi made it clear that she supported such a move. At that time, before the Rohingya crisis exploded with unprecedented implications, Aung San Suu Kyi's views still mattered enormously, both within the administration and on Capitol Hill, where there no doubt would be resistance to dropping sanctions. I arranged to meet with the state counsellor ahead of her September 2016 visit to Washington to discuss this and other visit-related matters.

I went to see Daw Suu at her Nay Pyi Taw residence. She had already heard from several of her economic advisors, who had made the argument for lifting sanctions. I explained to her how the SDN list worked, including the U.S. legal requirement that the president continue to declare that a "National Emergency" vis-à-vis Burma existed that provided the basis for including Myanmar individuals and companies on the list, and what the options were. She asked if we could keep some people/companies on the list. I said we could but pointed out that doing so would maintain the "odor" of sanctions that discouraged some investors. She thought about it and decided she preferred we lift all sanctions. There were risks in doing so, she noted, but also risks in not doing so.

I reported this back to Washington, adding to the growing momentum in the administration for dropping the sanctions completely. By the time of Aung San Suu Kyi's visit, President Obama was prepared to announce the lifting of sanctions. During Daw Suu's stop in London en route to Washington, Ben Rhodes called her to confirm her position on sanctions. She confirmed and did so once more upon arrival in Washington, where she began her official meetings on September 14, 2016.

Aung San Suu Kyi in Washington

She and President Obama had a good meeting in the Oval Office, with the president noting he would lift sanctions, specifically by ending the Burma Sanctions Program, which would remove from the global SDN list all of the people and companies that had been sanctioned under that program. He said the United States would grant Generalized System of Preferences (GSP) trade benefits to Myanmar, in an effort to boost Myanmar exports and create jobs. The two also announced the establishment of a U.S.-Myanmar partnership, a move I had pushed for as a way to signal that we had shifted to a new, much more positive chapter in the relationship that would include programs such as the Peace Corps in addition to stronger economic ties. In the meeting, they discussed the peace process, relations with the military, and the Rohingya issue, among other things. Aung San Suu Kyi asked if, now that we were dropping sanctions, we could help her government figure out how to regulate the jade industry, which in many ways had been a symbol of the corrupt, military-dominated resource-extraction economy of the past. China did not really come up, reflecting the reality that—for official Washington—engagement with Myanmar was fundamentally about promoting democracy and human rights, not countering Beijing.

The next day, there was some unnecessary and unhelpful drama. An administration official who had opposed lifting of sanctions suggested offline to Aung San Suu Kyi that there was a way—using another piece of legislation, the Jade Act, while lifting the National Emergency—that we could still sanction certain individuals and institutions outside of the former Burma Sanctions Program. This proposition confused Daw Suu, as it had not been broached with her previously. (In fact, it had not been discussed within the administration, nor reviewed by Treasury sanctions experts.) That confusion was reflected in some of her conversations on Capitol Hill later in the day and at an event that evening. Others in the administration discussed this with her in detail the following day. She reaffirmed her support for lifting all sanctions, but by then the damage had been done. She was clearly displeased by the sudden lack of consistency in messaging to her, specifically by the administration official who had contradicted the president's discussion with her.

This incident has given rise to a lot of revisionist history advanced by some members of the "Burma Lobby" who opposed lifting sanctions. This included suggestions that we had somehow misled Aung San Suu Kyi into agreeing to ask us to drop all sanctions. That is nonsense. I had gone through the options with her in detail, including the possibility of keeping some people or institutions on the SDN list. Suggesting that we instead sanction those same—or a similar group of—people and institutions via the Jade Act was a difference without meaning. Either way, this presumably small group would have remained sanctioned, and either way that fact would have discouraged Western investors. The banks and corporations were not holding back because people/companies were sanctioned under the Burma Sanctions Program rather than the Jade Act. They were holding back because the sanctions existed, period. Daw Suu had known that, and had stated multiple times, including with the president and with key U.S. senators and representatives, that she wanted us to drop all sanctions. It is perfectly legitimate to argue that dropping the sanctions was a mistake, but not to suggest that we somehow misled Aung San Suu Kyi on the options.

This mini drama took some of the glow off of what otherwise had been a very positive visit, which in turn capped a five-year period of remarkable change and achievement. Myanmar had gone from a harshly repressive military dictatorship and pariah state with little hope to a nascent, though flawed, democracy that had released political prisoners, established fundamental freedoms, implemented major economic reforms that were bringing benefits to many people, and ended its decades-long isolation. We had begun to build a new relationship and could now work inside the country to support all of the forces of reform, including a growing and impressive number of civil society groups and independent media players. Yes, huge problems and challenges remained, particularly the role of the military, the continuing conflicts with ethnic armed organizations, and the treatment of the

Rohingya. Success was by no means guaranteed. As I told my Washington colleagues, Myanmar had spent fifty years digging a very deep hole for itself. It had been climbing out for only five years. The Myanmar people could look down and marvel at how far up they had climbed, or they could look up and worry about how much further they still had to go. Both views were accurate, and it was critical to keep both views in mind as we assessed the state of the country.

We spent the few weeks after the visit explaining to both the Myanmar public and the U.S. business community the sanctions decision, as well as the benefits of GSP and the new partnership. The trip and these decisions had injected fresh momentum into the relationship, and we were hopeful that U.S. investment would increase. Parliamentarians, business executives, journalists, and many Myanmar activists welcomed the lifting of sanctions. To be fair, some activists, particularly from ethnic minority communities, expressed concern, fearing that it would let the military off the hook. Still, the overwhelming majority seemed supportive.

The First ARSA Attacks

On October 9, 2016, a small group of Rohingya calling themselves Harakah al-Yaqin (later renamed the Arakan Rohingya Salvation Army or ARSA) launched coordinated assaults on the Border Guard Police headquarters and two other bases in northern Rakhine State near the Bangladesh border, killing nine policemen and seizing weapons. The government cut off access to the region, while the military responded with extensive clearance operations against nearby villages, insisting that it had to recapture all of the weapons and ammunitions. When some of the troops involved in the operations came under attack, the military escalated their response. Over a period of several weeks, tens of thousands of Rohingya fled to Bangladesh or to other areas of Rakhine State, and numerous villages were burned amid widespread allegations of human rights abuses, including rape and extrajudicial killings, by the security forces.

We had a hard time getting good, verifiable information, given northern Rakhine's isolation and our lack of access. Still, the widespread reports of human rights violations—along with the military's well-earned reputation for brutality—made us fear the worst. There were reports that the initial ARSA attacks were linked to the drug trade, in which the government's Border Guards allegedly were involved. On the other hand, Harakah al-Yaqin, led by expatriate Rohingya, insisted they were fighting for Rohingya rights. There was much that we did not know. The diplomatic community pressed the government to give us access to the area, which it belatedly did in early November.

The government brought a group of ambassadors on a two-day visit through northern Rakhine via helicopter. We debated among ourselves the wisdom of taking the trip, given that we would have to rely on the government for transportation and would be accompanied by senior government officials. We decided to go nonetheless in the hope that our trip would give us at least some sense of what was going on and, more importantly, perhaps open the door to broader access for others, including the media and humanitarian organizations. We insisted that we be able to visit several of the villages that reportedly had been burned or suffered during the conflict, and the government agreed.

After receiving a police briefing on the attacks, we went to Kyee Kan Pyin village, which was very near the initial ARSA attacks and which we had heard had been badly damaged. We saw that it had been burned down and was empty, but we had no way to know for sure how it had happened. As we were preparing to leave for another location, a few hundred Rohingya emerged out of the nearby forest and made their way to us. It was a delicate situation, as we were accompanied by Border Affairs minister General Ye Aung and dozens of armed soldiers and police. One of the villagers spoke but was (understandably) reluctant to describe what had happened in detail. As we were speaking to him, a couple of policemen approached and started to detain him. I could not believe it. I told Minister Ye Aung that, if they detained this individual or anyone else who spoke with us, that would be the end of the trip, and we would go back to Yangon and tell the press what had happened. The minister said the man was thought to have been involved in the ARSA attacks and so had to be arrested. I repeated that arresting people who spoke to us was a deal-breaker. Other colleagues seconded my protest, and Ye Aung told the police to release the man. We learned later in the day that the police had returned to the area looking for him, but he had fled. The entire incident demonstrated the enormous gap in thinking between us and the military.

We visited several other Rohingya and Rakhine villages over the next day and a half. In a couple of villages we saw no signs of damage or conflict, and villagers indicated the situation had been calm. In a Rakhine village, a woman told us the Rohingya were a danger to them and that several men and boys from the village had disappeared in recent weeks. We had no way of confirming her account, but frankly it seemed staged. Our next stop was a Rohingya village, where—in sharp contrast to the extreme caution and reticence we encountered in other such villages—the residents were holding up signs, in English, saying things such as "End the Genocide against the Rohingya," or "End Rape of Rohingya Women." The villagers showed no fear of the military or police, which seemed strange. None of them spoke English or could tell us what the signs they were holding said. The stop raised questions in our minds.

At the end of the second day, we returned by helicopter to Sittwe, unsure what to make of what we had seen. We met with a large group of press that had come to hear about our visit. Some, particularly Western journalists, clearly expected us to confirm publicly the allegations of significant human rights abuses, including rape. We explained that we were not an investigative body, and that we had neither the capacity nor the mandate to "investigate" reported human rights abuses. We could confirm that some villages had been burned down and that many Rohingya had fled, but not much more than that. Our inability to tell the journalists what some of them clearly wanted to hear angered at least a few of them—that much was clear from the tone and substance of their questions. The government was equally unhappy, somehow thinking that after this quick visit we would corroborate their claim that the violence was all the result of ARSA attacks and that the security forces had not committed human rights violations. Of course, we could not say that either. Most of us believed the security forces had committed human rights violations and probably burned the villages, but believing it was one thing, providing evidence to prove it was another. We pressed hard for an independent investigation into the violence.

This brief visit provided a taste of what, sadly, was going to come in mid-2017, when the violence in the area again erupted on a massive scale. I came away from the trip feeling like all sides were playing us to some extent, and that we had to take much of what we heard with a grain of salt. That did not mean none of the accounts were true—without doubt there had been significant violence and human rights abuses, probably on a large scale—but it made me cautious about believing everything I heard. That caution would come back to haunt me in 2017.

I returned to Yangon believing more than ever that the Rakhine Advisory commission led by Kofi Annan was the only hope to find some way out of the awful situation facing the Rohingya community. Annan and his colleagues had decided early on that they would need to develop a set of recommendations that addressed the problem holistically, in the context of the much-debated history of Rakhine and the mistreatment of the Rohingya. I heartily agreed.

Making Sense of the Rohingya Issue

The history of the issue is complex, but if I had to summarize it, I would say it fundamentally revolves around demographics, complemented by Myanmar propaganda campaigns designed to exacerbate divisions and portray the Rohingya as illegal and dangerous interlopers. Rakhine State occupies a long, narrow coastal area along the Bay of Bengal, bordering Bangladesh in the northwest and separated from the rest of Myanmar by a mountain range. Of the estimated 3.2 million residents in 2016, the Muslim community that calls itself Rohingya—mostly descended from former migrants from the Chittagong region of Bangladesh—made up maybe 1.3 million, mostly in the state's north. Ethnic Rakhine Buddhists, also known as Arakan, made up most of the rest, though there were significant numbers of other minority communities, and a small group of non-Rohingya Muslims known as Kaman. The ethnic Rakhine constituted a majority in the state, but the Rohingya dominated (demographically) the northern three townships of Maungdaw, Buthidaung, and Rathedaung, accounting for some 80–90 percent of the population in those areas.[5]

There is heated debate in Rakhine and Myanmar about when the Rohingya arrived and outside scholarship is not conclusive. Many ethnic Rakhine (and many in Myanmar writ large) insist that the Rohingya are recent arrivals, mostly illegal immigrants, do not qualify for citizenship, and thus do not "belong" in the country. Furthermore, they argue that this "wave" of recent illegal immigrants has dramatically altered the demographic balance in Rakhine, especially the northern part of the state, making the ethnic Rakhine vulnerable minorities in their own land. For the more hardline ethnic Rakhine, this demographic

---

5 Population figures are estimates, as the official 2014 census failed to count anyone who attempted to identify as Rohingya. *The 2014 Myanmar Population and Housing Census: Rakhine State*, Census Report Volume 3–K, Myanmar Ministry of Immigration and Population, May 2015, https://myanmar.unfpa.org/sites/default/files/pub-pdf/Rakhine%20State%20Census%20Report%20-%20ENGLISH-3.pdf.

change—and the prospect of more "Bengalis" coming across the porous border—constitutes an existential threat.

Many Rohingya activists argue that their community has been in Rakhine for centuries and point to the history of the precolonial Arakan Kingdom, which included a Muslim population and boasted mosques. Many outside students believe that there was a small Muslim population during the Arakan Kingdom, and that the majority of Rohingya today descended from people who immigrated during the colonial period but are not "recent" immigrants by any reasonable definition of the word. In recent decades, cyclical violence, including military operations, has resulted in large-scale movements of Rohingya across the border into Bangladesh, with many returning to their homes in Myanmar when conditions permitted—one source of the argument that they were "recent immigrants." Put another way, the evidence, inconclusive as it is, suggests that the Rohingya community might not qualify as a "national race" (i.e., pre-1824) but has been resident in the country long enough that the vast majority qualify for citizenship, even under Myanmar's problematic citizenship law (which basically requires residence for three generations).

Because Myanmar's government has reasonably good records that go back quite far, one might think that the easy solution would be to use those records to determine conclusively which Rohingya have citizenship and which do not. That pragmatic and reasonable approach, however, runs headlong into the very intense emotional world of Rakhine and Myanmar politics, in which what should be fact-based decisions on citizenship status become intensely political and subject to enormous pressures.

The Rohingya and Rakhine communities have lived together for decades, mostly peacefully but largely segregated. During World War II, the Rohingya sided with the British, the Rakhine with the Japanese. There were clashes and massacres, which more than seventy years later still shape the views of people in the villages that were involved. Under military rule, the Myanmar military twice (1978 and 1991) conducted military operations to root out "illegal" residents, resulting in some two hundred thousand Rohingya fleeing to Bangladesh on each occasion. Subsequent agreements with Bangladesh resulted in the majority of those who fled returning, but under the 1982 Citizenship Law most Rohingya lost whatever citizenship status they had.

Over the next few decades, successive military governments gradually stripped away Rohingya rights, with the Thein Sein government striking a final blow in 2015 when it took away their so-called White Cards, which among other things had allowed them to vote. Along with these government actions, the Myanmar public was subjected to a barrage of propaganda that effectively rewrote the history of the Rohingya and portrayed them as illegal and dangerous immigrants, even though many had enjoyed citizenship and had served as civil servants, teachers, and even members of parliament. It is heartbreaking to talk with Rohingya in the IDP camps and hear their stories of how, for no reason other than that they are Rohingya, they have lost their businesses, their jobs, their political rights and freedoms, and—for many—their hope.

Slow Progress on Other Issues

After the immediate situation in Rakhine State calmed at the end of 2016, the government tried to shift its focus back to the peace process and building the economy, but by spring 2017—after a year in office—expectations of how much the government would accomplish had declined noticeably. It had yet to offer a clear economic strategy or set of policies, and as a result foreign investor interest was waning and the IMF and World Bank were lowering growth forecasts. The Myanmar government and business community expressed disappointment that our lifting of sanctions had not produced a flood of new U.S. investment, as most U.S. investors continued to view the overall investment environment as poor.

Hopes for constitutional and further political reform suffered a major blow in late January 2017, with the shocking assassination at the Yangon airport of prominent lawyer and Muslim community leader U Ko Ni, who had been working closely with the NLD government on potential constitutional changes. The investigation quickly led to several individuals with links to the military, confirming in many people's minds that the killing was intended to send a strong warning about the risk to anyone linked to efforts to challenge the military's power. More broadly, the assassination had a chilling impact on the NLD and both the pro-democracy and Muslim communities, as it indicated everyone and anyone was a potential target.

The peace process was not moving forward, either. Some of that was due to the substantial influence of the military, whose definition of peace seemed to the EAOs a lot like surrender on their part. Some of it, though, reflected the lack of engagement and negotiations by the government. Unlike her predecessor as leader of the country, Aung San Suu Kyi failed to delegate any real authority to her lead negotiator, Dr. Tin Myo Win, who—while a wonderful man who had served for decades as Suu Kyi's personal physician—was not really cut out for the job anyway. EAO representatives complained about the lack of informal dialogue, necessary to build trust and overcome obstacles, while ethnic communities as a whole lamented what they saw as Aung San Suu Kyi's condescending attitude toward them.

Meanwhile, the military was engaged in aggressive offensives against the KIA in Kachin and northern Shan states, causing significant damage and many civilian casualties and making it hard for people to go about their lives. The KIA fought back, but the Tatmadaw clearly was the aggressor. I met with the top generals in Nay Pyi Taw several times, urging them to work out a ceasefire with the KIA. I traveled to Chiang Mai, Thailand, to meet with KIA leader N'Ban La to encourage him to meet with the military. The two sides bickered over minor protocol matters and kept finding excuses not to meet. After one bloody clash, I again urged the military's deputy commander-in-chief General Soe Win to seek a ceasefire. He said he could not. How, he asked, could he agree to a ceasefire after so many of his soldiers had been killed? I suggested that his line of thinking would lead to a never-ending conflict like in the Middle East, where one side always had to stage one more attack to revenge the most recent loss of its soldiers. He was not impressed.

We continued to try to walk a fine line with the military, seeking to engage it sufficiently to build some relationships and an effective channel of communication, but avoiding any steps that would appear to embrace it, absent improvements in its respect for human rights. The military had taken some positive steps, such as working with the International Labour Organization to address the longstanding problem of child soldiers, but its overall behavior had not changed significantly. We tried to work more with the Myanmar Navy, which had traditionally been more open and had a less problematic human rights record than the rest of the armed forces. The high point was spring 2017 when the USNS *Fall River* visited, the first U.S. ship to visit the country in fifty years. We used all our engagements to press the military to address human rights concerns, support the peace process, and encourage steps to improve the situation for the Rohingya community.

Political reform and liberalization also stalled. Amending the constitution, an Aung San Suu Kyi campaign promise, went out the door in the face of military obstinance and the assassination of U Ko Ni.

Even where the NLD had control—the parliament—little was happening. In fact, Aung San Suu Kyi and her top lieutenants, longtime advisor U Win Htein and Speaker U Win Myint—imposed strict party discipline that gave NLD parliamentarians little room for maneuver or creativity. Some people longed for the more independent days of Thura Shwe Mann's speakership.

Even more worrisome was the government's increased use of existing laws to go after critics. Authorities charged dozens of individuals, including journalists, under the increasingly unpopular 66(d) provision of the Telecommunications Law, which outlawed "defamation" on social media. Myanmar journalists and activists, with strong support from the international community, lobbied hard for elimination of this provision that was inconsistent with Myanmar's new democracy. Many parliamentarians supported a change, but they faced great pressure from the NLD leadership (and the military) not to change it. In September 2017 parliament finally amended the law to remove some of its most repressive provisions (such as not being allowed to post bail upon being charged), but disappointed the media, activists, and much of the international community by maintaining the law's core. Senior NLD and government officials privately justified these measures and the strict control over NLD parliamentarians by pointing to the threat to the broader pro-democracy movement posed by the military, which they asserted could exploit cracks in NLD discipline, and which could likewise take advantage of division fomented on social media.

Despite these setbacks, we were able to make progress in some important areas. Responding to the state counsellor's request to President Obama, we developed a good partnership with the Ministry of Natural Resources and a number of NGOs and businesses to support development of new legislation and regulations to govern the rich but problematic gems sector. The ministry, with USAID support, organized a series of effective public consultations in mineral-rich regions and took advice from the NGOs and businesses in the development of the new legislation and regulations. These were some of the first genuine public consultations ever held in Myanmar. Our USAID-funded programs to support farmers and agriculture also were proving highly effective. Together with the liberalization of the microfinance industry, we saw a dramatic increase in the number of farmers using mechanized equipment and, as a result, significantly increasing production and income. In Shan State, farmers were quick to use new information and technology, as well as improved access to new markets, to boost production and begin to export to the West. These might seem like small matters, but they constituted a great example of "inclusive development."

Working Against Time on the Rohingya

As we worked on all of these issues and programs in the first half of 2017, our main priority—and that of the international community—remained that of addressing the Rohingya situation. A group of like-minded ambassadors worked closely with the UN team and the Annan commission to share information and develop common advocacy points vis-à-vis the government in Nay Pyi Taw as well as the authorities in Rakhine State.

The commission itself reached out widely to gather ideas, but the ethnic Rakhine community refused to cooperate with it, insisting that the issue was a purely domestic one. The Rakhine community's antipathy reflected its perception that the international community favored the Rohingya over them, a view that would only grow in intensity in the months to come. The Rakhine felt under attack from the Bamar, the Rohingya, and the international community. This sense of victimization—whether justified or not—would prove to be a huge obstacle to progress.

In response to international pressure, the Myanmar government established an "independent" commission to investigate the October 2016 violence. By naming as chairman Vice President Myint Swe, a former general who had played a key role in the 2007 suppression of the Saffron Revolution, the government virtually guaranteed the commission would have little credibility. The UN decided in early 2017 to establish its own investigation team, prompting Myanmar authorities to complain that the move would only increase tension.

While the various commissions worked, worries mounted in northern Rakhine State. ARSA members were active in Rohingya villages, recruiting, intimidating, and—on multiple occasions—killing Rohingya who defied them or whom they suspected of being informants. There were several incidents involving alleged ARSA militants in May through July 2017. In early August, after several ethnic Rakhine villagers were found killed in the Mayu mountain range of northern Rakhine State, ethnic Rakhine political figures traveled to Nay Pyi Taw to ask the military to send reinforcements. The military sent several hundred more troops to the area to search for "terrorists."

Also in early August, the Myint Swe commission delivered its final report, which was a pretty obvious whitewash of events. The report largely dismissed almost all of the allegations of atrocities, including murder, rape, and arson reportedly perpetrated by the security forces. Myint Swe himself told the press: "There is no possibility of crimes against humanity, no evidence of ethnic cleansing, as per UN accusations."[6] The conclusion not only failed the credibility test. It also highlighted how unwilling the authorities were to acknowledge even some human rights abuses, when it was clear to all that they had occurred on a significant scale.

The Annan commission finished its report and presented it to the government and the military on August 23, 2017. It was a good report, with an excellent analysis of the history and fundamental challenges in Rakhine State. It offered more than eighty specific recommendations to address the issues of Rakhine State holistically, ranging from enhanced efforts to address the widespread poverty and lack of access to government services that all communities in Rakhine faced, as well as accelerated work to verify and document Rohingya citizenship status. The commission stressed the importance of steadily expanding rights for the Rohingya community, including freedom of movement and elimination of IDP camps, as the citizenship verification process played out. Annan himself urged the government to act with urgency, warning, "Unless concerted action—led by the government and aided by all sectors of the government and society—is taken soon, we risk the return of another cycle of violence and radicalisation, which will further deepen the chronic poverty that afflicts Rakhine State."[7]

The Rohingya Crisis Explodes

The government officially welcomed the report and vowed to implement as many of its recommendations as possible. That mostly positive response, however, was overtaken by events. In the early morning of August 25, ARSA militants—in some cases joined by local Rohingya

---

6 "Burma: National Commission Denies Atrocities," Human Rights Watch, August 7, 2017, https://www.hrw.org/news/2017/08/08/burma-national-commission -denies-atrocities.

7 "Advisory Commission on Rakhine State: Final Report," Kofi Annan Foundation, August 24, 2017, https://www.kofiannanfoundation.org/mediation-and -crisis-resolution/rakhine-final-report/.

villagers—conducted thirty well-coordinated attacks on Rakhine security outposts, killing fourteen security officials. The security forces
responded aggressively, resulting in clashes between them and ARSA
militants over the next several days. Very quickly, things spiraled out
of control. As the military operations continued, dozens of Rohingya
villages were burned down, and thousands of Rohingya began fleeing
across the border into Bangladesh.

Every day for the next several weeks, the Rakhine violence and refugee flows dominated the headlines in the United States and much of the
world, with widespread accusations of substantial human rights violations by the military. For the first two weeks, we focused on convincing
Myanmar authorities to end military operations and on engineering the
safe evacuation of international humanitarian workers who were being
threatened by angry locals in Rakhine State (more on the latter below).
The military claimed it ended what it called "clearance operations"
on September 5, but troops remained in the area, Rohingya villages
continued to burn, and the exodus to Bangladesh continued. I flew to
Nay Pyi Taw two or three times a week for the first month or so of
the crisis, constantly pressing civilian and military leaders to cease the
military campaign, change their harsh anti-Rohingya public rhetoric,
and resume access for diplomats, the media, and humanitarian organizations. (Our work as diplomats was hindered, among other things, by
the government's requirement that we submit formal meeting requests
two weeks ahead of time, an impossibility in a crisis situation. We occasionally found ways around this requirement, but still had to shuttle
constantly between Yangon and Nay Pyi Taw, often with long delays
before we could get meetings.)

The military and the government denied the allegations of excessive
force and human rights violations, calling much of the reporting "false"
and arguing that the Rohingya had burned down their own villages and
fled as a way of making the government look bad. They highlighted examples in which the international press or foreign officials had pointed
to photographs of violence that turned out to be old pictures of violence and refugees fleeing from other countries and even other conti-
nents. Aung San Suu Kyi told Turkish president Tayyip Erdogan in an
early September telephone call that the situation in Rakhine was being
distorted by "a huge iceberg of misinformation."[8] This was all, the gov-

---

8 "Rohingya Crisis: Aung San Suu Kyi Says 'Fake News Helping Terrorists,'" BBC
News, September 6, 2017, https://www.bbc.com/news/world-asia-41170570.

ernment said, an orchestrated propaganda campaign designed to turn what in their view were serious terrorist attacks against them into a global story about Myanmar brutality against the Rohingya.

Because the government cut off all access to the region almost immediately, it was very difficult to obtain credible specific information that we could report to Washington. We knew there had been substantial violence and that Rohingya were fleeing, and we were confident that the security forces were committing human rights violations, probably on a significant scale. During the first week or so, however, I erred on the side of caution in our reporting, based on my experience the previous year when we had seen and heard false reports from all sides. We reached out to all of our trusted contacts and reported what we could verify or at least saw as credible, while noting that some other reports—perhaps true, perhaps not—could not be verified. Some in the administration privately criticized the embassy's initial caution, claiming we were in denial and insisting that the totality of allegations and the numbers of Rohingya fleeing proved that the military was trying to wipe out or push out all the Rohingya. We were even called "genocide deniers" by some of our colleagues. It was incredibly painful.

By the second week of September, it became increasingly clear that, while there was some propaganda and false reporting,[9] the totality of what was happening constituted a massively disproportionate and brutal response on the part of the Myanmar security forces. Our embassy reporting team performed brilliantly, being careful not to pass on hearsay but pulling no punches in describing credibly reported massacres and other violence by the security forces, and making it clear that the military, not the Rohingya, was burning the villages. From late August through September, more than three hundred Rohingya villages were burned to the ground, and there were numerous credible reports of the military engaging in massacres, rape, and other horrific abuses against the Rohingya. The government's refusal to allow access for humanitarian aid—on which a substantial share of the population depended—exacerbated the suffering and no doubt contributed to the decision of many Rohingya to leave. Over the next months, some 750,000–800,000 Rohingya fled to Bangladesh in one of the largest and most dramatic exoduses recorded in recent decades.

9 See, for example, "Rohingya Crisis: Aung San Suu Kyi Says 'Fake News Helping Terrorists.'"

At one point in early to mid-September, we received reports that only a few Rohingya villages remained in Rathedaung Township (the rest had been deserted). In one, Naung Pin Gyi, villagers reported being surrounded and threatened by ethnic Rakhine "vigilantes," while the security forces looked on. I reached out to ministers in Nay Pyi Taw to pass on these reports and to stress the need to protect the villagers. I, along with other diplomatic colleagues, made it clear that we had identified a specific village under threat and would hold the government responsible if anything happened to them. We later learned that they were safe—one of a precious few "wins" during that time.

Different Realities

International condemnation and pressure for action grew quickly. On September 11 Zeid Raad al-Hussein, UN High Commissioner for Human Rights, said the situation appeared to be "a textbook example of ethnic cleansing."[10] The State Department and UN ambassador Nikki Haley issued statements expressing serious concern,[11] and on September 13 the UN Security Council expressed concern about reports of excessive violence by the security forces.[12] Those were the most restrained voices; others, including in the media, were demanding urgent action.

In Myanmar, the military, government, and media were creating a different reality. From the moment the ARSA attacks took place, they were presented as a major terrorist operation, and ARSA was explicitly linked to ISIS. Aung San Suu Kyi said almost nothing publicly for a few weeks, leaving the field to military commander-in-chief General Min Aung Hlaing and government spokesman U Zaw Htay. Min Aung

---

10 "UN Human Rights Chief Points to 'Textbook Example of Ethnic Cleansing' in Myanmar," UN News, September 11, 2017, https://news.un.org/en/story/2017/09/564622-un-human-rights-chief-points-textbook-example-ethnic-cleansing-myanmar.

11 Heather Nauert, spokesperson, Department of State Press Briefing, September 7, 2017, https://2017-2021.state.gov/briefings/department-press-briefing-september-7-2017/index.html; and "Press Release: Ambassador Haley on the Current Humanitarian Situation in Burma's Rakhine State," United States Mission to the United Nations, September 8, 2017, https://usun.usmission.gov/press-release-ambassador-haley-on-the-current-humanitarian-situation-in-burmas-rakhine-state/?_ga=2.17899705.104728732.1612824474-1410681472.1612824474.

12 "U.N. Security Council Condemns Excessive Violence in Myanmar," Reuters, September 13, 2017, https://reut.rs/2fiqviP.

Hlaing traveled to Rakhine and elsewhere warning about terrorism and talking about the military's commitment to defend the "national races."[13] U Zaw Htay, incredibly, insisted that none of the human rights violations, including rape, were true, even though there had been no investigation.[14]

While the foreign press understandably focused on the violence, human rights allegations, and mass exodus of the Rohingya community, the Myanmar media reported a very different story. Toeing the government line, the local media was full of stories reporting that ARSA was linked to ISIS, that ARSA had choreographed the mass exodus of Rohingya—along with the allegations of abuse—to make Myanmar look bad, and that the reports of human rights abuses were "fake news." The state counsellor's Facebook page posted photos of USAID and World Health Organization (WHO) food rations found in ARSA camps (falsely implying we had delivered aid to ARSA), and authorities suggested international NGO workers had collaborated with ARSA. When a well-known foreign journalist working for the English-language *Myanmar Times* wrote a story reporting the rape allegations against the security forces, the government complained to the newspaper owner and the journalist was fired.[15] She, like others who questioned the official narrative, received threats and had to leave the country.

Fed by these stories and by longstanding prejudice and antipathy toward the Rohingya, the Myanmar public overwhelmingly supported the government and turned against anyone who questioned it. In Rakhine, long-simmering hostility toward the UN and foreign aid workers became palpable, with some organizations receiving serious threats. Our consular and security team worked quickly with the UN and others to secure the safe evacuation from Rakhine of a number of Americans and others, while I delivered a strong message to the defense minister and the civilian authorities about the very dangerous game they were playing by suggesting the UN, USAID, and international humanitarian workers were somehow in cahoots with ARSA.

13 Jurawee Kittisilpa, "Myanmar Army Chief Urges Internally Displaced to Return to Rakhine," Reuters, September 21, 2017, https://reut.rs/2fCCyrq.

14 Office of the State Counselor, "Information Committee Refutes Rumours of Rapes," news release, December 26, 2016, http://www.statecounsellor.gov.mm/en/node/551.

15 Oliver Holmes, "Myanmar Journalist Says She Was Fired Over Story on Military Rape Allegations," *The Guardian*, November 4, 2016, https://www.theguardian.com/world/2016/nov/04/myanmar-times-journalist-fired-fiona-macgregor.

But the problem was broader than Rakhine State. In Yangon, there was widespread fear and anger. One of our local staffers, who did not share the widespread animus toward the Rohingya, told me one morning she was afraid because "ISIS has come to Myanmar. We're not safe." Almost all of our Myanmar contacts, including many activists and human rights advocates, took the side of the government against the Rohingya. Most did it because they really believed the government line. A smaller number went along because anyone opposing the line risked being ostracized, or worse.

Underlying these views was a widespread and disturbing racism toward the Rohingya. Almost everyone loathed the Rohingya, even though most probably had never met one. They were the subject of many sickening comments, such as when a Myanmar diplomat called them "ugly as ogres" or a Rakhine state legislator claimed that allegations that the military had raped Rohingya women could not be true because the Rohingya were "very dirty."[16] It was difficult to find anyone who would offer support or even empathy for the Rohingya. Even in our own embassy, our support for the Rohingya caused a lot of grumbling among our local staff. One notable exception was the courageous Karen Women's Organization, which issued a strong statement condemning the military's atrocities against the Rohingya.[17]

In the face of growing international pressure, Aung San Suu Kyi finally decided to speak. She cancelled her trip to New York for the UN General Assembly meetings (she would have faced a very hard time had she gone), and instead gave a nationally televised address on September 18 to address the crisis. The diplomatic corps was invited to Nay Pyi Taw to attend, and in the brief pre-speech discussions there was some hope that she would show the leadership the government and the country really needed. Otherwise, they were going down a very deep, dark hole.

The state counsellor's speech disappointed. She "condemned" all human rights violations and offered the first hint of official empathy,

---

16 Shashank Bengali, "In Myanmar, Hatred for Rohingya Runs So Deep that a Diplomat Called Them 'Ugly as Ogres,' and Got Promoted," *Los Angeles Times*, December 26, 2017, https://www.latimes.com/world/asia/la-fg-myanmar-rohingya -hate-20171225-story.html.

17 "Karen Women's Organisation Press Statement on Burmese Military's Persecution of the Rohingya People," September 18, 2017, https://www.burmalink .org/karen-womens-organisation-press-statement-burmese-military-persecution -rohingya-people/

noting that "we feel sorry for the suffering of all the people caught up in the conflict." But she equivocated on who was responsible for the abuses, questioned why so many Rohingya had fled, and falsely claimed the Rohingya community had equal access to health and education. Overall, her speech failed to capture the magnitude of the crisis or suffering, or indicate any urgency on the government's part to address that suffering or the many allegations of human rights violations.[18]

The international press harshly criticized her remarks, while Myanmar citizens applauded and defended her. Less than a month after the violence began, the international narrative about what had happened could not have been more different than the Myanmar narrative. These starkly different narratives would persist, making it that much more difficult to make progress on what was an inherently very challenging problem.

Outrage and Denial

In early October, the government finally granted limited access to the diplomatic community in the form of a government-led visit by helicopter and vehicle. The authorities tried to use the trip to convince us of their version of events, but simply flying over miles and miles of devastated, burned-out Rohingya villages told a very different story, and one much closer to the international narrative than to the government's. We were able to visit Naung Pin Gyi village in Rathedaung, where we confirmed the Rohingya villagers were safe, if still fearful. We walked to the neighboring Rakhine village that bore the same name and were met by village "representatives" who told us they could no longer live with the "Bengalis." We visited a number of other villages, where the discussions with Rakhine and Rohingya reinforced my perception that the prospects for healing the wounds and rebuilding communal ties varied greatly village to village, depending on the local history and current community leadership. We also visited a Hindu village where dozens had been massacred in an attack that Amnesty International subsequently concluded had been carried out by ARSA.[19]

---

18 "Rohingya Crisis: Suu Kyi Speech Criticised by Global Leaders," BBC News, September 20, 2017, https://www.bbc.com/news/world-asia-41329662.
19 "Myanmar: New Evidence Reveals Rohingya Armed Group Massacred Scores in Rakhine State," Amnesty International, May 22, 2018, https://www.amnesty

Over the next several months, the situation on the ground in Rakhine stabilized, but that did not mean it was good. Rohingya communities continued to flee due to fear, a lack of access to livelihoods, and a loss of hope, not to mention the absence of fundamental rights. Following our October visit and intense international pressure, the government began to allow limited humanitarian assistance to flow, but humanitarian agencies continued to face constant bureaucratic and administrative obstacles.

More broadly, the international community maintained a high level of outrage, and Myanmar went from a democratic darling to a near-pariah state. Western tourists stopped coming. Western investors lost interest. Some pulled out. Aung San Suu Kyi's reputation plummeted as she faced harsh criticism for failing to speak out on behalf of the Rohingya and even appearing to take the military's side. The Myanmar press and most of the public remained defiant, insisting that the world did not understand the true situation and was being duped by a propaganda campaign and "fake news." The entire country appeared to be in denial. Over time, senior Myanmar officials and politicians latched onto bizarre conspiracy theories, egged on by a few Western Islamophobes, in which the Organization of Islamic Countries allegedly was orchestrating and funding an anti-Myanmar campaign.

Not surprisingly, Myanmar's relations with the West, including the United States, declined sharply, as Nay Pyi Taw leaned toward less-critical countries such as most of ASEAN, Japan, India, and especially China. We ended what little military-to-military engagement we had shortly after the crisis began, though we maintained limited channels of communication to top officers. From the embassy, we argued for continued high-level U.S. engagement with the country, not to "embrace" or even support the government, but rather to try to encourage Myanmar to acknowledge the human rights violations and change its approach toward the Rohingya. Our efforts were hampered by the lack of senior foreign policy officials in place during the first twelve to fifteen months of the Trump administration and by the understandably toxic environment surrounding any interaction with Myanmar. Officials who might have visited in some cases decided doing so would not be career-enhancing, so they went elsewhere.

.org/en/latest/news/2018/05/myanmar-new-evidence-reveals-rohingya-armed-group-massacred-scores-in-rakhine-state/.

Secretary of State Rex Tillerson made a half-day stop in Nay Pyi Taw in November 2016, meeting with Aung San Suu Kyi and General Min Aung Hlaing. Tillerson was effective in his meetings, highlighting the need for accountability and improved conditions for the Rohingya, while also reaffirming U.S. support for Myanmar's democratic transition. His diplomatic manner appeared to go over well. Aung San Suu Kyi said the right things, for the most part. General Min Aung Hlaing, however, took the opportunity to show Tillerson a series of gruesome photographs, purportedly of ARSA victims. He had shown me the same photos a few weeks earlier, apparently believing that the problem was simply a matter of convincing us that ARSA had carried out brutal attacks. We did not dispute that fact, and had strongly condemned those attacks, but of course that did not justify the military's brutal and excessive response. The general's presentation once again highlighted the enormous gap in thinking between Myanmar and the international community.

A few weeks after his visit, Secretary Tillerson announced that the United States had determined that the security forces' clearance operations constituted ethnic cleansing. The evidence overwhelmingly supported that determination, but the announcement nonetheless undid any momentum that his visit had generated. To be clear, when I speak about momentum, I am not suggesting that we wanted or should have wanted to pursue the bilateral relationship as if nothing had happened. Rather, I mean we needed to restore a level of engagement and sufficient trust so as to have some ability to influence Myanmar's thinking. At the end of 2017, we were not there yet.

How Do You Respond to Horror?

By that time, and frankly even earlier, the magnitude and horror of what had happened was weighing heavily on our minds at the embassy and within the broader diplomatic community. Some of my embassy colleagues were saying aloud that they had not signed up for this. They had come to Myanmar to try to help a country move forward down the democratic path, not to watch it carry out ethnic cleansing against a vulnerable community. Others asked pointedly, "Why are we still helping these people?" Some were depressed. Few of us slept much, as we would lie awake late at night wondering what we could or should have done differently. In Washington, our colleagues on the Burma desk had become virtual pariahs themselves, guilty by association.

We needed to rethink our approach. To me, the biggest challenge was to set aside our emotions—which were pushing us to walk away from the country—and ask ourselves what we could do that would have the best chance of helping the Rohingya, but also all the others in this country struggling for greater freedom, improved respect for human rights, and a brighter future? Some Washington visitors, from both the administration and Capitol Hill, castigated us for our apparently dispassionate analysis of the situation, which reflected both my failure to appreciate the need to show our anger and upset, and their difficulty in balancing emotion with a clear-eyed analysis of what actions might be most effective.

Working closely with NSC Asia and the EAP, we developed a revised strategy to reflect the new realities. We decided that our fundamental goals of trying to help Myanmar strengthen its nascent democracy, bring the military under civilian control, achieve peace and greater prosperity, and of course change its approach toward the Rohingya remained sound. What had changed, however, was the recognition that progress was going to take a lot longer and be much more difficult than we had hoped. Moreover, because so many of the country's leaders were trapped in the old mindset, progress also would require generational change. We should stay engaged with the existing government to try to maintain influence and encourage progress, as well as to counter China's efforts to gain excessive influence in Myanmar, but focus more of our efforts and resources on encouraging new thinking from the ground up, through civil society and the younger generation. While taking this longer-term approach, we of course had to continue to do everything possible in the near term to help the Rohingya.

The White House blessed this new approach, which was a major victory for those of us who did not want to give up on the country, but implementing it proved challenging on a couple of fronts. First, neither Washington nor Nay Pyi Taw made bilateral engagement a priority. The onus should have been on Myanmar, since its military had carried out the ethnic cleansing of the Rohingya, but the Myanmar authorities did not see it that way. They seemed to blame us (and much of the rest of the world) rather than accept responsibility for what had happened. In a 2018 meeting with Mandalay chief minister Zaw Myint Maung, the number two man in the NLD and a longtime democracy advocate and friend of the United States, he told me bluntly that the NLD was "deeply disappointed" that the United States had turned away from it. I told him that the NLD's disappointment mirrored that of Washington, where so many longtime supporters of the democracy movement had been shocked by developments in the country and by the NLD's response.

There was little engagement from the Washington end either. Secretary Tillerson's November 2017 stop in Nay Pyi Taw would turn out to be the only senior-level administration trip to Myanmar from January 2017 until the spring of 2018, when NSC senior director for Asia Matt Pottinger and USAID director Mark Green paid separate visits.

Second, to be effective in engaging the next generation and supporting reform-minded elements in Myanmar, we needed to maintain our assistance programs, which helped fund still-vibrant civil society and independent media, as well as agricultural programs aiding vulnerable ethnic minority communities and others in rural areas. In Washington, however, there was strong pressure—including from the USAID leadership—to cut or even eliminate assistance in response to the Rohingya crisis. Proponents of this approach argued that the Myanmar public's broad support for anti-Rohingya operations meant that the country as a whole was a lost cause and not worthy of our support. Frankly, some of this was politics—in Washington it always pays to show how tough one is on human rights violators. The reality, however, was that—if we really wanted to help the "good guys" in Myanmar, including the Rohingya—we needed to stay engaged and actually offer tangible support to reform-minded groups and individuals. I felt strongly about this and fought hard against those who wanted to "pull the plug" on Myanmar. In the end, with the support of key people on Capitol Hill, we were able to maintain our funding levels.

Third, the revised strategy glossed over the inherent conflict between pressing the government hard to create better conditions for the Rohingya and account for human rights violations on the one hand, and stepping up our engagement more broadly to enable us to counter China's aggressive influence efforts. We could do both, but it would require a willingness of senior Washington-based officials to visit and engage regularly, something few were willing to do because of the optics and likelihood of criticism from people back home.

China Steps into the Void

China, meanwhile, had stepped into the post–August 2017 void in a big way, constantly sending senior visitors, flying Myanmar officials (and others) to China to be wined and dined, promising to "defend" Myanmar in the UN Security Council, and offering substantial financing for Myanmar's much-needed infrastructure development. China's clout grew rapidly, as ours and that of other Western countries plummeted over our Rohingya-related criticism. During any number of meetings, Myanmar ministers would warn that our criticism was leaving them no choice but to turn to China. I would respond that they actually had another, perfectly feasible option—work with us and others to address the problems in Rakhine State, as they had committed to do, and pursue accountability for the human rights violations. Such an approach, I argued, was less threatening to their sovereignty than relying fully on China. Beijing, after all, interfered in Myanmar affairs on a daily basis (ask anyone in Kachin or northern Shan State) and was allowing its weapons to fall into the hands of insurgent groups.

China's top priority, it seemed, was to secure access to the Indian Ocean via construction of the Kyaukphyu port on the Bay of Bengal in Rakhine State. Chinese state-owned enterprises proposed a massive, $7.4 billion project that was dramatically bigger than what might be commercially warranted and offered few benefits to Myanmar. It also wanted to build a pipeline connecting that port to Yunnan, as part of a Myanmar-China Economic Corridor that would overwhelmingly benefit China. Also, while Beijing purported to support the peace process, it actually benefited from a fractious Myanmar, in which it could use its influence with various groups to advance its commercial and other interests.

Despite their unhappiness with our criticism over the Rohingya issue, many in Myanmar—including in the government and military—were wary of China. They did not want to become a vassal state any more than we wanted them to become one. So our role was not to drum up anti-China sentiment, but rather to share information about problematic Chinese behavior and to continue to support open public debate, independent media, and a strong civil society movement, including in the areas most under pressure near China's border. We also highlighted the benefits of quality investment, organizing, for example, a U.S.-Japan conference on responsible investment that emphasized the benefits of attracting quality investors, as opposed to those that would pay bribes and do nontransparent deals with shady business types on the Myanmar side.

Continued Diplomatic Efforts and Frustration

Throughout this period, we worked closely with like-minded governments, mostly from the West. We also coordinated constantly with Japan, which in its normal fashion had not been as publicly critical as we had and thus maintained greater access to key decision-makers in Nay Pyi Taw. Some criticized the Japanese for being too "soft," but in my view it was helpful that Tokyo maintained a higher level of engagement while also privately pushing the government to address the Rohingya issue. Having one more government screaming at Nay Pyi Taw was unlikely to help very much, and maintaining high-level access and good relations was helpful in many ways. I met or spoke with Japanese ambassador Ichiro Maruyama—a longtime Myanmar hand—at least once or twice each week to exchange information and ideas.

From mid-2017 until my departure in May 2020, the Rohingya/Rakhine crisis would remain both a humanitarian tragedy and an enormous weight that hung around Myanmar's ankles. The government committed to implement the Rakhine Advisory commission's recommendations, and those of us in the diplomatic community invested huge amounts of time and energy trying to achieve even modest progress. We would travel to Rakhine, whenever permitted, to assess the situation, and then fly to Nay Pyi Taw to relay our findings and recommendations to the government. We would fund small projects trying to create a better environment at the local level, which is where most of us thought the best hope for progress lay.

Much of the time, our government meetings were amicable, and ministers would commit to take at least small steps on citizenship verification, freedom of movement, and allowing greater access for international humanitarian organizations. At the same time, there was a steady undercurrent of animus from the government, which regularly criticized us for attacking it even as we constantly offered ideas that would help it get out of the mess it had created. Ministers and others would constantly tell us, "You don't understand." They were right. We did not understand how they could continue to deny the reality of a horrible ethnic cleansing campaign and blame the international community for what had happened.

Early in the crisis, a small group of us (the EU and UK ambassadors, the UN country representative, and I) were able to meet with Aung San Suu Kyi and a few of her top advisors a handful of times, usually at her residence, for in-depth and relatively open conversations in which we stressed the need for bold and urgent steps to address the violence and the humanitarian crisis. As the crisis and the international condemnation continued, Aung San Suu Kyi grew increasingly distant and cool toward me personally and toward the West in general. Access to her grew more difficult, and in the few meetings we had she quickly shut down any substantive conversation about the issue. Her top advisors, including Minister for the State Counsellor's Office Kyaw Tint Swe and National Security Advisor Thaung Tun, often sharply disagreed with the international community's view of the issue and were especially critical of the UN, but I at least was able to discuss the issue with them regularly and frankly.

Aung San Suu Kyi's approach toward the Rohingya crisis baffled her international supporters, as it stood in such stark contrast to her image as an advocate of human rights and a "democracy icon." I cannot pretend to know what she was thinking, but I attribute her stance largely to a handful of factors: (1) the fact that supporting the Rohingya was bad politics, domestically; (2) possibly, a wariness of crossing the powerful military; (3) her poor understanding of the situation facing the Rohingya, compounded by her apparent cognitive dissonance, in which she accepted inaccurate information provided by aides and the military but rejected conflicting accounts, particularly from the international community; and (4) her willingness, and that of her inner circle, to buy into conspiracy theories suggesting the crisis had been engineered by the Rohingya and their international supporters to harm Myanmar.

On the ground, progress was painfully slow. We asked ourselves whether it was a lack of government will or inability to deliver in the face of opposition from the Rakhine community and/or the military and hardline officials. It was both, but the government's inability to deliver at the local and state levels ranked as a huge problem. One well-intentioned minister told me privately that his own staff would not follow his orders in Rakhine State. Some of this was hostility toward the Rohingya, or fear of being ostracized for doing anything to help that community.

It also reflected the poor relations between the NLD government and its appointed chief minister in Rakhine State, on one hand, and the Rakhine community on the other. The Rakhine complained, justifiably, that the government neither consulted with nor listened to their views. In a meeting with an influential minister in early 2018, I stressed the need for the government to start a dialogue with the Rakhine political community, arguing that the Rohingya issue required a political solution that had buy-in from the Rakhine. He flatly rejected the suggestion, saying, "We can't trust the Rakhine."

In November 2017, Myanmar and Bangladesh reached agreement to facilitate the voluntary return of Rohingya who had fled since October 2016. We saw it as a useful step, but of course the Rohingya would only be willing to return to the extent that they felt the environment for them had improved. That would require at least some movement on implementing the Annan commission's recommendations. The Myanmar government, however, focused instead on building the physical infrastructure needed to process the returns, including a fenced-in return center that looked like a prison.

Over the next two years, the two governments several times indicated that major returns were imminent and then were disappointed when none of the Rohingya volunteered to come back. In meeting after meeting with senior officials, they would blame Bangladesh, or the UN High Commissioner for Refugees, or ARSA for blocking the returns. We would point out that the refugees were not coming back because there had been no meaningful improvement in the situation facing the roughly half-million Rohingya still in Rakhine. There had been no accountability for the human rights violations against them, and they still had almost no freedom of movement, no political or civil rights, extremely limited access to education and healthcare services, and no legal status. The citizenship verification process failed miserably, as only a few hundred Rohingya received citizenship documents of any kind over a couple of years.

The lack of progress was deeply frustrating for all of us, though of course our unhappiness was nothing compared to what the Rohingya community was continuing to suffer. Every time I traveled to Rakhine and spoke with Rohingya, often in IDP camps, I could see and feel the pain and hopelessness of the community. I remember one man with whom I spoke several times during visits. He projected great dignity, while lamenting that his children were growing up in a situation—an IDP camp—in which they not only felt no hope, but also were beginning to believe that it was normal not to work and not to have any contact with non-Rohingya communities.

Myanmar's treatment of the community was so fundamentally wrong and unjust that, after every trip, I would go through a couple of days of intense anger and wonder if we should cut off all assistance and disengage. Every time, however, I came to the same conclusion, which was that taking such steps would not help the Rohingya. In the end, we could not let anger drive our policy. We always had to ask ourselves what might help (or hurt) the Rohingya, as well as other vulnerable communities in the country.

The world continued to press Myanmar for accountability and justice for what had happened, amid growing calls to label it genocide. The UN had established a fact-finding mission to investigate alleged human rights abuses back in March 2017, but that effort took on renewed importance following the mid-2017 violence. The mission's report, released in August 2018, concluded that the military's abuses against the Rohingya called for an investigation for possible genocidal intent as well as other crimes against humanity.[20] UN special rapporteur for human rights in Myanmar, Yanghee Lee, continued her efforts as well, while the UN Security Council kept the issue on its agenda. Pressure grew in Washington for the State Department to make a determination of genocide, but that decision was put off a number of times until Secretary of State Antony Blinken announced such a determination in March 2022.

Based in part on a conversation I had in late 2017 with Mike Kozak, the senior official in the Bureau of Democracy, Human Rights, and Labor Affairs at the time, the State Department launched an initiative to document the human rights violations. That effort, which involved interviews with hundreds of randomly selected Rohingya refugees in Bangladesh, affirmed that the vast majority of refugees had either experienced or directly witnessed violence and abuse, including rape, at the hands of the military.[21]

The Myanmar government refused to cooperate with any of these investigations, arguing that they were all biased and constituted unwarranted interference in their domestic affairs. They refused to allow any of these entities—or otherwise independent observers—access to northern Rakhine State, while at the same time insisting that they were ready to investigate any allegations of human rights violations if presented with any evidence of such (they did not consider accounts by

20 "Myanmar Rohingya: UN Says Myanmar Military Leaders Must Face Genocide Charges," BBC News, August 27, 2018, https://www.bbc.com/news/world-asia -45318982.
21 "Documentation of Atrocities in Northern Rakhine State," Bureau of Democracy, Human Rights, and Labor, U.S. Department of State, September 24, 2018, https://2017-2021.state.gov/reports-bureau-of-democracy-human-rights-and -labor/documentation-of-atrocities-in-northern-rakhine-state//index.html.

refugees in Bangladesh to be "evidence.") It was a bizarre and counter-productive stance, but the authorities refused to budge. By the end of 2017, the government told Yanghee Lee she would no longer be allowed to visit. Privately, senior ministers told me Lee's failure to mention the ARSA attacks in her most recent public comments on the Rakhine crisis was the final straw, convincing them that she was biased. I told them they were making a huge mistake, but they did not listen. Surprisingly, both the government and the military agreed to receive briefings by the State Department team that had written the documentation report, but neither changed its approach to the issue as a result.

The government sought to counter international pressure by establishing its own "Independent Commission of Enquiry," which would include two international diplomats. This commission got off to a bad start when the government upon announcing its formation said its purpose would be to counter the "false allegations" made by the UN and others.[22] The commission members' own initial comments were not encouraging, but a few of us in the diplomatic community engaged with it in hopes of pushing it in the right direction. Some of our private conversations with members only added to our concerns, but the commission's last-minute effort to bring in credible analysts (informally and quietly) to help it gave us some hope. The commission's final report in early 2020 refuted allegations of "genocidal intent" but concluded that serious human rights violations, including war crimes, did occur.[23] Had such conclusions been announced eighteen to twenty-four months earlier, perhaps they would have influenced world opinion. By early 2020, however, anything short of admission of genocide would fail to change international views of Myanmar.

By that time, the world's focus had turned to the International Court of Justice (ICJ) at The Hague, where The Gambia had filed a genocide case against Myanmar. Interestingly, Nay Pyi Taw did not summarily reject the ICJ, deciding instead that it had sufficient legitimacy to warrant the government's engagement. Aung San Suu Kyi surprised us and her countrymen by going to The Hague herself to represent Myanmar. There, she denied the military had acted with genocidal intent while

---

22 "Myanmar Rejects UN Accusation of 'Genocide' Against the Rohingya," BBC News, August 29, 2018, https://www.bbc.com/news/world-asia-45338986.
23 "Myanmar Finds War Crimes but No Genocide in Rohingya Crackdown," Al Jazeera, January 21, 2020, https://www.aljazeera.com/news/2020/1/21/myanmar-finds-war-crimes-but-no-genocide-in-rohingya-crackdown.

for the first time acknowledging it might have used "disproportionate force." She vowed that Myanmar would hold human rights violators accountable, and even mentioned possible trials for "war crimes."[24] Again, had she made these comments a year or two earlier, she might have changed the world's perception of her and her country. But her comments came too late to affect world opinion, and in fact were widely criticized internationally.[25] At home, on the other hand, her "courage" in going to The Hague prompted mass demonstrations of support and almost certainly added to her still-immense popularity ahead of the November 2020 national elections.

Broader Impact of Rohingya Crisis on Reform

Looking back, I believe the Rohingya crisis not only was a disaster in its own right, but it also took the wind out of the sails of the broader NLD reform effort, such as it was. The government became even more conservative and intolerant of criticism. It is impossible to say how much political reform would have happened had the crisis not occurred. Perhaps not much, but the fact is that the government and Parliament implemented some political liberalization measures before the crisis and virtually none after. It began to use provision 66(d) of the Telecommunications Act and other laws more aggressively to pursue critics and even peaceful demonstrators, gradually restricting the space in which civil society, the media, and others could effectively dissent.

One of the most egregious cases of the government's intolerance of criticism related to the Rakhine crisis. I had just landed in Nay Pyi Taw on the morning of December 12, 2017, when the Reuters bureau chief called to say that two of his colleagues, Wa Lone and Kyaw Saw Oo, had been arrested the previous night in what appeared to be a police set-up. The two had been doing superb reporting from Rakhine, and apparently had a story in the works on a massacre of Rohingya at Inn

---

24 "Transcript: Aung San Suu Kyi's Speech at the ICJ in Full," Al Jazeera, December 12, 2019, https://www.aljazeera.com/news/2019/12/12/transcript-aung-san-suu-kyis-speech-at-the-icj-in-full.

25 See, for example, Marlise Simons and Hannah Beech, "Aung San Suu Kyi Defends Myanmar Against Rohingya Genocide Accusations," *New York Times*, December 11, 2019; and "Aung San Suu Kyi's Hague Performance Impresses Few Beyond Myanmar Loyalists," Radio Free Asia, December 13, 2019, https://www.rfa.org/english/news/myanmar/aung-san-suu-kyis-hague-performance-12132019180148.html.

Din village. I immediately raised the matter with two top advisors to Aung San Suu Kyi and urged them to find a way to resolve the matter quickly. Unfortunately, the government did the opposite, and pursued the case against the journalists with vigor, despite intense international criticism, until the two were convicted and imprisoned for violating state secrets. The case was outrageous, and simply dug the government and the country into an even deeper hole. The Myanmar public, however, supported the government, treating the courageous Wa Lone and Kyaw Saw Oo as traitors.

When their story came out, it included photos showing clearly that soldiers had detained and subsequently murdered several Rohingya villagers in cold blood.[26] It was awful. The government prosecuted the journalists for doing their jobs and for providing information that confirmed human rights abuses. We lobbied behind the scenes for months to secure their release (as did others), but Aung San Suu Kyi refused, insisting that "rule of law" must be followed. Eventually, they were released, but the case did untold damage to Myanmar, not to mention to the two journalists and their families. It also reflected the stubborn mindset that characterized Nay Pyi Taw's approach to the overall issue.

The government and military's approach to the peace process also was stuck. There were occasional meetings and initiatives that offered some hope, but none went very far. Much of the discussion focused on the process, including the lack of informal dialogue and the military's failure to honor elements of the Nationwide Ceasefire Agreement, such as the right of ethnic minority groups to hold national dialogues. It seemed the military often went out of its way to irritate the EAOs, who, by the way, varied greatly not only in size but in the extent to which they sought to represent and provide services to their communities. The NLD government, meanwhile, showed little or no initiative in the peace process and seemed to fade into the background over time. Because of the presence of so many parties—and the fact that men with guns dominated the negotiations, leaving the ethnic minority civilians on the outside—the peace process was inherently going to be very difficult. Nonetheless, I came to the conclusion that the fundamental problem remained the paternalist Bamar attitude toward ethnic minority communities and the Nay Pyi Taw approach of treating the EAOs like so

---

26 Wa Lone, Kyaw Soe Oo, Simon Lewis, and Antoni Slodkowski, "How Myanmar Forces Burned, Looted and Killed in a Remote Village," Reuters, February 8 2018, https://www.reuters.com/investigates/special-report/myanmar-rakhine-events/.

many wayward children. Ethnic minority communities, many of which had supported Daw Suu in the 2015 elections, gradually lost faith in her and the NLD.

The Rise of the Arakan Army

Nowhere was this truer than in Rakhine State, where the majority Arakan National Party had chafed under NLD rule since 2016. The community had largely welcomed the military's operations against the Rohingya in 2017, which after all had accomplished the goal of changing the demographic balance in the ethnic Rakhine's favor. By late 2018, however, many Rakhine were deeply frustrated with the government's failure to engage with them. In early 2019, the Arakan Army (AA), which had begun life as an instrument of the KIO in Kachin and northern Shan states, had shifted substantial forces to Rakhine and begun launching effective attacks against the military.

Over the next eighteen months, the AA would emerge as the most significant threat among all the EAOs. It conducted aggressive attacks that caused significant military casualties and also abducted officials. The military poured more troops into Rakhine and the government cut off internet service to the region, but the AA remained a potent force with what seemed to be widespread public support among ethnic Rakhine.

The problem called for a political solution. As a number of Rakhine political figures told us, young people were supporting and, in some cases, joining the AA because they did not see democracy as giving them a voice. The NLD, by insisting on appointing one of its party members as chief minister of Rakhine State and then failing to engage or consult with Rakhine political and community leaders, had alienated much of the public. The solution, it seemed, would be to engage with the Arakan National Party and others, make some political compromises so that the Rakhine would feel they had more of a voice, and in doing so gradually reduce support for the AA. The government took the opposite tack, labeling the AA a terrorist organization (which made it illegal for anyone to talk with them) and seeking to destroy it militarily. By mid-2020 that approach, predictably, was not working. The Union Election Commission's decision not to allow voting to proceed in much of the central and northern part of the state during the 2020 elections was sure to exacerbate the situation.

The November 2020 Elections

In many ways, it is remarkable that Myanmar succeeded in conducting largely peaceful and competitive elections in November 2020, despite conflict and the raging COVID-19 pandemic. The NLD again won overwhelmingly, enjoying an even bigger landslide than in 2015. The military-aligned USDP suffered a humiliating defeat, winning barely half as many seats as it had in 2015. Myanmar voters, including in ethnic minority areas, sent a clear signal that they supported the party (and the person) that to them represented democracy or at least civilian governance, and remained implacably opposed to the military and its allies playing anything beyond a minimal role in the country's political life. Unfortunately, election authorities had disenfranchised large numbers of ethnic minority voters by declaring significant areas of Rakhine and Shan states sufficiently insecure as to make voting impossible. The Arakan National Party nonetheless won a majority in the state parliament, reinforcing the Rakhine voters' message that they wanted to be governed by their own. Initially, the big post-election question was whether the NLD would take a more compromising, accommodating approach to the Rakhine and to other ethnic minorities than it had during its first term.

Of course, this and other questions would quickly be overtaken by events, specifically the military's February 1, 2021, coup, ostensibly based on the NLD government's refusal to take seriously the military's allegations of widespread electoral fraud. While the elections suffered from any number of problems, credible observers and analysts agreed that the military's claims were bogus and that the true reason for the coup was the military's thirst for power—or fear of a reelected NLD government chipping away at the political and economic power it still enjoyed—and military commander Min Aung Hlaing's personal ambition.

A Pre-Coup Assessment

I departed Myanmar in May 2020, after more than four years in the country and amid the COVID-19 pandemic, but well before the coup. To say I left disappointed would be an understatement, for all the reasons outlined above. After four or five years of unprecedented reform, the country under the NLD had taken some significant steps backward,

even if certain reforms continued and much of the population continued to enjoy substantial freedom and greater opportunity than in
the past. Moreover, the horrific abuses inflicted on the Rohingya community—and the government's failure even to acknowledge them, let
alone address them—ranked as a human rights and political disaster
of the first order. Some in the human rights community and the Burma
Lobby had taken to playing the "I told you so" game, arguing that we
had been fooled by the illusion of progress, duped by the military, and
had given up all our leverage—sanctions—too soon. Some even suggested the Obama administration had willfully turn a blind eye to the
Rohingya issue in its rush to engage and normalize with Myanmar,
or that the international community somehow was to blame for what
happened to the Rohingya.

Given how things have gone the past few years, all of us involved in
the policymaking need to be humble and open to legitimate criticism.
Things did not work out the way we had hoped, even before the coup.
That said, I take issue with many of the simplistic arguments noted
above. First, while it is true that in hindsight I and others were too optimistic about prospects for further reform, the fact is that Myanmar did
carry out dramatic reforms in 2011–16 that fundamentally changed
the country for the better. They did not solve all the problems, but we
all knew that it would take a generation or more to address all of the
systemic challenges the country faced. As I have said before, if you wait
to act until a country solves all its problems, you lose your opportunity
to influence developments.

Second, I see a lot of articles these days talking about how the West
had been "euphoric" and had rushed to embrace the military after the
initial reforms, when we should have focused on the military's continued substantial power and human rights violations. Some of the criticism is fair, but I certainly did not see—at least on the part of the United
States—a "rush to embrace" the military. I and probably others were,
in hindsight, more hopeful than we should have been that the military,
having accepted significant reform, would see it in its interest to go
along with further reform in return for the promise of greater engagement from the international community. That said, our engagement
with the armed forces remained extremely limited, involving mostly
discussions about what might be possible if the military accepted further reforms and improved its human rights record. In the end, the
military turned out to be even more obstinate than we had thought,

and the civilian "pro-reform" forces proved to be less reform-minded than we and many others had expected.

As for sanctions, people in Washington are too fond of them. Imposing them makes you look strong and principled, and they create the illusion of leverage. The reality, however, is that the sanctions did not give us much leverage in Myanmar. We had sanctions throughout the 1990s and 2000s, and that did not stop the military from rampaging through Shan and Karen states, killing, torturing and raping innocents with zero accountability. Nor did it stop them from throwing thousands of people in prison for decades for political crimes. I cannot prove that the military would still have conducted its brutal campaign against the Rohingya (or carried out a coup) if we had maintained our sanctions, but I would be willing to bet a lot of money it would have. Moreover, the broad sanctions we maintained in full until 2012 and in part until 2016 discouraged investment and caused a certain amount of suffering among the Myanmar people. I am not one of those who blames sanctions for the overall poor state of the economy under the military. It was largely the military's mismanagement and poor policy choices that held the economy back. That said, the breadth of our sanctions hit a lot of innocent people in the country.

Following the U.S. determination of ethnic cleansing of the Rohingya, we did impose targeted sanctions against certain military officials, including generals Min Aung Hlaing and Soe Win, less because we thought the sanctions would change behavior than to send a clear message that their actions were beyond the pale.

I also categorically reject the claim that the Obama administration turned a blind eye to the treatment of the Rohingya, or that it is somehow the international community's fault that the ethnic cleansing happened. President Obama himself had raised the Rohingya issue in a public speech during his historic 2012 visit to Myanmar. We were very aware of and concerned about the treatment of the Rohingya and constantly pushed, pleaded, and cajoled the Myanmar authorities to address it. Saying we should have withheld full normalization and assistance until Myanmar seriously addressed the problem is a legitimate argument. The question, in my view, is how best to respond when a country makes significant progress in several areas but not in another. Forgive the analogy, but if a student has been failing every class for several years, and then suddenly starts getting Bs and Cs in most classes, but an F in a very important class, do we engage and support or do we stay with the "stick" only until they improve that one grade? Again, one can argue it either way, but in my view, it is not an easy question.

The idea that the UN or the international community is to blame for the ethnic cleansing is absurd. The international community, including the UN, made an immense, concerted effort to persuade the Myanmar authorities to grant the Rohingya the rights they deserved. It was Myanmar—not the international community—that chose not to do so. And it was the Myanmar military—not the international community—that carried out the operations that killed thousands, caused untold suffering to thousands more, burned down hundreds of villages, and drove 750,000 Rohingya into Bangladesh. I am not saying the international community was perfect. I made mistakes and no doubt missed opportunities, and I am sure others did as well, but we should be honest about who was responsible for what happened.

Post-Coup: The Struggle Continues

The February 1, 2021, coup obviously constituted an enormous setback for Myanmar. The coup appears to have been motivated by three factors: (1) the military's fear that, having again won an overwhelming landslide victory, the NLD government would be in an even stronger position to try to chip away at the military's political and economic power (even if the military retained the seats in parliament to veto constitutional amendments); (2) the military's unhappiness or even anger that the NLD refused to take seriously its allegations of widespread electoral fraud, implying "disrespect" of the powerful military; and (3) Min Aung Hlaing's personal need, with mandatory retirement coming up, to land a powerful position in the state from which he could enjoy immunity from potential prosecution and also protect his substantial, ill-gotten family wealth. It was a power grab, fueled by ego and greed, and partly by the military's belief—perpetuated by years of operating in an echo chamber hermetically sealed off from society—that its political leadership was essential to keep the country from disintegrating, no matter what the people of the country might believe.

The NLD, for all of its faults and disappointments, had twice won landslide electoral victories and was trying to assert civilian control over the military, as well as to implement economic reforms. Many—probably most—people in the country were enjoying greater freedom and access to information, increased income, and more opportunities than they had a decade earlier. Just as importantly, there was a sense of hope that things would continue to get better.

The military, out of touch with the rest of the country, severely underestimated the opposition the coup would engender. Within days of the coup, huge numbers of people took to the streets in mass protests all over the country, while activists organized a powerful civil disobedience campaign, in which large numbers of people refused to work under the junta.

The military responded as it always does, brutally suppressing the protests, killing many demonstrators, and arresting many more. It shut down the internet, tried to shut down independent media, and detained anyone it considered a potential threat to its hold on power.

Those elected parliamentarians who avoided arrest quickly formed the Committee Representing Pyidaungsu Hluttaw (CRPH), which in turn established a National Unity Government (NUG) as an alternative to the junta's State Administrative Council (SAC). The CRPH also established a National Unity Consultative Committee, which aimed to bring together a broad spectrum of groups opposed to the coup.

Over time, the situation has developed into what can best be described as a national resistance against the junta, with small flash protests and the ongoing civil disobedience movement being supplemented by growing armed resistance in the form of dozens if not hundreds of locally formed People's Defense Units. Some ethnic armed organizations allied with the NUG and have fought against the military, while others have stayed largely neutral.

A year later, the coup arguably still has not succeeded. The military holds the critical levers of power, but faces widespread opposition and resistance that greatly limits its ability to govern. It has almost no domestic support and lacks international legitimacy and recognition. The junta basically is waging unbridled warfare against its own people, indiscriminately bombing, shelling, and burning villages and towns, and continuing to kill, arrest, and torture widely.

The resistance enjoys substantial popular support but lacks funding and international recognition, while having only a very limited ability to assert any kind of governing capacity. As of this writing, the outlook for the country is uncertain, though the most likely scenario is for continued violence, instability, and suffering for many months, if not years.

The Biden administration responded to the coup by immediately condemning it, calling for the military to return power to the elected authorities, and imposing a series of sanctions, including the February

2021 freezing of some $1 billion in Myanmar reserves held at the Federal Reserve Bank of New York. Over the following year, Washington imposed additional sanctions, sought to rally international support against the coup, and expanded humanitarian assistance to try to help those affected by the violence.

Washington has expressed sympathy for the Myanmar people and has engaged in a limited fashion with the NUG, while stopping short of recognizing it or offering direct financial or other support. The United States has not engaged directly with the junta, no doubt believing that such engagement would accomplish little other than to confer legitimacy on the SAC.

Generally, in this book, I have argued for dialogue and engagement even in the face of democratic backsliding. It is harder to make that argument in the case of the Myanmar military, partly because of their extreme brutality and tremendous unpopularity throughout the country, but also because they have shown little interest in dialogue with us or willingness to compromise. I will not comment on potential additional sanctions—beyond those already imposed by the Biden administration—against junta or military officials or other entities, as those likely will have been decided on by the time this volume is published.[27]

More importantly, the United States—to the extent circumstances allow—should strive to continue support for independent media and civil society, two important pillars of any future democracy. It also should continue funding for scholarships and education writ large, and, where possible, for assistance that benefits farmers, small businesses, and the like throughout the country.

The United States will also want to continue to engage and work with ethnic minority communities and in support of the long-term goal of creating a federal structure that most believe is the only viable way forward for the country. Washington should consider more funding for initiatives that facilitate dialogue about what a future federal system might look like, and that seek to build on the nascent discussion about how to build understanding and trust among the different ethnic communities in the country.

---

27 Note: Since the coup, many in Myanmar have stopped referring to the military as the "Tatmadaw," as it often was called in the past, believing that the term gives the junta and its soldiers unwarranted legitimacy and respect. Out of sympathy for that view, I generally am not using the term "Tatmadaw" in this book.

During the many years of military dictatorship, the people of Myanmar knew that the United States was on their side. Tragically, the U.S. criticism of Myanmar over the Rohingya crisis—which was fully justified in my view—changed that to a large extent. Now, in the aftermath of the coup, the Myanmar people once again will see that the United States is on their side. The coming months and perhaps years likely will be very difficult and frustrating, but Washington will do well by basing its policy on the long term and on the importance of staying on the side of the people.

IV. ASEAN, CHINA, AND THE UNITED STATES

CHAPTER ELEVEN

The Enigma of ASEAN

Although the Association of Southeast Asian Nations—ASEAN—has existed for more than a half-century, the reality is that few U.S. policymakers know very much about it or how best to work with it. Within the Washington foreign policy community, there is general recognition that the United States should work with ASEAN, balanced by modest expectations about what benefits such engagement actually might bring, especially in the short term.

ASEAN, administered by a thinly staffed headquarters in Jakarta, is a regional grouping of ten Southeast Asian nations—Indonesia, Malaysia, Thailand, Singapore, the Philippines, Brunei, Vietnam, Laos, Cambodia, and Myanmar. The member nations boast a combined population of some 670 million people and, collectively, would be the world's fifth-largest economy. Institutionally, however, ASEAN is relatively small and weak, not to be compared in size, budget, or mission with, for example, the European Union. ASEAN's founding members established the institution more than fifty years ago largely to manage disputes within the region and to discourage great power intervention. Since its inception, maintaining regional unity—even if paper-thin at times—has been paramount. Over time, ASEAN's size and role has grown, and it has asserted for itself a central role in regional diplomacy, including by convening annual summits that attract many of the region's and world's major powers.

In recent years, Washington policymakers have tended to view ASEAN mostly through the lens of how it responds to the challenge of an increasingly powerful and assertive China, particularly Chinese activities in the South China Sea. To many in Washington, ASEAN's inability to take a united position and its reluctance to speak out more forcefully against what seems to be obvious Chinese aggression and bad behavior has been disappointing. Southeast Asian officials, while not always thrilled with ASEAN's cautious approach and generally welcoming U.S. engagement, are also disappointed in some ways with the United States. They complain that Washington's demands for a tougher, united front are unrealistic, given the region's economic dependence on China, and fly in the face of ASEAN's nonaligned DNA. They also point out that the United States, for all its talk, has often failed to show up and has not proven itself a consistent, reliable partner that can be counted on in a crunch, including in the South China Sea.

The troubled situation in Myanmar, an ASEAN member, has from time to time been another source of difficulty in the U.S.-ASEAN relationship. Washington was not happy that ASEAN accepted Myanmar as a member and at times has pressed ASEAN to take stronger action to respond to human rights abuses there. ASEAN members, while often unhappy with the Myanmar authorities, have taken a softer approach and on occasion have questioned why Washington sometimes allows its intensive focus on the human rights situation there to overshadow its broader strategic agenda with the region.

There is a lot to unpack here, and that is even before we talk about all the other aspects of ASEAN's agenda, including economic integration, building an ASEAN community, and the broader issue of ASEAN centrality in a constantly evolving set of regional fora that bring together most of the world's major powers.

To understand where ASEAN stands now, it is essential to understand why it was created, how its goals have evolved, and what it can and cannot do. Also, this might sound like just semantics, but we need to remember the distinction between the institution of ASEAN and the region of Southeast Asia. We sometimes use the terms "ASEAN" and "Southeast Asia" interchangeably, but that is a mistake, because it implies a coherence that does not exist and suggests that the relatively small institution of ASEAN has much more power than it actually does. The reality is that ASEAN's ten nations are extremely diverse, generally uninterested in surrendering sovereignty to a regional institution, and will quickly swat down any organization or individual that seeks to speak out on behalf of the entire region. Compared with Europe, there is in Southeast Asia much less of a common identity or a sense of belonging to a broader community.

ASEAN's Origins and Purpose

In 1967 the foreign ministers of Singapore, Thailand, Indonesia, Malaysia, and the Philippines issued the Bangkok Declaration, establishing the Association of Southeast Asian Nations, with the stated objective of promoting "economic growth, social progress, and cultural development."[1] The five governments clearly saw value in a regional consultative mechanism that would allow them to work together to counter what, at the time, seemed to be the very real threat of communist expansion. In addition, just a few years after the *Konfrontasi* between Indonesia and Malaysia and a Philippine-Malaysia dispute over the creation of the Federation of Malaya, they hoped the new forum would enable them to tackle intraregional tensions and maintain the peace and stability they needed to pursue nation-building and economic development, while discouraging outside intervention. Bringing Indonesia into the group—possible only because the hyper-nationalist Sukarno had been replaced by the more pragmatic Suharto—was critical, given its massive size compared to its neighbors.

The five governments also saw ASEAN as a platform to assert their role in determining the direction and fate of their region. Put another way, it was a vehicle to prevent a regional diplomatic vacuum that, they feared, the big powers would be only too happy to fill. While Thailand and the Philippines were U.S. allies, Indonesia and Malaysia pursued a firmly nonaligned policy. All agreed, however, that the region needed to have a strong independent voice. To a large extent, whatever else one wants to say about ASEAN, one constant during its fifty-five-year history has been this emphasis on doing everything possible to ensure Southeast Asians, collectively through ASEAN, set the agenda and determined the ground rules for their region. In many ways, controlling the agenda in their own neighborhood and maintaining at least a minimal level of unity has been as important to the ASEAN member states as achieving substantive results on specific issues, if not more so.

Along these lines, the ASEAN members in 1971 signed a declaration designating Southeast Asia as a Zone of Peace, Freedom and Neutrality.

---

1 Jurgen Ruland, "From Trade to Investment: ASEAN and AFTA in the Era of the 'New Regionalism,'" *Pacific Affairs* 92, no. 3 (September 2019), https://doi.org/10.5509/2019923533.

The declaration offered an early example of how ASEAN would work: the issuance of the declaration by itself did not change any realities on the ground (or water); rather, it was a largely symbolic effort to try to create norms of behavior and make clear that ASEAN members did not want their region to be a superpower battlefield.

The original member states made ASEAN's scope and mandate modest. It was not to be a supranational organization or the beginning of an EU-like entity. Rather, it was a top-down diplomatic tool dominated by engagements among the various foreign ministries. The members did not write down formal rules or procedures but rather emphasized development of personal relationships and trust-building through informal meetings. There was an implicit understanding—which became firmer over time—that decisions would be made by consensus, and that they would avoid interfering in each other's domestic affairs. This understanding, along with the bloc's preference for quiet diplomacy and avoiding controversial issues, became known as the "ASEAN Way."

ASEAN Grows and Expands Its Mandate

Over the years, the members have been willing to allow ASEAN to evolve and grow in response to regional and global developments. For example, following the communist victories in Vietnam, Laos, and Cambodia in 1975 and the concomitant U.S. military withdrawal from much of the region, ASEAN members sought to strengthen cooperation on regional security. In February 1976 they held the first ASEAN summit meeting in Bali. They told their publics they intended to discuss economic cooperation, but security dominated the agenda. The summit produced the "Bali Declaration of ASEAN Concord" (often referred to as the "Bali Concord I"), which committed them to settle intraregional differences peacefully and to establish a secretariat for ASEAN. They also developed the Treaty of Amity and Cooperation (TAC), which set a standard of peaceful interstate behavior for members and for outside powers that wished to sign on.[2]

In response to Vietnam's late 1978 invasion of Cambodia, the ASEAN members unified behind a diplomatic strategy that—in coordination with the United States, China, and others—sought to deny recognition of the Vietnamese-imposed new Cambodian government and to create

---

2 Barry Desker, "Is ASEAN a Community," RSIS Commentary no. 145, August 2, 2017, https://www.rsis.edu.sg/wp-content/uploads/2017/08/CO17145.pdf.

incentives for Vietnam to withdraw. ASEAN's united approach helped keep the new government from taking a seat in the UN and put intense pressure on Vietnam. In 1988, U.S. secretary of state George Shultz praised ASEAN's firm stance, stating that "with each passing year, you (ASEAN) demonstrate new vitality and cohesion, earning the admiration of the international community."[3]

Over time Indonesia—wary of China's role—grew increasingly unhappy with the Thai-led approach of working with Beijing and the United States to exert maximum pressure on Vietnam. While maintaining superficial unity with its ASEAN partners, Indonesia engaged Hanoi directly, creating a two-track ASEAN approach that helped produce important breakthroughs. This effort, along with a broader diplomatic campaign and the end of the Cold War, helped created the conditions for Vietnam's eventual withdrawal by late 1989 and the signing of the Cambodian Peace Accords in October 1991.

In the early 1990s, the end of the Cold War, the Cambodian peace accords, the emergence of China, and changing global trade patterns led ASEAN to take several important initiatives, particularly at the fourth ASEAN summit in Singapore in 1992.

The leaders, who had previously devoted little energy to economic cooperation, announced that they would create an ASEAN Free Trade Agreement (AFTA) over fifteen years, beginning in January 1993. The initiative reflected two concerns: first, that China's rapidly emerging economy posed a competitive threat to Southeast Asian economies, which depended heavily for growth on foreign investment that now was increasingly drawn to China; second, that the rise of new trading blocs, particularly the North American Free Trade Agreement (NAFTA), and the potential for increased protectionism could close markets to their exports.

AFTA's goal was both to promote intraregional trade and to make Southeast Asia more attractive to foreign investment. Specifically, ASEAN members committed to reduce tariffs on all manufactured and processed goods produced in member states to 0–5 percent by 2008. ASEAN followed up in 1995 with the ASEAN Framework Agreement on Services, which called for liberalization of trade in twelve major service sectors.

---

3 Quoted in Donald E. Weatherbee, *ASEAN's Half-Century: A Political History of the Association of Southeast Asian Nations* (Lanham, Maryland: Rowman & Littlefield, 2019), 119.

The leaders also agreed to expand their discussions with their dialogue partners—key external players such as China, Japan, and the United States—on regional political and security issues. This led in 1993 to the establishment of the ASEAN Regional Forum (ARF), which was to be the first in what became a series of ASEAN-centered regional fora to discuss security and other issues. Members would include the ASEAN nations, plus the bloc's ten dialogue partners and other relevant nations that could be admitted by consensus decision.

With the end of the Cold War and the signing of the Cambodian peace accords, the leaders also could look forward to implementing their vision of an ASEAN that would include all ten Southeast Asian nations (East Timor did not become independent until 1999). Brunei had joined the original five members in 1984, once it gained full independence from the United Kingdom, but the eventual decision to bring in Vietnam, Laos, Cambodia, and Myanmar—which were significantly poorer and less integrated into the international economy—proved to be a much bigger step. ASEAN had, in theory, been open to such an expansion since its founding, but it was not a realistic option until the end of the Vietnam War, Myanmar's move away from socialist isolation, and then the 1991 accords that ended the Cambodia conflict and produced the withdrawal of Vietnamese troops.

By bringing in the four new members, ASEAN had at least on paper strengthened the region against unwanted great-power intervention or domination and created long-term opportunities for increased intraregional trade. On the other hand, expansion of the institution would make consensus decision-making that much harder, especially because the new members did not share the same values as the first six. In addition, the new members lagged far behind the others economically, which would complicate efforts at economic integration.

The Asian Financial Crisis, which hit the region hard in 1997–98, highlighted the vulnerabilities of Southeast Asian economies and spurred calls for accelerated economic integration. In 2000, the ASEAN nations, together with Japan, South Korea, and China, launched the Chiang Mai Initiative, a currency swap mechanism that would enable member countries to support each other in the case of future financial difficulties. Still, economic difficulties persisted, and—while several countries carried out important internal economic reforms—there was limited progress toward further economic integration.

ASEAN took another major step forward at the 2004 Bali Summit, at which the leaders produced the Bali Concord II (following on the important 1976 Bali Concord I). The new document, which came at a time of some frustration for several ASEAN members due, among other things, to the slow pace of economic integration, called for the development of a "people-centered ASEAN Community" by 2020 (later moved up to 2015), consisting of separate economic, security, and sociocultural pillars.

Thailand and Singapore, in particular, pushed for the ASEAN Economic Community (AEC) with the goal of creating a single, integrated market that, over time, would allow for the free flow of goods, services, labor, and capital. Proponents hoped that a more integrated region would attract increased foreign direct investment at a time of growing global competition for such funds. The AEC also sought to integrate ASEAN further into the global economic community, including via a series of trade agreements with major non-ASEAN trading partners.[4]

Indonesia led the effort to craft the vision for the ASEAN Political and Security Community (APSC), with Foreign Minister Hasan Wirajuda pushing for language that emphasized democracy and human rights and called for an ASEAN peacekeeping force, which would be a dramatic departure for ASEAN. In the end, more conservative elements within ASEAN pushed back, stressing the need for ASEAN to maintain its principle of noninterference and striking any reference to a peacekeeping force. Instead, the APSC offered a broad vision of an ASEAN that would work effectively both internally and with external partners to promote political development and democratic norms, and to tackle the wide range of security challenges—including relatively new problems such as terrorism—facing Southeast Asia, while maintaining ASEAN centrality. The language was all generalities, with little discussion of how to turn the goals into reality.

The third pillar, the ASEAN Socio Cultural Community (ASSC), also was vaguely defined. ASSC sought to reduce poverty, especially in rural areas, and promote human development, while building a true sense of community throughout the region. The decision to "build" this community reflected to some degree a recognition on the part of senior officials in the region that ASEAN had to date been largely elite-driven, and that more effort needed to be made to ensure the wider population in the region felt a sense of being part of a regional community.

In a series of follow-on meetings, ASEAN members agreed to create an ASEAN charter and approved action plans that sought to turn the

---

4 Ruland, "From Trade to Investment."

ASEAN community rhetoric into reality. The Vientiane Action Plan, approved by leaders in 2004, would be the key document outlining how ASEAN would seek to build the three pillars of its community.

By the time I took over the ASEAN portfolio for the State Department in 2007, the institution had expanded considerably in both membership and mandate. What had begun largely as a diplomatic consultation mechanism among five noncommunist nations had become a ten-member organization that sought to create an admittedly ill-defined regional "community" by 2015. Moreover, while it maintained its emphasis on discouraging big-power intervention, its approach had evolved to one of inviting external powers into the region to participate in ASEAN-hosted and ASEAN-centered regional security fora, ranging from the thirteen-member ASEAN Plus 3 (ASEAN plus China, Korea, and Japan) to the sixteen-member East Asia Summit (which consisted of the above thirteen plus Australia, New Zealand, and India), and the twenty-seven-member ASEAN Regional Forum (which included all ten ASEAN Dialogue partners, including the United States, plus others ranging from Russia to North Korea).

In 2007 ASEAN also was working to finalize the ASEAN Charter, which would provide the legal basis and operating guidelines for the institution, which had been working for decades based on the two-page Bangkok Declaration and any number of informal understandings. It also would offer more detailed blueprints for ASEAN's Political-Security, Economic, and Socio-Cultural communities. As of mid-2007, with the region feeling the global momentum behind greater democracy, there was also hope that the charter would set standards for democratic practice and respect for human rights. The charter also was expected to codify long-established ASEAN practices, including consensus decision-making and the principal of noninterference in the domestic affairs of members. There was a sense of ASEAN moving forward, but also concerns that, by expanding its mandate and membership, it would have a harder time achieving its goals and staying united.

U.S. Engagement with ASEAN

The United States had been working with ASEAN formally since 1977, when we held the first of many Dialogue Partner meetings. The United States is one of ASEAN's ten dialogue partners. There are a couple of meetings per year between individual dialogue partners and ASEAN members at the senior official level, and usually one at the minister level on the margins of the annual ASEAN and ARF Ministerial meetings. President Carter met with ASEAN foreign ministers in 1978, and the following year Cyrus Vance became the first U.S. secretary of state to lead a dialogue meeting with his ASEAN counterparts.

As noted above, Washington worked particularly closely with ASEAN in the 1980s to counter Vietnam's occupation of Cambodia. U.S.-ASEAN dialogues continued through the decade and into the 1990s, with the United States providing modest levels of technical assistance to ASEAN. In 1999 Washington increased technical assistance, and in 2002 Secretary of State Colin Powell announced the ASEAN Cooperation Plan, which provided aid to strengthen the ASEAN Secretariat and support the bloc's economic integration. In 2005 the United States and ASEAN launched the Joint Vision Statement on Enhanced Partnership, which largely consisted of expanded U.S. assistance. The following year, Washington and ASEAN signed a Trade and Investment Framework Agreement (TIFA), which provided a vehicle to discuss trade and investment relations.[5]

Since the mid-1990s, U.S. secretaries of state had regularly traveled to the region for the annual ARF Ministerial and U.S.-ASEAN Dialogue Partner meetings. In Washington and perhaps other capitals, these meetings were better known for the evening skits that the ministers were expected to perform than for the substance. For us, the skits were awkward if not embarrassing, and contributed to the sense in Washington that ASEAN was not a serious organization. For our Southeast Asian colleagues, they were meant to be humanizing, an icebreaker to facilitate closer personal ties.

The skits are no more, but the different attitudes toward them across the Pacific reflect a still very real difference in approach toward diplomacy in ASEAN-related meetings. The United States tends to focus on substance and results. Our Southeast Asian counterparts care just as much if not more about developing personal relationships and avoiding conflict. From their perspective, one of ASEAN's greatest achievements over its fifty-plus years of existence has been the development of a framework of personal relationships that arguably has facilitated resolution of disputes and helped avoid tensions and disagreements.

---

5 "U.S.-ASEAN Timeline," U.S. Mission to ASEAN, https://asean.usmission.gov/our -relationship/policy-history/u-s-asean-timeline/.

Southeast Asia's avoidance of interstate conflict over the past forty years suggests they have a point.

Although we had engaged consistently with ASEAN over the years and signed the Enhanced Partnership Framework in late 2005, the way we managed the relationship bureaucratically says a lot about how we viewed it. In the U.S. State Department's East Asia and Pacific Bureau, ASEAN matters were largely handled by one retired foreign service officer who had been brought back on a contract basis. I am not taking anything away from the quality of work this officer did, but in effect it was treated as a technical, mid-level matter 360 days out of the year, and something our secretary needed to attend to for about one week annually. Most of us working on Southeast Asia focused on our bilateral relationships and spent little time on ASEAN as an institution; it was not the subject of a lot of broad discussion, other than in the few weeks ahead of the annual summits.

We did not have a strategic vision for our relationship with ASEAN. Some of that reflected the lack of a broader strategic approach to Southeast Asia post–Cold War. It also was due in part to our view that ASEAN lacked strategic heft, largely because of its tendency to avoid tough issues and adopt the "lowest common denominator" approach to problems. Frankly, most of Washington found ASEAN to be an enigma. It was there, but few understood its role or value.

The Myanmar Problem

In the latter half of 2007, the most significant discussions we had in Washington about ASEAN concerned Myanmar. Myanmar—or Burma as we still call it—had been a problem for ASEAN from the outset. Malaysia had insisted on Myanmar's accession to the organization back in 1996–97, with then prime minister Mahathir Mohammed arguing that it would be inappropriate to exclude the country and that membership would help encourage Myanmar to move in a direction toward more democratic and economic reform.[6] At the time, Mahathir was pushing hard for pan-Asian institutions that kept the West at arm's length, which helps explain his strong support for expanding ASEAN membership. Some other members, particularly Singapore, were less enthusiastic, and the United States and EU objected because of the military

---

6 Qasim Ahmad, "Malaysia-Myanmar Relations 1997–2002: A 'Prosper Thy Neighbor' Strategy," https://jas.uitm.edu.my/images/2004_JUNE/4.pdf.

regime's terrible human rights record, but in the end the ASEAN member governments agreed by consensus to bring in Myanmar.

ASEAN settled on a policy of "constructive engagement," which involved rejecting harsh Western sanctions and isolation while also using quiet diplomacy to encourage Myanmar's military leaders to change course. In mid-1998, Thai foreign minister Surin Pitsuwan sought to push ASEAN into taking a more active approach, which he termed "flexible engagement," to deal with certain problems of its members, particularly in Myanmar, because they affected the entire region. "Perhaps it is time that ASEAN's cherished principle of non-intervention is modified to allow ASEAN to play a constructive role in preventing or resolving domestic issues with regional implications," he said.[7] Surin's proposal proved more than ASEAN could accept, but it fell in line with continuing behind-the-scenes efforts by Malaysia and Thailand, in particular, to encourage reform in Myanmar.[8]

In 2003, the "Depayin Incident," in which regime-associated thugs attacked Aung San Suu Kyi's convoy, killed dozens and nearly murdered her, prompted ASEAN to adjust its policy and even to criticize the military regime openly. Among other things, members demanded Aung San Suu Kyi's release. When Myanmar ignored its partners' requests, the other ASEAN members—facing tremendous international pressure and repelled by the regime's behavior—compelled Myanmar to relinquish its planned 2006 ASEAN chairmanship. This was dramatic action by ASEAN standards.[9]

When in 2007 the same military regime brutally suppressed widespread public protests led by monks, during the so-called Saffron Revolution, other ASEAN members again harshly criticized the government, expressing "revulsion" at the military's use of automatic weapons against peaceful protestors and demanding it desist.[10] Any number of Southeast Asian officials publicly complained that Myanmar's bad behavior served both to distract ASEAN from other important work and,

7 Girlie Linao, "Days of Sweet Talk Over for ASEAN?," *The Nation,* July 22, 1998, https://www.burmalibrary.org/reg.burma/archives/199807/msg00516.html.

8 Lee Jones, "ASEAN's Albatross: ASEAN's Burma Policy, from Constructive Engagement to Critical Disengagement," *Asian Security* 4, no. 3 (September 23, 2008): 271–93, https://doi.org/10.1080/14799850802306484.

9 Jones, "ASEAN's Albatross," 8–11.

10 "Statement by ASEAN Chair, Singapore's Minister for Foreign Affairs George Yeo, 27 September 2007, New York," National Archives of Singapore, September 27, 2007, https://www.nas.gov.sg/archivesonline/data/pdfdoc/20070927974.htm.

more importantly, to harm ASEAN's reputation around the world. Privately, several Southeast Asian diplomats told me they were appalled by the Myanmar junta's behavior and were frustrated by their inability to influence it positively. Several, however, also argued that "walking away" from Myanmar would not help, as it would only embolden regime hardliners, who would be delighted to be left isolated, and the country would inevitably move even closer to China.

Those arguments did not sway many in Washington, where there was widespread anger at the military regime's violent crackdown on the Saffron Revolution. Seeing monks and others mowed down on the streets of Yangon, the George W. Bush administration reacted forcefully. First Lady Laura Bush's personal interest in the country played a role, but the truth is that all of us were deeply upset by the military's ruthless suppression of the protests.

In the days and weeks after the violence, I attended almost-weekly meetings of the so-called Deputies Committee, an interagency group at the deputy secretary level, in the White House Situation Room to discuss the situation in Myanmar. Deputy National Security Advisor Jim Jeffrey, my old boss from my days in Turkey, chaired the meetings. Under Secretary of State Nick Burns, later replaced by Bill Burns, usually led the State Department team, but over time I found myself representing the department more and more.

Around the room, there was considerable disappointment over ASEAN's perceived unwillingness to take a tougher stance on Myanmar, or even to expel it from the organization. On one occasion, ahead of a U.S.-ASEAN Senior Officials meeting I was to host in Seattle, we even debated whether we should cancel the meeting over Myanmar. When I and others pushed back on the idea, saying we should not throw out the baby with the bathwater, NSC senior director for human rights Elliott Abrams suggested we tell ASEAN it had to choose between Myanmar and the United States. I responded that, if we put the ASEAN nations in that position, we would not be happy with their decision. The matter died, but Jim Jeffrey concluded the meeting with a firm instruction to me—only partially in jest—to "scowl" at the Myanmar delegation throughout the upcoming meeting.

In September 2007, Secretary Rice met with her ASEAN counterparts on the margins of the UN General Assembly meeting in New York. Perhaps anticipating what might happen, Myanmar sent a representative from its mission to the United Nations, rather than its foreign minister, to the meeting. After initial pleasantries, Secretary Rice turned to

the Myanmar official and, for two or three minutes, delivered a stinging rebuke of his government's human rights violations. It probably
was the harshest "diplomatic" message I ever witnessed. The ASEAN
foreign ministers were visibly uncomfortable throughout the tirade,
looking down and shifting in their seats. The tough message was justified but delivering it in a meeting with all ASEAN members was not
ideal. Rice's harsh reproval sucked all of the oxygen out of the room,
leaving little energy for the secretary to discuss other issues with her
ASEAN counterparts.

ASEAN's approach toward Myanmar at that time reflected some enduring realities about the institution and its members, which one can
still see today in ASEAN's response to the February 2021 Myanmar coup.
First and most importantly, they were concerned that Myanmar's behavior was damaging ASEAN's standing and its ability to play a central
role in regional diplomacy. That concern was sufficient to cause them to
act more forcefully than they normally would. Second, even when there
is obvious disagreement and unhappiness with a member, they will try
to manage it internally (within the ASEAN family) as much as possible,
rather than encourage outside parties to get involved. Third, they will
almost always choose patient engagement over punitive measures, as
maintaining the family—i.e., preserving regional unity—is often more
important than addressing specific problems or dysfunctionality.

Some ASEAN officials, while sharing our concerns about Myanmar,
privately questioned why Washington was so singularly focused on human rights problems in Myanmar. None said so openly, but it was clear
they saw inconsistency in this intense focus on Myanmar at the same
time the United States was continuing to strengthen its relationship
with communist Vietnam, which had a poor human rights record. They
had a point, to an extent, on the inconsistency. It reflected several factors that influenced U.S. policymaking: the emotional attachment many
Americans had to Vietnam due to the war, with some perhaps feeling a
sense of guilt or need to atone for what they viewed as an unjust war;
Vietnam's growing importance as an economic partner and a bulwark
against China's assertiveness, versus Myanmar's relative lack of strategic and economic importance; Hanoi's talent for working Washington,
and Myanmar's complete absence of such; the pure and naked brutality of the Myanmar regime; the presence and iconic status of Aung San
Suu Kyi, and the lack of anyone of similar stature opposing the regime
in Vietnam; and the influence of the so-called Burma Lobby, a collection of individuals and organizations that were personally invested in

Myanmar's struggle for democracy and that boasted significant influence in Washington.

The ASEAN Charter

While continuing to discuss Myanmar with our ASEAN colleagues, we also welcomed the organization's adoption of its charter in late 2007. To be sure, the final text proved to be weaker in key areas, particularly human rights, than many of us had hoped. Earlier drafts had included provisions that would have established a compliance monitoring mechanism for ASEAN agreements and even entertained the possibility of sanctions for violations, but several ASEAN members with poor human rights records insisted they be watered down or eliminated. The charter called for the establishment of a human rights commission, but—despite a strong push from Indonesia and the Philippines—it was left rather toothless, with no power to investigate or monitor transgressions. Critics such as Barry Desker, a prominent and respected ASEAN observer, lamented that the charter in effect only "codifies existing norms."[11]

We shared many of those concerns, but still saw the charter as a step forward. It had institutionalized ASEAN, established clear blueprints for progress toward an ASEAN community by 2015, and given the ASEAN secretary-general the authority for the first time to monitor and report on progress toward achieving the institution's goals. Maybe more importantly, we could feel a sense of momentum and a clear desire among many ASEAN members to build a stronger community that went beyond the elite. We also saw an effort to instill modest standards of more democratic behavior, or at least greater respect for human rights. In numerous discussions with ASEAN counterparts, I would note our disappointment at the weakening of the charter's language on human rights, and they would counter that, for a cautious, consensus-based ASEAN, even talking about human rights standards was a major step forward.

In an interview shortly after ASEAN adopted the charter, I emphasized that it reflected the political will among member countries to strengthen ASEAN as an institution, and that we saw it as a positive step. I did, however, also point to the challenges of turning its positive intentions into reality:

---

11 Quoted in Julie Ginsberg, "Backgrounder: ASEAN: The Association of Southeast Asian Nations," *New York Times*, February 26, 2009.

It still is going to take a lot of political will and political efforts to build upon the charter, use the charter as a platform to achieve progress, to create a dispute settlement mechanism that works, to create a human rights body that actually contributes to the development of human rights situation in the region. And a lot of work to overcome the inevitable protectionist pressure to move towards the integrated economic community by 2015.[12]

Surin Pitsuwan's energy and drive as ASEAN secretary-general added to my optimism. The previous ASEAN secretaries-general had been respected technocrats who tended to operate behind the scenes, more as senior staff than as leaders. Surin was cut from a different cloth. Born in southern Thailand, he had followed a political path, winning election to Parliament and then serving as Thailand's foreign minister before being named ASEAN secretary-general effective January 2008. Surin brought new energy and vision to the position just as ASEAN itself seemed poised to take important steps forward, with a new charter and a sense of purpose.

I met Surin for the first time at the ASEAN Secretariat in Jakarta in February 2008, a little more than a month after he took office. Coincidentally, President Bush had just nominated me to be the United States' first ambassador for ASEAN affairs, and the first such ambassador from any of ASEAN's ten dialogue partners. The nomination resulted from a significant push from Capitol Hill, particularly Senator Richard Lugar, who had long argued that we needed to engage ASEAN more effectively, including by appointing a U.S. ambassador to the institution. My appointment did not signal a shift in Bush administration priorities, but it would turn out to segue nicely into Washington's stepped-up engagement with ASEAN during the Obama administration.

Surin welcomed me, told me about his experience as a high school exchange student in Minnesota, and talked about his goals for ASEAN and his hope that the United States would do more to support the institution's transformation. He made clear that he wanted ASEAN both to become a more "people-based" community and a more effective regional body that could influence and shape the regional architecture of the entire Asia region. We talked at length about how we could work

---

12 "Asean 'To Clarify' Meeting Amid Turmoil," VOA Cambodia, December 1, 2008, https://www.voacambodia.com/a/a-40-2008-12-01-voa3-90165322/1354023 .html.

together to promote change in Myanmar and agreed to keep in close touch on that.

Cyclone Nargis

Just two months later, on May 3, 2008, Cyclone Nargis made landfall in Myanmar, killing some 140,000 people and devastating the entire Irrawaddy Delta region that abuts the Bay of Bengal in the country's southwest. Surin propelled ASEAN into action. On May 5, he publicly urged all ASEAN member states to provide urgent assistance through the ASEAN emergency response framework. He cajoled the reluctant Myanmar authorities into allowing an ASEAN Emergency Rapid Assessment Team, which included both government officials and NGO representatives, to travel to the affected area to do an assessment on May 9–19.

At the time, the Myanmar government was refusing to accept broader international assistance, insisting that it could manage on its own. Immediately after the cyclone hit, President Bush set aside his concerns about the regime and offered U.S. assistance. I flew to Yangon on May 12 with PACOM commander Admiral Tim Keating and USAID director Henrietta Holsman Fore to offer U.S. assistance, which the Myanmar authorities politely declined. The UN and international NGOs were having no more luck, and the prospects for an effective international relief effort seemed bleak. Meanwhile, people were suffering and dying.

Surin, to his credit, persisted, along with key ASEAN member states. He worked with the Myanmar authorities while keeping in close touch with the United Nations. He in effect used ASEAN both to pressure and to reassure the Myanmar generals, telling them that they needed to open the door to help, and that ASEAN would help them through the process and ensure external actors brought no hidden agenda.

ASEAN held a rare emergency Foreign Ministers meeting in Singapore on May 19, at which the ministers issued a public statement calling on Myanmar to accept international assistance and to facilitate the entrance of international experts. At the end of the meeting, Myanmar agreed to an ASEAN-led assistance coordination effort. They also agreed to a UN-ASEAN-Myanmar–hosted international pledging conference to be held in Yangon on May 25 that confirmed the ASEAN-led approach while offering the UN an important role. ASEAN, and specifically Surin, had succeeded in opening the Myanmar door to international assistance, which began flowing in large amounts. It was an important success.

We initially had planned to have our charge d'affaires in Yangon lead our delegation to the pledging conference. UN secretary-general Ban Ki-Moon, however, called our UN ambassador, Zal Khalilzad, on May 23, and impressed upon him the importance of the United States sending a senior Washington-based representative. That led to a Khalilzad call to Secretary of State Rice, who in turn called Under Secretary Bill Burns, who called me and asked me to go. It was late Friday afternoon ahead of the Memorial Day weekend. After having just returned from the region three days earlier and promised my family a quiet holiday weekend, I was not wildly enthusiastic. Nonetheless, I found a flight through Europe that left Washington Friday night and would get me to Bangkok Sunday morning, in time for a quick connecting flight to Yangon just ahead of the conference opening.

When I arrived at the Bangkok airport, I made my way to the Thai Airways lounge, where I ran into Surin. He was exhausted, but happy. I congratulated him and asked him how he had convinced the Myanmar authorities to sign off on the trilateral approach. He said they at first had been very resistant but had just enough trust in ASEAN as a "family" not to reject his proposal out of hand. Eventually, he said, some of the more forward-thinking officials in the government had convinced the hardliners that agreeing to this approach would help their international image, at minimal risk and cost.

"Talk Shops?"

Two months later, I returned to Singapore for the annual ASEAN Ministerial meetings, which Secretary Rice was to attend. I arrived feeling pretty gung-ho about our relationship with ASEAN. The institution had approved a new charter, achieved a breakthrough in engineering international assistance to respond to Cyclone Nargis, and seemed to be on a positive trajectory. ASEAN officials had warmly welcomed my appointment as ambassador for ASEAN affairs, because it signaled to them renewed U.S. interest and also prompted other dialogue partners to appoint their own ambassadors, bolstering ASEAN's international status.

During my first meeting with my ASEAN counterparts after my confirmation as ambassador, I had been struck by how big of a deal they had made of it. I had been to a number of such meetings before as deputy assistant secretary, but clearly my "promotion" to ambassador made a big difference to them. While always polite, they had clearly been unhappy about what they perceived to be U.S. neglect of the region during the Bush administration. We had not engaged consistently at high levels, and that matters in Southeast Asia.

Secretary Rice was not a fan of ASEAN. When Assistant Secretary Chris Hill and I went to her hotel suite to brief her ahead of her meeting with the ASEAN foreign ministers (the so-called ASEAN Plus One meeting), she looked at us and asked, "Why am I here?" In previous and subsequent discussions, she made it clear that the lack of substance in the meetings made them, in her view, of minimal value, particularly given the amount of time it took to fly to and from the region. I told her that the meetings themselves might not produce much in the way of concrete results, but in a region that relies so much on personal relationships and building confidence, her "showing up" was crucial. She was not convinced, but to her credit she joined the meetings and engaged effectively.

In the late 2000s, China and the South China Sea had not yet become dominant issues in the region or in our discussions with our ASEAN counterparts. That was good in many ways, but it also meant the discussions were often not of great substance. In the senior official meetings at my level, our discussions with ASEAN counterparts usually centered on ASEAN's own internal goals and how our assistance could support their efforts. In the discussions at the ASEAN Regional Forum, each official (whether at the senior official or ministerial level) would read written remarks, some of which were more interesting than others. More often than not, they would consist mostly of platitudes and recitation of ASEAN views on various mundane matters. Such limited substance had earned ASEAN meetings a reputation for being little more than "talk shops."

I remember one ARF Senior Officials meeting in particular, in which we discussed whether there was room to go beyond the forum's traditional focus on "preventive diplomacy" toward more active diplomacy. During a very long discussion, most representatives supported the idea of being more active, but a few were opposed. The chairman reminded us that, in ASEAN and ARF, we could only move forward at a pace with which all were comfortable. I jumped in to ask whether that really meant we could only move forward at the pace at which the slowest, most cautious member felt comfortable. My Singaporean counterpart, sporting a big smile, shouted out, "Yes, now you understand ASEAN," and they all laughed.

The Pivot/Rebalance and Stepped-Up Engagement with ASEAN

After the Bush administration's focus on the war on terror and the Middle East, the Obama administration took over in early 2009 intending to "pivot" to Asia. The move, later called the "rebalance," has been the subject of a lot of revisionist history. In brief, the president and his top foreign policy officials believed that Asia, because of its huge population, economic dynamism and overall positive trajectory, would have a significant impact on many if not most of the critical issues facing the world. It was, therefore, critical for the United States to pay attention to and engage with the region on everything from the global economy to climate change to security. The "rebalance" would return the United States, which after all was a Pacific nation, to what we viewed as a more appropriate level of engagement. It was not an anti-China strategy. It was an approach aimed at increasing engagement with a very important region. Incoming EAP assistant secretary Kurt Campbell had played a key role in developing and implementing the pivot.

Secretary of State Hillary Clinton wanted to highlight this pivot from the outset, so she decided to take her first official trip to the region, including Japan, China, South Korea, and Indonesia. Ahead of her trip, she explained that making Asia her first destination "demonstrates clearly that our new administration wants to focus a lot of time and energy in working with Asian partners and all the nations in the Pacific region, because we know that so much of our future depends upon our relationships there."[13]

I was thrilled that Clinton would travel to Jakarta. Doing so would highlight that we considered Southeast Asia important. I wondered aloud to Chris Hill, who was still assistant secretary pending Kurt Campbell's confirmation, whether we could convince her to stop at the ASEAN Secretariat. Chris looked at me like I was crazy and dismissed

---

13 Jill Dougherty, "Clinton Heads to Asia on First State Trip," CNN, February 15, 2009, https://www.cnn.com/2009/POLITICS/02/15/us.clinton.asia.trip/.

the idea. I had the greatest respect for him, so normally would have let it drop. It happened, however, that I ran into an aide to Secretary Clinton in the elevator. I could not resist saying that a brief stop by her at the secretariat would be huge, as it would immediately help us with all ten ASEAN member governments. I explained the rationale a bit more (literally making an elevator pitch), noting that just one meeting would have a big impact on how a region of more than six hundred million people viewed the United States. He asked how long it would take, and I optimistically said, "Ninety minutes tops, with travel time." He liked the idea and broached it with Clinton, who agreed. Now I just had to explain to Chris Hill how the meeting that he thought he had squelched had nonetheless been added to the schedule.

Ahead of the visit, a few colleagues and I pushed for the administration to consider using the occasion to announce its intention to accede to ASEAN's Treaty of Amity and Cooperation (TAC). The treaty is one of the pillars of ASEAN, though its actual substance is limited. We had debated this at my level late in the Bush administration but got nowhere because of opposition from some in the NSC who feared that the TAC's provisions against interfering in the domestic affairs of others might constrain our ability, for example, to impose sanctions against Myanmar. There were other concerns as well, but that was the main one. This time around, we were able to win more interagency support by pointing out that other signers, such as Australia, had not seen their freedom of action constrained. Moreover, we argued, the benefits of accession would be substantial: doing so would send a strong message to our Southeast Asian counterparts that we were serious about engagement and would also allow us to meet the one remaining condition for us to join the East Asia Summit, which was something else we were debating at the time.

A few weeks later, on February 16, 2009, Chris Hill and I accompanied Clinton to the ASEAN Secretariat, where the entire ASEAN staff had gathered and greeted her like a rock star, many holding up welcoming signs and shouting out her name. Secretary-General Surin greeted her warmly, in his engaging way, and the two had a long, productive conversation, in which the secretary highlighted Washington's interest in and support for ASEAN and agreed that we would pursue accession to the TAC (a move President Obama had blessed). Afterwards, she and Surin spoke to the press, with the always loquacious Surin slightly embellishing some of Clinton's private comments and commitments. He also pointedly noted, "Your visit shows the seriousness of the United States to end its diplomatic absenteeism in the region."[14]

Secretary Clinton was happy with the visit and afterwards gave clear instructions to move our relationship with ASEAN forward. She told me to do the needful so that she could sign the TAC at the July ASEAN Ministerial in Thailand. "Sure," I said, not realizing how much work was involved. It turned out we had to go through a lengthy process before we could sign. While the text of the treaty was set and nonnegotiable, we had to work with our dialogue partner at the time, the Thai government, to find wording acceptable to us and to ASEAN that clarified our understanding or interpretation of the various treaty provisions.[15] It was a lot of work, but we got it done in time.

In July 2009, I accompanied Clinton to Phuket for her first ASEAN Ministerial meeting. Her meeting with Russian foreign minister Lavrov (also there for the ARF Ministerial) ran very long, making her a good thirty minutes late for her meeting with the ASEAN foreign ministers. I was outside the Lavrov meeting, anxiously pacing and thinking about what a disaster her late arrival would be. Eventually, the meeting broke up, and we walked quickly to the ASEAN meeting.

I could see the foreign ministers were peeved that she was so late, but they nonetheless welcomed her politely. She quickly won them over by announcing that we were ready to sign the TAC, and then talked about how much we supported ASEAN and cared about Southeast Asia. As the ministers took turns speaking, Clinton turned to me to ask whether she really had to call Myanmar "Burma" in the meeting. My bureaucratic caution took over, and I told her she did. I should have been bolder.[16]

When it was Surin's turn to speak, he said something to the effect of, "We are all very impressed by your visit to the ASEAN Secretariat, your commitment to the rebalance, and your accession to the TAC. Now, if you can agree to a leaders-level meeting between the president and

---

14 Catherin Putz and Shannon Tiezzi, "Did Hillary Clinton's Pivot to Asia Work?" FiveThirtyEight, April 14, 2016, https://fivethirtyeight.com/features/did-hillary-clintons-pivot-to-asia-work/.

15 This agreement on the wording of the U.S. interpretation of certain clauses of the treaty would be put into side letters linked to our signing of the treaty.

16 When the military regime changed the country's name from Burma to Myanmar in 1989, the United States decided to continue to call it Burma, largely at the request of Aung San Suu Kyi, who argued that the regime lacked the legitimacy to change the country's name.

the leaders of ASEAN, we will really be convinced." Secretary Clinton looked at me and Assistant Secretary Kurt Campbell, and then looked back to NSC senior director for Asia Jeff Bader to ask if such a meeting was doable. To his credit, Jeff said, "Yes, I think we can make it happen." Clinton nodded and told Surin and the other foreign ministers that she thought she could make such a meeting happen. By then, everyone had forgotten that she had arrived to the meeting late.

On the margins of the Phuket meeting, I suggested to Kurt Campbell and Clinton's deputy chief of staff, Jake Sullivan, that we double down on our investment in ASEAN by establishing a diplomatic mission to ASEAN in Jakarta. Kurt, who always thought big, said, more or less, "Good idea, but you're thinking too small." He recommended we set up a mission *and* name a resident ambassador to ASEAN. I was ambassador *for* ASEAN but based in Washington and double-hatted as deputy assistant secretary. Jake agreed, and so did Clinton. Now we just had to convince the White House.

The Lower Mekong Initiative

That week in Phuket also saw our first ministerial-level meeting with a subgroup of ASEAN, as Secretary Clinton joined her counterparts from Thailand, Vietnam, Laos, and Cambodia to discuss opportunities to cooperate around the Mekong River area. Earlier in the year, I had read about separate Chinese and Japanese engagements with the so-called Mekong countries and asked myself why we were not doing anything along those lines. A U.S. Mekong initiative would give us an opportunity to engage more, especially with Cambodia and Laos, with whom we rarely met at senior levels. In addition, the Mekong River, which was the lifeblood of the region, faced significant threats due to unregulated dam construction and other developments. We had an opportunity to make a meaningful contribution while also bolstering our ties with key Southeast Asian countries.

I raised the idea with my colleagues in the State Department's Mainland Southeast Asia Office and asked them to work up a proposal for a Mekong initiative. A short while later, they proposed what was to become the Lower Mekong Initiative, in which we would work with the riverine countries on ways to protect and preserve the Mekong River ecosystem. They went even further, suggesting we ask Secretary Clinton to host a ministerial-level meeting. I thought that was more than the traffic would bear, but they convinced me. We put our ideas on paper, pushed it up the chain, and the secretary agreed.

That secretary-level meeting became an annual event, supplemented with some innovative partnership programs. Initially, we connected the Mekong River Commission, which was charged with coordinating discussions among the Mekong countries on dams and similar projects, with the Mississippi River Commission, which had a somewhat parallel role in the United States. We also engaged the U.S. Army Corps of Engineers, which could offer useful technical advice and assistance.

Solidifying Our Ties

As the administration's pivot or rebalance took shape, we remained focused on the importance of building strong, long-term links between the United States and Southeast Asia, including ASEAN specifically. We knew that it would take more than a few months of engagement to convince skeptical counterparts in the region that the United States' heightened engagement would last. In a region that has survived based on its ability to hedge and balance between the great powers, our opportunity to influence and shape decisions and relationships depended heavily on Southeast Asia's confidence in our long-term commitment.

On the margins of the 2009 APEC meeting in Singapore, several of us had a chance to discuss exactly this point at length with Secretary Clinton. Clinton's right-hand woman, Huma Abedin, had pulled us together at the secretary's request, after the APEC formal dinner, to talk strategy. We gathered around a small table in our hotel lobby—Clinton, Abedin, Jake Sullivan, Under Secretary for Economic Affairs Bob Hormats, Ambassador for APEC Kurt Tong, and me—and talked for a few hours about ASEAN, the East Asia Summit (EAS), and the Trans-Pacific Partnership (TPP).

ASEAN and EAS are part of the alphabet soup of what is known as the regional architecture, which is a technocrat's term for the institutions or fora that bring the relevant governments together to talk about regional security, political, and economic issues. East Asia had for many years boasted little in the way of architecture, other than ASEAN. The United States had, since the early 1990s, helped create and boost the awkwardly named Asia Pacific Economic Coordination (APEC) forum, which focused on trade and investment liberalization and brought in a number of Latin American countries.

In 1996, ASEAN and three powerful northeast Asian countries—China, Japan, and South Korea—had established the more pan-Asian ASEAN Plus 3 grouping, which met at the leaders' level every year. In 2005, amid growing concern that the ASEAN Plus 3 forum gave China excessive influence, ASEAN agreed to create a new forum, the EAS, that would add Australia, India, and New Zealand to the ASEAN Plus 3 group, thus diluting China's influence somewhat. It was not an anti-China move, but rather another example of the ASEAN states sensing a need to bring greater balance to the mix. Nonetheless, Beijing continued to advocate for ASEAN Plus 3 to play the key role on regional security.

As a result of this proliferation of fora, the annual "ASEAN meetings" now included an ASEAN Foreign Ministers Meeting, a total of ten meetings between ASEAN foreign ministers and individual dialogue partner counterparts, an ASEAN Regional Forum Ministerial meeting, an ASEAN Plus 3 Summit, and an EAS Leaders meeting. Because we were not members of either EAS or ASEAN Plus 3, the United States' participation was limited to the bilateral Dialogue Partner and ARF Ministerial meetings. Some in the Bush administration considered whether we should join the EAS as well, but there was never a strong push. Moreover, the U.S. Trade Representative's office in particular feared an expanded EAS would undermine APEC. Others raised concerns about ASEAN members' unwillingness to put tough security issues on the EAS agenda and questioned the viability of committing the U.S. president to attend both an EAS and an APEC Summit in the same year.

As we sat around the hotel table, Secretary Clinton asked whether we should join the EAS. Everyone said yes. The argument, in my view, was clear: some combination of EAS and ASEAN Plus 3 would determine the agenda and the rules for political-security matters in Asia for years, perhaps decades, to come. We needed to be at the table. We could not join ASEAN Plus 3, so the only option was to join EAS. APEC was great, but it was already losing influence and as an economic forum could not compete with the other two platforms on regional security matters. To me, it was a no-brainer. Others thought the same. Secretary Clinton probably already agreed, but she let us "persuade" her of the need to join EAS. The next year, she participated in the EAS as a guest of host Vietnam. In 2011 the United States officially joined the forum, along with Russia, and President Obama attended the summit.

She also asked about the TPP trade agreement, then under negotiation. The proposed trade agreement would sharply reduce trade barriers among the twelve partner nations, including the United States, that collectively accounted for 40 percent of the global economy. The agreement would have included four of the ten ASEAN countries—Singapore, Brunei, Malaysia, and Vietnam.

Again, the rest of us agreed that seeing the TPP through to the end was critical not only economically, but strategically. We explained that our engagement in the region needed a strong economic/commercial pillar, which the TPP—and nothing else—provided. Completing the negotiations and ratifying the agreement would cement our economic ties to the region, and thus strategically complement our membership in EAS and our beefed-up engagement with ASEAN. Clinton listened, nodded, and said, "I get it."

On November 15, 2009, a few days after our informal internal discussion with Secretary Clinton, President Obama sat down with the ten ASEAN leaders in Singapore for the first U.S.-ASEAN Leaders Meeting. We had delivered on Secretary Clinton's July commitment to make such a Meeting happen. It was a bit jarring, even for me, to see the president sit down with leaders such as Cambodia's Hun Sen and Myanmar's Thein Sein, both of whom would normally rank low on the list of global leaders the U.S. president would seek to meet. That aside, we could feel a sense of excitement and even optimism in the room, as this was a historic event. All the leaders were smiling and very welcoming of President Obama, and almost all remarked on how pleased they were that the United States was engaging at the highest level with ASEAN leaders.

The meeting did not break a lot of new ground substantively, but that almost did not matter. It was the fact that the meeting happened that counted. The leaders agreed to meet again in 2010. They also came together on a joint statement that highlighted the positive atmosphere and welcomed various efforts, including the Lower Mekong Initiative. Just as importantly, the statement emphasized the U.S. commitment to supporting ASEAN's agenda of building a community and a stronger, more prosperous region, including through a variety of technical assistance and educational programs. As I often told my ASEAN counterparts, the U.S. agenda vis-à-vis ASEAN was to help ASEAN achieve the goals it had set. This was not a platitude. It genuinely reflected our view that a strong, prosperous Southeast Asia benefited the United States, and that we therefore had a significant interest in supporting ASEAN's efforts. Importantly, this meeting was about the United States and ASEAN, not about China.

Three U.S. Objectives

Over the next several years, our approach toward ASEAN focused on three objectives: bolstering the ASEAN nations' confidence in our long-term commitment to the region; supporting ASEAN's own internal agenda of building a community and further integrating economically; and—as the South China Sea issue moved from simmer to high heat—encouraging a united and firm ASEAN front against provocative and problematic Chinese efforts to assert dominance over that disputed territory.

We felt we were off to a good start on the first goal. Signing on to the TAC, joining the EAS, holding the first U.S.-ASEAN Leaders Meeting, and stepping up our overall engagement with the region had changed perceptions in the region toward Washington. The ten ASEAN member states welcomed our increased efforts and commitment. To maintain the momentum, we announced that we would establish a U.S. mission to ASEAN in Jakarta, and in 2011 we sent out our first resident ambassador to the institution. President Obama and Secretary Clinton both showed up regularly, including for the summits, while also welcoming their counterparts to Washington numerous times. It helped that, coincidentally, Myanmar unexpectedly started to reform, and we responded enthusiastically, largely eliminating what had been an irritant in our ties with ASEAN. Also, while TPP negotiations included only four of the ten ASEAN nations and thus arguably weakened ASEAN centrality and the ASEAN Economic Community, our commitment to the trade deal reassured the always-nervous region that we were committed to Asia for the long haul.

We also did what we could to support ASEAN's own goals. We increased our technical assistance program. It was small, but we developed it in close consultation with our ASEAN counterparts and targeted it to issues and areas where they thought our aid could help the most. For example, we funded for several years assistance to help them develop the ASEAN Single Window, an essential part of their efforts to further economic integration by facilitating customs clearances. We worked with Brunei to develop an English-language training program for member state officials, focused on the poorest countries that most needed the skills. We continued our Lower Mekong Initiative, with ASEAN's blessing, doing what we could to encourage the lower riverine governments (and increasingly China) not to destroy the fragile ecosystem through uncontrolled dam construction.

President Obama also launched the Young Southeast Asian Leaders program in 2013. Modeled after a program we had implemented in Africa, it sought to develop a network of young "future leaders" in the ASEAN region through a series of leadership programs, mostly in the region. I will admit to being skeptical about the program, as it sounded like it lacked substance. I was wrong. The program became a big hit throughout the region, as thousands of self-identified future leaders jumped at the chance to participate. In doing so, they not only built their skills, but connected with counterparts throughout Southeast Asia, contributing—we hoped—to the development of a sense of ASEAN community.

We also took every opportunity to emphasize our support for ASEAN centrality. A lot of people did not really know what that meant. I had my own view. To me, it was less about ASEAN leading the way in regional diplomacy, which frankly it struggled to do, and more about supporting ASEAN's role as the one nonthreatening convening power in Asia and as an important voice in regional discussions. If Washington, Beijing, or Tokyo called a regional meeting or proposed an initiative, others would immediately suspect a particular agenda or feel threatened. If ASEAN (or, more accurately, the ASEAN chair at the time) called a meeting, it was neutral territory and nonthreatening. Now, admittedly, many in ASEAN might have a more ambitious definition of ASEAN centrality, implying that ASEAN would lead efforts to address regional issues. Surin Pitsuwan, for example, regularly called for ASEAN to serve a central role on substance, not just as a host. But more on ASEAN centrality later.

The South China Sea Begins to Heat Up

China, however, was working to insert itself into the discussion. After several years of relative calm in the South China Sea, China in 2009 began again to assert its claims of sovereignty more aggressively. It filed with the UN official, legal papers outlining its claims, which encompassed all of the land features as well as the sea within the so-called nine-dash line.[17] It stepped up its harassment of fishing and oil explo-

---

17 "China: Maritime Claims in the South China Sea," Bureau of Oceans and International Environmental and Scientific Affairs, U.S. Department of State, Limits in the Seas no. 143, December 5, 2014, https://www.state.gov/wp-content/uploads/2019/10/LIS-143.pdf.

ration vessels operated by other claimant nations, and also harassed a U.S. ship, the *Impeccable*, in March 2009.[18]

In the spring of 2010, Chinese officials warned visiting U.S. officials to stay out of the South China Sea dispute, insisting that it was none of our business and that it was one of China's core interests. We could not accept that, as we had a fundamental interest both in ensuring freedom of navigation through the world's seas and in preventing big powers from using force to assert their claims in territorial disputes.

At the July 2010 ARF Ministerial in Hanoi, Secretary Clinton spoke out forcefully on the South China Sea. She reiterated our position about not taking sides on the question of sovereignty but made it clear that the United States had an interest in preserving freedom of navigation and in peaceful dispute resolution. She even offered to facilitate multilateral talks, which seemed to infuriate Chinese foreign minister Yang Jiechi.

Ahead of the meeting, we had engaged in multiple detailed discussions in Kurt Campbell's office in EAP, as well as with other parts of the State Department, the Pentagon, and NSC to determine how best to respond to China's increasing assertiveness. We also had consulted extensively with our ASEAN counterparts and with other ARF participants, explaining our concerns and urging them to join us in speaking out. In every conversation, we stressed that we were not asking them to take an anti-China position, but rather to stand up for international principles. At the meeting, twelve of the twenty-seven participants—including several ASEAN members—spoke out on the issue, adding to Beijing's upset. The Vietnamese, who had lobbied hard ahead of the meeting for Clinton to raise the South China Sea, were very happy with her statement.

Some observers have cited Clinton's July 2010 statement at ARF as the moment the United States jumped into the South China Sea issue. That is not fully accurate, but it is fair to say that it was the moment when we first spoke out strongly at a very senior level about how U.S. interests and international principles were at stake. We did so because (1) China was acting more aggressively, and (2) the ongoing

---

18 Michael Green, Kathleen Hicks, Zack Cooper, John Schaus, and Jake Douglas, "Counter-Coercion Series: Harassment of the USNS *Impeccable*," May 19, 2017, Asia Maritime Transparency Initiative, CSIS, https://amti.csis.org/counter-co-harassment-usns-impeccable/.

China-ASEAN dialogue on the issue had failed to make much progress and was not preventing China from changing the status quo.

Understanding the South China Sea Issue

By 2012 or 2013, the South China Sea issue had begun to dominate the discussions, at least at senior levels in the Obama administration. We continued our other, important efforts to work with ASEAN, but it quickly became clear that the South China Sea—particularly China's increasingly assertive behavior—represented a fundamental challenge to the region, to ASEAN as an institution, and to fundamental issues of peaceful resolution of disputes and freedom of navigation.

Others have written about the South China Sea dispute in great detail. I will not try to replicate their work, but here in a nutshell is what it is all about (from Washington's point of view). The South China Sea is a critical international trading route, and also is believed to hold potential significant oil and gas reserves, not to mention abundant fisheries. It is also home to two island groups, the Paracels and the Spratlys. China, Taiwan, Vietnam, the Philippines, Malaysia, and Brunei all claim part or all of the area, including many of the islands, and their claims overlap. China's claim is the most ambitious—it has argued that it has historical rights to 80 percent of the area, including in areas that are well within other countries' exclusive economic zones.

Such disputes over territory and relevant seas are not uncommon. Ideally, they can be resolved through negotiation or international arbitration. Two main factors complicate the South China Sea dispute: the number of claimants, and the combination of China's power, its broad if vague claim to nearly all of the sea as well as the land features, and its aggressive efforts to assert its sovereignty through intimidation and deployment of vessels in contested areas.

Interpreting the UN Convention on the Law of the Sea (UNCLOS), the International Tribunal on the Law of the Sea (ITLOS) has ruled that China's maritime claims (as opposed to its claim of sovereignty over land features) have no basis in international law. It also ruled that none of the land features (with the possible exception of some of the Paracel Islands in the northern part of the sea) constitute "islands" in legal terms; hence, even if a country were determined to have sovereignty over one of these land features, it would not be entitled to an EEZ (a two-hundred-mile area around the feature in which it had exclusive rights to exploit resources) but only to a twelve-mile territorial sea. This is significant because, if accepted by all the claimant states, this ruling would dramatically reduce the area under dispute.[19] The United States has not taken a position on the land claims, other than that they should be resolved through negotiation, dialogue, or arbitration. Washington has also insisted that all nations should enjoy freedom of navigation through these waters.

The Search for a Code of Conduct

The ASEAN member states first began serious discussions on the South China Sea dispute in the early 1990s, when they produced a "Declaration on the South China Sea" that anticipated a binding agreement under which claimants would commit to resolve territorial disputes without the use of force. It is important to remember here that the dispute is not just between ASEAN claimants and China (and Taiwan). The ASEAN claimants themselves—Vietnam, Malaysia, Brunei, and the Philippines—also have overlapping claims with each other.

Beijing insisted through the 1990s that the disputes should be resolved via bilateral negotiations, and so refused to engage with ASEAN as a whole. When some of the ASEAN members started to express concern about China's role in the South China Sea late in the decade, China shifted its stance and agreed to talk about a China-ASEAN Declaration of Conduct (DOC). The two parties signed such a document in 2002, in which they committed to self-restraint. In reality it did little more than offer the hope of a more binding agreement, in the form of a Code of Conduct (COC), that would not resolve the underlying disputes but would provide rules for behavior pending a final settlement. China, however, kept finding reasons to delay negotiations on a COC. It was not until 2011 that China and ASEAN even reached agreement on draft guidelines for implementing the nonbinding DOC! I was in Indonesia in 2011, when talks produced President Yudhoyono's chairman's statement, which welcomed "commencement of a discussion in ASEAN to identify the possible key elements of a code of conduct in the SCS and

---

19 Gregory B. Poling, "Judgment Day: The South China Sea Tribunal Issues Its Ruling," CSIS, July 12, 2016, https://www.csis.org/analysis/judgment-day-south -china-sea-tribunal-issues-its-ruling.

anticipate a future engagement with China on the matter with a view to its timely realization."[20]

We were frustrated with the lack of progress and what we saw as ASEAN's passivity and wishful thinking. It was clear as day that China was stalling, had no intention of seriously negotiating and then adhering to a binding COC that would constrain its actions, and was engaged in the talks largely as a way of keeping us out of the issue. I discussed this matter on a number of occasions with Indonesia's able foreign minister, Marty Natalegawa. He insisted that the COC was the only viable way forward, given China's power, and urged patience.

While the talks continued, China worked to create a fait accompli by building artificial islands, stationing weapons on a few of them, and continually threatening or intimidating other claimants. We saw a steady pattern of China harassing fishing and oil exploration vessels, deploying vessels to areas well within the EEZs of other claimants, and of continuing to assert publicly that the area under dispute was indisputably theirs. China tended to use law enforcement vessels ("white hulls," versus navy ships, known as "grey hulls") for these operations, largely so they could accuse us of "militarizing" the issue when we deployed Navy ships to the area.

We tried to rally the ASEAN members, along with other international partners, to call out this Chinese behavior and present a united stance that imposed reputational costs on China, while staging freedom of navigation operations to challenge excessive maritime claims that could threaten freedom of navigation for all nations. We also stepped up assistance to the ASEAN claimants, particularly Vietnam and the Philippines, to bolster their ability to monitor and patrol their own territorial waters.

A Divided ASEAN

ASEAN struggled mightily with the issue. The member nations were (and are) divided, both by the extent to which the issue directly affected them and by their fealty to or fear of China. They knew they could not challenge China militarily and that Beijing would not hesitate to use its

---

20 Richard Javad Heydarian, "At a Strategic Crossroads: ASEAN Centrality Amid Sino-American Rivalry in the Indo-Pacific," Brookings, April 2020, https://www.brookings.edu/research/at-a-strategic-crossroads-asean-centrality-amid-sino-american-rivalry-in-the-indo-pacific/.

economic clout to punish them if they went too far. They generally welcomed U.S. involvement but were not sure how much they could count on Washington and also feared a potential U.S.-China clash. A few of the members also responded nervously to our decision to shift more military assets to the region. We knew our intentions were benign, but at least some in the region still had doubts.

The 2012 ASEAN meetings were a low point, as host Cambodia followed Beijing's wishes and blocked language Manila and Hanoi wanted on the South China Sea, even though China had just blatantly pushed the Philippines out of Scarborough Shoal in the Philippine EEZ. For the first and only time, the meeting failed to agree on a communiqué. Indonesian foreign minister Natalegawa, recognizing that this embarrassing failure threatened ASEAN unity, immediately made the rounds of ASEAN capitals and cobbled together six principles that the members agreed would guide their approach going forward. The principles were classic ASEAN, emphasizing the importance of concluding a COC, following international law, and avoiding the use of force. More important than the actual points, the agreement allowed ASEAN to show a face-saving sense of unity. As Natalegawa put it, "You can only have an ASEAN that is central in the region if ASEAN itself is united and cohesive. Last week we were tested, there have been some difficulties, but we have grown the wiser from it."[21]

As noted in chapter 2, the ASEAN failure at the summit in Cambodia contributed to Philippine president Aquino's decision to take a non-ASEAN approach, pursuing a legal case based on UNCLOS at the Permanent Court of Arbitration at The Hague. We pushed the other ASEAN members to support this legal case, arguing that it was consistent with ASEAN's own long-standing emphasis on peaceful settlement of disputes based on international law. Privately, a number of governments welcomed Manila's action, but publicly most remained cautious. Overall, the sympathy many members felt for the substance of what the Philippines was doing was offset by their concern about China's reaction and their unhappiness that Manila had broken with the rest of ASEAN to pursue this action unilaterally. When the court ruled largely in the Philippines' favor in 2016, the other ASEAN governments offered muted responses. Singapore, for example, issued a statement "taking note" of

---

21 Olivia Rondonuwu, "ASEAN to Claim 'Common Ground'" on S. China Sea, but No Communique," Reuters, July 20, 2012, http://reut.rs/OAWRB2.

the ruling, and reaffirming its support for peaceful resolution of competing claims, including through international law.[22]

Since the 2012 debacle in Phnom Penh, the tone of ASEAN statements on the South China Sea has varied from year to year, depending on the chair and the level of concern over China's most recent actions. For example, in 2014 and 2015, ASEAN issued relatively strong statements in response to concerns about increasingly assertive Chinese operations. Following the group's virtual summit in late June 2020, host Vietnam issued an even stronger statement, expressing concern about recent "serious incidents" and insisting—really for the first time—that the UN Law of the Sea should be the basis for sovereign rights and entitlements.[23] Philippine president Duterte, who had largely avoided directly challenging China, made his strongest statement to date at the UN General Assembly annual meeting on September 22, not long after the ASEAN summit in early September. He insisted that the South China Sea dispute had to be resolved in accordance with the 2016 ITLOS ruling.[24]

The bottom line, however, is that none of this has worked. China rejected and then ignored the 2016 ITLOS ruling, continued to build and militarize artificial islands, and has harassed and intimidated fishing boats and other vessels while blatantly deploying its own ships to the coastal waters of ASEAN claimants. In 2020 and 2021, despite (or maybe because of) the COVID-19 pandemic, China if anything became even more aggressive, sinking a Philippine fishing vessel off of Reed Bank and a Vietnamese fishing boat in the Paracel Islands, using a Coast Guard vessel to harass a Malaysian oil exploration project just forty-four miles off of Malaysia's coast, and deploying vessels in Indonesia's EEZ, off of Natuna Island.

22 "MFA Spokesman's Comments on the ruling of the Arbitral Tribunal in the Philippines v China case under Annex VII to the 1982 United Nations Convention on the Law of the Sea (UNCLOS)," Singapore Ministry of Foreign Affairs, July 12, 2016, https://www.mfa.gov.sg/Newsroom/Press-Statements-Transcripts -and-Photos/2016/07/MFA-Spokesmans-Comments-on-the-ruling-of-the-Arbitral -Tribunal-in-the-Philippines-v-China-case-under.

23 Jim Gomez, "ASEAN Takes Position vs China's Vast Historical Sea Claims," *The Diplomat,* June 29, 2020, https://thediplomat.com/2020/06/asean-takes-position -vs-chinas-vast-historical-sea-claims/.

24 Sebastian Strangio, "In UN Speech, Duterte Stiffens Philippines' Stance on the South China Sea," *The Diplomat,* September 23, 2020, https://thediplomat.com/ 2020/09/in-un-speech-duterte-stiffens-philippines-stance-on-the-south-china-sea/.

The Difficulties of Resolving the South China Sea Dispute

China's vast claims, its refusal to accept the ITLOS ruling, and its efforts to occupy and build up disputed land features, thereby creating a fait accompli, have been the primary driver of this issue. The United States has struggled to find an effective counter to China's approach. In dozens of discussions when I was principal deputy assistant secretary in 2013–16 (and no doubt dozens if not hundreds where I was not present), we spent more time on this issue than on anything else in Southeast Asia. We supported Manila's legal approach, enhanced our own security presence and initiated freedom of navigation operations, and constantly engaged with ASEAN and like-minded partners around the globe to build a diplomatic coalition that would push back against China's behavior. We wanted to avoid conflict, so chose not to intervene militarily when Beijing began island building, or when it failed to honor what we considered an agreement to pull back from Scarborough Shoal in 2012. We focused instead on ensuring freedom of navigation and imposing significant reputational costs on China. We thought, for example, that the 2016 UNCLOS ruling—which constituted a stinging rebuke of China's claims—might force China to rethink its approach. We realized after some time, however, that Xi Jinping was willing to accept much higher reputational costs than we had anticipated.

The ASEAN nations, and ASEAN itself, have borne a lot of criticism over their failure to take a strong, unified stance against China's behavior in the South China Sea. Many in Washington have found the group's timidity and lack of unity frustrating, especially when our Southeast Asian friends defend themselves by saying they do not want to get caught between us and China. My Stanford colleague, Don Emmerson, has argued that, in its more extreme forms, this position suggests a false equivalence between the United States and China,[25] as the United States—while having its flaws—is not building artificial islands or using its power to assert territorial claims.

Even more than official Washington, a number of U.S. academics and think tanks—and some elsewhere around the world—have

---

25 Shannon Tiezzi, "Donald Emmerson on Southeast Asia's Approach to China," *The Diplomat*, August 5, 2020, https://thediplomat.com/2020/08/donald-emmerson-on-southeast-asias-approach-to-china/.

criticized ASEAN's failure to respond to China's South China Sea behavior in a unified and firm manner, saying among other things that ASEAN cannot demand "centrality" and at the same time be unwilling to do anything. Some have called for it to abandon the consensus decision-making that is bogging it down. Others have suggested a "ASEAN minus x" approach, meaning that a subgroup of the membership—those with actual skin in the game—should be allowed to deal with the issue. [26]

My friends in the ASEAN world privately share some of these concerns, but they also point out the following: ASEAN is divided on the issue, and demanding a tougher stance will simply exacerbate and highlight the divisions; there is no support in the region for moving away from consensus decision-making, which in the Southeast Asian view has been essential to keep ASEAN together; and few in the region believe even a united ASEAN will be able to stop China from what it is doing. They also point out that there is no way—because of the group's genetic aversion to aligning with any outside power, its dependence on and fear of China, and the fact that they know China is staying but they are not sure if the United States will—that ASEAN is going to side with the United States openly against China on this issue. For many, that leaves continued pursuit of a binding COC as the only viable option for managing tensions.

These are fair points, but they do not change two facts: the ASEAN approach—waiting for a binding COC—is not working, at least not yet; and ASEAN's inability to adopt a united position or develop an effective strategy is undermining ASEAN centrality, or at least the more ambitious definitions of that centrality. One former colleague calls it the "ASEAN paradox." ASEAN wants to play a leading role in resolving issues in Southeast Asia, such as the South China Sea, but its lack of unity prevents it from taking a strong stance that might cause Beijing to rethink its aggressive approach. While even a united ASEAN would not necessarily succeed in resolving the issue, it would at least make it more difficult or costly for China to pursue its current strategy.

---

26 See, for example, Heydarian, "At a Strategic Crossroads," and "Remarks by Professor Don Emmerson, Head of the Southeast Asia Programme for the Shorenstein Asia-Pacific Research Centre of Stanford University," CPG's International Conference on Thailand's ASEAN Chairmanship 2019, March 1, 2019, http://www.cpg-online.de/2019/03/01/comments-by-professor-don-emmerson-head-of-the-southeast-asia-programme-for-the-shorenstein-asia-pacific-research-centre-of-stanford-university/.

ASEAN's Weaknesses

ASEAN's ineffectiveness on the South China Sea has highlighted its strategic weakness. The whole (ASEAN) is less than the sum of its parts (the ten member nations), at least on this issue. I understand why key players in the region insist that ASEAN unity and consensus are essential, and they might be right. The consequence, however, is that ASEAN does not carry the strategic heft that it otherwise might, making it harder to persuade American presidents to make the long journey across the Pacific every year to attend its meetings or to go to see ASEAN itself as a critical partner in resolving major political-security issues. As Donald Weatherbee put it back in 2012, "Another question that faces ASEAN is whether generalized good feelings about an ASEAN-centric agenda that does not address real regional political and security issues that engage the non-ASEAN participants will be enough to bring the American president to the summit on an annual basis . . . ."[27]

ASEAN's weakness in some cases frustrates individual member states to the point that they look for diplomatic options outside the ASEAN framework. I have no doubt that this factor helps explain why President Jokowi, when he took office in 2013, adopted a less ASEAN-centric approach to his foreign policy. I heard it directly from a few of his foreign policy advisors. It also explains why the Philippines went to The Hague in 2013, and perhaps why some in Hanoi are contemplating a similar unilateral legal challenge to China.

If ASEAN were going great guns in other areas and on other regional political and security issues, or if it were moving rapidly to integrate economically and build a strong, united community, it might be easier to convince top U.S. officials to see it as a serious strategic partner. Overall, however, its achievements in recent years have been modest. In foreign policy terms, ASEAN largely shrank from engagement in the 2008–11 Thai-Cambodian dispute over the Preah Vihear temple along their shared border until the UN Security Council delegated the issue to the organization in 2011. Only then did ASEAN act, with Indonesian foreign minister Marty Natalegawa leading an effort to mediate the dispute, which ended up being resolved between the two parties.[28]

---

27 Donald E. Weatherbee, "Southeast Asia and ASEAN, Running in Place," *Southeast Asian Affairs* (2012): 3–22, https://www.muse.jhu.edu/article/485123.
28 Julio S. Amador III and Joycee A. Teodoro, *The Role of the Association of Southeast Asian Nations in Post-Conflict Reconstruction and Democracy Support*

ASEAN also largely failed to deal with Myanmar's ethnic cleansing of the Rohingya minority in 2017. I was in Myanmar in 2016–20 and ASEAN did not distinguish itself. Malaysia and Indonesia spoke out, and Indonesian foreign minister Retno Marsudi traveled to Myanmar and Bangladesh a few times to offer an "Indonesian-style" diplomatic approach, as she put it to me during one of her trips, but ASEAN as a whole largely buried its head in the sand. The most it could do was send a humanitarian team to Rakhine State to look at the situation. Unfortunately, that team's report trumpeted the government's already-discredited line about treatment of the Rohingya, making ASEAN look bad.

ASEAN again faced a Myanmar dilemma in 2021, in the aftermath of a military coup and subsequent brutal crackdown against protestors. Although a few ASEAN members spoke out strongly against the coup, the member states remained divided and, at least initially, unable to offer a united front vis-à-vis the Myanmar military. The coup—and particularly the appalling and indiscriminate violence of the security forces against the population at large following the coup—posed (and continue to pose) a fundamental challenge to ASEAN and especially to the notion of ASEAN centrality. After much prodding by Indonesian president Joko Widodo, ASEAN held an emergency summit on April 24 to discuss the Myanmar situation. The meeting, which included Myanmar junta leader General Min Aung Hlaing, reached consensus on five points, including the need to end violence immediately and to name an ASEAN special envoy to attempt to mediate. The junta, however, ignored those points, saying only that it would consider them after the country returned to stability (i.e., after it had suppressed the opposition). As of this writing, ASEAN appears stuck, unable to act and unwilling to impose meaningful costs on the junta for ignoring its concerns.

Progress on what one might call ASEAN's internal goals—furthering economic integration and building the three pillars of the ASEAN community—also has been slow. The bloc has put the most effort into building its economic community, with mixed results. The AEC officially was launched, with much fanfare, in 2015. ASEAN officials have trumpeted the fact that member nations have eliminated tariffs on some 90 percent of goods, which is impressive. On the other hand, nontariff barriers

(Stockholm, Sweden: International Institute for Democracy and Electoral Assistance, 2016), https://www.idea.int/sites/default/files/publications/the-role-of-asean-in-post-conflict-reconstruction-and-democracy-support.pdf.

have persisted, if not increased. ASEAN has relied on member states voluntarily to reduce those barriers, with limited success. Nontariff barriers, plus the fact that many ASEAN economies produce similar items, has limited intra-ASEAN trade, which only grew from 19 percent of total ASEAN trade in 1993 to 23 percent in 2017.[29] Liberalization of services has also been slow, as several countries failed to meet their original commitments by 2015. There has been little movement on liberalizing capital flows, and almost no progress toward the goal of allowing free movement of labor across borders.

That said, the work continues. Five members—Vietnam, Indonesia, Thailand, Malaysia, and Singapore—took an important step in 2018 when they launched the ASEAN Single Window, which facilitates trade by simplifying customs processes.[30] The other five ASEAN members have since come on board as well.

ASEAN also introduced a "Master Plan on ASEAN Connectivity 2025" that aims to place ASEAN at the center of the region's effort to promote "connectivity" throughout the region via development of intrastate road, rail, and air networks. The purpose is to enhance economic integration, as well of course as to bolster the region's international competitiveness.[31] The ideas sound great, but they will rely on huge amounts of external financing, which is where China's Belt and Road Initiative comes into play. Early indications are that much of this infrastructure development will be negotiated and financed through bilateral deals, rather than by ASEAN itself. Still, if it promotes economic integration within ASEAN, it will have a major positive impact.

ASEAN has achieved greater progress in integrating into the global economy, negotiating free trade agreements with countries outside the bloc, including Australia, New Zealand, China, South Korea, Japan, and India. While these agreements are not as comprehensive as U.S. free trade agreements, they significantly reduced trade barriers, particularly tariffs. Then, in late 2020, ASEAN signed the Regional Comprehensive Economic Partnership, billed as the world's largest free trade

29 Eleanor Albert and Lindsay Maizland, "What Is ASEAN," Council on Foreign Relations, December 20, 2019, https://www.cfr.org/backgrounder/what-asean.

30 "Launch of the ASEAN Single Window Live Operation," ASEAN Single Window, November 1, 2018, https://asw.asean.org/index.php/news/item/launch-of-the -asean-single-window-live-operation.

31 Anna Funfgeld, "The Dream of ASEAN Connectivity: Imagining Infrastructure in Southeast Asia," *Pacific Affairs* 92, no. 2 (June 2019), https://doi.org/10.5509/ 2019922287.

agreement. In addition to ASEAN members, it includes China, South Korea, Japan, Australia, and New Zealand. There is some question how much the partnership will reduce trade barriers, but its signing signaled ASEAN's continued efforts to bolster its outside trade relationships. ASEAN also has increased its global share of inward foreign direct investment, more than doubling its share between 2007 and 2014.[32]

Progress on building the ASEAN Political-Security Community has been slow, in part because most ASEAN members have refused to move away from the bloc's "non-interference" principle, and also because the organization has struggled to turn rhetorical commitments into operational action. On security, ASEAN approved a Convention on Counter Terrorism, which established norms but did little to promote actual cooperation. As noted above, it also has made little progress on the South China Sea, arguably its most important security challenge, and early on shot down Indonesia's proposal for an ASEAN peacekeeping force. It has arguably fared even more poorly on the political side, where it failed to reach agreement on the idea of a regional human rights mechanism. As Donald Weatherbee has argued, there "is the huge gap between ASEAN's claims of promoting democracy and human rights in the APSC and the actual undemocratic political practices of what is the majority of ASEAN states that present ASEAN with its greatest credibility problem in dealing with its democratic dialogue partners."[33]

It is harder to quantify progress on building a sense of community within ASEAN. By that I mean building a sense among the populations in each member state that they are connected to the rest of ASEAN. Public polling on this issue presents a mixed picture. On the one hand, a significant majority of the population is aware of ASEAN, views it favorably, and even consider themselves to be "citizens" of ASEAN. On the other hand, polling also reveals that most in the region do not really know much about what ASEAN does or how it benefits them.[34] Some

32 Wolfgang Lehmacher, "The ASEAN Economic Community: What You Need to Know," World Economic Forum, May 31, 2016, https://www.weforum.org/agenda/2016/05/asean-economic-community-what-you-need-to-know/.

33 Weatherbee, *ASEAN's Half-Century*, chapter 11.

34 See, for example, Ponciano Intal and Lydia Ruddy, *Voices of ASEAN: What Does ASEAN Mean to ASEAN Peoples*, ASEAN@50 (Jakarta: Economic Research Institute for ASEAN and East Asia, 2017), https://www.eria.org/ASEAN_at_50_2.1_Integrative_final.pdf; and Candida Ng, "ASEAN Community, What's That Again?", Reporting ASEAN, August 17, 2015, https://www.reportingasean.net/asean-community-whats-that-again/.

observers have noted the large gap between the very positive rhetoric coming from officials about an ASEAN community and the reality on the ground and questioned whether a true community is realistic. One even called the goal of a community a "millstone" around ASEAN's neck, distracting it from the things it actually can do.[35] Perhaps the best way to put it is that progress toward building a true community is happening, but slowly. Nonetheless, ASEAN leaders in 2015 celebrated the establishment of a community by, among other things, approving another ambitious vision statement called "ASEAN 2025: Forging Ahead Together." The document foresees a stronger, more integrated, and more people-centered community by 2025, though again it is short on specific operational plans and commitments to turn the rhetoric into reality.

U.S. Mistakes

I have been critical here of ASEAN, but the United States has made mistakes too, usually due to a lack of understanding of how much emphasis ASEAN places on (1) doing things the ASEAN way, (2) avoiding taking sides with or leaning too much toward one of the big powers, and (3) partners such as the United States showing up and engaging at high levels consistently.

The high point of U.S. engagement came in early 2016, when President Obama hosted the ten ASEAN leaders at Sunnylands, California. The meeting did not produce any major breakthroughs, but it reaffirmed the U.S commitment to the region and further bolstered Southeast Asian confidence in the United States as a reliable partner. It also marked seven consecutive years when the United States and ASEAN had met at a high level, a growing relationship buttressed by consistent engagement at lower levels that supported ASEAN's own agenda.

The Obama administration's approach was not perfect, however. As I noted above, our decision to shift more military assets to the region, while welcomed by countries such as Vietnam and the Philippines, left others, including Indonesia, concerned. I was in Jakarta at the time, and even well-informed Indonesians not apt to fall for conspiracy theories

---

35 Muthiah Alagappa, "Community Building: ASEAN's Millstone?" Pacific Forum CSIS PacNet, Carnegie Endowment for International Peace, March 19, 2015, https://carnegieendowment.org/2015/03/19/community-building-asean-s-millstone-pub-59444.

actually wondered aloud whether the U.S. deployment of 2,500 troops to Darwin, Australia, presaged a U.S. intervention in troubled Papua. (President Obama, upon hearing this, laughed and pointed out that almost nobody in Washington even knew where Papua was.) We had let our Lower Mekong Initiative, which started off reasonably well, evolve into a series of programmatic seminars that were fine as far as they went but which cumulatively seemed like small potatoes, especially compared to the amount of money Beijing was throwing at the region. Also, at times the administration's criticism of China struck some in ASEAN as unnecessarily raising tensions. In contrast, at least some members—most notably the Philippines—blamed Washington for failing to put teeth into its tough rhetorical position on the South China Sea, and particularly for "allowing" China to assert control over Scarborough Shoal. Still, overall, one could see that the administration's consistent engagement had created significant positive momentum.

Unfortunately, the Trump administration failed to maintain that momentum. President Trump's withdrawal from the TPP eliminated a key strategic and economic pillar of our engagement and raised serious doubts about Washington's economic role in the region. Moreover, after showing up (briefly) at the first ASEAN/EAS Summit during his term, President Trump skipped the remaining three. He sent Vice President Pence to the summits in 2018, which was acceptable if not ideal, but then dropped U.S. representation even lower in 2019 and 2020. The nadir was in November 2019, when the president not only failed to attend, but did not even bother to send the vice president or the secretary of state. Instead, Trump sent National Security Advisor Robert O'Brien to represent him. O'Brien did a fine job, but to the Southeast Asians he was a senior staffer, and they felt snubbed. The disappointment, verging on anger, was palpable. O'Brien again represented the president in 2020, which in some ways was even worse, because the fact that it was a virtual summit (because of the COVID-19 pandemic) meant that the president could have piped in via video, with a minimal time commitment.

Washington's failure to appoint an ambassador to ASEAN reinforced the feeling in the region that we were not serious. Many in the region saw the Trump administration as unpredictable and largely disengaged. They also were concerned about the administration's tough rhetoric criticizing multilateralism and globalization, its "America First" mantra, its withdrawal from the Paris Climate Change Accords, and so on. Concerns about U.S. reliability grew; its poor handling of the COVID-19 outbreak exacerbated those worries. The Singapore-based ISEAS-Yusof Ishak Institute's annual survey of attitudes among ASEAN opinion leaders in 2020 found that less than 35 percent of respondents viewed the United States as a reliable strategic partner.[36]

Also, the Trump administration's increasingly tough rhetoric on China made Southeast Asians very nervous, even if they agreed with some of Washington's criticisms of Beijing. They feared they would be trampled in any major U.S.-China spat and also resented that some Washington officials appeared to attend ASEAN-hosted meetings only for the purpose of confronting China. In addition, some in the region did not react well to the Trump administration's new "Free and Open Indo-Pacific Strategy" and the development of the U.S.-Japan-Australia-India Quad, both of which they saw as aimed at or excluding China. Finally, the ASEAN member nations resented what they saw as the United States' tendency to try to speak for them, particularly on issues related to China, and on occasion to talk down to them.

With these concerns in mind, and also aware of the growing questions about ASEAN's role, some in the region tried to re-assert ASEAN centrality. Indonesia led the way, with President Jokowi and Foreign Minister Marsudi promoting the "ASEAN Outlook on the Indo-Pacific." Former foreign minister Natalegawa initiated this idea back in 2013, during a speech at CSIS in Washington, when he framed the Indo-Pacific region and proposed a TAC-like agreement that would bind the entire region to settle disputes peacefully, follow international law, and the like. It did not go anywhere, but his successor, Retno Marsudi, resuscitated the idea in 2018 in response to the Trump administration's launch of its Free and Open Indo-Pacific Strategy.

Officials in the region worried that the new U.S. strategy excluded China and thus would require them to choose between Washington and Beijing. For the Indonesians, coming up with an ASEAN framework for the Indo-Pacific would allow the group to avoid getting caught in this bind while thrusting ASEAN back into centrality, at least intellectually. After a few false starts, ASEAN leaders signed off on the concept in 2019. Unlike Marty Natalegawa's original idea, this approach is not

---

36 Sharon Seah, Hoang Thi Ha, Melinda Martinus, and Pham Thi Phuong Thao, *The State of Southeast Asia: 2021 Survey Report* (Singapore, ISEAS-Yusof Ishak Institute, 2021), 40, https://www.iseas.edu.sg/wp-content/uploads/2021/01/The-State-of-SEA-2021-v2.pdf.

legally binding. Rather, in true ASEAN fashion, it is a set of principles or precepts that are difficult to reject: peaceful resolution of disputes, cooperation, acceptance of international law, and so on. The trouble is that ASEAN has offered no ideas on how to turn these excellent principles into reality, though Foreign Minister Marsudi in particular continues to advance the concept and has gained some support among dialogue partners. It is less a policy or strategy document than it is an attempt to reaffirm ASEAN's centrality and keep the regional architecture inclusive, i.e., including rather than aimed at China.

By the end of the Trump administration, the U.S. performance on the three objectives noted above—restoring ASEAN confidence in America's long-term commitment to the region, effectively supporting ASEAN's own goals, and working effectively with ASEAN to counter China's aggressive approach in the South China Sea—was mixed at best. Confidence in the U.S. commitment was down substantially, and Washington and its Southeast Asian partners continued to struggle to counter China in the South China Sea. Arguably, Washington's assistance and support had helped ASEAN achieve some of its goals, particularly on economic integration (e.g., the Single Window initiative), but the initial U.S. failure to help the region tackle the COVID-19 pandemic had undermined even that success.

Joe Biden's election in November 2020 produced a surge of optimism in ASEAN that U.S. engagement would increase and Washington would be a more reliable partner. The 2021 ISEAS-Yusof Ishak Survey found that nearly 69 percent of respondents expected U.S. engagement to increase, and the percentage of those who had confidence in the United States as a strategic partner shot up from 34.9 to 55.4 percent.[37] As I write this, it is still too early in to say whether the Biden administration will meet the expectations in Southeast Asia. After a slow start, the administration stepped up its engagement with Southeast Asia in the latter half of 2021 and into early 2022, with the vice president and secretaries of state and defense all traveling to the region and the president joining the EAS Summit (virtually) in October 2021 and then hosting his ASEAN counterparts in Washington in May 2022. Washington offered millions of free COVID-19 vaccines to the region and began to fill vacant ambassadorships, though as this book goes to print it has yet to offer any substantial trade initiatives.

---

37 Seah et al., *State of Southeast Asia*, 39.

The Need to Put Disappointment Aside

Where does that leave us? ASEAN is what it is: cautious by nature, and these days divided over how to deal with China. Moreover, the bloc lacks leadership. In the past, that leadership generally has come from Indonesia, sometimes Thailand, along with Singapore and Malaysia. Indonesia, which packs the most heft, is less ASEAN-driven under President Jokowi than it was under President Yudhoyono. Thailand, which often has played a critical role, is too focused on domestic affairs to devote the time and energy needed to ASEAN. Singapore remains focused, but, as a small state that is somewhat resented in the region for its success and confidence, can only do so much. Malaysia, Vietnam, and to a lesser extent the Philippines play important roles, but they need help.

ASEAN members also have refused to give more authority and clout to the ASEAN Secretariat or the secretary-general. The late Surin Pitsuwan provided strong leadership during his tenure, but even then, I recall member state officials complaining that he was offering too much leadership. "Too much general, not enough secretary," was a regular refrain. His successors, as well as his predecessors, have been more secretary than general. As for the secretariat, it continues to be severely underfunded and understaffed, with a total budget of only some $20 million.[38] The member states presumably have made a deliberate decision to starve it of funds and, thus, of clout.

When we engage in the region, we often hear pleas for us to do more to support ASEAN, as if somehow ASEAN's weakness was due to a lack of external support. We should support ASEAN, but to use a cliché, we cannot want it more than the ASEAN members do. On the other hand, our perennial disappointment with ASEAN should not lead us to abandon or ignore it. ASEAN is a useful institution that has done much to keep the peace in the region, and over time there is some prospect it will facilitate the creation of more of a community and an integrated economy.

More importantly, even if ASEAN as an institution does not do as much as we would like, it is still very much in our interest to support and engage it. One reason: engaging with ASEAN helps our relationship with all ten of its members, for whom ASEAN is hugely important. As I

---

38 "'No Reforms' for ASEAN Anytime Soon," *Jakarta Post,* November 25, 2017, https://www.thejakartapost.com/seasia/2017/11/25/no-reforms-for-asean-any time-soon.html.

have been telling people for years, attending ASEAN meetings is like going to your spouse's family reunion. It might not be the most memorable thing you ever do, but joining the event will bring you rewards, and not showing up definitely will cost you. I was at the EAS in Bangkok in November 2019, and I promise you the fact that neither the president, vice president, nor the secretary of state showed up to represent the United States hurt us significantly (with all due respect to National Security Advisor Robert O'Brien). In a region that has long been skeptical of U.S. staying power in the region, showing up consistently at the highest levels is essential.

Also, it is not like ASEAN has no substantive value. First and foremost, it has largely succeeded in its original goal of preventing conflict among the Southeast Asian nations. It is hard to prove, but I am convinced the rich network of personal relationships that have developed at all levels among the ten governments has helped them resolve disputes and keep the peace.

In addition, there is value in ASEAN centrality, at least in terms of the group's ability to convene all the big players in the region. Imagine if ASEAN ceased to exist. There would be no regional forum that would include all of the key players, including the United States. The lack of such a forum would make it that much harder to resolve disputes and build the relationships upon which diplomacy depends. Also, ASEAN-hosted meetings provide a great opportunity for the U.S. president and secretary of state to conduct substantive meetings, not only with Southeast Asian counterparts, but with many other leaders who attend the summits.

Finally, despite its glacial speed, ASEAN is slowly moving forward on economic integration and building some sense of community. It is absolutely in the U.S. interest to support further progress, as a strong and increasingly cohesive Southeast Asia can better resist Chinese efforts to divide and dominate the region.

For ASEAN's ten members, there is a need to bolster the secretariat's budget and its clout. I understand that the Southeast Asian countries, many of which are still doing their own nation-building at home, are wary of surrendering much sovereignty or power to ASEAN. Still, there is a middle ground, in which the secretariat—and perhaps the secretary-general—could enjoy more influence and a greater role without undermining member nation sovereignty.

There are at least two other specific steps ASEAN might consider to boost its heft. First, there is a wealth of diplomatic talent in the region.

Why not ask a handful of senior or retired diplomats, or even former presidents and prime ministers, to serve as an ad hoc ASEAN diplomatic team, to be dispatched to member states that might need help? Such a grouping could have been very helpful during the Rohingya crisis in Myanmar, for example, as they could have given Aung San Suu Kyi some useful advice and ideas—quietly, in the ASEAN way—while the rest of the world was screaming at her. It might also have enabled ASEAN to move more quickly to address the Preah Vihear issue between Thailand and Cambodia or the more recent coup in Myanmar.

Second, as a number of others have suggested, ASEAN should try to facilitate a deal among the four member states that have claims in the South China Sea. China would hate this, but the failure of the four so far to have worked out their own deal greatly weakens all of them— and ASEAN—vis-à-vis China. There no doubt would be plenty of hurdles involved in negotiating some sort of acceptable outcome among the four, but if it is kept within the ASEAN family, there is some hope it could result in progress.

If there is one lesson I have learned from working with ASEAN, it is that—as a couple of my State Department colleagues have privately argued—the United States should accept and appreciate ASEAN for what it is rather than complain about what it is not. Washington should identify and work on a number of issues and areas where we and ASEAN have shared interests, rather than focus on our respective disappointments. Specifically, we should enhance our existing partnership on health (timely, given COVID-19) and on promoting ASEAN's economic integration, while bolstering efforts to address climate change and environmental issues, some of which are closely tied to strategic challenges. For example, protecting the Mekong River ecosystem is an environmental and ecological challenge, but doing so also has geostrategic implications, given China's ability to use its dams to influence the water flow downstream. In the South China Sea, China's island-building is prompting allegations of environmental destruction. Tackling the environmental and fisheries angles of the South China Sea together might create opportunities for us to deal also with the geopolitical issues, but in a way that the Southeast Asians might find more comfortable than the current approach. As I will describe in more detail in chapter 14, Washington might also look at a broader water initiative that would encompass the South China Sea, the Mekong, and other issues.

Last but not least, the United States needs to appoint a qualified ambassador to ASEAN and ensure the president attends ASEAN-hosted summits. We have lost credibility and trust in recent years. We can only rebuild it if we show up and engage consistently at senior levels.

For their part, the ASEAN member nations would do well to make a greater effort to show Washington that increased engagement pays dividends, whether by coming up with their own initiatives or taking stronger stances on critical international issues, such as the Russian invasion of Ukraine.

CHAPTER TWELVE

China's Role

China's growing power and increasingly assertive diplomacy have effectively ended the post–Cold War period in our relationship with Southeast Asia. I am not suggesting the dawn of a new Cold War, or that the world has become bipolar. Rather, China's rise has injected into regional diplomacy a significant geostrategic element that requires both Washington and the nations of Southeast Asia to think much more strategically and to redouble efforts to work together—not against China, but to protect and advance shared interests.

That is because this new, powerful China brings with it both many opportunities for the region—especially economically—but also significant challenges that go to the very heart of the origin of ASEAN more than fifty years ago. Remember, the original five members established ASEAN in 1967 both to manage the distrust among themselves and to ensure that they—collectively and individually—could defend their independence and dictate their own future in a world of big powers.

Others have written entire books—very good books—recently on China's relations with Southeast Asia.[1] I will not try to replicate these volumes or review all of China's actions and relationships in the region,

---

1 Three recent high-quality books include Murray Hiebert, *Under Beijing's Shadow: Southeast Asia's China Challenge* (Lanham, Maryland: Rowman & Littlefield, 2020); Sebastian Strangio, *In the Dragon's Shadow: Southeast Asia in the Chinese Century* (New Haven: Yale University Press, 2020); and Donald K. Emmerson, editor, *The Deer and the Dragon: Southeast Asia and China in the 21st Century,* (Stanford, CA: Walter H. Shorenstein Asia-Pacific Research Center, 2020); see also David Shambaugh, *Where Great Powers Meet: America & China in Southeast Asia* (New York: Oxford University Press, 2021).

but rather focus on some of the Chinese policies and behaviors that pose the most significant challenges to Southeast Asia and to U.S. interests. The intention is not to portray China as a bad actor overall, but rather to highlight those elements of its behavior that raise concerns.

China's greatly enhanced role in the region is in part the product of its own remarkable development and increased strength. China's military strength, including its navy and ability to project power beyond its borders, has increased dramatically over the past few decades, to the point that the United States no longer can assume military dominance vis-à-vis the mainland in the western Pacific. The gap between China's military and that of its Southeast Asian neighbors, which always existed, has expanded exponentially. China also has significantly increased its own defense diplomacy, selling weapons, providing training, and carrying out some joint exercises with Southeast Asian counterparts.

It is its economic muscle, however, that has most fundamentally altered the power equation in the region. Since the end of the Cold War, China has enjoyed sustained rapid economic growth that has catapulted it from a lower-middle-income nation to the second-largest economy and largest exporting nation in the world. Per capita income has risen twenty-fold, and China's top companies and banks now rival the biggest players in the world. At the end of 2020, China boasted foreign exchange reserves of more than $3.2 trillion, greater than the combined economic output of all ten ASEAN nations.[2]

This remarkable development also made China the most important—if not the dominant—economic player in Southeast Asia. The mainland's trade with the ten ASEAN member states skyrocketed from $7.5 billion in 1990 to $642 billion in 2018, pushing it past first the United States and then Japan to become Southeast Asia's top trading partner. China became the region's top source of foreign tourists, with 2,700 weekly flights bringing the lion's share of the nearly thirty million mainlanders who visit Southeast Asia annually (pre–COVID-19). Chinese investment in Southeast Asia also has grown sharply, though it still lags behind Japan and the United States.[3]

---

2 "China Foreign Exchange Reserves, 1989–2021" CEIC Data, https://www.ceic data.com/en/indicator/china/foreign-exchange-reserves.

3 "Flows of Inward Foreign Direct Investment (FDI) Into ASEAN By Source Country," ASEANStatsDataPortal, https://data.aseanstats.org/fdi-by-hosts-and -sources; Zhang Yunling and Wang Yuzhu, "ASEAN in China's Grand Strategy," in *Building ASEAN Community: Political-Security and Socio-Cultural Reflections*, ASEAN@50 vol. 4, ed. Aileen Baviera and Larry Maramis (Indonesia: Economic

Charm and Muscle

China's rise alone has guaranteed it significantly enhanced influence in the region, but Beijing also has made a concerted effort to use traditional diplomacy, soft-power tools, security engagement, its economic clout, and most recently vaccine diplomacy to make the most out of its increased power. In the late 1980s and early 1990s, many Southeast Asian nations still viewed China as a threat, in part due to its past support for communist insurgencies. By the mid-1990s, however, Beijing had renewed diplomatic relations with all ASEAN countries and began to move energetically to bolster its ties with the region. It joined the ASEAN Regional Forum in 1994 and became a full ASEAN dialogue partner in 1996, leading to the first China-ASEAN Summit and initial meeting of ASEAN Plus 3 in 1997. Beijing's decision not to devalue its currency during the Asian Financial Crisis—and in some cases to offer unconditional economic aid—drew praise in the region and helped maintain the momentum in the developing relationship.

China signed on to the ASEAN Declaration of Conduct in the South China Sea in 2002 and the ASEAN Treaty of Amity and Cooperation in 2003. Also in 2002, it signed a Framework Agreement on Economic Cooperation that was meant to produce an ASEAN-China Free Trade Agreement within ten years. Chinese trade with ASEAN tripled in 2000–05, exceeding $100 billion in 2004.[4]

When I returned to the region in 2005, China was in the midst of its so-called charm offensive, under which it was operating with restraint and emphasizing the economic benefits of growing trade and investment relationships. Beijing had just signed a "strategic partnership" with ASEAN and was investing heavily in its bilateral relations with individual Southeast Asian countries. It also was taking advantage of Washington's relative neglect of the region at the time, as the United States focused on the threat of global terrorism.

In the past fifteen years, China's engagement in and influence over the region has grown steadily, as Beijing has sought to position itself as

---

Research Institute for ASEAN and East Asia, 2017), 166, https://www.eria.org/ASEAN_at_50_4A.9_Zhang_and_Wang_final.pdf; and Strangio, *In the Dragon's Shadow,* chapter 1.

4 Names redacted, *China-Southeast Asia Relations: Trends, Issues, and Implications for the United States,* Congressional Research Service RL32688, February 8, 2006—April 4, 2006, https://www.everycrsreport.com/reports/RL32688.html.

the center of the Asia region, politically, economically, and institutionally. During that time, China's "charm" has increasingly been mixed with assertiveness, as a more confident Beijing under Xi Jinping has flexed its muscles as needed and made clear its view that Southeast Asia falls under China's sphere of influence.

This new assertiveness has presented itself first and foremost in the South China Sea. In 2009 Beijing formally made its claim to the area within the so-called nine-dash line, which encompasses nearly all the South China Sea and intrudes well into the exclusive economic zones of the Southeast Asian claimant nations. At the ASEAN Regional Forum Ministerial meeting in Hanoi in mid-2010, then foreign minister Yang Jiechi responded to Southeast Asian claimants' complaints about the nine-dash line with a remarkably blunt statement reminding them of the power dynamics in the region: "China is a big country and other countries are small countries, and that's just a fact."[5]

Then, in the spring of 2012, Chinese vessels basically kicked Philippine fishing boats out of the Scarborough Shoal, an area well within the Philippines' EEZ. As described in chapter 2, the United States brokered a deal under which China and the Philippines both agreed to withdraw their vessels from the Scarborough Shoal area. The Philippines implemented the agreement. China did not, and then denied there had been such an agreement. Since then, Chinese fishing and law enforcement vessels have maintained a regular presence in the area, threatening and intimidating Philippine fishing vessels and, according to some sources, doing significant environmental damage to the area.[6]

Manila first turned to ASEAN, which held its annual meetings in Phnom Penh in July 2012, but host Cambodia took China's side, blocking agreement on an ASEAN statement. Not coincidentally, Chinese president Hu Jintao had visited Phnom Penh just a few weeks prior to

---

5 Ian Storey, "China's Missteps in Southeast Asia: Less Charm, More Offensive," *China Brief* vol. 10, no. 25, December 17, 2020, Jamestown Foundation, https://james town.org/program/chinas-missteps-in-southeast-asia-less-charm-more-offensive/.

6 See, for example, "China's Most Destructive Boats Return to the South China Sea," Asia Maritime Transparency Initiative, Center for Strategic and International Studies, May 20, 2019, https://amti.csis.org/chinas-most-destructive-boats -return-to-the-south-china-sea/; and Jeffrey Maltem and Agence France-Presse, "Philippine Fishermen Protest Chinese Harvesting of Giant Clams on Scarborough Shoal in Further South China Sea Dispute," *South China Morning Post,* June 14, 2019, https://www.scmp.com/news/asia/southeast-asia/article/3014561/philippine -fishermen-protest-chinese-harvesting-giant.

the meetings and had promised millions of dollars in aid and investment to Cambodian prime minister Hun Sen.

When Philippine president Benigno Aquino filed a legal case with the International Tribunal on the Law of the Sea (ITLOS) in The Hague in January 2013, China preemptively rejected the case's legitimacy, made clear it would not abide by its findings, and stepped up its efforts to assert its control of disputed features. Between 2013 and 2015, through dredging and other engineering efforts, it turned several tiny land features in the South China Sea into artificial islands and then constructed airfields and other facilities on them, seeking to create a fait accompli. Beijing ignored the international outcry over the legal, military, and environmental consequences of its actions, and then—as it had promised—rejected the 2016 ITLOS ruling, which was a near total defeat for China's interests.

During that period and subsequently, Chinese vessels—a mixture of navy ships, law enforcement vessels, survey ships, and fishing boats— have routinely sailed throughout the South China Sea, often well within the EEZs of ASEAN claimant nations, intimidating, harassing and sometimes ramming vessels from other claimant nations. In 2020 alone, Chinese vessels harassed a Petronas oil exploration vessel off the coast of Malaysia, rammed Philippine and Vietnamese fishing boats operating in their own EEZs and engaged in a tense standoff with Indonesian ships in the Natuna Sea. As Gregory Poling, executive director of CSIS's Asia Maritime Transparency Initiative, concluded, "China's intent is to overwhelm the region" with vessels until the Southeast Asian claimants give up.[7] In April 2020 Beijing unilaterally announced the establishment of two additional administrative districts in disputed areas, one in the Paracel Islands and a second on an artificial island in the Spratly Islands.

Beijing has combined this aggressive behavior with just enough diplomacy to create the illusion that it is open to compromise. Namely, it has continued to express its willingness to negotiate a binding Code of Conduct (COC) that would set parameters for behavior among all the claimants pending a final resolution of the disputes. In practice, however, China has stalled, reflecting its lack of interest in compromising as

---

7 Frances Mangosing, "Analyst Says COVID-19 Pandemic Not Slowing China Conquest of South China Sea," *Inquirer.Net*, April 14, 2020, https://globalnation .inquirer.net/186834/analyst-says-covid-19-pandemic-not-slowing-china-conquest -of-south-china-sea.

long as it believes it can achieve 100 percent of its aims through asser-tive behavior. China and ASEAN reached a framework agreement on a COC in 2017, but it is not binding and has not translated into a change in behavior.

These COC negotiations have been important to China, even though they do not seem to be going anywhere, or at least not going anywhere quickly, because they facilitate China's work to keep ASEAN divided, unable to take a stronger, more united position on the issue. Whenever one or more claimant states become frustrated by China's actions and seek a stronger ASEAN stance, other Southeast Asian governments less interested in challenging their northern neighbor can point to the COC negotiations as a theoretical path forward, forestalling stronger con-sensus statements that might give Beijing pause.

Active and Pragmatic Diplomacy

China has effectively paired muscular diplomacy in the South China Sea with a softer approach overall toward the region and individual governments. Unlike the United States, it shows up consistently at se-nior levels at ASEAN-hosted regional meetings and maintains a brisk schedule of high-level visits between Beijing and all ten Southeast Asian capitals. To cite just one set of numbers, from 2016 through 2019, Southeast Asian heads of state or government made a total of forty-three official visits to China, while China's top leaders (President Xi Jinping or Premier Li Keqiang) made eleven visits to Southeast Asia.[8] This does not count the dozens if not hundreds of other senior visits by foreign ministers and the like.

Beijing also has not hesitated to offer support to governments and leaders facing domestic or international challenges and in fact has taken advantage of Western criticism of democratic backsliding and human rights violations to enhance its engagement and influence. After General Prayut Chan-ocha's 2014 coup in Thailand, the United States and many other Western countries responded critically. China, on the other hand, insisted the coup was an internal matter and sent Premier

8 Wooi Yee Tan and Chong Foh Chin, "High-Level Visits and the Belt and Road Initiative: The Case of Southeast Asia," *Contemporary Chinese Political Economy and Strategic Relations: An International Journal* 6, no. 1 (April-May 2020), 217–59.

Li Keqiang to Bangkok to reaffirm its support for the new government. Prayut paid a return visit a few days later, thanking Xi Jinping for China's support and offering general praise for Beijing's positive role in the region. Six years later, Foreign Minister Wang Yi visited Bangkok amid widespread youth-led protests against the Prayut government and the monarchy. He again reaffirmed Beijing's unconditional support for the Thai government. China's steady diplomatic efforts, combined with high levels of trade and a growing security relationship, have accelerated Thailand's movement from unusually close ties with Washington to a more balanced approach that arguably now tilts more toward Beijing.

Following Myanmar's brutal ethnic cleansing campaign against the Rohingya in mid-2017, China seized the opportunity presented by intense Western criticism to elevate its relationship with Aung San Suu Kyi's government and the Myanmar military. Beijing blocked potential UN Security Council statements and actions, and in November 2017 welcomed both military commander General Min Aung Hlaing and (separately) Aung San Suu Kyi to Beijing, where they heard no criticism over the mistreatment of the Rohingya. President Xi described Chinese-Myanmar military relations as the "best ever," while Aung San Suu Kyi lauded Beijing's empathy. "Myanmar values China's understanding of the Rakhine issue, which is complicated and delicate," she said.[9]

Cambodian prime minister Hun Sen has relied more than any of his counterparts on Beijing's diplomatic and political backing, turning to China time and again in the face of Western criticism and even sanctions. When the Hun Sen government engineered the arrest of opposition leader Kem Sokha and then disbanded his political party in late 2017, ahead of the country's 2018 national elections, the West criticized the government and pulled funding for the elections. China sent Foreign Minister Wang Yi to Phnom Penh, where he expressed support for Cambodia's efforts to "protect political stability." Beijing subsequently offered funds of its own to support the elections.[10] When the European Union threatened to withdraw Cambodia's trade preferences over human rights violations, China's ambassador to Cambodia

9 Jane Perlez, "In China, Aung San Suu Kyi Finds a Warm Welcome (and No Talk of Rohingya)," *New York Times,* November 30, 2017.
10 "China Supports Cambodia's Crackdown on Political Opposition," Reuters, November 20, 2017, https://reut.rs/2zTwXYF.

criticized the EU for mixing trade and politics and vowed that China would continue to support Cambodia and bolster economic ties.[11]

China's strong support for Hun Sen highlights its "pragmatic" approach, given the history between the two. In the 1980s, after the invading Vietnamese installed a pro-Hanoi government led by Heng Samrin and Hun Sen in Phnom Penh, China took the lead, along with Thailand and the United States, in blocking recognition of the new government and working to push it out of power. China funneled arms to the genocidal Khmer Rouge, which was fighting against the government and the Vietnamese. In the 1990s and 2000s, however, Chinese leaders recognized that Hun Sen had emerged as *the* political leader in Cambodia and so had begun to court him with visits and large amounts of aid.

China had taken an equally practical approach toward the emergence of a democratic government led by Aung San Suu Kyi in Myanmar. Beijing for years had backed the repressive, xenophobic military dictatorship that ran Myanmar, while the West had supported Aung San Suu Kyi as the leader of the democratic opposition. When her NLD party won a landslide victory in the 2015 national elections, China deftly altered course, acted as if it had supported democracy all along, and began courting Aung San Suu Kyi. Then, when the Rohingya crisis provided an opportunity, China redoubled its efforts, casting itself as the protector of Myanmar's sovereignty against a hostile world.

When the Myanmar military staged a coup in February 2021, China refused to call it a coup and readily accepted and engaged with the new junta, despite its near total lack of domestic support or legitimacy. Hedging its bets slightly, Beijing also has quietly urged the junta not to ban the NLD party.

One can look at this pragmatic diplomacy two different ways. One view is that Beijing is practicing smart diplomacy. Rather than trying to promote certain values or groups, it is willing to work with whomever is running the country, without political or ideological conditions. This approach allows China to engage consistently and to win the confidence of its Southeast Asian partners. The other way to look at this is to say China is reinforcing some of the behaviors and practices that many in the region oppose, including corruption, democratic backsliding, and human rights violations. This approach will provide

---

11 David Boyle, "Chinese Ambassador: EU Should Not Mix Politics, Trade in Cambodia," VOA News, July 19, 2018, https://www.voanews.com/a/chinese-ambassador-eu-should-not-mix-politics-trade-in-cambodia/4489291.html.

short-term benefits to Beijing, but it risks elevating anti-China public sentiment, which could affect longer-term relations.

Building Economic Influence and Leverage

Chinese leaders no doubt see their economic clout as a good insurance policy against this risk. Particularly under Xi Jinping, China has made a concerted effort to build and reinforce its growing economic influence and to turn its economic power into leverage. It signed a free trade agreement with ASEAN in 2010, further boosting already growing trade links, and joined negotiations for the Regional Comprehensive Economic Partnership (RCEP) trade agreement in 2012. In 2015, it launched the Asian Infrastructure Investment Bank (AIIB), which now counts seventy-six members, including all of ASEAN, to provide infrastructure financing. In 2013, it established the Belt and Road Initiative (BRI), which President Xi envisions supplying tens of billions of dollars in infrastructure investments in the greater region, including of course Southeast Asia.

Southeast Asians have largely welcomed China's expanding economic engagement. Growing trade, investment, and tourism have boosted their own growth and raised incomes, while Chinese assistance has supported any number of much-needed projects. The promise of Chinese funding of and investment in infrastructure—including via the BRI—has been particularly attractive to many governments that otherwise struggle to raise domestic funds or to attract Western or other international investment into these projects.

In Indonesia, for example, President Joko Widodo has made infrastructure development a high priority and often has turned to the Chinese government and Chinese companies to support projects that many other investors do not consider commercially viable. He joined AIIB and in his first two years in office met with President Xi five times. In 2018 Indonesia and China signed agreements for a total of $23 billion worth of BRI projects, including a number of important power plants.[12]

Malaysia has been one of the largest recipients of BRI funds (at least commitments) in Southeast Asia and in the world. Kuala Lumpur signed agreements with China for, among other things, a mammoth $16 billion East Coast Rail Link, which would travel from Port Klang

---

12 "Indonesia, China Sign $23.3b in Contracts," *Jakarta Post,* April 14, 2018, https://bit.ly/3sJVzww.

(the major port near the capital) to the Thai border, as well as a $10 billion port and industrial complex in the old city of Malacca.[13]

Myanmar has turned to China to finance numerous infrastructure projects. For example, China offered to fund Yangon chief minister Phyo Min Thein's ambitious Yangon New City project, a massive undertaking that struggled to attract any other foreign funding. When the Myanmar Energy Ministry put out several power project tenders in 2019, Chinese companies were the only ones willing to pursue them. Several Western and Japanese energy companies said bluntly that the projects were not commercially viable.

Trade as Leverage

China's economic engagement sometimes comes with high costs, however, something that many in Southeast Asia recognize. First, while the volume of China-ASEAN trade is very high, it is also skewed heavily in China's favor. China's exports to the region are significantly higher than its imports. At the ground level, one regularly hears local business executives in the region complain that they cannot compete against a flood of cheap Chinese imports.

Also, China uses trade as a political weapon on a regular basis around the world, giving it leverage vis-à-vis other nations. As the Center for Strategic and International Studies reported in early 2021, "To date, Beijing has used the threat and imposition of trade-restrictive measures to punish over a dozen countries for pursuing policies deemed harmful to Chinese interests."[14] During the China-Philippines struggle over the Scarborough Shoal in 2012, China suddenly changed its requirements for imports of Philippine bananas (the exports of which are very important for the Philippines), largely cutting them off in response to Manila's failure to accommodate China's interests in the South China Sea. It also banned Chinese tourists from traveling to the Philippines, cutting off another source of revenue for the island nation.

---

13 Mercy A. Kuo, "Malaysia in China's Belt and Road: Insights from Chow Bing Ngeow," *The Diplomat*, November 23, 2020, https://thediplomat.com/2020/11/malaysia-in-chinas-belt-and-road/; and Strangio, *In the Dragon's Shadow*, chapter 8.

14 Bonnie Glaser, "Time for Collective Pushback Against China's Economic Coercion," Center for Strategic and International Studies, January 13, 2021, https://www.csis.org/analysis/time-collective-pushback-against-chinas-economic-coercion.

In Myanmar, much of the bilateral trade with China travels overland through various border crossings. Chinese officials on a regular basis close border crossings for vague, undefined reasons, causing panic among Myanmar farmers and traders for whom the Chinese market often is the only feasible destination for their products. While it was not always easy to know in any particular case why China closed the border, Myanmar officials and businesses understood that Beijing was sending a political as well as an economic message through the closings.

More importantly, everyone in Southeast Asia knows that Beijing is willing and able to block imports or cut off tourism at a moment's notice for political reasons. Given the enormous size of the Chinese market, Southeast Asians—like others around the world—always must tread carefully in the bilateral relationship, for fear of incurring a high economic cost. This helps explain why Indonesia and Malaysia—in company with many other Muslim-majority nations in the world—have largely refrained from criticizing China's mistreatment of the Uighur minority in the country's west. They know—or at least have good reason to believe—that the Chinese authorities will respond to any criticism by imposing stiff economic penalties. China does not play by WTO rules, and everyone knows it.

Chinese officials as well as many in Southeast Asia might point out that China is not the first major power to use its economic clout to advance its broader interests. The United States, after all, has long used sanctions and other economic tools to pressure other governments to change policies and actions it views as problematic. That is a fair point, even if one believes that Beijing is quicker to use those tools than is Washington and often implements them without transparency.

Investments Welcome, but at What Cost?

Southeast Asian governments have generally welcomed Chinese investment, particularly the BRI and other programs that help meet huge demand for infrastructure. Southeast Asia's infrastructure needs are enormous—the Asian Development Bank estimated the region needed to invest some $200 billion per annum in infrastructure from 2016 to 2030.[15] With limited capacity to raise domestic funds, external

---

15 Asian Development Bank, *Meeting Asia's Infrastructure Needs* (Manila, Philippines: ADB, 2017), https://www.adb.org/sites/default/files/publication/227496/special-report-infrastructure.pdf.

financing is a must for most Southeast Asian nations, at least for the time being. Unfortunately, the region has struggled to access that financing, for a few reasons: (a) countries have had difficulty convincing private foreign businesses that their projects are commercially viable; (b) Western donors, with the exception of Japan, have largely shifted away from funding infrastructure; and (c) the multilateral development banks, while offering attractive financing in support of well-vetted projects, require an approval and disbursement process that is painfully slow and often heavily conditioned.

China's BRI—offering large amounts of money to fund large numbers of projects, some of questionable commercial viability, with relatively quick timelines—has therefore been very appealing to many Southeast Asian (and other) governments. China is filling a huge void, which is why its BRI conferences always attract a big crowd of Southeast Asian leaders and ministers. It is not that they are necessarily pro-China. It is that China has offered up hundreds of billions of dollars of funding for infrastructure projects these governments desperately need, and no one else is coming close to doing that.

Many China-backed projects turn out well. Southeast Asian nations have learned, however, that the reality of BRI is often less attractive— or brings greater hidden costs—than what was promised. The problems include the risk of excessive indebtedness, increased corruption, and the heavy use of Chinese contractors and laborers, which reduce the economic benefits of these projects to the host governments. Sri Lanka's 2017 decision to hand over its Hambantota Port to China for ninety-nine years (because of the heavy Chinese debt the project incurred) has become a standard talking point about the risk of excessive debt among Southeast Asian officials considering BRI projects. On the contractor/labor front, one study of thirty-four BRI-funded projects in Asia and Europe found that nearly 90 percent of contractors employed were Chinese, far above the norm.[16]

Another issue is China's difficulty in delivering quality projects on time. China often promises low costs and quick construction, but then fails to deliver on either score. Officials and business executives in Vietnam have complained that Chinese-backed projects, such as the Hanoi metro system and a major steel complex in Thai Nguyen Province,

---

16 James Kynge, "China's Contractors Grab Lion's Share of Silk Road Projects," *Financial Times,* January 24, 2018, https://www.ft.com/content/76bIbeOC-0113 -IIe8-9650-9CO-ad2d7c5b5, cited in Herbert, *Under Beijing's Shadow,* 40.

suffer from quality concerns, cost overruns, and delays that make their long-term costs substantially greater than promised.[17]

When Philippine president Duterte took office and prioritized the relationship with Beijing, he won Chinese promises of some $24 billion in financing and investments in Philippine infrastructure projects, in part by setting aside Philippine complaints about China's behavior in the South China Sea. Four years later, Philippine sources complained that only 5 percent of the promised resources had materialized, as China had taken a tough position in negotiating the terms of the various deals. Filipino analyst Richard Heyderian in late 2020 argued, "They're taking Duterte for a ride. . . . He's done a lot for China, and yet what did he get from China in exchange? Up until today, there are practically zero big-ticket infrastructure projects by China."[18]

When I was in Indonesia a decade ago, before BRI, Indonesian officials and analysts told me that China had only implemented a small percentage of the projects that Beijing had committed to complete. Several of the infrastructure projects China had implemented proved problematic. Most notably, Chinese-led consortiums had built all but one of a series of coal-fired power plants that President Yudhoyono's administration had pursued to add ten thousand megawatts to the country's power capacity. The plants ended up being delayed, with significant cost overruns, and then did not run properly when they were finally turned over to the government.

A 2019 Asia Society study[19] noted that many proposed BRI projects are rushed through to signature without adequate pre-feasibility and feasibility studies, consultations with affected communities, or due diligence. The study highlighted severe problems with the Chinese-funded Jakarta-Bandung high-speed rail project in Indonesia and the Malaysian East Coast Light Rail (ECLR) project. In the former, a 2018 Indonesian review concluded that the project had not received appropriate due

17 "China's Projects in Vietnam Earn Reputation for Poor Quality, Delays," *Nikkei Asia,* September 20, 2017, https://asia.nikkei.com/Economy/China-s-projects-in-Vietnam-earn-reputation-for-poor-quality-delays2.

18 Desmond Ng and Sumithra Prasanna, "They're Taking Him for a Ride: Has the Philippines Gained from Duterte's Pivot?," *Channel News Asia,* December 19, 2020, https://www.channelnewsasia.com/news/cnainsider/philippines-president-rodrigo-duterte-china-pivot-investments-13801780.

19 Daniel R. Russel and Blake Berger, "Navigating the Belt and Road Initiative," Asia Society Policy Institute, June 2019, https://asiasociety.org/sites/default/files/2019-06/Navigating%20the%20Belt%20and%20Road%20Initiative_2.pdf.

diligence and, as a result, was "deeply troubled." The Malaysian ECLR project likewise had been rushed through, using outdated exchange rates to calculate costs, and somehow making a sixty-five-kilometer error in calculating the length of the railway.

These two projects revealed additional, even more troubling Chinese practices. Indonesia initially had expected to award the Jakarta-Bandung railway contract to Japan, with which it had been working for years. China, however, came in late in the game with a lower-cost offer, which required no Indonesian government financing. The Chinese deal appeared too attractive to pass up. When it came time to implement, however, the project encountered any number of problems that resulted in delays and complaints of major environmental damage.[20] In effect, as it has done elsewhere, for political and strategic purposes China rushed in to underbid what was to be a Japanese-funded project, won the contract, and then could not deliver. Beijing is operating as a would-be monopoly supplier, seeking to undercut its competitors to gain strategic advantage. (China sought to do something similar in Myanmar in 2019, offering to build a high-speed rail line between Yangon and Mandalay to substitute for a long-planned Japanese-funded rail link between the two cities.)

China's role in the ECRL project is even more concerning. While a Malaysian consultancy had originally priced the project at under $7.5 billion, the deal announced by Prime Minister Najib Razak totaled an astonishing $16.4 billion, with some estimates that the figure could rise to $20 billion. Subsequent testimony indicated that Najib and those around him had agreed to inflate costs for this and other Chinese-backed infrastructure projects, allowing Najib to use the extra costs (borne by Malaysian taxpayers) to repay the debts of the government-owned 1Malaysia Development Berhad fund, which Najib had personally milked to the tune of hundreds of millions of dollars. In other words, China agreed to participate in a massively corrupt deal to bail out the Malaysian prime minister by vastly overcharging the Malaysian people for a BRI project.[21] It surely was no coincidence that

---

20 Emma Connors, "Off the Rails—Indonesia's Belt and Road Rail Mess," *Financial Review,* September 24, 2020, https://www.afr.com/world/asia/off-the-rails-indonesia-s-belt-and-road-rail-mess-20200917-p55wms.

21 Russel and Berger, "Navigating the Belt and Road Initiative"; see also Strangio, *In the Dragon's Shadow*, chapter 8.

Najib at the time opened secret talks with China that would allow Chinese naval vessels to dock at two Malaysian ports.

When Mahathir Mohammed took over for Najib after the 2018 elections, he canceled the ECRL project amid complaints about "unfair" deals and concerns that Malaysia could not repay the massive debt the project would incur. In early 2019, Malaysia and China agreed to resume the project, but at the much lower cost of $11 billion.[22]

Indonesia and Malaysia are relatively well-off and have plenty of skilled economists, financial experts, and lawyers who can do proper due diligence and negotiate reasonable deals with China, if given sufficient political backing. This is much less true in the poorer mainland Southeast Asian nations—namely Cambodia, Laos, and Myanmar—that also sit right at China's doorstep and thus lack the increased maneuvering room that comes with distance. These are the nations that most feel the weight of China's presence. Vietnam and Thailand also are near neighbors, but they boast sufficient economic and other strength to keep China at arm's length more easily.

The Unique Case of Cambodia

Cambodia's case is unique, in the sense that longtime prime minister Hun Sen appears to have agreed implicitly to an arrangement whereby his government supports China in the region in return for massive Chinese political and financial support. One can debate whether Western policy toward and pressure on Cambodia over human rights pushed him into Beijing's arms, but the fact remains that he has embraced China.

Cambodia's support for China has been most obvious in the South China Sea, where Phnom Penh blocked consensus on an ASEAN communiqué during its host year in 2012 and did Beijing's bidding again at the 2016 ASEAN summit. Hun Sen has consistently echoed China's argument that the South China Sea question is not an issue for ASEAN, but rather needs to be resolved through bilateral negotiations between Beijing and the various Southeast Asian claimants.

The cooperation goes beyond the South China Sea, however. As Sebastian Strangio has pointed out, between 2010 and 2015 China

---

22 "Malaysia, China Agree to Resume Railway Project After Slashing Cost," Reuters, April 11, 2019, https://reut.rs/2IuAXDg.

funneled some $5 billion in loans and assistance to Phnom Penh. For its part, the Hun Sen government blocked a proposed visit by the Dalai Lama and repatriated (to imprisonment or worse) twenty Uighur asylum seekers.[23]

Phnom Penh also approved a massive Chinese investment in the coastal city of Sihanoukville that largely turned it into a Chinese enclave. Identified as a prime target for BRI projects, the formerly quiet beach town saw a sharp increase in Chinese investment beginning in 2016. Chinese developers and investors poured into the Sihanoukville Special Economic Zone (SEZ), where Chinese firms accounted for 80 percent of all investors. The real draw, however, was the booming gambling and tourism business. Chinese businesses established dozens of casinos and guesthouses, all catering to the growing number of Chinese tourists who could gamble legally in Cambodia but not back home. By 2019, local authorities estimated there were anywhere from 62 to 88 casinos, nearly all Chinese-owned, and 156 guesthouses, all but six of which were Chinese-owned.[24]

Visitors to Sihanoukville were struck by the city's rapid growth, but also by how Chinese it had become. Chinese signs, Chinese money, and even Chinese payment systems dominated. While some local residents welcomed the increased job opportunities, many complained that they felt increasingly like strangers in their own town. They noted rising crime, increased prostitution, and growing inflation that was forcing many to move outside the city. Local business owners complained that the Chinese tourists only frequented Chinese restaurants and shops, where they paid via Chinese financial apps WeChat or AliPay, depriving the local economy of any benefits. Sihanoukville officials complained of growing crime, due at least in part to the large Chinese presence, while others talked of Chinese criminal syndicates and a sharp increase in money laundering.[25]

23 Strangio, *In the Dragon's Shadow*, chapter 4.
24 "How China Changed Sihanoukville," *ASEAN Post,* February 11, 2021, https://theaseanpost.com/article/how-china-changed-sihanoukville; and Chris Horton, "The Costs of China's Belt and Road Expansion," *The Atlantic,* January 9, 2020, https://www.theatlantic.com/international/archive/2020/01/china-belt-road-expansion-risks/604342/.
25 Chris Horton, "The Costs of China's Belt and Road Expansion"; "How China Changed Sihanoukville," *ASEAN Post*; and Sheith Khidhir, "China Crime Plaguing Cambodia?" *ASEAN Post* October 9, 2019, https://theaseanpost.com/article/china-crime-plaguing-cambodia.

The local backlash grew so severe that Hun Sen finally had to act. In August 2019, he temporarily banned online gambling, and then in December announced a permanent ban. The Chinese-driven boom in Sihanoukville, which some Cambodian officials had described as a miracle, had turned out to be a net negative for many Cambodians.

Nonetheless, other nearby Chinese infrastructure projects continue. Their massive scale and questionable commercial viability raise questions about their intended use. State-owned China Road and Bridge Corporation is funding and building a $2 billion four-lane expressway to connect Sihanoukville to Phnom Penh. Some twenty-five miles to the west of Sihanoukville, China's Union Development Corporation is building a huge airport, a seaport, and a luxury resort complex worth nearly $4 billion inside Cambodia's largest national park. Without any tender or transparency, it received a ninety-nine-year no-cost lease for 110,000 acres that cover some 20 percent of the country's coastline. This despite a Cambodian law that limits concessions to foreign companies to one-third of what Union Development Corporation received.[26]

U.S. officials have repeatedly expressed concern about the purpose of this project, with Secretary of State Mike Pompeo claiming in September 2020 that there was "credible evidence" that the facilities could be used to host Chinese military facilities. "If so, (this) would go against Cambodia's constitution and could threaten Indo-Pacific stability, possibly impacting Cambodia's sovereignty and the security of our allies."[27] That same day, the U.S. Treasury Department announced sanctions against Union Development and a Cambodian general linked to the project for illegally seizing land and displacing Cambodian families.

Washington has also expressed concern about another major Chinese project just to the east of Sihanoukville, the Sealong Bay National Beach resort. It is not the resort itself that is generating concern, but potential Chinese interest in its neighbor, Cambodia's Ream Naval Base. The *Wall Street Journal* reported in July 2019 that Cambodia and China had signed a secret agreement granting China exclusive access

---

26 Hannah Beech, "A Jungle Airstrip Stirs Suspicions About China's Plans for Cambodia," *New York Times,* December 22, 2019.

27 Men Kimseng, Hul Reaksmey and Aung Chhengpor, "U.S. Sanctions Chinese Company Developing Resort in Cambodia," VOA News, September 19, 2020, https://www.voanews.com/east-asia-pacific/us-sanctions-chinese-company-developing-resort-cambodia.

to dock its ships at the base.[28] Cambodian officials have angrily denied the allegation, but recent reports indicate that Cambodia has razed a couple of U.S.-constructed buildings on the base and welcomed Chinese support to construct new buildings, adding to Western concern.[29]

China and Laos

To Cambodia's north, impoverished, landlocked Laos also is receiving substantial Chinese interest, much of it welcome, but some of it concerning. Laos's secretive communist leadership has historically been aligned more with Hanoi than with Beijing, the product of the close relationship between the two during the Vietnam War. In recent years, however, China's economic largesse has pulled Vientiane's leaders closer to Beijing, which can offer funding and infrastructure development that is beyond Vietnam's reach.

China has funneled BRI resources to a series of projects in Laos, headlined by the $6 billion Kunming-to-Vientiane high-speed railway, which is meant to be one stage of an eventual Kunming-to-Singapore railway. China provided $4 billion of equity for the project, giving it a 70 percent ownership stake, and lent much of the money Laos needed to put up its 30 percent share. Laos's total GDP is less than $20 billion.[30] The Lao government inaugurated the rail line in December 2021.

The longer-term question is to what extent Laos will benefit from the existence of the rail line, beyond relatively modest transit fees. The Lao are hoping the project will enhance their economic competitiveness by reducing logistics costs, but many wonder if Lao companies will be

---

28 Jeremy Page, Gordon Lubold, and Rob Taylor, "Deal for Naval Outpost in Cambodia Furthers China's Quest for Military Network," *Wall Street Journal,* July 22, 2019, https://www.wsj.com/articles/secret-deal-for-chinese-naval-outpost-in -cambodia-raises-u-s-fears-of-beijings-ambitions-11563732482.

29 "Cambodia Defense Chief Defends Demolition of Second U.S.-Funded Building at Ream Naval Base," Radio Free Asia, November 10, 2020, https://www.rfa .org/english/news/cambodia/demolition-11102020164255.html; and "Update: China Continues to Transform Ream Naval Base," Asia Maritime Transparency Initiative, Center for Strategic and International Studies, October 12, 2021, https:// amti.csis.org/changes-underway-at-cambodias-ream-naval-base/.

30 Ashley Westerman, "In Laos, A Chinese-Funded Railway Sparks Hope for Growth—and Fears of Debt," NPR, April 26, 2019, https://www.npr.org/2019/ 04/26/707091267/in-laos-a-chinese-funded-railway-sparks-hope-for-growth-and -fears-of-debt.

able to compete with their Chinese counterparts. "The main problem is that the high-speed train is driven by a political economy agenda that serves the promoting nation much more than the recipient country," concluded Ruth Banomyong, a professor of supply chain logistics management at Thammasat Business School in Bangkok.[31] Moreover, Thailand's lack of enthusiasm for proceeding with the rail link through its territory has raised even more questions about the project's commercial viability, particularly for Laos.

In addition to official BRI projects, the Chinese presence in northern Laos is growing significantly through a combination of investment and migration across the porous border. According to author Sebastian Strangio, China has invested in new roads connecting Yunnan Province to the northern part of Laos. These roads have encouraged Chinese investments in hydropower, mining, and plantations, and also have facilitated the migration of thousands of Chinese across the porous border into northern Laos. In some northern towns, Chinese nationals now make up as much as 20 percent of the population.[32]

The Lao authorities have authorized the establishment of several SEZS near the border, and also approved multiple land-for-capital schemes, under which Laos offers Chinese investors substantial parcels of land in return for their investments. Many of these investments have been in agricultural plantations, where Chinese businesses use Lao land to grow crops—particularly bananas—for Chinese consumers back across the border.

Some Lao have benefited from the seasonal work these plantations offer, but there also have been widespread complaints about heavy pesticide use causing significant health and environmental problems, as well as displacement of Lao farmers. Radio Free Asia has reported consistently on Lao plantation workers complaining of health problems that they attributed to exposure to chemicals.[33] The Lao government

---

31 John Reed and Kathrin Hille, "Laos' Belt and Road Project Sparks Questions Over China Ambitions," *Financial Times,* October 30, 2019, https://www.ft.com/content/a8d0bdae-e5bc-11e9-9743-db5a370481bc.

32 Strangio, *In the Dragon's Shadow*, chapter 4.

33 See, for example, Radio Free Asia, "Lao Banana Workers Sickened by Chemicals Used on Farms," Mekong Eye, May 31, 2018, https://www.mekongeye.com/2018/05/31/lao-banana-workers-sickened-by-chemicals-used-on-farms/; and "Lao River Clogged with Trash from Chinese Banana Farms," Radio Free Asia, February 3, 2020, https://www.rfa.org/english/news/laos/banana-02032020151330.html.

banned new banana plantation licenses in 2017 because of these concerns, but many continue to operate.

Chinese investors also have opened casinos in northern Laos that, as in Sihanoukville, cater almost exclusively to mainland tourists and spawn a wide variety of illegal activities and social ills. The most well known and notorious is Kings Romans Casino, a tourist destination and gambling den that is the centerpiece of the Golden Triangle SEZ. The Lao government granted Kings Roman International a ninety-nine-year lease over a thirty-nine-square-mile SEZ along the Mekong River, near Laos' border with Myanmar and Thailand. Although the Lao government retains a 20 percent ownership stake, reports indicate it plays no active role in managing or administering the area.[34]

Zhao Wei, the company's owner, promised to build a five-star hotel, a casino, a golf course, and much more, and also committed to employ thousands of Lao workers. According to a Myanmar journalist who looked into the project, the company instead hired thousands of undocumented Myanmar workers, presumably because it could pay them lower wages.[35]

Kings Roman Casino reportedly welcomes hundreds of Chinese tourists every week. Visitors report that the area looks and feels like China, with street signs in Chinese and payment expected in yuan. The Myanmar journalist who visited reported that it felt like a "Chinese colony." He said even vehicle license plates were Chinese, as were taxi-cab drivers and many other employees.[36]

In early 2018, the U.S. Treasury Department slapped sanctions on Kings Roman Casino and Zhao Wei, claiming the operation was involved in illegal trafficking of people, drugs, and wildlife, as well as child prostitution. The Treasury Department statement alleged that the criminal network operating out of the casino had allowed the storage and distribution of heroin and other narcotics, and was engaged in

---

34 Sebastian Strangio, "The 'Lawless' Playgrounds of Laos," Al Jazeera, July 24, 2016, https://www.aljazeera.com/features/2016/7/24/the-lawless-playgrounds-of-laos.

35 Ye Ni, "A Visit to the Chinese Casino City in Laos Built By Myanmar Workers," *Irrawaddy*, October 21, 2019, https://www.irrawaddy.com/news/burma/visit-chinese-casino-city-laos-built-myanmar-workers.html.

36 Ni, "A Visit to the Chinese Casino City in Laos."

"horrendous illicit activities."[37] Zhao's involvement in such activities came as no surprise, as he had previously been forced to close down a similar operation in Myanmar's Mong La region due to his alleged involvement in illegal wildlife trade.

China's steady if informal encroachment into northern Laos is cause for growing concern among many Lao, but it is not the only threat to the country's sovereignty. Laos's rising debt to China—reportedly equal to more than one-half of its GDP—threatens to put the country even more under Beijing's influence. The World Bank has been warning that the country was likely to have to default on its debt obligations. A significant amount of that debt accrued to the state-owned power company, Electricite du Laos (EDL), which accepted Chinese financing to build a series of hydropower projects that, at least to date, have failed to generate the hard-currency earnings expected. To avoid a potential default, the government in September 2020 signed a power grid shareholding deal between EDL and China Southern Power Grid Co., under which the mainland firm would receive majority control of the newly spun-off EDL Transmission Company.[38]

One can argue that this Chinese takeover of Laos's electricity grid did not represent malign Chinese behavior, but rather the most practical, realistic way for Vientiane to avoid a debt default. That may be. Nonetheless, the fact remains that China has pushed any number of projects in Laos that have driven up that country's debt to unsustainable levels. More importantly, Beijing's increased control over the power grid gives it substantially more leverage over Laos's rulers than it had before, reducing the country's freedom of maneuver and, to a certain extent, its independence.

A Heavy Hand in Myanmar

China also has paid a lot of attention to neighboring Myanmar, with which it shares a 1,300-mile border. China's primary strategic interest

37 "U.S. Slaps Sanctions on Laos Golden Triangle Casino in Bid to Break Up Narco-Empire," Reuters, January 31, 2018, https://reut.rs/2rSVwTf.

38 Keith Zai and Kay Johnson, "Exclusive: Taking Power—Chinese Firm to Run Laos Electricity Grid Amid Default Warnings," Reuters, December 15, 2020, https://www.reuters.com/article/china-laos/exclusive-taking-power-chinese-firm -to-run-laos-electric-grid-amid-default-warnings-idUSL8N2FW068.

in Myanmar is gaining access to the Indian Ocean, which would enable it to reduce its reliance on the narrow Malacca Straits, which connects the Pacific Ocean to the Indian Ocean and through which most of its trade now flows. To accomplish this, China proposed in 2009 a series of major projects to build a deepwater port and SEZ at Kyaukphyu, on the Bay of Bengal in Myanmar's western Rakhine State, and to construct a railway and parallel oil and gas pipelines from there to Yunnan Province. China completed the oil and gas pipelines in 2015 but talks on the port/SEZ and railway stalled as Myanmar's reform-minded Thein Sein government grew leery of excessive debt and dependence on China.

State-owned Citic Group, the lead Chinese investor, had initially proposed a $7.3 billion port project, which would have made Kyaukphyu as big as the Port of Manila or southern California's massive Long Beach facility, along with a $2.7 billion SEZ. The enormous size of the project raised many red flags, with some suggesting China might have military use in mind. Given Myanmar's strong nationalist bent, that was unlikely, though not impossible. More likely, China was willing to spend big to ensure it had a quality alternative trade route.

For Myanmar officials, a key question was how the project would benefit their economy, beyond the possible short-term boost from construction. Kyaukphyu is probably Myanmar's best natural harbor, but there is almost no infrastructure connecting it to the rest of the country's economy. China's proposed railway would facilitate Chinese exports via Myanmar, but would do little to bolster Myanmar exports, unless the $2.7 billion SEZ developed extremely well.

Myanmar economic officials also worried about the risk of falling into a debt trap, à la Sri Lanka's Hambantota Port. Under the initial Chinese proposal, the Citic Group was to take an 85 percent equity stake, and China would loan the Myanmar government hundreds of millions of dollars to cover its 15 percent stake.

As China pushed Aung San Suu Kyi's government in 2016 and 2017 to proceed with the projects, Myanmar officials and the press vigorously debated the risks. Economic advisor Sean Turnell publicly warned that the project was overcapitalized, far larger than what Myanmar needed, and would saddle the country with excessive debt. Commerce minister Than Myint bluntly called the proposed deal "unfair" to Myanmar.[39]

---

39 "Green Light for Kyaukphyu," *Bangkok Post,* July 30, 2018, https://www .bangkokpost.com/business/1512470/green-light-for-kyaukphyu.

By late 2017, however, Nay Pyi Taw authorities found themselves relying heavily on China's political backing in the wake of the Myanmar military's ethnic cleansing operation against the Rohingya population. The economic officials charged with negotiating the Kyaukphyu port deal were mindful of the project's risks, but also felt growing pressure from above to move the projects forward to keep Beijing happy.

At the request of those officials, we were able to use an existing USAID economic program to provide a modest amount of funding that the officials used to engage outside, independent experts who could help them conduct proper due diligence of the project and better assess what made sense for their country. In the end, they succeeded in downsizing the project considerably, from $7.3 to $1.3 billion (for the first phase, with subsequent phases conditional on full use of the first phase). They also doubled Myanmar's equity participation to 30 percent without the need for additional government funding (or loans from China). Although some elements of the agreement raised concern among outside lawyers, overall the Myanmar authorities significantly lowered their risk.

The Yunnan-to-Kyaukphyu projects constitute the core of the broader, aspirational China-Myanmar Economic Corridor (CMEC), a complex of potentially dozens of projects that would connect Yunnan Province through the central city of Mandalay to both Kyaukphyu to the west and Yangon to the south. In Yangon, China's state-owned China Communications Construction Corporation has led the effort to fund a proposed but controversial New Yangon City project. Over the past few years, Chinese officials have been pressing Nay Pyi Taw to move ahead on turning this concept into a reality and to restart the highly controversial Myitsone Dam project, which Prime Minister Thein Sein suspended in 2011.

In January 2020, President Xi Jinping made a state visit to Myanmar, during which the two sides signed thirty-three CMEC-related agreements, including on the initial stage of the Yunnan-to-Kyaukphyu railway and on the proposed New Yangon City project. After the visit, Myanmar officials privately advised me and others not to read too much into these agreements, as Myanmar would continue to take great care to ensure any and all BRI-related projects were in the country's interest.

The Yunnan-Kyaukphyu railway project, for example, was receiving intense scrutiny from the Transportation Ministry and others. Senior officials there told me privately that, while they could see the economic justification for the Mandalay-Muse stage of the rail line (Muse being on the border with Yunnan), the initial cost estimate from the Chinese developer raised concerns. The ministry was seeking a third-party review of the pre-feasibility study to ensure the project made sense. They were even less sanguine about the Mandalay-Kyaukphyu stage, pointing out that the traffic for that section would seem to be nearly all Chinese exports, with little that Myanmar could ship back to China.

Meanwhile, the public debate over the Myitsone Dam project continued, with Chinese officials alternating between demanding it be revived and staying quiet about it. The project itself, which would have placed a hydropower dam in the upper reaches of the Irrawaddy River in Kachin State, near the Chinese border, was deeply unpopular. The Irrawaddy is in many ways the heart of Myanmar, and there is great opposition to building dams on it. Moreover, as initially envisioned, nearly all the electricity produced would have gone to China, a tough sell in Myanmar, where only one-third of households were connected to the power grid. A senior aide to Aung San Suu Kyi once told me that proceeding with the project would be "political suicide."

The NLD government, nonetheless, sought to avoid saying no to China, for fear Beijing would react harshly. So Nay Pyi Taw did the wise thing—it formed a committee to study the issue and looked for ways to delay a decision. Many observers thought China continued to push for the project less because it envisioned success and more as a means of maintaining leverage over Myanmar. Put another way, if Myanmar refused to proceed with Myitsone, it presumably would feel obliged to give the green light to some other projects that China wanted to pursue.

In many ways, the debate in Myanmar over BRI projects as a whole reflected this dynamic: China continually put intense pressure on the government to pursue BRI projects, constantly reminding the authorities how much Beijing was helping them (by, for example, protecting them in the UN Security Council). Myanmar officials insisted they would only pursue the projects that they wanted, but it was clear that they felt the political pressure to go beyond that.

In that sense, the government benefited from the wariness many Myanmar people, including in civil society and the media, felt toward Chinese investment and China in general. Based on experience, many people, especially but not exclusively in ethnic minority areas, equated Chinese investment with forced relocation, environmental damage, bribery and nontransparency, and a lack of benefits to the local communities. Opposition to the Myitsone Dam project might have been an extreme example, but it reflected widely shared concerns.

Several officials told me they felt more concern about Chinese activities outside of official BRI channels, specifically in border areas where government control was limited or nonexistent. If one looks around Myanmar's border areas, particularly those abutting China, one can see plenty of reasons to worry. Whether it is Chinese companies doing corrupt deals, Chinese investments damaging the environment or creating social ills, Chinese migrants flouting immigration rules, or Chinese officialdom supporting various armed groups for political reasons, the totality of Chinese activities in many of Myanmar's border areas raises important concerns.

Let us start in Kachin State in the country's northeast. The ethnic Kachin, who make up a sizeable share of the state's population but are not in the majority, have historically felt closer to the United States than to China, due to both their longtime bond with American Baptist missionaries and their World War II partnership with the U.S. military against Japan, as well as their concern about China's attitude toward religion. At the same time, with Kachin lying far from Yangon and nestled up against Yunnan Province, its people have long recognized the need to have a reasonably good relationship with their northern neighbor. Kachin farmers rely heavily on China's market, and the entire population depends on Chinese imports for many of their basic needs.

Beijing clearly sees Kachin as in its sphere of influence and has sought to limit U.S. and Western engagement there. Former Chinese ambassador to Myanmar Hong Liang told my predecessor, Derek Mitchell, that he should not travel to Kachin State. Hong Liang, with whom I was to develop a good relationship during the two years in which our assignments overlapped, told me the same thing when I first met him, saying the area was "too sensitive." I admired his chutzpah but ignored his advice, traveling to Kachin regularly, as had Derek Mitchell.

On at least two occasions, my travel to Kachin State prompted Ambassador Hong or his successor to visit within days of my trip. On one such occasion, a week after my joint visit with the UK ambassador in late 2018, Ambassador Hong Liang warned some of the Kachin politicians, religious leaders, and activists with whom I had spoken that they should be careful about meeting with me or others from our embassy or other Western missions. The warning backfired when several of his interlocutors publicly complained about his heavy-handed pressure.

Kachin Democratic Party president Gumgrawng Awng Hkam told the *Irrawaddy* that the ambassador had warned them not to develop close relations with Western diplomats or they would face "serious consequences." He and Reverend Hkalam Samson, president of the powerful Kachin Baptist Church, said that the Chinese diplomat had been bossy and threatening, and had warned them not to oppose Chinese projects such as the Myitsone Dam.[40] Later, a Kachin friend told me the Chinese officials had been very aggressive. He said the Kachin would not stop engaging with the United States, but he also added that they could not completely ignore Chinese demands, as Beijing could place massive pressure on them simply by closing the border gate for a while.

The Kachin also complained about Chinese-owned banana plantations, which increasingly dominated the landscape around Myitkyina and, reportedly, further afield from the state capital. As in Laos, locals complained that the Chinese used massive amounts of chemicals, polluting the streams and rivers, and causing myriad health problems. We also heard from some of the tens of thousands of people living in IDP camps—they had been displaced by the years-long conflict between the Kachin Independence Army (KIA) and the military—that, desperate for cash, they had sold their land cheap to corrupt local businesses that then partnered with Chinese investors to establish the banana plantations. It is hard to know how much the Chinese businesses were at fault on the latter point, but clearly the locals felt that they had taken advantage of their plight to make money.

The Chinese arguably are even more active and interested in neighboring Shan State, just south of Kachin. Myanmar's largest state, Shan State shares lengthy borders with both China and Thailand. It is home to a rich mosaic of ethnic minority communities, multiple ethnic armed organizations (EAOs) and militias, and one of the world's largest centers of methamphetamine production. The proposed CMEC would bisect conflict-ridden northern Shan State; it could create development opportunities, but already is exacerbating conflict among local armed groups fighting over control of land that they expect will increase in value due to the expected Chinese investments. One cannot blame Beijing for the existence of these conflicts, but a more sensitive investor

---

40 Nan Lwin, "Analysis: Behind the Threats and Warnings of Chinese Ambassador's Kachin Visit," *Irrawaddy*, January 9, 2019, https://www.irrawaddy.com/news/burma/analysis-behind-threats-warnings-chinese-ambassadors-kachin-visit.html.

might do more to consult with local stakeholders to try to minimize the negative effects of its projects.

The history of China's engagement and relations with the various groups along its border with Shan State is fascinating, but I will only highlight a handful of key points. Elements of Chiang Kai-shek's defeated Guomindang forces fled to the area in 1949 and for several years carried out insurgent activity, backed by the United States and often partly funded by opium trafficking. Later, the Beijing-backed Communist Party of Burma operated extensively in the area. In 1989, the party fell apart but spawned several armed groups that continue to operate to this day. They include the National Democracy Alliance Army (NDAA) in Mong La, the Myanmar National Democracy Alliance Army (MNDAA) in the Kokang region, and the United Wa State Army (UWSA) in the Wa State Special Administrative Region.

All three of these regions are more or less Chinese or at least China-dominated enclaves within Myanmar's borders. The Kokang themselves are largely ethnic Han Chinese but are a recognized ethnic group within Myanmar. In all three areas residents speak Chinese, use Chinese currency, and even set their clocks to Beijing time. All three are enjoying greater prosperity than most of the rest of Myanmar, based on close economic ties to China and revenues from casinos frequented by mainland gamblers. Wealth from the illegal narcotics trade—increasingly methamphetamines—has financed a lot of development, particularly in the Kokang and Wa regions (the Mong La region has by most accounts shifted away from narcotics).

In the past ten to twelve years, the MNDAA has twice engaged in major clashes with the Myanmar military, only to retreat into China. I do not know the details of the relationship between China and the MNDAA, but it is striking that Chinese authorities seem to tolerate the occasional presence of an armed insurgent group within their territory.

The Chinese relationship with the UWSA is more obvious and more problematic. The Myanmar government has no authority at all within the Wa area, which is protected by the thirty-thousand-person UWSA. The UWSA boasts a wide range of modern weaponry, all supplied by China, including artillery, drones, and missile-armed helicopters. There are regular reports of Chinese People's Liberation Army or intelligence officials working in the Wa area, without permission or knowledge of Myanmar authorities, and of Chinese officers training the UWSA.

These areas are also the regional—and maybe global—center for methamphetamine production, carried out by a combination of the armed groups and international criminal syndicates. There is no evidence that China is directly supporting this drug production, but Chinese authorities seem to be making little effort to stop the flow of precursor chemicals from the mainland into the region. There also is little evidence of Chinese pressure on these groups to stop their drug production.[41]

The Chinese also have been supporting the Arakan Army, which has become one of the most powerful and active EAOs in the country. The Arakan Army began as a small armed group, midwifed by the Kachin Independence Army, using ethnic Rakhine migrant workers to supplement KIA efforts in the northeast. By early 2019, however, the Arakan Army had shifted substantial forces to their ostensible home state of Rakhine, where with widespread popular support they launched an aggressive campaign against the Myanmar military. There have been widespread reports that the AA has been receiving arms from China (possibly through the UWSA), and the Myanmar military reportedly raised concerns about this directly with senior Chinese officials. Meanwhile, the Arakan Army has publicly supported controversial Chinese infrastructure projects in Rakhine State, shifting public opinion in the state noticeably. During a late 2019 visit to the Arakan National Party headquarters, I asked party officials why their office walls were now covered with posters praising the China-Myanmar Economic Corridor, something many of these same people had been deeply skeptical of when I had visited some months earlier. They laughed nervously and suggested they had just needed to put up something to cover their empty walls.

In eastern Kayin State, near the Thai border, Thai influence has historically exceeded that of China. The Chinese, however, are beginning to make inroads. In early 2018, the Myanmar Investment Commission approved a small ($22 million) joint venture between Hong Kong–based Yatai International and Saw Chit Thu, a Karen militia leader affiliated with the Myanmar military, for a twenty-five-acre development in Myawaddy Township, near the Thai border. Over the following months, reports filtered out that the project, known as Shwe Kokko, was dramatically larger than what had been approved. Yatai International itself boasted of a $15 billion, 180,000-acre development

---

41 To be fair to China, it was the Myanmar military that initially gave the green light to a number of EAOs to maintain their weapons and to engage in illegal activity, including the narcotics trade, in return for ending their armed struggle.

featuring everything from hotels and casinos to industry. Visitors to the area confirmed that construction already underway greatly exceeded the twenty-five-acre approved area, and that thousands of Chinese workers already were living in the area. Yatai claimed that its project had the backing of BRI.

Further investigation by the U.S. Institute of Peace,[42] among others, concluded that this project was not linked to the BRI. Furthermore, the main investors behind Yatai were the same sketchy characters who had been thrown out of Cambodia when Hun Sen cracked down on illicit and online gambling. It soon became clear that their intent, along with Saw Chit Thu, was to develop another huge gambling and entertainment complex, targeting Chinese tourists, inside Myanmar. Local Karen residents complained that this was not the kind of investment they wanted, as they understandably feared the rise of drug smuggling, prostitution, and other social ills. There were reports of tensions in nearby Myawaddy town between locals and Chinese migrants.

I raised concerns about these investments with civilian and military officials, noting that our concern was not about Chinese investment per se, but rather what seemed to be illegal investment that could have significant social and political implications in a very important part of the country. The officials, who already were aware of the controversy, said they were looking into the matter. Sometime later they reportedly suspended construction, but subsequent reports indicated the project was continuing. At a minimum, it was taking place in a deeply nontransparent fashion. Almost certainly, massive corruption was involved.

In many of these deals, whether in the Karen area or further north in Shan and Kachin states, it is hard to know how much the Beijing authorities have been involved or even aware. In some cases, it appears that Chinese businessmen are striking problematic deals with corrupt locals, with or without the support of Beijing or Yunnan authorities. Nonetheless, the result—for people in Myanmar—is the growing number of de facto Chinese enclaves on their territory, seemingly beyond the reach and authority of the Myanmar government.

The Chinese government's direct involvement was much more apparent in Myanmar's complex peace process, which aimed to end

---

42 Jason Tower and Priscilla Clapp, "Casino Cities: The Role of China and Transnational Criminal Networks," U.S. Institute of Peace, Special Report no. 471, July 27, 2020, https://www.usip.org/publications/2020/07/myanmars-casino-cities-role-china-and-transnational-criminal-networks.

fighting between the central authorities and some two-dozen EAOs. Although the February 2021 military coup largely halted the formal peace process, China's behavior until that time warrants attention. In addition to providing weapons to the UWSA and the Arakan Army, China provided political support for the Federal Political Negotiation and Consultative Committee (FPNCC), a coalition of EAOs operating near the Chinese border and de facto led by the UWSA. China portrayed itself as supporting the peace process, including by encouraging and pressuring the FPNCC groups to join the government's Panglong peace conferences and hosting various dialogue meetings between the parties to the conflict. On the other hand, its material support to some of the EAOs and its history of using its influence among them as leverage vis-à-vis Myanmar central authorities has made many observers question how much China really wants a full peace agreement that results in a federal democratic system.

Either way, China's direct involvement made clear that peace could not happen without Chinese support, even if Chinese support does not necessarily produce peace. That gave and perhaps still gives China enormous leverage over Nay Pyi Taw authorities. In addition, China sought to exclude other foreign government involvement in the peace process, putting pressure on the Myanmar government and on EAOs not to engage with us or other powers on the matter. The extent to which China was willing to go in this direction became clear during the mid-2018 Panglong Peace Conference in Nay Pyi Taw. China delivered FPNCC representatives to Nay Pyi Taw, put them up in hotels, and then kept close watch over them to prevent them from meeting with Western diplomats. Western diplomats were able to meet with one senior representative from the FPNCC coalition, but that individual confided that he had to sneak out of his hotel to see them.

China and the Mekong

One concern that all the mainland Southeast Asian countries share is China's control over water flows into the subregion. The Mekong, one of the world's largest and most important rivers, sources from the Tibetan Plateau in China and then flows downstream through Myanmar, Laos, and Cambodia before reaching southern Vietnam, where it forms a delta that empties into the Pacific Ocean.

The Mekong is the second-most biodiverse river (after the Amazon) and the largest source of freshwater catch in the world. It directly sustains some sixty million people, and its fisheries provides the overwhelming proportion of protein for many of those people.[43] It also waters the rich agricultural lands in Vietnam's Mekong Delta region, one of the world's largest producers of rice.

The river is under threat from development and climate change, but especially from the growing number of hydropower projects that have been and continue to be built on it and its tributaries. According to the Stimson Center, China has built eleven dams on the upstream Mekong and Laos has built two, with more than a dozen others planned for China, Laos, and Cambodia. In addition, hundreds of dams on Mekong tributaries have either been built, are under construction, or are planned.[44]

Numerous studies have found that these hydropower projects are having a severe economic and environmental impact downstream, reducing water and essential sediment flows and thus affecting both agriculture and fisheries.[45] The Mekong River Commission, established in 1995 to facilitate cooperation among the lower Mekong countries in managing the river, has played a useful technical role but so far has been unable to stem the rush to build dams, which provide electricity as well as export earnings, particularly for landlocked Laos.

There is plenty of blame to go around for the dam projects, but for purposes of this chapter the key issue is China's role. A 2020 Eyes on Earth scientific study found that, from April through November 2019, as the lower Mekong countries suffered from severe drought, China's portion of the upper Mekong received higher-than-average levels of

---

43 Stefan Lofgren, "Southeast Asia's Most Critical River is Entering Uncharted Waters," *National Geographic*, January 21 2020, https://www.nationalgeographic.com/science/2020/01/southeast-asia-most-critical-river-enters-uncharted-waters/.

44 Brian Eyler and Courtney Weatherbee, "Mekong Mainstream Dams," Stimson Center Mekong Policy Project, June 23, 2020, https://www.stimson.org/2020/mekong-mainstream-dams/.

45 Eyler and Weatherbee, "Mekong Mainstream Dams"; see also Yuichiro Yoshida et al., "Impacts of Mainstream Hydropower Dams on Fisheries and Agriculture in Lower Mekong Basin," *Sustainability* 12, no. 6 (2020), https://doi.org/10.3390/su12062408; and Ian Campbell and Chris Barlow, "Hydropower Development and the Loss of Fisheries in the Mekong River Basin," *Frontiers in Environmental Science*, October 19, 2020, https://www.frontiersin.org/articles/10.3389/fenvs.2020.566509/full.

rainfall, but China's dams held back a much-higher-than-normal amount of water. The study found that China's restriction of water flows prevented the annual rainy season rise in the Mekong's water level for the first time in recorded history.[46]

During monsoon season, the Mekong normally swells, irrigating cropland and pushing water up the Tonle Sap River in Cambodia into Tonle Sap Lake, which expands to four to six times its normal size. Brian Eyler, author of *Last Days of the Mighty Mekong*, calls Tonle Sap the "heartbeat" of the Mekong, because in its monsoonal expansion stage it serves as both a critical flood control feature and as host to millions of spawning fish.[47] In 2019, because of Chinese restrictions on the release of water, parts of the Mekong along the Lao-Thai border ran dry, and the Tonle Sap expansion—which normally lasts for five months—lasted only five weeks. Fishing production out of the Tonle Sap, which usually provides Cambodians with 70 percent of their protein, fell sharply as a result. The Chinese restrictions did not cause the drought, but they exacerbated its impact.

The study also found that, since China began operating its massive Nuozhadu Dam in 2012–14, China has been holding back an increasing amount of water. It also noted that China's occasional release of upriver water, without informing its downstream neighbors, explains a number of unexpected floods that have hit the lower Mekong countries.[48]

Stung by the criticism, China recently agreed to begin sharing water data with the Mekong River Commission year-round, rather than just for part of the year as in the past. It also emphasized cooperation on water management in its Lancang-Mekong Cooperation (LMC) forum, which it launched with the Lower Mekong countries in 2015. China has turned the LMC into a pillar of its broader BRI, funneling money through the LMC for a host of development projects in the Mekong

---

46 Alan Basist and Claude Williams, "Monitoring the Quantity of Water Flowing Through the Upper Mekong Basin Under Natural (Unimpeded) Conditions,," Sustainable Infrastructure Partnership, Bangkok, April 11, 2020, https://558353b6 -da87-4596-a181-b1f20782dd18.filesusr.com/ugd/bae95b_0e0f87104dc8482b99 ec91601d853122.pdf?index=true.

47 Brian Eyler and Courtney Weatherbee, "Sustaining the Heartbeat of the Mekong Basin," China Dialogue, March 11, 2019, https://chinadialogue.net/en/ energy/11126-sustaining-the-heartbeat-of-the-mekong-basin/.

48 Alan Basist and Claude Williams, "Monitoring the Quantity of Water Flowing Through the Upper Mekong Basin."

region. It is likely that Beijing saw the LMC as a means to enhance its influence in the Mekong subregion, and as a counter to earlier but less-well-funded initiatives like the United States' Lower Mekong Initiative.

I have not seen any evidence that China's restrictions on water flows out of the upper portions of the Mekong were driven by geopolitical interests or a desire to put pressure on its southern neighbors. More likely, China retained excess water to meet its own electricity-generation needs and to ensure its reservoirs remained full. That does not change the fact that China's control of the upper portions of the Mekong River give it enormous leverage over the Lower Mekong countries, which know that China can—if it wants—turn off the tap anytime. This power is one more reason these countries will be reluctant to challenge or oppose China on issues important to Beijing.

Conclusion

When one looks at the range of ways in which China is engaging in Southeast Asia, several points seem clear. First, China's economic engagement and intensive and pragmatic diplomacy, including all its soft diplomacy efforts, have borne fruit, bolstering its standing and influence in almost all ten ASEAN countries. Washington might not like this fact, but one can hardly blame Beijing for practicing vigorous diplomacy and for being an effective economic player.

Two developments in the 2017–20 time frame highlighted—at least in the eyes of many in Southeast Asia—Beijing's consistent, active engagement versus the United States' more episodic approach. First, while the United States was withdrawing from the TPP trade agreement, Beijing was rolling out BRI and negotiating the RCEP trade agreement. The contrast was not lost on anyone in Southeast Asia. Second, while the United States initially took steps to ensure that all U.S.-produced COVID-19 vaccines went to Americans rather than overseas and refused to join a WHO–led international vaccine effort, China moved quickly to offer its vaccines to the world, with a focus on Southeast Asia. China has been sending millions of doses—mostly sold but with some donated—to the region in regular shipments since December 2020.[49] Under the Biden administration, the United States belatedly re-

---

49 Khairulanwar Zaini, "China's Vaccine Diplomacy in Southeast Asia—A Mixed Record," *Perspective* no. 86, June 24, 2021, ISEAS Yusof Ishok Institute, https://

engaged with WHO and began donating millions of doses of vaccine, but only after several months during which it was seen as contributing little to help Southeast Asia. Time will tell how much the United States hurt its standing—and China helped itself—during those initial several months, but the contrast in the two countries' approaches could not have been starker.

That said, it is important not to overstate Beijing's success, as its often heavy-handed approach has also provoked concern and wariness in many countries. The 2021 ISEAS-Yusof Ishak Institute survey of regional attitudes found that, while a solid majority of respondents viewed China as the most influential outside power, the percentage of those who would choose it over the United States as a preferred partner—if forced to make such a choice—actually fell by eight percentage points compared to the previous year.[50] That same survey found that nearly three-fourths of respondents were concerned about China's rising economic influence, and an astounding 88 percent worried about its growing political-security influence in the region.

Second, some of China's actions are reinforcing harmful practices in the region. Its support for authoritarian leaders undermines efforts to build stronger, better-governed democracies. Its willingness to strike nontransparent deals, often with corrupt local officials and businesses, brings high economic (and environmental and social) costs to Southeast Asian countries and reinforces precisely those corrupt elites who are most opposed by their own countrymen.

Third, China has used its economic power (and control of water resources) to gain significant leverage vis-à-vis its Southeast Asian neighbors and has shown a willingness to use that leverage to pressure those neighbors. Whether it is large trade flows, investments, or growing debt, China's power and leverage are very real. Every Southeast Asian government knows that, if it confronts or opposes China on major issues, it risks significant economic retaliation that most cannot afford.

Fourth, the Belt and Road Initiative is bringing important benefits to the region, helping countries proceed with much-needed infrastructure projects. Western officials and analysts might not like it, but it is hard to argue with its popularity in the region. Nonetheless, the BRI clearly

---

www.iseas.edu.sg/articles-commentaries/iseas-perspective/2021-86-chinas-vaccine-diplomacy=in-southeast-asia-a-mixed-record-by-khairulanwar-zaini/.
50 Sharon Seah et al., *The State of Southeast Asia.*

involves some negatives. China has pressured countries—particularly the less-developed nations on its southern border—to sign on to deals that (a) seem to bring one-sided benefits (to China), (b) sometimes raise host country debt to concerning levels, and (c) are marked by nontransparency, a lack of consultation with affected communities, and a failure to address social and environmental consequences. Moreover, in some cases Chinese state-owned firms have engaged in predatory practices, deliberately offering below-market bids to win deals, and then often failing to implement them on time and at cost.

Additionally, China—or at least some Chinese businesses—have had no qualms about striking often-corrupt deals to set up de facto Chinese enclaves, particularly along its borders. These enclaves tend to feature large numbers of Chinese migrants, little transparency, gambling and other social vices, and minimal host government control. Calling them Chinese colonies might be going too far, but it would not be that far off the mark. One can accept that these enclaves are not all the result of Chinese government—as opposed to Chinese company—efforts, but they nonetheless result in Chinese actors gaining undue influence and in adding to crime and social problems.

Finally, in both the South China Sea and the Mekong, China has worked to present its neighbors with fait accompli situations that redouble Beijing's leverage. China's assertiveness and island-building in the South China Sea justifiably receives the most attention, but its success in gaining control over Mekong River water flows also warrants major concern.

The negative elements in China's overall approach pose a challenge both to U.S. and to Southeast Asian interests. For Washington, China's aggressive approach in the South China Sea potentially threatens freedom of navigation and even control over global trade routes, both of which are of huge importance to the United States (and much of the rest of the world). More broadly, the United States has an interest in ensuring that rising Chinese influence and growing Chinese relationships in Southeast Asia—which Washington should accept as a reality—do not infringe on Southeast Asian nations' sovereignty or ability to work with the United States and others on a wide range of issues.

For Southeast Asian countries, the threat is more to their freedom of maneuver or, put another way, their ability to act as independent, sovereign nations to the full extent they want. While it is true that many nations choose to accommodate big powers at times, the risk vis-à-vis China is that the Southeast Asians might feel they have little choice but to accept Chinese policies or actions most of the time. A secondary threat—to the publics if not necessarily to all the governments in the region—is those Chinese policies and actions that reinforce corruption, support authoritarian rulers, and bring negative social and environmental impacts.

Fortunately, the Southeast Asians are not helpless victims. While Cambodia's leadership and, to an extent, that of Laos have appeared willing to climb into China's pocket to a significant degree, overall the ASEAN member states are strongly committed to preserving their sovereignty and avoiding vassal state status. One sees this most clearly in Vietnam, of course, but it is present elsewhere. Following then prime minister Najib's downfall in 2018, the new Malaysian government renegotiated a number of BRI deals to reduce the risk of excessive debt. Myanmar did the same with the Kyaukphyu port and is pushing back on some other proposed BRI projects. In part thanks to pressure from domestic civil society groups, the Thai government has blocked China's proposed dynamiting of reaches of the Mekong River and stalled on Beijing's proposed extension of the high-speed railway between Vientiane and the Malaysian border. Even in Cambodia and Laos, public opposition to excessive Chinese influence (and presence) has forced the governments to think twice about moving ahead on some projects and even to backtrack on occasion (e.g., Hun Sen's prohibition of online gambling).

The challenge for Washington is to avoid conflating the region's healthy interest in avoiding undue Chinese influence with the notion that Southeast Asians share the U.S. view of China as a largely malign influence. While opinions vary, in general much of Southeast Asia sees both benefits and costs from engaging with China. Moreover, as relatively small nations next to a giant, they recognize that they must have good relations with Beijing, and that adopting an anti-China posture is a nonstarter. The corollary, not always appreciated in Washington, is that the Southeast Asians do not necessarily see the United States as many if not most Americans see it—as an unmitigated force for good.

Nonetheless, given China's growing clout in the region, the United States and Southeast Asia as a whole share a significant interest in working together—and with other like-minded partners—to bolster and protect the sovereignty of the ASEAN nations so that they maintain adequate maneuvering room and feel confident enough to push back (gently) on Chinese actions that they oppose or find concerning. Working together effectively toward this goal will require both a consistently high level of strategic thinking and careful, nuanced diplomacy in both Washington and Southeast Asian capitals.

CHAPTER THIRTEEN

Toward a Better Partnership

The relationships between the United States and the countries of Southeast Asia over the past several decades have produced many benefits for both sides, in the form of trade and investment, security and law enforcement cooperation, education and health, and strong bonds between people and institutions. ASEAN collectively is the United States' fourth-largest trading partner, while America ranks as ASEAN's third-largest market. U.S. direct investment in the ASEAN region exceeds that of U.S. investment in Japan, South Korea, and China combined, and ASEAN investment into the United States is growing rapidly.[1]

Historically, much of Southeast Asia has looked to the U.S. security umbrella to help keep the peace in the region, offer protection against rogue actors, and ensure trade flows remain uninterrupted. Security cooperation, including in law enforcement, has helped build the capacity of the region's militaries and police forces to deal with terrorism and other threats, while cooperative efforts have made some progress in tackling the illegal trade in narcotics, people, and wild animals.

More broadly, U.S. assistance and technical support have helped the nations of the region build key institutions, ranging from courts and parliaments to healthcare and education systems. U.S. assistance has

---

1 "Trade and Investment," U.S.-ASEAN Business Council, https://www.usasean.org/why-asean/trade-and-investment; see also "Association of Southeast Asian Nations (ASEAN)," Office of the United States Trade Representative, https://ustr.gov/countries-regions/southeast-asia-pacific/association-southeast-asian-nations-asean; and "Table 19: ASEAN Trade by Selected Partner Country/Region, 2015," ASEAN, https://asean.org/wp-content/uploads/2016/11/Table19_as-of-6-dec-2016.pdf.

bolstered private sector–led economies and provided critical relief to those affected by natural disasters and conflict, while also encouraging the development of an independent media and effective civil society.

Diplomatically, the United States and its ASEAN nation counterparts generally have enjoyed good relations and effective cooperation on regional and global issues, although of course the quality and intensity of ties with Washington has varied over time and among the different Southeast Asian countries. The United States has consistently supported ASEAN's own efforts, including to place itself at the center of the region's multilateral architecture. For their part, most Southeast Asian nations—at least since the end of the Vietnam War—have seen the United States as a friend that contributes to their efforts to promote economic development, peace, and stability.

Moreover, despite the perception—often highlighted in the media and public comments—that the United States is "losing" to China in the region, the fact remains that the United States still maintains a wide network of relationships in Southeast Asia, as well as a still-deep reservoir of goodwill among the peoples of those nations. David Shambaugh argues in his recent book, *Where Great Powers Meet*, that "the cultural, economic, diplomatic, and security footprint of the United States across Southeast Asia remains unprecedented."[2] Although Shambaugh might be somewhat overstating things, particularly about the U.S. economic role in the region, it is true that the United States remains a very significant and influential player.

Despite these many positives, in both Washington and Southeast Asian capitals, conversations about U.S. ties with Southeast Asia often highlight the imperfections or disappointments each sees in the other. Americans tend to complain about failings in individual countries related to democracy and human rights, or about the region's reluctance to confront or push back on problematic Chinese behavior. Many in the region point out that they cannot always count on the United States to engage or even show up, that U.S. engagement often consists of lecturing or criticism (often in public), that Americans do not "understand" them, and that the United States has unrealistic expectations about their desire or willingness to challenge China. In addition, while the region still clearly sees the United States as an important security partner,

---

2 David Shambaugh, *Where Great Powers Meet: America and China in Southeast Asia* (New York: Oxford University Press, 2021), 13.

its relative economic importance is declining, a trend reinforced by the Trump administration's withdrawal from the TPP.

We can agree that the United States and Southeast Asia have been imperfect partners. We should also be able to agree that the significant interests the United States and the nations of the region share, combined with the United States' continuing role as a leading power and Southeast Asia's growing economic and strategic importance, call for Washington and the region to redouble efforts to build a stronger and deeper set of partnerships going forward.

The United States and Southeast Asia share a deep interest in preserving and strengthening the sovereignty of all the nations in the region and encouraging closer intra-ASEAN cooperation and economic integration. Both believe in ASEAN playing a central role in addressing regional issues and in the nations of Southeast Asia being able to chart their own paths forward without undue outside interference. Both want to see the region integrate further into the global economy and achieve sustained broad-based growth, fueled by responsible investment, so that Southeast Asia can achieve its remarkable economic potential and be an even more robust commercial partner. The vast majority of Southeast Asians share with Americans the desire for better governance, reduced corruption, and greater justice. The United States and Southeast Asian nations have a common interest in working together to combat both traditional security threats and new ones, ranging from illicit trade to climate change, to terrorism and organized crime, to threats to the region's rivers and seas. Many in Southeast Asia appreciate America's longtime support for democracy and human rights and want greater access to U.S. higher education and technology.

China's rise adds a strategic component to this picture that was missing for many years. If policymakers in the region and in Washington look carefully, they will see that stronger and deeper ties between the United States and Southeast Asia—built on a positive agenda—would not only bring many direct benefits, but also bolster the ability of both individual countries and the region as a whole to preserve their full independence and freedom of maneuver in the face of a looming China. Similarly, good relations between Southeast Asia and other important partners—Japan, Korea, India, Australia, the EU, and others—will reinforce that independence and maneuvering room.

It bears emphasizing that this is not an anti-China perspective, but a pro–Southeast Asia one. This is a nuanced but important distinction.

It is essential that the United States' relationships in Southeast Asia not be all or even mostly about China. In other words, the United States should engage with Southeast Asia on its own merits, which are considerable, rather than through the lens of countering Beijing. China is going to be there, and it is going to have significant influence in Southeast Asia, no matter what Washington does.

I am not saying anything new or profound here. Virtually all my friends and professional contacts in Southeast Asia have been saying some variant of this for some time. They do not want to be pawns in a U.S.-China competition. They do not want every conversation with U.S. officials to be about China. They want and need to have good relations with China, and without exception also want to have good relations with the United States. As former Singaporean diplomat Bilahari Kausikan likes to say, Southeast Asians will be "promiscuous" in their relationships but will avoid aligning fully with any outside power.[3] They know that having close ties with the United States and with other major powers enhances their leverage vis-à-vis China, but that is different from wanting to line up with us against China.

So, what should the United States do? Broadly speaking, Washington should step up its investment of time and resources in Southeast Asia, recognizing the region's growing economic and strategic role, with the approach less one of limiting China's influence than of ensuring the region sees the United States as a consistent, reliable, and good partner. I outline below the key aspects of such an approach.

Presidential Engagement

The United States needs to show up and engage consistently at all levels, and that needs to start at the top. If it is to be taken seriously in the region and win the trust and confidence of its counterparts there, the president has to attend the key annual ASEAN-hosted East Asia Summit (EAS) every year, along with the U.S.-ASEAN Leaders Meeting, usually held the day before the EAS. The secretary of state must attend the annual ASEAN Regional Forum (ARF) meeting as well.

The United States did not join the EAS until 2010, so the ASEAN nations did not expect the president to attend until then, but they counted

---

3 Bilahari Kausikan, "Consistency Is Not Always a Virtue," Australian Outlook, Australia Institute of International Affairs, September 29, 2020, https://www.inter nationalaffairs.org.au/australianoutlook/consistency-is-not-always-a-virtue/.

on the secretary of state to join the ARF meetings and looked forward to President Bush's participation in the U.S.-ASEAN thirtieth anniversary summit in 2007, which would have been the first such leaders-level event. Secretary Condoleezza Rice skipped two of the four ARF meetings held during her tenure, and President Bush canceled his attendance at the 2007 anniversary summit. The White House tried to make up for this miss by inviting the Southeast Asian leaders to Texas, but at least some of them questioned why, if the president could not be bothered to fly to Singapore, they should all be expected to come to him. The meeting did not happen.

The Obama administration placed a higher priority on the region and demonstrated it by showing up. President Obama missed only one EAS meeting (because of a government shutdown) and hosted the ASEAN leaders in California. Secretaries of state Hillary Clinton and John Kerry consistently showed up at the ARF meetings, and secretaries of defense Chuck Hagel and Ash Carter attended sessions of the ASEAN Defense Ministers Meeting Plus, a forum established in 2010.

Sadly, the Trump administration failed to sustain that effort. The president attended the U.S.-ASEAN Summit in the Philippines in 2017, but then undermined his effort by skipping the East Asia Summit the following day. The following year, he sent Vice President Mike Pence. In 2019, neither the president, the vice president, nor the secretary of state attended the U.S.-ASEAN Leaders Meeting hosted by Thailand. Instead, the president sent National Security Advisor Robert O'Brien to represent him. I was at the meeting and can personally attest that the ASEAN representatives were not happy, as I have noted earlier. They felt offended and even insulted. In 2020, the president once again asked National Security Advisor O'Brien to represent the United States, even though it was a virtual meeting and required no travel. Meanwhile, China's premier Li Keqiang joined and witnessed the signing of the Regional Comprehensive Economic Partnership, a fifteen-nation trade deal that included China and all ten ASEAN nations, but not the United States.

It is difficult to overstate how much this failure by the most senior U.S. leaders to show up at Southeast Asia's most important annual meetings damages U.S. credibility and undermines all the other work we do to assure regional leaders of our commitment and reliability. That is especially true because the Chinese *do* show up, along with the Japanese, Koreans, Australians, and others. Southeast Asian leaders can accept the occasional well-excused absence—à la that of President

Obama in 2013, due to a government shutdown—but consistently failing to show up or to send the vice president if the president cannot attend sends the message that our commitment is only rhetorical. Showing up does not automatically produce understanding and agreement, but it is important for affirming the substantive U.S. commitment to the region and to ensure the U.S. president is at the table when important regional matters are discussed. Also, it is important to emphasize that, while the formal part of these ASEAN-hosted meetings often underwhelms, attendance gives the president (and secretary of state) unique opportunities to engage with a plethora of important players, including not only the ASEAN members but China, Japan, Korea, Australia, Russia, and India.

It will take many *years* of showing up consistently—and engaging constructively—to restore Southeast Asia's confidence in the United States, following the Trump administration's failure to treat ASEAN as a valued and respected partner. It is an early promising sign that President Biden attended the East Asia Summit in October 2021 and hosted the Southeast Asian leaders at the White House in early 2022.

Showing up also means making sure that the United States has ambassadors—the president's personal representatives—in all ten Southeast Asian countries and at the U.S. Mission to ASEAN. This should be obvious and easy, but it turns out to be neither. The United States did not have an ambassador in Singapore or to ASEAN during the entire Trump administration and in the past several years allowed lengthy gaps in filling ambassadorial positions in Thailand and Cambodia. Failing to fill these positions in a timely fashion harms U.S. interests in two ways: it reduces U.S. access to top host-government officials, and it sends a message that the United States is not serious about the relationship. Imagine not putting in place an ambassador to Singapore—one of Washington's closest friends and partners in Asia—for an entire administration!

Engage Consistently

In addition to showing up at the head-of-state level, the United States also needs to ensure consistent engagement at senior levels, through visits and calls. Beijing sends a steady stream of high-level officials to Southeast Asia, and just as regularly invites senior Southeast Asian officials to China. The United States does not need to match China visit for visit but needs to do more than it has. It is a tough task, given the distance and the United States' global commitments, but Washington can and should use technology to step up its interaction. Personal travel is still essential, but the United States can complement those time-consuming trips to Asia with virtual meetings, which the COVID-19 pandemic has taught us can be effective, and which many if not most Southeast Asian officials seem to be comfortable doing. Frankly, there is no reason Washington cannot organize at least monthly cabinet or subcabinet level virtual meetings with key Southeast Asian partners such as Indonesia, Thailand, Singapore, the Philippines, and Vietnam, and regular ones with the other countries of the region. Washington should make regular consultations and exchanges of ideas a habit—something it has done to some extent with European partners and a few others, but not with Southeast Asia. Of course, it is also incumbent upon Southeast Asian governments to do their part by making clear their interest in such regular consultations and in making them as productive as possible.

One of Washington's biggest challenges is maintaining adequate levels of engagement when countries take a step backward on democracy or protection of human rights. Since the end of the Cold War, the United States has developed a practice of pulling back from engagement with countries in the face of democratic backsliding or human rights problems. Just in the past several years, Washington distanced itself from Thailand after its 2014 military coup, sharply reduced engagement with Myanmar after its ethnic cleansing of the Rohingya, and threatened sanctions against Hun Sen's Cambodia in response to a number of anti-democratic developments.

These setbacks pose a dilemma for the United States. On the one hand, it is neither politically viable nor appropriate for the United States to conduct business as usual with governments that take profoundly negative steps. On the other hand, pulling back from diplomatic engagement (i.e., talking) or imposing sanctions often enhances China's relative influence, and—just as importantly—has not proven to be an effective way of engineering the positive behavior change Washington seeks.

It is time for the United States to consider anew how it should respond to such situations, given the changing international environment in which the United States is not the dominant player it was thirty years ago. A key issue is that many in the United States have come to equate engaging with endorsing or embracing. The criticism leveled at then U.S. ambassador to Thailand Ralph "Skip" Boyce for meeting Thai interim prime minister General Surayud Chulanont shortly after the Thai coup in 2006 is a perfect example. Boyce needed to meet Surayud to open a channel of communication and convey Washington's strong view that the country should return to democracy as quickly as possible. He even told the press immediately after the meeting that he had used the meeting to urge Surayud to restore democracy quickly. Yet for some in Washington, the mere fact that Boyce had met with the general constituted a form of endorsement.

The United States needs to take a more nuanced approach in these cases. Certainly, it should not and cannot ignore major human rights violations or anti-democratic actions such as coups. The United States' longtime, consistent support for democracy and human rights has won it a lot of appreciation and respect among many in the region, and is one of its greatest foreign policy assets. There are any number of ways that Washington can express its unhappiness or dissatisfaction when things go badly. That is different, however, from sharply curtailing or even eliminating senior-level discussions, or imposing sanctions, particularly if those sanctions might affect the welfare of the broader population. With rare exception, the United States should keep those high-level channels of communication open. Washington needs to recognize that practicing diplomacy, in an effort to influence other governments' next steps, does not constitute embracing or endorsing whatever those governments have done.

For example, it would not have been appropriate to invite General Prayut Chan-ocha to the White House following his 2014 coup in Thailand. Washington could, however, have sent a senior official—perhaps a deputy or under secretary of state—to Bangkok to meet with senior Thai officials to encourage them to move more rapidly back to democratic rule, while also sending an implicit message to the Thai people that the United States remained engaged. Or, given the risk that the Thai authorities would have spun such a visit to imply a U.S. embrace of the coup, or even used it to deliver a harsh public message to the U.S. visitor, another option would have been to arrange a senior-level bilateral meeting in a third country, on the margins of one of the many multilateral events. I have to confess that I was helping to shape our policy at the time of the 2014 coup and I did not push for such an engagement. I too was caught up in the mindset that we had to show Thai authorities our unhappiness and keep our distance.

The United States followed a similar approach in response to Myanmar's ethnic cleansing of the Rohingya in 2017. The country's treatment of the Rohingya was as bad a human rights situation as I have seen in my career. It was appalling and horrifying, to the point that the Biden administration eventually determined that genocide took place. For all kinds of reasons, the United States could not and should not have ignored it or gone ahead with business as usual. Washington needed to do everything possible to persuade the government and military to change their behavior. The United States issued many strong statements and pursued action in the UN Security Council, which sounded good but never was going to go anywhere given Beijing's veto power. What Washington did not do, however, was talk with the government and the military, beyond the efforts of the U.S. embassy in Yangon. Other than a half-day visit by Secretary of State Rex Tillerson in November 2017, for a full eight months during the most intense period of crisis no one in the administration above the deputy assistant secretary level visited the country. While the United States probably would have lost influence under any circumstances, it might have retained more—and had at least a somewhat better chance to shape behavior and help the Rohingya—if it had engaged in an intensive, high-level diplomatic campaign focused on the Rohingya issue during those crucial weeks and months.

There are exceptions to the appropriateness and efficacy of senior-level U.S. engagement, however. It is difficult to argue for such engagement with the Myanmar military in the aftermath of the February 2021 coup, for several reasons. First, even before the coup, in the aftermath of the Rohingya crisis, top Myanmar military officials showed little interest in dialogue with the United States. Second, the Myanmar public is overwhelmingly opposed to the military junta that took charge after February 1, and engaging the junta at senior levels risks inadvertently conferring legitimacy on it, with little chance of changing its behavior. Third, the Myanmar military's decades-long history of severe human rights abuses against its own people, its uncompromising approach to politics, and its refusal to change its behavior to meet even minimum international standards augurs poorly for any substantive benefits from engagement. (This was true during the Rohingya crisis as well, but the first two factors noted above—little or no interest in dialogue and public opposition to the junta—were not in place.) As longtime Myanmar observer David Mathieson recently wrote, the military is an "army of darkness."[4] Washington should not close the door on dialogue, and

---

4 David Scott Mathieson, "Myanmar's Army of Darkness," *The Nation,* February 12, 2021, https://www.thenation.com/article/world/myanmar-burma-coup-rohingya/.

should be open to low-profile opportunities for discussion, ideally out-side of Myanmar, but overall this might be an exception to my general policy guidance on engagement.

It will not be easy for any U.S. administration to shift to a more nuanced approach. The mindset that the appropriate U.S. response to setbacks should be disengagement is deeply embedded in the Washing-ton psyche, and there are plenty of institutional actors and individuals who will shout out loudly if an administration does not follow that ap-proach. Fair enough. But I am not talking about a 180-degree shift, just adding some nuance so Washington can actually engage in diplomacy during difficult periods. Failure to do so will reduce the United States' ability to influence governance and human rights developments on the ground, and will gradually cede influence to China.

The United States has many diplomatic tools at its disposal, not just sanctions, public criticism, and disengagement. I am confident that the United States can remain in the game while also making it clear to all concerned that the fact that it is meeting and talking does not consti-tute approval or willful neglect of democratic backsliding or human rights abuses. One way to do this is to ensure that high-level U.S. of-ficials consistently meet with civil society and human rights activists, as well as opposition politicians, where possible, in addition to govern-ment counterparts, during their visits.

The U.S. relationship with Vietnam can offer some hints on how to engage despite serious human rights problems. U.S. officials have consistently raised human rights issues with Vietnam over the past few decades, while also managing to engage with the leadership in Hanoi regularly at a high level. The lack of democracy and fundamental free-doms in Vietnam affects the bilateral relationship, but it does not define or dictate it. Some of the credit for this goes to the Vietnamese them-selves, who have made more of an effort than many of their Southeast Asian counterparts to reach out to Washington and offer reason for further engagement.

Strengthen Public Diplomacy

While the United States is very active in Southeast Asia and is widely engaged in a broad range of areas that, for the most part, bring benefits to the region, it does not do a good enough job telling its story. That contributes to a widespread perception that the United States is less active and engaged than it really is. The United States can change this perception by doing a better job of using public diplomacy to tell its story.

Specifically, Washington needs to devote more resources and manpower to bolster its understaffed public diplomacy teams in its Southeast Asia embassies. In my experience, most people in the region have little understanding or appreciation for all that the United States is doing, including by providing markets for host-country exports or by offering assistance to improve the public welfare or the quality of governance. Part of that is because U.S. assistance tends (rightly) to go toward programs to bolster health, education, governance, and economic policymaking, rather than toward highly visible projects such as roads and bridges. The key to overcoming that is to fund increased programming to explain exactly what the United States is doing and how it benefits local communities.

In addition, those public diplomacy programs that each of the U.S. embassies do run focus almost exclusively on U.S. activities in the particular host country. There is relatively little effort to tell the story about what the United States is doing in the region as a whole. It is true that most societies care mostly about what America is doing in their country, but the lack of information about how engaged the United States is in the broader region contributes to the sense of U.S. disengagement in all the countries. Incorporating greater regional messaging will require a concerted Washington effort, but it can be done and is critical to improving perceptions about the U.S. role.

Spend More Money

The United States needs to bring more resources to the game. Since the end of the Cold War, we have underfunded our engagement in Southeast Asia compared to other parts of the world, particularly when it comes to official aid. During the Obama years, the administration did shift some military assets to the region, which was a start. Despite the rhetoric about pivoting or rebalancing, however, it did not increase its aid levels. In 2008 total U.S. aid to Asia (most but not all of which went to Southeast Asia) equaled $1.7 billion, which was only 3 percent of our global aid. In 2016, at the end of the Obama administration, the amount for Asia remained $1.7 billion, still just 3 percent of all our aid around the world. In 2018, the United States provided \$1.6 billion in aid to Asia, still only 3 percent of the global total.[5]

There are some legitimate reasons why Asia gets a smaller share of U.S. aid than some other regions, starting with the fact that several major Asian nations are well off and do not need or qualify for official aid. Also, one can argue that the needs are greater in parts of sub-Saharan Africa or the Middle East and South Asia. Still, it is hard to justify such a significant discrepancy, given the size and strategic importance of Southeast Asia, which by itself is home to 10 percent of the world's population.

I am not arguing that aid equates interest or influence, but it plays two important roles: if programmed effectively, it can promote broad-based development, improved health and education, better governance, and enhanced security-force capacity; it also encourages host government officials and others in the host country to view the United States more positively and, in general, make them more open to cooperation with Washington. The level of aid shows an interest in and, to some extent, a commitment to the region's future.

If the United States wants to enhance its partnership with Southeast Asia, it should boost aid levels modestly. There is no correct number, but even shifting just one percent of Washington's global assistance budget from other regions to Asia (mainly Southeast Asia plus the Pacific Islands) would produce a 25 percent or \$400 million per year increase in aid. That amount would not necessarily be a game changer, but it would have a significant impact on the ground and would help convince skeptical Southeast Asians of the U.S. commitment to the region.

Bring a Positive Agenda

Showing up and engaging consistently are essential, but they only work if Washington attaches substance—a positive, cooperative agenda—to its engagement. That agenda needs to be broad, but the United States should place special emphasis on a handful of areas in which it enjoys a significant comparative advantage. It also needs to take action to reassert itself economically. Some of the ideas presented here might well be overtaken by events by the time this book is published, but I am hopeful most are broad and sufficiently long-term to enjoy some durability.

---

5 All figures from ForeignAssistance.gov, https://foreignassistance.gov.

Reinvigorate the U.S. Economic Role

In Southeast Asia, the substance of the U.S. agenda should begin with trade and the economy, where Southeast Asians generally see the United States losing clout and influence. While it remains an important investor and trading partner with Southeast Asia, as noted at the beginning of this chapter, it is losing ground in relative terms. Trade with ASEAN countries constitutes a steadily increasing share of China's global trade, but a declining share of U.S. trade. So, the United States is becoming a less important trading partner to one of the world's most dynamic and promising economic regions. At the same time, Washington has absented itself from the region's growing number of multilateral trade deals, ensuring that its role in trade will decline, absent new initiatives, and that the region will not look to Washington to play a key role in establishing trade rules and norms. Pulling out of the TPP set the United States back significantly, particularly given the emergence of RCEP (which, for all its faults, still will encourage trade among its members at the expense of nonmembers).

In addition, current U.S. trade and investment is heavily concentrated in four ASEAN countries: Singapore, Thailand, Vietnam, and Malaysia, with Indonesia and the Philippines occupying a second tier and the other four countries a third tier. In those latter four nations, the United States is a relatively small player. Moreover, it has struggled to play an effective role in one of the region's top economic priorities: building the infrastructure it needs to take it to the next level economically. China, Japan, and to some extent South Korea all are heavily involved in the infrastructure effort, while the United States plays a bit part. Finally, China is making important inroads in terms of building the digital infrastructure in the region, which will only grow in economic importance in the decades ahead.

In the 2021 State of ASEAN survey of opinion leaders, conducted by the respected ISEAS-Yusof Ishak Institute in Singapore, only 7.4 percent of respondents viewed the United States as having the most economic influence among outside partners, compared to more than 75 percent who viewed China as most influential.[6] While the United States remains much more influential on security and political issues, one wonders

---

6 Sharon Seah et al., *The State of Southeast Asia.*

how long that can persist if its role as an economic partner continues to decline, even in relative terms.

The question is what, realistically, the United States can do to generate some momentum and reinvigorate our economic partnership with the region. It does not need to match China dollar for dollar or investment for investment, but—if it is to maintain and even increase its overall influence—it needs to elevate the trajectory of its economic relationships. That will be challenging, given the U.S. government's traditional unwillingness to invest directly in other countries, its lack of tools to direct or even encourage more private investment, the U.S. private sector's strong preference for working in transparent, low-corruption, and reasonably well-regulated markets, and the increasing contentious politics on issues such as trade and globalization in the United States.

In a positive sign, in much if not all of Southeast Asia, there remains great interest in the U.S. market and tremendous respect for the quality and innovation of U.S. companies. What is needed is a trade and investment policy that solidifies our participation in the regional commercial network, and specific actions to ensure the United States can—alone or with like-minded partners—offer viable alternatives on infrastructure and in the digital space.

Ideally, the United States would move quickly to re-insert itself into the regional trade dynamic. It could do so in a big way by seeking to join the TPP successor agreement, known as the Comprehensive and Progressive Agreement for Trans-Pacific Partnership (CPTPP). Alternatively, it could begin by pursuing a series of smaller, more discrete deals with one or more Southeast Asian nations to promote trade in specific areas, such as environmental goods.[7]

Unfortunately, as of mid-2022, there is insufficient political support in the United States for any trade initiative that would grant partner countries increased access to the U.S. market (any such trade agreement would require congressional approval).

Recognizing this, the Biden administration has offered up the Indo-Pacific Economic Framework for Prosperity (IPEF), formally launched during President Biden's May 2022 visit to Japan. Rather than focusing on tariff reduction and market access like traditional trade agreements, the framework seeks to promote cooperation around four "pillars:

---

7 Environmental goods are those that enable sustainable growth or reduce pollution.

(1) fair trade (including in the digital realm); (2) supply chain resilience; (3) clean energy and decarbonization; and (4) "fair economy," which includes tax and anti-corruption efforts.

The good news is that twelve countries in Asia, including seven of the ten ASEAN member nations,[8] signed onto the framework's launch. Such initial participation suggests significant interest in the region in encouraging the United States' increased participation in Asian economic matters. On the trade side, early interest has focused on the possibility that IPEF could lead to a stand-alone digital trade agreement that might address issues such as cross-border data flows, data localization requirements, and privacy.[9]

The question going forward will be to what extent the United States and other participants will be able to turn this framework into concrete steps that bring about economic benefits and enhance the United States' economic engagement with the region. Perhaps the biggest concern at the outset is whether, in the absence of the promise of increased access to the U.S. market, other participants will see enough potential economic benefit to warrant serious and continued participation, including the adoption of standards that are high priorities for the United States but not necessarily for some of the other countries.

It is difficult to predict whether IPEF will in the end amount to much. It could become significant, or we might look back at it later as an initiative without substance. At a minimum, it will require intensive engagement between governments and business communities to identify and move forward on specific, practical arrangements and policy changes that reduce economic barriers and create or take advantage of opportunities.

Even if IPEF attains substantial success, it is hard to imagine that it will compensate for the lack of a major U.S. effort on the broader trade front. At some point, the Biden administration or its successor will need to fight and win the domestic political battle to allow for U.S.

---

8 The seven ASEAN members that signed onto the framework's launch were Singapore, Brunei, Malaysia, Indonesia, Vietnam, Thailand, and the Philippines.

9 For a fuller discussion of IPEF and the questions surrounding it, see Aidan Arasingham, Emily Benson, and Matthew P. Goodman, "Unpacking the Indo-Pacific Economic Framework Launch," Center for Strategic and International Studies, May 23, 2022, https://www.csis.org/analysis/unpacking-indo-pacific-economic-framework-launch.

entry into the CPTPP or another major trade initiative. If not, the United States almost inevitably will lose influence in the region.

It is difficult to find ways quickly to bolster U.S. investment in the region, since the primary factor there is the extent to which U.S. companies find the local investment environment attractive relative to other potential investment destinations. The United States should continue to support reforms designed to improve local investment environments, but that is a longer-term process and one that by definition Washington does not control.

One thing the United States *can* do is to continue to promote the concept of responsible investment, an area in which we have a comparative advantage. Some of the poorer nations of Southeast Asia, including Myanmar, Laos, and Cambodia, have suffered over the years from a series of problematic investments that brought more costs than benefits to local communities. In Myanmar, people in Kachin State have had such bad experiences with foreign investments (not just from China) that they told me during a 2017 visit that they did not want any investment at all. To them, investment meant displacement, environmental damage, corruption, and few if any benefits to their communities.

There is a growing appetite, consistently among the general publics and more intermittently among government officials, for higher-quality investments that follow local laws and rules, are transparent, and bring tangible benefits to local communities. For example, a U.S.-Japan Responsible Investment Seminar in Yangon in 2019 attracted Aung San Suu Kyi and hundreds of interested business executives, and prompted a series of media stories about the need to distinguish between responsible and poor-quality investments. Washington should work with the U.S. business community to develop a systematic campaign to highlight to the region the benefits of attracting transparent, rule-abiding, high-quality companies to their markets. These efforts do not directly bring U.S. investment, but they can over time bring about greater public pressure for policies and procedures that encourage and attract responsible investors.

The United States also should continue to support domestic efforts in Southeast Asia to enhance transparency and fight corruption. If there is one thing that unites all the publics in the region (and perhaps the world), it is anger at corruption. The United States cannot stop corruption, of course, but supporting domestic anti-corruption initiatives can help promote better governance and create an investment environment that is more attractive to U.S. firms. One assumes that Washington will use the IPEF "fair economy" pillar to advance this goal, though again it is hard to know how successful these efforts will be absent the incentive for other governments of increased access to the U.S. market.

One difficult task for the United States is to find ways to participate more effectively in infrastructure development, a top priority for most Southeast Asian governments. For a host of reasons, the United States has been a relatively small player in regional infrastructure relative to heavy Chinese and Japanese investment. In recent years, the U.S. government has launched a handful of initiatives—the BUILD Act, EDGE, and the Blue Dot Network, along with the establishment of the Development Finance Corporation (DFC)—to try to bolster U.S. competitiveness in the sector, but so far they have produced few concrete results. The IPEF touches on infrastructure via discussion of clean energy and technology, but it is not yet clear how the framework fits into these other efforts.

The DFC, which the BUILD Act created as a bigger, better Overseas Private Investment Corporation, seemed to be a good idea, as it brought increased capital, greater flexibility in its funding options, and a mandate to facilitate partnerships with like-minded countries. The DFC already has signed agreements with its counterpart organizations in Tokyo and Canberra to facilitate such partnerships, but so far it has been difficult to find actual deals. The Biden administration should reach out to U.S. businesses to hear their thoughts on how to make the DFC more effective. For starters, the DFC needs to avoid placing political conditions on its investments, such as the ill-advised late 2020 decision by the Trump administration to link possible increased DFC investment in Indonesia to Jakarta's establishment of diplomatic relations with Israel.[10] There was never a chance that Indonesia would agree to that, and even suggesting such conditionality no doubt angered many

---

10 DFC chief executive officer Adam Boehler was widely reported to have said in a December 21, 2020, interview in Jerusalem that Indonesian diplomatic recognition of Israel could result in the DFC funneling an additional $1–2 billion to Indonesia. See Ivan Levingston, "Indonesia Could Get Billions in U.S. Funding to Join Israel Push," Bloomberg, December 21, 2009, https://www.bloomberg.com/news/articles/2020-12-22/indonesia-could-get-billions-in-u-s-funding-to-join-israel-push?sref=BIAk2Vdl; and Tovah Lazaroff, "Indonesia May Receive $1 b. in US Financing If It Makes Peace with Israel," *Jerusalem Post*, December 23, 2020, https://www.jpost.com/american-politics/trump-prods-indonesia-to-recognize-israel-with-promise-of-2-billion-652959.

Indonesians and raised further doubt about U.S. reliability as an economic partner.

The Biden administration, like the Trump administration before it, recognizes the importance of playing a bigger role in helping to develop infrastructure in the region. In May 2021, the National Security Council's Kurt Campbell stated that the next Quad leaders meeting would focus on collaborative efforts to build infrastructure in Asia.[11] A year later, President Biden and the other Quad leaders announced a comment to extend more than $50 billion of infrastructure investment and assistance in the broader Indo-Pacific region over a five-year period.[12] This was a positive step, but at the time of this writing it was not clear whether this really constituted "new" money, where the funds would come from, or how they would be disbursed. Once again, intensive consultations with the private sector ahead of time can help ensure that any such initiatives are grounded in business realities.

Even where U.S. companies find it difficult to win infrastructure contracts, the U.S. government can still play an important role by helping countries in the region ensure they are signing on to quality deals that are in their interest. Some of the poorer countries in the region have limited capacity to conduct proper due diligence or to negotiate the best possible deals with foreign partners. To provide assistance to such countries, the Trump administration established the Transaction Advisory Fund (TAF), under which foreign governments can request assistance to obtain independent legal and professional support as they conduct due diligence and project negotiations. TAF is a great idea but would be more accessible and effective if Washington would house it in one specific office with a clear point of contact. As of the time I left Myanmar in mid-2020, it was not clear, even to those of us in government, who in Washington owned TAF. Also, USAID should complement TAF by providing each of its missions in the region with a modest sum that the mission director, with the ambassador's blessing, can use to respond quickly to host country requests. (We did exactly this in Myanmar—using funds from an existing economic program to support the

---

11 "Kurt M. Campbell and Laura Rosenberger on U.S.-China Relations | 2021 Oksenberg Conference," YouTube, May 26, 2021, https://www.youtube.com/watch?v=Hrm5Gthyoqg.

12 "Quad Joint Leaders' Statement," White House, May 24, 2022, https://www.whitehouse.gov/briefing-room/statements-releases/2022/05/24/quad-joint-leaders-statement/.

government's hiring of outside experts to help them assess and renegotiate a major Chinese-funded project proposal.)

Non-traditional Security Threats: Health, Climate Change, and Water Cooperation

Cooperation on health issues has been one of the best yet most underappreciated elements of U.S. partnerships with Southeast Asian countries. Since 2000, the U.S. government has invested $3.5 billion in health programs in the region, funding everything from joint research to the training of laboratory workers, nurses, and midwives, to health programs at the village level.[13] USAID has provided the bulk of the assistance, but the Center for Disease Control (CDC) also has assigned some of its top staff to work with national health officials to build public health capacity. In Myanmar, USAID helped fund a national program that reduced the incidence of malaria by an astonishing 86 percent. In other countries, too, U.S. assistance has contributed directly to reduced mortality and improved national healthcare capacity.

Going forward, there is every reason not only to maintain but to expand these health partnerships. It is a U.S. strength and the demand in the region is high. In light of COVID-19, pandemic preparedness is an obvious place to start. The CDC in particular has been working on this for years but going forward the United States should step up its efforts and its funding. Particularly considering America's initially poor handling of the pandemic at home, a sustained, well-funded "lessons learned" program with ASEAN and its member states could bring substantial benefits. The United States also needs to do a better job of informing the governments and general publics of all that it is doing, as U.S. health support is not very well known in Southeast Asia. The extent to which Washington, after a very slow start, is able to provide substantial amounts of vaccine to countries in the region to combat COVID-19 will also greatly influence perceptions of the United States, but that story likely will have been told, one way or the other, by the time this book is published.

Cooperation on climate change should be another key pillar of our positive agenda with ASEAN. During the Trump administration, this was a nonstarter, given President Trump's skepticism about climate

---

13 Office of the Spokesperson, "U.S.-ASEAN Health Futures," fact sheet, U.S. Mission to ASEAN, April 22, 2020, https://asean.usmission.gov/u-s-asean-health-futures/.

change science, but President Biden and his administration have a different view. Many of the countries of Southeast Asia, being either island nations or coastal states with rich agricultural deltas and large cities threatened by rising seas, are considered among the most vulnerable to climate change. A U.S.-ASEAN partnership on climate change should include both information and data sharing, assistance on mitigation measures, and programs to reduce greenhouse gas emissions, including through switching to cleaner energy sources. Such a regional partnership could potentially build on the U.S.-Indonesia Climate Change Partnership, discussions on which began in February 2021 and presumably would incorporate the IPEF's clean energy/decarbonization pillar. It would be a great opportunity to work together on something that is both meaningful globally and directly impacts the lives and livelihoods of millions of people in Southeast Asia.

Washington should also consider developing, in close consultation with its ASEAN partners as well as regional allies such as Japan, Korea, and Australia, an initiative to help Southeast Asian nations protect and preserve their waters, meaning both rivers and seas. Such an initiative could include a host of elements, such as protecting coastal and inland fisheries, which would involve both environmental regulations and law enforcement action against illegal fishing; protecting and preserving river and coastal ecosystems, which could be linked to hydropower, agriculture, tourism, and even navigation matters; and developing better and more reliable systems to provide clean water.

The initiative could be broad in design, perhaps involving regular dialogue with ASEAN itself, but flexible enough to allow for narrower, customized partnerships between the United States and individual Southeast Asian countries that focus on their particular needs and interests. The United States could provide training and capacity building, as well as equipment, especially ships and boats for law enforcement on rivers and in coastal seas. Given the huge international interest in this issue, there would be ample potential for cooperation with like-minded partners.

The United States is already working with Southeast Asian countries on some of these issues but pulling the currently disparate efforts together—and adding new ones and a substantial additional financial investment—under the broad rubric of water cooperation would bring a number of benefits. First, because of the breadth of challenges involved, it could generate more high-level interest and engagement, allowing issues that are now addressed at the technical level to be viewed more strategically. Second, it might encourage greater engagement and cooperation within ASEAN itself, as countries grappling with, say, river management, engage in dialogue with others trying to preserve off-shore fisheries.

Third, such an initiative would enable the United States and its part-ners in the region to discuss and cooperate on some more politically sensitive water-related issues, such as the South China Sea and the Mekong River, in a manner that would be less provocative—and thus perhaps more acceptable to the Southeast Asian governments—than, say, a proposal for U.S.-ASEAN cooperation on the South China Sea. For example, the U.S. provision of law enforcement vessels to combat illegal fishing (or pursue narcotics traffickers) would offer the same ca-pacity building as offering those same vessels to patrol the South China Sea, but without the explicit link to concerns about China.

Engage The Next Generation

Southeast Asia boasts a huge, dynamic, and plugged-in younger gen-eration whose interests and aspirations for the most part mesh well with America's strengths. For years, U.S. embassies have been reaching out and engaging the youth of Southeast Asia, but going forward there is more that Washington can and should do to empower and build re-lationships with the region's future leaders.

The U.S. higher education system constitutes one of its best diplo-matic assets. Tens of thousands of Southeast Asians already have stud-ied or are studying in the United States, and many more would if they had the opportunity. It is difficult to exaggerate the positive impact of such studies, both on the individuals involved and on U.S. interests. Each student who attends a U.S. college or university returns to his or her country with an enhanced ability to contribute to progress and, in many cases, greater appreciation for everything from diversity to trans-parency to fundamental freedoms. In most cases, students also return home with a positive view of the United States and a greater interest in and ability to engage with Americans and American institutions going forward. In other words, they are friends of the United States, and one can never have too many friends.

Bringing more Southeast Asian students to U.S. universities needs to be a major element of our strategy going forward. That means ramping up our marketing efforts, facilitating student visas, and offering more scholarships. People point out that scholarships are expensive. They are, but they are one of the best investments the U.S. government can make. The United States should begin an ASEAN scholarship program. Even if it were only funded at $20 million per annum—personally, I would argue for much more—such a program would allow us to bring approximately one hundred students from Southeast Asia to U.S. universities each year.

Going in the other direction, Washington should support the development of high-quality educational opportunities in the region, such as the Fulbright University in Vietnam. It should help address the lack of strategic thinking in some Southeast Asian countries by funding the study of China, regional affairs, and international relations, and by continuing to encourage the development of think tanks and research institutes.

The United States ought to supplement this by doing more to promote university-to-university partnerships and sharply increasing funding for short-term exchange programs, which any ambassador will tell you are worth their weight in gold in terms of building understanding and friendships. I cannot tell you how many alums of these programs I have met who considered even four-to-six week–programs in the United States life-changing, and who as a result feel a closer connection to America than they had before. Considering how valuable these programs are and how rich in absolute terms the United States is, Washington should be investing substantially more money in them.

Giving people—especially the younger generations—more opportunities to see and experience the United States is a great way of promoting U.S. values, such as democracy and respect for human rights. Even though the United States has its own failings in these areas, in my experience people from Southeast Asia who are able to spend time in America tend to come away with a deep appreciation for the freedom, rule of law, and diversity that have helped make the United States strong. Leading by example, sharing the American experience (good and bad), and supporting individuals and groups that are working to promote similar values and practices in their countries are great ways for the United States to encourage democracy and greater respect for human rights. Particularly these days, when developments inside the United States have resulted in a loss of U.S. credibility and prestige on these issues, leading by example is likely to be more effective than lecturing and adopting punitive measures. Washington also should continue and, if possible, expand support for civil society groups, the independent media, and others fighting for greater democracy, human rights, transparency, and good governance in their own nations. These groups, which include many young people, will play a critical role in encouraging further progress in the region.

Finally, Southeast Asia is a rising hotspot for tech start-ups, and many would-be tech entrepreneurs in the region look first and foremost to Silicon Valley as a model for and potential partner in their efforts; the United States should find a way to build an initiative to tap into this rapidly growing economic space. Already, Washington is funding programs to help Southeast Asian governments create a healthy regulatory environment for such start-ups. The next step would be to use a small amount of government funds to reinforce the nascent bond or connection between local entrepreneurs in the region and U.S. counterparts. Perhaps one element could be a program like the Young Southeast Asian Leaders Initiative, but specifically for those interested in launching start-ups, under which Southeast Asian entrepreneurs would participate in relevant U.S.-linked programs. Another might be annual or semiannual conferences featuring entrepreneurs from both countries. Such an initiative would also fit well with potential digital trade agreements. Washington should sit down with U.S. private sector representatives already active in the region, including the U.S.-ASEAN Business Council, to hear their ideas on how best to develop what seems to be a natural partnership.

Traditional Security Cooperation

I will not devote much space here to traditional security cooperation, not because it is unimportant, but because I do not see the need for dramatic changes in what the United States has been doing. The U.S. military has long played a critical role in Southeast Asia, providing an overall security umbrella, partnering with and often training regional militaries, and serving as a first responder to natural disasters. Many governments in the region look to the United States to continue to provide a regional security umbrella and for security cooperation, including training and education. While Washington wants to avoid reinforcing the view, held by some in the region, that they should look to China for economic partnership and to the United States for security, it does want to maintain its status as the security partner of choice. The

U.S. weakness, as it were, is much more on the economic and—to some extent—diplomatic fronts than in the security sector.

The U.S. military's steady presence, including continued freedom of navigation operations in disputed waters, will be a must for the foreseeable future, as will Cobra Gold and other cooperative military exercises with our key Southeast Asian partners (and other allies). Cobra Gold deserves special attention as the largest multilateral military exercise in all of Asia. In recent years, U.S. policymakers have adjusted the level of participation in the exercise in response to ups and downs in democracy and human rights in the region, particularly in Thailand, which hosts Cobra Gold. This is a bad idea. Cobra Gold, after all, benefits the United States enormously. Using the exercise as a political tool only makes some in Washington feel better, while undermining regional confidence and doing nothing to improve democracy and human rights in Southeast Asian nations. Going forward, the United States should endeavor to implement Cobra Gold fully and consistently and stop using it as a short-term political tool.

U.S. training and support for regional militaries, starting with allies Thailand and the Philippines, will also remain important, as will the United States' continued willingness to sell or otherwise provide appropriate military equipment. Washington also needs to find a way to enable the Pentagon's Indo-Pacific Command to engage regularly with the militaries from the more problematic countries in the region, including Cambodia and Laos. (I would have included Myanmar pre-coup, but that is now a longer-term question). The challenge is to find a mechanism to engage that does not suggest an embrace or endorsement and is acceptable to the U.S. Congress, and that we can sustain through the inevitable ups and downs of the relationship.

In my view, the best way to do this is through regular U.S.-ASEAN exercises and dialogues on humanitarian assistance and disaster relief, combined with programs that bring junior and mid-level officers from those countries to the United States for English-language training and for short programs such as those offered by the Asia-Pacific Center for Security Studies (APCSS) in Honolulu. A third and underutilized pillar should be regular senior-level meetings, at which U.S. flag-rank officers[14] can brief their Southeast Asian counterparts on Washington's view of regional security challenges and on how the United States mili-

---

14 Also referred to as "flag officers," these are senior officers at the rank of general or admiral.

tary is responding to those challenges. This could be a hard sell on Capitol Hill, but growing concern about China offers the possibility of compromise. The Biden administration might want to initiate an informal dialogue with key Capitol Hill members and staffers to try to come up with a politically feasible set of options.

On the law enforcement side, the U.S. government should focus on continuing to help key countries build their capacity to monitor and protect their maritime domains. The United States already has done some good work in this area, and the Quad in May 2022 announced a new initiative that will offer useful data to the region's governments on what is happening in their maritime areas. It will be important for Washington—and the Quad—to continue to build on this effort. The other primary area of focus should be counternarcotics. Southeast Asia—specifically northeastern Myanmar—is the world's largest producer and exporter of methamphetamines. This is a regional problem that needs a regional solution, but the ASEAN nations have been skittish about tackling it head-on, no doubt in deference to Myanmar sensitivities. (To be clear, most illegal narcotics production in Myanmar, even before the February 2021 coup, has been based in areas beset by conflict, over which the central government has limited control.) Washington should work quietly with the UN, Australia, New Zealand, India, and ASEAN members to identify a regionally acceptable forum or mechanism at which this issue can be discussed openly and fully. Whatever emerges will need to be primarily a product of the region. The United States will have to lead from behind, but leadership is needed.

South China Sea

In addition to these major strategy pillars, Washington will also need to pursue more specific approaches to a handful of key issues and countries. The South China Sea, of course, looms large. It is arguably the most fraught, given the inherent difficulty in pushing back against China's aggressive island-building approach without provoking major conflict or allowing China to achieve the territorial fait accompli it is seeking.

Unfortunately, there are no magic bullets on South China Sea policy. Lots of smart, experienced people from the United States and elsewhere have studied the problem intensively, and the best they have come up with is an approach that is more or less consistent with what the United

States has been doing, with perhaps a few minor adjustments. Going forward, U.S. strategy should focus on maintaining the maximum possible diplomatic and political support in the region for a firm stance against unilateral Chinese moves to assert sovereignty in disputed areas, and on preventing Beijing from using its island-building, militarization, and intimidation efforts to limit freedom of navigation or compel Southeast Asian claimants to surrender their rights. Specifically, that entails:

- Continuing to consult closely with the Southeast Asian claimant states. U.S. interests vary somewhat from those of the ASEAN claimants, but it is critical that as much as possible Washington consults and coordinates on all South China Sea matters.
- Continue freedom of navigation operations, ideally partnering with the Japanese, Australians, Indians, and others so it is not just a U.S. effort. Given China's extensive use of law enforcement vessels to assert its presence and claims, consider joint allied Coast Guard exercises and operations on a sustained basis in the South China Sea, ideally in conjunction with Southeast Asian claimants.

- Do everything possible to maintain and strengthen the alliance with the Philippines, which offers an irreplaceable strategic location but which requires consistent high-level attention.

- Redouble efforts to bolster the maritime awareness and presence capacity of Southeast Asian claimants as well as Indonesia. They are not going to take on China directly, but their presence and ability to monitor their maritime areas, particularly within their exclusive economic zones, makes it harder for China to use the presence of its ships to assert its claims.

- Maintain support for potential claimant state (e.g., Vietnamese) legal cases against China's excessive claims in the South China Sea.

- Raise the reputational cost to China by developing more systematic public messaging that consistently describes and calls out problematic Chinese behavior. This should be both for the U.S. public (to maintain public support for firm measures) and for publics in Southeast Asia.

- Consider ways, including public-private partnerships, to offer political risk insurance to U.S. (and maybe other) energy companies to encourage them to explore for oil and gas, in cooperation with Southeast Asian nations, despite Chinese threats and intimidation.

The Mekong

The Mekong River region also warrants greater attention, as the Trump administration recognized when it elevated the Lower Mekong Initiative to a full partnership, with additional funding. The United States has three goals vis-à-vis the Mekong: to create greater pressure on China to share water data with its downstream neighbors and to factor their concerns and needs into its own river management; to help the Lower Mekong countries manage and preserve the river's ecosystem as well as possible and reduce their vulnerability to any Chinese effort to use control of the river flow as leverage; and to parlay enhanced cooperation with the Lower Mekong countries into more consistent, higher-level engagement and improved bilateral relations, including with Laos and Cambodia.

The best way to pressure China into more responsible behavior is by internationalizing the issue, just as has been done with the South China Sea. Beijing would prefer to address issues bilaterally or, in the case of the Mekong, with a small group of relatively weaker countries. When an issue becomes internationalized, it becomes harder for China to use its leverage to compel others to accommodate it.

The first and most essential step in internationalizing the issue is for ASEAN to adopt and formally discuss it. To date, ASEAN has rarely discussed the Mekong issue, at least formally, but there is growing awareness in the region of the geostrategic and economic (not to mention environmental) implications of the issue for Southeast Asia. A recent survey of ASEAN policy elites found that nearly three-fourths of respondents supported ASEAN engaging on the issue.[15] Vietnam raised the Mekong during its 2020 chairmanship, but some of the other governments were lukewarm to the idea of ASEAN formally adopting it as an issue. In the past, they have argued that it is a "subregional" issue and thus not worthy of full ASEAN consideration.

Going forward, it would be good if Vietnam, perhaps joined by Thailand, Singapore, and possibly even Cambodia, continued to push the idea of ASEAN taking up the issue. They could cite the precedent of the

---

15 Sharon Seah et al., *The State of Southeast Asia,* xx.

late 1990s ASEAN adoption of the interstate haze issue (Indonesian forest fires causing air pollution in nearby states). An ASEAN discussion of the Mekong might create a confluence of interests between the South China Sea claimants—who (other than Vietnam) have no direct interest in the Mekong, and the Mekong countries, which (again, other than Vietnam) have no direct interest in the South China Sea. If one wanted to be optimistic, one could imagine the two groups of countries recognizing that they are facing similar challenges vis-à-vis China, and have at least some interest in supporting each other more than they have done to date.

For its part, the United States should continue to obtain and share information about what China is doing in the upper reaches of the river, particularly in terms of water flows. U.S. funding of the early 2020 Eyes on the Earth study of water flows served as a great example of how U.S. support for scientific-based evidence and data pushed China into becoming more transparent and cooperative. More recently, the State Department helped fund the private Mekong Dam Monitor, an online publicly accessible platform that provides timely data on dam operations and water flows along the Mekong. It promises an unprecedented level of transparency that should prove helpful to the Lower Mekong countries.

Thailand, Laos, Cambodia, and Vietnam have different interests and approaches toward the Mekong, which has hampered cooperation to date. Cash-starved Laos sees hydropower projects along the Mekong as one of the few ways to earn foreign exchange and promote development. Cambodia is also in the hydropower market, though not to the same extent. Vietnam, on the other hand, gains little and loses a lot from those very projects, though some of its businesses have been involved in specific projects. Thailand has a more nuanced position but appears increasingly concerned about the future of the river and its broader ecosystem.

The Obama administration tried to discourage big hydropower projects along the river, but its arguments about what was good for the entire Mekong ecosystem fell largely on deaf ears, at least in Vientiane and Phnom Penh. Perhaps a better approach would be to work with the Mekong River Commission and like-minded partners to provide the best possible information and analyses about different proposed projects and approaches to development that have minimal impact on the river and its ecosystem. In other words, rather than trying to push the countries to a particular conclusion, the United States can help them build their capacity to make the best possible decisions.

The United States also should provide relevant scholarships and training to help develop the Lower Mekong countries' capacity to study and evaluate the river and proposed projects. This can involve some training and study in the United States, perhaps combined with lower-cost programs in Thailand. Ideally, programs would include students and scientists from all Lower Mekong countries, so they can build their own network as they learn. This would fit well with the United States' existing commitment to invest in human capital development in the region.

Friends in the region have reminded me that China's Lancang-Mekong Cooperation Forum enjoys dramatically more funding than the U.S.-Mekong Partnership, and that the region suffers from a proliferation of Mekong fora organized by Japan, Korea, Australia, India, Europe, and others. One idea would be for the United States to reinvigorate and reimagine the former "Friends of the Lower Mekong Initiative" to create a multilateral forum for like-minded governments and NGOs to coordinate and engage with the Lower Mekong countries and with ASEAN as a whole. In other words, the United States might use its convening power to organize and make more efficient the plethora of Mekong-related fora. China probably would not want to join, but that would be up to Beijing.

The United States also should continue and ideally expand initiatives to partner with Japan, Australia, and others to promote cleaner and better energy solutions for the Mekong region. This could include smart, small hydropower projects, perhaps, but would also emphasize solar power, energy efficiency, and the like. The Japan-U.S. Mekong Power Partnership, launched in 2019, is a good start but more can be done. Convincing countries, particularly Laos, to shift away from big hydropower will be a challenge, though Cambodia already has canceled two proposed major dam projects. One idea would be for the international community, perhaps in partnership with the World Bank and/or Asian Development Bank, to pay Laos to forgo major dam projects. This could be in the form of direct budget payments or, preferably, funds to subsidize alternative income-generating projects.

Laos and Cambodia

The United States should take advantage of stepped-up efforts in the Mekong region to bolster its engagement and relationship with Laos and Cambodia. This is a tough sell in Washington, for a number of reasons. Laos "enjoyed" its last moment in the international spotlight nearly sixty years ago, when the "Laos Crisis" made the headlines and was one of the subjects of President Eisenhower's transitional discussion with incoming President Kennedy. When I served as the Laos desk officer thirty years ago, my colleagues assumed my career was heading nowhere. Laos is a small, sparsely populated country whose opaque communist leadership makes minimal effort to engage with the United States and is widely seen as largely in Beijing's pocket.

Cambodia gets much more attention, but most of it is negative, as discussed in chapter 6. Hun Sen's episodic anti-U.S. rants, his harsh treatment of the domestic opposition and strong support for China, and the continued disappointment of some key U.S. foreign policy players over Cambodia's failed democratic experiment combine to make the prime minister one of the less attractive interlocutors for U.S. leaders.

It is not realistic to ignore these problems or to think that, with a little effort, the United States can win over the Lao or Cambodian leadership. What is possible, however, is for Washington to engage more consistently, look for areas of common interest, and try to avoid emotional, punitive responses to democratic backsliding or other disappointments. I participated in several interagency dialogues with both the Lao and the Cambodian governments during the Obama administration, and both governments at fairly senior levels showed a lot of receptivity and interest. If the United States keeps its expectations modest but engages consistently and appropriately, there is some opportunity to build better, more durable relationships that over time will give the Cambodians and Lao more freedom of maneuver vis-à-vis China.

Thailand

The Mekong-U.S. Partnership also offers a great opportunity for the United States to restore some of the luster to its relationship with Thailand. Thailand has taken a great interest in the Mekong, including welcoming and encouraging the renewed U.S. engagement. Bangkok also is promoting its own Mekong-region economic development initiative, the Ayeyawady-Chao Phraya-Mekong Economic Cooperation Strategy (ACMECS), which has garnered interest and support from the United States.

I sense some disappointment among some Thai opinion leaders that Washington no longer looks to the kingdom as much for advice on how to navigate the shoals of Southeast Asian politics, a role it played for so long. To be fair, Thai diplomacy of late has done little to encourage Washington in this regard. In addition to engaging with and supporting ACMECS, the Biden administration might want to begin conversations in Bangkok on whether Thailand would be interested in taking up that navigator role again for the Mekong Partnership, with the understanding that times have changed, and Thailand will not want to be seen as working with the United States against China.

More broadly, as suggested in chapter 3, the United States and Thailand would benefit from further conversations to redefine the alliance relationship. It will be difficult as long as the Thai political scene remains so fraught and uncertain, but it makes sense at least to begin the dialogue (which, by the way, should include academics and other experts in addition to government officials). Chapter 3 goes into this question in more detail, but the bottom line is that such a dialogue would need both to re-frame the alliance itself (i.e., the security partnership) as well as to lay out ideas to reinvigorate the overall relationship, building on the already good people-to-people links, economic and health cooperation, and opportunities to work together on the Mekong and other regional matters. Critically, the United States also will need to find ways to assure the Thai that it considers the relationship special and that it will treat them accordingly, and the Thai should do the same vis-à-vis Washington.

The Philippines

The United States also should continue to invest in its alliance with the Philippines, despite the inevitable ups and downs and frustrations. The Philippines occupies a uniquely strategic location and also boasts a strongly pro-American public. Washington policymakers—myself included—sometimes have failed to appreciate these twin assets and have let their disappointment in Manila's unpredictable and raucous politics cloud their strategic analysis. The two countries took an important step in mid-2021, when after months of doubt they renewed the Visiting Forces Agreement, which is essential to the conduct of joint exercises and U.S. military access via the Enhanced Defense Cooperation Agreement. Over the previous eighteen months, the U.S. government had worked wisely and effectively to maintain this agreement, refusing to let President Duterte's threats and tilt toward China distract it from its longer-term strategic interests. It is critical that the Biden administration maintain this approach, continue to help the Philippines build its maritime capacity, and do everything possible to reinforce the very strong people-to-people ties that remain the essential pillar of the relationship. The Biden administration wisely moved rapidly to reaffirm the Trump administration's statement that the mutual defense treaty between the two countries applies to any attacks against Philippine forces, vessels, or aircraft in the South China Sea.

As Mike Green and Greg Poling of the Center for Strategic and International Studies recently suggested, Washington also needs to remain keenly aware of Philippine sensitivities about the historically asymmetrical bilateral relationship and look for ways to accommodate Manila's domestic political concerns over the defense relationship as much as possible.[16] As it did during the Duterte presidency, the United States will need to find ways to stay consistently and positively engaged, even when changes in leadership in Manila—such as the May 2022 election of Bongbong Marcos to the presidency—potentially bring about significant swings in policy and attitudes toward the alliance.

Vietnam

Over the years, the United States has managed its relationship with Vietnam as well as if not better than any of its other partnerships in the region. Washington-Hanoi ties remain on a positive trajectory and should continue to develop. Perhaps the biggest challenge for the United States will be to keep its expectations realistic. As noted in chapter 5, Vietnam is and should remain a good partner, but it is not going to become an ally. The United States should view and treat Vietnam much as it has Singapore—an effective and strategic and economic partner that is not going to serve as a model of democracy and which is most valuable if it is not seen as overly aligned with Washington.

Singapore

Singapore has been a tremendous success story and an incredibly valuable partner for decades. I have not written much about it in this book,

---

16 Michael J. Green and Gregory B. Poling, "The U.S. Alliance with the Philippines," Hard Choices: Memos to the President, CSIS, December 3, 2020, https://www.csis.org/analysis/us-alliance-philippines.

not because it is unimportant, but because it has been so steady and largely drama-free, as has the bilateral relationship. That does not mean Washington should ignore it or take it for granted. The Biden administration took an important first step by appointing Jonathan E. Kaplan as ambassador (he is now in place in Singapore) and another when it welcomed Prime Minister Lee Hsieng-Loong to Washington in spring 2022. Going forward, the United States should ensure regular dialogue with Singapore on both the bilateral relationship and on specific steps Washington can and should take to reinvigorate its role in the region.

Indonesia

Indonesia, of course, remains the giant of Southeast Asia, the one country in the region that by itself can push back against an overly assertive China (or the United States). The U.S.-Indonesian relationship over the past ten to fifteen years has been solid overall but has been held back by the lack of stronger economic ties. That is mostly due to Indonesia's reflexive protectionism and ambivalence about foreign investment, but the United States must continue to try to bolster commercial relations. The Trump administration's decision to maintain Generalized System of Preferences benefits for Indonesia marked a good step in the right direction, as did a series of letters of intent and memoranda of understanding between the U.S. Development Finance Corporation, Export-Import Bank, and Treasury Department with their Indonesian counterparts. It will take sustained engagement of this sort, along with greater Indonesian openness, to make progress, but it can happen.

More broadly, the United States should treat Indonesia as the world's fourth-largest country and third-largest democracy, biggest Muslim-majority nation, a G20 member, and the sixteenth-largest economy in the world—all of which it is. That means regular high-level engagement befitting our bilateral strategic partnership, continued support and assistance in improving governance, education, and healthcare, and a constant effort to persuade the still-skeptical Indonesian population that the United States is a good and worthwhile partner. It also means continued, steady efforts to build the growing security relationship, while recognizing and accepting that Indonesia is inherently nonaligned and thus unwilling to accommodate U.S. (or other major power) requests for anything that smacks of military basing or a security alliance.

Malaysia and Brunei

Malaysia poses its own challenges, with a wariness toward the United States, fueled by years of Mahathir Mohamad's anti-Western rhetoric. Nonetheless, Malaysia stands as one of the United States' best economic partners in the region, with very strong trade ties and significant U.S. investment. Although Kuala Lumpur enjoys good relations with China, Malaysia's fierce independence extends northward as well. The government and public are open to good relations—if not a particularly close partnership—with the United States. Malaysia definitely should be a key player in whatever trade and economic initiatives the Biden administration decides to pursue. So should Brunei, an easily neglected nation that (like Malaysia and Singapore) is part of the CPTPP. Also, while small, Brunei boasts some talented trade and foreign policy officials who can be good partners and excellent sources of advice and wisdom.

Myanmar

In the aftermath of the February 2021 coup, it is difficult to offer a detailed prescription for policy toward Myanmar, given the tremendous uncertainties of how things will play out in the years to come. The key points for Washington policymakers to keep in mind is that the struggle to reverse the coup and end the military's political power and impunity is one of the few things that unites this otherwise fractious country, and that struggle warrants strong U.S. support. In addition to putting maximum pressure on the junta to relinquish power, Washington's focus should be on assisting the longer-term effort by the people of Myanmar to build a sustainable democracy and a federal structure, which is the only hope for ending decades of internal conflict. The United States should focus on the younger generation, and—as much as the post-coup environment allows—continue to fund and support independent media, civil society, and others who are the long-term hope for the country. In Myanmar, as in the rest of Southeast Asia, the younger generation offers hope, and warrants as much U.S. attention and engagement—including plentiful scholarships—as possible.

A Note on the Quad

Washington has sought to promote cooperation among the four Quad members: Japan, Australia, India, and the United States. As noted in chapter 11, while some ASEAN members have welcomed this approach, several others see the Quad as too focused on countering China, and thus potentially raising tension and bringing major power competition more directly into Southeast Asia. Some also worry that the Quad could undermine ASEAN centrality.

The United States does not need to let ASEAN's concerns fundamentally alter its Quad strategy, but there are a couple of things Washington and other Quad members can do to address the region's concerns and, in doing so, build their influence. First, the Quad should consult regularly with ASEAN, formally or informally, to elicit ideas and to ensure Southeast Asians understand what the Quad is trying to do. Second, as a number of analysts have suggested, the Quad needs to have a positive agenda that contributes to the region beyond pushing back against an assertive Beijing. The Quad commitment to support expanded COVID-19 vaccine production and distribution out of India was a good start, as is the new maritime domain initiative, but there is more that can and should be done, including in some of the specific areas noted earlier in this chapter (e.g., infrastructure, water, climate change, healthcare).

Most importantly, the United States needs to remember that ASEAN exists to discourage big power intervention and conflict in Southeast Asia. The more Washington and other Quad members can keep this in mind in both its policies and its public statements, the better it will be able to address concerns about the Quad's role and build a more cooperative partnership with the countries of Southeast Asia.

In closing, building robust, sustainable, and cooperative relationships with ASEAN and with its ten member states will require Washington to find ways to bolster its economic engagement and to show that it is a consistent, reliable partner that brings a positive agenda, does not frame its engagement with the region in terms of China, and does not let short-term disappointments cloud its focus on the long-term strategic benefits of deeper ties with Southeast Asia.

Bibliography

Advisory Commission on Rakhine State. "Advisory Commission on Rakhine State: Final Report." Kofi Annan Foundation, August 24, 2017. https://www.kofiannanfoundation.org/mediation-and-crisis-resolution/rakhine-final-report/.

Ahmad, Qasim. "Malaysia-Myanmar Relations 1997–2002: A 'Prosper Thy Neighbor' Strategy." https://jas.uitm.edu.my/images/2004_JUNE/4.pdf.

Al Jazeera. "Myanmar Finds War Crimes but No Genocide in Rohingya Crackdown." January 21, 2020. https://www.aljazeera.com/news/2020/1/21/myanmar-finds-war-crimes-but-no-genocide-in-rohingya-crackdown.

———. "Military Government Chief Prayuth Chan-ocha Elected Thai PM." Al Jazeera, June 6, 2019. https://aje.io/2hf3b.

Alagappa, Muthiah. "Community Building: ASEAN's Millstone?" Pacific Forum CSIS PacNet, Carnegie Endowment for International Peace, March 19, 2015. https://carnegieendowment.org/2015/03/19/community-building-asean-s-millstone-pub-59444.

Alagappa, Muthiah. *The National Security of Developing States: Lessons from Thailand.* Dover, MA: Auburn House Publishing Company, 1987.

Albert, Eleanor, and Lindsay Maizland. "What is ASEAN." Council on Foreign Relations, December 20, 2019. https://www.cfr.org/backgrounder/what-asean.

Almonte, Jose. "The Philippines Rejoins Asia." Paper presented to the Singapore Institute of International Affairs and the National University of Singapore Society, June 11, 1993.

Amador, Julio S. III, and Joycee A. Teodoro. *The Role of the Association of Southeast Asian Nations in Post-Conflict Reconstruction and Democracy Support.* Stockholm, Sweden: International Institute for Democracy and Electoral Assistance, 2016. https://www.idea.int/sites/default/files/publications/the-role-of-asean-in-post-conflict-reconstruction-and-democracy-support.pdf.

Amnesty International. "Myanmar: New Evidence Reveals Rohingya Armed Group Massacred Scores in Rakhine State." May 22, 2018. https://www.amnesty.org/en/latest/news/2018/05/myanmar-new-evidence-reveals-rohingya-armed-group-massacred-scores-in-rakhine-state/.

———. "Philippines: Restore Respect for Human Rights on 46th Anniversary of Martial Law." Public Statement ASA 35/9139/2018, September 21, 2018. https://www.amnesty.org/en/documents/asa35/9139/2018/en/.

Andina, Swiny. "The United States Donates Additional 3.3 Million COVID-19 Vaccines to Indonesia." Reliefweb, December 19, 2021. https://reliefweb.int/report/indonesia/united-states-donates-additional-33-million-covid-19-vaccines-indonesia.

Arasingham, Aidan, Emily Benson, and Matthew P. Goodman. "Unpacking the Indo-Pacific Economic Framework Launch." Center for Strategic and International Studies, May 23, 2022. https://www.csis.org/analysis/unpacking-indo-pacific-economic-framework-launch.

Armstrong, David. "The Next Yugoslavia? The Fragmentation of Indonesia." *Diplomacy and Statecraft* 15, no. 4 (December 1, 2004): 783–808. https://doi.org/10.1080/09592290490886865.

ASEAN Post. "How China Changed Sihanoukville." February 11, 2021. https://theaseanpost.com/article/how-china-changed-sihanoukville.

ASEAN Single Window. "Launch of the ASEAN Single Window Live Operation." November 1, 2018. https://asw.asean.org/index.php/news/item/launch-of-the-asean-single-window-live-operation.

ASEAN Statistics. "Table 19: ASEAN Trade by Selected Partner Country/Region, 2015." November 2016. https://asean.org/wp-content/uploads/2016/11/Table19_as-of-6-dec-2016.pdf.

ASEANStatsDataPortal. "Flows of Inward Foreign Direct Investment (FDI) into ASEAN by Source Country." https://data.aseanstats.org/fdi-by-hosts-and-sources.

Ashwill, Mark A. "Vietnamese Student Enrollment in the U.S. Holds Steady." University World News, February 8, 2020. https://www.universityworldnews.com/post.php?story=20200205124654543.

Asia Group Advisors. "Indonesia's Omnibus Law on Job Creation." March 19, 2021. https://asiagroupadvisors.com/insights/indonesia's-omnibus-law-on-job-creation/70.

Asia Maritime Transparency Initiative, Center for Strategic and International Studies. "China's Most Destructive Boats Return to the South China Sea." May 20, 2019. https://amti.csis.org/chinas-most-destructive-boats-return-to-the-south-china-sea/.

———. "Update: China Continues to Transform Ream Naval Base." Center for Strategic and International Studies, October 12, 2021. https://amti.csis.org/changes-underway-at-cambodias-ream-naval-base/.

Asian Development Bank. Meeting Asia's Infrastructure Needs. Manila, Philippines: ADB, 2017. https://www.adb.org/sites/default/files/publication/227496/special-report-infrastructure.pdf.

Aye Thidar Kyaw and Claire Hammond. "Government Reveals 12-Point Economic Policy." Myanmar Times, July 29, 2016. https://www.mmtimes.com/business/21664-nld-12-point-economic-policy-announcement.html.

Baliga, Ananth, and Mech Dara. "U.S. Envoy Calls Government Claims 'Absurd.'" Phnom Penh Post, September 13, 2017. https://www.phnompenhpost.com/national/us-envoy-calls-government-claims-absurd.

Bangkok Post. "Green Light for Kyaukphyu." July 30, 2018. https://www.bangkokpost.com/business/1512470/green-light-for-kyaukphyu.

———. "Vietnam Soldier's War Diary Returned to Family." September 22, 2012. https://www.bangkokpost.com/world/313459/vietnam-soldier-war-diary-returned-to-family.

Barta, Patrick, and Vu Trong Khanh. "Clinton Presses Vietnam on Rights Record." Wall Street Journal, July 10, 2012.

Basist, Alan, and Claude Williams. "Monitoring the Quantity of Water Flowing Through the Upper Mekong Basin Under Natural (Unimpeded) Conditions." Sustainable Infrastructure Partnership, Bangkok, April 11, 2020. https://58353b6-da87-4596-a181-b1f20782dd18.filesusr.com/ugd/bae95b_0e0f87104dc8482b99ec91601d853122.pdf?index=true.

BBC News. "Aung San Suu Kyi: Reform Process 'Stalled.'" November 5, 2014. https://www.bbc.com/news/world-asia-29919094.

———. "Killer of Activist Kem Ley Sentenced to Life." March 23, 2017. https://www.bbc.com/news/world-asia-39362264.

———. "Myanmar Rejects UN Accusation of 'Genocide' Against the Rohingya." August 29, 2018. https://www.bbc.com/news/world-asia-45338986.

———. "Myanmar Rohingya: UN Says Myanmar Military Leaders Must Face Genocide Charges." August 27, 2018. https://www.bbc.com/news/world-asia-45318982.

———. "Rohingya Crisis: Aung San Suu Kyi Says 'Fake News Helping Terrorist." September 6, 2017. https://www.bbc.com/news/world-asia-41170570.

———. "Rohingya Crisis: Suu Kyi Speech Criticised by Global Leaders." September 20, 2017. https://www.bbc.com/news/world-asia-41329662.

———. "Suharto's Fortune." September 28, 2000. http://news.bbc.co.uk/2/hi/asia-pacific/864355.stm.

Becker, Elizabeth. "Vietnamese Invasion of Cambodia Draws Criticism by U.S." *Washington Post,* January 4, 1979.

———. *When the War Was Over: Cambodia and the Khmer Rouge.* New York: Simon and Schuster, 1986.

Beech, Hannah. "A Jungle Airstrip Stirs Suspicions About China's Plans for Cambodia." *New York Times,* December 22, 2019.

Bengali, Shashank. "In Myanmar, Hatred for Rohingya Runs So Deep that a Diplomat Called Them 'Ugly as Ogres,' and Got Promoted." *Los Angeles Times,* December 26, 2017. https://www.latimes.com/world/asia/la-fg-myanmar-rohingya-hate-20171225-story.html.

Bevins, Vincent. "What the United States Did in Indonesia." *The Atlantic,* October 20, 2017. https://www.theatlantic.com/international/archive/2017/10/the-indonesia-documents-and-the-us-agenda/543534/.

Biddle, Kurt. "Indonesia-U.S. Military Ties." *Inside Indonesia,* July 29, 2007. https://www.insideindonesia.org/indonesia-us-military-ties-2.

Bland, Ben. *A Man of Contradictions: Joko Widodo and the Struggle to Remake Indonesia.* Lowy Institute Paper. Australia: Penguin Random House Australia, 2020.

———. "Politics in Indonesia: Resilient Elections, Defective Democracy." Lowy Institute, April 20, 2019. https://www.lowyinstitute

.org/publications/politics-indonesia-resilient-elections-defective
-democracy.

Boardo, Alex S. "Enhanced Defense Cooperation Agreement: Aquino III's Balancing Strategy with the United States against China." Master's thesis, Naval Postgraduate School, 2017. http:// hdl.handle.net/10945/52958.

Bonner, Raymond. *Waltzing with a Dictator: The Marcoses and the Making of American Policy.* New York: Times Books, 1987.

Boyle, David. "Cambodia Arrest Opposition Leader, Alleges Treason." VOA News, September 2, 2017. https://www.voanews.com/a/cambodia-arrests-opposition-leader-alleges-treason/4013099.html.

———. "Chinese Ambassador: EU Should Not Mix Politics, Trade in Cambodia." VOA News, July 19, 2018. https://www.voanews.com/a/chinese-ambassador-eu-should-not-mix-politics-trade-in-cambodia/4489291.html.

Branigin, William. "'Crony Capitalism' Blamed for Economic Crisis." *Washington Post,* August 16, 1984.

———. "Shotgun Wedding." *Washington Post,* April 23, 1985.

Brunnstrom, David, and Arshad Muhammed. "Thai Coup Draws Swift Condemnation; U.S. Says Reviewing Aid." Reuters, May 22, 2014. http://reut.rs/1jaOisq.

Bueza, Michael, and Gloria Marie Castro. "MAP: Major Political Families in PH After the 2019 Elections." Rappler, August 30, 2019. https://www.rappler.com/newsbreak/in-depth/map-major-political-families-philippines-after-elections-2019.

Bui The Giang. "Vietnam-U.S. Political and People-To-People Relations: A Brief Overview." In *Dialogue on U.S.-Vietnam Relations Ten Years After Normalization,* edited by Catharin E. Dalpino. Washington, DC: Asia Foundation, 2005.

Bumiller, Elisabeth, and Norimitsu Onishi. "U.S. Lifts Ban on Indonesian Special Forces Unit." *New York Times,* July 22, 2010.

Bureau of Democracy, Human Rights, and Labor, U.S. Department of State. "Documentation of Atrocities in Northern Rakhine State." September 24, 2018. https://2017-2021.state.gov/reports-bureau-of-democracy-human-rights-and-labor/documentation-of-atrocities-in-northern-rakhine-state//index.html.

Bureau of Oceans and International Environmental and Scientific Affairs, U.S. Department of State. "China: Maritime Claims in the South China Sea." Limits in the Seas no. 143, December 5, 2014. https://www.state.gov/wp-content/uploads/2019/10/LIS-143.pdf.

Bureau of Population, Refugees, and Migration. "Refugee Admissions Program for East Asia." Fact sheet, U.S. Department of State archive, January 16, 2004. https://2001-2009.State.gov/g/prm/rls/fs/2004/28212.htm.

Burgess, John, and William Branigan. "Roman Catholic Bishops Condemn 'Fraudulence' of Philippines Election." *Washington Post*, February 15, 1986.

Byatnal, Amruta. "USAID Begins New Round of Agent Orange Cleanup in Vietnam." Devex, January 8, 2020. https://www.devex.com/news/usaid-begins-new-round-of-agent-orange-cleanup-in-vietnam-96222.

Caballero-Anthony, Mely. "Beyond the Iraq Hostage Crisis: Re-Assessing US-Philippine Relations." Institute of Defence and Strategic Studies, Commentaries, July 28, 2004. https://www.rsis.edu.sg/rsis-publication/nts/626-beyond-the-iraq-hostage-crisis/#.WQ1RiIiGPIU

Campbell, Ian, and Chris Barlow. "Hydropower Development and the Loss of Fisheries in the Mekong River Basin." *Frontiers in Environmental Science*, October 19, 2020. https://www.frontiersin.org/articles/10.3389/fenvs.2020.566509/full.

Campbell, Kurt M., and Laura Rosenberger. "Kurt M. Campbell and Laura Rosenberger on U.S.-China Relations | 2021 Oksenberg Conference." Shorenstein Asia-Pacific Research Center, May 26, 2021. https://www.youtube.com/watch?v=Hrm5Gthyoqg.

Campi, Alicia. "From Refugees to Americans: Thirty Years of Vietnamese Immigration to the United States." *Immigration Daily*. https://www.ilw.com/articles/2006,0313-campi.shtm.

CEIC Data. "China Foreign Exchange Reserves, 1989–2021." https://www.ceicdata.com/en/indicator/china/foreign-exchange-reserves.

Chanlett-Avery, Emma. *Thailand: Background and U.S. Relations.* Congressional Research Service RL32593, February 8, 2011. https://crsreports.congress.gov/product/pdf/RL/RL32593.

Chanlett-Avery, Emma, and Ben Dolven. "Thailand: Background and U.S. Relations." In *Thailand: Conditions, Issues and U.S. Relations*, edited by Kenny N. Kade. New York: Novinka, 2014.

Chauvel, Richard. *Constructing Papuan Nationalism: History, Ethnicity, and Adaptation, Policy Studies* 14. Washington, DC: East-West Center, 2005. https://www.eastwestcenter.org/sites/default/files/private/PS014.pdf.

Cheang, Sopheng. "Cambodia Marks 20 Years Since Deadly Grenade Attack." *Associated Press,* March 30, 2017. https://apnews.com/arti cle/027b9bb8504e40d48d83d695bfaefcbd.

———. "Cambodia's Leader Relieved Trump Doesn't Seek Regime Change." ABC News, November 27, 2019. https://abcnews.go.com/ US/wireStory/cambodias-hun-sen-tells-trump-welcomes-relations -67340590.

Cheesman, Nick. "How in Myanmar 'National Races' Came to Surpass Citizenship and Exclude the Rohingya." *Journal of Contemporary Asia* 47, no. 3 (May 27, 2017): 461–83. https://doi.org/10.108 0/00472336.2017.1297476.

Chestnut Greitens, Sheena. "The U.S.-Philippine Alliance in a Year of Transition: Challenges and Opportunities." Working paper, Brookings Institution, May 2016. https://www.brookings.edu/wp -content/uploads/2016/11/fp_20160713_philippines_alliance.pdf.

Chiang, Jeremy. "Philippine Foreign Policy in the 21st Century: the Influence of Double-Asymmetric Structure." Conference paper, ISA International Conference 2017, Hong Kong, China, June 15–17, 2017.

Childress, Richard T., and Stephen J. Solarz. "Vietnam: Detours on the Road to Normalization." In *Reversing Relations with Former Adversaries*, edited by C. Richard Nelson and Kenneth Weisbrode. Gainesville, FL: University Press of Florida, 1998.

Clymer, Kenton. *A Delicate Relationship: The United States and Burma/Myanmar since 1945*. New York: Cornell University Press, 2015.

CNN. "Thailand's King Gives Blessing to Coup." September 20, 2006. https://www.cnn.com/2006/WORLD/asiapcf/09/20/thailand.coup .king/.

———. "Vietnam Crash Kills 16, Pentagon Says." CNN, April 7, 2001. http://www.cnn.com/2001/WORLD/asiapcf/southeast/04/07/viet nam.crash.02/.

Committee for Development Planning. *Report on the Twenty-Third Session: Supplement No. 10*. E/1987/23, UN Economic and Social Committee, November 21–24, 1987. https://undocs.org/en/E/ 1987/23.

Committee on the Judiciary. *International Conference on Indo-Chinese Refugees: 1989, A Staff Report Prepared for the Use of the Subcommittee on Immigration and Refugee Affairs of the*

Committee on the Judiciary. Washington, DC: U.S. Government Printing Office, June 1989. https://babel.hathitrust.org/cgi/pt?id=pu r1.32754078877192&view=1up&seq=1.

Connors, Emma. "Off the Rails—Indonesia's Belt and Road Rail Mess." *Financial Review,* September 24, 2020. https://www.afr .com/world/asia/off-the-rails-indonesia-s-belt-and-road-rail-mess -20200917-p55wms.

Cooper, Mary H. "U.S.-Vietnam Relations: Should the U.S. Normalize Relations with Its Old Enemy?" CQ Researcher 3, issue 45, December 3, 1993. https://library.cqpress.com/cqresearcher/document .php?id=cqresrre1993120100.

Cropley, Ed. "Myanmar's Nutty Scheme to Solve Energy Crisis." Reuters, March 11, 2008. https://www.reuters.com/article/idUSBKK 16771520080312.

Crouch, Harold. "Indonesia: Democratization and the Threat of Disintegration." *Southeast Asian Affairs,* 2000: 115–133. https://www .jstor.org/stable/27912247.

Dalpino, Catharin E. "Indonesia at the Crossroads." Brookings Policy Brief 89, September 30, 2001. https://www.brookings.edu/research/ indonesia-at-the-crossroads/.

de Castro, Renato Cruz. "The Revitalized U.S.-Philippine Security Relations: A Ghost from the Cold War or an Alliance for the 21st Century." *Asian Survey* 43, no.6 (Nov-Dec 2003): 971–88. https:// www.jstor.org/stable/10.1525/as.2003.43.6.971.

———. "The 21st Century Philippine-US Enhanced Defense Cooperation Agreement (EDCA): The Philippines Policy in Facilitating the Obama Administration's Strategic Pivot to Asia." *Korean Journal of Defense Analysis* 26, no. 4 (December 2014): 427–44.

Dee, Liz. "In Politics, Pinatubo and the Pentagon: The Closure of Subic Bay." Association for Diplomatic Studies and Training, May 31, 2016. https:// adst.org/2016/05/politics-pinatubo -pentagon-closure-subic-bay-philippines/.

Defense POW/MIA Accounting Agency. "Progress in Vietnam." Factsheet, November 20, 2020. https://www.dpaa.mil/Resources/Fact -Sheets/Article-View/Article/569613/progress-in-vietnam/.

Demick, Barbara. "Rodrigo Duterte's Campaign of Terror in the Philippines." *New Yorker,* August 26, 2016. https://www.newyorker .com/news/news-desk/rodrigo-dutertes-campaign-of-terror-in-the -philippines.

Denton, Bryan. "With Joko Widodo's Re-election, Indonesia Bucks Global Tilt Toward Strongmen." *New York Times,* May 21, 2019.

Desker, Barry. "Is ASEAN a Community." RSIS Commentary no. 145, August 2, 2017. https://www.rsis.edu.sg/wp-content/uploads/2017/08/CO17145.pdf.

Dillon, Dana. "Arroyo's Policies Disappoint." Heritage Foundation, October 7, 2004. https://www.heritage.org/defense/commentary/arroyos-policies-disappoint.

Dohner, Robert S., and Ponciano Intal, Jr. "Debt Crisis and Adjustment in the Philippines." In *Developing Country Debt and World Economy*, edited by Jeffrey D. Sachs. Chicago: University of Chicago Press, 1989.

Dolan, Ronald E. "Martial Law and Its Aftermath (1972–86)." In *Philippines: A Country Study.* Washington, DC: GPO for the Library of Congress, 1991. http:// countrystudies.us/philippines/57.htm.

Dougherty, Jill. "Clinton Heads to Asia on First State Trip." CNN, February 15, 2009. https://www.cnn.com/2009/POLITICS/02/15/us.clinton.asia.trip/.

Earnest, Josh, and Ben Rhodes. "Press Briefing by Press Secretary Josh Earnest and Deputy National Security Advisor for Strategic Communications Ben Rhodes, 11/13/14." White House, November 13, 2014. https://obamawhitehouse.archives.gov/the-press-office/2014/11/13/press-briefing-press-secretary-josh-earnest-and-deputy-national-security.

Eklot, Stefan. *Indonesian Politics in Crisis: The Long Fall of Suharto 1996–98.* Copenhagen: Nordic Institute of Asian Studies, 1999. http://www.diva-portal.org/smash/get/diva2:842567/FULLTEXT01.pdf.

Emmerson, Donald K., editor. *The Deer and the Dragon: Southeast Asia and China in the 21st Century.* Stanford, CA: Walter H. Shorenstein Asia-Pacific Research Center, 2020.

———. "Remarks by Professor Don Emmerson, Head of the Southeast Asia Programme for the Shorenstein Asia-Pacific Research Centre of Stanford University." CPG's International Conference on Thailand's ASEAN Chairmanship 2019. March 1, 2019. http://www.cpg-online.de/2019/03/01/comments-by-professor-don-emmerson-head-of-the-southeast-asia-programme-for-the-shorenstein-asia-pacific-research-centre-of-stanford-university/.

Evans, Rowland, and Robert Novak. "The Philippines Struggle."
    Washington Post, February 22, 1986.
Eyler, Brian, and Courtney Weatherbee. "Mekong Mainstream Dams."
    Stimson Center Mekong Policy Project, June 23, 2020. https://www
    .stimson.org/2020/mekong-mainstream-dams/.
———. "Sustaining the Heartbeat of the Mekong Basin." China Dia-
    logue, March 11, 2019. https://chinadialogue.net/en/energy/11126
    -sustaining-the-heartbeat-of-the-mekong-basin/.
Farah, Douglas. "Foreign Policy: Something Wicked . . . This Way
    Does Not Come Often." NPR, August 12, 2009. https://www.npr
    .org/templates/story/story.php?storyId=111799310.
Freedom House. *Freedom in the World 2009*. Lanham, Maryland:
    Rowman & Littlefield, 2009. https://freedomhouse.org/sites/de
    fault/files/2020-02/Freedom_in_the_World_2009_complete_book
    .pdf.
Funfgeld, Anna. "The Dream of ASEAN Connectivity: Imagining Infra-
    structure in Southeast Asia." *Pacific Affairs* 92, no. 2 (June 2019).
    https://doi.org/10.5509/2019922287.
Garamone, Jim. "Philippines to Become Major Non-NATO Ally, Bush
    Says." American Forces Press Service, May 19, 2003.
Gelb, Leslie. "Marcos Reported to Lose Support in Administration."
    New York Times, January 26, 1986.
Gill, Indermit S., Ana Revenda, and Christian Zeballos. "Grow,
    Invest, Insure: A Game Plan to End Extreme Poverty by 2030."
    Policy Research Working Paper no. 7892, World Bank, November
    2016. https://openknowledge.worldbank.org/bitstream/handle/
    10986/25694/WPS7892.pdf.
Ginsberg, Julie. "Backgrounder: ASEAN : The Association of Southeast
    Asian Nations." *New York Times,* February 26, 2009.
Glanz, James. "Hostage Is Freed After Philippine Troops Are With-
    drawn from Iraq." *New York Times*, July 21, 2004.
Glaser, Bonnie. "Time for Collective Pushback Against China's Eco-
    nomic Coercion." Center for Strategic and International Studies,
    January 13, 2021. https://www.csis.org/analysis/time-collective
    -pushback-against-chinas-economic-coercion.
Gomez, Jim. "ASEAN Takes Position vs China's Vast Historical Sea
    Claims." *The Diplomat,* June 29, 2020. https://thediplomat
    .com/2020/06/asean-takes-position-vs-chinas-vast-historical-sea
    -claims/.

Gowen, Annie. "Burmese President Congratulates Aung San Suu Kyi on Her Party's Lead in Elections." *Washington Post,* November 11, 2015.

Green, Michael J., and Gregory B. Poling. "The U.S. Alliance with the Philippines." Hard Choices: Memos to the President, CSIS, December 3, 2020. https://www.csis.org/analysis/us-alliance-philippines.

Green, Michael, Kathleen Hicks, Zack Cooper, John Schaus, and Jake Douglas. "Counter-Coercion Series: Harassment of the USNS *Impeccable.*" Maritime Transparency Initiative, CSIS, May 19, 2017. https://amti.csis.org/counter-co-harassment-usns-impeccable/.

———. "Counter-Coercion Series: Scarborough Shoal Standoff." Asia Maritime Transparency Initiative, Center for Strategic and International Studies, May 22, 2017. https://amti.csis.org/counter-co-scarborough-standoff.

Greenhouse, Steven. "U.S. Open to Talks on Ties with Vietnam." *New York Times*, October 23, 1991.

Habito, Cielito F. "Divergent Twins: PH and Thailand." *Philippine Daily Inquirer*, September 2, 2017. https://opinion.inquirer.net/106791/divergent-twins-ph-thailand#ixzz6WMdXJBs3.

Harbin, Kenneth S. "The Expanding Sino-Thai Military Relationship: Implications for U.S. Policy in Thailand." Master's thesis, Naval Postgraduate School, December 1990. https://Calhoun.nps.edu/bitstream/handle/10945/27592/90Dec_Harbin.pdf.

Harding, Brian. "Moving the U.S.-Thailand Alliance Forward." CSIS commentary, August 7, 2018. https://www.csis.org/analaysis/moving-us-thailand-alliance-forward.

Heath, Timothy R. "The Ramifications of China's Reported Naval Base in Cambodia." RAND Blog, RAND Corporation, August 7, 2019. https://www.rand.org/blog/2019/08/the-ramifications-of-chinas-reported-naval-base-in.html.

Heer, Paul. "A Report on US-Vietnamese Talks on POWS/MIAS During the Nixon, Ford and Carter Administrations: Prepared for Richard Childress, National Security Council." September 23, 1985, declassified November 2007. https://www.cia.gov/readingroom/docs/DOC_0005359871.pdf.

Hewison, Kevin. "A Book, the King and the 2006 Coup." Review of *The King Never Smiles. A Biography of Thailand's Bhumibol Adulyadej,* by Paul Handley. *Journal of Contemporary Asia* 38, no 1 (February 2008): 190–211.

———. "Thaksin Shinawatra and the Reshaping of Thai Politics." *Contemporary Politics* 16, no. 2 (June 2010): 119–33.

Heydarian, Richard Javad. "At a Strategic Crossroads: ASEAN Centrality Amid Sino-American Rivalry in the Indo-Pacific." Brookings Institution, April 2020. https://www.brookings.edu/research/at-a -strategic-crossroads-asean-centrality-amid-sino-american-rivalry -in-the-indo-pacific/.

———. "A Revolution Betrayed: The Tragedy of Indonesia's Jokowi." *Al Jazeera,* November 24, 2019. https://www.aljazeera.com/ opinions/2019/11/24/a-revolution-betrayed-the-tragedy-of-indone sias-jokowi.

Hiebert, Murray. *Under Beijing's Shadow: Southeast Asia's China Challenge.* Lanham, Maryland: Rowman & Littlefield, 2020.

Hille, Kathrin, and John Reed. "US's Tougher Stance on South China Sea Undermined by Philippines." *Financial Times*, August 16, 2020. https://www.ft.com/content/853775 1f-2ffd-4d78-b6bb-2b3be b5230c3.

Hodal, Kate. "Coup Needed for Thailand 'To Love and Be at Peace Again'—Army Chief." *The Guardian*, May 23, 2014. https://www .theguardian.com/world/2014/may/22/military-coup-thailand -peace-general-prayuth-chan-ocha.

Holmes, Oliver. "Myanmar Journalist Says She Was Fired Over Story on Military Rape Allegations." *The Guardian,* November 4, 2016. https://www.theguardian.com/world/2016/nov/04/myanmar-times -journalist-fired-fiona-macgregor.

Horton, Chris. "The Costs of China's Belt and Road Expansion." *The Atlantic,* January 9, 2020. https://www.theatlantic.com/interna tional/archive/2020/01/china-belt-road-expansion-risks/604342/.

Human Rights Watch. "Burma: National Commission Denies Atrocities." August 7, 2017. https://www.hrw.org/news/2017/08/08/ burma-national-commission-denies-atrocities.

———. "Burma: 20 Years After 1990 Elections, Democracy Still Denied." May 26, 2010. https://www.hrw.org/news/2010/05/26/ burma-20-years-after-1990-elections-democracy-still-denied.

———. "Cambodia: Events of 2006." https://www.hrw.org/world -report/2007/country-chapters/cambodia.

———. "Indonesia: Abdurrahman Wahid's Human Rights Legacy." July 27, 2001. https://www.hrw.org/news/2001/07/27/indonesia -abdurrahman-wahids-human-rights-legacy#.

——. "Thailand's 'War on Drugs'." Human Rights Watch, March 12, 2008. https://www.hrw.org/news/2008/03/12/thailands-war-drugs.

Hunt, Luke. "Aun Pornmoniroth Emerges as Potential Future Cambodian Prime Minister." *The Diplomat,* November 24, 2020. https://thediplomat.com/2020/11/aun-pornmoniroth-emerges-as-potential-future-cambodian-prime-minister/.

Hutt, David. "Time to Boot Cambodia Out of ASEAN ." *Asia Times,* October 28, 2020. https://asiatimes.com/2020/10/time-to-boot-cambodia-out-of-asean/.

IDN Financials. "Jokowi Asks BKPM to Improve Indonesia's Ranking in EODB Index." October 31, 2019. https://www.idnfinancials.com/archive/news/29792/Jokowi-asks-BKPM-to-improve-Indonesias-ranking-in-EODB-index.

Indonesia Investments. "Asian Financial Crisis in Indonesia." https://www.indonesia-investments.com/culture/economy/asian-financial-crisis/item246.

Intal, Ponciano, and Lydia Ruddy. *Voices of ASEAN: What Does ASEAN Mean to ASEAN Peoples,* ASEAN @50. Jakarta: Economic Research Institute for ASEAN and East Asia, 2017. https://www.eria.org/ASEAN_at_50_2.1_Integrative_final.pdf;

International Crisis Group. "Myanmar's Peace Process: Getting to a Political Dialogue." Crisis Group Asia Briefing no. 149, October 19, 2016. https://www.crisisgroup.org/asia/south-east-asia/myanmar/myanmar-s-peace-process-getting-political-dialogue.

——. "Resuming U.S.-Indonesia Military Ties." International Crisis Group Indonesia Briefing, May 21, 2002. https://www.refworld.org/pdfid/3c21b11a4.pdf.

Jakarta Post. "Indonesia, China Sign $23.3b in Contracts." April 14, 2018. https://bit.ly/3sJVzww.

——. "'No Reforms' for ASEAN Anytime Soon." November 25, 2017. https://www.thejakartapost.com/seasia/2017/11/25/no-reforms-for-asean-anytime-soon.html.

Javad Heyderian, Richard. "Philippine President Duterte's Pivotal Visit to China." China-US Focus, October 26, 2016. https://www.chinausfocus.com/foreign-policy/philippine-president-dutertes-pivotal-visit-to-china.

Jenkins, David. *Suharto and His Generals: Indonesian Military Politics 1975–1983.* Monograph Series No. 64. Ithaca: Cornell Modern Indonesia Project, 1984.

Jerome Morales, Neil, and Simon Lews. "U.S. Joins Battle as Philippines Takes Losses in Besieged City." Reuters, June 9, 2017. http://reut.rs/2rbCIhe.

Jones, Lee. "ASEAN 's Albatross: ASEAN 's Burma Policy, from Constructive Engagement to Critical Disengagement." *Asian Security* 4, no. 3 (September 23, 2008): 271–93. https://doi.org/10.1080/14799850802306484.

Karen Women's Organisation. "Karen Women's Organisation Press Statement on Burmese Military's Persecution of the Rohingya People." September 18, 2017. https://www.burmalink.org/karen-womens-organisation-press-statement-burmese-military-persecution-rohingya-people/

Karnow, Stanley. "After Marcos, More of the Same?" *New York Times*, November 18, 1985.

———. "Reagan and the Philippines: Setting Marcos Adrift." *New York Times*, March 19, 1989.

Kausikan, Bilahari. "Consistency Is Not Always a Virtue." Australian Outlook, Australia Institute of International Affairs, September 29, 2020. https://www.internationalaffairs.org.au/australianoutlook/consistency-is-not-always-a-virtue/.

Keck, Zachary. "Second Thomas Shoal Tensions Intensify." *The Diplomat*, March 13, 2014. https://thediplomat.com/2014/03/second-thomas-shoal-tensions-intensify/.

Kessler, Richard J. "The Philippines: The Next Iran?" *Asian Affairs: An American Review* 7, no. 3 (Jan–Feb, 1980): 148–60.

Khidhir, Sheith. "China Crime Plaguing Cambodia?" *ASEAN Post*, October 9, 2019. https://theaseanpost.com/article/china-crime-plaguing-cambodia.

Kislenko, Arne. "A Not So Silent Partner: Thailand's Role in Covert Operations, Counter-Insurgency, and the Wars in Indochina." *Journal of Conflict Studies* 24, no. 1 (2004): 65–96.

Kittisilpa, Jurawee. "Myanmar Army Chief Urges Internally Displaced to Return to Rakhine." Reuters, September 21, 2017. https://reut.rs/2fCCyrq.

Kline, William E. "The Fall of Marcos." Case study, Kennedy School of Government, Harvard University, 1988.

Kuo, Mercy A. "Malaysia in China's Belt and Road: Insights from Chow Bing Ngeow." *The Diplomat,* November 23, 2020. https://thediplomat.com/2020/11/malaysia-in-chinas-belt-and-road/.

Kurlantzick, Joshua. "Keeping the U.S.-Indonesia Relationship Moving Forward." Council on Foreign Relations, Council Special Report no. 81, February 2018. https://cdn.cfr.org/sites/default/files/report_pdf/CSR81_Kurlantzick_Indonesia_With%20Cover.pdf.

Kyaw Phyo Tha. "Analysis: Kowtowing to the 'Prince of Evil.'" *Irrawaddy,* January 3, 2019. https://www.irrawaddy.com/news/analysis-kowtowing-prince-evil.html.

Kynge, James. "China's Contractors Grab Lion's Share of Silk Road Projects." *Financial Times,* January 24, 2018. https://www.ft.com/content/76bIbeOC-0113-IIe8-9650-9CO-ad2d7c5b5.

Laksamana, Evan. "Advancing the US-Indonesia Defense Relationship." East Asia Forum, January 19, 2021. https://www.eastasiaforum.org/2021/01/19/advancing-the -US-Indonesia-Defense -Relationship.

Landler, Mark, and Thomas Fuller. "Obama Prods Myanmar Back Toward Democracy." *New York Times,* November 13, 2014.

Laxalt, Paul. "My Conversations with Ferdinand Marcos: A Lesson in Personal Diplomacy." *Policy Review* 37 (Summer 1986): 2–5.

Lazaroff, Tovah. "Indonesia May Receive $1 b. in US Financing If It Makes Peace with Israel." *Jerusalem Post,* December 23, 2020. https://www.jpost.com/american-politics/trump-prods-indonesia-to -recognize-israel-with-promise-of-2-billion-652959.

Lee, Brianna. "During Clinton's Historic Visit to Burma, 'Flickers of Progress' Pave the Way for An End to Isolation." Need to Know, PBS, December 2, 2011.

Lehmacher, Wolfgang. "The ASEAN Economic Community: What You Need to Know." *World Economic Forum,* May 31, 2016. https://www.weforum.org/agenda/2016/05/asean-economic-community -what-you-need-to-know/.

Levingston, Ivan. "Indonesia Could Get Billions in U.S. Funding to Join Israel Push." Bloomberg, December 21, 2009. https://www.bloomberg.com/news/articles/2020-12-22/indonesia-could-get -billions-in-u-s-funding-to-join-israel-push?sref=BIAk2Vdl.

Lin, Judy, and Rodney Chan. "Singapore and Indonesia Lead in ASEAN Startup Scene, Says AppWorks Partner Jessica Liu." *Digitimes,* December 2, 2020. https://www.digitimes.com/news/a2020 1201PD212.html.

Linao, Girlie. "Days of Sweet Talk Over for ASEAN ?." *The Nation,* July 22, 1998. https://www.burmalibrary.org/reg.burma/archives/199807/msg00516.html.

Lindsey, Tim. "Is Indonesia Retreating from Democracy?" The Conversation, July 8, 2018. https://theconversation.com/is-indonesia -retreating-from-democracy-99211.

Lippman, Thomas W. "Albright Encourages Suharto to Leave Office." *Washington Post*, May 21, 1998.

Locsin, Teodoro L., Jr. "Statement of Secretary of Foreign Affairs Teodoro L. Locsin Jr. on the 4th Anniversary of the Issuance of the Award in the South China Sea Arbitration." Department of Foreign Affairs, Philippine National Government portal, July 12, 2020. https://dfa.gov.ph/dfa-news/statements-and- advisoriesupdate/27140-statement-of-secretary-of-foreign-affairs -teodoro-l-locsin-jr-on-the-4th-anniversary-of-the-issuance-of-the -award-in-the-south-china-sea-arbitration.

Lofgren, Stefan. "Southeast Asia's Most Critical River is Entering Uncharted Waters." *National Geographic*, January 21, 2020. https://www.nationalgeographic.com/science/2020/01/ southeast-asia-most-critical-river-enters-uncharted-waters/.

Lohman, Walter. "U.S.-Indonesian Relations: Built for Endurance, Not Speed." Heritage Foundation, March 5, 2010.

Lohman, Walter, and Renato De Castro. "U.S.–Philippines Partnership in the Cause of Maritime Defense." Heritage Foundation, August 8, 2011. https://www.heritage.org/asia/report/us-philippines-partner ship-the-cause-maritime-defense.

Lum, Thomas. *Cambodia: Background and U.S. Relations.* Congressional Research Service RL32986, April 30, 2009. https://crsre ports.congress.gov/product/pdf/RL/RL32986.

———. *Cambodia: Background and U.S. Relations.* Congressional Research Service R44037, updated January 28, 2019. https://fas .org/sgp/crs/row/R44037.pdf.

Lwin, Nan. "Analysis: Behind the Threats and Warnings of Chinese Ambassador's Kachin Visit." *Irrawaddy,* January 9, 2019. https:// www.irrawaddy.com/news/burma/analysis-behind-threats-warn ings-chinese-ambassadors-kachin-visit.html.

Mabaso, Roy. "Locsin to Call Washington if Filipino Vessel Attacked in West PH Sea." *Manila Bulletin*, August 26, 2020. https:// mb.com.ph/2020/08/26/locsin-to-call-washington-if-filipino-vessel -is-attacked-in-west-ph-sea/.

Maguire, Peter. "The Khmer Rouge Trials: The Good, the Bad, and the Ugly." *The Diplomat,* November 14, 2018. https://thediplomat

.com/2018/11/the-khmer-rouge-trials-the-good-the-bad-and-the
-ugly/.

Maltem, Jeffrey, and Agence France-Presse. "Philippine Fishermen
Protest Chinese Harvesting of Giant Clams on Scarborough Shoal
in Further South China Sea Dispute." *South China Morning Post,*
June 14, 2019. https://www.scmp.com/news/asia/southeast-asia/
article/3014561/philippine-fishermen-protest-chinese-harvesting
-giant.

Mangosing, Frances. "Analyst Says COVID-19 Pandemic Not Slowing
China Conquest of South China Sea." *Inquirer.Net,* April 14, 2020.
https://globalnation.inquirer.net/186834/analyst-says-covid-19-pan
demic-not-slowing-china-conquest-of-south-china-sea.

Mann, Zarni. "A Decade Later, Victims Still Seeking Depayin Massacre Justice." *Irrawaddy,* May 31, 2013. https://www.irrawaddy.com/
news/burma/a-decade-later-victims-still-seeking-depayin-massacre
-justice.html.

Manyin, Mark E. *The Vietnam-U.S. Normalization Process.* CRS Issue Brief for Congress, Congressional Research Service, updated
June 17, 2005. https://fas.org/sgp/crs/row/IB98033.pdf.

Marcus, Ruth, and Thomas W. Lippman. "Clinton Lifts Vietnam
Trade Embargo." *Washington Post*, February 4, 1994.

Maresca, Thomas. "Obama Visits Philippines." *USA Today*, April 27,
2014. https://www.usatoday.com/story/news/world/2014/04/27/us
-philippines-defense-pact/8299491/.

Martin, Michael F. *U.S. Agent Orange/Dioxin Assistance to Vietnam.*
Congressional Research Service R44268, updated February 21,
2019. https://crsreports.congress.gov/product/pdf/R/R44268/20.

———. *U.S. Agent Orange/Dioxin Assistance to Vietnam.* Congressional Research Service R44268, updated January 15, 2021. https://
fas.org/sgp/crs/row/R44268.pdf.

Mathieson, David Scott. "Myanmar's Army of Darkness." *The Nation,* February 12, 2021. https://www.thenation.com/article/world/
myanmar-burma-coup-rohingya/.

McCargo, Duncan. "Thaksin and the Resurgence of Violence in the
Thai South: Network Monarchy Strikes Back?" *Critical Asian
Studies* 38, no. 1 (2006): 39–71.

Mediansky, F. A. "The New People's Army: A Nation-Wide Insurgency in the Philippines." *Contemporary Southeast Asia* 8, no. 1
(June 1986): 1–17. https:/www .jstor.org/stable/25797879.

Men Kimseng, Hul Reaksmey and Aung Chhengpor. "U.S. Sanctions Chinese Company Developing Resort in Cambodia." VOA News, September 19, 2020. https://www.voanews.com/east-asia-pacific/us-sanctions-chinese-company-developing-resort-cambodia.

Mi, Tra. "Vietnam Plays Up U.S. Invitation to Communist Party Chief." VOA News, February 17, 2015, https://www.voanews.com/a/vietnam-united-states-invitation-communist-party-chief/2648251.html.

Mogato, Manuel. "Hagel Assures Philippines No New Permanent Bases." Reuters, August 30, 2013. https://www.reuters.com/article/philippines-usa/hagel-assures-philippines-no-new-permanent-u-s-bases-idINL4N0GV1OZ20130830.

Murphy, Dan. "Philippines Massacre: The Story Behind the Accused Ampatuan Clan." *Christian Science Monitor*, November 24, 2009. https://www.csmonitor.com/World/Global-News/2009/1124/philippines-massacre-the-story-behind-the-accused-ampatuan-clan.

Myanmar Ministry of Immigration and Population. *The 2014 Myanmar Population and Housing Census: Rakhine State*. Census Report Volume 3–K, May 2015. https://myanmar.unfpa.org/sites/default/files/pub-pdf/Rakhine%20State%20Census%20Report%20-%20ENGLISH-3.pdf.

Mydans, Seth. "11 Years, $300 Million, and 3 Convictions: Was the Khmer Rouge Tribunal Worth It?" *New York Times,* April 10, 2017.

———. "'People Power II' Doesn't Give Filipinos the Same." *New York Times*, February 5, 2001.

———. "Thai Parliament Selects New Prime Minister." *New York Times,* December 15, 2008.

Nachemson, Andrew. "Remembering Cambodia's 1970 Coup." *The Diplomat,* March 20, 2020. https://thediplomat.com/2020/03/remembering-cambodias-1970-coup/.

[Names redacted]. *China-Southeast Asia Relations: Trends, Issues, and Implications for the United States,* Congressional Research Service RL32688, February 8, 2006–April 4, 2006. https://www.everycrsreport.com/reports/RL32688.html.

Natalegawa, Andreyka. "Enhancing the U.S.-Indonesia Strategic Partnership." CSIS, July 9, 2018. https://www.csis.org/analysis/enhancing-us-indonesia-strategic-partnership.

National Bureau of Asian Research and Georgetown University. *The United States-Thailand Alliance: Reinvigorating the Partner-*

ship. U.S.-Thailand Alliance Workshop report, April 28, 2010. https://www.nbr.org/wp-content/uploads/pdfs/events/us_thai_alli ance_2010_report.pdf.

National Security Archive, George Washington University. "Memorandum of Conversation, Secretary's Meeting with Foreign Minister Chatichai of Thailand." November 26, 1975, declassified July 27, 2004. https://nsarchive2.gwu.edu/NSAEBB/NSAEBB193/ HAK-11-26-75.pdf.

Nauert, Heather. "Department Press Briefing – September 7, 2017." Department of State Press Briefing, September 7, 2017. https://2017-2021.state.gov/briefings/department-press-briefing -september-7-2017/index.html.

Neher, Clark D., and Wiwat Mungkandi. *U.S.-Thailand Relations in a New International Era*. Berkeley, CA: Institute of East Asian Studies, University of California at Berkeley, 1990.

Ng, Candida. "ASEAN Community, What's That Again?" Reporting ASEAN , August 17, 2015. https://www.reportingasean.net/asean -community-whats-that-again/.

Ng, Desmond, and Sumithra Prasanna. "They're Taking Him for a Ride: Has the Philippines Gained from Duterte's Pivot?" *Channel News Asia,* December 19, 2020. https://www.channelnewsasia.com/ news/cnainsider/philippines-president-rodrigo-duterte-china-pivot -investments-13801780.

Ni, Ye. "A Visit to the Chinese Casino City in Laos Built by Myanmar Workers." *Irrawaddy,* October 21, 2019. https://www.irrawaddy .com/news/burma/visit-chinese-casino-city-laos-built-myanmar -workers.html.

Nikkei Asia. "China's Projects in Vietnam Earn Reputation for Poor Quality, Delays." September 20, 2017. https://asia.nikkei.com/ Economy/China-s-projects-in-Vietnam-earn-reputation-for-poor -quality-delays2.

Niksch, Larry. *Indonesia: U.S. Relations with the Indonesian Military.* Congressional Research Service 98-677 F, August 10, 1998. https:// www.everycrsreport.com/files/19980810_98-677_ccc717c388e29ca ae32d5e71103fe52381077691.pdf.

Obama, Barack, and Daw Aung San Suu Kyi. "Remarks by President Obama and Daw Aung San Suu Kyi." White House, November 19, 2012. https://obamawhitehouse.archives.gov/the-press-office/2012/11/19/remarks-president-obama-and-daw-aung-san-suu -kyi.

Office of the Historian, U.S. Department of State. "Foreign Relations, 1969–1976, Vietnam, January 1969–1970." U.S. Department
of State Archive. https://2001-2009.state.gov/r/pa/ho/frus/nixon/
vi/64033.htm.

———. "Memorandum for the Record." January 19, 1961. In *Foreign
Relations of the United States, 1961–1963, Volume XXIV, Laos
Crisis, edited by Edward C. Keefer.* Washington, DC: United States
Government Printing Office, 1994.

———. "Telegram 14946 from the Embassy in Indonesia to the Department of State, December 6, 1975, 1000Z." Document 141. In
Foreign Relations of the United States, 1969–1976, edited by Bradley Lynn Coleman, David Goldman, and David Nickles. Volume
E–12, Documents on East and Southeast Asia, 1973–1976. Washington: Government Printing Office, 2010. https://history.state.gov/
historicaldocuments/frus1969-76ve12/d141.

Office of the Press Secretary, White House. "Fact Sheet: United
States-Vietnam Education Cooperation." May 25, 2016. https://
obamawhitehouse.archives.gov/the-press-office/2016/05/25/
fact-sheet-united-states-vietnam-education-cooperation.

———. "Fact Sheet: U.S. Response to Typhoon Haiyan." News release, November 19, 2013. https://obamawhitehouse.archives.gov/
the-press-office/2013/11/19/fact-sheet-us-response-typhoon-haiyan.

Office of the Spokesperson, U.S. Mission to ASEAN . "U.S.-ASEAN
Health Futures." Fact sheet, April 22, 2020. https://asean.usmis
sion.gov/u-s-asean-health-futures/.

Office of the State Counselor. "Information Committee Refutes Rumours of Rapes." News release, December 26, 2016. http://www
.statecounsellor.gov.mm/en/node/551.

Office of the United States Trade Representative. "Association of
Southeast Asian Nations (ASEAN)." https://ustr.gov/countries-re-
gions/southeast-asia-pacific/association-southeast-asian-nations
-asean.

———. "Indonesia." https://ustr.gov/countries-regions/southeast-asia
-pacific/indonesia.

———. "Vietnam." https://ustr.gov/countries-regions/southeast-asia
-pacific/vietnam.

Onishi, Norimitsu. "Corruption Fighters Rouse Resistance in Indonesia." *New York Times,* July 25, 2009.

———. "U.S. Updates the Brand It Promotes in Indonesia." *New York
Times*, March 5, 2011.

Open Doors, Institute of International Education. "All Places of Origin." https://opendoorsdata.org/data/international-students/all-places-of-origin/.

Owen, Taylor, and Ben Kiernan. "Bombs Over Cambodia." *The Walrus,* October 2006. https://gsp.yale.edu/sites/default/files/walrus_cambodiabombing_octo6.pdf.

Page, Jeremy, Gordon Lubold, and Rob Taylor. "Deal for Naval Outpost in Cambodia Furthers China's Quest for Military Network." *Wall Street Journal,* July 22, 2019. https://www.wsj.com/articles/secret-deal-for-chinese-naval-outpost-in-cambodia-raises-u-s-fears-of-beijings-ambitions-11563732482.

Parameswaran, Prashanth. "U.S. Policy on Myanmar Under Fire as Promise of Reform Dims." *World Politics Review*, October 7, 2014. https://www.worldpoliticsreview.com/articles/14148/u-s-policy-on-myanmar-under-fire-as-promise-of-reform-dims.

Parks, Thomas, and Benjamin Zawacki. *The Future of Thai-U.S. Relations: Views of Thai and American Leaders on the Bilateral Relationship and Ways Forward.* White paper. San Francisco, CA: Asia Foundation, August 2018. https://asiafoundation.org/wp-content/uploads/2018/08/The-Future-of-Thai-U.S.-Relations.pdf.

Parreño, Al A. *Report on the Philippine Extrajudicial Killings (2001-August 2010).* Manila: USAID/Asia Foundation, 2011. https://www.loc.gov/item/2012330478/.

Perlez, Jane. "In China, Aung San Suu Kyi Finds a Warm Welcome (and No Talk of Rohingya)." *New York Times,* November 30, 2017.

Pew Research Center. "America's Global Image." June 23, 2015. https://www.pewresearch.org/global/2015/06/23/1-americas-global-image/.

———. "Filipinos in the U.S. Fact Sheet: Filipino Population in the United States, 2000– 2015." https://www.pewsocialtrends.org/fact-sheet/asian-americans-filipinos-in-the-u-s/.

Poling, Gregory B. "Judgment Day: The South China Sea Tribunal Issues Its Ruling." CSIS, July 12, 2016. https://www.csis.org/analysis/judgment-day-south-china-sea-tribunal-issues-its-ruling.

Pongsudhirak, Thitinan. "The Geopolitical Ripples from Thailand's Coup." *Nikkei Asia,* July 31, 2014. https://asia.nikkei.com/Politics/Thitinan-Pongsudhirak-The-geopolitical-ripples-of-Thailand-s-coup.

Prak, Chan Thul. "Cambodian Leader Hun Sen Says Backs Eldest Son to Succeed Him." Reuters, December 2, 2021. https://www.reuters

.com/world/asia-pacific/cambodian-leader-hun-sen-says-backs
-eldest-son-succeed-him-2021-12-02/.

Priest, Dana, and Bradley Graham. "E. Timor Killings Renew Debate on U.S.-Indonesia Military Ties." *Washington Post*, September 14, 1999.

Purdam, Todd. S. "U.S. to Resume Aid to Train Indonesia's Military Forces." *New York Times,* August 3, 2002.

Putz, Catherin, and Shannon Tiezzi. "Did Hillary Clinton's Pivot to Asia Work?" FiveThirtyEight, April 14, 2016. https://fivethir tyeight.com/features/did-hillary-clintons-pivot-to-asia-work/.

Radio Free Asia. "Aung San Suu Kyi's Hague Performance Impresses Few Beyond Myanmar Loyalists." December 13, 2019. https:// www.rfa.org/english/news/myanmar/aung-san-suu-kyis-hague-per formance-12132019180148.html.

Radio Free Asia. "Cambodia Defense Chief Defends Demolition of Second U.S.-Funded Building at Ream Naval Base." November 10, 2020. https://www.rfa.org/english/news/cambodia/demolition -11102020164255.html.

———. "Lao Banana Workers Sickened by Chemicals Used on Farms." Mekong Eye, May 31, 2018. https://www.mekongeye .com/2018/05/31/lao-banana-workers-sickened-by-chemicals-used -on-farms/.

———. "Lao River Clogged with Trash from Chinese Banana Farms." February 3, 2020. https://www.rfa.org/english/news/laos/banana -02032020151330.html.

———. "Philippines Welcomes U.S. Presence to Maintain Order in South China Sea." August 26, 2020. https://www.rfa.org/english/ news/china/presence-08262020183240.html.

Ratcliffe, Rebecca. "Indonesian Names New Capital Nusantara, Re-placing Sinking Jarkarta." *The Guardian*, January 18, 2022.

Ratner, Ely. "Learning the Lessons of Scarborough Shoal." *National Interest*, November 21, 2013. https://nationalinterest.org/ commentary/learning-the-lessons-scarborough-reef-9442.

Raymond, Gregory V. "Strategic Culture and Thailand's Response to Vietnam's Occupation of Cambodia, 1979–1989: A Cold War Epi-logue." *Journal of Cold War Studies* 22, no. 1 (Winter 2020): 4–45.

Reed, John, and Kathrin Hille. "Laos' Belt and Road Project Sparks Questions Over China Ambitions." *Financial Times,* October 30, 2019. https://www.ft.com/content/a8d0bdae-e5bc-11e9-9743 -db5a370481bc.

Reston, James. "Washington: A Gleam of Light in Asia." *New York Times,* June 19, 1966.

Reuters. "China Supports Cambodia's Crackdown on Political Opposition." November 20, 2017. https://reut.rs/2zTwXYF.

———. "Clinton and Suharto Talk." *New York Times,* February 22, 1998

———. "Malaysia, China Agree to Resume Railway Project After Slashing Cost." April 11, 2019. https://reut.rs/2IuAXDg.

———. "U.N. Security Council Condemns Excessive Violence in Myanmar." September 13, 2017. https://reut.rs/2fiqviP.

———. "U.S. Slaps Sanctions on Laos Golden Triangle Casino in Bid to Break Up Narco-Empire." January 31, 2018. https://reut.rs/2rSVwTf.

Richburg, Keith B. "Cashing in on Years in Power." *Washington Post,* May 22, 1998.

———. "Suharto Resigns, Names Successor." *Washington Post,* May 21, 1998.

Rollett, Charles. "PM Gets His Photo-Op with Obama as Cambodian-Americans Protest." *Phnom Penh Post,* February 17, 2016. https://www.phnompenhpost.com/national/pm-gets-his-photo-op -obama-cambodian-americans-protest.

Rondonuwu, Olivia. "ASEAN to Claim 'Common Ground" on S. China Sea, but No Communique." Reuters, July 20, 2012. http://reut.rs/ OAWRB2.

Ruland, Jurgen. "From Trade to Investment: ASEAN and AFTA in the Era of the 'New Regionalism.'" *Pacific Affairs* 92, no. 3 (September 2019). https://doi.org/10.5509/2019923533.

Russel, Daniel R., and Blake Berger. "Navigating the Belt and Road Initiative." Asia Society Policy Institute, June 2019. https://asiasoci ety.org/sites/default/files/2019-06/Navigating%20the%20Belt%20 and%20Road%20Initiative_2.pdf.

Sambhi, Natalie. "Generals Gaining Ground: Civil-Military Relations and Democracy in Indonesia." Brookings Institution, January 22, 2021. https://www.brookings.edu/articles/generals-gaining-ground -civil-military-relations-and-democracy-in-indonesia/.

Santos, Reynaldo Jr. "Looking Back: Daniel Smith and the Subic Rape Case." Rappler, December 1, 2015. https://www.rappler.com/ newsbreak/iq/looking-back-daniel-smith-subic-rape-case.

Schaefer, Peter F. "Setting the Record Straight on Marcos's Fall." *Asian Wall Street Journal Weekly,* February 19, 1996.

Schnabel, Chris. "Beyond the Numbers: How Aquino Fueled the Economy." Rappler, June 17, 2016. https://rappler.com/business/economy/president-aquino-economy-legacy.

Schwarz, Adam. *A Nation in Waiting*, 2nd ed. Boulder, Colorado: Westview Press, 2000.

Scott, Austin. "U.S., Vietnam Set Talks to Establish Normal Relations." *Washington Post*, March 24, 1977.

Seah, Sharon, Hoang Thi Ha, Melinda Martinus, and Pham Thi Phuong Thao. *The State of Southeast Asia: 2021 Survey Report*. Singapore: ISEAS-Yusof Ishak Institute, 2021. https://www.iseas.edu.sg/wp-content/uploads/2021/01/The-State-of-SEA-2021-v2.pdf.

Searight, Amy. "Jokowi 2.0: Policy, Politics, and Prospects for Reform." CSIS, October 18, 2019. https://www.csis.org/analysis/jokowi-20-policy-politics-and-prospects-reform.

Shambaugh, David. *Where Great Powers Meet: America & China in Southeast Asia*. New York: Oxford University Press, 2021.

Shan Human Rights Foundation and Shan Women's Action Network. "License to Rape: The Burmese Military Regime's Use of Sexual Violence in the Ongoing War in Shan State." May 2002. https://www.peacewomen.org/sites/default/files/vaw_licensetorape_shrf_swan_2002_0.pdf.

Shawcross, William. *Sideshow: Kissinger, Nixon and the Destruction of Cambodia*. New York: Simon and Schuster, 1979.

Sherlock, Stephen. "Crisis in Indonesia: Economy, Society and Politics." Parliament of Australia Current Issues Brief 13 1997–98, April 8, 1998. https://www.aph.gov.au/About_Parliament/Parliamentary_Departments/Parliamentary_Library/Publications_Archive/CIB/CIB9798/98cib13;

Simandjuntak, Deasy. "Indonesia's Democracy Under Challenge." EastAsiaForum, January 30, 2020. https://www.eastasiaforum.org/2020/01/30/indonesias-democracy-under-challenge/.

Simons, Marlise, and Hannah Beech. "Aung San Suu Kyi Defends Myanmar Against Rohingya Genocide Accusations." *New York Times,* December 11, 2019.

Singapore Ministry of Foreign Affairs. "MFA Spokesman's Comments on the Ruling of the Arbitral Tribunal in the Philippines v China Case under Annex VII to the 1982 United Nations Convention on the Law of the Sea (UNCLOS)." July 12, 2016. https://www.mfa.gov.sg/Newsroom/Press-Statements-Transcripts-and-Photos/2016/07/

MFA-Spokesmans-Comments-on-the-ruling-of-the-Arbitral-Tribu
nal-in-the-Philippines-v-China-case-under.

Siregar, Kiki. "Indonesians Should 'Love Local Goods, Hate Foreign
Products'": President Jokowi." Channel News Asia, March 4, 2021.
https://www.channelnewsasia.com/news/asia/indonesia-love-local
-hate-foreign-products-jokowi-growth-14331276.

Slodkowski, Antoni. "New U.S. Ambassador to Myanmar Says He
Will Keep Using Term 'Rohingya.'" Reuters, May 10, 2016. http://
reut.rs/1OdLIIh.

Smith, Anthony L. "Reluctant Partner: Indonesia's Response to U.S.
Security Policies." Asia Pacific Center for Security Studies, March
2003. https://apps.dtic.mil/dtic/tr/fulltext/u2/a592297.pdf.

Spetalnick, Matt, and Jeff Mason. "Obama Offers Praise, Pressure on
Historic Myanmar Trip." Reuters, November 18, 2012. http://reut
.rs/XUfFRR.

Steinberg, David Joel, ed. *In Search of Southeast Asia: A Modern History*. Honolulu: University of Hawaii Press, 1985.

Stern, Lewis M. "Diverging Roads: 21st-century U.S.-Thai Defense
Relations." *Strategic Forum* 241 (June 2009). Institute for National
Strategic Studies, National Defense University. https://ciaotest.cc.
columbia.edu/wps/inss/0017418/f_0017418_14900.pdf.

Stimson War Legacies Working Group. "The U.S.-Vietnam Relationship and War Legacies: 25 Years into Normalization." Virtual meeting, July 15, 2020. Highlights at https://www.stimson.org/2020/
the-us-vietnam-relationship-and-war-legacies-looking-to-the-future/.

Stolen Asset Recovery Initiative (STAR). "Asset Recovery Watch Database." http://star.worldbank.org.

Storey, Ian. "China's Missteps in Southeast Asia: Less Charm, More
Offensive." *China Brief* vol. 10, no. 25, Jamestown Foundation,
December 17, 2020. https://jamestown.org/program/chinas-mis
steps-in-southeast-asia-less-charm-more-offensive/.

Strangio, Sebastian. *In the Dragon's Shadow: Southeast Asia in the
Chinese Century.* New Haven: Yale University Press, 2020.

———. "In UN Speech, Duterte Stiffens Philippines' Stance on the
South China Sea" *The Diplomat*, September 23, 2020. https://the
diplomat.com/2020/09/ in-un-speech-duterte-stiffens-philippines
-stance-on-the-south-china-sea/.

———. "Indonesia Breaks Daily COVID-19 Record as Omicron Surge
Continues." *The Diplomat*, February 16, 2022. https://thediplomat

.com/2022/02/indonesia-breaks-daily-covid-19-record-as-omicron -surge-continues/.

———. "The 'Lawless' Playgrounds of Laos." Al Jazeera, July 24, 2016. https://www.aljazeera.com/features/2016/7/24/the-lawless -playgrounds-of-laos.

———. "The World According to the CPP." *The Diplomat,* July 23, 2020. https://www.sebastianstrangio.com/2020/07/23/the-world -according-to-cambodias-cpp/.

Suu Kyi, Aung San. "Transcript: Aung San Suu Kyi's Speech at the ICJ in Full." *Al Jazeera,* December 12, 2019. https://www.aljazeera .com/news/2019/12/12/transcript-aung-san-suu-kyis-speech-at-the -icj-in-full.

Tan, Wooi Yee, and Chong Foh Chin. "High-Level Visits and the Belt and Road Initiative: The Case of Southeast Asia." *Contemporary Chinese Political Economy and Strategic Relations: An International Journal* 6, no. 1 (April-May 2020): 217–59.

Thant, Myint-U. "Myanmar, An Unfinished Nation." *Nikkei Asia,* June 17, 2017. https://asia.nikkei.com/Politics/Myanmar-an-unfin ished-nation.

———. *River of Lost Footsteps: Histories of Burma.* New York: Farrar, Straus and Giroux, 2006.

The Guardian. "U.S. Defies Myanmar Government Request to Stop Using Term Rohingya." May 11, 2016. https://www.theguardian .com/world/2016/may/11/us-defies-myanmar-government-rohingya -muslims.

———. "Vietnam Declares US-Based Activist Group is a Terrorist Organization." October 7, 2016. https://www.theguardian.com/ world/2016/oct/07/vietnam-viet-tan-terrorists-dissent.

Thoburn, John. "Vietnam as a Role Model for Development." Research Paper No. 2009/30, United Nations University–World Institute for Development Economics Research, May 2009. http:// citeseerx.ist.psu.edu/viewdoc/download?doi=10.1.1.395.5645&rep =rep1&type=pdf.

Tiezzi, Shannon. "Donald Emmerson on Southeast Asia's Approach to China." *The Diplomat,* August 5, 2020. https://thediplomat .com/2020/08/donald-emmerson-on-southeast-asias-approach-to -china/.

Time. "The Face of Buddhist Terror." July 1, 2013. http://content.time .com/time/covers/asia/0,16641,20130701,00.html.

Tower, Jason, and Priscilla Clapp. "Casino Cities: The Role of China and Transnational Criminal Networks." U.S. Institute of Peace, Special Report no. 471, July 27, 2020. https://www.usip.org/pub lications/2020/07/myanmars-casino-cities-role-china-and-transna tional-criminal-networks.

Transparency International. "Suharto's Family 'Must Return Looted Wealth.'" May 24, 1998. https://www.transparency.org/en/press/ suhartos-family-must-return-looted-wealth#.

U.S. Census Bureau. "Trade in Goods with Vietnam." https://www .census.gov/foreign-trade/balance/c5520.html#2000.

U.S. Chamber of Commerce. "The Next Stage of US-Vietnam Rela-tions: A Blueprint to Deepen Trade and Investment Ties." May 8, 2019. https://www.uschamber.com/report/the-next-stage-of-us-viet nam-relations-blueprint-deepen-trade-and-investment-ties.

U.S. Chamber of Commerce. "U.S. Chamber and AmCham Indonesia Convene Public and Private Sector Leaders for 8th Annual U.S.-Indonesia Investment Summit." December 11, 2020. https://www .uschamber.com/press-release/us-chamber-and-amcham-indonesia -convene-public-and-private-sector-leaders-8th-annual.

U.S. Department of Defense and Department of State. *Final Inter-agency Report of the Reagan Administration on the* POW/MIA *Issue in Southeast Asia.* January 19, 1989, Washington, DC.

U.S. Department of State. "Ask the Ambassador." U.S. Department of State Archive, January 11, 2008. https://2001-2009.state.gov/r/pa/ ei/ask/99222.htm.

———. "*Country Reports on Human Rights Practices for 2017: Cambodia.*" April 20, 2018.

———. "Southeast Asia." U.S. Department of State archives. https:// 2001-2009.state.gov/g/prm/108723.htm.

U.S. Embassy & Consulate in Vietnam. "Number of Vietnamese Stu-dents in the U.S. Increases for 18th Straight Year." November 19, 2019. https://vn.usembassy.gov/number-of-vietnamese-higher-educa-tion-students-in-the-united-states-increases-for-18th-straight-year/.

U.S. Embassy & Consulates in Indonesia. "Fact Sheet: U.S.-Indonesia Education Partnership." https://id.usembassy.gov/our-relationship/ policy-history/embassy-fact-sheets/fact-sheet-u-s-indonesia-educa tion-partnership/.

U.S. Embassy in Indonesia. "U.S. Signs Millennium Challenge Cor-poration Compact with Indonesia to Support Economic Growth."

November 22, 2011. https://www.povertyactionlab.org/sites/de
fault/files/Embassy%20of%20US%20Jakarta%20-%20MCC%20
signs%20contact%20to%20support%20economic%20growth
.pdf.

U.S. Mission to ASEAN. "U.S.-ASEAN Timeline." https://asean.usmis
sion.gov/our-relationship/policy-history/u-s-asean-timeline/.

U.S.-ASEAN Business Council. "Trade and Investment." July 22, 2019.
https://www.usasean.org/why-asean/trade-and-investment.

United Nations Human Rights Council. Promotion and Protection of All Human Rights, Civil, Political, Economic, Social and
Cultural Rights, Including the Right to Development: Report of
the Special Rapporteur on Extrajudicial, Summary or Arbitrary
Executions, Philip Alston. Addendum. Follow-Up to Country
Recommendations— Philippines, A/HRC/11/2/Add.8. April 29,
2009.

United Nations. "UN Human Rights Chief Points to 'Textbook Example of Ethnic Cleansing' in Myanmar." UN News, September 11,
2017. https://news.un.org/en/story/2017/09/564622-un-human
-rights-chief-points-textbook-example-ethnic-cleansing-myanmar.

United Press International. "Aid for Indonesia Barred in Senate; Sukarno Scored in Debate on Tower's Amendment." *New York Times*,
August 14, 1964.

U.S. Embassy & Consulate in Thailand. "History of the U.S. and
Thailand." http://th.usembassy.gov/our-relationship/policy
-history/io/.

United States Holocaust Memorial Museum. "Cambodia 1975–
1979." April 2018. https://www.ushmm.org/genocide-prevention/
countries/cambodia/case-study/introduction/cambodia-1975.

———. "Day One: April 17, 1975." https://www.ushmm.org/
genocide-prevention/countries/cambodia/case-study/violence/
day-one.

———. "International Response to Khmer Rouge Rule." https://www
.ushmm.org/genocide-prevention/countries/cambodia/case-study/
violence/international-response.

United States Mission to the United Nations. "Press Release: Ambassador Haley on the Current Humanitarian Situation in Burma's
Rakhine State." September 8, 2017. https://usun.usmission.gov/
press-release-ambassador-haley-on-the-current-humanitarian
-situation-in-burmas-rakhine-state/?_ga=2.17899705.104728732
.1612824474-1410681472.1612824474.

Unson, John. "ARMM Mourns Dimaporo's Death." *Philstar Global*, April 22, 2004. https://www.philstar.com/headlines/ 2004/04/22/247143/armm-mourns-dima poro146s-death

Varagur, Krithika. "Declassified Files Provide Insight into Indonesia's Democratic Transition." Voice of America, July 24, 2018. https:// www.voanews.com/east-asia-pacific/declassified-files-provide-in sight-indonesias-democratic-transition.

Vasandani, Chandni, and Amanda Hodge. "Indonesia Moves Closer to One-Party Rule as Jokowi Aide Takes Over Opposition." *The Australian*, March 8, 2021. https://www.theaustralian.com.au/ world/indonesia-moves-closer-to-oneparty-rule-as-jokowi-aide -takes-over-opposition/news-story/3b880e108efaaef3d996cac36a1 27942.

Vatikiotis, Michael R. J. *Indonesian Politics Under Suharto: The Rise and Fall of the New Order*. New York and Oxon: Routledge, 1993.

Vietnamese Embassy, Washington, DC. "Nguyen Co Thach: Breaker of Deadlocks, Builder of Ties." Webinar. August 28, 2020.

Villacorta, Wilfrido V. "The Curse of the Weak State: Leadership Imperatives for the Ramos Government." *Contemporary Southeast Asia* 16, no. 1 (June 1994): 67–92. https://www.jstor.org/stable/ 25798233.

VOA Cambodia. "Asean 'To Clarify' Meeting Amid Turmoil." December 1, 2008. https://www.voacambodia.com/a/a-40-2008-12-01 -voa3-90165322/1354023.html.

VOA News. "Kerry: China's Oil Rig in South China Sea 'Provocative.'" May 13, 2014. https://www.voanews.com/a/kerry-chinas-oil-rig-in -south-china-sea-provocative/1913329.html.

Voice of America. "Analysts Review Megawati's First Year in Office." July 23, 2002. https://www.voanews.com/a/a-13-a-2002-07-23-35 -analysts-66291942/541271.html.

Wa Lone, Kyaw Soe Oo, Simon Lewis, and Antoni Slodkowski. "How Myanmar Forces Burned, Looted and Killed in a Remote Village." Reuters, February 8, 2018. https://www.reuters.com/investigates/ special-report/myanmar-rakhine-events/.

Wai Moe. "Junta Pushes the 'Seven-Step Roadmap" Forward Despite Flaws." *Irrawaddy,* December 3, 2007, https://www2.irrawaddy .com/article.php?art_id=9500.

Wain, Barry. "Manila's Bungle in the South China Sea." *Far Eastern Economic Review* 171, no. 1 (Jan/Feb 2008): 45–48.

Walker, Peter. "Man Who Crossed Lake to Aung San Suu Kyi Home Leaves Burma." *The Guardian,* August 16, 2009. https://www.the guardian.com/world/2009/aug/16/john-yettaw-leaves-burma.

Warburton, Eve. "Deepening Polarization and Democratic Decline in Indonesia," Carnegie Endowment, August 18, 2020. https:// carnegieendowment.org/2020/08/18/deepening-polarization-and -democratic-decline-in-indonesia-pub-82435.

Washington Post. "U.S., Indonesia Rebuilding Military Ties; Meetings on Terrorism, Piracy Are First Since Sanctions for E. Timor Violence." April 25, 2002.

Wayne, Leslie. "Free to a Good Country." *New York Times*, October 31, 2006.

Weatherbee, Donald E. *ASEAN's Half-Century: A Political History of the Association of Southeast Asian Nations.* Lanham, Maryland: Rowman & Littlefield, 2019.

———. "Southeast Asia and ASEAN, Running in Place." *Southeast Asian Affairs* 2012 (2012): 3–22. https://www.muse.jhu.edu/ article/485123.

Wehrle, Edmund. F. "'A Good, Bad Deal': John F. Kennedy, W. Averell Harriman, and the Neutralization of Laos, 1961–1962." *Pacific Historical Review* 67, no. 3 (1998): 349–77. http://www.jstor.org/ stable/3641753.

Westerman, Ashley. "In Laos, A Chinese-Funded Railway Sparks Hope for Growth—and Fears of Debt." NPR, April 26, 2019. https://www.npr.org/2019/04/26/707091267/in-laos-a-chinese -funded-railway-sparks-hope-for-growth-and-fears-of-debt.

White House. "NSDD 163 United States Policy towards the Philippines." National Archives Catalog, February 20, 1985. https://cata log.archives.gov/id/6879758.

White House. "Quad Joint Leaders' Statement." May 24, 2022. https://www.whitehouse.gov/briefing-room/statements-releases/ 2022/05/24/quad-joint-leaders-statement/.

Wintle, Justin. *Perfect Hostage: A Life of Aung San Suu Kyi, Burma's Prisoner of Conscience.* New York: Skyhorse Publishing, 2007.

World Bank. "World Bank Open Data." https://data.worldbank.org.

———. *World Development Report 1990: Poverty.* New York: Oxford University Press, 1990. https://openknowledge.worldbank.org/ bitstream/handle/10986/5973/WDR%201990%20-%20English .pdf.

Wroughton, Lesley. "Suu Kyi Calls for 'Space' to Address Myanmar's Rohingya Issue as Kerry Visits." Reuters, May 21, 2016. http://reut .rs/1qBUJ2H.

Ye, Htut. "Myanmar's Long Journey to Peace Starts in Panglong." Straits Times, August 31, 2016. https://www.straitstimes.com/ opinion/myanmars-long-journey-to-peace-starts-in-panglong.

Yeo, George. "Statement by ASEAN Chair, Singapore's Minister for Foreign Affairs George Yeo, 27 September 2007, New York." National Archives of Singapore, September 27, 2007. https://www.nas .gov.sg/archivesonline/data/pdfdoc/20070927974.htm.

Yoshida, Yuichiro, Han Soo Lee, Bui Huy Trung, Hoang-Dung Tran, Mahrjan Keshlav Lall, Kifayatullah Kakar, and Tran Dang Xuan. "Impacts of Mainstream Hydropower Dams on Fisheries and Agriculture in Lower Mekong Basin." Sustainability 12, no. 6 (2020). https://doi.org/10.3390/su12062408

Zai, Keith, and Kay Johnson. "Exclusive: Taking Power—Chinese Firm to Run Laos Electricity Grid Amid Default Warnings." Reuters, December 15, 2020. https://www.reuters.com/article/china -laos/exclusive-taking-power-chinese-firm-to-run-laos-electric-grid -amid-default-warnings-idUSL8N2FW068.

Zaini, Khairulanwar. "China's Vaccine Diplomacy in Southeast Asia— A Mixed Record" Perspective no. 86, ISEAS Yusof Ishok Institute, June 24, 2021. https://www.iseas.edu.sg/articles-commentaries/ iseas-perspective/2021-86-chinas-vaccine-diplomacy=in-southeast -asia-a-mixed-record-by-khairulanwar-zaini/.

Zhang, Yunling, and Wang Yuzhu. "ASEAN in China's Grand Strategy." In Building ASEAN Community: Political-Security and Socio-Cultural Reflections. ASEAN@50 vol. 4. Edited by Aileen Baviera and Larry Maramis. Indonesia: Economic Research Institute for ASEAN and East Asia, 2017. https://www.eria.org/ASEAN _at_50_4A.9_Zhang_and_Wang_final.pdf.

Congressional Hearings

Administration Review of U.S. Policy Toward the Philippines: Hearing Before the Committee on Foreign Relations, 99th Cong. October 30, 1985.

Agent Orange: What Efforts Are Being Made to Address the Continuing Impact of Dioxin in Vietnam? Hearing Before the

Subcommittee on Asia, the Pacific and the Global Environment of the Committee on Foreign Affairs, 111th Cong. First session, June 4, 2009. Serial No. 111-39. https://www.govinfo.gov/content/pkg/CHRG-111hhrg50112/pdf/CHRG-111hhrg50112.pdf.

Burma in the Aftermath of Cyclone Nargis: Death, Displacement and Humanitarian Aid: Hearing before the Subcommittee on Asia, the Pacific and the Global Environment of the Committee on Foreign Affairs, 110th Cong. Second session, May 20, 2008. Serial No. 110-229. https://www.govinfo.gov/content/pkg/CHRG-110hhrg42477/pdf/CHRG-110hhrg42477.pdf.

Burma's Saffron Revolution: Hearing before the Subcommittee on East Asian and Pacific Affairs of the Committee on Foreign Relations, 110th Cong. First session, October 3, 2007. S. Hrg. 110-505. https://www.govinfo.gov/content/pkg/CHRG-110shrg44490/pdf/CHRG-110shrg44490.pdf.

East Timor: A New Beginning? Joint Hearing Before the Subcommittee on Asia and the Pacific of the House Committee of International Relations and the Subcommittee on East Asian and Pacific Affairs of the Committee on Foreign Relations, 106th Cong. Second session, February 10, 2000. Serial No. 106-98. https://www.govinfo.gov/content/pkg/CHRG-106jhrg67455/html/CHRG-106jhrg67455.htm.

Extrajudicial Killings in the Philippines: Strategies to End the Violence. Hearing before the Senate Foreign Relations Full Committee, 110th Cong. First session, March 14, 2007. S. Hrg. 110-290. https://www.govinfo.gov/content/pkg/CHRG-110shrg40811/html/CHRG-110shrg40811.htm.

Human Rights Concerns in Vietnam: Hearing of the Subcommittee on International Organizations, Human Rights and Oversight of the House Committee on Foreign Affairs, 110th Cong. First session, November 6, 2007. Serial No. 110-117. https://www.govinfo.gov/content/pkg/CHRG-110hhrg38819/pdf/CHRG-110hhrg38819.pdf.

Indonesia in Transition: Recent Developments and Implications for U.S. Policy, Hearing before the Subcommittee on Asia and the Pacific of the Committee on International Relations, 109th Cong. March 10, 2005. Serial No. 109-41. https://www.govinfo.gov/content/pkg/CHRG-109hhrg99826/html/CHRG-109hhrg99826.htm.

Indonesia: Confronting the Political and Economic Crises: Hearing Before the Subcommittee on Asia and the Pacific of the Committee on International Relations, 106th Cong. First session, February 16,

2000. Serial No. 106-99. https://www.govinfo.gov/content/pkg/
CHRG-106hhrg64418/html/CHRG-106hhrg64418.htm.

*Our Forgotten Responsibility: What Can We Do to Help Victims
of Agent Orange: Hearing before the Subcommittee on Asia,
Pacific, and the Global Environment Subcommittee of the Committee on Foreign Affairs, 110th Cong.* Second session, May 15,
2008. Serial No. 110-231. https://www.govinfo.gov/app/details/
CHRG-110hhrg42425/CHRG-110hhrg42425.

*An Overview of Cambodia and Debt Recycling: How Can the U.S.
Be of Assistance? Hearing Before the Subcommittee on Asia, the
Pacific, and the Global Environment of the Committee on For-
eign Affairs, 100th Cong.* First session, February 14, 2008. Serial
No.≈110–198. https://www.govinfo.gov/content/pkg/CHRG-
110hhrg40746/pdf/CHRG-110hhrg40746.pdf.

*The Philippine Bases Treaty: Hearing before the Subcommittee on
Asia and Pacific Affairs of the Committee on Foreign Affairs, 102nd
Cong.* September 25, 1991.

*POW/MIA's: Report of the Select Committee on pow/mia Affairs.
103rd Congress.* First session, January 13, 1993. Report 103-1.
https://fas.org/irp/congress/1993_rpt/pow-exec.html.

*Thailand: A Democracy in Peril: Hearing Before the Subcommittee
on Asia and the Pacific of the Committee on Foreign Affairs, 113th
Cong.* Second session, June 24, 2014. Serial No. 113-191. https://
www.govinfo.gov/content/pkg/CHRG-113hhrg88457/html/CHRG
-113hhrg88457.htm.

*U.S.-Indonesia Relations, Hearing before the Subcommittee on East
Asian and Pacific Affairs of the Committee on Foreign Relations,
109th Cong.* September 15, 2005. https://www.foreign.senate.gov/
imo/media/doc/JohnTestimony050915.pdf.

*United States Security Agreements and Commitments Abroad: King-
dom of Thailand. Hearings Before the Subcommittee on United
States Security Agreements and Commitments Abroad of the Committee on Foreign Relations, 91st Cong.* November 10, 1969.

Index

The authorized representative in the EU for product safety and compliance is:
Mare Nostrum Group
B.V Doelen 72
4831 GR Breda
The Netherlands

* 9 7 8 1 5 3 8 1 7 8 9 5 9 *